PENGUIN BOOKS

THE PENGUIN GUIDE TO THE MONUMENTS OF INDIA

VOLUME TWO: ISLAMIC, RAJPUT, EUROPEAN

Philip Davies read history at Queens' College, Cambridge, before taking a post-graduate diploma in town planning. He worked first in the G L C Historic Buildings Division and is now a principal historic buildings adviser to Westminster City Council. He is the author of the highly acclaimed *Splendours of the Raj*, which is also published by Penguin.

BY THE SAME AUTHOR

THE PENGUIN GUIDE TO THE MONUMENTS OF INDIA

VOLUME ONE: BUDDHIST, JAIN, HINDU

by George Michell

D1627847

0140 084 258 0 172 75

THE PENGUIN GUIDE TO THE

MONUMENTS OF INDIA

VOLUME TWO

ISLAMIC, RAJPUT, EUROPEAN

PHILIP DAVIES

PENGUIN BOOKS

PENGUIN BOOKS
Published by the Penguin Group
27 Wrights Lane, London W8 5TZ, England
Viking Penguin Inc., 40 West 23rd Street, New York, New York 10010, USA
Penguin Books Australia Ltd, Ringwood, Victoria, Australia
Penguin Books Canada Ltd, 2801 John Street, Markham, Ontario, Canada L3R 1B4
Penguin Books (NZ) Ltd, 182–190 Wairau Road, Auckland 10, New Zealand

Penguin Books Ltd, Registered Offices: Harmondsworth, Middlesex, England

First published 1989
Published simultaneously in hardback by Viking
1 3 5 7 9 10 8 6 4 2

Copyright © Philip Davies, 1989
All rights reserved

Typeset in Bembo by Goodfellow & Egan Ltd, Cambridge
Made and printed in Great Britain by
Butler & Tanner Ltd, Frome

Frontispiece: Municipal buildings designed by F. W. Stevens, Bombay

DEDICATION

For Liisa

'Jesus Son of Mary (on whom be peace) said:
The world is a bridge, pass over it,
but build no houses on it. He who hopes for an hour
may hope for eternity. The world endures but an hour.
Spend it in prayer, for the rest is unseen.'
(Inscription on the Buland Darwaza, Fatehpur Sikri)

'The unseen is the cause of the seen.'
(Esoteric aphorism)

'There is but one treasure that will forever last;
but few seek for it and fewer find it.'
(Sufi aphorism)

CONTENTS

ACKNOWLEDGEMENTS

In writing such an ambitious work as *The Penguin Guide to the Monuments of India* the author has relied on the support, encouragement and goodwill of a large number of individuals and organizations.

At Penguin general editorial direction was provided first by Catriona Luckhurst, under whom the project was conceived and initiated, and then by Tessa Strickland, who ably steered the two volumes through the complex editorial and production stages. Lesley Levene performed the herculean task of checking all the text, and of ensuring that the two volumes worked together effectively.

Particular thanks are due to Liisa Davies, who selflessly devoted unlimited hours of her time for over three years to typing and correcting the manuscript. Melanie Gibson offered constructive criticism and advice and scrutinized the entire manuscript. Many other individuals have also offered advice, support or assistance or have provided me with photographs, material or useful leads, principally: Mildred Archer, Margaret Carlyle-Lancaster, Jane Davies, Virginia Fass, Fiona Jackson, Dieter Klein, Rosie Llewellyn-Jones, S. Muthiah, Foy Nissen, Jessica Smith, Robert Sykes, Giles Tillotson and Theon Wilkinson.

Special thanks are also due to the British Association for Cemeteries in South Asia, the British Council, INTACH and Thomas Cook; and to the staff of the following libraries and institutions: British Architectural Library/RIBA, British Library (India Office Records and Prints and Drawings Collection), National Army Museum, School of Oriental and African Studies, Trustees of the Victoria Memorial Library (Calcutta) and the libraries of Westminster City Council, Camden Council and Barnet Council.

The preparation of the maps and plans of the various sites and monuments was a daunting task, using diverse material drawn from a wide variety of sources. Many are appearing in print for the first time here. In London Nigel White worked tirelessly to turn the most basic material into intelligible standardized maps. K. S. Ravindran was responsible for the building plans.

Without the enthusiasm, efficiency and organizational skills of George Michell, author of the first volume of *The Penguin Guide to the Monuments of India*, I would never have had the stamina or incentive to complete the book. His support, interest and constructive advice have proved invaluable throughout the project.

Although many individuals helped to prepare this comprehensive volume, the author does not hesitate to accept full responsibility for any inaccuracies or inconsistencies which may have occurred. These are inevitable given the size and complexity of the task and the nature of available historical evidence. In the interests of accuracy the author would appreciate notification of any particular errors. Correspondence may be directed to the publisher in London.

PREFACE

To write a guidebook to India's historic buildings and monuments is to cover an area and a time-span almost equivalent to those that would be necessary for a treatment of the whole of Western European architecture from the time of Charlemagne to the present day! While few authors would venture to cover such a huge spectrum in a single volume, guidebooks on India do not hesitate to attempt such an ambitious task. A comparison of the state of Karnataka with West Germany gives an idea of the scale of the undertaking. They are equivalent in size, and probably have the same large number of historic buildings and sites. Because of the sheer scale and volume of work involved, most guidebooks on India have given even the major monuments inadequate coverage, often using sources over 100 years old. Other less familiar, but not necessarily less interesting, sites are generally omitted altogether. For some monuments there are detailed scholarly studies; other sites still await a professional publication. Much of the information in this volume is presented for the first time in a format intended for the traveller. The regional maps are the most detailed yet to appear in a work of this kind; many of the site maps have been specially commissioned.

Overall Aims

The two volumes of *The Penguin Guide to the Monuments of India* are intended as comprehensive handbooks to all the major monuments and sites. Volume I describes sacred Hindu, Buddhist and Jain buildings and their art, while this volume covers the Islamic, Rajput and European buildings and the principal Hindu secular buildings. In both volumes the entire country is covered, from Kashmir and the Himalayas in the north to Kanyakumari at the southernmost tip of the subcontinent, and from Assam in the east to Dwarka on the westernmost promontory of Gujarat. The time-span is equally comprehensive. Volume I runs from the earliest sacred monuments of the 3rd century BC up to those which have been erected in the present century. There is a chronological overlap between the two guides. This volume, dealing with the secular and sacred architecture of the Muslim, Rajput and European periods, includes forts, public buildings and monuments from the earliest traces of Islamic influence in India to independence and beyond. Much of the coverage of the European buildings reflects the radical reassessment of the architecture of British India which has taken place in recent years.

11

The two volumes have been designed to complement more conventional travel books, the best of which are *India: A Travel Survival Kit* (Melbourne: Lonely Planet Publications, 1987) and *India in Luxury* by Louise Nicholson (London: Century, 1985). In those books the visitor will find essential information on hotels, restaurants and shopping, as well as on the logistics of travel throughout the country. *The Penguin Guide to the Monuments of India* is unique in that it presents information about sites and buildings which are only sketchily covered, if at all, in other publications.

The first part of this volume is a general introduction to the religious, architectural, historical and artistic heritage of Islamic, Rajput and European India. The aim is to provide sufficient information to permit the traveller to appreciate the buildings, sculptures, paintings and monuments with a wider comprehension of their historical and social context. Obviously, these chapters are condensations of a vast and complex subject that encompasses a considerable diversity of cultural practices and beliefs. However, an attempt has been made to cover all the relevant aspects, without engulfing the reader in too many unfamiliar Indian names or technical terms. In general, place names have been spelt using the most popular current form – Varanasi rather than Benares, for instance. Elsewhere, anglicized spellings or names have been used where these would be more familiar to the reader – Jumna rather than Yamuna, Ganges rather than Ganga. Similarly, it is difficult to separate precisely references to the English and the British. Generally English refers to the period before the Act of Union of England and Scotland in 1707, and British to after, but where this would necessitate a change within a single section, usage has been standardized. For those who wish to pursue their interests in more detail, a list of important publications is also included.

The bulk of the information is contained in the second section, which is a gazetteer of the monuments. This is divided into six regions, each of which has an historical summary in which the chronological development of the sites is described. The town or site descriptions are arranged alphabetically and a map for each regional section indicates the location of the monuments, towns and sites. The maps have been fully annotated to indicate access roads and the nearest town from which transport can be obtained. So that the traveller can plan his itinerary in conjunction with the sites described in Volume I, these have also been indicated.

Visiting the Monuments

Many historic buildings and monuments of all periods come under the protection of the archaeological authorities, either of the Government of India or of the State, whose custodians are often in attendance. Some monuments are enclosed, and occasionally a small fee may be charged for admission. Visiting hours vary widely, depending on local situations and circumstances. It is common for these to be altered without warning, so it is prudent to check in advance. There are cases where visitors will need to show persistence to obtain access to local monuments, such as certain churches, but usually resident caretakers or custodians are only too pleased to accommodate the polite and interested traveller.

Photography is usually permitted, but many public buildings and monuments, such as law courts, government offices, military installations, stations and bridges, have strict security provisions, which should always be respected. Accredited local guides are available at most major sites. It is customary to give a small gratuity.

Monuments which are currently in use for worship, such as mosques, have specific regulations, which need to be respected. Like other worshippers, visitors will be required to dress appropriately. Shoes, hats and other proscribed articles may have to be deposited at the gateway, where a responsible custodian will charge a small fee. The times of visiting may be governed by the hours of worship. Visitors may be discouraged from entering during the main ceremonies or during certain festivals. In some areas buildings may also close at the hottest time of the day.

Museums are mentioned in this volume where they have notable collections from relevant buildings or sites. Generally they are closed on one day of the week and on public holidays. There is a small entrance charge and perhaps also an additional fee for taking photographs. Guidebooks are sometimes, but not always, available.

PART ONE

INTRODUCTION

Ceremonial Elephants

ONE

THE LAND AND THE PEOPLE

India is comparable in size to Western Europe. It has a total area of 3,287,782 square kilometres and a population of over 750 million, greater than the combined peoples of Africa, South America and Australia. Every four weeks the population increases by a further million. India's greatest achievement is to have survived over forty years of turbulent post-war history as a free nation, the world's largest democracy.

Each region of India is in itself a country, with strong ethnic and cultural characteristics. Although the regional basis of the country's population, languages and history prevented any overall cultural uniformity, the early growth of common social and religious systems acted as a cohesive supra-regional force. The continuing tension between these diversifying and unifying cultural tendencies is a common theme of Indian history and one which dominates the current political scene, as constituent parts of the modern Indian nation strive to assert their individual identity.

The Land

Divided by the Tropic of Cancer, the Indian peninsula protrudes into the ocean which bears its name. Isolated from the rest of Asia by the encircling ranges of the Himalayas, it extends from the Tibetan plateau in the north, across the great Gangetic plain and the Deccan, to the tropical shores of the Indian Ocean in the south. It is subcontinental in scale, no less than 3,200 km (2,000 miles) from north to south, and almost the same distance from east to west. Notwithstanding the great variety of terrain, from desert to jungle, there is the common climatic experience of a violent monsoon in the months from June to September. India's summer, from March to May, is hot, dry and dusty. In June the intense heat over the northern plain acts as a furnace as the air currents rise and move north of the mountains drawing the violent monsoon rains across the entire country.

The Indian Himalayas contain the highest mountain peaks in the world and comprise a continuous chain of ridges which defines the northern boundary of the subcontinent. Nanda Devi (7,816 m: 25,412 ft) is the highest mountain in India. Narrow valleys intrude into these mountains, some of which open up to form isolated self-contained regions, such as central Kashmir. The lowest valleys of the foothills, the Terai, are hot and sultry in summer, with a heavy rainfall in July. Other higher and more remote valleys extend into the Tibetan region further north.

17

Two great continental river systems have their origins in the Himalayas. The Indus flows southwards through Pakistan to the Arabian Sea, while the Ganges and Jumna flow eastwards, eventually joining the Brahmaputra in one great waterway that ends its journey in the Bay of Bengal. These riverine landscapes are flat and featureless. The Indus crosses the sandy desert of Pakistan, part of which extends into western India, the country's most arid region. Here in the Great Indian Thar Desert, in Rajasthan, is an area of haunting natural beauty. The Brahmaputra and lower Ganges flow through the wettest zone, which is in the east.

Central India has large expanses of low, wooded ridges, bordered on the north by the Vindhya hills and on the south by the westward-flowing Narmada and Tapti rivers. South of this region is the Deccan, an elevated plateau dramatically punctuated by granite and sandstone outcrops. This plateau is cut off from the Arabian Sea to the west by forested ridges known as ghats. On the east another line of ghats descends to the Bay of Bengal. The Deccan is traversed by the eastward-flowing Godavari and Krishna rivers. Their fertile coastal deltas contrast sharply with the dry plateau.

Southern India is generally wetter and more varied in elevation than the Deccan, counterpointed by rugged granite hills. The Cauvery, which is the principal river of the region, fans out into a fertile delta along the eastern Coromandel coast. The western Malabar coast, the wettest zone in the south, is bounded by wooded mountains, which define the limits of coastal Kerala and Kannara. The Coromandel and Malabar coasts meet at Kanyakumari, the southernmost tip of the Indian peninsula.

The People

A recurrent theme of Indian history is persistent invasion by peoples from the north-west, but ethnic and cultural differences also existed among the indigenous people, due to the regional basis of the country's population. India's densely populated river valleys and coastal deltas are separated from each other by vast expanses of mountains, forests and arid zones, which do not offer hospitable areas for habitation and settlement. In general much of the population has always been separated into these different fertile regions, each with its own distinctive language, religious practices and artistic traditions.

Peoples of northern, central, eastern and western India, as well as parts of the northern Deccan, speak languages which belong to the Indo–Aryan group. These can be traced to a common origin in the language introduced by the Aryans. These languages have given their names to some of the modern states of India, such as Bengal, Gujarat and Maharashtra. Urdu and its derivative, Hindi, reflect centuries of Persian influence in northern India. In contrast, southern India is dominated by indigenous languages of the Dravidian group. These have given their names to the modern states of Karnataka and Tamil Nadu.

There is a proliferation of religious traditions, some of them tribal in origin, which focus on local deities. In the ancient religious context of India hills, trees or caves have been revered for generations as auspicious places where divine forces are likely to manifest themselves. Each region has its own sacred geography, which is often overlain by countless layers of religious or sectarian devotion. It is not uncommon for the tombs of respected British officers to be worshipped as sacred, or for Muslims, Hindus and Buddhists to revere a common shrine.

For almost 2,000 years India's artistic traditions have been dominated by regional techniques and styles. With the advent of Islam in India, this diverse regional tradition continued. The dominating influence of Delhi and central Imperial power was never strong enough to suppress vigorous local traditions in the arts. Regional and provincial styles of architecture affected not just the form and appearance of buildings but often their layout as well. For instance, the mosques of Kashmir are wholly different from those of Golconda. Architectural forms also reflected the impact of local climate. Painting, literature and music displayed local influences, owing to the activities of long-established guilds of artists and craftsmen in different parts of the country.

Although considerable differences exist between the regions of India, there has always been a steady movement of people and ideas from one part of the country to another. Over the centuries this has fostered an intermingling of beliefs, cultures and artistic traditions and a remarkable tolerance of other creeds and races. With the establishment of Muslim rule under the Sultanate and later the Mughal Empire, and with the rise of British rule under the East India Company and the Raj, there was a major unifying influence which helped to counterbalance the tendency towards political and social fragmentation. In many ways the history of India can be seen as the perpetual interaction between central and regional authority and between cohesive and fragmentary forces.

Islam is based on the surrender of the self to the will of God. Daily devotional prayer is one of the pillars of the faith.

TWO

RELIGIOUS THEMES

Islam

Islam is a way of life, a transaction based on surrender of the self to the will of God. In India there are about 75 million Muslims, comprising approximately 10 per cent of the population. This makes them the largest religious minority.

Conceived in the early years of the 7th century, Islam is the youngest of the world's three great Semitic religions. Its founder, the Prophet Muhammad, was born in Mecca in about 570, the posthumous child of Abd Allah of the Hashim line. (Hashim is the name still carried by the royal family of Jordan.) His mother died when he was four, and he was raised by his grandfather and later by his uncle. Little is known of his childhood, but it is thought that he was influenced in his outlook by an early monotheist.

Muhammad is believed to have had his first mystical experience at the age of about forty in a series of visions of the archangel Gabriel, who hailed him as the rasul or the one who is sent, the Messenger of God. He preached in and around Mecca for about ten years, acquiring a considerable number of followers. He denounced idolatry and paganism, and conveyed his overriding conviction that there was one God alone and that there should be but one community of believers. His tremendous uncompromising vision of the majesty and unity of God was an open challenge to the polytheism which flourished in Arabia at this time, especially in Mecca, where the main temple, the Kaaba, housed more than 300 idols. Opposition to Muhammad grew so intense that in 622 he was forced to migrate from Mecca to Medina, an event known as the hijra. It is from the hijra that the Islamic calendar is dated.

At Medina Muhammad consolidated his new religion, Islam (literally Submission to God). He had left Mecca as a persecuted citizen, but returned in 630 as the leader of a religious community acknowledged to possess divine authority. There could be no compromise with idolatry. He was convinced that his message was for all Arabs and that those who refused to accept Islam had to be quelled, if necessary by force. By the preaching of war as a sacred duty or jihad, Muhammad induced his followers to attack Mecca.

Within two decades the Muslims (literally Those who have submitted) had conquered Syria, Iraq, Egypt and Turkey. By 670 the Arabs were in control of Iran. By the early 8th century they had reached the borders of southern France in the west and India in the east.

The Quran is a written record of what Muhammad said in his states of revelation. Much was recorded in haphazard fashion or passed on orally.

21

Tradition associates the collation of all this contemporary material with Abu Bakr, the first caliph, or his successor, Umar, but like the Bible, the text was arranged in an arbitrary manner, lacking any coherent chronological sequence. To Muslims the Quran is a faithful and unalterable reproduction of the original scriptures, which are preserved in heaven.

The God of Islam is seen as compassionate, rahman, and merciful, rahim. There is a strong connection between the Old Testament and the teachings of Muhammad. God is the sole creator of the universe. He who gave life will renew man's life after death, when the body will rise from the grave. The dominating theme is the warning of hell that awaits all idolators, the unjust and the selfish rich. For the faithful, the luxuries of Paradise are eulogized in flowing verses. God will forgive lesser crimes, but major sin will meet with divine retribution.

The basic spiritual tenets of Islam are summarized in the Five Pillars. A true Muslim must accept that 'There is no God but Allah, and Muhammad is his Prophet.' Prayer is the remembrance of the absolute sovereignty of God on earth, and its ritual symbolizes the humility of man in the presence of God. Therefore, a Muslim must pray five times a day. He must also perform acts of charity, like alms-giving; observe a fast from dawn to dusk during Ramadan, the month in which Muhammad received his divine revelation; and make a pilgrimage or hajj to Mecca at least once in his lifetime.

Notwithstanding its unique characteristics, Islam claims to be a continuation of the earlier religions of western Asia, particularly Christianity and Judaism. Indeed, the ritual code of Islam is based on that of Judaism as practised in Arabia at the time of Muhammad. Some festivals, for instance, include the celebration of Old Testament events, such as the sacrifice of Isaac (or Ismail, in the Islamic version), while Adam, Abraham, Moses and Jesus all recur frequently throughout the Quran. Jesus, in particular, is referred to as the spirit of God. Although many miracles are ascribed to him, he is regarded as just one of a series of prophets sent to all nations to show them the true path.

As Muhammad left no heir, when he died in 632 claims were pressed on behalf of his son–in–law and cousin Ali, but senior members of the community elected as their leader or caliph the Prophet's companion, Abu Bakr, one of his earliest converts. Religious schisms in Islam began at its very birth, leading to the formation of two principal sects: the Sunni and the Shia.

Sunnis and Shiites

Among the orthodox Sunni Muslims the caliph was regarded as the head of the community, responsible for the administration of justice through the sharia or law, and for the defence of the realm of Islam. He owed his position either to the choice of the community or to the nomination of his predecessor.

The Shia or Shian-i-Ali (partisans of Ali) Muslims maintained that in every age there was an infallible imam who alone was trusted by God with the guidance of his servants. The Shia taught that the faithful must believe in all the imams. This belief was made an additional pillar of the faith. The imam is regarded as a divinely appointed ruler and teacher of the faithful, the direct successor to the Prophet himself.

To the Muslim, idolatry in any form is an unforgivable sin. Wine and pork are eschewed; pride, arrogance and ostentation are reviled. The Quran expounds at length on many ethical and moral issues, including the position of women. For instance, the primary object of marriage is the procreation of children, and because of this, and for other reasons, a man is allowed four wives at a time. It is laid down that wives must be treated with kindness and strict impartiality. A dowry is paid to the woman at the time of marriage and this money or property remains her own. The husband may divorce his wife at any time, but he cannot take her back until she has remarried and been divorced by a second husband.

In India the first wave of Muslim rule was aggressive and uncompromising but gradually it adapted to the social and cultural context of the country and assimilated many local customs and traditions. Today it is not uncommon to find shrines or monuments revered by both Muslims and Hindus.

Sufism

The mystical thread in Islamic thought, Sufism, had a profound influence in India because it echoed many of the spiritual truths of Buddhism and Hinduism. The doctrines of Sufism are based on the importance of individual personal communion with God rather than on received wisdom and the strict laws of orthodox Islam. This mystical ideal, which arose in the 10th century, maintained that in order to reach God one needed to release the dormant intuitive spiritual force latent in all men and to 'travel the path'. The journey to God began with a spiritual awakening, a profound realization that the phenomenal world was a veil which concealed the divine. In India Sufis played an important part in disseminating a message of universal brotherhood and love which was often startlingly at variance with the more strident tone of conventional orthodox thought.

Early Sufi missionaries to India accompanied the first Muslim armies. The term 'sufi' probably derives from the simple woollen garments worn by these ascetic mystics, in contrast to the rich apparel of the wealthy; in Arabic 'suf' means wool. They were not a separate sect, but more a spiritual movement focussed around various gifted holy men, who formed specific religious orders. There were a large number of orders with different customs and traditions, but all accepted the necessity of submission to a guide. Many Sufis occupied powerful positions at court and served in both a spiritual and political capacity as guides and advisers to local magnates. For example, it was a Chishti saint who prophesied the birth of Akbar's son, Prince Salim, later the Emperor Jahangir, and this led to the founding of the city of Fatehpur Sikri in celebration.

The Chishti is the oldest of the Sufi orders in India. Begun in 966, it was introduced to India by the Sufi saint Khwajah Muin al-Din Chishti, who came to Delhi in 1192 with the army of Shahab-ud-Din Ghuri. He was buried at Ajmer in Rajasthan, where his tomb is an important centre of pilgrimage during the festival which commemorates the anniversary of his death in 1236. In the Deccan the Qadiri order was influential, named after its founder, Abd-al-Qadir al Gilani, who died in 1166. At Delhi Nizam-al-Din Auliya was revered in a similar fashion.

Sufi guides and spiritual counsellors were used by rulers to consolidate and strengthen their temporal power. Large endowments were made in exchange for moral and spiritual support, but this reliance on saints for their goodwill compromised the spiritual integrity of the Sufi mystics, who were taught to abhor political power. 'My room has two doors,' declared the Chishti saint Nizam-al-Din Auliya, whose order laid particular emphasis on avoiding temporal power: 'If the sultan comes through one door, I will leave by the other.' The only way a king could consult a Sufi was to visit the holy man's dwelling in complete humility, a popular theme in Indian Muslim painting.

For devout Muslims there are a number of sources of spiritual guidance. The first is the Quran, the word of God. It is omniscient, as God is indivisible. There is a right path which Man must follow if he hopes to reach Paradise.

The second source of guidance is the hadith, the body of traditions relating the Life of the Prophet, initially oral but later written, to support competing partisan interests. Out of the Quran and the hadith evolved the sharia or laws (literally The path leading to the water, i.e. the source of life). This body of theological law grew up as early Muslims tried to wrestle with the social and political problems which confronted them. There were four legal schools. In India the Hanafi school of law generally prevailed. The sharia is an all-embracing theocratic code covering all human activities, defining Man's relations both with God and his fellow-man. Its intention was to direct man along the true path. Human actions were classified on a five-point scale: obligatory, meritorious, indifferent, reprehensible and forbidden.

Early Sufi claims that their inner way was the true path leading to annihilation of the self and absorption in God brought them into direct conflict with the ulama or orthodox men of learning, who insisted that knowledge of God came through study of the Quran, the hadith and sharia. A complete schism was avoided by the work of one man, al-Ghazzali, the most influential Muslim figure after Muhammad, who died in 1111. His autobiography, *The Deliverer from Error*, charted his personal search for God. In it he demonstrated that it was possible to reconcile both paths in one man. As a result Sufism gathered enormous momentum, adding new elements to Islamic life and culture.

By 1500 most Indian Muslims approached God along the Sufi path, as the sharia struggled to come to terms with the spread of Sufi thought. Through Sufism many popular local religious customs were assimilated: singing, dancing and mystic feats such as walking on fire.

Belief in miracles performed by saints was widespread. The countryside was dotted with their tombs, which became venerated as shrines. The veneration of a disciple for his shaikh was the key to the transmission of mystical knowledge down the centuries. For much of the time in Islamic society the balance between spiritual and temporal power was maintained effectively. This can be seen as one of its greatest strengths.

The Rise of Islam in India

The history of India is dominated by the recurrent theme of foreign invasion. For centuries waves of invaders swept through the vulnerable passes of the north-west and across the fertile plains of the north, before the tides of conquest ebbed and died on the boundless plains of Hindustan.

The Aryans arrived in the middle of the 2nd millennium BC, followed by the

Kushanas in the 1st century AD, and then in the 6th century, the Hunas. But most significant of all were the Muslim invasions, which began as early as the 8th century. Each wave brought its own distinctive cultural practices and religious beliefs, yet eventually each was absorbed by the vast mass of the indigenous population. Layer upon layer of successive generations left rich cultural deposits in the stratified soil of Indian society.

Islam was first implanted in the lower Indus valley by the Arab governors of the Umayyad caliphs. In 711 Sind was conquered by Muhammad ibn Qasim on the crest of the earliest wave of Arab success, as Muslim armies drove west into Spain and the heartland of Christian Europe, and east into Persia, Transoxiana and Central Asia.

Qasim had been sent by the Governor of Iraq to combat piracy on the sea routes between the Arab lands and the west coast of India and Ceylon. He stormed the pirate stronghold of Debal, defeated the Brahmana king Dahir and reached the west bank of the Indus, before extending his conquests with the capture of the cities of Alor and Bahmannadad.

This initial wave of conquest was significant. For the first time it implanted Islam on Indian soil. It also brought the Arabs large numbers of slaves for use in the conquered lands, enabling the economic potential of the agricultural heart-lands of the Fertile Crescent to be fully exploited.

These early Muslims were instructed not to interfere with local religious customs or traditions and to tolerate Hindu practices. Unfortunately, only fragments of their ancient mosques survive. The remains of one from the early 8th century has been discovered 40 km (25 miles) east of Karachi at Bhambore, which may be the site of ancient Debal, scene of Qasim's victory.

After Muhammad ibn Qasim there was no large-scale Arab immigration. Arab influence gradually declined, although Sind and Multan, in what is now Pakistan, maintained links with Iraq and Egypt. This early Arab conquest had important repercussions for the future, for the political system introduced by Qasim provided the basis for later Muslim policy in India. In accordance with Muslim practice, Qasim treated the idolatrous Hindus with religious tolerance, as 'people of the book'. He conferred on them the status of zimmis or the protected. By the time of the establishment of Muslim supremacy at Lahore and Delhi, this liberal tradition was already well entrenched, diluting the stringent provisions of the sharia with regard to idol-worshippers and non-believers.

This initial contact was sustained for over 300 years, a local event in the history of Islam but a significant one in the history of India.

Although these early traces of Islam in India were eradicated almost entirely by subsequent raids, and, in particular by the multiple invasions of the Turks and Afghans, in the coastal areas of Gujarat and the Deccan there was extensive peaceful contact with the Islamic world, as there had been with the west in classical times.

At Bhadreshwar in Kutch, the Solah Khambi Masjid predates the great wave of Muslim invasions of the late 12th century and provides a tangible historical link with the remote coastal trading enclaves of early Muslim settlement in India. It was from these coastal colonies at ports such as Cambay and Chaul, and those further south on the Malabar coast, that Muslim missionaries travelled east to spread Islam to Malaya and Indonesia.

The full shock of Muslim military might hit India in the early 11th century when the Turkish Ghaznavids under Mahmud of Ghazni subjugated many of the Rajput rulers of the north-west, penetrated as far as Varanasi in the east, and sacked the legendary shrine of Somanatha in Saurashtra on the west coast in 1026. These annual raids only ceased when the Seljuk Turks took Ghazni in 1038.

With the rise of the Ghurids under Muhammad of Ghor in the 12th century, a large part of northern India was absorbed into an Islamic empire extending as far as the Caspian Sea.

The Ghurids dominated the inaccessible central region of Afghanistan. Their pugnacious zeal carried them both west and east, absorbing the remains of the Ghaznavid Empire. In 1192 they overthrew Prithviraj Chauhan, the legendary Rajput ruler of Ajmer and Delhi, on the battlefield of Tarain, where the mighty 'Hindu host tottered and collapsed in its own ruins'. Two years later the Hindu Gahadavala king of Varanasi and Kanauj succumbed.

The mounted archers of the Muslim armies were formidable shock troops. Time and again they wreaked havoc among the Hindu and Rajput forces, who were hampered by their reliance on ponderous elephants and battle trains. Within twelve years of the death of Prithviraj Chauhan, the Hindus of northern India were reduced to tributary status under the rule of the Muslim Slave dynasty.

The spearhead of the Muslim invasion, Qutb-ud-Din Aybak, was the most successful of all the commanders of Muhammad of Ghor. Appointed viceroy and placed in charge of all his master's conquests in India, he used his semi-autonomous position to carve out an extensive empire. He laid permanent foundations for the establishment of Muslim power in northern India.

Initially he consolidated his hold on the Punjab; then, in rapid succession, he seized Ajmer, stormed the fortress of Gwalior and conquered Delhi and Kanauj, reaching the distant stronghold of Kalinjar in the remote territory of Bundelkhand in 1203. Another Ghuri general, Ikhtiyar-ad-Din Muhammad Khalji, penetrated Bihar and Bengal, seized the ancient city of Gaur and attacked Assam.

With the death of Muhammad of Ghor in 1206, Qutb-ud-Din Aybak assumed power at Lahore. When the Afghan parts of the empire were severed from India by the Mongols, an independent dynasty was created, based on Delhi, the ancient capital of Prithviraj Chauhan, a strategic centre which controlled the corridor between the Himalayas and the Thar Desert. It was a great trading city, commanding the region between the Ganges and Jumna.

The Delhi Sultanate was the first major centralized Muslim kingdom in India. The Slave dynasty, begun by Qutb-ud-Din Aybak and maintained by his successors until 1290, was so called because three of its most important sultans – Aybak, Iltutmish and Balban – were former slaves who had received manumission before achieving royal power.

The power of the Sultanate was acknowledged throughout the north and west, although in many of the regions away from Turco-Afghan military control, the influence of the local Hindu and Rajput chiefs remained formidable.

The Architecture of Islam

As Islam developed in India, a complex interaction took place at all levels between the Muslim faith and established Hindu culture and practices, a two-way cross-fertilization of ideas and beliefs that wrought perceptible changes in both cultures. This process of interaction is obscure, but it had enormous repercussions for the development of the religious and cultural traditions of modern India.

One of the most obvious reasons for the success of the Islamic conquest of India and the spread of the faith at a popular level was the significant advantage which an open, dynamic and cosmopolitan society enjoyed when it met the static, closed societies of northern India, which had ceased to be receptive to alien influences.

In Bengal, for instance, the appeal of Islam for the depressed classes, with its emphasis on equality, was enormous. Here, the religion of the conquerors offered a powerful attraction, a prospect for advancement and liberation from the stifling restrictions of caste and class. Islamic missionaries capitalized on this. In a similar way to the early Christian tradition, by identifying ancient Hindu and Buddhist stories of miracles with Muslim saints, the older religions were fused with the new to maximize popular appeal. New mosques arose on the sites of ancient temples. This cultural interplay between the two societies was given its most tangible form in the architecture and monuments of the period.

Of all the civilizations encountered by the Muslims, none was more alien or diametrically opposed to their ideals and beliefs than that of Hinduism. This fundamental conflict was expressed most eloquently in the respective places of worship, the mosque and the temple. Each symbolized the innermost theological perceptions of its religion. The temple was mysterious, elusive, and complex – a dark sanctum coruscating with iconography and images and focussed on a central shrine. In contrast, the mosque was wholly intelligible – open, functional and devoid of imagery, with wall surfaces broken up by vividly painted or glazed surfaces, enriched with decorative calligraphy taken from the Quran.

Given this profound antithesis of spiritual and aesthetic ideals, it seems extraordinary that any sort of fusion could occur, yet in spite of fundamental differences of outlook and belief, a syncretism did develop. Each society was able to make its own contribution to the evolution of Indo-Islamic architecture.

On the one hand lay the ancient tradition of the Indian masons, who had built their great stone temples to the very limits of their artistic and structural abilities but, owing to the static nature of society, never developed new techniques or methods of construction. On the other lay the energetic, pluralistic traditions of the Muslim conquerors, who had absorbed new architectural principles and technical practices in their expansion east and west.

Stylistically, the Indian tradition was based on trabeated principles of construction using posts and beams, in contrast to the Muslims, who employed arcuated styles and introduced the arch to India. The Muslims also brought with them mortar masonry, which offered far greater versatility in design than the primitive method of placing one stone upon another. As Muslim influence spread, the ancient pointed spire or shikhara of Hindu temple architecture was counterpointed in the cities and countryside of India by the distinctive silhouette of the bulbous Islamic dome.

By the time the first Muslim buildings were raised in India, the constructional principles of Islamic architecture had been well established in the great mosques of Cairo and Damascus and elsewhere in the Islamic world. However, in India the presence of a large labour-force skilled in masonry building enabled widespread use to be made of stone construction rather than the plaster and rubble more commonly employed in the Middle East.

Mosques

The mosque or masjid (literally the place of prostration) is the principal social, political and religious centre of Islam, intended for daily prayers, one of the five pillars of the faith. Essentially, its form is derived from the humble house of the Prophet at Medina, an open courtyard surrounded by a colonnade of palm trunks covered with palm leaves. As the faith developed there was a need to develop an enclosed building where worship could be conducted in a separate environment. This dictated the form and plan of the mosque, which was maintained with relatively minor changes for centuries. In India the principal form and structure of the mosque were imported from Persia during the period of the Sultanate, with iwans or vaulted halls open at one end, enriched with highly decorated façades and domes.

Usually a mosque has a rectangular courtyard or sahn with the four sides enclosed by three shallow pillared cloisters and one deep portico, which serves as a covered hall of prayer and offers protection from the sun. In the centre lies a fauwwara or fountain or tank for ritual ablutions. To create a focal point for prayer, the cloisters on the Mecca side were enlarged into a sanctuary with a wall containing a recess or alcove, the mihrab, indicating the qibla or direction for prayer. To the right of the mihrab is the mimbar or pulpit, while part of the sanctuary is often screened off for the exclusive use of women. Many mosques have minarets, to provide a high platform from which the muezzin can summon the faithful to prayer. Most towns and cities of India have a Jami Masjid, a large congregational mosque, where the faithful assemble for Friday prayers.

An idgah is a mosque reduced to its bare essentials: an open praying area with a qibla and a mihrab intended for communal prayer on the festivals of the Breaking of the Fast and the Sacrifice of Abraham.

Architecturally, it was never easy to assemble these traditional requirements into a balanced, integrated composition. The treatment of the internal areas and, in particular, the courtyard, was always a problem in Indo–Islamic architecture. Given the significance of the mihrab as the direction for prayer, it was inevitable that this would be developed into the main architectural element. Usually, this was achieved by the development of a façade screen to the sanctuary and the creation of a large dome above, but the difficulty of reconciling the façade and dome was rarely overcome in India. As a result, most mosques enjoy an uneasy, unresolved duality whereby the dominating element of the dome is compromised by the parapet of the façade screen.

Tombs

There was no indigenous tradition of tomb building in India. The ashes of the dead were carried away by the sacred rivers. Even in Islam, tomb building was prohibited. For many centuries it was forbidden to glorify a grave by constructing a building over it, as this would run counter to the equality of all men in death. Veneration of tombs was regarded as an improper habit derived from

Christian and Jewish customs. However, by the time of the Muslim invasions of India in the 12th century, the proscription against tomb building was widely ignored. It seems ironic that a creed which began with stringent restrictions against all forms of monumental funerary art should develop in such a way as to produce the most splendid examples in the world.

In India a Muslim tomb or qabristan usually comprises a single vaulted domed chamber or huzra, in the centre of which is the cenotaph or zarih. Underneath lies the mortuary chamber or maqbara, with the grave or qabr in the centre. Sometimes the west wall contains a mihrab. Often some larger tombs have mosques attached as separate buildings, the whole ensemble being contained within an enclosure or garden and called a rauza.

The tombs of men and women may be distinguished easily. Generally, the former have a long, arched ridge along the top which slopes slightly north to south, while the latter have flat tops. The body lies with the head to the north, lying on the right-hand side, with the face towards Mecca. A vault is considered essential so that the body can sit up and reply to the angels of the grave.

Some particularly notable tombs are called dargahs, a Persian word meaning a court or palace. Often these contain the remains of Sufi shaikhs and are places of pilgrimage on the anniversary of the death of the saint, the urs. As spiritual descendants and disciples of the shaikh sought to be buried near their master, dargahs often contain a great concentration of tombs and graves, which militates against any sort of architectural cohesion. Sometimes a whole series of monuments in different styles and forms ranging over a period of 500 years can be found juxtaposed, obscuring the principal tomb.

The reason for this crowding against the qibla wall is the belief in baraka, a spiritual energy emanating from the grave of a saint or holy man. Great importance is attached to this psychic force.

The tombs of Humayun, Akbar, Jahangir and, above all, Shah Jahan rank with the Pyramids as the greatest funerary monuments in the world, but the concept of the tomb in a walled enclosure predated the Mughals. The word 'paradise' is a transliteration of the old Persian word 'pairidaeza', which means a walled garden. The location of a monumental tomb at the centre of an enclosed garden alluded to basic cosmological ideas. In essence it was the Garden of Eden that was lost to man through original sin, but it was also the Garden of Paradise. Inscribed over the entrance to Akbar's tomb at Sikandra are the words: 'These are the Gardens of Eden: enter them to dwell therein eternally.' The garden was a microcosm of the physical world, organized symmetrically and axially in accordance with contemporary cosmological beliefs. At the centre lay the tomb, the material universe, crowned by a dome, the symbol of eternity.

Madrasas

The concept of the madrasa as a separate institution from the mosque first developed in Central Asia. Essentially madrasas were teaching institutions set up by strictly orthodox Sunni Muslims to fight the Shia heresy and to maintain and transmit the central traditions of the faith. Their architectural form was not dissimilar to that of an Oxford or Cambridge college, with four axially placed iwans or vaulted halls disposed around a central courtyard. The iwans, flanked by

29

cells and rooms for students and teachers, were almost always on two storeys, although at Bidar and in Delhi some have three.

Madrasas were endowed by pious or public-spirited rulers to perpetuate the true faith. The main subjects which were taught seem to have been religious: tafsir, the interpretation of the Quran; hadith, tradition; and fiqh, jurisprudence. The intellectual vitality of the schools owed much to the influx of refugee scholars from Central Asia and Persia in the 13th century in the wake of the Mongol invasions. In the Deccan, where contact with Persia and Egypt was maintained through maritime links, intellectual activity was broader, encompassing scientific subjects such as botany, astronomy, geometry and logic. The madrasa of Mahmud Gawan at Bidar is a magnificent example of this type. In the north, other than religious subjects, literature, history, mysticism and ethics were the principal topics taught. Medicine also received widespread attention in all schools.

Khanqahs

With the development of Sufism as a popular movement, organized monastic brotherhoods of mendicants appeared: faqir in Arabic or darwish in Persian. All Sufi orders believed in the absolute importance of a pir or shaikh, a spiritual guide, who would gather about him a brotherhood. The pir's residence was the centre of a particular order, and khanqahs or monastic mosques or retreats were established by endowment all over India and the Islamic world for kindred souls.

Decorative Arts

Decorative art plays a crucial role in Islamic architecture. It envelops buildings like a mantle, with the intention of concealing rather than revealing the structure. The key elements are geometry, calligraphy and foliation.

The façades of Islamic buildings are rigorously controlled by primary and secondary grids, which create frames within which elevations are strictly organized. The most famous example is the Taj Mahal, with its central pointed arch contained within a rectangle, a motif which is repeated in a reduced form on the flanking niches. The repetitive use of this simple but powerful motif imparts a basic unity to the entire composition.

Geometry plays a crucial role in Islamic architecture, not only in the form and massing of a building but also in its surface treatment. In India this achieved its most sophisticated expression in the pietra dura work of the Mughals, whereby inlaid multicoloured stones were employed to create surface patterns of dazzling profusion and richness. Occasionally these were offset by changes of texture as well as colour, by the use of mirror work or by carved or incised patterns which accentuated the overall play of light and shade. Arcuated, circular and complex stellate patterns were all employed to impart richness and variety. Vivid colour, repetitive motifs, symmetrical composition and dramatic changes of scale were guiding principles. Often the treatment was extended to ceilings and floors. The Tomb of Itmad-ud-Daula at Agra, for instance, has a marble floor which reproduces the designs of Mughal carpets of the period.

Given the Muslim proscription against figurative art, calligraphy was incorporated into many Islamic buildings. It was regarded as the highest of the arts. 'Good writing makes the truth stand out' runs an ancient Muslim saying. The words of the Quran were an important unifying decorative theme in Islamic architecture. Arabic lettering was developed to a high degree of sophistication, with scripts varying from flowing cursive forms to the angular kufi. The famous Qutb Minar in Delhi has deeply carved bands of Quranic epigraphy around the base, framed by ribbons of foliated decoration.

Foliated decoration is a central theme of Islamic art. Classical vine and scroll designs offered an infinite repertoire of sinuous forms. Flowers, leaves, stalks and stylized foliage had been popular accessory themes in Hindu sacred art for centuries. Vegetal ornament evoked the generative forces of nature. To the Hindu the lotus floating on water served as a ubiquitous emblem of perfection, while animals and birds symbolized essential aspects of the divine personality.

Frequently, lotuses were combined with geometric motifs or multi-lobed designs to create elaborate fantasies. In the Hindu cosmos dense sprays of foliation or scrollwork were symbols of nature's fecundity. In Islamic India this ancient tradition was manipulated by the Muslims to create exquisite ornamental patterns to enrich the exteriors of buildings. One of the most famous examples is the delightful stone screen in the mosque of Sidi Sayyid in Ahmadabad, where the curling tendrils of intertwined leaves and flowers form sinuous abstract shapes in a wonderful synthesis of the Islamic and Hindu traditions. More generally, foliated ornament and arabesques were used by the Mughals both in carved relief and in decorative polychromy.

The interplay of light and shade was another vital component of Islamic architecture, not merely externally but also in the internal treatment of spaces. The most popular device for regulating temperature and atmosphere was the pierced stone screen or jali. In India some superb examples were created using repetitive geometric designs, often carved from a single block of marble. The screens at the tomb of Shaikh Salim Chishti at Fatehpur Sikri or at the Rang Mahal in the Fort at Delhi are some of the finest in existence.

Coupled with the manipulation of light and shade, water provided an essential complement to Islamic buildings, offering an additional, dynamic perspective. In the gardens of Mughal India water was employed not only to reflect the buildings and to multiply their decorative themes but also to enhance their overall impact and to accentuate visual axes and symmetry. Long rectilinear pools of water and channels provided an additional framework of control for the architecture and added a whole new perspective. In some Mughal buildings, such as the Rang Mahal at Delhi, water was an integral part of the actual building, channelled under screens and across floors to provide a unifying directional sequence and theme for the entire building.

Other Religious Influences

The theological doctrines of Buddhism, Jainism and the vast amalgam of cults and devotional movements which make up the religion known as Hinduism are set out in Volume I. However, there are several other significant religious groups which form influential local minorities.

Parsees

The Parsees fled their native Persia in the face of persistent Muslim persecution and arrived in India around 766. They brought with them the ancient Persian religion of Zoroastrianism, one of the world's oldest religions and one of the first to postulate belief in a single, omnipotent and invisible God. Based on the teachings of the Prophet Zarathustra, it can be traced to the 6th century BC. Today there are only about 85,000 Parsees in the world, concentrated in and around Bombay, but they form an influential and powerful minority, dominating commercial and industrial life with a long and august tradition of philanthropy.

Theologically they endeavour to follow the 'path of Asha', a path of action in good thoughts (humata), words (hukta) and deeds (huvarshta), hence their philanthropic tradition. Their scripture is the Zend Avesta, which describes the eternal conflict between the forces of good and evil in a dualistic universe. The god of light, Ahura Mazda, is symbolized by fire.

The focus of religious life is the fire temple. Within these agiaries the sacred flame is always kept burning. The office of priest or dastur is hereditary. Parsees believe in the purity of the elements. They do not cremate or bury their dead, as this would pollute the earth, air, fire or water, but leave their bodies on the Towers of Silence, where they are stripped of their flesh by vultures. Physically many Parsees retain their Persian features. Their numbers are slowly diminishing.

Jews

There are two ancient Jewish communities in India: the Marathi-speaking B'nai Yisroel and the Malayam-speaking Jews of Cochin. Although their numbers have never exceeded 30,000, their survival is a testimony to the tolerance of successive generations of Hindus and Muslims, among whom they have lived for over 1,000 years.

The Jews of Kerala are reputed to have settled there as early as 567 BC, after the destruction of the Temple at Jerusalem. Today there are only about 5,000 remaining but synagogues exist in Calcutta, Pune, Delhi, Cochin and other great cities.

Christians

There are about 25 million Christians of a multitude of denominations in India. The earliest communities were the result of the ancient evangelization of St Thomas the Apostle in southern India from 52 onwards. Later, a Christian connection developed with the see of Seleucia–Ctesiphon in Mesopotamia from about 450, but active Christian missionary work really began with the Portuguese and, in particular, St Francis Xavier, from 1542.

In the 18th century Protestant missionaries from Denmark, Holland and Germany, such as the famous Frederick Christian Schwartz, were active in India, but the establishment of English supremacy gave the Anglican church a distinct advantage. The work of William Carey and his followers, Joshua Marshman and

William Ward, at Serampore was particularly important, as they established the first printing press and newspaper in Bengali.

Missionaries were usually regarded with suspicion by the British authorities as they tended to disturb the deeply conservative basis of Indian life and culture, but the influence of Christian thought was profound. In some tribal areas, such as Mizoram or Nagaland on the North-East Frontier, Christians now form a majority of the population, and both Rabindranath Tagore and Mahatma Gandhi were deeply influenced by Christianity.

The Tomb of Ghiyath-ud-Din Tughluq, Delhi

THREE

THE SULTANATE STYLE

The Sultanate style is a generic term covering the architectural heritage of five successive Muslim dynasties which ruled from Delhi in a continuous display of centralized power for over three and a half centuries. The surviving examples of this form of Indo-Islamic architecture demonstrate every stage in the development of the style, from the early use of salvaged temple masonry to the stately tombs of the Lodi dynasty.

The style can be divided into five distinct phases, corresponding to the respective ruling dynasties: the Slave, 1206–1290; the Khalji, 1290–1320; the Tughluq, 1320–1414; the Sayyid, 1414–45; and the Lodi, 1451–1526. Sometimes these are referred to as Early Pathan, 1206–1320, Middle Pathan, 1320–1414, and Late Pathan, 1414–1557. For details of the dynasties, see the dynastic tables on pages 585–91.

The Slave Dynasty, 1206–1290

With the assassination of Muhammad Ghuri of Ghor in 1206, control of his Indian possessions passed to his slave governor, Qutb-ud-Din Aybak, who made no new conquests but consolidated Muslim dominion by an even-handed policy of conciliation and patronage. He converted the old Hindu stronghold of Qila Rai Pithora into his Muslim capital and commenced two magnificent mosques at Delhi and Ajmer.

The Quwwat-ul-Islam mosque at Delhi, begun in 1193, has arcaded aisles of richly carved salvaged Hindu masonry taken from twenty-seven temples disposed around a central courtyard, in the centre of which lies the famous Iron Pillar. Architecturally, the overall effect was one of confused improvisation, until in 1199 it was articulated by an expansive arched screen erected across the sanctuary. This noble, richly carved edifice of pointed arches was a major attempt by indigenous craftsmen to turn their hands to a wholly new and alien architectural concept.

In the same year Aybak commenced the remarkable Qutb Minar, a huge tower 73m (238 ft) high, proclaiming the prestige and authority of Islam to the world and intended, according to the inscriptions, 'to cast the shadow of God over the East and over the West'. Although minars and towers recur across the Muslim world, the Qutb is unique in Islamic art both in its size and its conception, a perpetual memorial to the creative genius of its patron.

At Ajmer Aybak was responsible for the Arhai-din-ka Jhonpra mosque, an important early Indo-Islamic building commenced in 1200, also using salvaged temple masonry but in a more composed fashion than the rather chaotic juxtaposition of elements employed at Delhi.

The second great architectural patron of the Slave dynasty, Shams-ud-Din Iltutmish (1211–36), was responsible for four major works, including the first example of a monumental tomb, erected over the remains of his son Nasir-ud-Din Muhammad in 1231.

His first great project was the construction of an ornamental screen across the sanctuary of the mosque at Ajmer. Only twenty-five years separated this from the work of Aybak at the Quwwat-ul-Islam mosque in Delhi, but the stylistic changes are pronounced. The main arch is less curved, almost four-centred, while four of the smaller side arches are multifoil. However, it is the change in surface decoration and ornament which is so significant. The exquisitely carved floral decoration applied to the screen at Delhi by Hindu masons has been eschewed in favour of more stylized conventional patterns, a direct result of the Islamic rejection of imagery.

The remaining works of the reign of Iltutmish can be found at Delhi. Here a large extension was added to Aybak's original mosque by enlarging the arched screen and enclosing the entire composition within a grand courtyard. While this is relatively conventional in form, the tomb of his son was revolutionary, a major development of Indo-Islamic funerary architecture.

The culmination of the architecture of the Slave dynasty was the Tomb of Iltutmish, built around 1236, just outside the north-west angle of his mosque extension in the Qutb complex. The most startling aspect of this building is the lavishly carved interior, inlaid with white marble and Quranic inscriptions, but it is also an early instance of attempts by Hindu masons to construct a dome over a rectangular compartment by the use of a squinch or angled arch in each of the corners of the hall.

With the death of Iltutmish the Sultanate suffered severe reverses. The Hindus reasserted themselves and the Mongols pressed forward to attack Lahore in 1241. With the accession of Nasir-ud-Din Mahmud Shah I, this period of confusion ended, but real power was vested in the hands of Ghiyath-ud-Din Balban, a member of a noble family of Ilbari Turks, who eventually became sultan in 1266. Balban's main efforts were concentrated on consolidating his dominion and enhancing royal status. Architecturally, the most significant building of his reign was his own tomb, built around 1280. Now a ruin, it is the earliest instance in India of a building containing a true arch, produced by radiating voussoirs, an indication of the increasing sophistication of the local masterbuilders of the day.

The Khalji Dynasty, 1290–1320

With the end of Balban's highly personalized autocratic rule, power passed to a number of ineffectual or wayward sultans who were unable to control the fierce rivalries of the factions struggling to seize power. Eventually Jalal-ud-Din Firuz Shah II was proclaimed sultan in 1290.

The Khalji people were one of a number of Turkish clans who had lived for generations near Ghazni in Afghanistan. Rivals of the aristocratic Ilbari Turks, their seizure of power marked a major social revolution as Muslim government ceased to be the preserve of the old Turkish ruling families. This generated considerable social momentum, leading to further expansion and conquest in the south.

Jalal-ud-Din was murdered by his nephew Ala-ud-Din Muhammad Shah I, a bold and decisive military leader, whose twenty-year reign witnessed an enormous resurgence of Muslim power. His reign can be divided into three phases.

Between 1296 and 1303 he defeated the Mongols, reconquered Gujarat and seized the great fortress of Ranthambhor. In 1303 he reduced Chitor and the remaining Hindu strongholds in Rajasthan. Over the next four years he consolidated his position. Two years later he annexed Malwa, then conquered Ujjain, Chanderi and Mandawar in quick succession. From 1307 to 1313, he completed the conquest of south India, where, with the exception of Daulatabad, the conquered territories were ruled by local rajas who paid an annual tribute to Delhi.

Ala-ud-Din Khalji was essentially a fighting soldier with exceptional delusions of grandeur. He saw himself as the new Alexander. His court attracted a dazzling array of Muslim luminaries such as the poet Amir Khusrau and the historian al-Baruni. His architectural projects not only reflected his own ambitions but also the grandiloquent view he had of himself and his place in the world.

In the field of architecture little progress had been made since the death of Iltutmish in 1236, but in the dynamic atmosphere of Ala-ud-Din's court a decisive advance took place. A scheme was devised to build an enormous congregational mosque around the Qutb complex by enclosing the existing buildings in a gigantic new arcaded courtyard. In the centre was planned the Alai Minar, a colossal tower designed to dominate even the neighbouring Qutb Minar.

Only one part of this great project was completed, the Alai Darwaza or Gateway of Ala-ud-Din, in 1305. Here it is possible to trace a much more assured relationship between the dome and the cube beneath than had been seen hitherto in India. For the first time since Balban's tomb twenty-five years earlier, the squinches of corner arches and the dome are all built of true arches. It is a delightful composition, with a spearhead fringe to the central arch invigorated by the use of red and white marble. The jali screens to the windows, enriched with star and hexagon patterns, are early examples of one of the greatest joys of Muslim architecture.

It was Ala-ud-Din who founded the second city of Delhi at Siri. Today these remains are so fragmentary that little can be discerned, the ruins having been ravaged for building materials over centuries. The Jamaat Khana Masjid at the Dargah of Nizam-ud-Din Auliya is the only other notable building of the period, less successful than the Alai Darwaza but important for several innovations, such as the transformation of the liwan into one uninterrupted hall.

The architectural achievements of the Khalji dynasty were not just confined to the capital. At Chitorgarh the bridge below the fortress was built at this time by Ala-ud-Din. At Bayana the Ukha Masjid is a late example of the Khalji style, built by Qutb-ud-Din Mubarak Shah (1316–20), but in a diluted and rather provincial manifestation of the Sultanate style.

The Tughluq Dynasty, 1320–1414

In 1320 Khalji rule was usurped by Khusraw Shah in a bloody palace coup. Its success was shortlived, owing to the resistance of the military governor of Multan, Ghiyath-ud-Din Tughluq Shah I, who became sultan in the same year. His father was Turkish, but his mother was a Hindu. Later he took a Hindu wife and introduced large numbers of Hindus into government service.

The Tughluq dynasty established the strongest and most creative state in the history of the Delhi Sultanate. It laid the foundations of a distinctive, unitary Indo-Muslim culture which was to provide the bedrock of later Mughal rule.

Of the eleven rulers of the Tughluq dynasty, only three were interested in architectural patronage: the founder of the dynasty, Ghiyath-ud-Din Tughluq (1320–25); his son Mahmud Tughluq Shah II (1325–51); and Firuz Tughluq Shah (1351–88). Each added his own capital city to those already in existence at Delhi.

In this period Indo-Muslim architecture was transformed from a provincial version of Ghurid forms into an assertive, self-generating style of its own. Materials and techniques were standardized and royal involvement organized through a hierarchy of engineers and architects. It was a period of fertile eclecticism and energetic experimentation which marked a watershed in the history of India's Islamic architecture.

Ghiyath-ud-Din Tughluq Shah I was an old man when he ascended the throne. His efforts were concentrated on the creation of a formidable new defensive fortress at Tughluqabad, the third city of Delhi.

The fortifications of the city are in two parts: the central citadel and the main city and outer walls. The most distinctive feature of the Tughluq style is the use of battered or sloping walls which rake back at an angle of about 75 degrees, an echo of the old mud-brick walls of ancient Arab cities, carried eastward and reproduced here in massive masonry construction. Initially the Sultanate looked west for its architectural forms. Ghiyath-ud-Din was familiar with the brick tombs of the Multan region, where the most characteristic feature was the use of sloping walls, and it is likely that the precedent was taken from his experience there.

The outer walls of Tughluqabad are over 6·5 km (4 miles) long, reinforced with immense, sloping, battlemented circular bastions. Architecturally, the most important monument is the famous tomb of Ghiyath-ud-Din, which stands in an irregular pentagonal enclosure forming an outwork to the main city. It was built *circa* 1325 and is 19 m (61 ft) square, with distinctive angled walls set at a 75-degree camber. Here, for the first time, two further architectural developments took place. Each arch is complemented by a lintel installed beneath the springing-point, a curious combination of elements that became the hallmark of the Tughluq style. The second innovation is the dome, which is crowned by a kalasha finial, commonly used on Hindu temples.

Muhammad Tughluq Shah II, the son of Ghiyath-ud-Din, is ascribed with the construction of the fourth city of Delhi, Jahanpannah or 'World's Refuge'. In reality he merely enclosed the area between the first and second cities by means of fortified walls, most of which have disappeared since. However, the Bijai Mandel, a remnant of a wider complex, suggests that the art of good building was being maintained if not developed. It was Muhammad Tughluq II whose

38

disastrous attempt to move the capital from Delhi to Daulatabad almost destroyed the city. It was left deserted and desolate, and it was only through the energy and dynamism of his successor, Firuz Tughluq Shah III (1351–88), that Delhi revived and the Tughluq style came to fruition.

Firuz Tughluq Shah III was a prolific builder, but the misguided actions of his predecessor in relocating the capital dispersed the reservoir of skilled masons and masterbuilders which had once been concentrated at Delhi. This hampered its subsequent development.

Accordingly, many of the buildings of his reign, particularly of the early part, comprise random rubblework and render rather than dressed stone or ashlar. The ornament is inscribed in plaster rather than carved. None the less, the influence of the Multani tombs persisted, with battered walls accentuated by tapering turreted buttresses at the quoins and projecting conical towers crowned by low domes.

When the water supply around the Qutb area became unreliable, the decision was made to move the capital to the north, on the banks of the Jumna.

Begun in 1354, Firuzabad became the fifth city of Delhi, a more sophisticated elaboration of the fortified capital of Tughluqabad. It was intended to be a fully self-contained and comfortable royal residence. The Firuz Shah Kotla is now in ruins, but originally its range of private palaces facing the river and its impressive public halls and gardens must have provided a fitting and noble setting for the sultan and his Imperial administration. Towards the centre of the complex, raised high on a curious stepped pyramidal structure, is one of Ashoka's famous pillars, relocated here from Ambala, an architectural totem identifying the Tughluq dynasty with the great Imperial ruler of the Mauryas.

Firuz Tughluq Shah III was also responsible for the founding of the fortified cities of Fathabad, Hissar and Jaunpur. Literally hundreds of mosques were built during his reign. The most characteristic in Delhi are the Kali Masjid (1370), Kalan Masjid (1375) and Begumpura Masjid (1370). They all share common traits, with tapering walls and circular quoins at the entrances and corners in the rear wall of the maqsura. The most prominent feature is the massive arched and buttressed pylon, which dominates the entire composition, including the dome.

Two of the tombs of this period are of major significance. The tomb of Firuz Tughluq Shah III is situated within the Hauz-i-Khas, a beautiful complex of palaces built by Ala-ud-Din Khalji some seventy-five years earlier around an ornamental lake. Firuz Shah built a mosque at the northern end of the tank and a madrasa along the northern and western banks. At the junction of the two wings of the madrasa, he built his own tomb, executed in characteristic Tughluq style: powerful, restrained and austere, with sloping masonry walls crowned by a parapet of merlons and a handsome contoured dome. The tomb of Khan-i-Jahan Tilangani, his Prime Minister, who died in 1369, is remarkable because it was a prototype which influenced tomb building in India for over 200 years. Unlike its massive predecessors, the tomb is a more elegant conception, octagonal in shape with a projecting eaves cornice or chajja and a series of eight small cupolas over the parapet, prefiguring many of the more opulent compositions which were to develop later in northern India and elsewhere. The use of the chajja was a new departure, adding a fresh dimension to Islamic architecture in India. Culled from Hindu sources, these projecting sun-breaks cast deep shadows, introducing new opportunities for manipulating light and shade on the façades of buildings.

Unlike their predecessors, the Tughluqs did not make lavish use of architectural epigraphy. The number of extant religious inscriptions is very limited.

Firuz Shah Tughluq is credited with the building of over 200 towns, 100 mosques, thirty madrasas, more than 150 bridges, as well as countless dams, reservoirs, hospitals and baths. The preservation and restoration of the monuments of earlier kings, such as the Qutb Minar, were also accorded high importance. The price of this enormous expansion in Imperial infrastructure was the administration itself.

Royal taste and patronage were key factors in the dissemination of Tughluq rule and architectural style. The creation of such an enormous corpus of buildings, Islamic institutions, towns and cities spread Imperial styles far beyond Delhi. The monuments of the Sharqi dynasty of Jaunpur and the Bahmanis in the Deccan owed much to Tughluq antecedents, while the tomb developed into the creative focus of Muslim architecture in India.

On the death of Firuz Shah civil war broke out between his son and grandson. The Hindu chiefs threw off their allegiance and the provincial governments asserted their independence. This chronic weakness at the heart of the Sultanate led to its downfall.

In December 1398 the fearful Timur, the ferocious grandson of Ghengis Khan, swept across India and sacked Delhi in an orgy of destruction. Timur created a 'wilderness adorned with pyramids of skulls of those he had slain', before he defeated Mahmud Tughluq Shah II outside Delhi.

With the collapse of Tughluq resistance, Timur resolved to flatten Delhi, so that his own capital of Samarkand should be without rival in any country. Delhi was to be left desolate, so that 'no craftsman, of whatever craft he be, shall be found any more in thee'. He released 15,000 seasoned Turks on the city to slay and plunder at will. It is said that over 100,000 Hindu inhabitants were 'despatched to hell by the proselytizing sword' of the Mongol hordes. Timur looted what remained and carried off hundreds of craftsmen, masons and materials to enrich Samarkand. As the dust settled on his retreating hordes, the sacked and looted capital was devastated by a famine so severe that for two months 'not a bird moved a wing in Delhi'.

Although Mahmud Shah II returned and ruled until 1414, he was unable to perpetuate the Tughluq succession.

The dispersal of the craftsmen and masterbuilders from Delhi forced those who had escaped enforced service in Samarkand to look elsewhere for patronage and commissions. With the collapse of centralized rule from Delhi, many of the erstwhile governors of provinces such as Bengal, Gujarat, Jaunpur and Malwa proclaimed independence and began their own provincial dynasties. Each had its own distinctive architectural flavour. These are examined in more detail in Chapter 4.

The Sayyid and Lodi Dynasties, 1414–45 and 1451–1526

In the century between the collapse of the Tughluq dynasty and the emergence of the Mughals in the early 16th century, two significant historical processes can be traced in Muslim India.

The first was the slow but inexorable disintegration of the centralized Imperial power of the Sultanate. The second was the consequent rise of a number of independent regional kingdoms.

Imperial power shrank to a mere shadow of its former self. Under the diminished influence of the Sayyid and Lodi dynasties the only significant architectural developments were in funerary architecture. Because of its Imperial association, countless tombs and mausolea were raised in and around Delhi. Three large and stately octagonal tombs demonstrate the manner in which the prototype of Tilangani's tomb was adapted and refined over the ensuing century. These are the tomb of Mubarak Sayyid (1435), the tomb of Muhammad Sayyid (1445) and the tomb of Sikander Lodi (1517).

The most characteristic and accomplished example is that of Sikander Lodi. The dome was constructed with an inner and outer shell of masonry with a space between the two. This was intended to achieve a loftier silhouette and a more imposing impact without destroying the proportions of the internal chamber below. The tomb lies in an elaborate formal garden rather than on the barren plain of the surrounding countryside, and thus it anticipates the great garden tombs of the Mughals.

Another distinctive characteristic of this period was the popularity of the more conventional 'cube and hemisphere' type of tomb, with 'boat-keel' domes. These became so common that they were called 'gumbads' (literally domes). Most are isolated structures without enclosing walls. The most notable are the Bara Khan-Ka Gumbad (1497), the Chota Khan-Ka Gumbad and the Bara Gumbad (1497), the latter with traces of coloured tile decoration. All are impressive for their size and for the robust confidence of their lofty domes.

Although no large public mosques were built during this period, several private structures were raised which incorporated interesting changes from established practice and these paved the way for the great mosques of the Mughal period. In the two Delhi mosques, the Moth-Ki-Masjid (1505) and the Jamala Masjid (1536), the Tughluq device of a large central pylon was discarded in favour of a more open, arcuated style, albeit in a very bold and bare manner, unadorned by any modelling or refinement of the vast mass of masonry.

Architectural styles do not fit neatly into an overall dynastic framework. The Lodi style continued into the Mughal period for some time. The Jamala Masjid was actually built in the reign of Humayun, while as late as 1564 the tomb of Muhammad Ghaus at Gwalior embodied all the elements of the Lodi style, even though the ornamental features were derived from Gujarat. Indeed, it is possible to regard the great tombs of distant Bihar, erected by Sher Shah Sur in the mid-16th century, as part of the evolution and continuing development of the Lodi tradition.

Sikander Lodi was a patron of learning who attracted many scholars and poets to his court, including the famous mystic Jamali. Although Sikander has been accused of religious bigotry, it is evident that many Hindus began to adjust to new conditions. Many started to learn Persian. This period was one of constructive mutual exchange as both Hindus and Muslims became interested in each other's culture and learning.

Sikander was succeeded in 1517 by his son Ibrahim Lodi II, but he alienated many of his Afghan nobles and military commanders, with the result that Daulat

Lodi Khan, governor of the Punjab and the Sultan's uncle, invited Babur, the ruler of Kabul, to invade India.

Babur's victory over Ibrahim Lodi at Panipat on 21 April 1526 was a major turning-point in the history of India. With an army only one-tenth the size of his opponent, Babur devastated Ibrahim's ponderous force of 100,000 men and slew the last scion of the Lodi dynasty on the field of battle. The age of the Mughals had begun.

FOUR

THE PROVINCIAL STYLES

With the disintegration of the power and authority of the Delhi Sultanate on the collapse of the Tughluq dynasty in the early 15th century, the rise of provincial independent kingdoms prevented the eclipse of Muslim power in India. Ironically, in many ways it was strengthened, as the loose suzerainty of Delhi was replaced by a much more effective administration under the aegis of local rulers.

The rise of these kingdoms gave renewed impetus to the spread of Islam and Muslim culture. While under the Sultanate, Delhi was the major seat of Islamic learning and religion, in the 15th century and onwards Ahmadabad, Gaur, Gulbarga, Jaunpur, Pandua and other provincial capitals also became centres of Muslim life and culture. It was in these provincial kingdoms, where Muslims were not in a majority, that a much greater synthesis with indigenous cultures occurred.

Unlike the Imperial government in Delhi, the provincial kingdoms were not preoccupied with the Mongol incursions or the problems of central administration. They were able to nurture literary and cultural activities, which flourished in many of the provincial capitals. Music was actively patronized, for instance, in Gujarat, Jaunpur, Kashmir, and Malwa. Provincial languages developed in place of Persian. But it was in the field of architecture that vernacular and Imperial influences intermingled to form a whole host of provincial styles.

A decisive factor in this process was the character of the indigenous arts which prevailed in each region. Where these were strong, local artisans and master-builders turned from producing temples to designing and building elegant mosques and tombs.

Seven major provincial styles developed between 1150 and 1650. These are indicated in the Historical Chronology of Key Events on pages 581–4. Although the provincial style of the Punjab, centred on Multan and Lahore, was influential, particularly for the architectural designs of the Tughluqs, virtually all the major sites are now in Pakistan and they therefore lie outside the scope of this book. Full details of the buildings designed in the other provincial styles are set out in the gazetteer. In order to relate these to the wider context, the following brief résumé of the major styles might be helpful.

Bengal, c. 1336–1576

Independent Bengal was ruled by a succession of dynasties. Two are significant: the Ilyas Shahi, which ruled from 1345 to 1414 and from 1437 to 1487; and the

The Chowkhandi at Bidar

Husain Shahi, which ruled from 1494 to 1539. In particular, Sayyid Ala-ud-Din Husain Shah (1494–1519) and his son Nasir-ud-Din Nusrat Shah (1519–32) were competent liberal rulers and great patrons of the arts. Both left magnificent buildings at Gaur and Pandua and both encouraged the development of Bengali language and literature.

The Islamic heritage of Bengal is strongly conditioned by the geography and climate of the region. In the flat delta region of Bengal, the entire world seems impermanent. The land is subject to devastating floods. Water courses silt up. Cultivated land is submerged by erratic changes in patterns of fluvial drainage. Coupled with the extreme humidity and high rainfall, this encouraged the development of more transient vernacular forms of buildings, which could be replaced as and when necessary, using cheap local materials such as thatch and bamboo. The characteristic curved roof of the Bengali huts was a direct response to the demands of the climate, but it became a vernacular convention which was taken up by the Muslim overlords and reproduced in a more permanent form in brick and plaster, terracotta and, sometimes, stone.

The development of Islamic architecture in Bengal is set out in the introduction to the various regional of the section. Several characteristics can be discerned; the common use of brick, often intricately carved, the characteristic curved roof and cornice, the decorative use of terracotta, the popularity of the 'drop' arch and constant allusions to the simple vernacular buildings of the region. The chased detail on the Eklakhi tomb at Pandua, for example, echoes the framework of a timber-framed hut.

In many ways the history of Islamic architecture in the region revolves around the technical adaptations employed by Muslim artisans and builders to devise architectural forms which could express the spiritual tenets of Islam. The dependence on brick, and sometimes on basalt, for columns dictated a robust form of architecture which never achieved true elegance or refinement.

Jaunpur, *c.* 1394–1479

Jaunpur was an important dependency of the Sultanate under the Tughluq dynasty. It became the centre of a powerful Muslim state in the 15th century under the Sharqi Sultans. With the collapse of Imperial power following Timur's invasion of India and the sack of Delhi, they seized independence and assumed the insignia of royalty.

A particularly fine provincial school of architecture developed here. With the demise of Delhi, Jaunpur became a major cultural centre, the resort of poets, sages and men of letters. For over a century, it was known as the 'Shiraz of the East'. Although devastated by the Lodis at the end of the 15th century, five mosques were reprieved. Sufficient survived to suggest a vigorous local style.

Stylistically, one major influence was the militaristic form of Tughluq architecture, with its steep sloping walls and formidable bastions. These were taken and adapted by the Sharqi rulers to create a powerful new vocabulary for mosque design, which reached its apogee in the Jami Masjid, built around 1470.

The principal hallmark of the Jaunpur style was the appearance of the massive arched pylon in the centre of the façades of the mosques. This feature does not occur in any other manifestation of Indo–Islamic architecture. These dominant pylons with their tapering walls rose high above the dome behind. The huge gateways and depressed four-centred arches enriched with ornamental fringes of spearheads created a vigorous and assertive local style.

Gujarat, *c.* 1396–1583

Situated on the shores of the Indian Ocean, Gujarat enjoyed a long and illustrious maritime tradition which brought it into contact with a diverse range of overseas influences and fostered a cosmopolitan culture. The rich revenues of maritime trade had been employed for centuries on public and private building projects, so that a large and skilled workforce of artisans existed, well equipped in ancient traditions of construction.

With the advent of Muslim rule under the Khaljis and their successors from 1290 onwards, this self-confident body of craftsmen were able to adjust their architectural vocabulary to suit the new conventions of their overlords by employing the pointed arch and by omitting figurative sculpture. It is hardly surprising, therefore, that the provincial style of architecture which flourished in Gujarat embodied more indigenous Indian elements than any other regional manifestation of the Indo-Islamic style.

For over 250 years, from the early impact of the Khalji governors, through the splendour of the independent Ahmad Shahi dynasty, to the absorption of the country into the Mughal Empire in the late 16th century, an unparalleled heritage of Islamic architecture was created which constitutes the largest and most significant regional style in India.

The evolution of the style is outlined in the gazetteer in the introduction to the western region. Beginning with the customary initial phase of improvisation using salvaged Hindu and Jain masonry, by the mid-15th century the style had developed with massive arcuated brick structures of great power and sophistication.

This process of refinement reached its final expression between 1458 and 1511 in the reign of Mahmud Begada at Ahmadabad and in his own great city of Champaner. At the Siddi Sayyid mosque (*c.* 1515) in Ahmadabad the entire façade of the mosque iwan is treated as an arcuated composition, with beautifully contoured arches springing from slender columns. In the exquisite jali screens of this building some of the highest standards of Indo-Islamic art were attained. Here the discipline imposed by Islamic requirements for non-figurative decoration was complemented by the Hindu capacity for producing a sensual and sinuous design of deceptive simplicity and transcendental grace. The best of the two traditions united to surpass the sum of their constituent parts.

Another distinctive aspect of the region was the artistic treatment given to the step-wells or vavs, which are common in western India. The embellishment of these with cascades of steps and lavishly carved subterranean passages reached its most sophisticated limits under Muslim rule.

So vigorous and self-confident was the Gujarati style that its influence permeated way beyond the region into Rajasthan and central India. Its most influential feature was intricate stone latticework and the use of carved jali screens. It was in this field that Gujarati architecture made its greatest contribution to Indian architecture.

Malwa, 1401–1531

Muslim rule in Malwa was only secured after a bloody and protracted struggle for supremacy with the local Rajput princes of Chitor and Ujjain. After being subjugated by Ala-ud-Din Khalji in 1305, Malwa was administered by governors despatched from Delhi, until the shock of Timur's invasion of 1398–9 and the consequent collapse of Imperial power provided an opportunity for the local governor, Dilawar Khan, to declare independence and assume control. In many ways the rise of Malwa was similar to that of the Sharqi Sultans at Jaunpur.

The provincial style which developed in Malwa was concentrated virtually entirely within the heavily defended fortress of Mandu and at the ancient capital of Dhar, where a whole series of splendid buildings were erected.

In the absence of any strong local architectural tradition, the Ghurid dynasty of Dilawar Khan and his successors looked to Delhi for inspiration, relations with neighbouring Gujarat being strained. Several characteristic elements were borrowed from the capital and used at Dhar, and later at Mandu: in particular, the use of battered walls, the pointed arch with spearhead fringe, the unusual combination of arch and lintel and the familiar 'boat keel' dome and pyramidal roof of the Lodis.

These characteristic features were adapted to local needs and complemented by several innovations. Many Malwa buildings are distinguished by high plinths approached by steep flights of steps. Colour was also employed as an important part of the overall composition. Although much has been eroded or lost with the passage of time, sufficient remains for its importance to be appreciated – particularly, the structural deployment of different coloured stone or marble and also the use of encaustic tiles. Some of the interiors boast marble inlaid with semi-precious stones, such as jasper, agate and carnelian, and brightly decorated glazed friezes.

The buildings at Dhar and Mandu exhibit the same three phases which can be traced elsewhere. There is the initial reuse of temple masonry, denoting the fragmentation and supersession of the old indigenous system, followed by a more ordered, formalized architecture, characterized by massive elegance. In the third and final phase the style reached fruition in a more romantic and flamboyant form. Kiosks, cupolas, turrets and pavilions evoked the sybaritic luxury of an exotic Oriental court, before it fell in 1531 to Bahadur Shah of Gujarat, and then to Humayun.

A local outcrop of the Malwa style also occurred at Chanderi, a dependency of the Malwa sultans. Here the buildings also show evidence of other outside influences, particularly those of Gujarat.

The Deccan, 1347–1686

Muslim armies first raided south to the Deccan in 1294. These raids persisted for over twenty years. Islamic influence was reinforced with the transfer of the Imperial capital from Delhi to Daulatabad by Muhammad Tughluq in 1328. The only significant architectural repercussions were fairly crude reassemblies of Hindu and Jain masonry at Bodhan and Daulatabad with little compositional flair.

As the authority of Muhammad Tughluq waned, the newly conquered lands of the Deccan fell away from Imperial control. In the extreme south the local governor proclaimed a sultanate at Madura. Far more important was the foundation of the Bahmani dynasty at Gulbarga by a Persian adventurer, Ala-ud-Din Hasan Bahman Shah, in 1347.

The rise of the Bahmanis created a virile and aggressive Muslim power in the heartland of India, capable of confronting the two great Hindu kingdoms of Warangal and Vijayanagara. The eventual subjugation of Warangal and the checking of Hindu power in the region brought the Bahmanis considerable kudos throughout the Islamic world. Their court was transformed into a major seat of learning and patronage of the arts. Under their tutelage a specific style of Muslim architecture evolved which owed a great deal to external influences, particularly Persia, as artisans, engineers and skilled craftsmen flocked to the Deccan capital. Although the general course of Islamic architecture in the Deccan is set out in the regional introduction to the gazetteer, certain salient characteristics should be mentioned here.

In some buildings, such as the madrasa of Mahmud Gawan at Bidar, the Persian influence on architectural design was extremely strong. Virtually unadulterated by any local nuances, they were the product of imported Persian craftsmen intent on reproducing faithfully the style of their native land.

However, there is also a whole series of monuments which demonstrate the way in which the Deccani style of architecture evolved. These are the great royal tombs at Bidar, Golconda and Gulbarga. The mid-14th-century mausolea of the Sultans of Gulbarga were strongly influenced by the design of the Tughluq tombs at Delhi, with massive sloping walls. At Bidar, the Bahmani tombs incorporated Persian forms and motifs, most noticeably in the proportion and shape of the dome and in the beginning of the constricted neck over the octagonal drum. At Bidar, in the tombs of the Barid dynasty, and also at Golconda, in the royal mausolea of the Qutb Shahis, the voluptuous bulbous dome so characteristic of Deccani architecture reaches its most accomplished form.

Perhaps the most eloquent expression of the Deccani style is the Char Minar at Hyderabad. This is a monumental gateway of graceful exuberance. Elegant minars soar heavenwards from each of the four corners.

In 1489 the Bahmani kingdom fragmented into five independent dynasties: the Imad Shahi at Berar, 1490–1577; the Nizam Shahi at Ahmadnagar, 1490–1633; the Adil Shahi at Bijapur, 1490–1686; the Qutb Shahi at Golconda, 1512–1687; and the Barid Shahi at Bidar, 1487–1609.

The Adil Shahis at Bijapur claimed Turkish descent, but their architecture developed directly from the early Bahmani buildings in a very distinctive way. The style was characterized by full bulbous domes arising from bands of petal-like ornament at the neck, a treatment which continued on the corner turrets to create an evocative and romantic silhouette. The four-centred arches were more curved and graceful than their Bahmani prototypes, offset by huge projecting chajjas carried on ornamental brackets. The surface ornament was also unusual, with interlaced symbols, rosettes and running patterns incised into the stucco.

With the erection of the great Gol Gumbad at Bijapur by Muhammad Adil Shahi in 1656, the structural ingenuity and skills of the Deccani masons reached their culmination in one of the finest architectural triumphs of the age – a dome which spans the largest area of uninterrupted floorspace in the world. The architectural achievements of the masterbuilders of Bijapur were of a very high order. This was reflected in the outstanding quality of their workmanship. Their masterly use of a structural system of intersecting arches was the result of decades of trial and error, while their brickwork and masonry can truly be said to be unsurpassed.

Between 1425 and 1650 the small but influential state of Khandesh (Land of the Khans) arose in the valley of the River Tapti between the Bahmani kingdom and Malwa. Here, a pronounced local style developed which borrowed inspiration not only from the Deccan but from Gujarat and Malwa. Under the Faruqi Sultans the buildings of Burhanpur and Thalner expressed a distinctive local architectural idiom.

Kashmir, 1346–1589

The last of the major provincial styles, the Kashmiri could hardly be more different from that of the Deccan. High up in the valleys and foothills of the Himalayas, a unique local style evolved, derived in a great measure from long-established principles of vernacular construction.

Islam spread across the region in the late 14th century. It was not fully consolidated until 1586, when Kashmir was incorporated into the Mughal empire by Akbar. The Mughal heritage of the region falls within the wider context of Mughal architecture, but prior to this there existed a significant number of Islamic mosques and tombs constructed from timber. These share several common features: rectangular base structures crowned by pyramidal roofs and capped by thin spires. The ready availability of local supplies of good building timber, particularly deodar, and the existence of an ancient and refined indigenous tradition dictated that, even with the introduction of stone architecture by the Mughals in the 17th century, the indigenous timber style continued to flourish in the service of the Muslim conquerors.

The Pearl Mosque in the Red Fort at Delhi

FIVE

THE MUGHAL PERIOD

'Hindustan is a country that has few pleasures to recommend it . . . The people are not handsome. They have no idea of the charms of friendly society, of frankly mixing together, or of familiar intercourse. They have no genius, no comprehension of mind, no politeness of manner, no kindness or fellow-feeling, no skill or knowledge in design or architecture . . . There is an excessive quantity of earth and dust flying about.'

Babur's jaundiced view of India seems to have been dictated more by homesickness for the lush gardens of his native Kabul than by any objective insight into the nature of Indian society and culture. However, after his crushing victory at Panipat in 1526, the Great Mughal found himself master of Delhi, and successor to the decaying symbols of Imperial authority.

Babur (1483–1530) was an intelligent, charismatic and dynamic personality who, in his comparatively short reign of five years, laid the foundations of Mughal power in India. He was descended through his father from Timur and through his mother from Ghengis Khan.

Babur died a death as romantic as the life he had lived. At the age of forty-seven with his eldest son, Humayun, on his deathbed, Babur pledged his own life in the hope of saving that of his son. 'O God. If a life may be exchanged for a life, I who am Babur give my life and body for Humayun.' Soon after, it is alleged, Babur contracted a heavy fever, and as he slipped away into unconsciousness, so the life spirit returned to his son and heir.

If Babur laid the foundations of Mughal supremacy across northern India, his son Humayun came close to losing it. Dissolute and wayward in his early years, Humayun was overthrown in 1540 by the brilliant Sher Shah Sur, an Imperial vassal of Afghan lineage who ruled Bihar. Harried and defeated, Humayun fled to Persia in 1544.

The Suris quickly established a firm grip on the administration and created a vigorous, centralized bureaucracy, reviving the Imperial idea but under Afghan control. However, after more than a decade in exile, Humayun was able to re-establish himself as the Suri dynasty succumbed to factional disputes. In 1555 he regained the throne. Six months later he was dead – from a fall down the stairs of his library at the Sher Mandel, a fitting end for a man who did much to foster learning and culture.

After the Suri interregnum, Mughal fortunes improved under the gifted Akbar, the greatest of the dynasty. Crowned at the age of fourteen, within ten years he had reasserted Imperial authority over many of the petty regimes on his borders.

By 1569 Rajputana was subdued, with the exception of Mewar, where the prince was forced into hiding. Gujarat fell in 1572. Four years later Bengal followed, then Kashmir (1586), Orissa (1592) and Baluchistan (1595). By Akbar's death in 1605, the Deccani kingdoms of Berar and Khandesh were tributaries of the empire. Under Jahangir (1605–27) and Shah Jahan (1628–57), the north-west frontier was strengthened, while in the south Mughal authority and power rolled relentlessly forward at the expense of the independent Muslim kingdoms of the Deccan. Under Aurangzeb (1658–1707), the empire reached its greatest extent. Bijapur was seized in 1686, followed a year later by Golconda, although by this date the empire was weakened by internal rebellion and strife. Aurangzeb's death began a period of agonizing decline for the Mughals, as a series of ephemeral rulers proved unable to resist the mounting forces of separatism within the empire.

Babur, 1483–1530

During his short five-year reign, Babur took considerable interest in building, particularly secular works. Little has survived. One of his earliest projects was the layout of a beautiful garden on geometric lines at Dholpur, near Agra, depicted in a miniature in the *Baburnama*. Unfortunately, only the excavated ruins can be seen.

It is reputed that Babur summoned master-craftsmen and pupils of the famous Albanian architect Sinan from Constantinople to work on his ambitious building schemes in India. Regrettably, the only legacy of this energetic phase of construction is an unexceptional mosque at Panipat and another at Sambhal, outside Delhi, both erected in 1526.

During the early years Mughal domination of the country was too unsettled to produce any works of great distinction, but the seeds of architectural inspiration which were to germinate to such magnificence under Akbar and Shah Jahan were planted by Babur and Humayun.

The remarkable flowering of Mughal art and architecture in the late 16th and early 17th centuries is one of the greatest expressions of man's creative genius. There were several factors responsible for this extraordinary burst of artistic energy.

First, the empire itself provided a powerful and secure framework within which artistic genius could flourish. Secondly, it commanded wealth and resources on a scale unparalleled in Indian history and, thirdly, and perhaps most important, the Mughal rulers themselves were remarkable patrons of the arts. Their intellectual calibre, cultural outlook and enthusiasm for painting, music, literature and architecture reflected a latent dynastic interest in aesthetic matters which was expressed in the most refined taste.

Both architecturally and administratively the empire owed a profound debt to the Suri dynasty, which laid the groundwork on which the Mughals built.

The Suri Dynasty, 1540–55

The architectural heritage of the Suri dynasty may be divided into two separate and distinct periods.

The first phase emerged at their capital, Sasaram, in Bihar, under the audacious Sher Shah Sur between 1530 and 1540, where a group of tombs was built which took the Lodi style to its ultimate expression. The second phase occurred between 1540 and 1545, when Sher Shah Sur wrested control from Humayun. Under his active patronage a number of architectural innovations were adopted and these represented an important development in the gestation of the subsequent Mughal style.

The first phase of tomb building at Sasaram clearly reflects the ambition of Sher Shah Sur to create a monument grander than anything found in Delhi. In order to give inspiration to his dreams, he procured the services of Aliwal Khan, a masterbuilder trained in the Imperial tradition, who began with the construction of the tomb of Hasan Sur Khan, Sher Shah Sur's father, in 1525. This is a fairly conventional exercise in Lodi design, but his subsequent work, the tomb of Sher Shah Sur, is an extraordinary building, an architectural masterpiece, a huge and noble composition set in a beautiful tank approached by a causeway. This remarkable monument, constructed of the finest Chunar sandstone, had a major impact on the architectural evolution of Indo-Islamic funerary architecture.

The second phase of development occurred at Delhi, where Sher Shah Sur built the Purana Qila or Old Fort, a defensive citadel intended to provide the focus of his sixth city of Delhi, Shergarh. Today, only two isolated gateways survive.

Far more influential in the subsequent development of Mughal art was the Qila-i-Kuhna Masjid, the royal chapel of Sher Shah Sur, built about 1542, which illustrates graphically the skill, confidence and expertise of the Suri craftsmen. The mosque is a convincing and eloquent essay, a disciplined and balanced composition with firmly contoured four-centred arches set in well-defined rectangular frames, offset by delicate spearhead fringes and merlons and articulated by the horizontal line of the projecting chajja into a well-integrated whole. The interior too is equally accomplished.

Sher Shah Sur's declared ambition was to build 'with such architectural embellishments, that friend and foe might render their tribute of applause, and that my name might remain honoured upon earth until the day of resurrection'. The product of his extraordinary egotism was a major advance in the development of an architectural style which reached its culmination under the rule of his successors.

On the death of the great Sher Shah Sur, his son Salim succeeded to the throne. With the exception of the Salimgarh, a defensive outwork to the Red Fort in Delhi, the architectural impulse which so motivated his father waned. With his death in 1554, civil war ensued and Humayun seized the opportunity to re-establish Mughal pre-eminence.

Humayun, 1530–56

Humayun's return was shortlived, but it was fruitful for a number of reasons.

Most important, the Mughal dynasty was re-established firmly at the helm of the ship of state. Secondly, after fifteen years in exile, Humayun had drunk deep at the well of Persian culture. He had imbibed many aspects of that culture, including the Shia faith, if only temporarily. On his return he imported Persian artists, who set up the royal atelier or school of painting. Finally, in the field of

53

architecture, his tomb at Delhi was an outstanding landmark in the development and refinement of the Mughal style. It was designed in 1564, eight years after his death, as a mark of devotion by his widow, Haji Begum, who had lived with him in exile in Persia and who, undoubtedly, was influenced by the architecture which she saw there.

The architect was Mirak-Mirza Ghiyath; the site selected was not far from the Jumna. It is clear that imported Persian craftsmen contributed many of their skills and techniques, for the building is an Indian rendition of a Persian concept.

The plan comprises a central octagon surrounded by four corner chambers, a distinctly Persian element. The great central arch to each side and the shape and technical construction of the dome, with its double shell, also reflect the strong influence of Persia. Conversely, the elevation of the entire tomb on to an arched plinth or stylobate, the beautifully finished red sandstone and marble inlays, and the romantic silhouette of kiosks and cupolas are pure India, so that the whole tomb is a wonderful synthesis of two great traditions, the Persian and the Indian.

This exercise in architectural miscegenation between two great building traditions was of vital significance for the development of Indian architecture. It presaged the development of a mature and sophisticated style which reached its highest expression almost seventy years later in the incomparable Taj Mahal.

Akbar, 1556–1605

Akbar vies with Ashoka, the ancient Mauryan emperor, as the greatest of Indian rulers. He created an effective administrative and political system which brought strength and durability to the empire. Building on the framework laid down earlier by Balban and the Suri dynasty, Akbar created an efficient government which affected every part of the realm, down to village level.

The entire framework of Mughal government depended on Hindu cooperation. Most of the officials responsible for the daily administration of the empire were drawn from Hindu castes. Even the Rajputs, once defeated, were drawn into the network of Imperial rule and government, sharing the same status and privileges as the Muslim nobility. With the marriage of Akbar to Rani Jodha Bai, a Hindu princess from Jaipur, this process of cultural and political interdependence was sealed at the highest level. Their son, Jahangir, became the living synthesis of the august traditions of the two societies.

Under his enlightened finance minister, the Hindu Todar Mal, a fair and accurate revenue assessment was fixed. This fostered cultivation and production and also brought a regular flow of revenue into the Imperial treasury. It was this sound political and financial base which enabled the dynasty to finance its steady expansion and some of its greatest building projects, and which later formed the bedrock of British administration in the 19th century.

The style of architecture which evolved under Akbar was distinctive. Executed in red sandstone, often with marble inlay, it made widespread use of trabeated or post and lintel construction. Arches were used, but in a decorative rather than structural form, as arcades, for instance. Domes tended to follow earlier Lodi forms. Pillars were multi-faceted with capitals in the form of bracket supports. In terms of decoration, boldly carved or inlaid patterns were commonplace, complemented by brightly coloured painted patterns on interior walls and ceilings. One of the first major building projects of his reign was the construction of a huge fortress-palace at Agra, one of a number he built across India. The massive sandstone ramparts of the Red Fort were one of the wonders of the age. 'From top to bottom the fire-red stones, linked by iron rings, are joined so closely that even a hair cannot find its way into their joints,' wrote one contemporary. The massive walls, battlements, machicolations and loopholes combined to convey an overall effect of tremendous power. This combination of dynastic power and aesthetic discernment was one of the great hallmarks of Mughal rule, creating monuments of unsurpassed beauty and elegance.

Within the walls of the fort it was recorded that over '500 edifices of red stones in the fine-styles of Bengal and Gujarat' were erected. Virtually all were demolished by Shah Jahan as part of a later phase of remodelling. Only the Jahangiri Mahal survives, an interesting asymmetrical range of apartments which marks a transition in palace design from the Hindu type, exemplified by the Man Mandir at Gwalior, to the more domestic requirements of the Mughal rulers.

The most ambitious architectural exercise of Akbar's reign, and one of the most glorious examples of Indo-Islamic architecture, was the creation of an entirely new capital city at Fatehpur Sikri to commemorate the successful birth of Prince Salim, later Emperor Jahangir.

Straddling a barren rocky ridge outside Agra, Fatehpur Sikri comprises a spectacular complex of palaces, houses and religious buildings, a magnificent architectural heritage of unparalleled splendour. In its design and layout the pragmatic but decisive hand of Akbar can be seen; a city without streets, where the public areas, like the courtyards, Diwan-i-Am and Jami Masjid, form a coherent group around the private palace apartments.

The sandstone ridge on which the city was constructed runs from north-east to south-west, but the majority of its buildings are oriented to face north and south to respect the fixed east–west alignment of the great mosque. The main approach from Agra leads straight to the Hall of Public Audience or Diwan-i-Am. Other than this general grouping of buildings according to function and the skilful use of multiple axes, there is little evidence of any conscious overall plan; instead, in a series of pragmatic decisions, buildings were sited to relate successfully to each other and to their surroundings, with the principal compositions sited on the strategic intersections of the main axis.

The city was built with astonishing speed from local red sandstone. This dictated the use of trabeated principles of construction whereby pillars, lintels, brackets, tiles and posts were cut from the local rock and assembled without the use of mortar.

The most significant of the administrative buildings in the city is the Diwan-i-Khas or Hall of Private Audience. Here the elusive character of Akbar can be discerned in its extraordinary internal layout. Inside is a single chamber, dominated by a central pillar with a colossal capital made of a series of pendulous Jain brackets carrying a circular stone platform. Four diagonal aerial bridges connect this to an outer gallery. Here, 'the Emperor, like a god in the cup of a lotus flower, sat in the centre of the corbelled capital', while his ministers or representatives of the different religious communities sat in each angle, the architectural embodiment of Akbar's 'dominion over the Four Quarters'.

As a result of the city's size, and the speed with which it was built, Akbar employed craftsmen and builders from all over India, and they brought with them their own individual techniques and traditions. It is possible to trace the workmanship of particular provincial schools, such as those of Gujarat or Bengal, and to see these diverse influences expressed in the architecture of the city. It is thought that the Panch Mahal, for instance, with its diminishing storeys was inspired by the multiple-storeyed Buddhist viharas of antiquity.

However, the architectural climax of the city is a remarkable concentration of religious buildings focussed on the Jami Masjid.

The Great Mosque, commenced in 1571, was the original part of the scheme. This is a vast conventional structure with a wide-open courtyard surrounded on three sides by arcaded cloisters, the fourth forming the sanctuary, which is enriched with carved, inlaid and painted ornament of outstanding quality.

Twenty-five years after its completion Akbar commenced the mighty Buland Darwaza, to commemorate his conquest of the Deccan. It is one of the most forceful and majestic buildings in India. This great 'Gate of Magnificence' is a masterpiece of structural ingenuity and aesthetic composition, for, at the point of entry, it successfully reconciles an awesome monumentality with human scale. From the outside it is approached by a massive flight of steps, above which the gateway soars heavenwards, the central framed arch flanked by lofty minarets. From the courtyard it provides a fitting centrepiece to the colonnaded southern cloister. The Buland Darwaza is one of the great buildings of India, 'a miracle of art, combined with an element of thought, veneration and melancholy that makes up one of those rare sensations of completeness which times cannot impair'.

Within the mosque itself, the Tomb of Shaikh Salim Chishti provides a perfect counterpoint to the great Buland Darwaza. Originally built in sandstone, the entire edifice was clad in marble, probably in the time of Jahangir. It is an exquisite architectural gem, with sinuous, serpentine brackets of astonishing delicacy and diaphanous marble jali screens of ethereal beauty.

In 1585, just fourteen years after building the city, Akbar deserted Fatehpur Sikri for good, probably because the water supply was drying up. He ruled for another twenty years. Much of the rest of his life was spent consolidating the eastern and northern frontiers of his expanding empire, but the years he spent at Fatehpur Sikri were the richest and most creative of his entire reign. He laid the foundations of a culture and lifestyle which would endure for another century.

In fifty years Akbar had turned a small regional foothold into an effective empire controlling the whole of Hindustan.

'Let not difference of religion interfere with policy, and be not violent in inflicting retribution. Adorn the confidential council with men who know their work. If apologies be made, accept them.' By adopting a policy of conciliation with defeated enemies and by welding the empire together under the benign autocracy of his own person, a dynamic, efficient and stable administration was created, run by a trusted body of officers and civil servants.

Jahangir, 1605–27

Before becoming emperor, for the last five years of Akbar's reign, Prince Salim was repeatedly in rebellion against his father. After a week of mourning, Salim

56

ascended the throne as Emperor Jahangir, 'Seizer of the World', on 24 October 1605.

Judging him to be spineless, decadent and debauched, history has accorded Jahangir a bad press. In reality he was one of the most sympathetic and cultured of all the Mughals. With the aid of his able wife, the Empress Nur Jahan, and with the continuity provided by a competent civil administration, he was able to pursue his own interests in painting, literature and scientific inquiry. As a result a magnificent heritage of Mughal painting, depicting historical scenes, flora and fauna, was assembled under royal patronage. Yet in spite of his preference for other art forms, one of the most remarkable buildings of the Mughal period was created during his reign.

The Mausoleum of Akbar at Sikandra, outside Agra, was built to plans which had been approved by Akbar and which drew inspiration from a wide variety of sources, including ancient Buddhist traditions. Nevertheless, extensive variations were carried out by Jahangir. This accounts for its curiously unresolved character and for the lack of unity and cohesion. It was conceived on a grand scale, the tomb at the centre of a vast enclosed garden approached through a monumental gateway of exceptional elegance. This was inlaid with geometric marble patterns and crowned by four perfect marble minarets, precursors of those on the famous Taj Mahal. The tomb itself, a tiered, truncated pyramidal structure, was raised on a massive arcaded platform. Inside, in a plain chamber devoid of any ornamental detail, was placed the tomb of Akbar, like a pharaoh at the centre of his pyramid.

Architecturally, the mausoleum stands at a major crossroads in Mughal history, as the vigorous sandstone compositions of Akbar were adapted and softened by his successors into opulent marble masterpieces of exquisite craftsmanship.

For all his indifference towards architecture, Jahangir is the central figure in the development of the Mughal garden, the best of which lie in Kashmir, his first and greatest love. For several years he made an annual journey there. The incomparable Shalimar Bagh on the banks of Lake Dal, the most famous and most secluded, was completed by his son. Shah Jahan shared his father's interest in garden art. There at the head of a canal one of the loveliest gardens in the world was created, a paradise of all-pervading peace and calm, with glimpses of the encircling mountains captured through the breaks in the trees. Here the undulating topography and abundant supply of water introduced stunning new dimensions into the art of the Mughal garden. The adept use of axial vistas, unfolding panoramas and cascading waterfalls interspersed with elegant pavilions, cool fountains and lush vegetation took the art of the landscaped garden to its highest expression.

The only other significant architectural productions of Jahangir's reign must be attributed to the perseverance and devotion of his wife, Nur Jahan. One is the tomb of Jahangir at Lahore, now in Pakistan, and the other is the tomb of her father, Ghiyath Beg, Itmad-ud-Daula, 'pillar of the empire'.

Both have a pronounced feminine character and mark a transitional phase between the styles of Akbar and Shah Jahan. The tomb of Itmad-ud-Daula at Agra has stumpy, ungainly corner minarets, but what it lacks in compositional elegance is more than compensated for by its stunning surface treatment in white marble from Makrana, inlaid with pietra dura work of semi-precious stones –

topaz, onyx, jasper and carnelian. Although the inlay work is executed to the highest standards, the geometric and linear patterns resemble a patchwork quilt unrelated to the overall composition, with the result that the overall impact is ambiguous and disorganized. What is important is that the technique of pietra dura work had superseded the earlier craft of opus sectile or different-coloured marble inlay. For this reason the buildings of Jahangir's reign prefigure the sumptuous creations of the last and greatest phase of Mughal architecture, which flourished in the reign of Shah Jahan.

Shah Jahan, 1628–57

Addicted to opium, alcohol and a life of excess, Jahangir succumbed to chronic asthma en route to his beloved Kashmir. His favourite son and successor, Prince Khurram, was proclaimed emperor in Lahore on the last day of 1627. A month later he ascended the throne as Emperor Shah Jahan, 'Ruler of the Universe'. The golden age of the Mughal Empire had begun.

Even as a boy Shah Jahan was interested in architecture, and this enthusiasm remained with him for life. Under his patronage a major change was wrought in the substance and form of Mughal architecture, as the experiments of his predecessors were brought to full and glorious bloom.

The single most important change was the use of marble rather than sandstone. This dictated significant stylistic refinements. The arch developed a distinctive form with foliated curves, usually with nine cusps. Marble arcades of engrailed arches became a hallmark of the period. The typical Bengali roof, with its curvilinear form and sloping lines, was adopted by Shah Jahan's builders as an elegant visual device to enrich the silhouette and profile of many buildings. The dome developed along Persian lines into a full, voluptuous, bulbous form with a constricted neck constructed on the double-dome principle. Other notable features were the use of pillars with tapering baluster shafts, voluted bracket capitals, foliated plinths and a sensuous fluidity of line which imparted softness and femininity to the style.

During the earliest part of his reign Shah Jahan resided in the Red Fort at Agra. He demolished the austere sandstone structures that Akbar had built and replaced them with a sumptuous group of marble buildings. The earliest, the Diwan-i-Am, was begun in 1627. Lustrous white Makrana marble was employed to create a large rectangular hall of elegance and simplicity on an open grid of engrailed arches and columns with sparing use of ornamentation. Unlike the fussy inlaid ornament of the tomb of Itmad-ud-Daula, here it was used to accentuate and enhance the architectural form and contours of the building in a perfect fusion of art and architecture.

About ten years later this was followed by the Diwan-i-Khas, which boasts some of the most graceful columns of the period. The exquisite Moti Masjid or Pearl Mosque was not completed until 1654, a miniature marble gem and a matchless example of the Mughal style at its zenith. Between the erection of these two major buildings a whole series of chaste marble palaces and pavilions were built.

The improvement of the fort at Agra was merely a preliminary exercise for the magnificent architectural projects which were to follow. The first of these was the emperor's decision to move the Imperial administration from Agra to Delhi, where in 1638 he began to lay out the city of Shahjahanabad beside the Jumna. The city was the last of the great citadels of Muslim power in India. Although it was laid out on fairly conventional lines, it was unusual because it was built under his personal direction, the product of one mind executed to the requirements of a single authority. At the centre of the new city lay a palace-fortress for his own use, larger and more formidable than anything which had been produced before.

The Red Fort at Delhi represents the culmination of centuries of experience in the construction of Muslim palace-forts. It contains a range of marble buildings and formal ornamental gardens. A sumptuous array of palaces, pavilions and balconies was erected along the eastern wall, capped by turrets and kiosks which imparted a romantic silhouette to the entire edifice.

Almost all the structures took the form of one-storey open pavilions with façades of engrailed arches shaded by chajjas and punctuated by corner domed kiosks – the fabled marble tents of Shahjahanabad. Today they resemble deserted husks. The resplendent life of the court can only be gleaned from the countless contemporary miniature paintings, which depict it in its heyday, with palaces hung with carpets, brocades, canopies and Muslims, and gardens planted with exotic shrubs, interspersed with cool fountains and sparkling cascades.

The Rang Mahal was described by one contemporary as: 'In lustre and in colour . . . far superior to the palaces in the promised paradise.' This was rivalled for sheer splendour by the Diwan-i-Khas, with its elegant perforated tracery. The common use of polished marble, the lavish but ordered use of inlaid ornament and the pulsating rhythm of internal perspectives of engrailed arches with flowing sensuous curves combined to create a complex of buildings of exuberance and grace. The Diwan-i-Am was not as lavishly treated; its use for public audience as opposed to private pleasure dictated a more restrained, dignified treatment. Within this structure is the alcove where the emperor sat in state on the famous Peacock Throne, a scene illustrated in some Mughal miniatures of the period.

Outside the fort Shah Jahan built the famous Jami Masjid, one of the largest mosques in the country, an impressive building situated on a raised plinth and executed in a lucid and coherent manner for maximum visual impact. It was the last of the great mosques of Islamic India, the culmination of a heritage which began almost 500 years earlier with the Quwwat-ul-Islam mosque and which developed in fine examples at Ahmadabad, Bijapur, Jaunpur, Mandu, and elsewhere. Another distinguished mosque, the Jami Masjid at Agra, was built by Shah Jahan in 1648 in honour of his daughter Jahanara Begum, but architecturally the most impressive was the mosque of Wazir Khan, built in 1634 at Lahore, now in Pakistan.

With the death of Mumtaz Mahal during a campaign in the Deccan in 1629, Shah Jahan resolved to build his favourite wife the most magnificent tomb ever erected. The Taj Mahal represents the architectural climax of Indo-Islamic architecture. It is a monument of unique perfection. Undoubtedly, its sources can be seen in Humayun's tomb, in the tomb of Akbar at Sikandra and in the proportions of the Khan Khanan's tomb at Delhi, but the Taj Mahal transcends the sum of its constituent parts to express that rare moment of perfection in an architectural style which is heralded by so much promise but rarely ever achieved.

The tomb forms the architectural focus of a large formal garden which was designed to provide a perfect frame and setting for the central structure. Planned as the climax of an axial vista, the tomb stands as the centrepiece of a symmetrical group of buildings, flanked on the west by a mosque and on the east by its replica, the jawab or answer, as it is known. The scale is awesome – taller than a modern twenty-storey building. The internal plan of the Taj is clearly modelled on that of Humayun's tomb, but its crowning glory is the exterior which produces a completely coherent effect. Each part is perfectly related to the whole. The dome appears to float over the arched façade beneath within a perfect frame created by the four corner minarets. Its transcendental beauty arises from the translucent Makrana marble from which it is built, and from the wonderful pietra dura work, with its disciplined floral patterns of semi-precious stones.

Shah Jahan intended to duplicate the entire composition in black marble on the opposite side of the river, to accommodate his own remains, and then connect the two by a bridge. This was not to be. Although work began, it was stopped by the war which broke out between the emperor and his son, Aurangzeb.

No account of the reign of Shah Jahan would be complete without reference to his interest in landscape architecture and gardening, an enthusiasm he shared with his father, Jahangir, and which can be traced back to Babur. Ornamental gardens and enclosures were commonly used around many major buildings, but the Mughals developed the idea of spacious gardens purely as retreats for pleasure and relaxation. The most famous were in Kashmir, although Shah Jahan was responsible also for the Shalimar Bagh at Lahore, which he laid out in 1637 as a series of descending terraces and cascades on a rigid symmetrical axial plan. The aim was to discipline nature and not to imitate it. A favourite device was the chahar bagh or fourfold plot, accentuated by linear pathways and water channels.

The last years of Shah Jahan's reign were marked by increasing dynastic strife, as Aurangzeb outmanoeuvred his brothers and finally imprisoned his father in the fort at Agra. Here Shah Jahan spent his last years, gazing wistfully across at the tomb of his beloved Mumtaz Mahal from the ramparts of the fort he had done so much to embellish. After he was deposed by Aurangzeb in 1658, Shah Jahan lingered on for eight unhappy years, comforted by his eldest daughter, Jahanara, and spending long hours studying the Quran. He never met his son again. On 22 January 1666, while listening to verses from the Quran, he died. The next morning his body was taken by water to the Taj Mahal, where he was buried beside his wife in perpetual union beneath the most perfect building ever created by the hand of man.

Aurangzeb, 1658–1707

With the accession of Aurangzeb as emperor, it is possible to trace the beginning of the decline of the Mughal Empire in its architecture, but this trend should not be overstated. Aurangzeb has been denigrated by historians for his bloody rise to power, the destruction of his brothers and the imprisonment of his father, but in this he was no different from others of his race, including his father. He was to govern India for forty-eight years and under his tutelage the empire grew to its widest extent.

His reign can be divided into two periods. The first twenty-three years were largely a continuation of Shah Jahan's administration, based in Delhi, with annual visits to Kashmir, but from 1681 he virtually transferred his capital to the Deccan, where he concentrated his attentions on reducing the two remaining Deccani kingdoms and on combating the Maratha rebellion.

Aurangzeb was an able and ruthless politician. As he grew older he acquired a reputation as a religious ascetic and sage, but his enormous strength of character and fierce reputation enabled him to dominate India for almost half a century. By 1690 he was 'lord paramount of almost the whole of India – from Kabul to Chittagong and from Kashmir to the Kaveri', but his uncompromising character and unremitting religious bigotry provided an arid climate for fine art and architecture.

Shah Jahan's genius for extravagant ceremonial and architectural indulgence had been achieved at great expense to the realm. The peasants and artisans were squeezed of their wealth by Imperial taxes. By the time of Aurangzeb's accession, the empire was in a state of insolvency and the opportunity for grandiloquent architectural projects severely diminished.

Perhaps the most obvious expression of the rapid decline in architectural design can be seen in a comparison between the Taj Mahal and a similar tomb, the Bibi-ki-Maqbara, built over the grave of Aurangzeb's wife, Rabi Durrani, at Aurangabad forty years later, in 1678. While the design was inspired by the Taj Mahal, the entire composition was only half size, the proportions compressed and the ornamental detail clumsily executed, verging on the decadent, a sterile exercise in architectural plagiarism and a travesty of its original prototype.

The decline of the Mughal style can be seen through comparisons with other buildings of the period. The Moti Masjid or Pearl Mosque in the fort at Delhi is a delightfully chaste work, erected for the emperor's personal use, but the three crowning cupolas lack the suave confidence which was the hallmark of the best Mughal buildings. Similarly, the Badshahi mosque at Lahore, built twelve years later, shows a comparable indecision and lack of vitality, indicative of a waning creative impulse.

It is not quite true that 'not a single edifice, finely written manuscript or exquisite picture commemorates Aurangzeb's reign', for there are monuments of the period scattered across upper India, such as the mosque at Varanasi and the Jami Masjid at Mathura, but neither exhibits any spark of originality to suggest that the period was anything other than one of inexorable architectural decline.

After the death of Aurangzeb in 1707, the dissolution of the empire was only a matter of time, and the few significant buildings of the period all express the decadent political context. The tomb of Safdar Jang at Delhi, completed in 1753, stands in marked contrast to the great tomb of Humayun built 200 years before. Although conceived on a monumental scale and set in a large ornamental garden, it is the melancholy expression of an architecture gone to seed, 'the last flicker of the lamp of Mughal architecture'.

With the decline and eclipse of Mughal power in India, the centre of power moved from Delhi to Lucknow. The Nawabs of Oudh became the most active patrons of Indo-Islamic architecture. The skilled architects, builders and draughtsmen who had served the Mughals with such distinction were dispersed to the courts and palaces of provincial magnates. There a new mix of architectural styles developed as Hindu, Muslim and European forms and motifs collided in promiscuous forms of free expression, often bordering on the outrageously decadent.

The court of the Nawabs of Oudh marked the last phase of Mughal art and culture. In general Nawabi religious buildings such as mosques, imambaras and temples represented a continuation of earlier building traditions. The Bara Imambara at Lucknow was perhaps the most celebrated example, a vast building with huge foliated arches intended for the Shia ceremony of Muharram. Nawabi mausolea share certain common features – foliated arches to the windows and doorways, perforated arcades on the parapets, domed roofs and the use of brick and stucco. The mausoleum of Safdar Jang at Delhi, Saadat Ali's tomb at Lucknow and the Gulab Bari at Fyzabad are probably the most notable examples.

However, it is the secular buildings of the period which show the finest and most innovative architecture in a free association with European styles. This unconstrained mix of European and Indian forms and motifs generated florid buildings of enormous exuberance. Great gateways like the Bara Imambara Gate or the Rumi Darwaza exhibit a distinctly Baroque trend. Palaces such as the Chattar Manzil (1814–27) and the Kaisar Bagh (1848–50) boast elements which are classical in style but thoroughly Indian in execution.

With the increasing popularity of European styles, bizarre houses such as the Farhad Bakhsh and Constantia, built for the European adventurer Claude Martin, and incoherent compositions, like the Begum Kothi or Roshan-ud-Daula Kothi, arose. By the mid-19th century the inventive blend of styles and forms which had characterized the earliest compositions had given way to the reckless use of classical features in an undisciplined, chaotic jumble of debased elements, symptomatic of the wider breakdown in understanding between the two societies on the eve of the Mutiny.

SIX

FORTS, PALACES, COURTLY LIFE AND ART

Forts

Given the vulnerability of Hindustan to successive waves of invasions, it is not surprising to discover an ancient tradition of fortification for the protection of settlements against hostile attack and marauding wild animals. The origins of some forts are lost in the mists of time. Many were transformed or reconstructed after the Muslim invasions of the 12th century.

The earliest treatises on Indian architecture and fortification can be found in the Shilpa Shastras and in ancient Indian literature such as the Puranas and Epics. This vast repository of knowledge throws considerable light on the development of fortification in India. 'Pur', a word which recurs repeatedly in the Vedas, means a rampart, fort or stronghold. Elsewhere forts 'with 100 walls' are mentioned.

In the 4th century BC, Kautilya wrote at length about protective fortifications. He classified forts according to the preferred types of site. Water and mountain fortresses were regarded as best for the defence of populous towns. Desert and forest sites were regarded as 'habitations in the wilderness'. Where a fort had to be located on an open plain, then water was introduced and the land cleared to form a maidan or open field of fire. The nara durg, a fort protected by men, describes the Aryan correlation of a fort with a town. A variety of plans were used for defensive works, usually based on a rectangle.

Ancient Shastra and Vedic rules for town planning were reflected in Kautilya's works. Generally, two major axial roads were aligned with the cardinal points, intersecting at a central crossing. Here the gods were placed. The king's house lay to the north, while the outer ring behind the ramparts reflected the path around the sacred sacrificial enclosure. Later, with the impact of the Bactrian invasions in the north-west, Hellenistic ideas of town planning became influential, with a grid pattern layout around an isolated central citadel or acropolis. Another vital component of the fort complex was the temple and, after the 12th century, the mosque. Water was always an overriding consideration to ensure self-sufficiency during times of siege or duress. Most forts have natural or artificial tanks within their protective ramparts and some have underground supplies of extraordinary sophistication.

After the Muslim invasions fortifications in India reflected many of the developments which had taken place in Europe. The central citadel was kept isolated and secure from the expansive outwork of curtain walls. Usually the citadel was sited on a naturally defensible outcrop of rock. The great Maratha forts of western India – Purandhar, Raigarh and Sinhagarh, for instance – all

A Mughal miniature depicting the three great Mughal Emperors – Akbar, Jahangir and Shah Jahan

manipulated natural terrain to their strategic advantage. Where this was not possible, as at Gulbarga, in the Deccan, the central stronghold followed the practice of the Crusader castles of the Near East, with a robust donjon or inner redoubt at the heart of the defence.

Two other distinctive elements can be discerned. The importance of defence in depth had been appreciated for centuries. Accordingly, many forts have concentric rings of moats and walls, with advanced gateways or outworks dominating the approach. Also, considerable ingenuity was employed in manipulating the approach to thwart an enemy's advance. The use of right-angle bends, zigzag causeways and serried ranks of fortified gateways reinforced with anti-elephant spikes provided a formidable barrier to any hostile army.

With the advent of artillery, the entire nature of fortification changed. High, thick walls were superseded by broad, low, sunken ramparts, protected by ditches to offer a minimal target for cannon fire. As firearms became more sophisticated, massive angular, battered bastions with interlocking fields of crossfire replaced the curvilinear forms of the mediaeval strongholds. With the impact of European rule, the great fortresses of the Portuguese at Diu and Goa, or the English at Fort St George, Madras, or Fort William, Calcutta, were designed on European principles, based on the ideas of Scamozzi and Vauban but adapted to an Indian context.

Palaces

The great forts of India were not just strategic centres of defence. Some, such as the Maratha forts, were always intended primarily for military purposes but many were the architectural and social centrepiece of an entire state. This is particularly true of the Mughal and Rajput forts, which comprised concentrations of opulent public and private palaces of great splendour.

Few Hindu palaces or secular buildings have survived from before the mediaeval period. While it is evident from literary and documentary sources that these existed, the tradition of the perpetual reconstruction and recycling of existing masonry militated against the effective repair and conservation of secular buildings. One of the earliest is the great Man Mandir palace at Gwalior, begun in about 1486 and representative of a distinctively independent thread in Indian architecture.

There were two great periods of palace building in India. The first corresponded to the period of Mughal supremacy, from the mid-16th century to the mid-18th century, and the second to the British Raj. In both cases the provision of an overriding central authority kept local rulers in check and fostered the growth of a provincial elite who gained power and prestige as their local representatives.

The great Rajput palaces represent the development of a distinct architectural style of very considerable sophistication. In general, they share many common features.

Most major Rajput cities boast a principal palace, which was the main residence of the raja and his court. Usually, the palace was divided into two parts – the zenana or women's quarters and the mardana or men's quarters. The zenana was approached by a separate entrance and was generally closed to all men, other than selected courtiers or eunuchs. Intricately carved jali screens to the windows and balconies combined seclusion and privacy with the conditions of purdah.

The mardana was divided into state apartments and the private rooms of the raja. Most boasted a Diwan-i-Am or Hall of Public Audience, where the raja held court with his subjects or visitors. The Diwan-i-Khas or Hall of Private Audience was a chamber where he could confer with his advisers on state affairs. Often this doubled up as a private bedroom or apartment. Usually, the private rooms included a picture gallery or chitra shali, a bedroom and a temple. Where the private room was enriched with inlaid mirror work, it was called a sheesh mahal. The public rooms commonly included the sileh khana or armoury and the daulat khana or treasury.

Contemporary miniatures depict life in these palaces in great detail. They show rooms furnished with carpets, awnings, cushions and brocades, with embroidered canopies carried on poles, all enriched with sumptuous patterns and colours. There was very little solid furniture until the 19th century, when European patterns of taste began to prevail.

The courtyards were used for a wide range of activities from royal audiences to religious festivals, while the roof tops and highest courtyards were employed as outdoor bedchambers in hot weather. This interplay of indoor and outdoor space was one of the hallmarks of the Indian palace, where great importance was attached to the cool flow of air. Similarly, all the main apartments were designed for a versatility of use, so that each apartment or chamber could serve a variety of functions. Often, at Bundi or Udaipur, for instance, they were linked by narrow labyrinthine corridors with right-angle bends so that any insurgent enemy would be forced to advance in single file through the tortuous palace complex.

In most Rajput cities the principal palace was also the central fortified citadel. Some were known as garh palaces – that is, a fort-palace defended by vertiginous walls and impregnable gates. At Chitorgarh, Gwalior, Jaisalmer and Jodhpur, the fort-palace is situated on a high hill which dominates the entire area. On the exterior the lower storeys have few openings and little ornamentation, but above, these palaces break out into a spectacular skyline of balconies, kiosks, cupolas, turrets and crenellations, the product of incremental additions and accretions over many generations.

In some of the later palaces, modelled on those of the Mughal emperors at Delhi and Agra, the complex was designed as one overall composition, with a vast outer wall enclosing several groups of buildings and gardens. At Alwar, Dungarpur and Jaipur, dispersed city palaces of this nature were copied by the local rulers from Mughal prototypes. Elsewhere, at Amber, Bundi or Deeg, for instance, the garh palace forms part of a wider complex of fortifications. These great military citadels became symbols of the power and prestige of their respective rulers in much the same way as the English country house was an expression of the social and political power of the English gentry.

In addition to the main palace complex, subsidiary secular buildings were erected for particular purposes. Pleasure palaces were built for shooting and picnics, or as hot-weather retreats. Usually, these comprised a sequence of open pavilions linked by gardens or ornamental pools. They were always comfortable – elegant expressions of royal power and patronage.

Within the principal towns of Rajasthan, nobles and rich merchants resided in courtyard houses or havelis. These sophisticated houses, such as those at Jaipur and Jaisalmer, express the same architectural spirit as the great garh palaces.

The four principal palaces of Bundelkhand, built during the 16th and early 17th centuries at Datia and Orchha, were significantly different from the majority of the Rajput garh palaces in that they were conceived symmetrically both in their massing and plan form. Some have attributed this to the influence of Indo-Islamic architecture, others to the symbolism of an ancient Hindu mandala or Indian cosmic diagram. In reality they were a distinctive local manifestation of Rajput palace architecture.

Elsewhere in India, surviving examples of palace architecture are comparatively rare. In Kashmir the early palaces of the local rulers tended to reflect the simple vernacular style of the region. In the south, examples of palace architecture at Cochin and Padmanabhapuram were also derived from local architectural styles and idioms. The Marathas were more interested in the construction of isolated, inaccessible forts than in monumental palace architecture. Only two palaces of any significance were built, at Berar and Pune. Both were executed in carved teak and subsequently burnt down, so that the style was never copied.

The second great era of palace building occurred under the British. With the establishment of British paramountcy, many rulers aspired to European ideals and consciously cultivated European and, in particular, English social habits. This led to significant changes in palace design. The old halls of audience were superseded by Durbar halls, where a ruler could receive his British overlords or representatives in an opulent setting. Guest-rooms were designed for European visitors with magnificent collections of European furniture and art. Facilities were provided for their entertainment. Billiards rooms, dining-rooms, ballrooms, swimming-pools and tennis courts reflected the interests and predilections of a new Western-educated generation of Indian rulers. Suites of English and French furniture and vast collections of antiques replaced the comfortable soft furnishings of the old garh palaces.

Many of these new palaces were designed by European architects or military engineers. Some, such as the Lallgarh Palace at Bikaner, by the accomplished Sir Samuel Swinton Jacob, were designed as scholarly interpretations of existing native styles. Others were full-blown essays in European styles. The Elysée palace at Kapurthala was modelled on Versailles. Italian Renaissance designs were employed at Cooch Behar, Gwalior, Indore and Porbandar, while the gifted Henry Lanchester built the colossal Umaid Bhawan palace for the Maharaja of Jodhpur as a monumental exercise in civic classicism. Sometimes a curious distorted romanticism prevailed. At Bangalore the Maharaja of Mysore built a palace reminiscent of Windsor Castle, while another, the Lalitha Mahal, now a hotel at Mysore, boasted a centrepiece based on St Paul's Cathedral.

With the growth of Indo-Saracenic styles of architecture in the late 19th century, many patrons felt there was no need to stick to one particular style. Sometimes this led to a highly inventive blending of Western and Oriental design. The buildings of Major Charles Mant and, in particular, his palaces at Kolhapur and Baroda were ingenious attempts at an intermingling of forms and styles, but not all were characterized by either discipline or restraint. The most outrageous – the Amba Vilas palace at Mysore, by Henry Irwin, and the Laxhmi

Vilas palace at Baroda, completed by Robert Chisholm – have been described as 'orgiastic shopping sprees in the bargain basement of architecture'. The best, the Viceroy's House in New Delhi, by Sir Edwin Lutyens, is simply one of the finest buildings of the 20th century, the ultimate resolution of a series of stylistic experiments in the blending of Eastern and Western architecture which produced an extraordinary heritage of palace buildings unparalleled anywhere in the world.

Courtly Life and Art

Royal patronage provided a perpetual spring which irrigated the fertile soil of Indian art and culture. The Imperial and provincial courts of India were centres of artistic and literary endeavour, attracting talented scholars, artists and craftsmen from all over Asia.

After the sack of Baghdad in 1258, Delhi was one of the most important cultural centres in the Muslim East. With the destruction of centres of learning in Central and Western Asia by the Mongols, a stream of talented refugees sought sanctuary in India, but without libraries only those activities which were not dependent on accumulated stores of knowledge, such as poetry, art, architecture and music, flourished.

The Sultanate

Under the Delhi Sultanate important developments were made in music as Indian and Arab forms intermingled with the traditions of Persia and Central Asia. This syncretism led to the creation of a new type of music in north India quite different from traditional Indian music, which maintained its hold in the south. Much of the credit for this synthesis can be attributed to Amir Khusrau, the poet whose fame gave prestige to the new music, and also to the interest of the Chishti Sufis. At the independent court of Jaipur, music received special attention. At Jaunpur the last Sharqi king, Sultan Husain, was regarded as the founder of the Khiyal or romantic school of music, which later blossomed under the Mughals. At Gwalior under Raja Man Singh the chief musician was a Muslim who systematized Indian music in the light of the changes it had undergone since the advent of the Muslims.

In the field of education little is known about the detailed curriculum of the madrasas, but it appears that medicine was accorded high importance. The earliest surviving work, written in 1329 by Zia Muhammad, *Mazmua-i-ziai*, is based on Arabic and Indian sources, and gives local equivalents of Arab medicines. Others followed with combinations of Arab, Greek and Indian works, bringing together the medical knowledge of three cultures. Very few literary works have survived from the period of the Sultanate. With the exception of some major pieces by poets such as Amir Khusrau or Hasan, the only enduring works were those included in general histories, like the poems of Sangreza, the first poet of eminence born in India, or Ruhani's poem of the conquest of Ranthambhor by Iltutmish.

Perhaps the most important literary contribution during the Sultanate was in the field of history. Ancient Indian culture produced no historical literature, so surviving Muslim works are vital primary sources. These works are richly varied. While many glorify or exaggerate the role of their royal patrons, the basic historical facts are sound. The historian Baruni is particularly notable for his fascinating insights into the political philosophies of different monarchs and for his portrayal of individual personalities.

With the disintegration of the power of the Sultanate in the 15th century, the rise of the provincial kingdoms fostered the growth of regional languages. While Hindu rulers had patronized Sanskrit as the language of religion and the Epics, Muslim rulers supported the common languages of the people. Ironically, it was the Muslims who were responsible for the first translations of the Sanskrit Epics into the provincial languages.

The Mughals

The synthesis of Indo-Muslim culture reached its height under the Mughals in all fields of artistic endeavour. In music the syncretic tradition was maintained by men such as Fuqir Allah, whose analysis of musical composition, *Rag Darpan*, was derived from Sanskrit origins.

In the field of language the Mughal court spoke Persian and patronized the finest Persian poets of the day, but in the interaction between the court and the wider world a new language grew up – Urdu. This was a north Indian dialect using Persian vocabulary and metaphor and it rapidly became a favourite language of Indo-Muslim society.

Painting

It was in the field of painting that the greatest advances were made. Although Babur had some painters in his service, he made no attempts to foster art in his newly won empire. This was left to Humayun. During his exile in Persia and Afghanistan he encountered many painters who had studied under the illustrious Bihzad, and he persuaded a number of masters, such as Mir Sayyid Ali and Abdal Samad, to join him in Delhi, where they formed the nucleus of the Mughal school.

There was an earlier indigenous, non-Islamic tradition of miniature painting in India, the importance of which has often been understated. Generally, these were sub-miniature book illustrations painted on palm leaves or thin horizontal leaves of paper, quite unlike the rectangular format of Mughal painting. There was a flourishing school at Malwa, for instance. However, under the Mughals Indian painting in the form of albums and manuscripts achieved a grandeur and sophistication which has never been surpassed.

One of the first major productions of the Mughal studio was begun under Humayun. It was completed between 1562 and 1577 under Akbar. This was the *Romance of Amir Hamza* or the *Hamza-nama*, comprising over 1,400 paintings on cloth. Each painting was over 60 cm (2 ft) high, with the text on the reverse, so that it could be read aloud while the illustrations were displayed to the court.

Akbar was the true father of Indian painting. The school was placed under his direct supervision, with Khwaja Abdul Samad, a master-painter from Persia, as the head of an establishment of over 100 artists from 1572 onwards. There were a small number of Persian artists and later a preponderance of Hindus who had been trained in manuscript and mural painting. They joined with Persian painters in decorating the walls of Akbar's new capital at Fatehpur Sikri between 1570 and 1585. This collaboration soon gave rise to a distinct style of Mughal painting. In addition to the imported Persian masters, there were local gifted Hindu artists, such as Basawan Lal, Daswant and Kesu Das.

Artists collaborated on a single composition. One man was responsible for the design, another for the painting and often a third, a specialist in colour or portraiture, was called in to complete the picture. However, this system was abandoned after about 1590 with the end of the production of large-scale manuscripts.

The Akbari style was a blend of Persian art with native Indian elements, distinguished by an extended sense of space and action. The best examples were not only vigorous and realistic but contained elements of individual portraiture, a development which was to permeate Rajput painting as well.

When Akbar died in 1605 his library contained over 24,000 illustrated manuscripts. Although he could not read, others read to him. It was not only the great Persian classics that were illustrated but Hindu Epics like the Ramayana and the Mahabharata, and great dynastic sagas of the Mughal house itself, the *Timurnama, Baburnama* and *Akbarnama* – wonderful pictorial records of contemporary life and culture.

In 1578 a delegation of Portuguese Jesuit priests visited Akbar at Fatehpur Sikri and presented him with sets of illustrated Bibles and religious pictures. Akbar was so impressed with these that he instructed his own painters to emulate their qualities. European realism was added to the embryonic Mughal style. Subjects included scenes of contemporary life, historical incidents, animals, birds and portraits. Some of the finest and most interesting depict scenes from Akbar's life, such as the Birth of Prince Salim or the Construction of Fatehpur Sikri, painted about 1590. Another album depicts Akbar's courtiers.

The centre of manuscript production at Fatehpur Sikri was the Kitabkhana or Imperial library, which was divided into several parts. Often copies of the same manuscript or scene were made over a period of years.

Akbar's enthusiasm for portraiture was opposed by many orthodox Muslims at court. Traditionalists smeared the faces on miniatures with moist thumbs to comply with the Quranic prohibition against portraying any creature possessing a soul, but gradually a greater realism in portraiture did develop.

A distinct trend can be traced in Mughal painting from its early origins based on flat, delicate decoration in the Indo-Persian style, through a blending with Rajasthani styles, to a confident realism fostered by contact with the West, with golden haloes placed over the emperor's head, fine line shading on faces and more natural landscapes using accurate perspective.

Great care was taken in the choice and preparation of materials. Paper was made from bamboo, jute and cotton, or sometimes flax. This was then burnished with an agate pebble to give a uniform surface. Brushes were made of camel, squirrel or monkey hair; pigments from natural substances mixed with gum or sugar. Bookbinders and calligraphers also played a vital role in the production process.

Jahangir was an even more enthusiastic patron than his father. He was a connoisseur who prided himself on his discerning eye and he formed great collections of manuscripts. Under his patronage Mughal art reached its full range of expression and mood – allegorical, realistic, sensual and naturalistic. Jahangir loved nature. His artists were instructed to record animals, birds and flowers from all over the empire and, in particular, from his beloved Kashmir. He regarded the talented Ustad Mansur as the 'wonder of the age' for his accurate depiction of animals and birds. Everything was recorded: hunts, women, elephants and the pomp and splendour of courtly life.

Under Shah Jahan painting continued to flourish. A technique known as Nim Kalam or line drawing with a tint of colour became very fashionable. This had first been used under Akbar and later more widely under Jahangir, but the vigour and creative energy which characterized the work of Jahangir's reign began to wane. Although technically perfect, many miniatures seem cold and rather stiff. Figures were usually depicted in profile with garments richly painted in mosaic colouring enhanced with gold. Shah Jahan's greatest interest was architecture. He reduced the numbers of court painters, retaining only the best. The remainder were dispersed to provincial courts and palaces, where a flourishing provincial Mughal school developed.

With the accession of Aurangzeb, Imperial patronage was virtually withdrawn from the arts. Although the Imperial atelier was not completely disbanded, many drifted into the service of petty magnates or to the courts of Rajasthan.

In the 18th century Mughal painting entered a new phase. Under Muhammad Shah (1719–48) the style was revitalized. Painting grew popular outside court circles as the rich merchant classes also patronized the fine arts. With the disintegration of the empire, a shadow of the old Imperial style was maintained at the courts of Lucknow in Oudh and at Murshidabad in Bengal, but the innovative artistic impulse had disappeared.

Deccani Painting

In parallel with the development of Mughal painting under Akbar, a separate art form developed in the late 16th century in the Muslim kingdoms of the Deccan.

The styles which developed there were marked by a love of decorative detail, the sensitive use of colour and an overall refined elegance, which mixed Hindu, Persian, Turkish and European influences in a distinctive amalgam. The strong maritime links which the kingdoms maintained with the Middle East provided a cosmopolitan influence. Deccani artists tended more towards idealized imagery than realism. Many were probably Hindu artists displaced by the fall of Vijayanagara in 1565. Ibrahim Adil Shah II of Bijapur was one of the greatest patrons and an accomplished artist and musician in his own right.

Concurrent with the Mughal and Deccani schools of painting, there coexisted an indigenous Hindu school with deep roots in Indian history. There are two main subdivisions, Rajasthani and Pahari. Although both were influenced by Persian painting, their favourite themes were the great Hindu Epics and, in particular, the legend of Krishna.

Rajasthani Painting

Rajasthani painting evolved out of an earlier school of western Indian painting. It received an enormous boost with the renaissance of Hinduism in the 14th century. As religion found new life, so the arts expanded under its revitalizing impulse. Rajasthani miniatures are crowded with poetic metaphors and symbolism illustrating popular themes which people knew well, depicted in the vivid colours which they loved. While Mughal art was essentially realistic, Rajput painting was primarily symbolic. Different colours expressed different meanings – for instance, red for anger or brown for eroticism. In the ragamala paintings these artists illustrated musical modes, so that in a subtle blending of the arts, a particular painting was associated with a specific poem or melody.

By the early 17th century certain regional styles developed – at Bundi, Kishangarh, Kota and Malwa. By the mid-18th century schools such as those at Bundi and Kota had absorbed Mughal influences, the latter cruder and more exaggerated than the elegant style of Bundi. An unusual feature of the Kishangarh school, which flourished between about 1757 and 1770, was the large size of the miniatures, over 45 cm (1½ ft) or more. At Jaipur a hybrid style evolved, characterized by outstanding draughtsmanship.

Pahari Painting

The origins of the Pahari school are unknown, but it is possible that the Hindu courts of the Himalayan foothills were not as isolated from the mainstream of Indian life as has been thought hitherto. Some of the earliest miniatures date from about 1650, but the sack of Delhi in 1739 provided a significant impetus for the refinement of Pahari art. The first development, the Basohli school, is characterized by the use of bold, intense colour and strong profile. It was popular in the valleys of Chamba, Guler, Kulu and Mandi. Both Rajput and Pahari artists enjoyed detailing jewellery, clothing and landscape for their subjects. Over thirty-five Himalayan hill states produced miniature paintings. Each developed its own distinctive characteristics, often delicate in outline and pale in colour. One of the most distinguished was the Kangra school, which flourished between 1780 and 1805, and again between 1810 and 1823 under Raja Sansor Chand. Many of the best examples depict the Krishna legend in all its languorous, sensual symbolism. The Kangra school exerted considerable local influence on the art of Garhwal, where paintings in the Kangra school were produced as late as 1860.

With the expansion and consolidation of British power over much of India, the art of miniature painting died. Some artists found employment painting for the British. Pictures of flowers, birds and exotic scenes became popular in Anglo-Indian circles. These 'Company paintings' achieved high standards. Recently they have become appreciated for their own merits.

In the late 18th century European artists such as Chinnery, Zoffany and the Daniells travelled widely throughout India. Their portrayal of the exotic landscape and buildings of India had a significant, if limited, impact on European taste, where Orientalism in both painting and architecture became fashionable.

SEVEN

THE IMPACT OF EUROPE

Early Connections

It is a popular fallacy that the European connection with India began with the arrival of Vasco da Gama in 1498. This is untrue. The relationship is far older and deeper. It can be traced back to classical antiquity.

As early as 327 BC Alexander the Great crossed the borders of India and left social and cultural traces which survive to this day, high up in the Hunza valley on the north-western fringes of the subcontinent. The Romans enjoyed regular links with the west coast of India, trading direct in jewels, ivory, fragrant woods, perfumes and spices. Spices were not a luxury but an essential requirement of European life. A Roman cohort was maintained at Calicut on the Malabar coast. Roman coins, pottery and other artefacts have been unearthed at Madurai and elsewhere in southern India, suggesting that the link was not a tenuous one, and when Alaric sacked Rome in 410 the attack was mitigated not by Roman arms but by the promise of 3,000 lbs of Indian pepper.

There is no architectural legacy surviving from the Roman period, but Indian sources suggest that even at this early date the foreign community occupied a distinctly separate area in the coastal ports, a common thread which can be traced right through to the 20th century. These early settlements were probably little more than defensive timber palisades surrounding thatched huts, but they were sufficiently robust to protect the occupants from marauding beasts and hostile local forces.

The Portuguese

This ancient pattern of social and economic intercourse was severed by the fall of Rome and the rise of Islam, but it resumed with the arrival of the Portuguese in 1498.

The Portuguese were set on the road to India by Prince Henry the Navigator in a concerted effort to break the Venetian and Levantine monopoly of the spice trade. They were also impelled by the proselytizing zeal of the Catholic Church.

The Portuguese impact on India was immediate but never extensive. In 1505 Almeyda arrived as first viceroy at Cochin. Five years later the pugnacious Captain Affonso D'Albuquerque captured Goa from the Sultan of Bijapur. A series of strongholds was established, dominating the Eastern trade with Europe. By the mid-16th century Bassein, Daman and Diu were all well-established settlements, laid out on grid patterns and heavily protected in European style

Triumphal Gateway to Victoria Memorial, Calcutta

with polygonal walls, embrasures and central redoubts. In 1680 Bassein could boast a cathedral, five convents, thirteen churches and an asylum for orphans constructed over an underground network of bomb-proof caverns and tunnels.

When the Portuguese arrived on the Malabar coast, they found a flourishing Christian community governed by bishops sent out by the Eastern patriarchs, or by their own metrans or metropolitans. Tradition attributes the first conversions to St Thomas the Apostle in 52, but after the condemnation of the Nestorian heresy by the Council of Ephesus in 431, these early Christians were joined by waves of Syrian refugees seeking sanctuary.

Initially, the Portuguese made little attempt to interfere with established doctrines or rituals, but with the introduction of the fearful Inquisition in Goa in 1560, the Catholic authorities attempted to sever communications between the Syrian Christian Maronites and their distant Patriarchs. Ultimately, this led to the first great fissure in the Christian Church in Malabar in 1663.

The Portuguese attitude to the Indian people was ambivalent. Socially they encouraged intermarriage for political ends – to create a self-perpetuating Catholic elite – but culturally they were very intolerant, banning Hindu temples from Goa, for instance. Today the former Portuguese enclaves exert a peculiar fascination, with their heritage of Catholic Baroque architecture and beguiling Mediterranean charm. The great monuments of Goa, such as the See Cathedral (the largest Christian church in Asia) or the historic Basilica of Bom Jesus, together with the historic buildings of Diu and Daman, bear eloquent witness to a fascinating chapter of Indian history.

The Portuguese were undermined by their own reputation for cruelty and untrustworthiness, and when they were defeated by the English off the Swally river in 1612, they were displaced as the naval auxiliaries of the Mughal Empire. The Dutch, Danes, French and English followed in their wake. All established factories and trading stations in fierce competition with each other. Over time the Dutch concentrated at Chinsura, the Danes at Serampore and Tranquebar and the French at Pondicherry, Mahé and Chandernagore.

The Rise of the East India Company

The English were latecomers to India. The East India Company was granted its charter by Queen Elizabeth I on 31 December 1600, 'as much for the honour of this our realm of England as for the increase of our navigation and advancement of trade'. Rebuffed by the Dutch after failing to break their monopoly of the East Indies, the English turned to the less attractive consolation of India.

In January 1616, Sir Thomas Roe, the ambassador of James I of England, was received with 'courtly condescension' by the Mughal emperor Jahangir at Ajmer. This was one of those great moments of history when two cultures collide and acknowledge each other formally for the first time.

English influence spread rapidly at the expense of their European rivals. The first factory or trading post was established in 1613 at Surat, where some of the earliest English monuments in India can be found in the cemetery. By 1647 there were twenty-three factories, of which Madras and Surat were pre-eminent. In 1661 the Company acquired Bombay as part of the dowry of Catherine of

Braganza when she married Charles II, but as it was notorious for its insalubrious climate, for many years it remained subordinate to Surat.

The east coast always enjoyed a much healthier reputation. For this reason in the early years it was the centre of English influence. The early European settlements were all established peacefully either under Imperial firman or by local agreement, and not by force of arms.

In 1639 a new station was founded at Madraspatam on the Coromandel coast by Francis Day. Within sixty years, Day's small settlement had grown into a thriving city of over 300,000 people. It was from Madras that early ventures were made to the north and to Bengal. Here the Portuguese had founded Hooghly as early as 1537. The English presence did not commence until 1651, and then only tentatively. The foothold was not consolidated until 1690, when the persistence of Job Charnock led to the foundation of the city of Calcutta.

In the early 18th century both Madras and Calcutta enjoyed a long period of quiet prosperity, as the East India Company developed and expanded its trading links with England. Both developed into elegant cities.

At Madras settlement was concentrated within Fort St George, which underwent a process of continuous expansion throughout the late 17th and early 18th centuries. The development of Madras, with its distinctive grid pattern of streets, is the earliest example of English town planning in India. Similarly at Calcutta, all the principal European buildings were concentrated within the ramparts of old Fort William: the Governor's house, barracks, factors' houses, writers' quarters and warehouses. Only St Anne's Church, with its tall steeple, and a few European houses stood outside the walls. The only building of any architectural distinction was the Governor's House, a symmetrical classical range raised high on a podium to dominate the fort. At this stage European buildings resembled English town houses, with few concessions to the climate.

By the 1740s the Mughal Empire was in terminal decline, leaving a dangerous political vacuum. The great days of Babur, Akbar, Jahangir and Shah Jahan had long since passed. The unifying power of Delhi over much of the subcontinent began to shake and then crumble as the constituent parts of the empire broke away or formed regional alliances against each other, often in conjunction with the European trading companies. For all their efforts, the Mughals failed to establish the Imperial idea sufficiently deeply, so that when their power weakened, it was not followed by a revival under other leaders but by a release of those elemental forces which periodically threw the entire subcontinent into a paroxysm of internecine warfare.

It is important not to see India as a country or nation state at this stage. It was a patchwork quilt of kingdoms, fiefs and petty states, rather like mediaeval Germany, with the Mughal emperors on the Peacock Throne in Delhi exercising an overall suzerainty over large parts of the country, in much the same way as the Holy Roman Emperor once did in Europe. Within this ethnic melting-pot there were numerous martial races – the Sikhs, the Rajputs, the Jats, the Marathas, the Rohillas and the fearful Pindaris, marauding freebooters who lived off plunder and pillage – so when the Mughals lost their mission to rule there was no shortage of parties pushing to succeed them.

In 1739 the Persians swooped on Delhi. The Marathas, broken by Aurangzeb, regrouped into a confederacy under their hereditary minister, the Peshwa, and

76

re-established themselves across western and central India. In time, this confederacy fragmented into five areas of control: the Peshwa in Pune and Maharashtra, the Gaekwar in Baroda and Gujarat, the Bhonslas in Nagpur and central India, Holkar at Indore and Scindia at Gwalior. Power passed to their descendants and in time these five separate army commands developed into a mother state and four autonomous dependencies. In 1757 the Afghans under their brilliant leader Ahmad Shah Abdali cut through the north-west and sacked Delhi. The Mughals called in the Marathas for help. Four years later at the great Battle of Panipat, the Marathas were trounced by the Afghans, but the latter, threatened with mutiny, withdrew, leaving a power vacuum at the very heart of India.

India in the aftermath of Panipat has been described as 'a swirling sea at high tide, angry and tumultuous, but divided and lacking direction'. The concept of unity and central authority remained, but in reality it had vanished. No single faction was powerful enough to assert its authority over the whole.

It is likely that this anarchy would have persisted indefinitely had it not been for foreign intervention. The conditions favouring European intervention existed long before it actually occurred, and these conditions were self-induced. India was saved from herself, but not for altruistic, deliberate or even planned reasons. It was almost accidental, the product of European rivalries.

In the War of Austrian Succession, Britain and France were on opposite sides in rival coalitions. In the Seven Years War, from 1756 to 1763, the alliances were reversed, but the two countries remained opposed. In the simple distant struggle between the rival British and French companies in India, both were drawn into local alliances which eventually cleared the field for the British. The Indians were ready to call in European help as a decisive factor in any dispute. The door wasn't forced. It was held wide open, but to a power interested in trade not dominion.

In 1760 French power in southern India was broken at the Battle of Wandiwash. In Bengal, Clive had established British supremacy at Plassey three years earlier and given the merchants of the East India Company a free rein throughout Bengal. In 1764 at the Battle of Buxar the able Sir Hector Munro won a far more decisive victory than that at Plassey. He defeated the combined forces of the king of Delhi and wazir of Oudh, thereby consolidating the power of the East India Company throughout the entire region.

With the defeat of the French in the south and mastery of Bengal, increasing security provided impetus to the expansion of both Madras and Calcutta.

The Neo-classical Age

At Madras greater security encouraged wider growth outside the confines of the fort walls. This gave rise to the spread of Madras 'flat-tops', garden houses set in large, landscaped compounds. These houses, with deep verandahs to provide shade, were adapted from Palladian prototypes. Pedimented centrepieces and curved bays to the garden frontage were common themes, imparting a sense of grandeur and presence as well as providing a welcome respite from the unremitting sun. Notable survivals include the Adyar Club, Brodie Castle, the old Madras Club and Government House, Guindy.

With the resumption of British control of Calcutta by Clive in 1757, after the sacking of the city by Suraj-ud-Daula and the notorious incident of the Black

77

Hole, a major change occurred in the form and pattern of European settlement. A gigantic new fort was built, based on Vauban's 17th-century concepts of fortification. The new Fort William was the most important symbol of British military power in Asia. It took thirteen years to build and cost over £2 million.

In contrast to Fort St George, where all the principal public buildings were contained within the fort, at Calcutta the new public buildings were placed outside the ramparts. This was a significant change. The static form of development based on defensive strongholds gave way to a much more dynamic form of dispersed settlement, one more conducive to unrestricted growth and expansion. This was a reflection of growing power and security and increased wealth.

The new fort altered the entire layout of Calcutta, for in order to command an unrestricted field of fire, a huge open space, the Maidan, was cleared. This not only rendered the fort unassailable but created a magnificent setting around which an elegant collection of public and private buildings arose.

The formation of the Maidan in 1780 provided an opportunity for European merchants to express their newly found wealth in a more visible form. The old thatched bungalows were swept away, to be replaced by grand classical houses which reflected the aspirations and status of their European owners.

These fine Indian mansions, designed in an accomplished classical style, mark the first stage in the adaptation of European forms of architecture to an Indian context. Most are similar to the garden houses at Madras – a well-proportioned cube of two or three storeys set in a garden compound with the inner rooms screened by a colonnaded verandah or portico.

The siting of the houses in separate garden areas was prompted as much by good planning – it encouraged a cool flow of air and reduced the risk of disease – as by a desire for exaggerated individual impact. As a result, settlement was widely dispersed, with considerable distances between the houses. Transport was either by carriage or palanquin. Entrance porches became portes-cochères, often of enormous proportions, to accommodate the elephants of visiting grandees arriving by howdah.

The materials used were always the same: a rough brick core covered with Madras chunam, a form of lime stucco made from burnt seashells and polished to a high sheen, although in the harsh climate of Bengal this deteriorated to reveal the sham beneath the façade.

As development gathered momentum, the more central districts, such as Chowringhee and the Esplanade, acquired a continuous street frontage of boundary walls, screens and gates, which complemented the fine classical architecture of the houses. The serial construction of these houses over many decades was a process of continuous refinement and adjustment to local conditions. Intercolumniation was exaggerated to provide greater shade; proportions were bastardized to suit the context and louvred screens of wooden ribs or cane tatties of moist plaited grass were hung between the columns of the verandahs to provide a cool flow of air. Oversailing hoods and fretwork valances were added to the window openings to provide additional relief from the climate. In time, these became ornamental art forms in their own right, a recurrent theme in Anglo-Indian architecture.

Although many of these fine houses have been demolished or submerged in the encroaching bazaars, a number of well-preserved examples can still be found in

Chowringhee, Alipur and Garden Reach. Warren Hastings's house at Alipur, described as a 'perfect bijou' when built in 1777 and reputedly haunted by his ghost, is a notable example, together with nearby Belvedere, now the National Library. Other survivals, such as the Tollygunge Club or the Royal Calcutta Turf Club and Loretto Convent in Chowringhee, offer a rewarding insight into the 'city of palaces'.

As European architecture came to dominate the image of the city, so native merchants adopted European styles for their own houses and mansions in a curious process of hybridization. It is not uncommon to find European houses enriched with Hindu-style capitals or a compendium of strange motifs highlighted in gaudy colours. This cross-fertilization of architectural styles even affected the mosques. The mosque of Tipu Sultan, for instance, is a fascinating example of European forms and details being applied to a functional Islamic building.

By 1770, Calcutta had become the effective capital of British India, and the East India Company began to erect public buildings which echoed this newly found self-confidence. These were designed and built by military engineers or amateur dilettanti rather than by recognized architects, using available architectural reference works and technical pattern books. The books of Gibbs, Chambers, Stuart and Revett and the Adam brothers were freely plundered for inspiration and guidance. Interested amateurs such as C. K. Robison, J. P. Parker, James Prinsep and Claude Martin were all self-taught enthusiasts with considerable personal skill. It was men of taste and discernment such as these who were responsible for the transformation of Calcutta into a 'city of palaces', evoking the visions of Greece and Rome which so inspired the 18th-century cities of British India. These allusions to classical antiquity were not accidental. In part they were a product of the same movement in Europe, but in India they were a deliberate attempt to identify the expanding British Empire with the civilizing values of the Ancient World. This adaptation of classical architectural vocabulary to the climate was remarked upon at the time.

Maria Graham arrived in 1809 and wrote: 'On landing I was struck with the general appearance of grandeur in all the buildings; not that any of them are according to the strict rules of art, but groups of columns, porticos, domes and fine gateways interspersed with trees, and the broad river crowded with shipping, made the whole picture magnificent.'

The transformation of Calcutta and Madras from commercial trading enclaves into elegant neo-classical cities coincided with changing perceptions of British activity in India. Trade remained important, but the conscious reflection of the values of Greece and Rome in the monumental civic architecture of the period reflected a growing awareness of a wider political and Imperial role.

This was expressed in various buildings throughout India. In Madras, the ambitious remodelling of Government House by the second Lord Clive and the construction of a huge monumental basilica as a Banqueting Hall proclaimed this change in British perceptions. The grand pedimented ends of the Hall were enriched with arms celebrating British triumphs at Plassey and Seringapatam. In Calcutta the arrival of Marquess Wellesley, elder brother of the future Duke of Wellington, as Governor-General marked a profound change in British self-awareness. He, more than any other individual, stamped an Imperial dimension on Company rule.

The most significant manifestation of this change was the erection of Government House in 1803 to the designs of Captain Charles Wyatt. Modelled on Kedleston Hall in Derbyshire, the house was set in its own large compound at the north end of the Maidan. The main approaches were adorned with monumental entrance screens crowned with lions and sphinxes, recalling Robert Adam's screen at Syon House.

Once this Imperial dimension had been created, it was quickly taken up and copied elsewhere in India – particularly in the native states. Grand classical British residences approached through monumental entrance arches were built at Hyderabad, Lucknow and Mysore. Here architecture was used as an instrument of political policy. It was cheaper than sepoys in a country where power was judged by its outward expression. In 1811 the Resident of Hyderabad remarked: 'They can judge power and authority by no other standard than the external marks of it . . . the keeping up of an outward appearance of power will in many instances save the necessity of resort unto the actual exercise of it.'

Although Wellesley was recalled for his extravagance, the momentum towards an Imperial role was unstoppable.

As Calcutta grew, it blossomed into a city of palaces, a magnificent expression of rising British power. A whole series of classical perspectives was formed, with vistas terminated by prominent public buildings and monuments, such as the Town Hall, the Mint, Metcalfe Hall and the La Martinière schools. European ideas of townscape, planning and layout were imposed on an Asian city on a scale which had never been witnessed before.

The same process can be discerned elsewhere in British India. In Bombay a spectacular new Greek town hall was commenced in 1820, the finest neo–classical building in India. At Murshidabad a fine new palace was designed by General Duncan Macleod for the Nawab, based on Government House, Calcutta, while at Madras the shoreline boasted a range of classical buildings which provoked comparison with the Mediterranean in the age of Alexander.

Churches and Cemeteries

The prototype for many British churches in India is St Martin–in–the–Fields, London. In numerous early colonial churches the influence of great architects such as Wren and, in particular, James Gibbs was visible, and this was not just confined to India. St Martin's provided an appropriate model for use throughout the British Empire. Its plan, elevations and distinctive tiered spire recur again and again from Australia to North America and from South Africa to India. It continued to be used long after the Baroque style had been superseded by neo–classicism and the Gothic Revival.

St Martin's was used for various reasons. Symbolically, it lay at the heart of the Empire, and, after St Paul's, it was the grandest church in London. More importantly, its details were reproduced in Gibbs's *Book of Architecture* of 1728, thus its plan form and dimensions were readily available to remote colonial engineers. Functionally, it was an excellent prototype, with a long nave of three bays and a single chancel at the east end, but with a grand portico and handsome tower and spire, which conveyed an image of grandeur and Christian dignity.

St Mary's, Madras, the oldest complete Anglican church in the East and one of the earliest surviving British buildings in India, was commenced in 1678. Therefore, it predates the influence of Gibbs. It is of outstanding importance in the history of the British Empire and a repository of evocative monuments of considerable historical interest.

The first major church to use the Gibbs precedent was St John's, Calcutta, built by Lieutenant James Agg in 1787 at the heart of the old city. Although the spire was not built as Agg intended (an entire tier was omitted), it was widely admired and copied throughout India. The nearby Scottish Kirk of St Andrew's is a better rendition, and similar examples can be found in many of the cantonments and stations of upper India at Agra, Allahabad and Varanasi, for instance. The best are in Madras – St George's Cathedral and St Andrew's Kirk. St Andrew's is the finest early-19th-century church in India, based on Gibbs's plan for a circular church but adapted to the climate and conditions. It is crowned by a shallow dome. Both St George's and St Andrew's are sophisticated essays in the Baroque style, distinguished designs which owe a great deal to the structural ingenuity of the military engineer who built them, Thomas Fiott de Havilland. The façade of the chancel of St Andrew's is flanked by two enormous British lions and a frieze inscribed with the motto of the East India Company: '*Auspicio Regis et Senatus Angliae*', an overt statement of British political and religious supremacy.

So pervasive was the influence of St John's, Calcutta, and Gibbs's London prototype that it is a surprise to discover the occasional aberration, such as St James's Church, Delhi, designed by Colonel Robert Smith and built between 1828 and 1835 in memory of the famous Colonel James Skinner in fulfilment of a vow he made when wounded on the battlefield. This was designed on a Greek Cross plan and crowned by a Baroque dome, with each arm terminated by a Doric portico, but such exercises remained the exception rather than the rule.

Many of these churches contain splendid examples of funerary sculpture by leading sculptors of the day, such as John Flaxman and John Bacon. These were commissioned from India and sent out from London as ballast in the ships. Elegant marble monuments in crisply executed neo-classical designs expressed deep sincerity of feeling. Common repetitive themes were used in India and in England: the pedimented stele with draped figures in low relief mourning beside a pedestal or urn representing 'Resignation', or draped female figures contemplating the Bible or the heavens. Some are spectacular compositions in high relief. St Thomas's Cathedral, Bombay, St Mary's, and St George's, Madras and St John's, Calcutta, have outstanding collections of mural monuments which should not be missed.

Notwithstanding the surface grandeur and prospects for rapid wealth, life for Europeans was precarious and constantly overshadowed by the prospect of sudden death. For many life was just two monsoons. In Calcutta, European residents met on 15 November every year until 1800 simply to celebrate having survived the seasonal rains.

The cemeteries of British India are one of the most poignant reminders of the price of British rule. There are over 2 million European graves in India. Park Street Cemetery, Calcutta, is of outstanding interest, a fascinating repository of funerary architecture in the form of pyramids, pavilions and temples, resembling an Imperial city of the dead. Virtually every town and city in India has its old European cemetery, where ancient Dutch, Portuguese, French and British tombs

81

can be found. While many are overgrown and neglected, a number, including Park Street, have been restored with assistance from local firms and British commercial interests under the energetic guidance of the British Association for Cemeteries in South Asia, a charity which has done much to foster the effective conservation of a unique aspect of European colonial history.

Cantonments

By the late 18th century, the British enjoyed unprecedented security and power. Large areas of the subcontinent were under direct or indirect control. A new military strategy was evolved, based on the rapid deployment of troops and artillery, which had profound consequences for the form and layout of towns and cities. The concentration of European troops in city strongholds was replaced by the growth of separate military camps or cantonments on the periphery.

This marked a major change in the pattern of European settlement, separating the ruling European elite from the Indian masses. Their evolution marked another step in the physical separation of the rulers and the ruled. Insulated from the teeming bazaars of the native quarters and cushioned from the chaos and squalor of local life, the British created a wholly separate existence, which became increasingly distant from the real India of the masses. Although this promoted aloof, disinterested government motivated by the highest ideals, it also fostered arrogant concepts of racial superiority in contrast to the easy relationship which had characterized the earlier years of Company rule.

The concept of the cantonment arose from the Mughal practice of mobile government. The cantonment was merely an ossified military camp and was laid out accordingly. Most have a simple grid pattern of avenues lined with classical bungalows, counterpointed with the great institutions of British India – the club, the church and the racecourse. Virtually every major town and city in British India has its cantonment area, divided into civil and military lines.

Barrackpore, outside Calcutta, is unusual. It was the summer residence of the Governor-General. Originally favoured by Wellesley, it remained a favourite hot-weather retreat and boasts a number of interesting monuments, in particular the Temple of Fame, a Greek temple dedicated as a war memorial to the officers who fell in the conquest of Java and Mauritius in 1811. Varanasi (Benares) has an interesting cantonment area with a number of early houses, including the old Mint and the Nandeswar Kothi. Perhaps the most unexpected is at Patna, where the entire area is dominated by a huge beehive structure called the Gola, built in 1786 to the designs of Colonel John Garstin as a storehouse for grain in time of famine, one of the most extraordinary buildings erected in the British Empire.

Bungalows

Bungalows originated in Bengal. In Hindustani the word 'bangla' or 'bangala' referred to local village huts. It was from these crude prototypes that the bungalow developed. With the arrival of Europeans the word was soon corrupted and applied to any single-storey building with a verandah. The increasing numbers of officials, planters and soldiers residing in up-country locations stimulated demand for a form of housing that could be quickly built

82

from available local materials. The British adopted the bungalow as the ideal form of tropical housing and exported it all over the world.

From the crude early vernacular prototypes, bungalows soon acquired elements which reflected the social status of the occupants. Masonry and tiles replaced thatch and bamboo. Tuscan and Doric columns replaced wooden posts. Ornamental balustrades, arcaded verandahs and louvred screens were added to provide additional sunbreaks and to embellish the external appearance.

Common devices were used to control temperature and light: Venetian shutters to windows and doors, cane tatties suspended from verandahs and latticework screens. Internally, the ceilings were often just stretched muslin, which could be soaked with water in hot weather. Air circulation was provided by a large fan or punkah, although mechanical fans were introduced from as early as 1780 in Calcutta.

Most bungalows have a similar plan form, with the entrance through a colonnaded porch or porte-cochère leading to an arcaded verandah, part of which was sometimes enclosed to form a study or office. Usually the drawing-room led straight off the verandah, with the dining-room beyond. The rear verandah was used for household activities. The kitchens were kept away from the house in a separate outbuilding. This was common practice to minimize the heat and smells and to reduce the risk of fire. At Government House, Calcutta, this was taken to extremes. The kitchens were located completely outside the estate in the city. Food was carried to and fro on 'dhoolies' – wooden boxes on long poles. The Vicereine Lady Dufferin lamented: 'The kitchen is somewhere in Calcutta, but not in this house.'

By the 1870s the popularity of classical designs for bungalows gave way to more romanticized Gothic styles. Often the two styles overlapped to create delightful hybrids of considerable charm. Some of the most interesting examples are those in Bangalore and Mysore, where a distinctive local style with elaborately carved bargeboards, fretwork canopies and trelliswork known as 'monkey-tops' emerged.

Hill Stations

Between 1815 and 1947 the British built over eighty hill stations in the foothills of the mountain ranges of India at altitudes between 1,230 km (4,000 ft) and 2,460 km (8,000 ft). They were intended to provide rest and relaxation for the European population of the great cities during the hot weather, and sanatoria for recuperation after ill-health. They fall into four major regions. The foothills of the Himalayas contain the greatest number – Dalhousie, Mussoorie, Naini Tal and Simla were among the most popular, although in later years the ornate houseboats of Kashmir offered a popular alternative. In the north-east, Darjeeling and Shillong in Assam remained favourite resorts for Calcutta. In the west Pune and Mahabaleshwar served Bombay, while in the south, the stations of the Nilgiri Hills – Coonoor, Kodaikanal and Ootacamund – catered for Madras. All shared the same characteristics: an Arcadian setting, an informal layout and a strict social hierarchy, a nostalgic recreation of English upper-class values in the Indian Hills.

From the mid-19th century until the Second World War, the entire government retreated from Calcutta to Simla, where for almost six months of the year the British ruled one-fifth of mankind in celestial isolation from a remote Himalayan village. Until the forbidding new Viceregal Lodge was built in 1888, the seat of government was a small ramshackle house called Peterhof, which at least one Viceroy, Lord Lytton, considered to be a pigsty.

Generally, the architectural form of many Himalayan hill stations simply reflected long-established local practices and techniques. Heavy winter snowfalls dictated pitched roofs, while oversailing eaves and fretwork bargeboards were employed to protect the houses from wind and spring melt-water. The British merely adapted these indigenous structural features to their own architectural experience, and employed whimsical Gothic, Arts and Crafts or Alpine cottage styles. Prefabrication was important. Widespread use was made of cast-iron components and corrugated-iron sheeting.

In the south, Ootacamund was the principal hill station for Madras, but unlike Simla, it never succumbed entirely to the onslaught of the great offices of state. It retained its style and ambience as a select resort – 'Snooty Ooty', as it was known. Numerous maharajas retained summer retreats there: the Maharaja of Jodhpur at Aranmore, the Maharaja of Mysore at Fernhill Palace and the Gaekwar of Baroda at Baroda Palace.

While the hill station was a welcome consolation for those who lived their lives in exile, they were always pale imitations of life at home in Britain. For this reason, a sense of nostalgia and melancholy seems to pervade them, although today they are nearly all in active use. Ootacamund is a major centre of the Indian film industry; Simla a popular honeymoon location.

The Mutiny, 1857

The events of 1857 marked a watershed in the history of India. By the early 1850s, India was undergoing a period of acute social stress as the sweeping changes of the past thirty years pressed hard upon the traditional social structure of the country. In the mid-19th century the British were faced with a moral dilemma. Was it right to intervene and impose Western standards and values on an alien culture or should local customs and practices be tolerated and left alone? The Evangelical Radicals, such as Macaulay and Bentinck, and other great reformers had no doubts. Thuggee and suttee, for instance, were abolished as abhorrent heathen practices. Such widespread changes altered native perceptions of British rule and posed a threat to a whole host of vested interests. The Company was no longer a disinterested instrument of government, but one driven by all the remorseless moral convictions of the Victorian social conscience. Company rule was seen to be partial, bestowing patronage and favours on those who collaborated with the forces of change and new technology.

The introduction of the telegraph and railway and the development of irrigation and road works disturbed the ultra-conservative basis of Indian society. The great revenue assessments of northern India displaced many traditional communities and landholders. At a political level Dalhousie's Doctrines of Lapse extended British rule to those native territories without a direct heir. Persistent mismanagement became a valid excuse for annexation. In the huge Muslim state of Oudh, the activities of the British alarmed the entire ruling class.

The Indian Mutiny was not a war for Indian independence, nor a religious conspiracy, nor even a populist revolt based on agrarian grievances. It occurred at a point when the British were powerful enough to disturb the traditional structure of Indian society but lacked an effective means of social control. It provoked a wild atavistic spasm of communal violence against the advancing new order of Western values and institutions. It marked the death throes of old India and the dawn of the nation state.

The reaction when it came was compartmentalized, reflecting the uneven impact of colonial rule and the different stages of development of different social groups. It involved only parts of upper India and split the decaying fabric of Indian society into bloody civil war. Often tensions were greater in areas that did not revolt and remained loyal to the British.

The spark came not from the peasantry, nor from the dispossessed nobility displaced by the British, but from within the Company's own army, inflamed by rumours that cartridges for the new Enfield rifles were smeared with pig's and cow's fat – an affront to both Muslims and Hindus alike.

The flashpoint occurred at Meerut on 8 May 1857. The British were taken unawares. There was a fatal delay in responding. Within a month, the British were dislodged from Delhi and most of the surrounding area, and were invested in Lucknow and Kanpur (Cawnpore). Although the Bombay and Madras presidencies held, Bengal went up in flames.

Today the historical monuments associated with the events of 1857 offer a poignant insight into a tragic and bitter struggle. The ruins of the Residency at Lucknow, the memorial church and the commemorative screen at Kanpur, and the famous monuments along the Ridge at Delhi bear silent witness to the epic events.

The suppression of the Mutiny took almost two years, resistance petering out into the sporadic lawlessness of 1859. The defence and subsequent relief of Lucknow, the storming of Delhi and the ferocious campaigns fought across upper and central India rank as some of the boldest achievements in the annals of British military history. As in the days of Clive, time and again small units of ill-equipped and isolated British and Indian troops routed vast numbers of organized and well-equipped hostile forces.

In the aftermath of the Mutiny, a sea-change occurred in British relations with India. Company rule was abolished. The Crown assumed direct control through the instrument of the Viceroy. This new personal relationship accounted for the close bond which was to develop between Queen Victoria and her Indian subjects. Far greater emphasis was placed on respect for India's complex social and religious systems. British policies of Westernization and social engineering were thrown into sharp reverse. The *ancien régime* of Indian princes and maharajas, who had once been regarded as a barrier to change, became the main bulwark of the Raj. This was unfortunate in the long term because the Raj became identified as reactionary and backward-looking, reluctant to come to terms with the great forces of the age. More importantly, it denied the newly emerging, self-confident Westernized middle classes an effective voice in the new India. With the full weight of the Raj thrown behind the princes and in favour of the status quo, the aspiring professional classes were increasingly brought into confrontation with the government as they demanded a more substantial say in the administration of the country. Having been inculcated with Western values and ideals, they suddenly felt their rightful inheritance slipping away. With the old landed aristocracy discredited as saviours of India because of their collaboration with the British, the Westernized professional classes acquired a new respect in the eyes of traditional India. These were the men of the future.

The Buildings of the Raj

After the traumatic events of the Mutiny, the balance of British commercial interests changed. Calcutta remained pre-eminent, but Madras became less important. The centre of activity shifted to the west coast and to the emerging city of Bombay, which in less than three decades exploded from a forgotten backwater to a great Imperial city – 'Urbs Prima in Indis'.

The rapidity of its growth was phenomenal. In 1864 there were thirty-one banks, sixteen financial associations and sixty-two joint stock companies. Nine years earlier there had been none. This sudden economic boom owed much to the slump in supplies of American cotton to the Lancashire textile mills on the outbreak of the American Civil War. Overnight Bombay became 'cottonopolis', a vast clearing-house for Indian produce. Prices climbed to staggering levels. Land values rose fourfold. Speculation in land became frenetic.

This influx of unprecedented wealth coincided with the arrival of a new Governor, Sir Bartle Frere. Under his enlightened and energetic direction the city was transformed into the Gateway to India. The old town walls were swept away. A new city began to take shape in the latest fashionable Gothic style. Frere was determined to give the city a series of public buildings worthy of its wealth, power and potential. He stipulated that the designs should be of the highest architectural calibre, with conscious thought given to aesthetic impact.

The great neo-classical town hall, built by Colonel Thomas Cowper between 1820 and 1835, was, of course, already there, together with the venerable St Thomas's Cathedral. Frere nurtured this image of Imperial power. As a result Britain's finest heritage of High Victorian Gothic buildings now lies in Bombay.

Here, in a great phalanx facing the Maidan lie the Secretariat, University Library and Convocation Hall, the Rajabai Tower, the Law Courts, Public Works Office and Telegraph Office – 'a truly Imperial vision, monolithic, awe-inspiring and supremely self-confident'. Today, owing to land reclamation, they no longer face out across the sea, but they coalesce to form a splendid romantic skyline.

Although St Paul's Cathedral, Calcutta, was the first major church in India to break the mould of Gibbs's derivatives, it was designed in a whimsical English Perpendicular Gothic style. The first church in India to be designed in accordance with the new principles of 'correct' Gothic architecture, laid down by Pugin and the Ecclesiological Society, was the Afghan Memorial Church of St John the Evangelist at Colaba in Bombay, commenced in 1847. Its tall spire was a local landmark and its revolutionary principles infected the city with an enthusiasm for Gothic architecture which continued for over fifty years.

The architectural prototypes for the great public buildings of Bombay were the Victorian Gothic buildings then in the course of construction in London. The designs were readily available to the local military engineers of the Public Works Department in the pages of professional journals like the Builder. George Gilbert

86

Scott, who designed the university buildings in the city from his office in London, provided a clear source of inspiration for many. His competition design for the Foreign Office, with its central tower, symmetrical façade and Venetian inspiration, was highly influential. His design for the Rathaus in Hamburg, modelled on the great mediaeval Cloth Hall at Ypres, provided a direct source for the Law Courts at Calcutta, the most important Gothic building in a city of classical palaces.

Parsees and Sephardic Jews had resided in Bombay for generations. They associated freely with the British and invested heavily in the commercial life of the city. Some, such as Sir Jamsetjee Jeejeebhoy, Sir Cowasjee Jahangir Readymoney and the Sassoon family, devoted their energies to philanthropic endeavours. Many of the great civic buildings of Bombay were paid for from private sources and built from a range of readily available local building stone. Following designs by able military engineers such as General Sir Henry St Clair Wilkins and General James Augustus Fuller, the rage for Gothic buildings spread unabated across the city. They reached their climax in the great railway stations, which epitomized the expansive spirit of the age.

The Victoria Terminus, Bombay, or VT, as it is known, is the finest Victorian Gothic building in India. Erected between 1878 and 1887, it was inspired by Scott's St Pancras Station, but it is a highly original work, rooted firmly in the High Victorian Gothic tradition.

Bombay had been in the forefront of railway building. The Great Indian Peninsular Railway reached Thana in 1853, and the railway system played a significant role in the economic success of the city, particularly after the opening of the Suez Canal in 1879. Bombay VT is a 'paean of praise to the railway, the supreme example of tropical Gothic architecture; a riotous extravaganza of polychromatic stone, decorated tiles, marble and stained glass'. The colossal masonry dome over the huge internal staircase is crowned by a symbolic statue of progress. Flanking the main entrance stand the Imperial lion and the Indian tiger, twin sentinels of the Raj.

The architect, Frederick William Stevens (1848–1900), was one of the most gifted, resourceful and inventive practitioners of Victorian Gothic architecture, although he is virtually unknown in England. It was Stevens who designed the rival Churchgate Terminus in 1894–6, with its large domed lantern, but his real *tour de force* was Municipal Buildings, built between 1888 and 1893 opposite VT, a vertiginous mass of masonry capped by a glorious Islamic dome. For sheer controlled ebullience, it is unsurpassed in British India. It exudes the twin qualities of Imperial and civic pride, self-confidently symbolized by the crowning figure on the gable – '*Urbs Prima in Indis*'. With its intermingling of Gothic and Indo-Saracenic architecture, it is one of the great buildings of India.

Although Stevens's works represent the architectural climax of Victorian Gothic architecture in the city, the style continued to develop under his successors and, in particular, in the work of George Wittet, consulting architect to the Government of Bombay. Wittet was a more committed Orientalist, responsible for the Prince of Wales Museum and also the great Gateway to India, which became an architectural metaphor for the entire city and the symbolic point of departure for the last British troops to leave India after independence.

Elsewhere in India, Gothic architecture made a significant impact in the character of the Raj. At Varanasi, Queen's College was one of the earliest secular buildings in the 'correct' Gothic manner, built by Major Kittoe in a Perpendicular style between 1847 and 1852. At Allahabad a whole sequence of Gothic buildings was erected, including the Cathedral and Mayo College by William Emerson, future President of the Royal Institute of British Architects. Even the 'city of palaces', Calcutta, succumbed, with its Gothic High Court by Walter Granville. All over India churches and public buildings arose, influenced by popular Gothic taste. The cathedral church of All Saints, Nagpur, was remodelled to designs sent out from England by G. F. Bodley, while as late as 1914 Lahore Cathedral was being completed in a 13th-century style to designs prepared thirty years before by John Oldrid Scott.

The search for a definitive Imperial style preoccupied the British for the duration of the Raj. What sort of architecture should there be in India? The aesthetic Imperialists advocated an uncompromising approach. British architecture should be imported along with British law, order, justice and culture, not just out of duty but for the glory of the Empire. Civic architecture should be the physical expression of the highest Imperial ideals. Pure Gothic architecture was considered to be appropriate as a Christian national style. Later, the style of Wren and the English Renaissance was favoured as the quintessential expression of English values. The revivalist school respected local traditions and techniques. They advocated that the truest path was to eschew all imported forms and styles and to develop indigenous crafts and skills.

In the later 19th century the revivalists gained ground. There was a good reason for this. Victorian Indo-Saracenic buildings were part of the British response to rising Indian nationalism. Paradoxically, they helped to foster it by reviving a cultural awareness of India's past. They were sophisticated symbols of the Imperial presence. The external camouflage may be Indian and Indian labour may have been used, but the designs, plans and overall control remained British, in much the same way as the British remained the power behind the princely states. This transmutation of a national Gothic image into Indo-Saracenic forms is an indication of how the Raj began to adapt its image to make itself more palatable to the rising Indian middle classes.

Examples of Indo-Saracenic architecture can be found all over India. Many of the 19th-century palaces in the native states were designed in this style by accomplished practitioners, like Major Charles Mant at Kolhapur or Sir Samuel Swinton Jacob at Bikaner. One of the most prolific architects in this style was the versatile Robert Fellowes Chisholm, who designed the Presidency College and Senate House at Madras and the vast, rambling Laxhmi Vilas Palace at Vadodara (Baroda). However, the greatest Indo-Saracenic building in Madras is not by Chisholm but by his successor, W. Brassingham, and Henry Irwin, the architect of Viceregal Lodge, Simla. The Madras Law Courts, built between 1888 and 1892, were one of the high points of Indo-Saracenic architecture in India – 'a Romantic confection of multi-coloured Mughal domes, Buddhist shapes, canopied balconies and arcaded verandahs, crowned by a bulbous domed minaret which forms a lighthouse'. Irwin also designed the exquisite Victoria Memorial Hall and Technical Institute, based on the great Buland Darwaza, Akbar's great gateway at Fatehpur Sikri.

At Hyderabad the English architect Vincent Esch adorned the city with a large number of elegant public buildings, including the High Court and Osmania General Hospital. Here, a blending of Hindu and Muslim styles was used to symbolize the harmony between the two communities when the risk of sectarian strife was a constant worry.

In the south, at Mysore, Henry Irwin designed the incomparable Amba Vilas Palace for the maharaja, with an onion-dome and minaret which closely resembled those on the Law Courts at Madras. But the most scholarly exponent of revivalist architectural styles was Colonel Sir Samuel Swinton Jacob, who did an enormous amount of work in Ajmer, Jaipur and throughout Rajasthan, building on the pioneering work in Indian Arts and Crafts at Bombay by John Lockwood Kipling, the father of Rudyard. The effective conservation of many Indian monuments was one of the most enduring legacies of the British Raj. The Archaeological Survey of India was founded in 1861, but as early as 1808 the government had concerned itself with the preservation of the Taj Mahal. It was Lord Curzon who established the present framework of statutory control with the Ancient Monuments Preservation Act of 1904.

Not all cities succumbed to the blandishments of the Gothic school. Bangalore, for instance, remained firmly in the classical tradition, with its elegant Public Offices designed by Colonel Richard Sankey and its beautiful 'garden city' layout studded with charming bungalows enriched with 'monkey-tops'. It is a tradition that has continued through to the present day, with the completion of the Windsor Manor Hotel in 1985 in a colonial classical style.

Notwithstanding the High Court and Hogg Market, Calcutta also clung to its patrician image, with the construction of the General Post Office, East India Railway Office, Royal Exchange and other civic buildings all in the classical style.

By the early 20th century, Baroque civic classicism began to supersede Gothic as the most appropriate expression of the Imperial ideal. At Allahabad the new High Court by Frank Lishman (1916) was a sophisticated essay in Baroque architecture, cleverly adapted to the demands of an Indian setting, but the most potent intermingling of grand civic classicism with Indian forms was the Victoria Memorial, Calcutta.

Conceived at the very climax of the Empire, the building itself is the architectural climax of a city which owed its very existence to the Imperial mission. It dominates the whole of Calcutta. It is one of the most important buildings to be erected in the 20th century because it stands as an historical symbol to the Queen-Empress, completed at the very moment that the Imperial impulse was waning.

Intended to be an Imperial Valhalla of British achievements in India, its construction was entirely due to the influence of Lord Curzon, who specified the style and selected the architect, Sir William Emerson. The design was consciously influenced by English civic Baroque architecture of the period and, in particular, by Belfast City Hall. It was Lord Curzon too who insisted on the use of Makrana marble from the same quarries that supplied material for the Taj Mahal, for he saw his own Queen-Empress as equal in stature to the great Mughal consort.

It took almost twenty years to complete. Not until December 1921 was the entire monument finished and opened by the Prince of Wales. The crowning dome, with its huge bronze revolving Angel of Victory, proclaimed to the world the supremacy of the British Empire in the aftermath of the Great War.

In 1911 at the Delhi Durbar the new King-Emperor, George V, announced the momentous decision to move the capital from Calcutta to Delhi. The idea had been current for many years, but it was seized on as a political device to defuse the mounting tension and violence in upper India and Bengal. The British move was subtle if transparent. By identifying Imperial rule with Delhi they placed themselves in a direct historical continuum, stretching back through the Mughals and the Sultanate to the ancient empire of Ashoka. Despite the virulent opposition of vested interests, including Lord Curzon, who envisaged his great Victoria Memorial Hall as the focus of an Imperial capital at Calcutta, the move went ahead.

New Delhi combined 20th-century architecture with town planning on a grandiloquent 17th-century scale, a pure expression of political power. Every single building and vista reflected the hierarchy of the society which built it. At New Delhi the social structure of the British Raj was ossified for future generations to see. Land plots were allocated according to status. Within the vast hexagonal grid pattern, five areas were allocated according to race, occupational rank and social status. A clear pattern of social segregation was established.

The passionate pursuit of system and symmetry in the new city represented a final attempt by the British to impress order on the chaos of Indian society. The city which arose under the transcendent influence of Sir Edwin Lutyens and Sir Herbert Baker represents the culmination of over 200 years of persistent endeavour to achieve a true architectural synthesis of Eastern and Western styles. To Sir Herbert Baker, the new city was 'the spirit of British sovereignty . . . imprisoned in its stone and bronze'. In Lutyens's magisterial Viceroy's House, the architectural experiments which began to create a distinct Anglo-Indian architecture in its own right in the late 18th century reach their culmination. It is one of the great palaces of the world, a masterpiece, larger than Versailles, combining the grandeur of Bernini and the subtlety of Palladio with the colour, shade and water of the Oriental architectural tradition. Like all great works of architecture, it has a total unity and integrity and does not rely on a single façade for architectural effect. It dominates the entire city and is itself dominated by a monumental dome, which came to be regarded as an architectural metaphor for the British Empire, as Imperial in spirit as the solar topee which it resembles.

The great east front faces the principal axis, Rajpath (formerly Kingsway), the architectural climax of the entire city, approached along a vast triumphal route almost 3·2 km (2 miles) long and embellished with Imperial monuments. Even the notorious flaw in the gradient between the two great Secretariats could not diminish the magnitude of the overall achievement.

Lutyens was not just responsible for the overall plan and its spectacular centrepiece, the Viceroy's House; he also built two fine mansions for the princes of Hyderabad and Baroda and supervised the erection of many other buildings. However, it was the concerted efforts of his colleagues and subordinates which transformed the dream into reality. To Sir Herbert Baker can be attributed the two Secretariats and the Council House – bold and determined exercises in civic design; but the greatest number of buildings in New Delhi were designed by a largely unknown Englishman, Robert Tor Russell, who was responsible for the great circular concourse at Connaught Place, the Eastern and Western Courts, Flagstaff House (later the house of Nehru) and countless police stations, post offices, bungalows and public buildings.

The careful disposition of buildings within the city, and their relationship to the supreme symbol of authority, the Viceroy's House, applied also to the ecclesiastical buildings. God too knew his place.

Lutyens had prepared sketches for a great new Anglican cathedral in the city, but the money was never forthcoming, so in 1923 a competition was held and Lutyens chose an entry submitted by Henry Medd, one of his ablest young acolytes.

The Cathedral Church of the Redemption was completed in 1935, a splendid building exuding spiritual strength and power in a heathen land, a powerful, controlled mass of masonry with an interior kept cool by small windows, high barrel-vaulted ceilings and intersecting lateral arches. Medd went on to build the Roman Catholic Cathedral of the Sacred Heart, the product of the same architectural inspiration but compromised by the intervention of the Catholic authorities, who insisted on twin towers and demanded that an oval cartouche of St Francis be included.

St Martin's Garrison Church was designed by another follower of Lutyens, Arthur Shoosmith, between 1925 and 1930. It is an extraordinary composition, a massive gaunt monolith of 3½ million bricks looming straight out of the flat Indian plain. The walls, which are battered, rise in a series of setbacks and are pierced by deeply shaded openings cut straight through the outer mass.

St Martin's is important because it represented the end of a process which had begun over 200 years earlier: the search for an architectural form and style which would be comfortable, dignified and perfectly adapted to the rigours of the Indian climate. With independence in 1947, this architectural tradition did not die. The architect Walter Sykes George, for instance, who worked with Lutyens, stayed on and practised in India, but the mood changed. The International Modern style of Le Corbusier and other modernists was perceived as the answer to India's urban planning problems. Futuristic cities such as Chandigarh and Gandhinagar were built to express the spirit of a new age.

For much of the duration of the Raj, successive governments were obsessed with the threat from Russia. For decades the Great Game was played out high in the snow-clad mountains of Central Asia and across the burning deserts of Afghanistan. Ironically, when the real test came, it was not from Russia but from Japan, Britain's old ally in Asia, and not on the blood-soaked North-West Frontier but through the impenetrable jungles of the little-known North-East Frontier and Burma.

Empires, like people, tend to have the weaknesses of their strengths and the strengths of their weaknesses. As soon as the subjects of the Raj started to appeal to the innate sense of freedom for which it stood, the whole edifice began to crumble. Ultimately, there was a fundamental conflict between the two concepts of dominion and freedom. It was this moral contradiction between the high Imperial mission and the British liberal tradition that was seized upon and exploited so brilliantly by Gandhi, Nehru and the Indian nationalists.

By 1939 the British Empire was hopelessly overstretched. On the field of battle at Imphal and Kohima, the British and Indian armies not only atoned for the massacre of Amritsar but forged a lasting bond between the two nations which endures in the special relationship which exists to this day.

PART TWO

GAZETTEER OF MONUMENTS

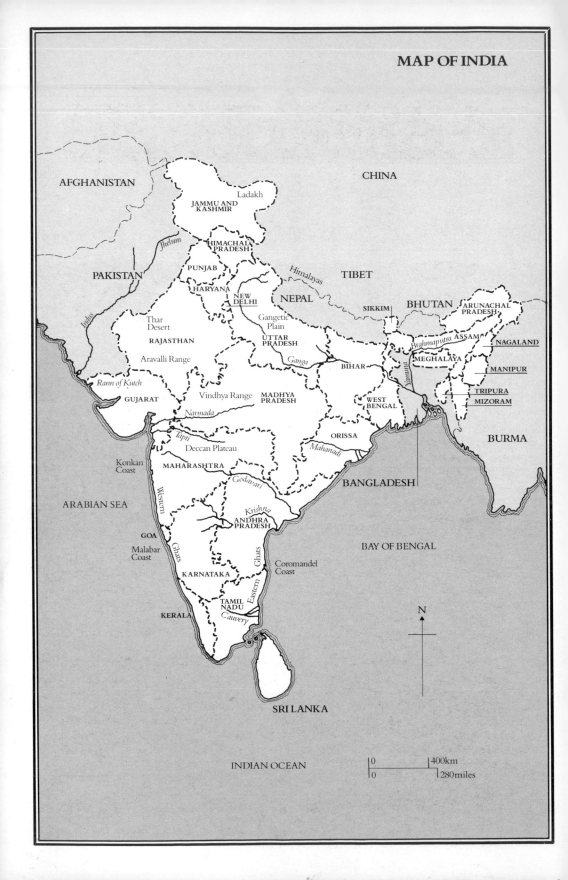

MAP OF INDIA

HOW TO USE THE GAZETTEER

The sites included in the gazetteer are grouped into six regions, beginning with northern India and ending with southern India. These regions coincide only partly with modern state boundaries since they are based on geographical and historical divisions. Each region is preceded by an illustrated introduction that surveys the development of regional architecture and art over a period of 1,000 years. Sites indicated in **bold** are marked on the detailed regional map that follows the introduction. This map shows modern roads, railways and airports, as well as nearby cities and towns where accommodation is available.

The sites marked in **bold** are also described separately in the regional gazetteers, where they are organized alphabetically. Over 340 cities, towns and sites have been selected according to the importance of their monuments, from the earliest surviving examples up to the present day. The selection of monuments is intended to be representative of all significant regional forms and historical styles. Even within a single site, there has often been a choice of monuments. The relative interest of sites is indicated by the length of their gazetteer entries.

Throughout, there is an emphasis on basic information. City maps and site plans have been provided where possible. Generally, individual buildings are described in detail, especially their architectural characteristics. Wherever possible terminology has been simplified. The glossary explains English, Islamic and Indian terms.

Islamic and Indian names of kings, rulers and saints have been spelt without diacritical marks to facilitate pronunciation. Cities, towns and sites are spelt according to prevailing modern convention or popular usage. Dates have been indicated as accurately as possible, based on the most reliable sources.

An Historical Chronology of Key Events records major events related to the principal Islamic dynasties from 1190 onwards and throughout the British period to 1947. The chart is divided into the six regions of the gazetteer. Complete lists of all the major Islamic dynasties of India and of British Governors-General and Viceroys are set out in separate dynastic tables.

Important museums are included in the gazetteer entries. In general, cities and towns are treated much more fully in this volume, which deals with the Islamic, Rajput and European monuments, than in Volume I. The sacred Hindu, Buddhist and Jain sites covered there tend to be more remote and isolated. Cross-references between the volumes are indicated in the relevant gazetteer entries, and those sites marked with an asterisk (*) in the index also appear in Volume I.

NORTHERN INDIA

EIGHT

NORTHERN INDIA

New Delhi, northern Uttar Pradesh, Punjab, Haryana, Himachal Pradesh, Jammu and Kashmir

Introduction

This region embraces Delhi and the territory to the north, including Jammu and Kashmir. To the west is the border with Pakistan and to the east, the foothills of the Himalayas and Nepal.

As one of the most ancient and historic cities of the world, **Delhi** is of outstanding importance, having witnessed the passage of mighty empires and powerful kingdoms since time immemorial. Repeatedly sacked by rapacious invaders, time and again the city has risen, like a phoenix from the ashes, to dominate the history of Hindustan. Each succeeding generation has left its mark. There have been at least eight major cities on the site, including **New Delhi**, and countless smaller fortified settlements and strongholds between Shahjahanabad, the Old Delhi of today, and the famous Qutb Minar.

The area is associated with the Mahabharata Epic, which was written over 3,000 years ago, but the first mention of the name 'Dilli' is by Ptolemy, the geographer of Alexandria, who visited India in the second century AD. Little is known of the history of the area prior to the Muslim conquest, although tradition assigns the founding of the city to the Tomaras, a Rajput clan, in 736. It was reputedly the threat of the Muslim invasions that led the Tomara ruler Anangpal to build a fort at Lal Kot in the 11th century, the first known defensive work in Delhi.

In 1192 Muhammad Shahab-ud-Din of Ghor defeated Prithviraj Chauhan, the last Hindu ruler of Delhi, and opened a chapter of continuous Muslim occupation. Every stage of the development of the Imperial style of Islamic architecture can be seen here, from the initial conversion and reuse of Hindu temple masonry to the accomplished compositions of the Mughal emperors.

Because of its commanding strategic location, Delhi rapidly grew in importance at the expense of Lahore. Under Qutb-ud-Din Aybak, the Slave dynasty was founded, producing some of the earliest Muslim buildings in India. The famous Quwwat-ul-Islam (literally Might of Islam) mosque was commenced in 1193, using the salvaged masonry from over twenty-seven Hindu and Jain temples. The celebrated Qutb Minar was started in about 1200.

This earliest phase of Muslim architecture, between 1193 and 1320, is characterized by the adoption and then adaptation of Hindu materials and styles to Islamic forms and functions. Later elaborate decorative features were developed from Hindu prototypes, with arches and domes rising from pendentives. The Tomb of Iltutmish (1236) is a notable example. Under Balban (1266–87) Persian etiquette and ceremonial were introduced to impart dignity and splendour to the court. The dynasty ended in 1290, when Shams-ud-Din was deposed

Overleaf The foothills of the Himalayas contain some of the most dramatic mountain scenery in the world

by Jalal-ud-Din Firuz Shah II, the first of the Khalji monarchs.

The Khaljis were a dynasty of Afghan Turks from a village near Ghazni. Under the third of their line, Ala-ud-Din Muhammad Shah I (1296–1316), virtually the entire subcontinent was subjugated. The Delhi Sultanate conquered the Deccan, defeated the Rajputs, checked the Mongols and transformed Delhi into an Imperial centre. In architecture a decisive advance took place with the erection of the Alai Darwaza in the Qutb complex, a splendid gateway built in 1305 with a sophisticated self-assurance and flair unseen before in India. This was probably due to the cultural influence of the Seljuk Turks, many of whom had sought refuge and protection at the royal court.

In 1320 Khusraw Shah was ousted by the provincial governor of the Punjab, Ghiyath-ud-Din Tughluq Shah I, founder of the Tughluq dynasty, which held sway until 1393. Only three of the Tughluq kings were interested in architecture; the founder, Ghiyath-ud-Din Tughluq Shah I (1320–25), his son Muhammad Tughluq Shah II (1325–51) and Firuz Tughluq Shah III (1351–88). Each built a new capital at Delhi.

Initially, local stone or red sandstone was employed, with sloping or battered walls and limited use of marble dressings. Later, buildings were plastered and carried on rough columns. Mosques were raised high on elevated platforms. The tomb of Ghiyath-ud-Din Tughluq Shah I at Tughluqabad is a good example of the earlier style, while the Kalan Masjid and the Hauz Khas tomb are representative of the more severe later style.

Ghiyath-ud-Din was an old man when he came to the throne. He reigned only five years. His successor, Muhammad Tughluq Shah II, 'one of the most accomplished princes and furious tyrants that ever adorned or disgraced human nature', was responsible for the disastrous attempt to move the capital and population to Daulatabad, a grandiose plan which caused widespread suffering and ended in ignominious failure.

Firuz Tughluq Shah III, who ascended the throne in 1351, was a prolific builder and a man of peace who did much to atone for the damage of his predecessor. It was he who built Firuzabad, the 'Windsor of Delhi', as a flourishing city on the river frontage, 13 km (8 miles) from Old Delhi at the Qutb.

As the Tughluq dynasty petered out in a succession of weak rulers, the decaying fabric of Imperial rule was torn apart by the devastating invasion of the Mongol Timur. In 1398 Delhi was sacked and the inhabitants put to the sword or enslaved. The great body of craftsmen and builders who had made Delhi the locus of Islam for over 200 years lay dead or were exiled to Timur's capital at Samarkand.

In the aftermath of Timur's invasion, Delhi recovered slowly, first under the rule of the Sayyids (1414–51) and later under the Lodis (1451–1526). The kingdom maintained its independence, but Imperial power was a mere shadow of its former self. This was reflected in the architecture. No great building projects were undertaken. No mosques, public buildings, palaces or strongholds were built. The only major monuments of this period are tombs, symbolically expressive of the dissolution of the empire.

Under both dynasties scores of large tombs arose in and around Delhi, so that the entire neighbourhood resembled a necropolis. This obsession with funerary architecture fostered a process of continuous development and refinement. Over fifty monuments of size and importance can be traced. The style expressed in the tombs of the Sayyid and Lodi kings was the outcome of two separate building conventions. There was the one-storey type, octagonal in plan, surrounded by an arched verandah or colonnade oversailed by projecting eaves, and there was the two or three-storey tomb, square in plan with no verandah. In both cases the

99

tomb was crowned by a large dome and often had a range of kiosks at parapet level, over each side on the octagonal plan, and at each corner on the square variety. The octagonal tomb type had originated at the close of the previous dynasty and can be seen in the tomb of Khan-i-Jahan Tilangani, but it developed as the recognized design for a royal tomb, that of Sikander Lodi (1517) being the most notable complete example.

It was the Mongols who once again intervened with such devastating effect on Indian history, and brought to an end the Lodi dynasty. Babur, a descendant of Timur, exploited the confusion in Indian affairs and invaded. At Panipat in 1526, Ibrahim Lodi was routed and the first of the great Mughal (Mongol) emperors seized control. The reign of his son Humayun (1530–56) was interrupted by the interregnum of the great Afghan monarch Sher Shah Sur, who established control over northern India in 1540 and put Humayun to flight.

Notwithstanding his comparatively short reign, Sher Shah Sur made a major impact on the development of Islamic architecture in India. His building projects at the Purana Qila, including the Qila-i-Kuhna mosque and Sher Mandel, and his tomb at Sasaram in Bihar demonstrate how brilliantly the torch of architecture burned in his hands.

However, when Humayun regained control in 1555, the foundations were laid for the supreme development of Islamic architecture under the Great Mughals. The cultural achievements of the Mughal Empire were almost entirely dependent on royal patronage and under the five great emperors – Babur, Humayun, Akbar, Jahangir and Shah Jahan – a distinctive Mughal style developed in two main phases.

In the earlier phase the buildings were generally constructed of red sandstone, in a robust, 'masculine' style, with sparing use of marble dressings. In the later period, under Shah Jahan, the style

reached its apogee. White marble was employed with stunning success, the domes became more bulbous, the minarets higher and more prominent and the style softer and more 'feminine'. In the later Mughal period, after the reign of Aurangzeb, the style became overelaborate and decadent, lacking the vigour and balance of the earlier compositions.

Although the Mughal Empire reached its greatest extent under Aurangzeb, on his death in 1707 it entered a period of rapid decline. In 1739 Delhi was sacked by Nadir Shah, the Persian, who massacred the inhabitants and carried off the Peacock Throne as well as the famous Koh-i-Noor diamond. Although the empire recovered, seventeen years later the Afghan Ahmad Shah Durani attacked the city and, in spite of orders to the contrary, it was plundered. For twenty years control was disputed between the Rohillas and the Marathas, but in 1771 the Maratha chief Daulat Rao Scindia captured Delhi and held it for over thirty years. During the Maratha War of 1803 it fell to the forces of the East India Company under General Lake, after which the Mughal emperors became mere figureheads.

Elsewhere in the region a wholly different provincial form of Islamic architecture developed. In Kashmir a distinctive style evolved constructed almost entirely of available local materials, principally wood and usually deodar, a form of cedar.

The technique of timber-framed construction was not dissimilar to that used in the vernacular buildings of Scandinavia or Austria, with logs laid horizontally one above the other and single tree trunks acting as piers. The log bridges or kadals across the Jhelum river in **Srinagar** are built on this simple cantilever principle with layers of logs placed transversely in alternate courses standing on a low masonry cutwater.

Islam was not widely accepted in

Kashmir until the latter part of the 14th century. In 1532 Mirza Haidar of Ladakh seized control, but it was not until 1586, with the incorporation of Kashmir into the Mughal dominions by Akbar, that the region was brought into the mainstream of Muslim life.

The most typical wooden buildings of Kashmir are the mosque and the tomb. The latter, known as a ziarat, often contains the holy remains of a local saint or figurehead and can be found outside many local towns and villages. The design and form of the ziarat and local mosques are broadly similar: a low, cubic structure containing a hall or chamber and a tiered, pyramidal roof crowned by a flèche spire. In many mosques a square pavilion was added between the apex of the roof and the base of the spire, acting as a gallery from which the muezzin can call the faithful to prayer. The mosque of Shah Hamadan in Srinagar, although extensively reconstructed on several occasions, is typical of this architectural vocabulary.

In the 16th and 17th centuries the Mughals attempted to revive the art of stone building in the state. At Srinagar the Fort of Hari Parbat, the Pattar or Stone Masjid (1623) and Mosque of Akhun Mulla Shah (1649) all exhibit typical Mughal features, with a common use of local grey limestone.

However, the greatest expression of Mughal art in Kashmir was achieved in the wonderful series of formal gardens which were designed around Lake Dal: the Nazim Bagh, Nishat Bagh and the incomparable Shalimar Gardens, some of the most spectacular garden landscapes ever created by man, set against the towering backcloth of the Himalayas.

The love affair of the Mughal emperors with Kashmir started when Akbar ordered the construction of a road through the mountains after he began his Imperial pilgrimages there in 1588. Jahangir was particularly enamoured with the valley. In 1620 he commissioned the court painter Mansur to depict more than 100 Kashmiri flowers to mark his first spring visit. By the middle of the 19th century a notable school of mural painting had developed in the towns of the region, such as **Chamba** and **Kulu**.

With the establishment of British control of Delhi after the Anglo-Maratha War of 1803, British influence increased steadily. After the Nepal War of 1815 the foothills of the Himalayas were opened up. Ten years later the first house had been built in **Simla**, later the summer capital of the Raj. Other hill stations followed at **Dalhousie, Dharamsala, Mussoorie, Naini Tal** and elsewhere, as the British found cool, hot-weather retreats on the rolling lower slopes of the Himalayas. With the subjugation of the Punjab in the fierce Sikh Wars of the 1840s, greater security was obtained throughout the region.

On the outbreak of the Mutiny at **Meerut** in 1857, the mutineers streamed to Delhi, where the aged Mughal emperor Bahadur Shah became a puppet rebel figurehead. Delhi played a crucial role in the course of the Mutiny. After being ousted by the rebels, the British stormed the city in September 1857 in one of the most memorable military actions in the history of British India.

With the transfer of the capital from **Calcutta** to **Delhi** in 1911, a huge new Imperial capital was planned by Sir Edwin Lutyens to enshrine the spirit of British sovereignty in bronze and stone. The new city was undoubtedly the finest architectural achievement of British India. With its spacious plan, vast avenues, vistas, rond-points and magnificent buildings designed in a synthesis of Eastern and Western styles, **New Delhi** represented the culmination of generations of architectural experiment to find a truly Imperial style. Viceroy's House is, quite simply, one of the greatest buildings of the 20th century, but it should not be allowed to eclipse the totality of the scheme as a whole.

Ironically, the eighth and greatest city of Delhi reached its completion just as the Imperial impulse was waning and the days of the Raj were numbered, but it provided a splendid focus for the feder- ated government of independent India and, arguably, a more compelling state- ment of Western values than the sterile, modern aesthetic of **Chandigarh**.

All India War Memorial, New Delhi

Right The Qutb Minar, Delhi

Below The Quwwat-ul-Islam Mosque, Delhi

Above The Tomb of Humayun, Delhi

Above right The Jantar Mantar, or Observatory, Delhi

Below right Lahore Gate, Red Fort, Delhi

Above Jami Masjid, Delhi

Above right The Cathedral Church of the Redemption, New Delhi

Below right St James's Church, Delhi

Above Viceroy's House, now Rashtrapati Bhavan, New Delhi

Below Christ Church, Simla

Right Mutiny Memorial, Delhi

Left Viceregal Lodge, Simla

Above High Court and Secretariat, Chandigarh

Below Elysée Palace, Kapurthala

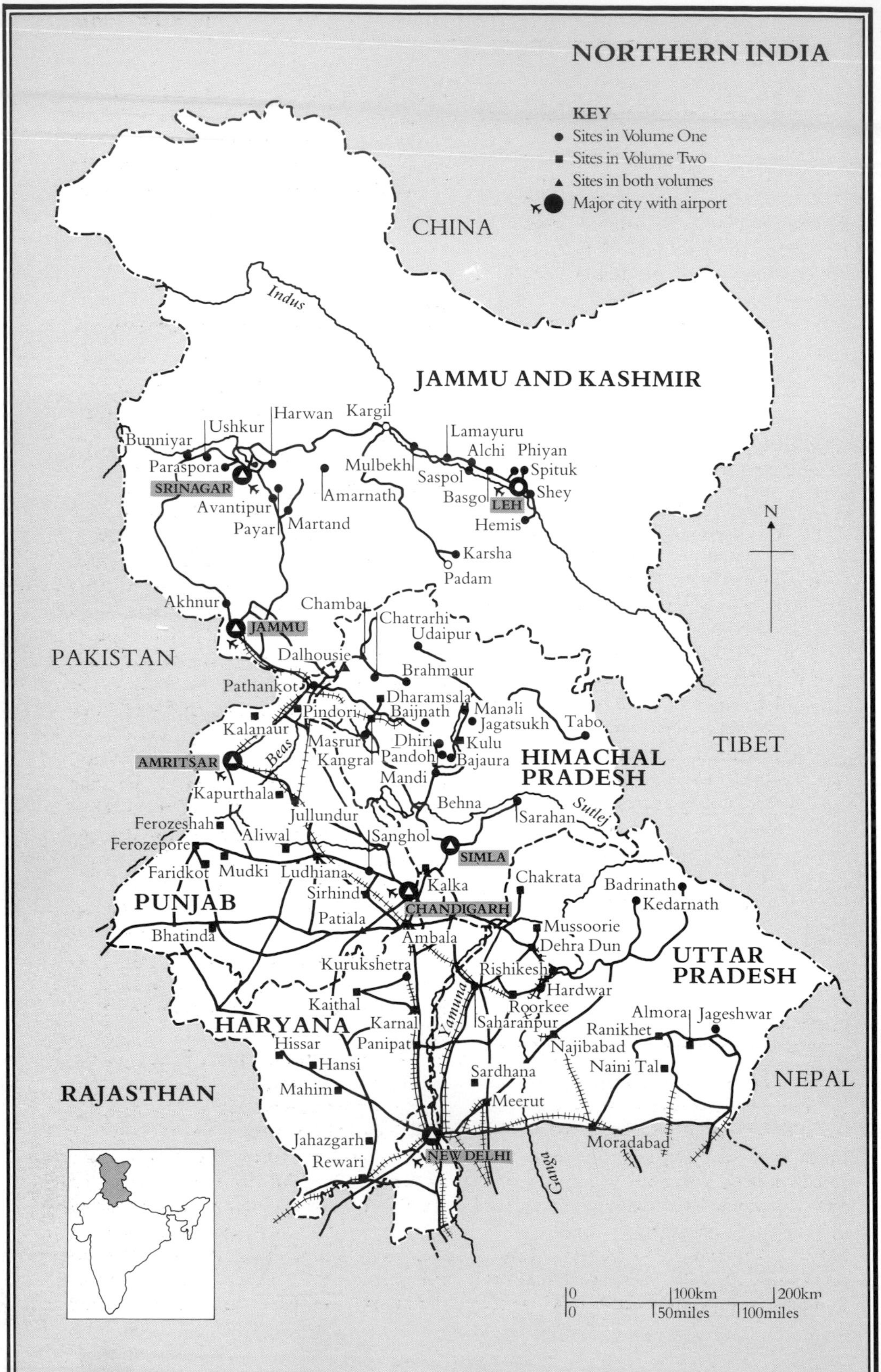

NORTHERN INDIA

KEY
- ● Sites in Volume One
- ■ Sites in Volume Two
- ▲ Sites in both volumes
- ⬤ Major city with airport

CHINA

Indus

JAMMU AND KASHMIR

Bunniyar
Ushkur
Harwan
Kargil
Lamayuru
Alchi
Phiyan
Paraspora
Mulbekh
Saspol
Spituk
SRINAGAR
Amarnath
Basgo
LEH
Shey
Avantipur
Hemis
Payar
Martand
Karsha
Padam

Akhnur
Chamba
Chatrarhi
Udaipur
JAMMU
Dalhousie
Brahmaur

PAKISTAN

Pathankot
Dharamsala
Manali
Tabo
Pindori
Baijnath
Jagatsukh
Kalanaur
Masrur
Dhiri
Kulu
Kangra
Pandoh
Bajaura
HIMACHAL
AMRITSAR
Beas
Mandi
PRADESH
Kapurthala
Behna
Sutlej
Ferozeshah
Jullundur
Sarahan
Ferozepore
Aliwal
Sanghol
SIMLA
Faridkot
Mudki
Ludhiana
Chakrata
Badrinath
Sirhind
Kalka
Kedarnath
PUNJAB
Patiala
CHANDIGARH
Bhatinda
Ambala
Mussoorie
Kurukshetra
Rishikesh
Dehra Dun
UTTAR
Hardwar
PRADESH
Kaithal
Roorkee
Almora
Jageshwar
HARYANA
Karnal
Saharanpur
Ranikhet
Hissar
Panipat
Najibabad
Hansi
Sardhana
Naini Tal
NEPAL
RAJASTHAN
Mahim
Meerut
Jahazgarh
Moradabad
Rewari
NEW DELHI
Yamuna
Ganga

TIBET

N

0   100km   200km
0   50miles   100miles

ALIWAL

One of the three great battlefields of the First Sikh War, Aliwal lies about 25 km (16 miles) west of Ludhiana. Here, on 28 January 1846, a British force under Sir Harry Smith defeated a large body of Sikhs commanded by Ranjit Singh. A later plain obelisk carries the name and date of the engagement in three languages.

ALMORA

Situated on the crest of a ridge 1,674 m (5,494 ft) above sea level, for centuries Almora formed one of the major strongholds of its native rulers. In 1744 a Muslim force invaded the area and Almora was plundered. In the Gurkha War of 1815 it formed an important strategic centre, suffering heavy bombardment by the British under Colonel Nicholls. After its fall, Almora recovered and became a prosperous little town, the local headquarters of the Kumaon district.

Today it is a picturesque hill station with a population of 23,000. It is a good centre for hill walking, with numerous pleasant routes through isolated woods. The view from the Kasar Devi Temple is lovely.

AMBALA

Ambala lies astride the route from Delhi to Simla, strategically sited on the borders of the Punjab. There is a huge cantonment area covering over 78 sq km (48 square miles), attractively laid out from 1843 onwards in a classic example of colonial grid planning.

Paget Park and the Maidan are pleasant open spaces, but the most notable British building is **St John's Cathedral** (1857).

Faced in brick and designed in a 14th-century Gothic style by Captain Atkinson, the local military engineer, it was a conspicuous local landmark until it was bombed during the Indo-Pakistan War of 1965. Only the shell now remains.

AMRITSAR *Map overleaf*

Amritsar, holy city of the Sikhs, was founded in 1579 by Ram Das, the fourth Guru. It takes its name from a sacred tank, the Pool of Nectar, by which the famous Golden Temple was built. (For details of the temple see Volume I.)

In 1761 Ahmad Shah Durani sacked the city, destroyed the temple and devastated the shrines. The temple was rebuilt in 1764. In 1802 the roof was covered with gilded copper plates by Ranjit Singh and the building acquired its popular name. It was Ranjit Singh who enclosed the city with a massive wall, most of which is now demolished, and who built the fort of Govindgarh.

The Islamic and European sites are generally of secondary importance to the Sikh shrines. The **Old City** is now enclosed by the circular road. Eighteen of the gates still survive, but only the gate to the Ram Bagh gardens is original.

The road from the railway station passes several sarais and mosques and goes on through an archway to the Kaisarbagh. The **Saragarhi Memorial** is here, erected to commemorate the Sikh soldiers who died defending the Saragarhi Fort on the Samana Ridge on the North-West Frontier in 1897.

The **Clocktower** marks the entrance to the Golden Temple. The road to the east leads to the **Jallianwala Bagh**, scene of the appalling Amritsar Massacre on 13 April 1919. Here, under a state of martial law, a large crowd was dispersed by General Dyer with heavy casualties. In this single incident the British surrendered the political initiative to the

113

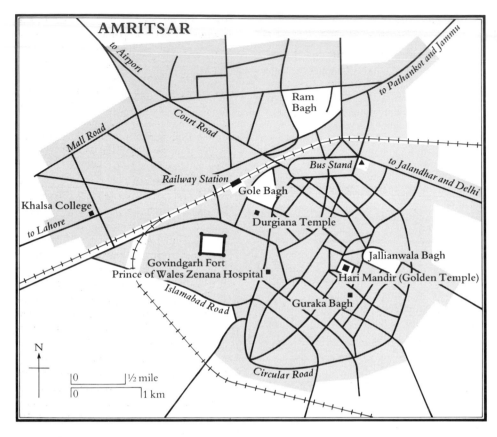

nationalists, which they never subsequently lost.

The **Rambagh Public Gardens** were laid out by Ranjit Singh around a summer pavilion. They offer a medley of walks and fountains in a 16-hectare (40 acres) garden. The journey from the Rambagh Gate passes the Mosque of Muhammad Jan, which has three white domes and elegant minarets. To the north is the Idgah and close to that is the Mosque of Khan Muhammad.

A short distance to the south-west of the city is the **Govindgarh Fort**, completed by Ranjit Singh in 1809 with the assistance of French officers in his service. French names can be seen on the fortified walls.

In the civil station are St Paul's Anglican Church, several missionary institutions and the Roman Catholic Church.

On the Grand Trunk Road is **Khalsa College** (1882), a large institution affiliated to the East Punjab University of Arts and Science. The future King George V visited here in December 1905.

BHATINDA

Bhatinda, 296 km (185 miles) from Delhi, was an important town during the rule of the Pathan Suri dynasty. There is a large fort, Govindgarh, with towering masonry walls almost 36·5 m (120 ft) high, which can be seen from the railway.

Within the town is the shrine of **Baha Ratan** (c. 1200), a Hindu convert and Muslim saint, which dates from the reign of Shahab-ud-Din Ghuri.

CHAKRATA

A small hill station lying 64 km (40 miles) west of Mussoorie at a height of 2,438 m (8,000 ft), Chakrata has distinct charm but few buildings of any note: a club, a library and three small churches.

CHAMBA

56 km (35 miles) from Dalhousie, Chamba lies high above the River Ravi at an altitude of 926 m (3,038 ft). It is the centre of the Gaddis, local shepherds who move their flocks up to the high pastures in summer and down to the Kangra and other lower levels in the winter.

The **Bhuri Singh Museum** has an interesting collection of art and culture from the region. Chamba is renowned for its school of miniature painting.

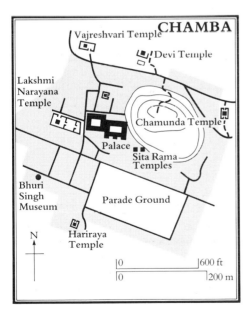

There are two centres. The older paintings are found in the Temple of Deviri-Kothi, but the most famous and accomplished lie in the Rang Mahal

Palace, in the upper part of the town. However, since the palace was damaged by fire, some of the best murals have been transferred to the town museum.

The **Rang Mahal Palace** was built by Raja Umed Singh (1748–64). He had been a prisoner of the Mughals for over sixteen years, which may account for the architectural form of the palace, which appears to be late Mughal in style. However, the original composition has been eroded by additions made by Jit Singh (1794–1804) and then by Charat Singh (1808–44). The Rang Mahal was the residence of the women of the Rajas of Chamba until 1947.

The fine miniature paintings date from the mid-19th century and were executed in the reigns of Charat Singh and Siru Singh (1844–70). They comprise one of the largest collections of wall paintings in the hills. Generally they depict spiritual themes, illustrating the religious eclecticism of the period, and legends of Shiva, Rama and Krishna are prominent also. The romance of Krishna's life seems to have been particularly popular and four of the best paintings portray secular themes.

At the north end of the chaugan or maidan is the Raja Sham Singh Hospital (1904). At the other end is the Old Residency, used as a state guest-house. The Presbyterian Church and Mission House of the Church of Scotland lie opposite the Museum.

(Details of the fine carved temples in the town are to be found in Volume I.)

CHANDIGARH *Map overleaf*

With the partition of the Punjab in 1947, the decision was taken to build a new, modern capital. The master plan was conceived by the French architect Le Corbusier and in its time it was considered the summation of accepted principles of town planning and civic design

115

based on the tenets of the International Modern Movement.

Today it is deemed to be a rather sterile exercise in Western planning, unsuited to the needs or requirements of the people, although in India it remains a popular place in which to live. Laid out on the grid principle, the spaces between the sectors and buildings are ugly, derelict stretches of wasteland which do little to enhance or soften the brutal modernism of much of the architecture.

Many of the principal buildings were designed by Le Corbusier, while the English architects Maxwell Fry and Jane Drew designed most of the neighbourhood sectors, with their schools, shopping bazaars and government housing. It makes a rather sorry comparison with the spectacular civic grandeur of New Delhi, but the High Court, Secretariat, Assembly, Governor's Palace and Museum, are all interesting examples of International Modern architecture designed by Le Corbusier. (For details of the Government Museum and Art Gallery see Volume I.)

DALHOUSIE

83 km (52 miles) north-west from Pathankot, at an elevation of 2,035 m (6,678 ft), lies Dalhousie, a hill station

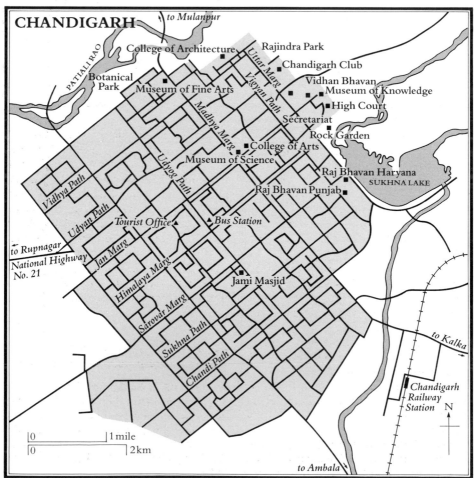

116

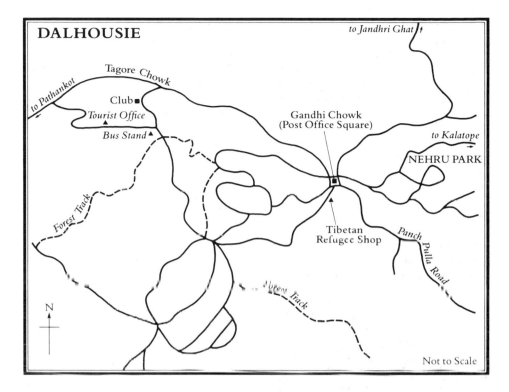

DALHOUSIE

and sanatorium in the Chamba Hills named after the Governor-General.

The station occupies the summits and upper slopes of three peaks of the main Himalayan range east of the Ravi river. It owes its inception to Lieutenant-Colonel Napier, then Chief Engineer of the Punjab and later Lord Napier of Magdala, who selected the site in 1851. In 1856 Captain Fagan was employed to mark out supply lines, plots and roads. By 1867 it was a municipality in its own right. It reached its high point in the 1920s and 1930s, when it offered an attractive, cheaper alternative to Simla, but since independence and partition its popularity has diminished.

Today the town is the gateway to Chamba state. Chamba town is some 56 km (35 miles) away through wonderful mountain scenery.

Post Office Square (now Gandhi Chowk) is the centre of Dalhousie. There is a convent school, college, hospital and Anglican church. Many of the houses are designed in the usual gimcrack Gothic and neo-Gothic styles which are the hall-mark of Indian hill stations. 2·4 km (1½ miles) from the square is **Martyr's Memorial**, commemorating Ajit Singh, supporter of the Indian National Army and Subhash Bose during the Second World War, who died on 15 August 1947, the day of Indian independence.

Jandhri Ghat, the old palace of the rulers of Chamba state, is set among tall pine trees.

DEHRA DUN *Map overleaf*

Dehra Dun (pronounced Doon) lies 79 km (49 miles) from Lhaksar and is the rail head for Mussoorie, which is 22·5 km (14 miles) away. The town is beautifully situated in a mountain valley 695 m (2,282 ft) above sea level in the Siwalik Hills.

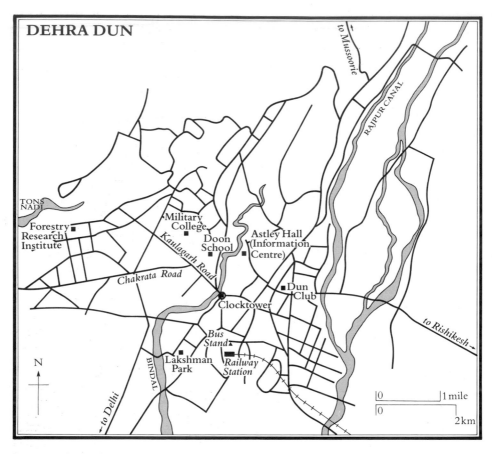

It was founded by Ram Rai in the 17th century after he had been driven from the Punjab because of doubts over his legitimacy. From 1770 onwards the area was devastated by marauders and invaders, including the Gurkhas. At the end of the Gurkha War of 1815, the country was ceded to the British, who had stormed the hillfort of Kalanga, 8 km (5 miles) away, during the fighting. It was at Kalanga that the British general Sir Rollo Gillespie fell. He is buried at Meerut. North-east of the town is a monument to the fallen.

The **Royal Indian Military College** (1922) is located here in a large complex of buildings designed by James Ransome. The architectural style chosen for the military station is distinctly Tudor, with half-timbering, leaded lights and dormer windows in a wistful Arts and Crafts idiom. Although the buildings were designed to resemble English cottages, in reality the upper windows act as clerestories to the large space within. Note the unusual dormer windows, which are recessed into the roof line and carried on timber posts. The viceregal residence is **Doon Court. Lakshman Park** is the residence of His Holiness Shri Mahant Lakshman Das. Other buildings include a Forestry Research Institute (1914), situated on the Chakrata Road; the Survey of India, founded in 1767; an Agricultural Institute; and a Laboratory of the Archaeological Chemist. The centre of the town is marked by the clocktower.

The famous Indian public school, Doon School, lies across the river from the clocktower.

118

DELHI

Delhi is one of the great cities of the world, with a tradition which recedes into the legendary age of the Mahabharata Epic over 3,000 years ago. Situated at an altitude of 216 m (709 ft), it lies between the Aravalli Hills and the River Jumna, a route centre and strategic location. That there have been no fewer than eight major cities at Delhi testifies to its historical pre-eminence.

The earliest mention of Delhi as a city of that name occurs in the songs of the Hindu Bards. It is alleged that a city called Indraprastha was founded by the

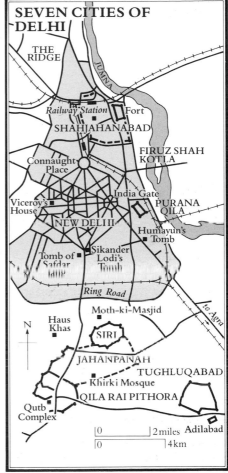

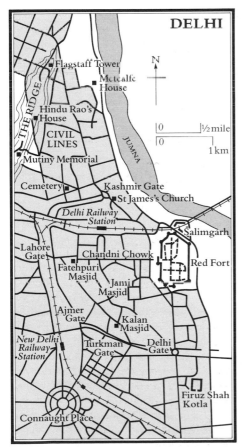

ancient king Yudhishthir on the site of the Purana Qila, but no archaeological evidence has been discovered to support this. Lal Kot, the Rajput citadel, was built by the Tomar king Anangpal in about 1060. Later, in 1180, Rai Pithora Prithviraj Chauhan enlarged the defences. After the capture of Delhi in 1193, the great Quwwat-ul-Islam mosque was begun in the same year by Qutb-ud-Din Aybak. Six years later, in 1199, he commenced the construction of the famous Qutb Minar.

The second city, Siri, was established by Ala-ud-Din Khalji in 1304 near the

119

present-day Hauz Khas. The city was founded as an entrenchment during the Mughal invasions of 1303 and it grew into a prosperous and flourishing centre. The third Delhi, at Tughluqabad, was created by Ghiyath-ud-Din Tughluq in 1321. Standing on a rocky escarpment, it is a vast complex of ruins with impressive fortified walls. It was occupied for only five years; Ghiyath-ud-Din's son Muhammad Tughluq built the new city of Jahanpanah (literally world's refuge), which lay between Lal Kot and Siri. It was intended to protect the vulnerable open plain between Old Delhi and Siri, but it too was soon abandoned. In 1328 Muhammad Shah decreed the transfer of the capital to Daulatabad in the Deccan. After a forced march and fearful hardship, the move was a failure and the citizens of Delhi returned to their homes.

When Firuz Shah Tughluq established himself on the throne, an era of peace and prosperity returned. In 1354 he constructed the city of Firuzabad, about 7 km (4 miles) to the north-east of Siri. He repaired the Qutb Minar and built canals, roads and pavilions. Situated on the banks of the river, Firuzabad was a thriving and populous city with splendid monuments, mosques and gardens. Today only the Ashoka pillar rising from the ruins of the Firuz Shah Kotla marks the site of the fifth city.

Under the Sayyid and Lodi dynasties a whole series of monuments, tombs and mosques were built across the surrounding countryside. In 1504 Sikander Lodi established his court at Agra and for over 150 years the capital alternated between the two royal cities, Delhi and Agra.

After the Mughal conquest Humayun built the Purana Qila in 1534. With his expulsion by Sher Shah, a sixth city, Shergarh, was founded around the Purana Qila within the confines of the ruins of Firuzabad. Of the fortifications, only the Kabuli Darwaza and Lal Darwaza remain from this period, although within the old city the Purana Qila and

Qila-i-Kuhna Masjid survive intact.

Under Akbar the capital moved to Fatehpur Sikri for a few brief, brilliant years. It was not until 1638 that Shah Jahan decided to move back to Delhi, where within ten years he built the huge new city of Shahjahanabad, now known as Old Delhi. Much of the building material for the new capital was taken from the ruins of Firuzabad and Shergarh.

With the decline of the Mughal Empire, Delhi once more fell victim to the periodic invasions which had so often devastated the city. In 1739 Nadir Shah, Emperor of Persia, swept across north India, defeated Muhammad Shah and seized the throne of Delhi. After a local riot the entire city was sacked and the inhabitants massacred. When he returned to Persia, the fabled treasures of the Mughal Empire were taken with him, including the Koh-i-Noor diamond and the Peacock Throne.

In 1857 it was to Delhi that the mutineers streamed, to the figurehead of the last Mughal emperor, Bahadur Shah. As a result of the ferocious storming of the city by British troops, further devastation was caused, but just twenty years later it was the scene of the durbar at which Queen Victoria was proclaimed Empress of India.

In 1911 King George V announced the removal of the capital from Calcutta to Delhi, and on the plains outside Shahjahanabad the eighth and greatest city of Delhi was raised to symbolize the enduring might of the British Raj.

The Old City: Shahjahanabad

The **Red Fort** or Lal Qila was commenced on 19 April 1639 and took over nine years to build. Conceived by the emperor Shah Jahan, in plan it is an irregular octagon with high battlemented walls carried around the city side to terminate in three-storey towers at the

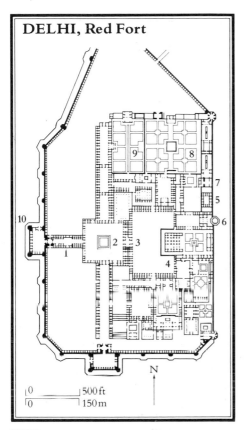

DELHI, Red Fort

```
0 _____ 500 ft
0 _____ 150 m
```

KEY

1. Bazaar
2. Nakkar Khana
3. Court of Public Audience
4. Diwan-i-Am
5. Diwan-i-Khas
6. Samman Burj
7. Royal Bath
8. Bakhsh Bagh
9. Mehtab Bagh
10. Lahore Gate

north and south ends of the river frontage. On the city side there is a deep moat, dry since 1857. The principal gates are the Lahore and Delhi gates, the Water Gate (at the south-east corner), a small postern in the centre of the river face and the Salimgarh Gate, which opens on to a bridge of twelve arches leading into an

outwork. Originally, the moat was spanned by wooden drawbridges, but these were replaced by stone bridges in 1811. The walls of the fort are faced in red sandstone with a succession of bastions, kiosks and turrets which create a powerful but picturesque profile.

Facing Chandni Chowk is the **Lahore Gate**, with side towers and a great central arch. The outer barbican was added by Aurangzeb to protect the main entrance of the fort, impairing the original conception, 'like a veil drawn across the face of a beautiful woman'. Prior to its erection there was a great square here where Hindu nobles camped and cavalcades of elephants and horses were ridden by the court nobility.

The **Delhi Gate** is a noble structure with lofty, flanking towers and a barbican, also by Aurangzeb.

The Lahore Gate leads directly into the **Chhatta Chauk** or vaulted arcade, which is flanked by thirty-two rooms. This vaulted hall, with a central octagonal court open to the sky, provides an imposing entrance to the fort. In Mughal times it was a bazaar humming with the activity of goldsmiths, jewellers, carpet makers and silk weavers who catered for the most sumptuous court in the world. Today the court jewellers and traders have been replaced by shops and souvenir kiosks. From the central octagonal court steps lead up to rooms over the Lahore Gate where the collector, commissioner and magistrate of Delhi and other Europeans were killed at the outbreak of the Mutiny on 11 May 1857. The rooms were formed by enclosing the once-open pavilions with stonework.

The Chhatta Chauk leads to a square measuring 164 m (540 ft) by 109 m (360 ft) from which the side arcades and central tank have now been removed. Around the edge of this tank over fifty Europeans, who survived the rebellion of 11 May, were killed on 16 June 1857.

In the east wall of the old enclosure is the **Nakkar** or **Naubhat Khana**, a music

121

gallery measuring 30·4 m (100 ft) by 24·3 m (80 ft). Music was played here five times a day. All visitors except royal princes had to dismount at this point and proceed on foot. Note the fine carved sandstone dado on the gateway.

Beyond the Nakkar Khana lay an inner court, the Am Khas, once surrounded by arcades, where the great feudatories mounted guard over the palace. Today it is a clear lawn on the far side of which is the **Diwan-i-Am** or Hall of Public Audience. The emperor made a daily appearance here until the custom was abolished by Aurangzeb. Designed for ceremonial audience, it stands on a raised plinth and is open on three sides. The façade is an impressive arcade of nine bays of engrailed arches three aisles deep. The whole hall was originally covered with ivory polished chunam. In the raised recess on the back wall was the emperor's throne. Below is the marble seat of the wazir around which are twelve inlaid panels by Austin of Bordeaux, including that of the artist as Orpheus, returned from the South Kensington Museum by Lord Curzon. In 1909 the hall was restored on Lord Curzon's instructions. Signor Menegatti, a Florentine mason, was imported to renew the pietra dura work to the throne recess.

In Mughal times the hall was hung with rich awnings, carpets and tapestries, and enclosed by gold and silver railings. Brocade canopies concealed the roof and silk carpets were spread on the floor. The original effect can be seen in contemporary miniatures. Here justice was dispensed rapidly: malefactors were crushed to death by elephant, put to the sword or bitten by poisonous snakes.

In the wall to the right of the throne are two doors which were once guarded by eunuchs. Behind the Diwan-i-Am lay the Imtiaz Mahal, one of the garden courts given over to the women. A gate on the north side of the hall led to the inner sanctum of the palace, the Diwan-i-Khas or Hall of Private Audience. This was where the famous Peacock Throne stood.

The **Peacock Throne** (1634), the seat of the Mughal emperors, no longer exists but it is depicted in several miniatures. It was seized by Nadir Shah in 1739 and carried off to Persia. On his death in 1747 it was broken up and the fragments dispersed, some being used for the throne at the royal palace in Teheran. It is alleged to have taken the royal goldsmith Bebadal Khan seven years to make. It was 3 m (9 ft 9 in) long by 2·28 m (7 ft 6 in) wide by 4·57 m (15 ft) high. The exterior was completely inlaid with sapphires and rubies. The twelve pillars were set with emeralds. On the crown two peacocks gazed upon flowers of jewels, and a tree studded with rubies, diamonds, emeralds and pearls. Between the peacocks was a figure of a parrot carved from a single emerald.

The **Diwan-i-Khas** was the most exclusive and splendid of all the pavilions in the palace. The arcaded courtyard or Jilau Khana, which once enclosed the hall, has been removed, adversely impairing the setting. The privilege of entering the court was accorded only to high nobles and officers of state. The hall measures 27·4 m (90 ft) by 20·4 m (67 ft) and is built entirely of white marble. The dados of the interior walls and columns are inlaid with precious stones. The hall is actually a baradari, a twelve-pillared pavilion with typical scalloped Mughal arches. The ceiling, once enriched in silver but removed by the Marathas, has been restored in timber. In the centre of the hall the empty marble dais marks the position of the Peacock Throne. Over the outer two arches in gold is the famous Persian inscription attributed to Saadullah Khan, Prime Minister of Shah Jahan:

If there is a Paradise on the face of the earth, It is this, Oh, it is this, Oh, it is this.

Above, over the four corners of the roof, are marble chatris; water flowed in a marble channel beneath. At night it was lit by scented candles and hung with brocades, silks and fine carpets.

Here, in the splendour of the Diwan-i-Khas, Nadir Shah received the submission of the Mughal emperor Muhammad Shah in 1739. On this spot in 1788 the emperor Shah Alam was blinded by the brutal Rohilla leader Ghulam Kadir, and in 1803 Lord Lake was received and celebrated for having saved the empire from the Marathas. Here also the rebel forces proclaimed Bahadur Shah as Emperor of Hindustan after the expulsion of the British in 1857.

Immediately to the north are the royal baths or **Hammams**, consisting of three principal chambers separated by corridors with canals to carry water to each room. The floors are inlaid with pietra dura work and the windows are embellished with coloured glass. The western apartment provided hot vapour baths, while the eastern chamber was used as a dressing-room, with a fountain which sprayed scented rose-water. It is reputed that four tons of wood were required to heat up the baths.

The **Moti Masjid** or Pearl Mosque lies close by to the west. It was built by Aurangzeb in 1662 for his own personal use and for the ladies of the zenana. It is a tiny marble building with three domes enclosed by a high red sandstone wall. A bronze gate leads to a small courtyard with a central fountain and a covered prayer hall at the west end. The floor is divided into small sections or musallahs, resembling individual prayer carpets. The marble domes replace the originals of gilded copper, which were destroyed during the Mutiny.

The passage through the baths leads to the river terrace. Here stood the Moti Mahal or Pearl Palace, a sandstone range covered with marble and gilded and painted, but it was demolished shortly after 1857. The small Hira Mahal was built by the last titular emperor, Bahadur Shah.

To the north lies the **Hyat Bagh** or Life-giving Garden, a courtyard 61 m square (200 ft square) with the Shah Burj bastion in the north-east corner and the Bhadon and Sawan pavilions on the north and south sides. The tank and channels were restored by Lord Curzon. Beyond, the road leads to Salimgarh, an outwork built by Salim Shah in 1546 and now bisected by the railway line. It contains no buildings of any interest and was once used as a state prison. Nothing remains now of the Mahtab Bagh or Moon Garden, which lay to the west and was once filled with fragrant white flowers.

To the south of the Diwan-i-Khas is an impressive group of buildings. The **Khas Mahal** (1639-48) was the imperial residence and place of private worship. The three apartments are known as the Tasbih Khana or House of Worship, facing north, the Khwabagah or sleeping-chamber in the centre and the Baithak or drawing-room to the south. The Musamman Burj is an octagonal tower, similar to that at Agra, over which a later balcony, added in 1810, projects. It was from this bastion that the emperor showed himself daily to his subjects on the river bank below. King George V and Queen Mary followed the same custom in 1911. At the entrance to the water gate below the tower an elephant was always stationed on guard. The marble dome replaces one of copper-gilt.

At the northern end of these rooms is a water channel. In the open central bay is an exquisite inlaid and pierced marble screen, translucent in its upper parts. Spanning the 'Channel of Paradise' the screen depicts the sun, moon and stars and the scales of justice; the lower part is carved like lace. Over the screen are four verses.

South of the Khas Mahal is the **Rang Mahal**, sadly defaced after it was used as an officers' mess after 1857. Once it was the royal zenana, surrounded by a garden court, the Imtiaz Mahal. Arcades used to enclose the court crowned by 2,000 gilded turrets. The richly decorated pillared building has a central hall of fifteen bays with small compartments at each end. Once the ceiling of the hall was silver, gilded with flowers, which reflected in the flower-shaped marble pool below, but the silver was used by Emperor Farrukhsiyar and replaced by copper and later again by wood. In the small end chambers are tiny reflecting mirrors inlaid into the ceiling. The most important feature is the central fountain – a marble, inlaid basin was fed via the Shah Burj pavilion from a branch of Ali Mardan's canal with water brought from the River Jumna.

The Daria or River Mahal has been demolished. Beyond is the **Mumtaz** or **Little Rang Mahal**, built in the same style as the Rang Mahal and probably used by the princesses. It has five openings to the river. After the Mutiny it was used as a guardroom and cells. Since 1912 it has been used as the **Museum**, with exhibits of textiles, weapons, carpets, imperial swords, jade and metal work, depicting life in the fort. Of the Khurd Jahan, shown on early plans, no trace remains. The entire area to the south was filled with humble quarters for domestic servants and other ancillary buildings, including a 'Silver Palace' of which little is known.

In the south-east corner, near the **Asad Burj**, are a water gate and some underground baths. In the south-west corner is the **Delhi Gate**. Between the inner and outer gates are two stone elephants, reinstated by Lord Curzon, the riders representing Jaimal and Patta, two Rajput chiefs. The gates are studded with elephant spikes. In front of the Delhi Gate is the elegant Sonehri Masjid or Golden Mosque, built in 1751 by Nawab Kudsia Begum and repaired in 1852 by Bahadur Shah.

The Red Fort is a national symbol of Indian freedom, for it was here on 15 August 1947 that Pandit Nehru unfolded the National Flag of India. There is a *son et lumière* every evening after sunset which re-creates some of the dramatic history of the fort.

Chandni Chowk is the principal axis of the city and its main commercial thoroughfare. The original bazaar comprised an octagonal court laid out in the vicinity of the present clocktower by Jahanara Begum, the favourite daughter of Shah Jahan, in 1648. The channel excavated in the centre of the road by Ali Mardan to supply water to the palace was built over after 1857. Today the whole street is a vibrant Oriental market of silver, jewellery and textile shops. The eastern end is marked by the Digambar Jain Mandir, built in 1656 with a bird hospital in its compound. The Dariba Kalan is a narrow, crowded lane of silversmiths. Along the street are a number of historic buildings. Near the central square and fountain is a Sikh shrine, the Gurudwara Sisganj. Adjoining is the **Kotwali**, the Police Station. Here many rebels were hanged after the recapture of Delhi in September 1857 and the bodies of the three royal princes shot and hanged by Captain Hodson were exposed for public view.

The Town Hall (1886) is an imposing colonial structure. The building occupied by the Bank of India was once the home of Begum Samru of Sardhana, who married the notorious Walter Reinhardt, the European adventurer. The Beresford family were murdered here on 11 May 1857. Opposite the Town Hall stood the **Clocktower**, designed by E. J. Martin but now demolished.

The **Sonehri Masjid** or Roshan-ud-Daulah Mosque, with its copper-gilded domes, was built in 1722 by a nobleman for Shah-Bhik, a local saint. It was here that Nadir Shah gave the signal for the massacre of the people of Delhi in March 1739.

Terminating the western end of the bazaar is the **Fatehpuri Masjid**, built in 1650 by Fatehpuri Begum, one of the queens of Shah Jahan. An imposing gateway leads to a wide courtyard with cloisters to three sides. The main prayer hall has a façade of seven bays and flanking minarets, crowned, unusually, by a single dome.

To the south of the mosque a street leads to Lal Kuan Bazaar, and to the north, to the Lahore Gate, and the smaller Sarhandi Mosque. A road from the Fatehpuri Masjid passes the west end of Queen's Gardens, the central park of Old Delhi, and the Cambridge Mission Church, and leads to Queen's Road and the **Kabul Gate**. Nearby a section of the old wall has been retained to mark the spot where Brigadier-General John Nicholson fell mortally wounded during the storming of the city on 14 September 1857. The gateway and main wall were removed in 1904.

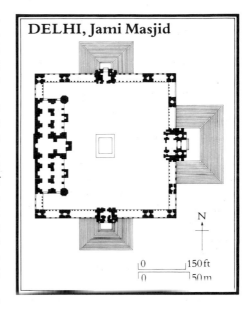

DELHI, Jami Masjid

The **Ajmer Gate** was built out of older masonry and survives intact. It is protected by an outer hornwork, built in 1805, in which lies the **Mausoleum of Ghazi-ud-Din Khan** (1710). He was the father of Asaf Jah of Hyderabad, whose son, also called Ghazi-ud-Din, is buried here, and whose grandson played a major role in the decline of the Mughal Empire. A Mosque and college are situated here.

The **Jami Masjid** (1644–58) is the largest mosque in India, the last great architectural work of Shah Jahan. It was designed by Ustad Khalil. The mosque has three huge gateways, four angle towers and two 39 m high (130 ft) minarets built of red sandstone inlaid with white marble strips. It stands on a natural outcrop of rock and dominates the city and views from the fort. It took 5,000 workmen six years to build. The approach is from the north or south, via broad flights of steps which lead through gateways into a massive courtyard measuring over 99 m (325 ft) square, with a central basin and fountain. The eastern gateway was opened only for the emperor or later, the Governor-General.

The massive doors are overlaid with brass arabesques. The prayer hall on the western side is capped by three bulbous domes flanked by minarets, which can be ascended. The domes, relieved by a thin line of black marble, rise above a façade of eleven bays. The present imam is a direct descendant of the imam appointed by Shah Jahan.

In the north-east corner of the courtyard is a small pavilion containing relics of the Prophet. To the east is the tomb of the Muslim leader Maulana Shaukat Ali (1873–1938).

From the Jami Masjid, Chaura Bazaar leads south-west to the Qazi Hauz and Lal Kuan Bazaar. South from the Qazi Hauz a main street leads past the Kalan Masjid to the Turkman Gate.

The **Kalan Masjid** or Black Mosque was built by Emperor Firuz Shah Tughluq in 1386 and was once the principal mosque of the city of Firuzabad. It is an imposing structure of two storeys, the lower forming a plinth. The upper walls have stone screens, now much mutilated, and the arcades are carried on square stone columns. It is a plain, austere building with a square cloistered court

125

and a prayer hall covered by a large number of plain domes.

To the east lies the tomb of the saint Turkman Shah, who died in 1240. Near the gate is Holy Trinity Church, erected by the Society for the Propagation of the Gospel in 1904. North of the saint's tomb is the **Tomb of Sultana Radiyya**, daughter of Shams-ud-Din Iltutmish, the only Muslim queen of India, who ruled from 1236 to 1240.

The Civil Lines and the Ridge

The area now known as the Civil Lines was where the early British residents settled in the city. It became the focus of European life and in 1857 was the scene of ferocious fighting as the British stormed the walls of Delhi.

The **Kashmir Gate** was built in 1835 by Major Robert Smith and later, early in 1857, it was made into a double gateway. It was here that the famous assault leading to the blowing of the gateway took place in September 1857. A plaque installed by Lord Napier of Magdala in 1876 was replaced with a memorial by Lord Minto in 1910.

Inside the gate lies **St James's Church**, commissioned by the famous Colonel Skinner. Work commenced in 1826 and took ten years to complete. The church was designed by Major Robert Smith, who built it to the top of the entablature, and finished by Captain de Bude.

James Skinner was born of a Scottish father and Rajput mother and had a distinguished military career. While lying wounded on the field of battle, he vowed that if his life was spared he would build a church in thanksgiving. St James's is the result. Later he raised his own cavalry regiment, Skinner's Horse, known as the Yellow Boys because of the distinctive colour of their uniforms.

The church is unusual in India. It has a cruciform plan, modelled on Venetian precedents, around an octagonal central enclosure with projecting porches on three sides. During the Mutiny the church was damaged by shellfire, but it was restored in 1865. Crowning the dome is a copper ball and cross, used for target practice by sepoys in 1857. Inside the church are some interesting memorials and brasses.

In the **Graveyard** are some notable tombs, including the vault of the Skinner family, the grave of William Fraser, murdered in 1835, and that of Sir John Theophilus Metcalfe, joint magistrate of the city in 1857.

Skinner's House lies just to the east of the church. It is a spacious colonial bungalow with wings on either side of a domed centrepiece. Here Skinner entertained William Fraser and Thomas Metcalfe. The entrance is via the central gate in Sultan Singh Mansions at the Kashmir Gate.

St Stephen's College (formerly the Cambridge Mission) has been transferred from this area to the north ridge. Part of the High School on the left was the library of Prince Dara Shukoh. At a fork in the road is a memorial obelisk to the officers of the Telegraph Department who fell in 1857. Beyond stand the gateways of the old **Magazines**. Here in May 1857 nine men defended the arsenal for as long as they could before blowing the magazine. Over the central gate is a memorial to Lieutenant Willoughby and his gallant men. In the south-east corner at the rear are the steps by which the survivors escaped. Under the south wall of the magazine is the old cemetery, with numerous old tombstones. One under a canopy was erected by Colonel James Skinner to the memory of Thomas Dunn. The cemetery closed in 1855.

The Dufferin Bridge crosses the railway and leads to Mori Gate and the Civil Lines. The **Mori** or **Shah Bastion** lies 183 m (595 ft) west of the gate and offers excellent views of the south end of the

126

Ridge and the north wall before the Kashmir Gate. The great walls of Delhi were built by Shah Jahan, but many of the bastions were strengthened by the British in 1809 after the attack on the city by Jaswant Rao Holkar. At this memorable engagement in October 1804 a small British force under Colonel Burn defeated over 70,000 Maratha troops with 130 guns.

Outside the Kashmir Gate is the **Qudsia Garden**, laid out in 1748 by the empress Qudsia Begum, who was born a slave but became the wife of Muhammad Shah. During the siege of 1857 a British battery was placed here. The imposing garden gateway still stands, together with pavilions, a small mosque and a river platform, opposite the **Cemetery**. The **Grave of Brigadier General John Nicholson**, who fell in the hour of victory and died on 23 September 1857, is here.

1·6 km (1 mile) further, past Maidan's Hotel, is a high mound, the site of Timur's camp. Beyond, in the grounds of Metcalfe Park, are the temporary buildings erected for the Houses of Parliament and Imperial Secretariat in 1912, pending the completion of New Delhi. They were designed by E. Montague Thomas and are now used by the University of Delhi. Close by the river is **Metcalfe House**, on Mahatma Gandhi Marg. It is a fine colonial bungalow (1844), once the residence of Sir Thomas Metcalfe, the Commissioner of Delhi from 1835 to 1853. One room was devoted to memorabilia of Napoleon, and the library contained over 20,000 books. Unfortunately, the house was looted in the Mutiny and the collection destroyed.

Shamnath Marg proceeds north for 1·2 km (¾ mile) before turning sharply west to meet the Ridge, which it enters via the 'Khyber Pass'.

The road leads to the **Flagstaff Tower**. Here, on 11 May 1857, the confused and agitated European survivors of the massacres in Delhi assembled. A fine view can be obtained from the roof. Along the Ridge between the tower and Hindu Rao's house, the British forces consolidated prior to retaking the city four months later.

To the west of the tower is a large house now used as the University Office. It was built for the Coronation Durbar in 1903 for use by the Viceroy, and was used as the Viceregal Lodge until 1931. Beyond is the old cantonment, which covers an extensive area to the Najafgarh Canal. St Stephen's College is here. Long lines of 'bells of arms', where the arms and accoutrements of the sepoys were locked up, can still be seen. The canal provided valuable protection during the siege. Near the canal is the **Rajpur Cemetery**, in which there are many Mutiny graves, including that of Sir Henry Barnard, and a memorial cross of Aberdeen granite.

3·2 km (2 miles) beyond, to the north side of the road, is the Plain of Barwari. Here the Imperial Assemblage of 1 January 1877 and the two Coronation Durbars of 1903 and 1911 were held. The site of the thrones occupied by King George V and Queen Mary in 1911 is marked by a granite column. An amphitheatre of earth formed for the 1903 Durbar remains.

6·4 km (4 miles) out on the Karnal road is the battlefield of **Badli-Ki-Sarai**, where the British under Sir Henry Barnard defeated a rebel force on 8 June 1857. There is a memorial to the 75th Foot in Sarai Pipal Thela village. 1·6 km (1 mile) to the west lie two old gateways and a grove of trees, all that remains of Shah Jahan's famous Shalimar Gardens, laid out in 1653.

From the Flagstaff Tower the road runs south down the Ridge past the Chauburji Masjid, a mosque built by Firuz Shah Tughluq as part of his hunting-lodge. This marked the left of the British position on the Ridge. Traces of trenches and breastworks can still be seen. About 800 m (½ mile) further south is the Observatory, probably a hunting-tower built in the 14th century.

Hindu Rao's House is now used as a hospital. It was built for William Fraser, agent to the Governor-General in Delhi, in about 1820. After his murder in 1835 it was bought by a Maratha nobleman, Hindu Rao. It was the key to the British position on the Ridge and was held by Major Reid and a force of Gurkhas, who suffered heavy punishment from rebel artillery.

At the rear of the house on the west side is an old baoli, which once provided water for the Hunting Palace of Firuz Shah. At the bottom of the well an underground passage leads to the Ridge.

The famous **Ashoka Pillar** was erected 228 m (740 ft) to the south of the house. Originally from Meerut, it was recovered from ruins close to the baoli.

The **Mutiny Memorial** is a lofty, octagonal, Gothic memorial cross which stands on the site of the right batteries of the British position. In panels around the base are recorded the 2,163 officers and men who were killed, wounded and went missing between 8 June and 7 September 1857.

Further west is the **Sabzi Mandi** or Vegetable Market, through which the British were attacked repeatedly. West of this are the **Roshanara Gardens**, laid out in 1650 by Roshanara, a daughter of Shah Jahan, who was buried here in 1671. In the centre of the garden is an original summer house, but only one of the four channels survives. The garden was saved from neglect by Colonel Cracroft in 1875. Part is now a Japanese Garden.

**South of the Old City:
Monuments along the River**

This tour commences at the Delhi Gate. To the right on the Circular Road is Irwin Hospital. Beyond, in Sikandra Road, is the Lady Irwin College for Women. To the left is the **Lal Darwaza**

or Red Gate (c. 1540). This was the northern entrance into Sher Shah's city. Also known as the Khuni Darwaza, it was from here that the sons of the last Mughal emperor were shot and hanged by the British in 1857.

Bahadur Shah Zafar Marg leads to the **Firuz Shah Kotla** (1351–88), once the citadel of the city of Firuzabad, founded by Firuz Shah Tughluq in 1354, the fifth city of Delhi. It was a populous capital which extended from Hauz Khas in the south to the north of the Ridge and eastward to the River Jumna.

Little remains of the glories of Firuzabad. The principal ruins are the Kushk-i-Firuz or Palace of Firuz on the river bank. The most distinctive feature is a monolithic tapering column of polished sandstone from the 3rd century BC, the Ashoka Column, brought here by Firuz Shah from Ambala to grace his new palace. It is the second column of Ashoka, 13·1 m (42 ft 7 in) high, and the first to be deciphered, by James Prinsep in 1837. Nearby is a circular baoli, with two storeys of arches, and a ruined **mosque**, which must have been imposing in its original state for it was said to have accommodated over 10,000 people. It is alleged that Timur, the Mongol, worshipped here and was so impressed that he used the same model for his own mosque at Samarkand.

The royal palaces and private apartments were situated on the river front to the south of this masjid. A low, roofed terrace with an arcaded front once faced out across the river. There were three underground passages, one leading to the river, the second to the Ridge and the third to the Qila Rai Pithora. Most of the complex was designed by Malik Ghazi Shahna, the chief architect, and his deputy, Abdul Hakk.

North of the Kotla is **Raj Ghat**, where Gandhi was cremated on 31 January 1948. In the centre of a walled enclosure is a low, square platform of black marble on which are inscribed Gandhi's last words. Opposite is the Gandhi Memorial Museum, inaugurated in 1961, with a vast library. To the north of this, at Shanti Vana, is the spot where Jawaharlal Nehru was cremated in 1964.

The road continues south past Tilak Bridge to the Purana Qila. En route, off the Mathura Road, is the **Supreme Court**. Designed in the Lutyens manner with a lofty dome and colonnaded frontage, architecturally it is part of New Delhi.

The **Purana Qila** or Old Fort lies on the site of the legendary city of Indraprastha, home of the heroic Pandavas in the Mahabharata Epic. The Old Fort is the work of Humayun and Sher Shah. The formidable walls and bastions were built by Humayun, who called it Dinpanah. Sher Shah strengthened the citadel, built the Qila-i-Kuhna Masjid and the Sher Mandel, and renamed the fort Shergarh. Once the river flowed along the eastern base of the fort, feeding the moat on the other three sides. Today only a wide ditch remains.

The citadel is rectangular in shape, with massive corner bastions. The entrance to the fort is through the north gate, the **Tallaqi Darwaza** or Forbidden Gate. Note the relief panels, including two depicting a man engaged in mortal combat with a lion and a carving of the sun. Over the gateway are three small pavilions, which were originally covered with coloured tiles. The southern gate has similar panels with elephants and faces the Delhi Zoo. The three gateways reveal an interesting mixture of Hindu and Muslim styles of architecture. For instance, the pointed arch is blended with Hindu chatris and brackets.

Inside, there are some notable buildings and excavated areas. The **Sher Mandel** is a small octagonal tower of red sandstone relieved with white marble dressings and crowned by a pavilion. Built by Sher Shah, it was used as a library by Humayun. Here, on its steep steps, on 24 January 1556, hurrying to obey the call of the muezzin, he slipped and died.

On the incline to the south, excavations have revealed stratified levels showing continuous settlement on this site from the Mauryan dynasty to the Mughal period. The finds are displayed in the **Museum**.

The **Qila-i-Kuhna Masjid** (1541) is the finest monument of the reign of Sher Shah. Built in the Afghan style, it was influential in the development of Indian Islamic architecture and is a splendid, balanced composition. The rear corners have fine stair turrets with oriel windows carried on brackets. The façade of the prayer hall is divided into five arched bays, the central one larger than the others, each with an ogival archway recessed within it. It is richly carved in black and white marble and red sandstone, and the central arch is flanked by narrow, fluted pilasters.

Inside, the mosque has five elegant mihrabs set in the western wall. The arches are lavishly ornamented with arabesques and Quranic inscriptions, and the central bay is crowned by a low dome. The juxtaposition of different materials, the composed treatment of the constituent parts and the elegant arches and pendentives combine to create a distinguished architectural statement.

Facing the western gateway across the Mathura Road is the **Khair-ul-Manzil Masjid** (1561), built by Maham Anga, wet-nurse of the infant Akbar, and a powerful influence at court in the early years of his reign. A large sandstone gateway leads to a cloistered courtyard, once used as a college or madrasa. The prayer hall lies on the western side, comprising three bays capped by a single dome. Once the façade was embellished with green and gold enamelled tiles.

Alongside is **Sher Shah's Gate**, similar to the Lal Darwaza and built of grey ashlar and red sandstone. This was the southern gateway to Sher Shah's city, the Qila standing outside the actual city limits. On the south-west side of the Purana Qila, covering a vast area, lie the **Zoological Gardens**. Among the sundry attractions are the rare white tigers from Rewa and a harmonica-playing elephant.

Further south Mathura Road leads to **Nizam-ud-Din**, a mediaeval village which grew up around the Dargah or shrine of Shaikh Nizam-ud-Din Chishti, the fourth in line of the Chishti saints, who died here in 1325. From the 14th century this area became a burial ground for Muslim nobility, and even today it retains a distinctive, introverted local character. Two entrances lead to the village and the main shrine. From Mathura Road a narrow road leads from near the Police Station to an arched gateway. From Lodi Road the entrance is via a modern gate.

At the northern end of the Dargah enclosure is a baoli. Legend asserts that the emperor Ghiyath-ud-Din Tughluq attempted to prevent workmen from building the shrine because it diverted labour from his own city of Tughluqabad, then being built, but that he was killed before he could enforce his orders.

The **Dargah of Nizam-ud-Din Auliya** was built in 1325 and comprises a small square chamber with verandahs on all four sides. This was renovated by Firuz Shah Tughluq, who added the arches and lattice screens in the inner sanctum, and at various stages, alterations and additions have been carried out. Much of the present structure is due to Faridun Khan, a high-ranking noble, who reconstructed the tomb in 1562 and added the octagonal drum and dome. The actual **Tomb of the Saint** is enclosed by a marble rail and covered with a canopy of mother of pearl. The Dargah is the focus of an annual festival in November and is one of the most revered shrines in the city.

South lies the **Tomb of Princess Jahanara**, eldest daughter and favourite of Shah Jahan. It is enclosed by marble screens but is otherwise plain, with a hollow space at the top filled with grass to comply with her own epitaph:

Let naught cover my grave save the green grass
For grass suffices as the covering of the lowly.

East of this tomb is a similar marble enclosure containing seven graves, one of which is that of Emperor Muhammad Shah (1748). East again in another enclosure lies Prince Jahangir, eldest son of Akbar II. Both of these enclosures have elaborately carved screens and doors.

Beyond the central court of the Dargah is another called the **Chabutra-i-Yaran** or Seat of the Friends, where the saint used to sit with his disciples. To the right, surrounded by two pierced stone screens, is the **Tomb of Amir Khusrau**, a great poet and principal disciple and friend of the saint. He is reputed to have died of a broken heart when he heard of the saint's death six months later. Celebrated as the first poet in the Urdu language, he helped considerably in the development of Persian and Hindi literature. An inscription on the walls refers to him as 'Tuti-i-shakar maqal' or sweet-tongued parrot.

To the west of the tomb is the **Jamaat Khana Masjid** (1325), built in red sandstone by Khizr Khan, the son of Ala-ud-Din Khalji. The central chamber, in typical Khalji style with lotus bud fringes, horseshoe arches and a large bulbous dome, is the oldest part. The three splendid arched bays are faced in sandstone and surrounded by three low domes. Stylistically it resembles the Alai Darwaza near the Qutb Minar. The side chambers are later additions, from the Tughluq period.

To the east of the tank in the northern part of the village is the **Tomb of Atgah Khan** (1566–7). This lies on a rocky outcrop with a white marble dome, a replica of that on the tomb of Humayun. It comprises a compact cube of sandstone with deep recessed arches to each side.

Coloured tiles and inlaid marble decorate the façades. It is a gem of early Mughal architecture, built by his son, Mirza Aziz Kokaltash. Atgah Khan rescued Humayun at Kanauj in 1540 and became Imperial Chancellor under Akbar. He was murdered in May 1562 by Adham Khan, the son of Akbar's wet-nurse, as a result of palace intrigue.

Nearby and to the east is the **Chausath Khamba** or Sixty-four Pillars (1625), an elegant marble pavilion which forms the final resting-place of Azam Khan and his family. It was built by Aziz Kokaltash and is inscribed with the date. The marble columns are enriched with carved foliated patterns. The outer pillars are linked by marble screens.

The **Chini Burj** or Tower of Tiles lies to the west of the baoli. Decorated with coloured tiles and incised plaster on the interior, it dates from the Lodi period.

The **Tomb of Mirza Ghalib** (1796–1868) lies just outside the Chausath Khamba in a courtyard flagged with red sandstone. Within stands the tomb of the great Urdu poet, recently rebuilt in marble. Adjacent is the Ghalib Academy, established to foster the research and study of Urdu literature.

Bahadur Shah Zafar's Palace is known as Lal Mahal. It lies near the Chausath Khamba, a central domed room surrounded by flat-roofed verandahs. It is now a private residence.

Across the Mathura Road from Nizam-ud-Din village is the **Tomb of Khan-i-Khanan** (c. 1627), a huge sandstone monument on an arcaded podium. It is the grave of the great Mughal general, poet and humanist Abdur Rahim Khan-i-Khanan, the son of Akbar's regent. It is built in two storeys, crowned by a double dome, and it set a precedent for the Taj Mahal. The interior has incised and painted plaster ornament to the ceiling, but the original external facings of marble and sandstone were removed in the 17th century for the Tomb of Safdarjang.

The **Tomb of Khan-i-Jahan Tilangani** (c. 1370), not to be confused with the above, is in a dilapidated condition but is important because it was the first octagonal tomb to be built in Delhi and had enormous influence on Islamic funerary architecture. It stands near the Kali or Sanjar Masjid (1370–71) and marked the beginning of a new phase of Muslim architecture for the royal tombs of the Sayyid and Lodi dynasties.

To the east of the Mathura Road a short road leads to the Humayun Tomb complex. The road passes the **Mausoleum of Isa Khan**, which is located to the right, just south of the western entrance to the first garden enclosure. It was built in 1547. Octagonal in form, it stands on a low platform and is crowned by a squat dome and finial. Raking buttresses provide structural support to the outer walls. Note the distinctive Hindu elements in the design, such as the projecting eaves over the verandah and the domed kiosks around the central dome. This synthesis of Hindu and Muslim styles is typical of Lodi architecture of the 15th and early 16th centuries. Within the octagonal garden enclosure is a small mosque with pointed arches to the three bays of the façade, enriched with brilliantly coloured inlaid tiles.

The path proceeds into **Bu Halima's Garden**, restored in 1914. Little is known about her; her rubble-built tomb lies to the north of the central garden.

In front of the garden forecourt of Humayun's Tomb, a small gateway to the south leads to another enclosure, which embraces the ruins of **Afsarwala's Mosque and Tomb** (1566–7). Over on the eastern wall are a series of chambers and an arched gateway. This is the **Arab Sarai**, allegedly built by Humayun's widow, Haji Begum, as a caravansarai for 300 Arab priests she brought back to India from her pilgrimage to Mecca. It is more likely that it housed the Persian craftsmen who worked on the emperor's mausoleum. The main pathway enters the garden forecourt of **Humayun's Tomb** through an impressive gateway which has a deep, octagonal recessed bay.

The tomb was built by Humayun's wife, Haji Begum, and completed in 1565, nine years after his death. The Mughal architecture design has been attributed to the Persian architect Mirak Mirza Ghiyath. It is the first great example of a new distinctive style which developed to become the hallmark of the dynasty. It is the first sophisticated development of the garden tomb complex, a symmetrical, monumental composition set in a landscaped garden enclosure.

The tomb is raised high on an arcaded sandstone platform with steps providing access to the terrace above. Octagonal in plan, it is crowned by a dome which rises over 38 m (125 ft) high. It is actually a double dome, the inner shell forming the vaulted ceiling to the tomb chambers and the outer shell creating a majestic external impact. The red sandstone is counter-pointed with white marble. To the centre of each side is a porch 12·2m (40 ft) high with a pointed arch flanked by outer bays, each with a similar, smaller arched entrance. The windows are recessed and filled at the lower level with carved lattice screens of stone and marble.

Inside is the emperor's cenotaph, the actual graves being in the basement, which is entered via a passage in the south face of the plinth. In the north-east corner of the main chamber lies Haji Begum. Steps provide access to the gallery and then up to the neck of the dome, from where magnificent views of the countryside can be obtained. The structures around the terrace once formed a religious college.

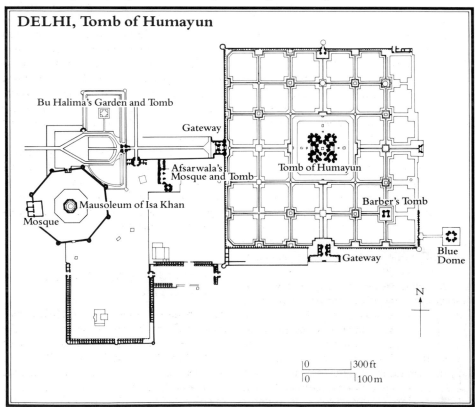

DELHI, Tomb of Humayun

132

The garden enclosure retains its original Persian form and layout, with paved stone avenues on the Persian chahar bagh plan, divided into four by water channels.

Architecturally the tomb is important because its plan and form are precursors of those at the Taj Mahal. Historically it is notable as the burial place of the royal house of Timur, containing many scions of the Mughal dynasty, including Dara Shukoh, eldest son of Shah Jahan, and the emperors Farrukhsiyar and Aurangzeb. It was to here that Bahadur Shah fled in 1857 and from here that he eventually surrendered ignominiously to the British under Major Hodson.

Across the river a grove of trees marks Patparganj, where Lord Lake defeated the Marathas in 1803.

Towards the south cast are two small tombs. The **Blue Dome** is octagonal in shape and is reputed to contain the bones of Fahim Khan, who was employed by Akbar's general Khan-i-Khanan. The other, a two-storey square tomb of red sandstone, is double-domed. This is the **Barber's Tomb** (1590–91).

The **Tomb of Muhammad Shah** (1450) is the tomb of the third of the Sayyid rulers. It has sloping buttresses, an octagonal plan, projecting eaves and lotus patterns on the ceiling.

North-east of this tomb is the **Bara Gumbad Mosque** (1494). Built in the reign of Sikander Lodi, it is a three-sided range with a prayer hall to one side and a fine domed gateway. The mosque is built of grey ashlar with some of the finest plaster decoration in India. Note the beautiful filigree work and profusely decorated façade.

On rising ground nearby is the **Sheesh Gumbad** (late 15th century), square in plan with a distinctive dome, once covered in glazed blue tiles that glittered in the sunlight, conferring the name Glass Dome. The interior comprises a single chamber rising through two storeys to a high dome enriched with stucco and painted ornament. It contains a large number of unknown graves of the Lodi period.

The **Tomb of Sikander Lodi** (1517–18) lies in a walled enclosure in the north-west corner of the gardens. There is a mosque on the west wall. It is octagonal in plan, with a Persian double-dome and Hindu decoration of lotus motifs.

Just to the east is the **Athpula**, a fine Mughal bridge (16th century) with seven arches and eight piers built by Nawab Bahadur.

This route terminates at the **Tomb of Safdarjang** (1753–74), who was the Wazir of Emperor Ahmad Shah and the Nawab of Oudh. The title Safdarjang means Disperser of the Battle Ranks, but unfortunately for him it was usually his own troops that he had to disperse, in ignominious flight.

The building represents the last example of the Mughal garden tomb complex. Set on a high podium, the mausoleum is topped by a high bulbous dome with four corner polygonal towers inlaid with marble. It is built of red and buff-coloured sandstone embellished with marble panels, but the whole composition lacks the solidity and power of the Humayun complex and is indicative of the decay of Mughal art.

Flanking the mausoleum are pavilions used by the family of Shia-ud-Daulah when they visited Delhi. Immediately to the south is the battlefield upon which Timur routed Muhammad Shah Tughluq in December 1398.

The Old Cities of Delhi and the Southern Tracts

The massive ruins of **Tughluqabad** straddle the rocky defiles to the west of the Mathura Road. This was the third city of Delhi, built by Ghiyath-ud-Din Tughluq, founder of the dynasty. Here, between 1321 and 1325, he built a vast range of formidable fortifications comprising a city,

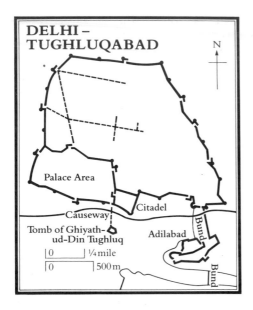

DELHI –
TUGHLUQABAD

Palace Area

Causeway
Citadel
Tomb of Ghiyath-
ud-Din Tughluq
Adilabad

palace precincts to the **Tomb of Ghiyath-ud-Din Tughluq** (*c.* 1325), which once stood within a large artificial lake. The mausoleum is an irregular pentagon in plan with a battlemented wall fortified at the angles by bastions. A massive gateway leads into the walled enclosure. The white marble dome crowning the building rises from a low octagonal drum. Architecturally it is important as the earliest Muslim building in India to have sloping walls, 'a warrior's tomb unrivalled anywhere, and a singular contrast with the elegant and luxuriant garden tombs of the more settled and peaceful dynasties that succeeded'.

palace precincts, citadel and fortified tomb which retain an aura of lonely grandeur.

The **Fort** is a half-hexagon in shape. The outer curtain walls follow the contours of the area and are defended on the north, east and west sides by a deep ditch and on the south by a lake. The walls are built of massive masonry and slope inwards to a height varying between 9 m (30 ft) and 15·2 m (50 ft), rising to 29·8 m (98 ft) around the citadel. The battlemented parapets are loopholed and there are large bastions at intervals pierced by thirteen gateways and three more to the inner citadel. It was defended in depth by three tiers: an external gallery, then a mural gallery and then the battlements. Inside are seven water tanks and extensive ruins.

Legend asserts that the fort was abandoned because of a curse by the saint Shaikh Nizam-ud-Din Auliya, who prophesied that the city would be inhabited by Gujars or be abandoned: 'Ya base Gujar, ya rahe ujjar.' In the north part of the fort are the ruins of the Jami Masjid.

A bridge and causeway, originally fortified, lead from the south gate of the

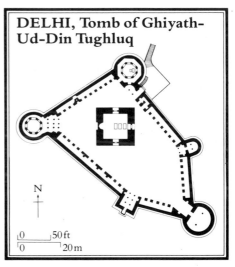

DELHI, Tomb of Ghiyath-
Ud-Din Tughluq

In the arcade to the left of the entrance is a small grave which is reputed to contain the bones of the emperor's favourite dog, a high honour for the animal as dogs are normally considered unclean by Muslims. Inside the mausoleum are three graves: those of Ghiyath-ud-Din Tughluq Shah I, his wife and their son Ghiyath-ud-Din Muhammad Shah II.

From the south-east corner of Tughluqabad and connected to it by a causeway lies **Adilabad**, built by Muhammad Tughluq. It is similar to the main fort,

134

with sloping walls of huge stones. Within was once the famous Qasr-i-Hazar Satun or Palace of a Thousand Pillars, which had a vast audience chamber carried on columns of varnished wood. The southern gateway retains its original vaulted corridor and passage flanked by guardrooms. Inside is a right-angled turn, once closed by secondary gates to protect the entrance to the fort. Eastward lies an isolated outwork, the Barber's Fort.

Architecturally this complex of buildings is a fine example of the early Tughluq style, with typical characteristics: severe battered walls, austere bare surfaces, squinch arches and crenellation.

Westward along the Mehrauli – Badarpur road lie the remains of the fourth city of Delhi, **Jahanpanah**. This was constructed by Muhammad Shah Tughluq in about 1328. Originally there were six gates in the western wall and seven in the eastern, but most of the stone ruins have disappeared. Only remnants survive.

The **Khirki Mosque** was built in 1380 by Khan-i-Jahan Tilangani, Prime Minister of Firuz Shah Tughluq. It lies in the heart of Khirki village and comprises an interesting covered mosque with four open courts. The entrance is from the east and leads to a cruciform courtyard; the upper storey is perforated with windows or khirkis, hence the name. The roofs are carried on massive monolithic columns, typical of the period, and the gateways and prayer niche are flanked by sloping towers.

Adjacent to the east is a weir, the **Satpula** or Bridge of the Seven Openings (c. 1380), built by Muhammad Shah Tughluq for irrigation purposes. At each end are octagonal cells, once used as an Islamic college or madrasa.

About 1·2 km (¾ mile) north-east is the Dargah of Chiragh Delhi (1356) and the **Tomb of Bahlul Lodi** (1488), which has twelve doors and five domes and was probably used as a summer house during his lifetime.

The **Tomb of Shaikh Yusuf Katal** (1500) lies just north of the village. It is a little pavilion with a dome carried on twelve pillars enclosed by sandstone screens. Encaustic tiles encircle the dome. The Tomb of Kabir-ud-Din Auliya lies to the north-west and is called **Lal Gumbaz** or Red Dome. Nearby is a well dated 1410.

At Begumpura village is the **Begumpur Mosque** (1387), built by Khan-i-Jahan in typically severe Tughluq style with a vast courtyard surrounded by arcaded cloisters. The mosque is raised on a high podium with a prayer hall three bays deep and a façade of twenty-four arched openings. On each side there are battered minarets tapering in typical Tughluq style. Note the central part of the façade, which is similar to the Jaunpur mosques and unique in Delhi.

A short distance from the mosque is the **Bijai Mandal**, a huge octagonal structure set on a high platform with sloping walls. Adjacent are the remains of a structure possibly used by Ghiyath-ud-Din Muhammad Shah II for reviewing his troops.

Siri, the second city of Delhi, was built by Ala-ud-Din Khalji (1296–1316) in about 1304. Once a flourishing city, little now remains except crumbling ruins. After it was plundered by the armies of Timur, it declined rapidly. Under Sher Shah the walls were dismantled for use as building stone. Only a few bastions survive.

The **Shahpur Jat Mosque** has an old walled enclosure. The whole area of Siri is now dominated by the Asian Games Village Complex.

Moth-ki-Masjid was built in 1505 by Miyan Bhoiya, Prime Minister of Sikander Lodi. It is arguably the finest specimen of the Lodi style, the largest mosque of its age with storeyed towers and finely proportioned arched openings. The materials – white marble, red sandstone and coloured tiles – coalesce to create an impressive structure.

The first city of Delhi, **Lal Kot**, was raised by Anangpal, one of the first Tomar Rajputs to settle in Delhi, in 1060. When the Chauhan Rajputs seized control in the 12th century the fortifications were extended. Massive ramparts were built around the city, **Qila Rai Pithora**. Once pierced by thirteen gates, only fragments survive. The Hauz Rami, Barhka and Budaun gates still exist.

The Qutb complex lies in the middle of the east side of Lal Kot.

The **Quwwat-ul-Islam Mosque** (literally the Might of Islam) is the earliest surviving mosque in India. It was begun by Qutb-ud-Din Aybak in 1193 and completed four years later on the site of Rai Pithora's Hindu temple. Subsequent additions were made by Iltutmish in 1230 and Ala-ud-Din Khalji in 1315. Twenty-seven Hindu and Jain temples were levelled to provide enough masonry for the new structure and the Hindu influence permeates the whole complex. Hindu motifs – tasselled ropes, bells, tendrils, cows and leaves – can all be clearly traced on the masonry in richly carved detail.

Steep steps up to the entrance arch lead to a dramatic courtyard enclosed by cloisters built from carved temple pillars. The prayer hall stood to the west. Today only three archways survive, the central one over 6·15 m (20 ft) high, profusely carved with sinuous ornamental details in one of the earliest and finest combinations of Hindu and Islamic art.

The mosque is important because it demonstrates how Hindu art was used to create a Muslim edifice. Note how the later screenwork and other extensions carried out by Iltutmish in 1230 are fundamentally Islamic in design. The flowers and leaves have been replaced by diapered arabesque patterns and Quranic inscriptions.

Ala-ud-Din Khalji added a further eastern courtyard, entered by his great gateway, the Alai Darwaza.

In the centre of the courtyard is the celebrated **Iron Pillar**. It consists of a solid shaft of wrought iron 7·2 m (23 ft 8 in) long and 37 cm (16 in) in diameter. It is an ancient monument of the Gupta age, possibly brought and set up here before the Islamic invasions. It is inscribed with a Sanskrit text dated to the 4th or 5th century.

There is a local tradition that people who can encircle the column with their arms behind their back will have their wishes come true. Try it.

The **Qutb Minar** is one of the most famous monuments in India. It dominates the entire area and is visible for miles. It was commenced by Qutb-ud-Din Aybak as a tower of victory, similar to that at Ghazni, but it also served as a minaret and was used by the muezzin to summon the faithful to prayer.

DELHI – QUTB MINAR COMPLEX

Qutb-ud-Din built the first storey and his son-in-law Iltutmish built the next three. It is 72·3 m (238 ft) high (over 24·4 m [80 ft] higher than Nelson's Column in London) and rises in five successive storeys with twenty-seven flutings broken by four projecting balconies decorated with inscriptions. The diameter at the base is 14·4 m (47 ft 3 in) and at the top about 2·7 m (9 ft). The lower storeys are of red sandstone with semicircular and angled flutings; the two highest storeys are mainly Makrana marble and were rebuilt by Firuz Shah Tughluq in 1368, when a cupola was added. In 1782 and again in 1803 it was damaged by an earthquake and the cupola destroyed. It was restored in 1828 by Major Robert Smith of the Bengal Engineers, so successfully that it withstood two subsequent tremors in 1829 and 1905.

Note the beautifully carved honeycomb detail beneath the balconies, which are reminiscent of the Alhambra. Access is no longer possible to the interior following an accident some years ago, but around the tower there are carved mouldings containing the names and praises of the patron builder, Qutb-ud-Din Aybak, and Kufic inscriptions. The cylindrical upper stages are quite different from the fluted lower parts.

There has been some speculation that the tower was the work of Rai Pithora, but there is no evidence that the tower is anything other than an Islamic construction.

The **Tomb of Iltutmish**, built in 1236, lies in the north-west corner of his extension to the mosque. It is the first surviving tomb of an Islamic ruler in India. Built in a blend of Hindu and Muslim styles, it comprises a square chamber of red sandstone. The lower parts of the interior are covered with beautiful Islamic carvings and arabesques, and in the centre of the west side there is a marble mihrab. The tomb is in the centre on a raised platform and the whole structure was probably covered by an overlapping dome, now gone.

The **Alai Darwaza**, to the south-east of the Qutb Minar, was erected by Ala-ud-Din Khalji in 1311 as an entrance gateway to his southern extension of the mosque. Built in red sandstone, it is richly carved in low relief and is the first building in the complex conceived on Islamic principles, the Hindu masons having adapted their decorative style to imported forms.

It is a small domed square block with lofty doorways and pointed horseshoe arches to three sides and a rounded arch on the inner side. Massive lattice screens enclose the corner windows. It was poorly restored in 1828.

The **Alai Minar** stands to the north of the Qutb enclosure. This is the base of a second tower, 26·5 m (87 ft) high, begun by Ala-ud-Din Khalji. He intended to emulate the Qutb, with a tower of twice the diameter and proportionally higher (over 152 m [500 ft]), but he died before the project reached the first storey.

South-west of the Quwwat-ul-Islam Mosque is a complex of rooms which was probably **Ala-ud-Din's Madrasa**, founded to teach Islamic scripture, and which includes his tomb, a massive unfinished square block.

South-east of the Qutb is **Dilkusha**, a country retreat of Sir Thomas Metcalfe, the Commissioner of Delhi from 1835 to 1853. Originally a Muslim tomb, it was converted by him into a small country house in 1844, but it is now in ruins.

Outside the complex is the **Jamali Kanali**. There is a mosque (1528) and, in a separate enclosure, the Tomb of Shaikh Fazl-ullah (1535), a traveller, poet and saint. The tomb is flat-roofed with an enriched ceiling, painted plaster and encaustic tile work. Among the inscriptions are Jamali's own verses. There are two tombs, those of Jamali and his brother, Kanali.

About 182 m (592 ft) to the east of the Jamali Mosque is the **Tomb of Balban** (1287). Architecturally it is notable for its use of the true arch rather than the earlier crude corbelled arches devised by Hindu builders.

The road from the Qutb to the village of Mehrauli passes a number of interesting monuments.

The Yog Maya Temple is a distinctive 19th-century Hindu temple. High on a podium, south-east of the Qutb Minar, is the **Tomb of Adham Khan** (1526). On the south wall of Lal Kot, known as the

Bhul Bhulaiyan or labyrinth, it was built by Emperor Akbar for his wet-nurse, Maham Anga, and her son, Adham Khan. Adham Khan was eventually executed for his cruel excesses and over-weaning ambition.

Architecturally the tomb, an octagonal drum of grey sandstone with a low round tower to each angle, is one of the last in the Lodi style. Around the central chamber is an arcaded verandah, above which rises the corona of the dome, in which there is a sort of labyrinth.

A short way to the south-east, past an old well, is an entrance to the **Dargah** or shrine of **Qutb-ud-Din Bakhtiar Kati** in the village of Mehrauli. He died in 1235. Iltutmish is reputed to have pre-sided over the funeral. An enclosure was made in 1541 at the foot of the hill. The grave of the saint stands in the open, protected by an awning.

Beyond the gateway is a long marble screen, the gift of Emperor Farrukhsiyar in the early 17th century. Close to a third gateway are the graves of the Nawabs of Jhajjar. In an adjoining court there is a baoli together with two graves; one is that of Zabita Khan, a Rohilla Pathan, and the other is reputedly that of Ghulam Kadir, who blinded Shah Alam, though this is unlikely.

To the left of the entrance gate is the Tomb of Motamid Khan, historian of Aurangzeb, and to the left of this is the entrance to the **Moti Masjid** (1709), built in white marble but of no great interest. Beyond, in an enclosure, are the simple **Graves of the Kings of Delhi**: Akbar Shah II (d. 1837), the blind Shah Alam (d. 1806) and Bahadur Shah I (d. 1712). The space between the last two was reserved for Bahadur Shah II, who died in Rangoon in 1862, exiled for his part in the Mutiny.

The area around Mehrauli village was once the preserve of the first Muslim kings of Delhi and their nobles. Numerous wells, tanks, pavilions and palaces survive.

West of the Dargah is the Mahal Sarai, a gateway, and beyond that is a mosque raised on a high plinth built by Ahsa-nullah Khan, physician to the last king of Delhi. Going southwards, the route along the main street leads to the **Hauz Shamsi**, a vast reservoir built by Iltut-mish in 1230 after a prophetic dream. In the centre is a domed pavilion built in 1311 by Ala-ud-Din Khalji.

On the east bank is the **Jahaz Mahal**, a pleasure palace built of grey and red sandstone and glazed blue tiles. Today it is the centre of an annual flower carnival celebrated by Hindus and Muslims alike. Nearby is the **Auliya Masjid**, where tradition holds that prayers were offered for the capture of Delhi in 1193. Across the road is the delightful Jhirna or Spring Garden, through which the overflow from the Hauz Shamsi runs to Tugh-luqabad.

The **Tomb of Sultan Ghori** (1230) is probably the first example of a Muslim tomb in India. It was built by Iltutmish for his eldest son and heir, Nasir-ud-Din Mahmud. It is a peculiar octagonal struc-ture, sunk beneath a raised courtyard with rubble walls and domed corner bastions. Note the extensive reuse of Hindu masonry, including sculpted 7th-century panels and lintels from a Hindu temple.

On the road from Mehrauli to Delhi the village of Hauz Khas lies to the west. The area takes its name from the special reservoir built by Ala-ud-Din Khalji in 1305, for the use of the citizens of Siri, the second city of Delhi.

The Hauz Khas is now dry but the steps and surroundings remain, complete with garden pavilions. The chambers to the north and west were built in 1354 as a college.

Adjoining the tank is the **Tomb of Firuz Shah** (1390), an austere, plain block of grey sandstone with a decorated interior of finely patterned carved plasterwork. Of the four graves in the tomb, the one in the centre is that of

Firuz Shah. The others are believed to be his sons and grandsons.

The **Bagh-i-Alam Ka Gumbad** is probably the most impressive of the tombs in the area. Tradition asserts it is the grave of Miyan Shaikh Shihabud din Taj Khan, a Muslim saint, built in 1501 in the reign of Sikander Lodi. It follows the established pattern of Lodi tombs, with a huge dome or gumbad.

Of the other tombs in the area, two major ones are called the **Dadi** and **Poti Ka Gumbad**. The larger is known as the Bibi (wife) or Dadi (grandmother) gumbad, and the smaller the Poti (granddaughter) gumbad. They are in typical Lodi style, square in plan with openings on three sides.

New Delhi

The great capital of New Delhi is one of the triumphal achievements of the British Empire. The transfer of the capital from Calcutta to Delhi was announced at the Delhi Durbar in December 1911 by the King-Emperor George V. Twenty years later, on 15 February 1931, it was inaugurated.

The form and layout of the city owe much to the magisterial genius of Sir Edwin Lutyens and to his collaboration with Sir Herbert Baker. However, many of the buildings were designed by their staff and assistants, principally Robert Tor Russell, who was responsible for Connaught Place and all the government housing, bungalows, hospitals, police stations and other official buildings. The entire layout was designed on a hierarchical basis, which underscored the supremacy of the British Raj, and the complex geometrical plan, dominated by the huge central axis of Kingsway (Rajpath), was designed expressly to exalt the power and position of the Viceroy on his throne in the Durbar Hall of Viceroy's House.

It is the last of the great Imperial cities of the world.

The most appropriate starting-point for any tour of New Delhi is the **All India War Memorial**, popularly known as India Gate. Situated at the east end of Rajpath, it is a huge stone memorial arch designed by Sir Edwin Lutyens to commemorate more than 70,000 Indian soldiers who fell in the First World War. An additional 13,516 names engraved on the arch and foundations form a separate memorial to the British and Indian soldiers killed on the North-West Frontier and in the Afghan War of 1919. The foundation stone was laid by HRH The Duke of Connaught in 1921 and the dedication took place ten years later under the Viceroy, Lord Irwin. Another memorial, 'Amar Jawan Jyoti', was added under the arch in January 1972 to commemorate losses in the Indo-Pakistan War of December 1971.

The entire arch stands on a low base of red Bharatpur stone and rises in stages to a huge cornice, beneath which are inscribed Imperial suns. Above on both sides is inscribed INDIA, flanked by MCM. Immediately below to the left is XIV and to the right, XIX. The shallow domed bowl at the top was intended to be filled with burning oil on anniversaries.

Facing the arch is an open cupola which once contained a statue of the King-Emperor George V by C. S. Jagger. The **King George V Memorial**, designed by Sir Edwin Lutyens, is an elegant baldachino of cream and pink stone set in a rectangular pool and adorned with allegorical sculpture and symbols of kingship. The nautilus shells symbolize British maritime dominion.

To the east is the National Stadium (formerly the Irwin Amphitheatre). Just to the north, flanking Kasturba Gandhi Marg, are two impressive houses, now used as offices.

Hyderabad House was built for the Nizam of Hyderabad by Sir Edwin Lutyens in collaboration with Abdulla Peermahomed. Designed on a classical

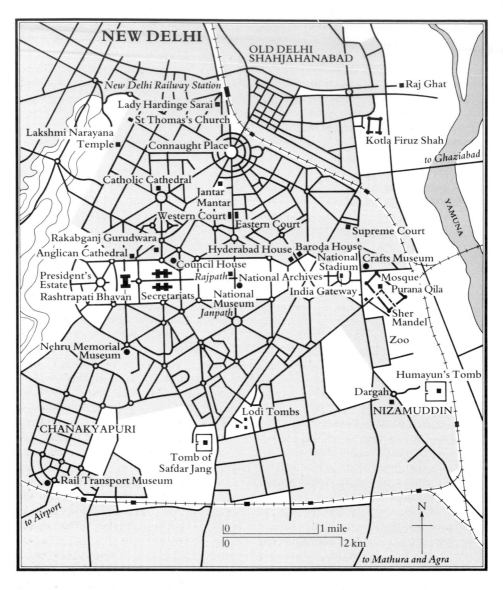

English butterfly plan, it is an elegant and impressive range in cream stucco with stone dressings, accentuated by a shallow dome over the concave corner entrance bay. Note the obelisk on the parapet.

Baroda House, opposite, built for the Gaekwar of Baroda, is similar in plan, with a concave porte-cochère crowned by a shallow dome and delicate carved stone panels of pierced jali work. Here the parapet is adorned with urns. Both

houses were located carefully in the overall plan to be subsidiary to Viceroy's House, symbolizing the paramountcy of the British Raj over the princely states.

Rajpath leads eastwards to Janpath. Immediately to the north on Janpath are the **National Archives** (formerly the Imperial Record Office), with over 72,000 bound volumes, a central reference library of India's political, social and economic history. Designed by Lutyens, the National Archives are a fragment of a much more ambitious plan for a series of public buildings at the intersection. Only the National Archives were completed.

South of the intersection is the **National Museum**. The foundation stone was laid by Nehru in 1955 and it was completed in 1960. The galleries are on three floors. Gallery III, on the first floor, has a good collection of Deccani paintings and miniatures from Rajasthan, Persia and western India. Galleries IV and V contain the results of Sir Aurel Stein's Central Asian expeditions of 1901, 1906–8 and 1913–16. (For further details see Volume I.)

Rajpath continues to the **Great Place**, now called Vijay Chowk, at the foot of Raisina Hill. It is a great plaza on a monumental scale, marking the transition from the axial processional route to the great complex of the Secretariats and Viceroy's House. From here one can see the flawed vista of Viceroy's House, which Lutyens later referred to as his 'Bakerloo', due to Sir Herbert Baker's miscalculation of the gradient between the Secretariats. Note how the façade of Viceroy's House disappears from view as you approach the gradient.

The **Secretariats** lie each side of a wide avenue, dominating the new acropolis. Designed by Sir Herbert Baker, they are reminiscent of his Government Buildings of Pretoria, two huge ranges of classical buildings with projecting colonnades and large Baroque domes dominating the composition. Both are derived from Christopher Wren's Royal Naval College at Greenwich. Although criticized by comparison with Lutyens's work, they are magnificent pieces of civic design. The towers flanking the entrance from the Great Place were designed to be twice the height, to act as obelisks guarding the way to the inner sanctum, but these were reduced in scale and lost their impact. The domes are embellished with lotus motifs and elephants. On the north and south eleva-

tions are huge Mughal gateways centred on the horizontal axis between the domes. Note the condescending inscription on the North Secretariat: 'Liberty will not descend to a people: a people must raise themselves to liberty. It is a blessing which must be earned before it can be enjoyed.'

In the Great Court beyond the Secretariats are the four **Dominion Columns**, donated by the governments of Canada, Australia, New Zealand and South Africa, each crowned by a bronze ship symbolizing the maritime power of the British Empire and bearing the arms of the dominion on the base. In the centre of the court is the **Jaipur Column**, given by the Maharaja of Jaipur, a thin red shaft of sandstone, carrying a white egg and bronze lotus from whose calyx arises the six-pointed glass star of India. Across the entrance to the Great Court is an ornate iron entrance screen 205 m (666 ft) long, broken by stone aedicules and piers carrying elephants and wreathed urns.

Viceroy's House, now called Rashtrapati Bhavan, straddles the crown of Raisina Hill and is used as the official residence of the President of India. Larger than Versailles, it is one of the most important buildings of the 20th century. It was designed by Sir Edwin Lutyens as a synthesis of Eastern and Western styles of architecture and was completed by 1929. It is dominated by a monumental copper dome which rises over a vast colonnaded frontage. The main entrance is approached by a broad flight of steps which leads to a dodecastyle portico. The capitals are wholly original, a fusion of acanthus leaves and pendant Indian bells. Note the enormous projecting cornice or chajja, a Mughal device, which provides a strong unifying element and throws a band of deep shadow around the perimeter. The palace is a masterpiece of symmetry, discipline, silhouette, colour and harmony.

Access can be obtained to the interior on occasions by prior arrangement. The

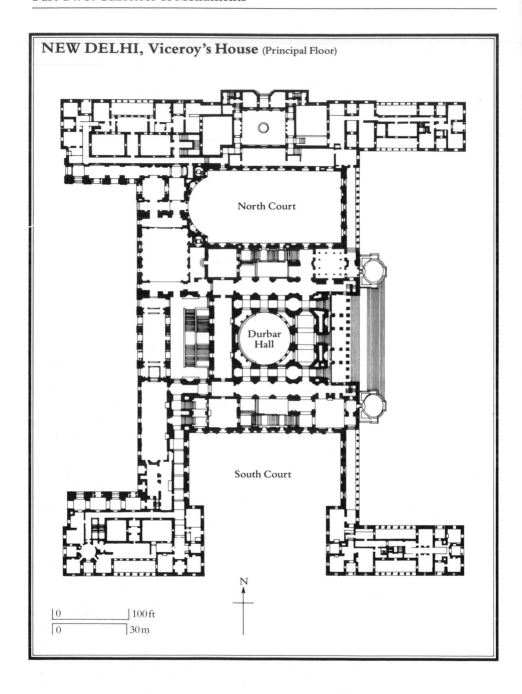

NEW DELHI, Viceroy's House (Principal Floor)

North Court

Durbar Hall

South Court

N

| 0 | 100 ft |
| 0 | 30 m |

principal floor comprises a magnificent series of state apartments. Beneath the dome is the circular **Durbar Hall** 22·8 m (75 ft) in diameter. The Viceroy's throne faced the main entrance and commanded a view along the great axial vista of Kingsway, the focus of the entire city. The coloured marbles used in the hall

142

come from all parts of India. The State Drawing-Room is barrel-vaulted and plainly treated with domestic fireplaces. The State Ballroom is enriched with Old English mirror glass. The State Library is based on the form of Wren's St Stephen's, Walbrook. The State Dining-Room is lined with teak panelling enriched with the Star of India. The concept of Imperial order and hierarchy permeates the entire house. Marble staircases flanking the Durbar Hall provide access to the private apartments above. There are fifty-four bedrooms together with additional accomodation for guests.

To the west the palace overlooks an enormous garden designed by Lutyens. Here the principles of hierarchy order, symmetry and unity are extended from the house into the landscape. A series of ornamental fountains, walls, gazebos and screens combine with scores of trees, flowers and shrubs to create a paradise so delightful that Indians called the garden 'God's own Heaven'. On the outer radials to the south-west are extensive quarters for the viceregal staff and body-guards, known as Schedule B. Both villages in plastered brick reflect the order and hierarchy of the city as a whole. Even ranges of servants' cells and houses are grouped to create an overall grandeur. The **Band House**, visible from Willingdon Crescent, has a distinctive attenuated dome resembling Horse Guards Parade in Whitehall, and the other ranges are thoughtfully disposed to avoid monotony and to enhance the impact.

The Viceroy's court, which frames the main entrance to the house, has lateral entrances on the axis of the Jaipur Column. Here the levels were reduced artificially and cascades of steps are flanked by huge sandstone elephants and ranks of Imperial lions modelled by the sculptor C. S. Jagger.

The **Nehru Memorial Museum** (formerly Flagstaff House, the Commander-in-Chief's House) or Teen Murti closes another main vista, directly to the south from Viceroy's House. Situated at a major rond-point, it was designed by Robert Tor Russell and completed in 1930 in a grand manner. It is a handsome building faced in stone and stucco in an austere classical style, carefully placed in the city to reflect the importance of military power to the Viceroy. In 1948 it became the residence of India's first Prime Minister, Jawaharlal Nehru. On his death in May 1964 it was preserved as a museum and research library in his memory. The house retains many of his personal belongings. Note the watch on the bedside table. The gardens are beautifully maintained. Nearby is the Jawahar Jyoti, the eternal flame, lit on his birth day in 1964. Adjacent on a rock is his epitaph.

The circular **Council House** was added to the layout at a later stage, following the Montagu–Chelmsford reforms of 1919, which created a large Legislative Assembly. The site chosen terminated a major axis from the Old City. It comprises three semicircular chambers for the Legislatures and a Central Library crowned by a 27·4-m-high (90 ft) dome to the designs of Sir Herbert Baker. It is 173 m (570 ft) in diameter and covers 2·02 hectares (5 acres) in area, with colonnaded verandahs enclosing the entire circumference.

Terminating the northern vista from the Jaipur Column and west of the Council House is the **Cathedral Church of the Redemption** (1927–35), by H. A. N. Medd, the result of an architectural competition. It is a fine building redolent of Palladio's Il Redentore in Venice and strikingly similar to Lutyens's Free Church, Hampstead Garden Suburb. Built in coursed rubble masonry with split red sandstone roofing, it has an aura of monumental dignity entirely appropriate to its function. Consecrated on 15 February 1931, its construction was largely due to the energy of Lord Irwin,

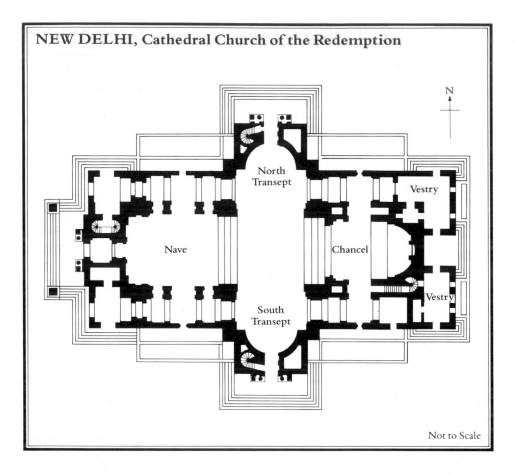

NEW DELHI, Cathedral Church of the Redemption

N

North Transept

Vestry

Nave

Chancel

Vestry

South Transept

Not to Scale

who presented the picture at the east end as a thanksgiving for his escape from an attempt to blow up his train in 1929. The altar was donated by the Dean and Chapter of York to mark the thirteenth centenary of York Minster.

To the north, in Alexandra Place, is the **Roman Catholic Church of the Sacred Heart** (1930–34), also designed by Medd in a competition held in 1927. It closes the vista from the North Secretariat at a strategic intersection between Connaught Circus and Raisina Hill. It is a bold and elegant design in the Lutyens tradition with an Italianate south front enriched by an oval mosaic cartouche of St Francis.

The major commercial centre of New Delhi is **Connaught Place** (1928–34),

the focus of its entertainment, shopping and business activities, named after the visit of the Duke of Connaught to India. It comprises two huge concentric circles of colonnaded terraces in plastered brick designed by Robert Tor Russell in collaboration with W. H. Nicholls and is a noble exercise in Imperial town planning. Flanking the approach to Connaught Place from Janpath are **Eastern and Western Courts**, also by R. T. Russell, a dignified pair of classical buildings with colonnaded Tuscan verandahs.

There are a few other notable European buildings located in the new city. At Paharganj on the northern outskirts is **St Thomas's Church**, by Walter Sykes George (1930–31). Built for Indian sweepers, it is a delightful little brick

144

structure with deeply recessed windows and a simple Romanesque entrance portal. Unfortunately, it is now afflicted by severe subsidence, probably due to the lack of steel or concrete in its construction.

The **Garrison Church of St Martin** (1928–30), by Arthur Shoosmith, lies west of the Ridge, looming over the cantonment area, which was laid out to the designs of John Begg. It is an extraordinary building of great architectural significance. Built from over 3½ million red bricks, it is a vast, gaunt monolith with a high square tower of battered walls and small, deeply recessed window openings reminiscent of Dutch and German Expressionist architecture. Internally, it is austerely treated, with a high concrete and rib barrel vault.

Another work by Shoosmith is the **Lady Hardinge Sarai** (1931), a plastered range of buildings with a high tower capped by the familiar Lutyens cupola close to the railway station.

The Lady Hardinge College and Hospital for Women lies to the west of Connaught Place.

Within the confines of the new city on Parliament Street lies the **Jantar Mantar** or Observatory, the first of several built by Maharaja Jai Singh II, in 1724. Jai Singh was a keen astronomer entrusted by the Mughal emperor Muhammad Shah with the task of revising the calendar and astronomical tables. The instruments are all made of plastered brick.

The Samrat Yantra or supreme instrument, a sun-dial, is the largest structure. The Jai Prakash is a complicated instrument invented by Jai Singh showing the sun's position at the vernal equinox. South is the Ram Yantra, two circular buildings with a pillar in the centre of each. The walls and floors are calibrated for reading horizontal and vertical angles of the moon and stars. The Misra Yantra or mixed instrument has four devices. The central or Niyata Chakra includes meridians at Greenwich, Zurich, Notkey and Serichew

for comparison with noon in Delhi. The two pillars south-west of the Misra Yantra are used to determine the shortest and longest days of the year. More detailed information can be obtained from the site guide.

In Barakhamba Road is the **National Museum of Natural History**, the first of its kind in the country.

Chanakyapuri is the large diplomatic enclosure housing the main embassies and missions of East and West. The **Rail Transport Museum** stands on a large site on Shantipath, close to the Turkish and Czech embassies. It has a splendid collection of old locomotives including the 'Fairy Queen', the oldest surviving engine in India, built in 1885 in Leeds by Kitson, Thompson and Hewitson. The coach in which the Prince of Wales (later Edward VIII) travelled during his visit to India, built in 1875, is also here.

DHARAMSALA *Map overleaf*

Founded in 1855, Dharamsala is one of the most spectacular hill stations in India. Perched under the shadow of the great rock wall of Dhaula Dhar, which rises to a height of over 4,876 m (16,000 ft), the town is surrounded by forests of giant trees set against a background of snow-capped mountains which encircle the town on three sides. There is a strong Tibetan influence here, reinforced by the presence of His Holiness, the Dalai Lama, who fled to Dharamsala after the invasion of his country by the Chinese in October 1950.

The station is divided into the upper and lower towns, with a difference between the two of 457 m (1,500 ft). In 1852 it became the capital of the Kangra District and it still retains a strong aura of Imperial days, particularly in McCleod Ganj and Forsyth Ganj in the upper town.

The principal building of interest is the

145

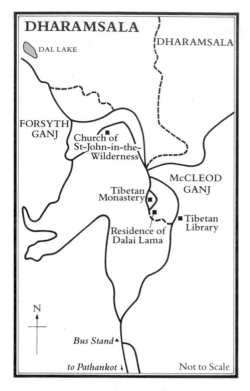

Raja Bikram Singh in the 1870s and 1880s retired British officials were brought in to reorganize the state administration.

The Palace or **Raj Mahal** is a jolly stucco colonial bungalow with cast-iron verandahs built by a local master craftsman, Mistri Jagat Singh, in the 1880s. Painted Eton blue with white dressings, it stands in a large park.

The **Fort** was built in the 13th century by the Rajput warrior Mokalsai and named after Bawa Farid-ud-Din, a local saint. The present Raja is a progressive farmer and the state is renowned for the **Davies Model Agricultural Farm** and farmer's house.

FEROZEPORE (FIROZPUR)

Ferozepore, 384 km (239 miles) from Delhi and close to the border with Pakistan, is a town and military cantonment. The town was founded by Firuz Shah Tughluq III, Emperor of Delhi from 1351 to 1388. In the 19th century, under Sir Henry Lawrence and his successors, this declining town was revived into a thriving commercial centre, aided by the opening of the Sirhind Canal and irrigation works along the Sutlej which were completed in 1878.

The **Fort** (1858) lies 1·6 km (1 mile) west of the cantonment station. It was strengthened in 1887. The cantonment is spacious and well maintained. The **Memorial Church** to those who fell in the Sutlej Campaign of 1845–6 was destroyed in the Mutiny but later restored.

There is a **Memorial** (1933) to the Sikh garrison of Saragarhi, which fell defending the outpost in 1897.

The **Cemetery** on the Grand Trunk Road towards the border contains several important British tombs, including those of Major George Broadfoot, General Sale and General Dick.

Church of St John-in-the-Wilderness (1860), a short distance below McCleod Ganj. The church contains some splendid stained-glass windows, a memorial to Lord Elgin, the Viceroy, who died here in 1863. Elgin loved the area, which reminded him of his native Scotland, and he left instructions for his burial here.

FARIDKOT

Faridkot lies about 96 km (60 miles) south-west of Ludhiana, close to the border with Pakistan. One of the cis-Sutlej states, the dynasty was founded in the 16th century. By the mid-17th century it was an independent state and, in spite of seizure by Ranjit Singh in 1809, it was restored to the family. After generations of family feuding, the state prospered with British support, and under

146

FEROZESHAH

One of the three great battlefields of the First Sikh War, Ferozeshah lies 17·7 km (11 miles) east of Ferozepore, about 19 km (12 miles) from the left bank of the Sutlej river. On 21 December 1845 British forces under Sir Hugh Gough and Sir Henry Hardinge attacked a formidably entrenched Sikh encampment. After two days of severe fighting the position was carried and the enemy routed, but the British lost 2,415 men.

No trace of the old entrenchments remain, but a plain obelisk marks those who fell in one of the bloodiest engagements of the war.

HANSI

26 km (16 miles) east of Hissar, Hansi is famous as the place where the celebrated Colonel Skinner of Skinner's Horse died in 1841. It is an old settlement, founded in the 8th century by Anangpal Tomar, King of Delhi, and was once the capital of ancient Haryana. Desolated by the famine of 1783, the town's fortunes revived when the sailor and adventurer George Thomas made Hansi his headquarters between 1798 and 1802. With the establishment of British rule in 1803 the town enjoyed a long period of quiet prosperity, until the Mutiny, since when it has fallen into decay.

HISSAR

164 km (102 miles) west of Delhi, Hissar is an old Muslim town founded in 1354 by Firuz Shah, who constructed what is now a branch of the West Jumna Canal to supply it with water. It was the emperor's favourite residence and was preferred to Hansi.

The town is studded with ruins which attest to its former importance. The **Gujari Mahal** is an old Muslim edifice built from Jain remains within the original fort. In the citadel are the Lat and Mosque of Firuz Shah (14th century). The **Jahaz**, an extraordinary building shaped like a ship, lies to the east of the city. Most of the Muslim monuments are in an advanced state of dilapidation.

In 1796 George Thomas settled here and built a fort before moving his headquarters to Hansi, 26 km (16 miles) away.

JAHAZGARH

Jahazgarh, a corruption of the name Georgegarh, lies near the town of Jhajhar in the Rohtak area of the Punjab. It is alleged that the town was built by the military adventurer George Thomas in the late 18th century. In 1801 the Marathas besieged the fort and Thomas escaped to Hansi, where he was defeated. Abandoning his conquests he retired to the comparative safety of British territory and died at Berhampur.

JAMMU

Jammu, the winter capital of Jammu and Kashmir, lies at a height of 343 m (1,127 ft) in the foothills of the Himalayas.

The city is reputed to have been founded by Raja Jambu Lochan as early as 2,700 BC, but this is unlikely. Until the late 18th century the history of Jammu was bound up closely with the turbulent history of the Punjab. Under Ranjit Singh the Dogras of Jammu were allowed virtual semi-autonomy under their enterprising leader Gulab Singh. With the collapse of Sikh power, Gulab Singh offered to relieve the British of the problem of Kashmir and, as a result of the treaty of 1846, he became the independent ruler of the combined states of Jammu and Kashmir. The Dogras are the Rajput clans of the hill states north of the Ravi river.

Jammu has two distinct areas. The old town lies at the top of the hill overlooking the River Tawi; the new town is at the bottom.

The **Mondi Palace** (1880s) now houses the High Court. Perched high over the river, it is entered via a large quadrangle, to the right of which is a huge reception room. The verandah outside the small reception room commands fine views across the river.

The **Amar Singh Mahal** (early 20th century), off the Srinagar Road, was built by Maharaja Sir Pratap Singh in a classical Art Deco style, as a successor to the Mondi Palace. The palace museum has a portrait gallery and an important collection of paintings.

Other buildings of consequence include the **Dogra Art Gallery**, which has a notable collection of miniatures from local schools of painting. It is situated in the Gandhi Bhavan, next to the New Secretariat.

North of this is the Prince of Wales College, commemorating the visit of George V in 1905 before he became king. Close by is the parade ground.

A long flight of steps leads from the Gumit Gateway down to the river.

(For the temples see Volume I.)

JULLUNDUR (JALANDHAR)

This is an ancient settlement with historical connections which predate the invasion of Alexander the Great, but only two ancient tanks survive to attest to the existence of the primitive Aryan city. It was conquered by Ibrahim Shah of Ghazni and later, under the Mughal Empire, it was a town of considerable importance.

The present city comprises a cluster of distinct, separate wards, each originally enclosed by its own wall but now connected by later development. The caravansarai built by Shaikh Karam Bakhsh in 1857 is noteworthy.

The **Church** (1852) lies 800 m (½ mile) south-east of the artillery lines and is an unusually long building without a tower. The cantonment, established in 1846, covers an area of 19·5 sq km (7½ square miles).

KAITHAL

Kaithal is an old town picturesquely located on the edge of the artificial Bidkiar Lake, which has bathing ghats. Under Akbar's rule it was a place of some importance. In 1767 it passed to the Sikh leader Bhai Desu Singh, whose descendants, the Bhais of Kaithal, were high among the cis-Sutlej chiefs before the territory lapsed to the British in 1843. The ruins of the fort or palace of the Bhais overlook the lake.

KALANAUR

Kalanaur, 26 km (16 miles) west of Gurdaspur, is the spot where Akbar received news of his father's death and ascended to the Imperial throne. A **Monument** marks the place where he was proclaimed emperor.

The town was a thriving centre from the 14th to the 16th centuries. The **Jhulna Mahal** is a peculiar arched wall, 12 m (40 ft) long and 3 m (10 ft) high, which is alleged to sway under a person sitting on it.

KALKA

Kalka, 16 km (10 miles) from Chandigarh, is a small town and terminus of the Kalka-Simla narrow-gauge railway, one of the delights of the Indian rail network.

Built in 1903 by the British engineer H. S. Harington at a cost of over £1 million, it was one of the outstanding feats of British Imperial engineering. It runs for 96·5 km (60 miles) in a series of tight reverse curves with gradients of over 3 feet in every 100. 8 km (5 miles) lie underground in a series of 107 tunnels. 3·2 km (2 miles) run over vertiginous viaducts. Both the railway carriages and electric railcar are wonderful period pieces, a perfect way to travel up to the former summer capital of the Raj.

21 km (13 miles) south-east of Kalka is an old Mughal summer house at Pinjor, set in a landscaped park with fountains and pavilions. It was built by Fidai Khan, foster brother of Emperor Aurangzeb and builder of the famous Badshahi Mosque in Lahore.

KANGRA

Kangra is situated on a hill overlooking the Banganga torrent. Known in the past as Nagarkot, Kangra passed to the British in 1845 at the end of the First Sikh War.

A Rajput fort crowns a formidable rock which rises sheer from the Banganga. Once it was the strategic key to the entire area and was considered impregnable until the advent of modern artillery. However, it was largely destroyed in an earthquake of 1905. Little survives. The **Temple of Devi**, one of the oldest and wealthiest shrines in India, was reconstructed after the earthquake.

Under the walls of the old fort is an interesting British cemetery.

KAPURTHALA

The capital of a former Sikh state, Kapurthala is located 19 km (12 miles) from Jullundur. It has been the chief town of the Ahluwalia family since the conquest and consolidation of various scattered possessions by Jassa Singh

between 1747 and his death in 1783.

In spite of an early alliance with the British in 1809, Kapurthala troops fought against the British at Aliwal during the First Sikh War. During the Second Sikh War and the Mutiny the forces of Randhir Singh remained unswervingly loyal and for this he was well rewarded. The subsequent ruler turned Kapurthala into a model city-state.

The most magnificent monuments date from the time of Jagatjit Singh, who ascended the throne in 1890. Educated in London and Paris, he was an ardent francophile and on his accession turned the city into 'a scrap of Paris laid at the foot of the Himalayas'.

The **Jalaukhana** or **Elysée Palace**, now a boys' school, is a spectacular French château built between 1900 and 1908 in red sandstone, but completed in pink stucco once the money began to run out. Designed by a French architect, M. Marcel, the palace comprises a central bay, cribbed from Fontainebleau, with a high pavilion roof and oeil-de-boeuf windows, flanked by two symmetrical wings with blind arcades terminated by secondary pavilions. The interior is treated lavishly in the same opulent French manner, with Louis XIV furniture, Gobelin tapestries, enriched plasterwork, Carrara marble chimney pieces and Aubusson carpets specially woven for the rooms. The gardens are embellished with fountains and statuary in the French style, and the entire area is designed to resemble a French estate. Surrounding buildings are designed in other European styles.

The **Villa Buona Vista** (1894), by the local engineer J. O. S. Elmore, is in Italianate style with a low corner tower crowned by a pyramidal roof. After the Maharaja's marriage to a Spanish dancer, other buildings were laid out in a Spanish style. The entire complex of buildings is a fascinating example of the strong influence of European taste on the Indian ruling classes of the period.

149

KARNAL

Karnal is inextricably linked with the legendary sites of the Mahabharata. According to tradition, the town was founded by Raja Karna, the champion of the Kauravas in the national epic. The town was the site of the catastrophic defeat of the Mughal emperor Muhammad Shah in 1739, when victorious Persian troops under Kuli Khan, Nadir Shah, killed over 20,000 Indian soldiers with little loss. The Persians captured many more prisoners and seized virtually the entire Mughal camp and all its treasure before entering Delhi. The town was occupied by the Rajas of Jind from 1763 and seized in 1797 by the Irish adventurer George Thomas, from whom it was wrested later by the Sikh Raja of Ladwa. In 1803 Lord Lake conferred the district on the Mandil Pathans. From 1811 to 1841 a British cantonment was established here, but only the old church tower remains in the civil station as the cantonment was abandoned as insalubrious and malarial.

In 1840 Dost Muhammad Khan, Amir of Afghanistan, was confined in the fort for six months en route to Calcutta as a state prisoner. The town is surrounded by a 3·6-m (12-ft) wall, which forms the back of many of the houses.

The King Edward VII Memorial Hospital was built in 1910–11. There is an important Dairy Farm.

KULU

Situated at an altitude of 1,200 m (3,937 ft), Kulu is the headquarters of an entire district. It is an interesting town, which sprawls along the western bank of the River Beas. The town has a spacious feel created by the large, grassy maidans which lie on the south side, where every October the colourful Dussehra festival is held.

Kulu was the centre of a school of miniature painting characterized by simple rustic scenes and pictures of yogis meditating. The emphasis on rural simplicity is probably a reflection of the fact that the nomadic tribes in this area lacked the sophistication of an urban civilization and their drawings were influenced by the wild, rugged grandeur of the local landscape of the Kulu region.

Some of the finest murals were found on the walls of the **Sultanpur Palace**. These wall paintings, first discovered in 1953, were executed under the patronage of Raja Pritam Singh (1776–1806). The most important, the Devi Mural, has now been moved to the National Museum in New Delhi. It comprises a large panel of the goddess Tripurasundari, an aspect of Devi. Many of the smaller panels show scenes of common people engaged in daily tasks and considerable local detail.

KURUKSHETRA

156 km (97 miles) from Delhi, Kurukshetra is a holy tract and place of pilgrimage for Hindus (see Volume I). Most of the sites and shrines are Hindu, but of the Muslim sites there is a fort and the **Tomb of Shaikh Chilli Jalal** (*c.* 1585). The tomb is built of white marble in the form of an octagon, with exquisitely carved trelliswork windows. It is raised on an octagonal podium, set on a square platform, and embellished with cupolas. On the west side is a small pavilion which forms a tomb.

To the south-west is the **Lal Masjid**, a small red sandstone mosque with carving on the domes reminiscent of details at Fatehpur Sikri.

LUDHIANA

Ludhiana is a major town and district headquarters on the south bank of the

Sutlej river. It was founded in 1480 by Yusaf and Nihang, princes of the Lodi dynasty of Delhi. In 1760 it fell into the hands of the Rais of Raikot, who held it until expelled by Ranjit Singh. In 1809 it was occupied by Colonel Ochterlony as political agent following the Treaty of Amritsar, and for twenty years from 1834 it was an important military station. Shah Shuja settled here after his expulsion from Afghanistan between 1816 and 1833 and again between 1834 and 1838. Nearby lie the great battlefields of the First Sikh War: Aliwal, Ferozeshah, Mudki and Sobraon.

The Fort, to the north-west of the city, embraces the **Shrine of Piri-i-Dastgir** or **Abdul Kadir Galani**, a Muslim saint who attracts an annual religious gathering of Hindus and Muslims. Other notable public buildings include the Small Causes Court, the jail, the Christian Medical College and Hospital, the American Presbyterian Mission and School and the railway station. The church and public gardens lie to the south of the city. The old European cemetery dates from 1809.

MAHIM

Mahim, an ancient and decayed town, lies 32 km (20 miles) west of Rohtak. It was once a town of considerable significance. The original settlement was destroyed by Shahab-ud-Din Ghuri. It was restored by Peshora, a bania or money-lender, in 1266. Akbar bestowed the town on an Afghan, Shahbaz Khan, under whose family it attained great prosperity, but in the desultory war waged by the Rajputs against Aurangzeb the town was plundered and went into decline.

The most significant monument is a fine well with steps built in 1656 by Saidu Kalal, mace-bearer to Shah Jahan. Several other interesting Muslim ruins surround the town, including tombs and mosques. The town itself, with high walls and brick houses, is picturesque.

MEERUT

Meerut, 72 km (45 miles) north-east of Delhi, is the capital of the district, a large city of considerable importance which was the scene of the outbreak of the Mutiny of the Bengal Army on Sunday, 10 May 1857.

It is an ancient settlement with a history which can be traced back to the time of Emperor Ashoka. By the early 19th century it was a depopulated town with little trade, but with the establishment of British cantonments here in 1806, the population expanded and trade flourished.

The **Military Cantonment**, lying to the north of the old city, is very extensive in area, 5·6 km (3½ miles) across, running from the railway on the west to the police lines on the east. The principal thoroughfare is the **Mall**, one of the finest examples in India, a wide, tree-lined drive flanked by bungalows set in garden compounds. The Club and Roman Catholic Church can be seen here. **St John's Church** (1821) is in the classical style, with a handsome spire visible from the foothills of the Himalayas. It was in this church that the British were at evening service when the outbreak of the Mutiny occurred. The interior contains a large number of memorial tablets to British officers killed in Upper India.

North-west of the Church is the **Cemetery**, which is divided into two parts. The old part is studded with cupolas, pyramids and obelisks. A large column, 15 m (50 ft) high and set on a square base, commemorates Sir Rollo Gillespie, who subdued the Vellore mutiny of 1806. General Sir David Ochterlony, whose memorial column stands in Calcutta and who served in every Indian war from the time of Clive onwards, culminating in the conquest of Nepal in 1816, was buried here in 1825. His tomb comprises a large cenotaph of ornamental brickwork carrying a marble slab and inscription. Another memorial is dedicated to those officers and privates of the 14th Regiment of Foot who fell in the storming of Bharatpur in 1825–6. **Victoria Park** marks the site of the old Central Jail, notorious during the events of 1857.

The earlier antiquarian remains of Meerut are notable. The **Suraj Khund** or Monkey Tank lies to the west of Victoria Park. It was built by a rich merchant, Jowahir Mal, in 1714 and its sides are lined with small temples, sanctuaries and suttee pillars. The **Baleswar Nath Temple** predates the Muslim conquest.

Near the Collector's Office is the **Tomb of Makhdum Shah Wilayat**, which was reputedly built by Shahab-ud-Din Ghuri. The **Tomb of Shah Pir**, a fine red sandstone structure, was erected in 1628 by the wife of Emperor Jahangir, Nur Jahan, in memory of a pious fakir. The **Jami Masjid** (1019) was built by Hasan Mahdi, Wazir of Mahmud of Ghazni, and repaired by Humayun.

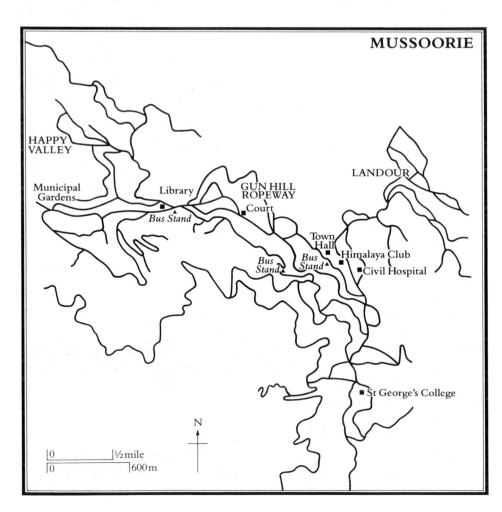

MUSSOORIE

152

Qutb-ud-Din Aybak is alleged to have built the **Maqbara of Salar Masa-ud Ghazi** in 1194. The mausolea of Abu Muhammad Kamboh (1658) and Abu Yar Khan (1577) are also of interest, together with an **Idgah** on the Delhi Road dating from 1600, and the **Mosque**, built by Nawab Khairandesh Khan in the Saraiganj. There are at least sixty-two other mosques and sixty temples of no specific interest.

MUDKI

On 18 December 1845 a fierce engagement was fought between the British and the Sikhs at Mudki in the opening battle of the 1st Sikh War. With a small force the British under Sir Hugh Gough met a much larger Sikh army, which had crossed the Sutlej two days earlier. The British lost 872 men. A plain obelisk marks the site of the battlefield.

MUSSOORIE

Mussoorie is a popular hill station about 22·5 km (14 miles) from Dehra Dun, situated at a height of 2,002 m (6,570 ft) on an outer spur of the Himalayas. The scenery is very beautiful, with deep, wooded gorges and fine views.

The **Anglican Church** (1837) was founded by Bishop Wilson. There are the usual library, club and Catholic Church and a large number of European-style bungalows. The **Municipal Gardens** to the west of the town have a good collection of botanical specimens. There is a ropeway to Gun Hill.

A narrow spur 180 m (585 ft) long leads to Landour. Landour Hill rises 273 m (900 ft) above Mussoorie, with bungalows and barracks built on the ascending spur.

NAINI TAL *Map overleaf*

A picturesque hill station lying 1,934 m (6,346 ft) up in the Kumaon Hills of the Himalayas, Naini Tal is easily accessible from Bareilly via Kathgodam. To the north lies the peak of China, 2,611 m (8,568 ft) high, to the west lies Deopatha, 2,434 m (7,987 ft), and to the south lies Ayarpatha, 2,274 m (7,461 ft), but the most impressive feature is the sacred lake which forms the focal point of the station.

The town was founded in 1841 and the first house was erected a year later. The **Church of St John-in-the-Wilderness** (1846), in a pretty picturesque Gothic style, lies 400 m (¼ mile) south-west of the club. It has a dark-coloured timber roof and two stained-glass windows. A brass records the life of Cuthbert Bensey Thornhill. Another memorial records those who perished in the landslip of 1880.

The finest building in the station is **Government House** (1899), by F. W. Stevens, the architect of many of the best Gothic buildings in Bombay. It stands at the lower end of the station on Ayarpatha. St Nicholas and St Mary's stand close to Government House. Other notable buildings include the Government Secretariat, the District Offices, the American Methodist Mission and the Ramsey Hospital.

Naini Tal is best remembered for the catastrophic landslip which occurred after heavy rains at 1.45 p.m. on 18 September 1880. Over 150 people were buried when the hotel, assembly rooms, library and other buildings were engulfed in a sea of mud.

NAJIBABAD

This small town, 50 km (31 miles) south-east of Hardwar, was founded by Nawab

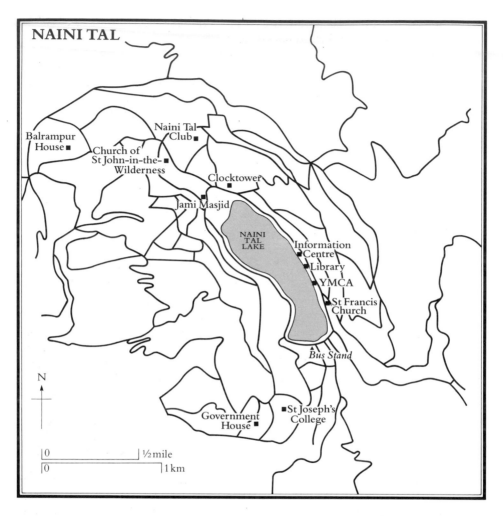

Najib-ud-Daula, who erected a fine stone fort at Pathargarh, 1·6 km (1 mile) east of the town, in 1755. A number of Islamic monuments remain.

The **Tomb of Nawab Najib-ud-Daula** (mid-18th century) is a handsome edifice surrounded by numerous chambers. To the north stands the tomb of his brother Jahangir Khan (late 18th century). Within the town the **Kothi Mubarak Banyad**, now a rest-house, is a monument to its founder. The best surviving local example of Sultanate architecture is a **baradari** or twelve-pillared pavilion, once the summer house of the ruling family.

PANIPAT

Panipat is a town of great antiquity situated 85 km (53 miles) north of Delhi, near the old bank of the Jumna. The town lies on high ground made up of the accumulated detritus of centuries, overlooking the old course of the river.

Three great battles have been fought here, although few signs remain of Panipat's role in the historical destiny of India or in the establishment of Mughal supremacy.

The First Battle occurred on 21 April 1526 between the small veteran army of

Babur and the forces of Ibrahim Lodi, King of Delhi, at the head of 100,000 troops. The battle was strongly contested for the entire day, but by evening Ibrahim Lodi lay dead with 15,000 of his followers, and the victorious Mughal army under Babur entered Delhi to establish the Mughal dynasty.

The Second Battle was fought thirty years later, on 5 November 1556, between Babur's grandson Akbar and Himu, the Hindu general of the Afghan Sher Shah. It was a fierce affair, but Himu was wounded by an arrow in the eye, captured and executed. This vital battle re-established the fortunes of the Mughal dynasty, which had been challenged with some success by the Pathan dynasty of Sher Shah.

The Third Battle, which took place over two centuries later, on 14 January 1761, was equally as decisive, for it shattered the unity of Maratha power and laid the Empire open to the Afghan conquerors. A small monument marks the spot where the Bhao, the Peshwa's cousin and overall commander of the Maratha forces, watched the fight. The battle was on an epic scale, with the combined Maratha forces, having been cut off from supplies from Delhi for many months, desperate to break through the smaller Afghan forces of Ahmad Shah Durani. After a shattering charge into the Afghan ranks, the prospect of victory was within their grasp, but the Afghans rallied and the Marathas were pursued from the field in complete disorder, leaving thousands dead and dying.

In 1885 the British held manoeuvres on the plain of Panipat, simulating the advance of an invading army on Delhi.

PATHANKOT

Pathankot, a flourishing town on the main route from India to Srinagar and the focus of numerous local trade routes, lies 37 km (23 miles) north-east of Gurdaspur.

12.8 km (8 miles) to the north, on the banks of the River Ravi, is the **Shahpur Kandi Fort** (16th century), once the stronghold of the Rajas of Pathan, who rebelled repeatedly against Mughal authority and who were driven into the hills. The fort is a picturesque building with numerous bastions, one of which accommodates a rest-house.

A spectacular mountain railway built in 1928 runs from Pathankot to Jogindarnagar in Mandi state.

PATIALA *Map overleaf*

Patiala is a large town and was the capital of the most important of the cis-Sutlej states. The ruling Sikh families of Patiala, Jind and Nabha, are called 'the Phulkian houses', because they trace their origins from Phul, an agrarian leader, who founded a village in Nabha in the mid-17th century.

Ala Singh was the grandson of Phul, and it was he who established local supremacy over the Bhattis and other rivals. He built the fort at Patiala, but was crushed by invading Afghan forces under Ahmad Shah Durani at the Battle of the Barnala in 1762. Appointed Raja by the Afghans, he seized the first opportunity to rebel and sacked Sirhind, killing its Afghan governor. By 1765 the foundations of the state were established. Although it suffered at the hands of the famous European freebooter George Thomas, it survived to be consolidated under Ranjit Singh, who entered into treaty arrangements with the British in 1809.

In the Nepal War of 1815, again in 1845–6 and during the Mutiny, the Maharaja remained loyal to the British and offered valuable support, a policy which continued through the two world wars.

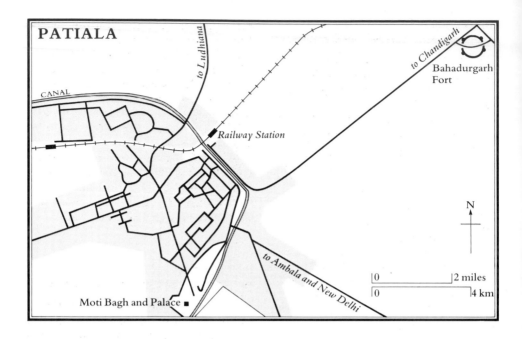

There are a number of interesting buildings in the town, which has a clean, well-kept appearance and beautiful gardens.

The **Old Motibagh Palace** (late 19th century) is, quite simply, one of the largest residencies in Asia, a vast rambling building situated in the middle of manicured lawns and tree-lined vistas. The central block is flanked by enormously long wings, which seem to last for ever but are actually symmetrical around the central axis. Architecturally, it is an eclectic Victorian mixture of Rajput and Mughal styles, all in rose-pink sandstone, a spectacular setting for a maharaja whose lavish lifestyle and reputation for self-indulgent eccentricity enlivened the social scene in the early 20th century. The Durbar Hall has over 100 chandeliers. There are fifteen dining-rooms and a vast central saloon, once furnished with English chairs and sofas and signed portraits of European dignitaries, but now the National Institute for Sports.

There are numerous outbuildings, including the **Sheesh Mahal** or Hall of Mirrors, for senior ladies of the family, and the **Baradari**, a smaller white marble pleasure pavilion in a walled Mughal garden.

The **New Motibagh Palace** was built in 1959 and, by comparison, it is a more modest affair, with a plain arcaded façade crowned by a simple cupola. It accommodates many of the furnishings and family mementos from the Old Palace.

The **Fort** is a huge and impressive exercise in late-18th-century defensive fortification, a vast concentric model citadel set behind a formidable moat. The entrance is across an intermediate island in the moat and through a great semi-circular outer bay before the main stronghold is reached. It is a classic example of a fort on the plain, a 'nara durg'. In 1794 a fierce Maratha attack was repulsed from here.

Other buildings of interest include the King Edward Memorial Hospital, the Clinical Research Laboratory, the Fort Museum and the Temple of Mahakali and Rajeswari.

(For the sacred shrines see Volume I.)

156

PINDORI

About 10 km (6 miles) from Gurdaspur is the Pindori Darbar or gaddi of Bhagwan Narayana Das, built by Jahangir in 1679. Within the building is Raghunathjis Temple, which is covered with mural paintings, stylistically dated to the period 1816–30. They are advanced in technique and composition and are rendered in a dramatic manner using perspective with a distinct Mughal influence.

One remarkable series of paintings illustrates Krishna's marriage to Rukmini. Although most of the paintings portray religious scenes, two interesting secular paintings can be seen, one of which shows a beautiful rani smoking a hookah. In another two female angels can be seen in Muslim-style clothes and caps playing stringed instruments.

Within the Darbar compound the Baba Mahesh Das Ki Samadhi also contains some fine painted murals.

RANIKHET

Ranikhet is a small but once important military hill station, 79 km (49 miles) north of Naini Tal, at a height of over 1,800 m (6,000 ft). There are few buildings of any note but its greatest asset is the spectacular vista of the Himalayas which can be obtained, particularly the view of the twin peaks of Nanda Devi, 7,816 m (25,402 ft), 96·5 km (60 miles) away.

REWARI

Rewari, 51 km (32 miles) south-east of Gurgaon, is an old town built on the ancient debris of an earlier settlement. The present town was founded around 1000 by Raja Rawat, who named it after his daughter. On the collapse of the Mughal Empire, Rewari fell first to the Marathas and then to the Jat Rajas of Bharatpur. In 1805 it came under direct British rule, which boosted its prosperity. It remains a prosperous centre for the manufacture of iron and brass vessels.

The main streets are well laid out, with a circular drive surrounding the town. To the south-west is an attractive tank built by Rao Tej Singh with bathing ghats and temples. The main buildings of consequence are the Town Hall, the Government Courts and the school.

ROORKEE

Situated on an elevated ridge overlooking the Solani river, Roorkee lies 35 km (22 miles) east of Saharanpur. It has grown in importance in recent years as a centre for the Corps of Engineers and the Ganges Canal workshops.

The **Thomason Engineering College** (1847) is now a university catering for military engineers. There is a church, observatory and mission school.

SAHARANPUR

Saharanpur, 67·5 km (42 miles) from Dehra Dun, was founded by Muhammad Tughluq around 1340, and later became a favourite resort for the Mughal court. A palace was built here by the consort of Jahangir and during the reign of Shah Jahan a royal hunting-seat, the Badshah Mahal, was erected by Ali Mardan Khan, the architect of the Eastern Jumna Canal, which, with the decline of Mughal power, fell into disuse. It was reconstructed by Sir P. Cautley (1802–71).

The **Government Botanical Gardens**, founded in 1817, are based here, exporting seeds and specimen fruit trees

157

all over India. The gardens contain small Hindu temples, wells, chatris and suttee monuments.

The **Anglican Church** (consecrated 1858) is worth a visit, together with the **Mosque** (mid-19th century), based on the plan of the Jami Masjid in Delhi, and the old Rohilla fort of Ghansgarh (mid-18th century).

Saharanpur was the base for Rollo Gillespie during the Gurkha War of 1814. It was also the centre for the Trigonometrical Survey of India when it extended operations into the Himalayas in 1835.

SARDHANA

Sardhana, 19 km (12 miles) north-west of Meerut, is a fascinating town with romantic historical associations which epitomize the freebooting nature of many of the European adventurers drawn to India in the late 18th century. Two in particular are connected with Sardhana: Walter Reinhardt and George Thomas.

Reinhardt, appropriately a butcher by profession, came to India with the French army in about 1750, but later deserted and joined a band of European deserters and sepoys which he forged into a fierce group of mercenaries. Known as Samru or Sombre for his swarthy complexion, he entered the service of Mir Kasim, Nawab of Bengal, and was responsible for the massacre of English prisoners at Patna in 1763. He escaped to Oudh and followed various native chiefs before serving Najaf Khan of Delhi, from whom he received Sardhana for the support of his troops. He died here in 1778 and was succeeded by Begum Samru, his formidable widow, who took command of his forces.

In 1781 she became a Roman Catholic and in 1792 married another French adventurer, Levassoult, whom she later

tricked into suicide to be rid of him. Her troops rendered excellent support at the Battle of Gokalgarh in 1788, when a charge of Sardhana troops under George Thomas saved the day. When she was usurped by her European officers in 1795, it was Thomas who restored her position, which she retained until her death in 1836.

The **Kothi Dilkusha** (1834), the Begum's former residence on the east of the town, is a fine colonial mansion in the classical style, with a cascade of steps to the main entrance. Situated in 20·2 hectares (50 acres) of gardens, it is currently used as a school and orphanage. The collection of paintings from the palace is now at Government House, Calcutta, and includes a picture of the Begum by W. Melville.

Outside the town to the south is the imposing **Roman Catholic Cathedral** (1822), enclosed by an ornamental wall. Nearby **St John's Roman Catholic College** was once the residence of the Begum.

SIMLA (SHIIMLA)

Simla, the former summer capital of British India, is now the capital of Himachal Pradesh and is a major administrative centre and hill station. Situated 1,898 km (1,180 miles) from Calcutta and 362 km (225 miles) from Delhi, it is perched on a transverse spur of the central Himalayan system at a height of 2,159 m (7,084 ft) above sea level.

English attention was drawn first to the area during the Nepal War of 1815, and in 1822 Captain Charles Kennedy was appointed Superintendent of the Hill States. It was he who erected the first house in 1825. Owing to the pleasant climate, the station rapidly acquired a reputation as a sanatorium. In 1827 the Governor-General Lord Amherst visited the town and five years later his succes-

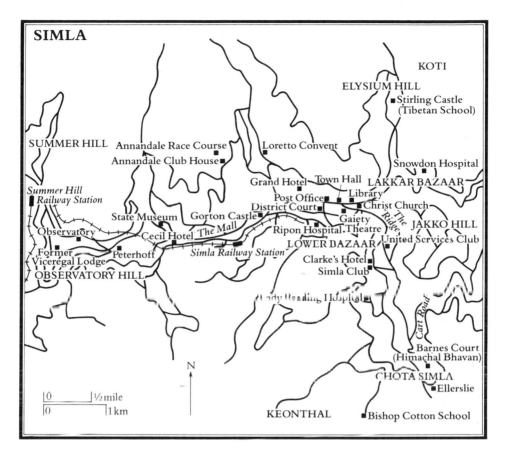

sor, Lord William Bentinck, spent the summer here, establishing the tradition of Simla as the hot-weather headquarters of the government of India, one which continued until 1947. During the Second World War the exiled Government of Burma resided here. In 1946 the Simla Conference prepared the way for independence.

The town is a curiously ramshackle affair built largely of timber, corrugated and cast iron and now much in need of repair. It has been called the Indian Capua, Mount Olympus and the 'Abode of the Little Tin Gods', yet for well over 100 years the British ruled a fifth of mankind from this remote hill station, an astonishing gesture of Imperial self-confidence. Sir Edwin Lutyens remarked: 'If I had been told it had all been built by monkeys, I would have said, what wonderful monkeys, they must be shot in case they do it again.'

The approach to Simla is via Kalka, at the foot of the hills, a distance of 93 km (58 miles). By road it takes about 3½ hours, by train 6 hours and by railcar 4½ hours.

The **Kalka–Simla Narrow-gauge Railway**, completed in 1903, is one of the most impressive railways in the world, an outstanding feat of British Imperial engineering. It cost over £1 million and was designed by H. S. Harington, the chief engineer, on a 2 ft 6 in gauge. It runs over 96·5 km (60 miles) in a series of tight reverse curves with gradients of over 3 feet in every 100. 8 km (5 miles) are underground in a series of 107 tunnels, while 3·2 km (2 miles) are

159

out across precipitous viaducts balanced over yawning chasms. At Barog there is a refreshment room in a delightful Edwardian station with wooden fretwork canopies.

Simla is built across a range of hills and connecting ridges. This imparts a distinct identity to the different quarters. The principal hills are Jakko, 2,453m (8,050ft); Prospect Hill, 2,176m (7,140ft); Observatory Hill, 2,148m (7,050ft); Elysium Hill, 2,255m (7,400ft); and Summer Hill, 2,103m (6,900ft). But most of the houses and major buildings are concentrated on and around the Ridge, the outstanding feature of the town, which runs east to west in a crescent from Jakko Hill and Chota Simla to Prospect Hill and Boileauganj. Spectacular views can be obtained to the north: rows of snow-capped mountain peaks disappearing in the distance. To the south are the Kasauli Hills and the valley of the Sutlej.

The town is dominated by the silhouette of **Christ Church**, which can be seen on the skyline for miles around. Designed by Colonel J. T. Boileau, it was commenced in September 1844, consecrated in January 1857 and subsequently extended. The porch was added in 1873. The clock was donated by Colonel Dumbleton in 1860. The five stained-glass windows depict Faith, Hope, Charity, Fortitude, and Patience and Humility. No trace now remains of the frescoes around the chancel window designed by John Lockwood Kipling. The church was never large enough for the seasonal influx of Europeans. In 1860 the vicar berated the ladies in the congregation because their crinolines occupied so much space at the expense of other worshippers. Note the interesting brasses and plaques.

Adjacent is the **Library** (*c.* 1910), designed by James Ransome with half-timbered gables. The original external staircase has been removed. Around the open space on the ridge are the bandstand and Gandhi's Statue. To the north, the highest peak in the vicinity is Shali, 2,865 m (9,400 ft), with Elysium Hill in the foreground.

Facing the church the path to the right leads to the Ritz cinema, the YMCA and the Masonic Hall. Between the Library and Church is the most direct path to Jakko Peak, where there is the well-known Monkey Temple.

To complete the 9·6 km (6 miles) circuit of Jakko, start to the extreme left. The road leads to Lakkar Bazaar, where fine carved wooden toys, sticks and other goods are made. At the entrance to the Bazaar another road to the left leads to Elysium Hill, named in honour of Emily and Fanny Eden, Lord Auckland's sisters, who lived in Auckland House, which still survives in a much-altered form as a girls' school. It was here that the first Durbar for the hill chiefs was held, on 8 May 1838. Beyond Lakkar Bazaar the main road leads to Sanjouli via the Government College and Civil Hospital.

At the entrance to Sanjouli Bazaar the road turns to the right to the Ladies' Mile, at the end of which a road runs straight back to the Ridge past the Convent of Jesus and Mary and St Bede's College for girls. Above the Ladies' Mile is Lovers' Walk.

The main road then descends to Chota Simla, passing Ellerslie, formerly **Barnes Court**, a large rambling building with half-timbered gables, once the residence of the Lieutenant-Governor. Lord Napier of Magdala, Sir Colin Campbell and Sir Hugh Rose all lived here. John Lockwood Kipling added a Moorish-style ballroom. Today it is the offices of the State secretariat.

From Chota Simla Bazaar a road leads to Kasumpti village. Another leads west to the Bishop Cotton School (1859), which has a chapel with excellent stained glass, and St Edward School.

The main road continues westwards past the Lady Reading Hospital to

160

Clarke's Hotel, a fine range in the distinctive local vernacular style. This marks the beginning of the Mall. Beyond is Combermere Bridge. By the Post Office a path leads up to the United Services Club. Above is the Ladies' Park. The **Gaiety Theatre** (1887) is well worth a visit. It is a delightful little theatre, the home of the Simla Amateur Dramatic Society. There are photo albums depicting old productions which are highly evocative. In a room behind the auditorium is a small vaulted ballroom with fireplaces.

Opposite is a good range of vernacular buildings, in particular a central group with half-timbering, Begg Parade, reminiscent of London suburbia. Scandal Point is marked now by a statue of the Punjabi nationalist Lala Lajpat Rai at the junction of the Ridge and the Mall.

Just behind the Gaiety Theatre and facing the Mall and the Ridge is the Town Hall (c. 1910), a fine piece of civic design in a distinctive Arts and Crafts style with half-timbered gables and projecting window bays.

Cascading down the hill from Scandal Point is Lower Bazaar, a warren of steep alleys, passages and iron and timber buildings. 'A man who knows his way there can defy all the police of India's summer capital, so cunningly does verandah communicate with verandah, alley-way with alley-way, and bolt-hole with bolt-hole,' wrote Kipling in *Kim*. The model for Lurgan's curio shop run by the mysterious Mr Jacob lay down the Mall towards Clarke's Hotel.

To the west of Scandal Point lies the **General Post Office** (1886), a fine range of timber buildings in a style best described as Wild West Swiss, now sadly neglected and altered. Nearby are the YWCA, the old St Andrew's Church (1885), now a college, and the Telegraph Office. Beyond is the Grand Hotel.

The main road descends and joins the Mall at the State Bank of India. From here another path leads to Kaithu and on to Annandale, the pleasure ground of Simla, where there is the **Racecourse and Cricket Ground**. Close to Kaithis Bazaar is the Loretto Convent.

The main road westward is dominated by the spires and turrets of **Gorton Castle**, a gaunt, romantic pile designed by Sir Samuel Swinton Jacob for the Civil Secretariat but considerably modified during its construction by Major H. F. Chesney. By the entrance of Gorton Castle a road to the left leads to the Railway Station. Another to the right goes to Annandale.

In the district known as Chaura Maidan is **Cecil Hotel** (1877; modified in 1902), a fine old building which clings to the side of a precipice. The entrance is at roof level and run the second to the principal rooms.

From the Cecil Hotel it is only 800 m (½ mile) to **Viceregal Lodge**, now Rashtrapati Niwas and used as an Institute of Advanced Study. It was built for the Viceroy Lord Dufferin, who himself suggested the plan and interfered at every stage. Designed by Henry Irwin and Captain H. H. Cole, with F. B. Hebbert and Hon. L. M. St Clair as executive engineers, it was completed in 1888 in a gaunt Elizabethan style in light-blue limestone dressed with light-grey sandstone.

The site was entirely appropriate for the Lords of the Indian Empire as the hill is a natural watershed, with water flowing down to the Sutlej and on to the Arabian Sea on one side and on the other into the Jumna and out into the Bay of Bengal.

It resembles an English country house or Scottish sanatorium, but the garden enjoys spectacular views of the Himalayas. Externally, it is dominated by a high central tower containing the water tanks and an octagonal corner bay crowned by a cupola.

Internally, there is a fine entrance hall and staircase and a huge central gallery executed in teak. At ground-floor level is

161

the State Ballroom and State Dining-Room, the latter enriched with teak panelling which once carried the armorial bearings of the Governors-General and Viceroys of India. Only the inscriptions now remain. The original furniture is by Maples. The mirrors over the chimneypieces come from King Thebaw's palace at Mandalay. At first floor level are the Viceroy's and Vicereine's bedrooms, surprisingly spartan considering that half of Asia was ruled from here. In a small room at first floor level the treaty leading to Indian independence was signed by Mountbatten, Nehru and the Indian nationalists.

In the garden area is an inscribed bronze plate indicating the names of the distant peaks, a sundial and other memorabilia. The outbuildings, including the nursery and gate lodge, are also of interest. The little Chapel of All Saints (1885) lies within the grounds.

The earlier residence of the Governors-General was Peterhof, which is passed en route. Unfortunately, this was burned down in 1981. Only the ruins remain. Below is a covered tennis court erected by Lord Dufferin, a model of the one he built at Rideau Hall in Ottawa.

From Viceregal Lodge, the upper road leads to Summer Hill, the lower to Boileauganj. From Summer Hill there is a precipitous path down to Chadwick Falls.

From Boileauganj the Mall leads back to the centre of Simla past the **GHQ Building**, a prefabricated iron range, east of which is the **Roman Catholic Church of St Michael and St Joseph**, a Gothic building completed in 1900 by the addition of a steeple and belfry. There is some good stained glass. Nearby are the District Courts and St Thomas's School. This leads back to the Telegraph Office, with its prominent clock. From here there is a road down to Lower Bazaar, in which the most notable building is the **Ripon Hospital**, designed by Henry Irwin in 1885 and built by Campion and Learmouth. This is an

excellent, well-preserved building with inventive Gothic detailing adapted to timber materials.

The principal mosque, the Sandagaron Ki Masjid (1910), is an undistinguished building in Middle Bazaar.

It is alleged that cuttings from the tree over Napoleon's grave on St Helena were sent to Simla to the nephew of the emperor's medical attendant. Several real St Helena willows survive, so the story may be true.

The road beyond Elysium Hill passes **Snowdon**, once the residence of the Commander-in-Chief, and turned by Kitchener into a grandiose personal shrine. It is now a modern hospital. The road leads to Mashobra. **St Crispin's Church** (1920) is here, just like an English village church, built to commemorate the fallen of the First World War, with fine stained-glass memorial windows. The Retreat nearby was once the residence of Sir William Henry, the Commissioner of the Hill States. Often it was rented to the Commander-in-Chief as a refuge. Lord Roberts stayed here.

SIRHIND

Sirhind, 251 km (156 miles) north-west of Delhi, was once a very important town and the capital of the Pathan Sur dynasty. The name Sirhind, which was applied to a wide tract of territory, was derived from 'Sar-i-hind', Frontier of Hind. In 1191 it was taken by Shahab-ud-Din Ghuri and it was later besieged by Prithvi Raja.

The **Fort** once formed part of a strategic quadrilateral. Built by Sher Shah Sur, little now survives of the magnificence of the old city. Mounds of debris and ruins testify to the former splendour of the place, which flourished between 1556 and 1707. In 1709 the city was seized by the Sikh Banda, who executed the Mughal governor in an act of

162

revenge. Banda was then executed in retaliation and in 1763 Sirhind was attacked and laid to waste.

The best surviving buildings are the **Tomb of Mir Miran** (15th century), a fine specimen of Sultanate architecture with a large dome carried on an octagonal base and four smaller domes to each corner. The walls are clad in bright-blue enamelled tiles. Other tombs in the same complex include a large plain brick mausoleum with a dome 12·1 m (40 ft) in diameter attributed to Sayyid Khan Pathan and another, attributed to Khoja Khan, with a dome 10·9 m (36 ft) in diameter. Both are probably 15th century in date.

The **Tomb of Pirbandi Nakshwala** (17th century) can be recognized by its distinctive Mughal dome. The building is lavishly ornamented, with flowers and glazed green and blue tiles The **Mosque of Sadan Kasai**, with a dome 13·7 m (45 ft) in diameter, lies to the north of the town.

One of the most interesting buildings is the **Haveli of Salabat Beg**, perhaps the largest and best-preserved example of domestic Mughal architecture. It comprises two large brick structures, 18·2 m (60 ft) square and 24·3 m (80 ft) high, linked by high walls. The old **Sarai** of the Mughal emperors lies to the southeast of the city and is now used as a public hall.

SRINAGAR *Map overleaf*

Srinagar (literally Shri Nagar, beautiful city) is the capital of Kashmir. It stands at a height of 1,593 m (5,227 ft) on the Dal Lake and River Jhelum, which divides the town in two. It is a popular resort in itself and is also used as a stepping-stone to Leh and Ladakh. Roughly equidistant from Jammu, Rawalpindi, Leh and Gilgit, it stands at the head of the passes leading to the Indian plains from Central

Asia. It is therefore a commercial and strategic centre. (For the Museum and temples see Volume I.)

The river is crossed by nine famous old wooden bridges or kadals, built on an ancient cantilever principle, together with some more recent constructions. The embankment and stone revetments contain old carved masonry from demolished temples. The city is criss-crossed by canals and narrow lanes. These are extremely picturesque and contain many fine old timber houses in a distinctive local vernacular style, with sloping earth roofs.

Crowning Sharika Hill and clearly visible for miles around is **Hari Parbat Fort**, built between 1592 and 1598 by the Pathan Governor Aalin Khan. The outer walls, now much restored, were built by Akbar. There is a Persian inscription on the domed Kathi Darwaza commemorating the work. Much of the present construction is 18th century. Access is restricted, but permission can be obtained from the Director of Tourism.

On the southern side of the hill is the Muslim **Shrine of Makhdum Sahib**, with a modern mosque. Below is the **Mosque of Akhund Mulla Shah** (1649), built by Shah Jahan's son with a stone lotus finial over the pulpit, the only surviving example of its kind in Kashmir. Built in stone rather than wood, externally it has rectangular panels enclosing cusped arches. Internally the plan is very unusual. Outside the southern gate of the fort is a Sikh shrine.

The **Jami Masjid** lies in the centre of the city beneath Hari Parbat. It has four arched openings in the centre of each side covered with pyramidal roofs. There are three pagoda-shaped minarets used by the muezzin to call the faithful to prayer. Over 370 pillars support the roof, each made of a single deodar tree trunk. The present mosque was rebuilt to the original design after a fire in 1674. The mosque was first built in 1385 by Sultan Sikander Butshikan and enlarged by his

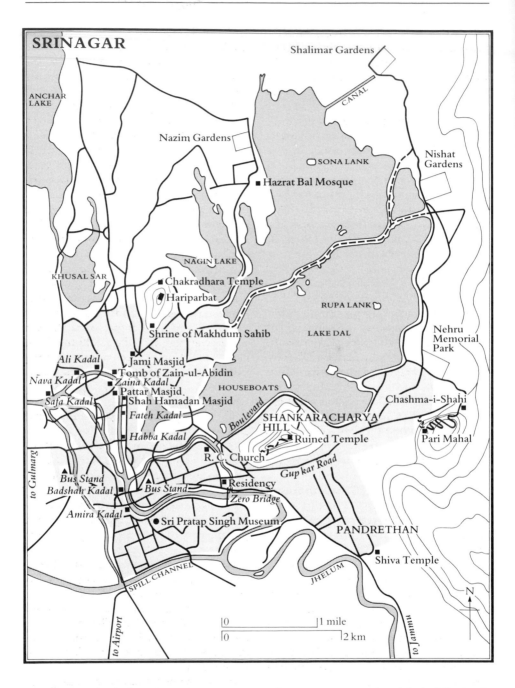

son, Zain-ul-Abidin, in 1402. It was destroyed by fire in 1479, rebuilt in 1503 and destroyed again in Jahangir's reign.

The building was restored to the Muslims in 1841 by Maharaja Sher Singh.

The inner courtyard is delightfully landscaped and very peaceful. Architecturally the building is a fine example of the hybrid Muslim style of Kashmir but with an orthodox mosque plan.

164

Immediately to the south, on the right bank of the river, is another fine mosque, the **Shah Hamadan**, typical of the wooden architecture of Kashmir. Originally erected in 1395, it was destroyed by fire in 1479 and 1731. The masonry plinth is composed of old temple fragments while the body of the mosque is a simple cube crowned by a pagoda-like roof. This has a low pyramidal roof over which rises an open pavilion for the muezzin and a flèche spire. Note the heavy eaves cornice made of corbelled logs. The view of the mosque with the timber bridge in the foreground should not be missed.

Opposite, across the river, is the old **Pattar Masjid** (1623), built in provincial Mughal style for Empress Nur Jahan under the supervision of the architect Malik Haidar Chaudara and now used as a granary. Below the fourth bridge is the tomb of the widow of Sikander Butshikan, which has an earlier 9th-century Hindu plinth.

The **Tomb of Zain-ul-Abidin's Mother** (c. 1430) is built on the foundations of an old Hindu temple. It has an Islamic superstructure with pronounced Persian influence in its domed construction and glazed tiles.

On the right bank, by Zaina Kadal, are the ruins of Bad Shah, a mosque and tomb from the 15th century enclosed by an old stone wall. Stones from here are reputed to cure smallpox sores.

The fifth bridge, Ali Kadal, is a recent reconstruction below which is the Mosque of Budul Shah, the first Muslim fakir, who established Islam in the valley. Nava Kadal or New Bridge was built by Saif Khan in 1664. At Safa Kadal is the old Yarkand sarai, where traders from Yarkand and Central Asia used to stay with their merchandise.

The Sri Pratap Singh Museum is south of the river between Zero Bridge and Amira Kadal. It has an interesting collection of Kashmiri exhibits.

The Sher Garhi, once enclosed by the walls of the city fort, was the summer residence of the maharaja, until it was replaced by the now abandoned classical Baradari Palace on the banks of the Jhelum.

The greatest attraction of Srinagar is Lake Dal, which lies to the east of the town. It is 6·4 km (4 miles) long and 4 km (2½ miles) broad. The western side is dotted with flat willow-covered islands called demb, separated by narrow channels, the chief of which is the Mar, which drains down from a high mountain lake and enters Lake Dal to the north. The English willows here are used to make cricket bats.

The lake is divided into three parts by two causeways. The eastern portion is called Lokut or Small Lake, the other Bod or Large Lake. In the west is an inlet called Sodura Khon, which is the deepest part of the lake, over 12 m (40 ft) deep. Here are many of the famous **houseboats**, with decorated fretwork canopies, interspersed among groves of chinars, willows and poplars and orchards of apricots, quince, almond and pear trees.

The two islands in Lake Dal, the Rupa Lank and Sona Lank (the Silver and Gold Lanka) are ancient, artificial creations. The northern island, the Sona Lank, is just above water level and the vegetation appears to float on the water. Shah Jahan planted a tree symmetrically in each corner.

Hazrat Bal (literally Majestic Place) lies 10 km (6 miles) from Srinagar and has an excellent view of the lake. It contains a modern mosque which is the repository of a hair of the Prophet. The view of the mosque on its lakeside setting with the snow-capped mountains beyond is magnificent.

Just to the north lies **Nazim Bagh** or Garden of the Morning Breeze, the earliest of the Mughal gardens of Kashmir. Little remains of the original work laid out by Akbar, except for some terrace walls and some small ruined lakeside buildings. Some of the chinars are over 380 years old. Most of the present layout dates from the time of Shah Jahan, who planted hundreds of chinars on a regular grid. It is now used by an engineering college. Viewed from the lake in an autumn sunset it is deeply impressive.

High in the distance is the peak of Mahadiv, 3,966 m (13,013 ft) high, the water from which drains into the lake via the Tel-Bal-Nala. The Dachigam valley, which skirts the foot of the mountain, is one of the most beautiful in Kashmir.

The famous **Shalimar Gardens** lie about 5 km (3 miles) away. They were built for the empress Nur Jahan by her husband, Jahangir, from 1616. They are the most secluded of the Lake Dal gardens and some of the loveliest in the world. The approach along the canal from Lake Dal is through tightly packed lotus plants, and at the head of the canal lies one of the most delightful gardens imaginable. The design is simple. At the centre of the garden a broad, shallow canal leads to a wide, rectangular basin in which is set a black marble pavilion surrounded by fountains and jets of water. The pavilion is the focal point and climax of the garden composition, a subtle combination of axial planning, proportion and planting. Behind the cascades above the black pavilion are double rows of chini-kanas or pigeon holes, in which lights were placed behind the sheets of falling water. From May to October a *son et lumière* is held here.

The eastern shore of Lake Dal is full of springs, the most important of which is Gupta Ganga, a sacred spring situated in Ishibor village.

Nishat Bagh, the Garden of Gladness, lies between the mountains and the lake. It was laid out by Asaf Khan, brother of Nur Jahan, in 1632. Designed on a monumental scale, it is a set-piece intended to be viewed from water level, rising in a series of spectacular terraces to the backdrop of the mountains beyond. Approached by boat, the entrance is

under an angled pyramidal bridge with a single arched opening. Beyond lies a pavilion reflected in the lake, with the terraces rising majestically behind. The pavilion is sited with less effect than that at Shalimar, but the view from the highest zenana terrace is breathtaking. The main feature is the central watercourse, a series of channels cascading into the terrace below, punctuated by fountains. Each change of level is marked by stone thrones across the water. The retaining wall of the zenana terrace is arcaded, terminating in small gazebos at either end. Note the carved patterns on the chadars or stone channels to create rippling of the water as it passes through the garden.

The **Chashma-i-Shahi** or Royal Spring was built in 1632 for Shah Jahan by Ali Mardan Khan, the Mughal Governor. In its present form it combines the work of many periods. Originally, it was a small axial enclosure moulded by the natural contours of the mountain, derived from a small spring which bubbled up through a marble lotus basin set in the floor of the upper pavilion. Today the garden has been extended and restored, with many dramatic changes in level, rich planting and a degree of asymmetry. Only the bases of the two pavilions are Mughal; the remainder is Kashmiri in design. Visit in the late afternoon or evening, for the panorama of the lake in the setting sun is an unforgettable experience. High up on the Bren Nullah is the Shrine of Baba Ghulam Dink, the brother of Shaikh Nur-ud-Din.

Amid a grove of chinars and mulberry trees, just to the right of Chashma-i-Shahi, is the Chashma-i-Sahibi, a delightful clear spring.

The **Pari Mahal** or Palace of Fairies (*c.* 1635) was built by the eldest son of Shah Jahan, Dara Shukoh. It was reputed to have been a school of astrology but is now in ruins. Five terraces can still be seen, together with the remains of fountains and tanks behind the ruined façade which lie on an inaccessible spur of rock with the mountains looming behind.

At the village of Zithair is a Hindu shrine. The road back into Srinagar passes Shankaracharya Hill, once called Takht-i-Sulaiman or Throne of Solomon. From the summit, marked by a TV mast, are fine views of the lake. At the foot of the eastern slope is a ziarat to the Shias beside a cluster of stunted pines.

Nehru Park lies on the opposite side of the Gagribal Spur.

Anchar Lake lies 11·2 km (7 miles) north of Srinagar and is a popular excursion. It is about 5·6 km (3½ miles) long and 3·6 km (2¼ miles) wide, with numerous small willow-clad islets, wildfowl and swans. However, from here a journey up the Sind river leads to Ganderbal.

Achabal (literally Peaceful Place) lies close by the old direct road to Srinagar from Pahalgam. Here the gardens were laid out in 1640 by Nur Jahan around a natural spring. On the west side are the ruins of an old hammam from which warm water once flowed. The water was

warmed by a candle under an iron pan. During excavations it was extinguished and could not be relit. The water from the natural spring runs into three canals, which cascade over three terraces. The main canal has several fountains. On the upper terrace are three pavilions. Little remains of the original Mughal structures; most of the present buildings are Kashmiri. The stone platforms or chabutras may once have provided a base for tents and awnings.

Verinag or Nila Nag is one of the largest springs in India, the source of the River Jhelum. Originally circular in plan, the spring was altered by Jahangir into an octagonal basin in 1620. It is surrounded by a brick wall and vaults. According to Jahangir, 'in the whole of Kashmir there is no sight of such beauty and enchanting character'. It was a favourite haunt of his empress, Nur Jahan. The subtle combination of landscape, geometry, light and shade combines to create an imposing garden of exceptional beauty.

Little survives of the original buildings. The main canal is over 304 m (1,000 ft) long.

CENTRAL INDIA

NINE

CENTRAL INDIA

Madhya Pradesh, eastern and central Uttar Pradesh

Introduction

This region comprises the heartland of India, two huge states, Madhya Pradesh (literally the Middle Land) and Uttar Pradesh or U.P. (literally the Northern Provinces). This vast area of central India bears witness to over 2,000 years of continuous religious activity. Here Buddhism and Jainism were first established in the 5th century BC. But the ancient centres of Hindu, Buddhist and Jain art are also overlain with the monuments of later periods of occupation – deserted palaces, haunted by the shades of departed princes, impregnable hill fortresses, which lie brooding over the forests below, and spectacular ruined cities, studded with the evocative ruins of mosques and tombs of generations long since passed.

Madhya Pradesh, the ancient land of Malwa, is India's largest state. Geographically it separates the desert areas of Rajasthan from the fertile Indo-Gangetic plain and the great lava tableland of the Deccan. The stony, inhospitable landscape of Malwa, Bundelkhand and Rewa, is drained by the Chambal, Ken and Betwa rivers and is broken into rugged plateaux and deep ravines which have always enjoyed a reputation for lawlessness, dacoity and banditry.

While the northern part of the state lies on the unrelenting plain of the Ganges, the upland areas of the south are clad in a carpet of rich forest, providing a sanctuary for wildlife and some of the best deciduous hardwood in the world. This is the land of Kipling's *Jungle Book*. A high proportion of India's tribal population live here. The Gonds, who inhabit the Satpura and Kymore ranges, gave their name to the central region of the state: Gondwana. The colourful Bhils, a warrior tribe, live in the west and the Christian Oraons live in the eastern part of the state.

Between the 12th and 16th centuries the region was the scene of a continuous struggle for local supremacy between successive waves of Muslim and Hindu invaders. Of greatest significance was the rise of Muslim rule in Malwa, which was established only after a bloody, protracted conflict with the local Rajput rulers of **Chitorgarh** and **Ujjain**. Malwa was invaded initially by Shams-ud-Din Iltutmish early in the 13th century, but in 1305 Ala-ud-Din Khalji, the Sultan of Delhi, sent an army to subjugate the area. Later, with the waning of the power of the sultanate, the provincial Governor, Dilawar Khan, declared his independence and commenced his own dynasty. This independent kingdom flourished from 1401 to 1531, at which time it was conquered by Gujarat, and later by Humayun.

The capital was created at the remote fortress of **Mandu**, where a magnificent series of palaces and other buildings, designed in a distinctive provincial style, was erected over many generations.

Overleaf The Taj Mahal 'A tear drop on the face of eternity'

Local Hindu architectural traditions were far less important here than the strong influence of Delhi, from where many of the local craftsmen came after the devastation wrought by Timur. Stylistically, the pointed arch with the spear-head fringe, battered or sloping walls and arch and lintel doorways are derived from Khalji and Tughluq sources, while the 'boat-keel' dome and pyramidal roof are reminiscent of the Lodi tombs. Distinctive original features were also introduced, such as the use of high plinths approached by flights of steps, perforated screens, carved window brackets and the ornamental use of coloured encaustic tiles and semi-precious stones.

The style passed through three specific phases. The earliest can be seen in the mosques at **Dhar**, the old capital of Malwa under the Paramara kings, and in the mosques of Dilawar Khan and Malik Mughith at **Mandu**. Most of the principal buildings at **Mandu**, such as the famous Hindola Mahal and the Jahaz Mahal, belong to the second and most sophisticated phase, the final stage being confined to the pleasure palaces, pavilions and hammams erected in the mid 16th century. **Chanderi**, the old northern capital of Malwa, has interesting remains in the same provincial style.

South of Malwa, in the valley of the Tapti river and north of the Bahmanid kingdom of the Deccan, lay Khandesh, the land of the Khans. In the 15th and 16th centuries under the Faruqi dynasty this small independent kingdom produced a number of buildings which displayed original and distinctive features, if not a specific local style. The Jami Masjid and Bibi-ki-Masjid at **Burhanpur** are typical examples.

The chronic insecurity of the region, coupled with its strategic location, fostered the construction of a series of formidable hillforts. **Ajaigarh** sits perched on a granite outcrop. Nearby is the ancient, awe-inspiring fortress of **Kalinjar**, one of the oldest fortified sites in India, venerated by successive generations of invaders. At **Asirgarh** there are traces of settlement from as early as 1600 BC. East of **Jhansi** lies **Garhkundar**, dominating a forbidding tract of Bundelkhand, but the greatest and most formidable of all is the spectacular hilltop fortress at **Gwalior**, 'the pearl in the necklace of the castles of Hind'.

Here, the Man Mandir palace is of outstanding architectural significance, one of the most important pre-Mughal palaces to survive intact in central India. With its copper-gilt cupolas glinting in the sunlight and its bold carved relief work of elephants, birds, trees and coloured ornament, the exterior demonstrates how the great Hindu princes could emulate the finest Muslim monuments in a controlled exercise of architectural exuberance and vitality.

During the 16th and 17th centuries an architectural movement arose in Bundelkhand which achieved its most eloquent expression in the two great palace complexes at **Datia** and **Orchha**. In each case the square plan with corner towers and the composed silhouette with arrays of kiosks and cupolas imparted a romantic dignity and elegance to a formidable mass of masonry.

The central and eastern parts of Uttar Pradesh cover the flat alluvial Gangetic plain and contain some of the greatest concentrations of population in the country. The region is drained by the mighty river system of the Ganges, Jumna, Ghagra, Gandak, Gomati, Ramganga and Chambal. To the north lies Nepal and the foothills of the Himalayas; to the south, the low Vindhyan Hills. At the junction of the two sacred rivers, the Ganges and Jumna, stands **Allahabad**, the ancient Prayag, and one of the holiest places in the country. Here lies Akbar's fort and palace and the Khusrau Bagh, where the brother of Shah Jahan is buried.

To the east is the holy city of **Varanasi**, with its world-famous river

171

frontage of temples and bathing ghats. Looted by successive waves of Muslim invaders, there are several notable Muslim buildings, including the historic mosque of Aurangzeb, who was responsible for the wholesale destruction of most of the ancient Hindu shrines and temples in the city.

To the north of **Varanasi** lies the old town of **Jaunpur**, once the capital of the independent Sharqi sultans, before it succumbed to Sikander Lodi and then to the Mughals. Founded in 1359, it became known as the 'Shiraz of the East' for the number and quality of its colleges and for its interest in the arts. By the 15th century it had become the centre of a powerful Muslim state situated between the sultanates of Delhi and Bengal.

A particularly fine provincial style of architecture developed at **Jaunpur**, but many of the monuments were destroyed later by Sikander Lodi. Although the mosques were built to a conventional plan, they possess a unique local character. Tapered minarets, battered walls to the propylons and the use of four-centred 'Tudor' arches with decorative fringes are derived from Tughluq prototypes. The buildings are characterized by stucco ornament and the rough but effective use of carved stone ceilings, lattice screens and panels and arches in geometrical floral designs. The hallmark of the Jaunpur style is the propylon – a tall screen with battered sides concealing the dome and raised in front of a gateway or the entrance to the prayer chamber of a mosque. The Atala Masjid and the Jami Masjid are the most significant examples of this style, together with the tombs of the Sharqi sultans.

Lucknow, the capital of Uttar Pradesh, rose to importance initially under the Mughals but later flourished as the fabled capital of the Nawabs of Oudh, who were Shiite Muslims. It is one of the finest cities in India, with a magnificent heritage of buildings mostly dating from the mid-18th century onwards. At its height this wonderful city of palaces, mosques and tombs rivalled Peking as the most opulent royal court in the East. The Great Imambara and the Rumi Darwaza are two of the most famous monuments in India, but the city boasts a whole series of sumptuous palaces, such as the Kaisarbagh and Chhatar Manzil, which were renowned for their splendour and extravagant architectural style.

Lucknow evolved its own peculiar style in the early 19th century, originally based on Mughal sources but later overlain with many European motifs, including a free and imaginative use of the classical orders. Constantia, the mausoleum of Major General Claude Martin, now La Martinière Boys' School, is typical of the hybrid eclecticism which pervaded the city.

For Europeans, however, the city will always be associated with the events of 1857 and the heroic siege and defence of the British Residency, the ruins of which stand as a perpetual reminder of one of the most stirring chapters in British military history. Similarly, **Kanpur** retains many sites with poignant memories of the Mutiny, such as All Souls' Memorial Church, the remains of Wheeler's entrenchment and the Sati Chaura Ghat.

In the extreme west of the state lie **Agra** and **Fatehpur Sikri**. They contain the finest concentration of Mughal buildings in India.

Agra was the capital of Sikander Lodi, who died there in 1517, but it was under Akbar that the city rose to international pre-eminence as a centre of civilization and culture. The massive fort contains a whole series of splendid Mughal monuments, including the Diwan-i-Am, Diwan-i-Khas and the Moti Masjid, which no visitor to India should miss. It was here that Shah Jahan, imprisoned by his son, passed his last years, gazing across the Jumna to the Taj Mahal, the last resting-place of his beloved wife, Mumtaz Mahal, and the supreme achievement of Mughal architecture, arguably the most perfect building ever erected.

In and around the city are various buildings which show the gradual evolution of the design that culminated in the Taj Mahal. On the opposite bank lies the Tomb of Itmad-ud-Daula, a beautiful marble sepulchre inlaid with semi-precious stones and arabesques, a low square building with four corner towers. To the north of the city at **Sikandra** is Akbar's tomb, approached through four great sandstone gateways inlaid with polygonal marble patterns. Both were important in the development of the Mughal style.

35 km (20 miles) south-west of Agra is the deserted city of **Fatehpur Sikri**, Akbar's capital for a brief but brilliant period of twelve years. The Imperial ruins of this matchless city are a fascinating repository of fine Mughal buildings. The huge Buland Darwaza, set high on the ridge and approached by a cascade of steps, is one of the greatest monuments in India, while within the Jami Masjid

the tomb of Shaikh Salim Chishti, with its sinuous serpentine brackets and delicately-carved diaphanous marble screens, is an architectural masterpiece.

The region also has a rich heritage of European buildings from the more recent past. In addition to the monuments associated with the Mutiny at **Lucknow** and **Kanpur**, the British also left an indelible mark on the country. At **Ghazipur** Lord Cornwallis is commemorated by a stately cenotaph. **Agra**, **Allahabad** and **Varanasi** all have extensive cantonments of very considerable interest. At **Allahabad** there is the great Cathedral of All Saints and a fine group of civic buildings designed in a vigorous tropical Gothic style, while the palaces at **Indore** and **Gwalior** are European in conception and design. But perhaps the most pervasive influence of all is at a local level, in the simple bungalows and public buildings of the up-country towns and villages, and in the forgotten cemeteries, where the British left an enduring legacy of dominion in both life and death.

The river ghats at Varanasi

Left Badal Mahal, Chanderi

Right Hindola Mahal, Mandu

Below Tomb of Hoshang Shah, Mandu

Left The Jahangir Mandir Palace at Orchha

Right The Govind Mandir Palace at Datia

Below The great walls of the Man Mandir, Gwalior

Tomb of Shaikh Salim Chishti, Fatehpur Sikri

Above right Gateway to Akbar's Tomb, Sikandra

Below right Tomb of Itmad-ud–Daula, Agra

Constantia, now La Martinière Boys' School, Lucknow

Above right The Rumi Darwaza, Lucknow

Below right The Residency, Lucknow

180

Left The Mutiny Memorial Church, Kanpur

Below Allahabad Cathedral

Right Marochetti's mournful seraph commemorates the fallen at Kanpur

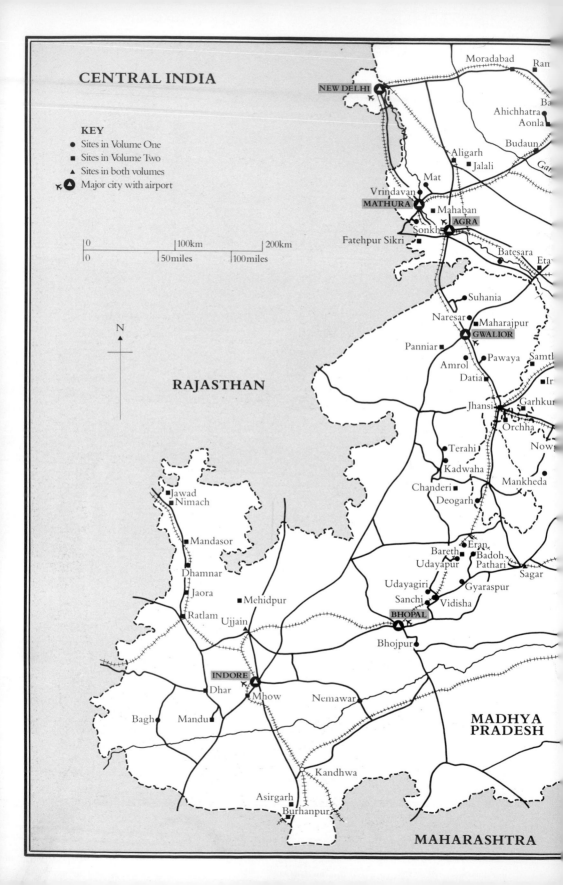

CENTRAL INDIA

KEY
- Sites in Volume One
- Sites in Volume Two
- Sites in both volumes
- Major city with airport

Scale: 0 — 100km — 200km / 0 — 50miles — 100miles

N

RAJASTHAN

MADHYA PRADESH

MAHARASHTRA

Moradabad, Ran, Ba, Ahichhatra, Aonla, Budaun, New Delhi, Aligarh, Jalali, Mat, Gan, Vrindavan, Mathura, Mahaban, Sonkh, Agra, Fatehpur Sikri, Batesara, Eta, Suhania, Naresar, Maharajpur, Panniar, Gwalior, Amrol, Pawaya, Samth, Datia, Ir, Jhansi, Garhkur, Orchha, Terahi, Now, Kadwaha, Mankheda, Chanderi, Deogarh, Jawad, Nimach, Mandasor, Eran, Bareth, Badoh, Udayapur, Pathari, Dhamnar, Udayagiri, Gyaraspur, Sagar, Jaora, Mehidpur, Sanchi, Vidisha, Ratlam, Ujjain, Bhopal, Bhojpur, Indore, Dhar, Mhow, Nemawar, Bagh, Mandu, Kandhwa, Asirgarh, Burhanpur

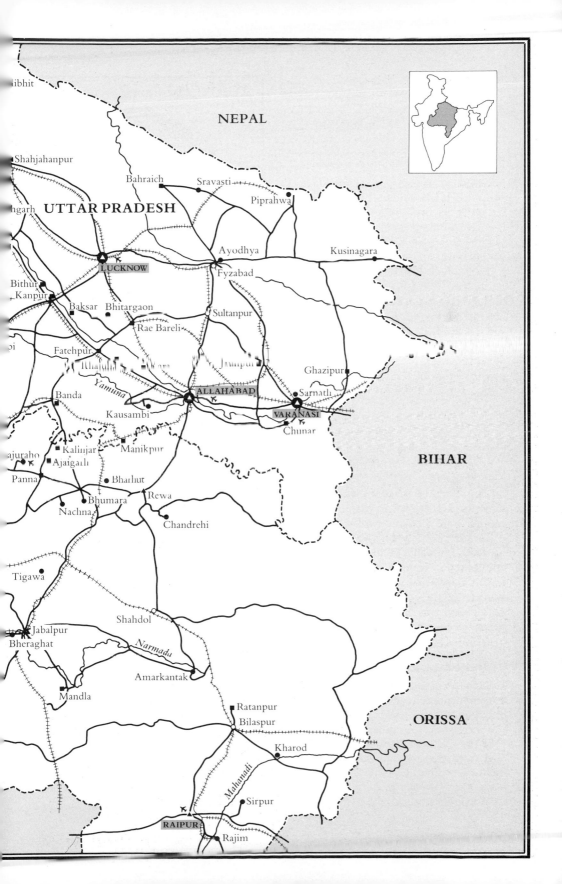

AGRA

Agra lies on the west bank of the River Jumna, 482 km (300 miles) above its confluence with the Ganges at Allahabad and 223 km (139 miles) south-east from Delhi.

The ancient history of the city is shrouded in obscurity. There was reputed to be a legendary city on the east or left bank in the legends of Krishna. Agra became the capital of Sikander Lodi, the penultimate ruler of the Afghan dynasty, in 1501. He died here in 1517 and Sikandra, 8 km (5 miles) outside the city, the burial place of Akbar, is named after him. With the death of Sikander Lodi's son Ibrahim Lodi at Panipat in 1526, Agra became one of the principal cities of the Mughal Empire, which was founded by the victorious Babur.

The superb Mughal monuments, for which the city is renowned throughout the world, made it an outstanding centre of civilization, comparable in artistic pre-eminence to Rome. In addition to the incomparable Taj Mahal, there are the Fort, the fabled city of Fatehpur Sikri, the tomb of Akbar at Sikandra and other magnificent Mughal monuments which should on no account be missed.

Akbar resided here in the early years of his reign and founded the Fort. His capital was at Fatehpur Sikri from about 1571 to 1585, when he transferred to Lahore. But in 1599 he returned to Agra, where he died and was buried in 1605. Jahangir never returned here after he left Kashmir in 1618. It was Shah Jahan who did so much to enrich the city with spectacular monuments, conceived at the very highest point of Mughal architectural achievement, renaming the city Akbarabad after his grandfather. He was deposed and imprisoned by his son Aurangzeb in 1658 and lived seven years in captivity. In 1761 Agra was sacked by the Jats under the Raja of Bharatpur. Later it was seized by the Marathas, from whom it was taken by the British under Lord Lake in October 1803.

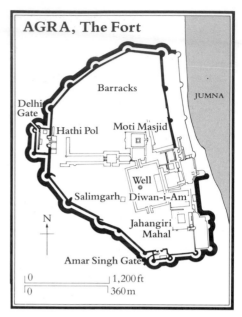

AGRA, The Fort

The **Fort** dominates the centre of the city. Within are some of the finest Mughal buildings in India. The present Fort, on the site of an older one built by the son of Sher Shah, was erected by Emperor Akbar between 1565 and 1573 under the supervision of Muhammad Qasim Khan. It lies on the right bank of the Jumna, about 1·6 km (1 mile) above the Taj Mahal. Akbar was responsible for the walls and gates and Aurangzeb for the ramparts and outer fosse, while most of the principal buildings were erected by Shah Jahan.

The Fort takes the form of an irregular triangle with its base along the river bank to the east. The overall circuit of about 2·4 km (1½ miles) is a continuous sandstone rampart, punctuated at regular intervals by gracefully curved bastions.

There are four gates. The **Amar Singh Gate** to the south is the main entrance for visitors. The Delhi Gate to the west and Water Gate to the east are now closed. The fourth gate, to the north-east, is also closed.

The **Tomb of Jangi Saiyid**, on the bed of the inner ditch, is said to predate the fort.

186

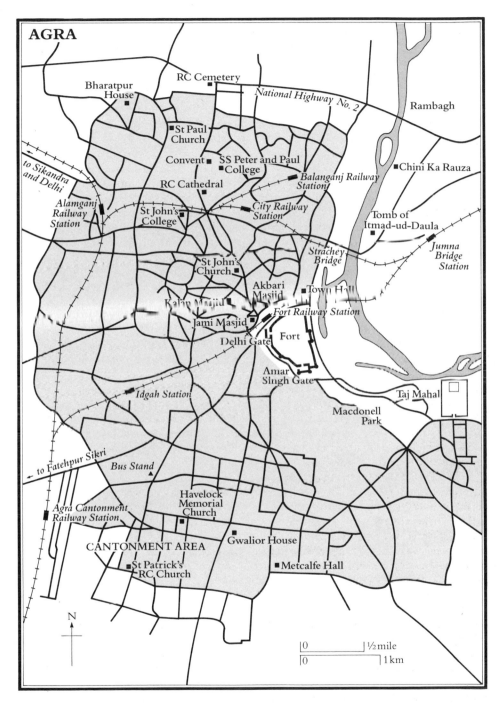

AGRA

Bharatpur House · RC Cemetery · National Highway No. 2 · Rambagh · St Paul Church · Convent · SS Peter and Paul College · Balanganj Railway Station · Chini Ka Rauza · to Sikandra and Delhi · RC Cathedral · Alamganj Railway Station · St John's College · City Railway Station · Tomb of Itmad-ud-Daula · Jumna Bridge Station · St John's Church · Strachey Bridge · Akbari Masjid · Town Hall · Kalan Masjid · Fort Railway Station · Jami Masjid · Delhi Gate · Fort · Amar Singh Gate · Taj Mahal · Idgah Station · Macdonell Park · to Fatehpur Sikri · Bus Stand · Havelock Memorial Church · Agra Cantonment Railway Station · Gwalior House · CANTONMENT AREA · St Patrick's RC Church · Metcalfe Hall

N

0 ½ mile
0 1 km

Originally, the principal entrance was via the **Delhi Gate**, nearly opposite the Jami Masjid. Formerly, there was a walled enclosure, the Tripulia, in front of this gate, but it was removed in 1875. The inner archway carries the date 1600.

187

Inside, a paved incline leads to the **Hathi Pol** or Elephant Gate. This is an impressive inner gateway flanked by two octagonal towers of red sandstone dressed with white marble.

Two stone elephants with riders once stood guard outside the gate on the raised guard platforms to either side, but these were demolished by Aurangzeb. The identification of these colossal statues is disputed, but they may have been erected by Akbar to commemorate the vanquished Rajput adversaries, Jaimal and Patta, at the capture of Chitorgarh in 1568. The inner elevation is well-detailed, a fine example of early Mughal style. There are good views of the Jami Masjid from the crest of the gateway, which can be reached via an inner staircase. The pavilions on the top of the octagonal towers bear traces of tilework and painting. Descending, one can reach balconies on the front of the gate.

At Hathi Pol the road bifurcates. To the left it loops around, past 19th-century barrack buildings, to the Moti Masjid or Pearl Mosque. To the right it leads to the Amar Singh Gate and the court of the Diwan-i-Am.

The **Amar Singh Gate** is a fine portal, enriched with glazed tiles, similar in form to the Delhi Gate. It too was erected by Akbar. It was via this gate that the victorious Lord Lake entered the Fort in 1803.

The Fort is enclosed by a double wall of rubble faced in sandstone, crowned by embattled parapets with ramparts and loopholed merlons. On the east frontage part is occupied by palaces and other buildings. These are protected by the **Shah Burj** and **Bengali Burj**, at the north and south extremities respectively. The distance between the double walls is about 12·2 m (40 ft). In this space is a paved ditch, from the base of which the outer wall is 19·8 m (65 ft) and the inner about 32 m (105 ft) away. The area between the walls on the river frontage is called the East Enclosure.

The **Moti Masjid** or Pearl Mosque, built by Shah Jahan from 1648 to 1655, stands at the highest point in the Fort. The projecting entrance gateway on the east façade is approached by a double staircase. The exterior is built in red sandstone, the interior in veined marble. The building relies for its impact on proportion, materials and that elusive characteristic of cohesive harmony which is the hallmark of the best Mughal architecture. It is a building of sublime simplicity.

The courtyard has a square marble tank in the centre, south-east of which is an ancient sundial comprising an octagonal marble pillar. To the east, north and south arcaded marble cloisters surround the main courtyard, punctuated on the north and south sides by two gateways. The Mosque comprises a marble prayer-chamber 50 m (159 ft) by 17 m (56 ft), surmounted by three elegant marble domes resting on three aisles, each of seven bays. Over the centre of each arch is a kiosk. Each dome is beautifully contoured and rises from the roof like a flower-bud on the point of unfolding. The floor is marked with prayer spaces bordered by yellow marble strips. To either side are screens of white marble lattice-work dividing the chambers for women worshippers. In each corner of the prayer chamber is an octagonal tower crowned by a marble cupola. Over the east face is a Persian inscription inlaid in black slate recording the date 1648–55.

Nearly opposite the mosque is an inclined passage which leads to an old gateway. This was probably the Dersane Darwaza, part of Akbar's original buildings.

Beyond is the crossroads to the Mina Bazaar, now demolished. To the left is the descent to the Water Gate. Ahead is the **Diwan-i-Am** or Hall of Public Audience. To the north and south are great arched gateways of red sandstone, that to the north being the Akbari Darwaza, where ambassadors, ministers and nobles entered the Diwan-i-Am.

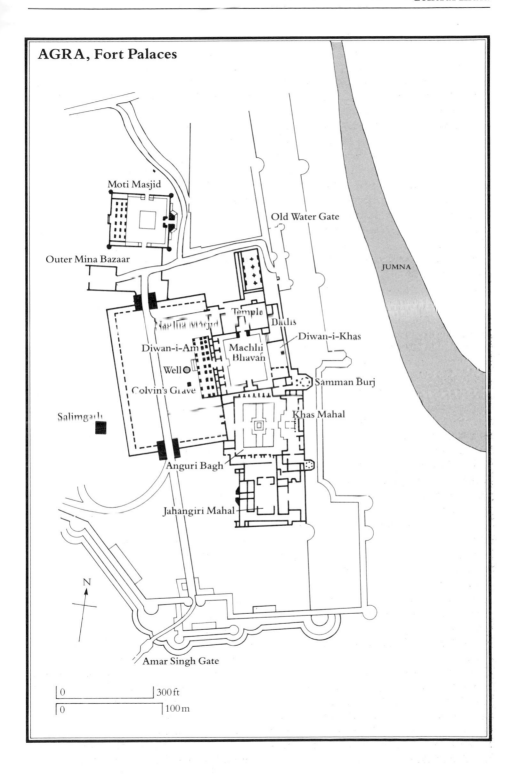

AGRA, Fort Palaces

Moti Masjid

Old Water Gate

Outer Mina Bazaar

JUMNA

Temple

Naubat Masjid
Dalus

Diwan-i-Khas

Diwan-i-Am

Machhi
Bhavan

Well

Colvin's Grave

Samman Burj

Salimgarh

Khas Mahal

Anguri Bagh

Jahangiri Mahal

N

Amar Singh Gate

| 0 | | 300 ft |
| 0 | | 100 m |

The hall was built by Shah Jahan to replace an earlier wooden structure. It was restored in 1876 by Sir John Strachey. It consists of three aisles of nine bays, open on three sides, with beautifully enriched peacock arches carried on columns of red sandstone. At the back of the hall is a richly decorated alcove of inlaid marble connected to the royal apartments beyond. This was the **Throne of the Emperor**, where he gave daily audience to his court. At the base of the alcove is a small block of marble on which ministers stood to receive petitions to the emperor. On either side are perforated marble screens, which enabled the ladies of the zenana to view the proceedings. On festivals and special occasions the Diwan-i-Am was enriched with gold brocades, satin canopies and magnificent silk carpets. The great nobles each decorated a bay of the arcade around the great courtyard, vying for the emperor's attention.

In the centre of the great colonnaded courtyard is a Gothic Christian tomb. This is the **Grave of Mr John Russell Colvin**, Lieutenant-Governor of the North-West Provinces, who died here during the Mutiny of 1857. Close by is **Jahangir's Hauz** or cistern, cut from a single block of porphyry in 1611 with a Persian inscription on the outer rim.

A passage and steps to the north of the Diwan-i-Am lead to the inner courts of the Palace. The first enclosure is the **Machhi Bhavan** or Fish Square, now heavily altered. Originally, it was laid out with tanks, channels, fountains and flower beds. Much of the original mosaic and marble fretwork was auctioned by Lord William Bentinck. Today it is enclosed on three sides by a two-storey cloister. The fourth side is an open terrace.

To the left of the throne-room in the north-west corner is the **Nagina Masjid** or Gem Mosque, a beautiful white marble mosque with three domes built by Shah Jahan for ladies of the zenana.

Beneath is the **Inner Mina Bazaar**, overlooked by a splendid marble balcony with carved geometric screens and peacock arches. Here the ladies of the zenana sat and watched merchants display their silks, brocades and jewellery in the courtyard below.

The furthest corner of this courtyard leads to the **Chitor Gates**, trophies brought by Akbar to commemorate his capture of the Rajput fortress in 1657. The two bronze gates provide the principal entrance back to the Machhi Bhavan courtyard. Beyond is another quadrangle, containing a Hindu temple built by the Bharatpur Rajas, who sacked Agra in the mid-18th century.

On the riverside lies the **Diwan-i-Khas** or Hall of Private Audience, one of the most elegant of Shah Jahan's buildings. It was built in 1637 and is smaller than the Diwan-i-Khas at Delhi, though equal in beauty. It consists of an open colonnade in front and an enclosure at the rear measuring 19·8 m (65 ft) by 10·36 m (34 ft) by 6·7 m (22 ft) high. The marble is inlaid with semi-precious stones such as jasper, carnelian and lapis lazuli in charming floral patterns of pietra dura work relieved by exquisite carving.

On the terrace in front of the Diwan-i-Khas are **two thrones**, one in white marble facing the Machhi Bhavan and one of black slate on the riverside. The black pedestal had the reputation of being able to test the quality of gold. The black throne is inscribed, indicating it was made for Prince Salim when he was made heir to Akbar and assumed the name Jahangir in 1603. Here he watched elephant fights on the plain below.

The throne has a long fissure, reputed to have appeared when the Jat Raja, Jawahar Singh of Bharatpur, usurped the throne in 1761. It is alleged that blood spurted from the throne in two places leaving red stains as evidence. Jawahar Singh was assassinated shortly after.

On the terrace opposite the Diwan-i-Khas is the **Hammam** or royal bath.

190

Water was brought up from a well 21·3 m (70 ft) below.

One of the most beautiful of the baths was broken up by the Marquess of Hastings and sent to the Prince Regent in England. Other remnants were used to ornament the garden at Government House, Barrackpore.

A staircase at the back of the Diwan-i-Khas leads to the **Samman Burj** or Jasmine Tower, a beautiful two-storey pavilion capped by an octagonal domed cupola standing on one of the largest circular bastions. Probably built by Jahangir, it was here, in full view of the famous Taj, that Shah Jahan lay on his death-bed attended by his faithful daughter, Jahanara. As night closed in to hide the Taj from view, with a few consoling words to his daughter, Shah Jahan went to join his beloved Mumtaz Mahal, the Lady of the Taj and the ruling passion of his life.

In front of the pavilion is a little fountain and a raised platform laid out in marble squares for pachisi, a form of chess. Just to the right is the **Mina Masjid**, possibly the smallest mosque in existence, for the private prayers of the emperor.

The route leads into the zenana and on to the **Khas Mahal** (1636), the model for the Diwan-i-Khas at Delhi. This beautiful hall was restored in 1895. It once contained niches with portraits of the Mughal emperors, looted by the Raja of Bharatpur in 1761. Beneath is a labyrinth of underground chambers, used as a tykhana or hot-weather retreat and also as dungeons. In the south-east corner is a well-house or baoli.

The large quadrangle facing the Khas Mahal is the **Anguri Bagh** or Grape Garden, 85·3 m (280 ft) square with arcades on three sides. Originally, it was laid out with geometric flowerbeds and terraced walks radiating from a central stone platform.

On the north side is the **Sheesh Mahal** or Hall of Mirrors, once the bath-house of the zenana. It comprises two dark rooms with fountains and an artificial cascade, the walls enriched with badly renovated glass mosaic and pounded talc.

Flanking the Khas Mahal are the **Golden Pavilions**, with Bengali roofs covered with gilded copper plates. They were used as ladies' bedrooms, with deep holes in the walls, so narrow that only a woman's hand could retrieve the contents. Jewels were concealed here.

Before the entrance of the Jahangiri Mahal, in one corner of the Anguri Bagh, are the erroneously named **Gates of Somnath**, reputed to have been carried away from the Hindu temple by Mahmud of Ghazni in 1025. They were captured by the British in the Afghan Expedition of 1842 and brought back to India amid great pomp and ceremony. They are of deodar, finely carved, about 3·6 m (12 ft) high, but are of a later Muslim design and are certainly not from a Hindu temple.

The **Jahangiri Mahal**, notwithstanding its name, was probably built by Akbar. Robustly conceived, it is in sharp contrast to the sensual luxury of Shah Jahan's buildings. The upper east façade, faced in bright tiles and pierced by an entrance gateway, leads to a domed hall with an elaborately carved ceiling. Beyond, a corridor leads to a central court which is Hindu in character but has exquisite Saracenic surface details. Originally, it was brightly coloured and gilded.

On the north side of the quadrangle is a pillared hall of Hindu design. Great piers and cross-beams with serpentine brackets carry the roof. It is believed that Jodh Bai, one of Jahangir's wives, lived here. A gallery runs around the hall at the upper level. On the south side is a smaller, similar hall known as Jodh Bai's Drawing-Room. On the east a set of chambers leads to a recessed portico in the centre of a quadrangle which faces the river. The portico opens into a large, beautiful room known as the Library, restored in 1900. On the roof are two pavilions and various cisterns, while underground are extensive vaulted chambers for use in summer.

Of the **Akbari Mahal** (*c.* 1571) only a few traces remain to the south of the Jahangiri Mahal. Once it consisted of spacious courts surrounded by capacious chambers, but now only the excavated foundations, a gateway and tower remain, outlined by shrubberies.

On rising ground behind the Diwan-i-Am stands the **Salimgarh**, reputed to be the spot where Salim Shah Sur built his palace in 1545–52 but more probably erected by Prince Salim, later Emperor Jahangir (1605–27). It is a delightful early-Mughal two-storey pavilion with fine carving on the outside.

Outside the Amar Singh Gate is a **stone horse**, half-buried in red sandstone on the glacis of the fort. It probably marks the grave of a favourite horse of someone from the Mughal period. Legend asserts it was the noble horse of the Maharaja of Jodhpur which leapt from the battlements and prayed to be turned to stone to commemorate the murder of its master in the presence of Shah Jahan. To the south-west are some old cemeteries.

At the north end of Macdonnel Park stood a huge statue of Queen Victoria by Thorneycroft. This has now been removed.

Nearly opposite the Delhi Gate of the Fort is the **Jami Masjid**, close to the Fort railway station. An inscription over the gateway records that it was built by Shah Jahan in 1648 in the name of Jahanara, his favourite eldest daughter, who was imprisoned with him by Aurangzeb. The mosque is raised on a high plinth approached by flights of steps on the south and east sides. The main elevation has five arched entrances to the courtyard, crowned by three large sandstone domes with zigzag bands of marble.

The eastern archway was demolished by the British in 1857.

To the poet Tagore it was 'a tear on the face of eternity'; to others, 'a tender elegy in marble', 'a lustrous pearl', the 'ultimate expression of earthly love'. The **Taj Mahal** is quite simply one of the wonders of the world. To Shah Jahan, who built it, it 'seems to proclaim to the world that in spite of all Man's greatness, the last word in this life and the ultimate triumph is not Man's, but only the Creator's'.

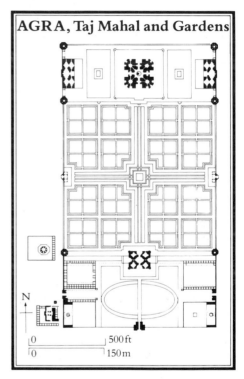

AGRA, Taj Mahal and Gardens

0   500 ft
0   150 m

The Taj stands to the east of the Fort and is clearly visible from its ramparts. It should be viewed at different times of the day, particularly by moonlight, as the Makrana marble from which it is made assumes incredibly subtle variations of light, tint and tone, so that it is never actually the same. The colour values vary from soft dreaminess at dawn to dazzling whiteness at noon to cold ethereal splendour in the moonlight, when the dome hangs among the stars like a huge iridescent pearl.

192

The tomb was built by Emperor Shah Jahan for his favourite wife, Arjumand Banu Begum, better known by her titles Mumtaz Mahal (Chosen of the Palace) and Taj Mahal (Crown of the Palace). She married Shah Jahan, then Prince Khurram, in 1612 to become his second wife and inseparable companion. She bore him fourteen children before she died in childbirth at Burhanpur on campaign with the emperor in 1629. On her death-bed she entrusted responsibility for her husband to her eldest daughter, Jahanara, to whom the Jami Masjid is dedicated.

The entire kingdom mourned her death. Shah Jahan was inconsolable and never fully recovered, the shock of her death turning him prematurely grey. The court went into mourning for over two years and the emperor contemplated abdication in favour of his sons.

The dead queen was brought to Agra and, according to Tartar custom, she was laid in a garden on the banks of the Jumna river. A council of the best architects and craftsmen in the kingdom was assembled to prepare designs for her tomb. One of them, Geronimo Verroneo, was an Italian in Mughal service and this has led some to attribute the design to him, but evidence suggests it was designed by Ustad Isa Khan Effendi, a Persian masterbuilder from Shiraz, who assigned the detailed work to his gifted pupil Ustad Ahmed. The dome was designed by Ismail Khan.

The tomb, which is higher than a modern twenty-storey building, took twenty-two years to complete with a workforce of 20,000. Craftsmen and masterbuilders came from all over Asia to join in the great work – from Baghdad, Shiraz, Delhi, Samarkand and Turkey. The marble, India's finest, was quarried at Makrana near Jodhpur. Precious and semi-precious stones were imported from distant lands: jasper from the Punjab, jade and crystal from China, turquoise from Tibet, lapis lazuli from Afghanistan and Ceylon, chrysolite from Egypt, amethysts from Persia, agates from the Yemen, malachite from Russia, diamonds from Golconda and mother of pearl from the Indian Ocean.

The colossal structure was raised using brick scaffolding. A 3·2 km (2 miles) slope was built to lift material up to the level of the dome. It is alleged that on its completion the emperor ordered that the chief mason's right hand be cut off so he could never repeat his marmoreal masterpiece.

In addition to the lavish expenditure on the tomb, lakhs of rupees were spent on providing sumptuous fittings and furnishings, including rich Persian carpets and gold lamps and candlesticks. Originally, the sarcophagus was enclosed by a screen of gold studded with gems, but this was replaced by a delicate marble screen in 1642. Two wonderful silver doors to the entrance were looted and melted down by the Jat freebooter Suraj Mal in 1764. A sheet of pearls made to cover the sarcophagus was carried off by Amir Husein Ali Khan in 1720.

It is alleged that Shah Jahan intended the Taj to be merely one half of a wider composition, with a black tomb for himself on the opposite bank. A bridge over the river was to connect the two, but this never went beyond the laying of foundations.

The approach to the Taj from the city passes the Circuit House and Gardens.

The surroundings of the Taj have been restored close to the original designs of Ali Mardan Khan, one of the nobles at Shah Jahan's court. The formal landscaping provides a perfect setting for this outstanding masterpiece of Mughal art. The water supply to the fountains and channels is from a series of reservoirs which lie above the rooms in the garden walls and which are fed from the river, originally by bullocks but today by electricity.

The principal vista is accentuated by a red sandstone channel set between rows of cypress trees and punctuated in the middle of a low marble platform. The original geometric patterns inlaid into the pathway still survive. At regular intervals marble and stone benches are provided, from which one can contemplate the mysteries of the Taj and admire the perfect symmetrical reflection in the central channel.

The main entrance is from the west, but there are two other entrances – from the east and from the south of the Jilo Khana, the courtyard.

The east gateway leads to Fatehbad. Close by, to the south, is the **Mausoleum of Sirhindi Begum**, one of Shah Jahan's wives, an octagonal domed tomb in poor repair but with fine mosaics.

The south gateway or **Sirhi Darwaza** provides a view of Taj Ganj, where the workmen once lived.

The main gateway is a large, three-storey sandstone structure with an octagonal central chamber with smaller two storey rooms to each side, crowned by domed pavilions. It was here that the great silver doors, looted in 1764 by Suraj Mal, once hung. The walls are inscribed with verses from the Quran.

The approach via the **Taj Ganj Gate** opens into the Jilo Khana, a large arcaded courtyard 268 m (880 ft) long and 134 m (440 ft) wide. This was once a caravansarai for travellers, with rooms in the arcades.

Just outside the main gateway, on an elevated platform, is an octagonal domed building containing two uninscribed marble tombs. These are reputed to belong to Mumtaz Mahal's Maids of Honour. Opposite is the Fatehpur Mosque, with a paved courtyard built in red sandstone. Immediately to the right, beyond the gate, is the Mausoleum of Sati-un-Nisa, Maid of Honour to Mumtaz and later governess to Jahanara. The tomb lies in an octagonal hall with traces of finely painted walls and ceilings. The sides of the tomb are enriched with arabesques.

The grand portal to the Taj enclosure, the **Great Gateway** (1648), faced in red sandstone, is a splendid example of Mughal architecture, finer than the gateway to Akbar's tomb at Sikandra. The stonework is inscribed with passages from the Quran inviting the pure of heart to enter the Gardens of Paradise. The gateway is crowned by twenty-six marble chatris.

The **Taj Museum** (1903) lies above and comprises a main hall and three side galleries. In the main hall are two fine marble columns, believed to have come from the Fort, as well as portraits of Shah Jahan, Mumtaz Mahal and other Mughal emperors. Gallery I has various architectural drawings of the Taj. Gallery 2 displays porcelain and examples of the elaborate inlay work for which Agra is famous. Gallery 3 has a collection of 17th-century Mughal coins and calligraphy.

Flanking the Great Gateway on the garden frontage is a fine arcaded gallery of red sandstone. From the balcony some spectacular views of the Taj can be obtained, closing the axial vista of the garden. Originally, the crowning finial of the dome aligned with the Pole Star.

The view of the Taj from the Great Gateway is one of the most famous in the world, an ingenious perspective carefully devised for maximum architectural impact.

A double staircase provides access from the garden level to the mausoleum, which is set on a huge raised marble platform 6·7 m (22 ft) high and 95 m (313 ft) square, paved in a black-and-white chequerboard pattern. At each corner is an elegant, slender, three-storey minaret of white marble inlaid with black lines, 41·6 m (137 ft) high, reminiscent of those of 17th-century Samarkand. Each tapers at the top, crowned by a shallow umbrella dome, providing a perfect spatial frame for the tomb and a measure of scale.

The main tomb is square with bevelled corners. Each side is 56·6 m (186 ft) long with a large central arch flanked by two pointed arches, one placed above the other. At each corner smaller marble domes rise, while in the centre is the great majestic central dome, 56·9 m (187 ft) high, crowned by a brass finial which rises another 17·1 m (56 ft). Around the central arches which dominate each side are Quranic inscriptions recited by the faithful on the death of a loved one. The calligraphy is skilfully graduated in size so that the letters over the main portal are one and a quarter times larger than those on the sides at ground level, to give the illusion of uniformity throughout. All the inscriptions were designed by Abdul Haq Shirazi.

The surface ornament is of three main types. The screens within the tomb are of the finest moucharabya work – intricate filigree resembling lacework carved from slabs of solid marble. The delicate sculptured ornament on the body of the tomb is in low relief. The real glory of the Taj is the spectacular pietra dura work involving the excision of tiny fragments of marble and their infilling with semi-precious stones in beautiful floral patterns. In a single leaf of one flower there are thirty-five different variations of carnelian.

The centre of the main tomb is an octagonal chamber lit through double screens of filigree work, creating a soft, luminescent glow. Directly beneath the main dome is an exquisite enclosure of carved marble filigree work, inside which are replica tombs. The actual tombs lie in the basement vault beneath, which can be reached by a flight of steps. Mumtaz Mahal lies in the centre, Shah Jahan to the left. The replica tombs were for common view, the actual sepulchres beneath being reserved for members of the royal household and chosen nobility. The original gold screen, embellished with precious stones, was replaced by Aurangzeb with a filigree screen carved from a single block of marble, which is a wonder to behold.

Originally, the Queen's sepulchre was elaborately inlaid with precious stones, but many of these have been replaced with semi-precious varieties. The inlay work is magnificent. Shah Jahan's tomb is the only asymmetrical element in an otherwise perfect symmetrical composition. He was never intended to lie here, having planned his own black marble mausoleum on the opposite bank. Over the tombs is a fine Cairene lamp, installed by Lord Curzon.

The inscription on the Queen's tomb bears the ninety-nine names of Allah and the words 'The resplendent Grave of Arjumand Banu Begum, called Mumtaz-i-Mahal, died in 1040 AH [1629 AD]'.

At the head of the tomb is the inscription 'He is the everlasting; He is sufficient', and a passage from the Quran: 'God is He, besides whom there is no God. He knoweth what is concealed and what is manifest. He is merciful and compassionate.'

Shah Jahan's tomb carries the words:

The illustrious sepulchre and sacred resting-place of His Most Exalted Majesty dignified as Razwan [the Guardian of Paradise], having his abode in Paradise, and his dwelling in the starry heaven, inhabitant of the regions of bliss, the second Lord of the Qiran [the conjunction of Venus and Jupiter, when both he and Timur were born], Shah Jahan, the King valiant. May his tomb ever flourish, and may his abode be the heavens. He travelled from this transitory world to the world of eternity on the night of the 28th of the month of Rajab 1076 AH [1666 AD].

Flanking the Taj to either side are two mosques of red sandstone in a similar style to the entrance gateway, the interiors enriched with fine cut plasterwork, arabesques and frescoes. To the west is a mosque, intended entirely for prayer, with a panelled floor marked out for each devotee. To the east is its jawab (answer), the **Jamaat Khana** or assembly hall for the congregation. The pavement here is inlaid with floral patterns and a representation of the finial from the tomb. The two mosques provide a symmetrical frame for the entire composition.

The view from the east bank, which can be reached by a ferry, is very striking. The preservation of the Taj owes much to the British, and in particular to Lord Curzon, who did much to stimulate interest in the proper conservation of India's architectural heritage. Today it is threatened by atmospheric pollution.

On the left bank of the Jumna are three major sites of interest. About 228 m (741 ft) north of the Jumna railway bridge is the **Tomb of Itmad-ud-Daula** (1622–8), a jewel box in marble.

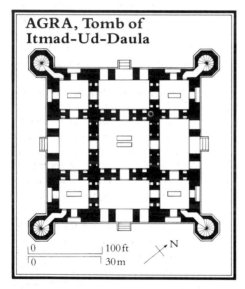

AGRA, Tomb of Itmad-Ud-Daula

The mausoleum was built by the empress Nur Jahan as a gesture of love for her father, Mirza Ghiyath Beg, the grandfather of Mumtaz Mahal, the Lady of the Taj. Mirza was Lord High Treasurer and later Wazir to Jahangir.

The tomb is beautifully conceived, standing on a low platform 1·22 m (4 ft) high. At each corner four octagonal minarets with domed roofs frame a central roof pavilion enclosed by beautiful marble tracery.

The enclosure is approached from the east via a red sandstone gateway enriched with marble mosaics. Sandstone path-

ways lead to the main tomb, the platform of which is inlaid with bright marble decoration.

The main tomb is built of the finest Indian marble embellished with mosaics and pietra dura inlay work of semi-precious stones. The central chamber contains the yellow marble tomb of Itmad-ud-Daula and his wife. The side rows are decorated with painted floral decorations. Fine marble screens of geometric lattice work suffuse the interior in a soft light.

The tomb is important as it marks a change in architectural style from the robust 'masculine' buildings of Akbar's period to the softer, more sensuous architecture of Shah Jahan. However, the roof pavilion retains a distinctive Hindu feeling, with its curved Bengali roof and broad eaves. Within the pavilion are replica tombs of those in the main chamber below. The tomb is the earliest example of this particular type of architecture and it was influential throughout north India. A similar design was adopted for Jahangir's tomb at Shahdara, near Lahore. The art of inlaying stone in marble had been practised for many years, but this was the first attempt to imitate Persian pottery decoration and tilework.

800 m (½ mile) to the north on the east bank of the river lies the **Chini Ka Rauza** or Tiled Tomb (c. 1635), reputed to be the mausoleum of Afzal Khan, a Persian poet and later Prime Minister to Shah Jahan. Now partly ruined, it takes its name from the glazed tiles used on the exterior. It is an octagonal structure with a large bulbous dome. The central chamber contains the tombs of Afzal Khan and his wife. Built during his lifetime, the tomb is entirely Persian in concept. It is renowned for its exquisite enamel and plaster polychrome decoration in elaborate floral patterns.

Further to the north lies the **Rambagh**, reputed to have been one of the pleasure gardens laid out by Babur and

196

the resting-place of his body before its interment at Kabul. It is believed to be the first Mughal garden in India. Now in ruins, only traces of the old watercourses and terraces remain. Vestiges of the original plasterwork and frescoes can still be discerned. The tall octagonal cupola of red sandstone carried on thirty-six pillars is called the **Battis Khamba**.

The **Zuhara Bagh** is another garden enclosure between the Chini-Ka-Rauza and Rambagh, named after Zuhara, one of Babur's daughters. Little of interest survives.

The old European quarter of the city lies to the north-west and west of the Fort. The main cantonment lies to the south. On Drummond Road is **Agra University**, founded in 1796 by Daulat Rao Scindia and established here under the auspices of the East India Company, in 1823. Immediately to the north lies a fine range of buildings, including a hall and library designed by Sir Samuel Swinton Jacob: **St John's College**, now part of the University, but originally founded by the Church Missionary Society. Nearby are large Christian schools for boys and girls. To the east is a complex of hospitals, including the Dufferin Hospital Medical Schools (1854).

To the south of the Sarojini Naidu Hospital is the **Kalan Masjid** or Black Mosque (*c.* 1600), built in early Mughal style by the father of Shah Jahan's first wife, the Khandari Begum. Nearby is the Lady Lyall Hospital, on Nuri Gate Road.

The road to Mathura leads to the **Roman Catholic Cathedral, Convent and Schools**. The Cathedral is a local landmark, with a tower about 46 m (150 ft) high, the focal point of an ancient Catholic mission which was founded in the time of Akbar. The St Peter and St Paul's College lies to the east.

About 1·2 km (¾ mile) to the north, at Lashkaspur, is the **Catholic Cemetery**, one of the oldest in India, with some fine monuments. The tomb of General Hessing, the Dutchman who served with Scindia and died in 1803, is a curious miniature version of the Taj Mahal in sandstone. The earliest Christian tomb in north India is here – that of John Mildenhall (1614), envoy of Elizabeth I. Here also is buried the notorious Walter Reinhardt, or Samru, as he was known, the European adventurer.

Beyond St Paul's Church, at the end of Church Road, is Bharatpur House or Kandahari Bagh, where Shah Jahan's first wife was buried. Close to St Paul's is the Protestant Cemetery, containing three early tombs of English factors; Offley (1627), Drake (1637) and Purchas (1651).

In the Nai ki-Mundi quarter is the Mosque of Shah Ala-ud-Din Majzub, known as the **Alawal Bilawal**, a Muslim saint of the time of Sher Shah. In Hipitolla Street lies the **Hammam** or Baths of Ali Vardi Khan, built in 1620.

The **Cantonment** area to the south-west of the Fort is spaciously laid out on the usual grid-pattern lines. **St George's Church** is a typical cantonment church of Upper India, designed by Colonel J. T. Boileau in 1826, a pretty building of yellow ochre stucco with white dressings. The tower and spire were added later.

The **Havelock Memorial Church** (1873) replaced an earlier Baptist Church. The Roman Catholic Church is a typical classical exercise in stucco. The Central Post Office was designed by John Begg (*c.* 1905). There is the usual club, avenues of bungalows and **Metcalfe Hall**, a handsome Greek Revival hall used for public meetings.

Sikandra

9 km (5½ miles) along the road to Mathura lies Sikandra and the **Mausoleum of Akbar**. The village takes its name from Sikander Lodi (1489–1517), one of the last kings of the Delhi Sultanate. Along the road can be seen a number of Kos-minars, pillars erected every 4 km (2½ miles), and several tombs.

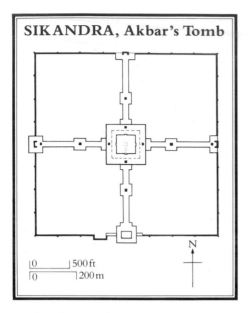

SIKANDRA, Akbar's Tomb

6·4 km (4 miles) from Agra, on the left-hand side of the road, is a curious sculptured horse, alleged to commemorate one of Akbar's favourite animals which died nearby. Opposite is the Kachi-ki-Sarai, approached via an ancient arched gateway.

About 800 m (½ mile) beyond is the **Guru Ka Tal**, a large red sandstone tank marked by octagonal towers. Broad flights of steps on the south side provide access to the tank, which is now dry.

The **Mausoleum of Akbar** lies at the centre of a huge garden, which is enclosed by high, battlemented walls pierced on each side by four 21·3 m (70 ft) gateways built of local red sandstone with arched recesses inlaid with marble mosaics. The main entrance to the south is inlaid with white marble enriched with a scroll of Quranic writing, the Surah-i-Mulk. Crowning each corner of the gateway are four marble minarets, each of three storeys, forerunners of those on the Taj and the first of this type to appear in northern India. In the centre is a lofty pointed arch flanked by smaller arches on either side, a perfectly symmetrical composition.

A wide sandstone causeway leads to the mausoleum. It stands on a low marble platform, above which rises an orderly arrangement of red sandstone pavilions in three tiers, crowning which is an open court surrounded by a marble screen. The ground storey is a superb composition of arched recesses. In the centre is a tall, rectangular gateway with a recessed alcove, above which rises an elegant marble kiosk in silhouette on the skyline. The burial chamber is reached by a corridor which leads deep into the heart of the building. The vaulted ceiling of the crypt carries ornamental frescoes in blue and gold. Akbar's grave is plain and devoid of inscription. Flanking the main vault a number of bays are enclosed and contain several family tombs with beautiful inscriptions.

Above the first tier is a large platform, over which rises the rest of the building. The second storey of red sandstone is punctuated with richly decorated kiosks and marble domes of Hindu design. The third and fourth storeys are similar, but the top storey comprises only tall marble screens of different designs. Each screen has thirty-six arches, each divided into panels carrying Persian eulogies. In the centre lies a replica tombstone directly over the actual grave in the chamber below. It is carved from a single block of marble with finely chased floral patterns and the ninety-nine names of Allah. On the north side of the tombstone are the words 'Allahu Akbar' (God is great) and on the south side 'Jalla Jalalahu' (May his glory shine). About 1·2 m (4 ft) away is a small marble pedestal, once covered in gold, on which the Koh-i-Noor diamond reputedly lay.

The mausoleum was one of the most ambitious building projects undertaken by the Mughals, but it lacks cohesion and discipline and is typical of the transition in style at the end of Akbar's reign.

Just to the east of the tomb is the **Kanch Mahal**, a rare and fine example of Mughal domestic architecture. Probably built for Jahangir, it is elaborately detailed with inlaid stone and enamelled tiles. The building was restored under Lord Curzon's orders.

A short distance beyond the **Suraj-Bhan-Ka Bagh** is another two-storey building of the same period facing the Agra road. Beyond, towards Mathura, lies **Mariam Zamani's Tomb**, supposedly the baradari or garden house of Sikander Lodi, where one of Akbar's wives is buried. The baradari was built in 1495. In 1838 the Church Missionary Society took over the building as an orphanage, but in 1912 it was purchased by the government as a protected monument.

AJAIGARH

26 km (16 miles) from the awe-inspiring hill fortress of Kalinjar is Ajaigarh, lying in rugged country, perched 531 m (1,744 ft) above sea level on a granite outcrop and crowned by a 15·2 m (50 ft) perpendicular scarp. The fort stands on the southern crag and of the five main gates only two are now accessible to the intrepid traveller. A continuous outer rampart encircles the hill, varying in breadth every few yards, studded with the ruined fragments of ancient Hindu sculpture and carvings which were placed here by the Muslims to strengthen the outer walls. The huge cliff face is enriched with a wealth of elaborate Hindu rock carvings.

The fort was built around the 9th century by the Chandela kings, who lost control to the Chauhan emperor of Delhi in 1182. It is covered with carved masonry ruins: suttee pillars, palm prints, lotus petals and other divine Hindu motifs.

In the 18th century Ajaigarh formed part of the territory ruled by the Bundela chieftain Chhatar Sal. On his death in 1734 the area descended into factional conflicts until the Marathas under the Nawab of Banda seized the fort in 1800.

In 1809 a British force under Colonel Martindell bombarded the fort, compelling the marauding local chieftain Lakshman Daowa to capitulate. Great masses of masonry were demolished during the bombardment. Today little is changed and the debris from the British artillery barrage remains scattered where it fell, among the encroaching teak forests which clothe the hill.

ALIGARH

Aligarh (literally the high fort), 135 km (84 miles) south-east of Delhi, is a large and important town which embraces the ancient settlement of Koil. Before the first Muslim invasion, the town was a noted Rajput stronghold, but from 1194 it was administered by Muslim governors. The great minaret erected by Ghiyath-ud-Din Balban in 1252 was demolished in 1862. Between 1401 and 1440 Koil remained a strategic stronghold in the confrontation between the forces of Ibrahim Sharqi of Jaunpur and the Delhi armies. With the death of Aurangzeb and the collapse of Mughal authority, Koil was contested by the Jats, Marathas, Afghans and Rohillas. In 1784 Scindia seized control. It remained in Maratha hands until 1803, with the exception of a brief interregnum during which a Rohilla garrison was placed here.

It was at Koil that Scindia drilled his armies in European tactics, aided by the Frenchman de Boigne, but in the war of 1803 the French leader, Jean Perron, surrendered ignominiously to the British forces under Lord Lake. On 29 August 1803, in a brilliant assault on the fort at Aligarh, Lord Lake carried the day and captured over 280 guns. During the Mutiny the local sepoys rebelled and British control was not reimposed until 5 October 1857, when a column under Colonel Greathed occupied Koil.

The **Fort**, built during the reign of Ibrahim Lodi in 1524, was strengthened subsequently by French engineers and later, after 1803, by the British. Situated 3·2 km (2 miles) north of the town, it is reinforced by a wide ditch 5·5 m (18 ft) deep. The main entrance is from the north. **Perron's House** or the Sahib Bagh, now the University Medical Institution, lies 800 m (½ mile) to the south of the main fort. Approached through a square entrance arch with a guardroom over, the garden compound has a well with a dedication in Persian. Close to the Fort is the Old Cemetery.

Koil is a handsome and interesting native city. Situated at the crown of a long, steep slope, the Bala Kila is the principal **Mosque**, built in 1728 by Sabit Khan on the site of earlier Hindu and Buddhist temples. To the south-east is the Moti Masjid or Pearl Mosque (17th century). The Achal is a large tank surrounded by Hindu temples interspersed with beautiful landscaping.

The **Civil Station** lies to the north-east of the city, beyond the railway. It embraces the old cantonment, which was abolished in 1869, and is laid out on classic colonial lines, a simple grid pattern with tree-lined avenues around a central maidan. The maidan was the old cantonment parade ground.

The principal buildings of interest are concentrated along Anupshahr Road: the Judges' Court, District School, jail and cemetery. Opposite the Judges' Court an avenue links Crosthwaite Hall with the Harrison Clocktower (late 19th century). The **Lyall Library**, founded in 1889, is a distinguished building in Indo-Saracenic style.

Aligarh Muslim University, formerly the Anglo-Oriental College, is a major international centre of Muslim education and theology. It was founded by Sir Saiyad Ahmad Khan and laid out from 1875 in the manner of the Oxford and Cambridge colleges, in beautiful landscaped gardens.

ALLAHABAD

Allahabad is one of the largest towns in Uttar Pradesh, the former capital of the North-West Provinces and the celebrated ancient city of Prayag. One of the religious centres of Hindu India, it stands symbolically at the confluence of the Ganges and Jumna.

The city has always been of strategic importance. It was held successfully during the Mutiny and in 1858 it was the scene of Lord Canning's famous Durbar, at which Queen Victoria's proclamation announcing the transfer of the government of India from the East India Company to the Crown was read. Later, in 1885, the first Indian National Congress was held here. There is an annual Hindu religious festival, the Magh Mela, between 15 January and 15 February, when thousands of pilgrims converge on the city.

Most visitors from Calcutta or Bombay arrive at the railway station, which provides a useful starting-point for a tour of the city. The bridge over the Jumna (1865), just above the confluence with the Ganges, is a great feat of British engineering, over 1,006 m (3,300 ft) long.

Immediately to the south of the station is the **Khusrau Bagh**, on the city side of the railway. The enclosure is entered through an old archway, 18 m (60 ft) high, overgrown with creepers. It was once the pleasure ground of Jahangir, son of Akbar. Khusrau was the elder brother of the future Emperor Shah Jahan. He died in 1615 and the tomb was completed seven years later, a large, handsome, domed structure in the Mughal style. The actual burial chamber is underground, enriched with plasterwork painted with birds and flowers and flowing Persian inscriptions. West of the tomb is another, resembling that of Islam Khan at Fatehpur Sikri and believed to be the tomb of Khusrau's sister. West again is a quaint, four-sided, two-storey tomb – that of his mother, a Rajput lady of high birth.

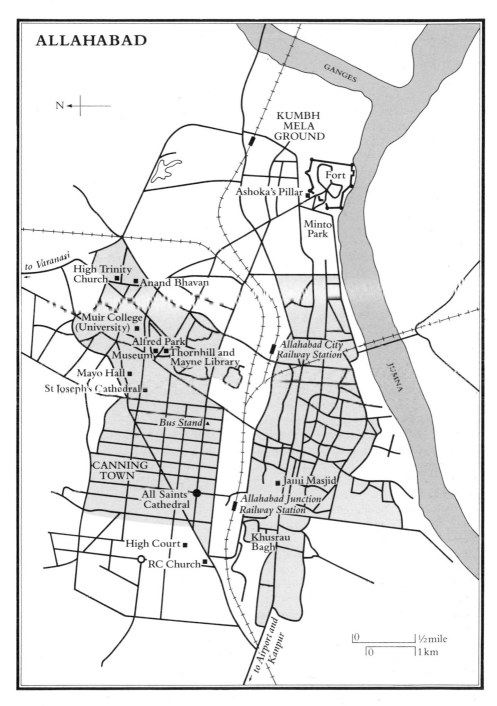

ALLAHABAD

North of the railway is **Canning Town**, the civil station and European quarter, designed and laid out on a grid pattern by Cuthbert Bensey Thornhill in the 1860s. It is an attractive cantonment with wide tree-lined streets. Among the principal buildings are the **Old High Court and Public Offices**, four two-storey blocks of sandstone and ashlar in classical style built by Colonel Piele in 1870.

All Saints' Cathedral, designed by William Emerson (later President of the Royal Institute of British Architects) in 13th-century Gothic style, was commenced in 1877. Standing in a pleasant grass compound at a major intersection, it is faced in white stone from Surajpur with red sandstone dressings. The five lower openings of the apse are enclosed by geometric patterns copied from Fatehpur Sikri. The pavement to the choir and sanctuary is pure Jaipur marble. The cathedral was not consecrated until 1887. Six bays of the nave were completed, after a private bequest of £20,000, in 1891. Emerson's original concept of two west towers was never completed owing to shortage of funds.

At the east end of the civil station lies **Alfred Park**, founded in 1870 to commemorate a royal visit by the Duke of Edinburgh. At the edge of the park is the **Thornhill and Mayne Memorial** (1878), by R. Roskell Bayne, a public

library in a highly accomplished Gothic style reminiscent of the work of William Burges. The memorial has a lofty tower and arcaded cloisters enriched with structural polychromy.

Nearby in the park stands an open limestone canopy which once sheltered a large statue of Queen Victoria, removed in 1957.

To the north of the park, **Muir College**, by William Emerson, is an excellent, imaginative essay in Indo-Saracenic architecture. Commenced in 1874 and opened in 1886, it comprises an arcaded quadrangle which is dominated by a 61-m-high (200 ft) minaret tower in cream-coloured sandstone from Mirzapur with marble and mosaic floors. The domes are clad in glazed tiles from Multan and the whole exercise is a wonderfully well-digested commingling of Gothic and Islamic details from many sources, including the mosque of Kait Bey in Cairo.

To the west of the College is the **Mayo Memorial Hall** (1879), also by R. Roskell Bayne, comprising a large hall with a tower 54 m (180 ft) high; it is an extraordinary, ill-disciplined pile, far less composed

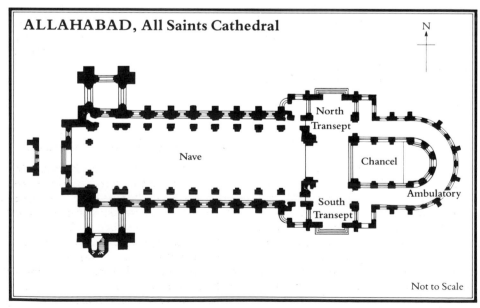

ALLAHABAD, All Saints Cathedral

N

North Transept

Nave

Chancel

Ambulatory

South Transept

Not to Scale

than the nearby Thornhill and Mayne Memorial, again by Bayne. The interior is ornamented with designs by Professor Gamble of the South Kensington Museum, London. In the Vizianagram Hall is a bust of Lord Mayo by Boehm.

West of Alfred Park, between Edmondstone Road and Thornhill Road, are **St Joseph's Roman Catholic Cathedral** (1879), in the Italian style, and the Bishop's Palace, Convent, Girls' and Boys' Schools. The **Anand Bhavan**, formerly the home of the Nehru family, is now a national monument.

Holy Trinity Church (early 19th century), on the road to the Fort, is a fine composition based on Gibbs's prototype of St Martin-in-the-Fields, London, with interesting memorials and tablets from the Gwalior Campaign of 1843 and the 1857 Mutiny. Kydgunge Cemetery also retains some good memorials.

The **Fort**, built from 1583 onwards by Akbar, stands at the junction of the two great rivers. It was the largest of Akbar's forts, and although its original form has been much impaired by poor early restoration work, the splendid **Zenana Palace** survives. This is a fine baradari or pavilion, with a central square hall carried on sixty-four columns surrounded by a deep verandah of double columns with clusters of four in each corner. Note the exceptionally fine capitals.

Under the wall of the palace is the so-called **Undying Banyan Tree** or Akshai Vata. Contained in a dark underground chamber, it is the object of Hindu veneration. In front of the gateway to the Fort is the **Ashoka Pillar**, 10.7 m (35 ft) high, of polished stone and reputedly brought from Kausambi. On it are inscribed the Edicts of Ashoka (242 BC) and later inscriptions. The restoration of the pillar by Captain Edward Smith in 1838 was a dismal failure. The antiquarian James Prinsep thought 'the animal on the top . . . not unlike a stuffed poodle stuck on top of an inverted flower-pot'.

A number of other buildings are of architectural interest. The Law College and University Library (1911), in Indo-Saracenic style by Sir Samuel Swinton Jacob, stand in Church Road. The new **High Court** (1916), by Frank Lishman, is one of the best expressions of Edwardian Baroque architecture in India, subtly adapted to the climate. Conceived in the grand manner, it has a domed, pedimented centrepiece, but the arcaded wings have pierced stone balustrades and engrailed arches in a very sophisticated synthesis of Eastern and Western influences.

Out to the west of the Fort is **Minto Park**, with a memorial pillar to the Royal Proclamation of the Assumption of Rule by the British Crown in 1858; 'the Magna Carta of India the golden guide to our conduct and aspiration' (Lord Curzon). The pillar is enriched with royal medallions and four lions carrying the Imperial coronet.

The **Municipal Museum** is a treasure house of remarkable archaeological artefacts with a fine collection of early Indian coins. The exhibition of terracotta works is unique. (See Volume I.) There is also a fascinating display of paintings by the Russian artist Nicholas Roerich depicting his haunting landscapes of Central Asia. Adjoining the Museum is the Library, which contains thousands of ancient Sanskrit manuscripts.

AONLA

This small, ancient town, 26 km (16 miles) south-west of Bareilly, was once the capital of the Rohilla court, between 1748 and 1774, but with their overthrow it sank into insignificance. The town contains the splendid **Tomb of Ali Muhammad** (1752), the Rohilla leader, and numerous other masonry buildings of the period, now fallen into disrepair, together with tombs and other relics.

ASIRGARH

This famous hill fortress is situated on a bluff precipice on an isolated outcrop of the Satpura range, about 11·2 km (7 miles) from the railway station.

The access is long and difficult. The north approach leads up a ravine defended by an outer rampart which contains four casements with embrasures 5·5 m (18 ft) high. The easier approach, from the south-west, proceeds through five stone gateways, protected by double lines of works, which could be blocked in time of emergency. A third line, called the Lower Fort, embraces the outcrop over the village.

Asirgarh is reputed to be one of the oldest forts in India. There are traces of settlement as early as 1600 BC. According to the historian Ferishta, the fort was built in 1370 by the herdsman Asa Ahir, whose ancestors had held the rock for over 700 years. On 18 August 1600 it was surrendered to Akbar by the Faruqi princes of Khandesh. He was so elated by its capture that the event was commemorated on the walls of the Jama Masjid at Burhanpur and on the rock of Asirgarh itself.

The strategic location of Asirgarh prompted Wellesley to take it in 1803, prior to his great victory at Assaye, but later it was restored to Scindia. In 1819 it was besieged again by the British under General Malcolm, who captured it after a twenty-day siege. A number of Mughal cannon survive, but the best piece now stands before the Governor's House at Nagpur.

BAHRAICH

Bahraich is a small town about 61 km (38 miles) from Lucknow. It is notable for the **Tomb of Syad Salar Masud** (mid-11th century), nephew of Mahmud of Ghazni, a warrior-saint who invaded Bahraich and met his death here in 1033. The **Daulat-Khana** (*c.* 1785), a handsome range, now ruined, was built

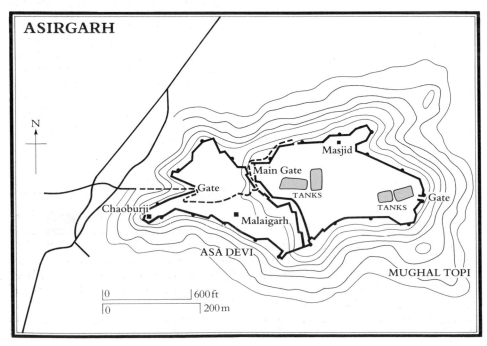

by Asaf-ud-Daula, the grandiloquent fourth Nawab of Oudh.

BAKSAR

This small village on the left bank of the Ganges, 55 km (34 miles) south-east of Unao, is famous as the landing-place of the single boatload of fugitives who escaped from the massacre at the Sati Chaura Ghat in Kanpur (Cawnpore) in 1857. Of the fourteen who landed, only five survived the subsequent fight to reach safety.

BANDA

Situated 160 km (16 miles) south-west of Allahabad on the right bank of the Ken river, Banda is a small, modern town which owed its importance to the residence here of the Nawab of Banda, who traced his lineage back to a Maratha general who served at Panipat in 1761. The Nawab took a prominent part in the Mutiny and was stripped of his position in 1858.

The Nawab's Mosque lies in the eastern district of the town. The palace is largely demolished, but other historic buildings include a ruined palace built by the Ajaigarh Rajas, the tomb of Guman Singh, Raja of Jaitpur, and the remains of old Bhuragarh Fort, which was stormed by the British in 1804.

BAREILLY

Bareilly is the capital of Rohilkhand. It lies about 84 km (52 miles) from Lucknow and was founded in 1537 by Bas Deo and Barel Deo, from whom the name is derived. After a period of Mughal suzerainty it passed to the Rohilla Pathans, who in turn ceded it to

the British in 1801. In 1857 it became the centre of disaffection for the entire area.

The city has little architectural pretension, but a number of monuments survive. The ruins of the ancient fortress of Barel Deo can still be traced. There is a later British fort in the cantonment.

The chief mosques are the **Mirza Masjid**, built by Mirza-Ain-ul-Mulk in 1600, and the **Jami Masjid**, erected in 1657. The **Mosque of Ahmad Khandar** has a Persian inscription of 1284.

In the cantonment is **Christ Church**. There are a number of interesting graves in the churchyard, in particular that of Mr Thomason, Lieutenant-Governor of the North-West Provinces in 1843–53, who founded the land revenue system of northern India. In **St. Stephen's Church** are a tablet and chancel windows commemorating those who were murdered in the Mutiny at Bareilly in June 1857. A palace of the Nawab of Rampur lies outside the city.

BARETH

This small town, 6·4 km (4 miles) east of the small village of Udayapur in Gwalior state, has a spectacular Indo-Aryan temple of Shiva built by Udayaditya, a Paramara, in 1059. (See Volume I.)

There are numerous Islamic monuments in the immediate vicinity, including the **Mosque of Sher Khan** (1488) and the Shahi Masjid.

BHOPAL *Map overleaf*

Bhopal is the capital of Madhya Pradesh, a large sprawling city made notorious by the Union Carbide disaster of 1984. The city, which is enclosed by a masonry wall, stands on the north bank of a large lake. A bridge separates this from the lower lake.

The name of the city is alleged to derive from Raja Bhoj, who is supposed to have created the surrounding lakes by building a dam or pal, hence Bhoj-pal. The city was laid out by the founder of the dynasty, Dost Muhammad, an Afghan in the service of Aurangzeb. In 1778 Bhopal was the only Indian state which aided General Goddard in his famous march across India, and in 1809 it sought British protection. The state had a continuous history of support for the British and remained loyal during the Mutiny.

The **Palace of the Nawab** is a large, impressive building with sheer walls rising from the lake. To the south-west, on a large rock, is Fatehgarh, a fort from which excellent views can be obtained across the lake. Within the fort is an armoury.

The **Jami Masjid** (1837), built by Qudsia Begum, stands in the bazaar. The **Moti Masjid** (1860) was built by Qudsia

Begum's daughter, Sikander Jahan Begum. It is similar in style to the Jami Masjid in Delhi, with two tall red minarets capped with gilt finials. The most impressive structure is the **Taj-ul Masjid**, commenced by Shah Jahan Begum in the late 19th century. It is one of the largest mosques in India, a huge pink structure with two colossal white-domed minarets and three bulbous domes, a striking local landmark visible for miles around.

Other buildings worth a visit are the **Mint**, the **Arsenal** and the Gardens of Qudsia and Sikander Begums. The Alexandra High School for Boys is in the old Be-nazir Palace; the Sultania Girls' School, not to be outdone, is in the Taj Mahal Palace. The Lady Landsdowne Hospital should also be noted. (For the museums see Volume I.)

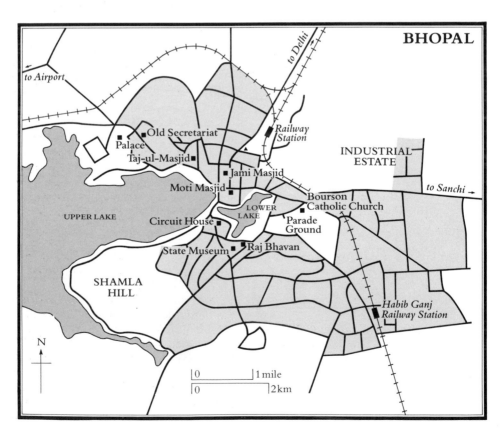

206

BITHUR

Bithur, 24 km (15 miles) north of Kanpur, is an isolated town notorious as the residence of Nana Sahib, the instigator of the massacre at Cawnpore during the Mutiny.

The river front, with numerous ghats and pavilions, has a picturesque aspect. The principal ghat, built by Raja Tikait Rai, a minister of the Nawab of Oudh, has an imposing Islamic arcade and is sacred to Brahma.

During the Mutiny the town was captured by General Havelock on 19 July 1857. The Nana Sahib's palaces were obliterated in retaliation for the massacre, but the culprit escaped capture after the Battle of Bithur on 16 August 1857.

BUDAUN

This ancient city, situated 48 km (30 miles) south-west of Bareilly, is associated in legend with Raja Bharat, who was the predecessor of the heroes of the Mahabharata. In 1028 it was the object of Muslim invasions when it was attacked by Masud Ghazni, nephew of Mahmud of Ghazni. In 1186 it was conquered by Qutb-ud-Din Aybak.

The principal Islamic monuments here – the Jami Masjid, the Hauz-i-Shamsi and the Idgah – were all built by Shams-ud-Din Iltutmish.

The **Jami Masjid** is the most important building. Built in 1223, it is one of the oldest and largest mosques in India, measuring 85·3 m (280 ft) from north to south and 68·9 m (226 ft) from the outer face of the west wall to the front of the east wall. In 1571 a fierce fire ravaged the city and damaged the impressive dome. Thirty-three years later it was repaired, since when it has undergone a sequence of changes and alterations. The original courtyard cloisters have disappeared and

been replaced by later arcades. The central propylon of the façade was built by Shaikh Khubu, foster-brother of Jahangir, in the reign of Akbar. Although the building, with its large central dome, is impressive, little of the original fabric now survives after extensive 19th- and 20th-century restorations.

BURHANPUR

Situated on the north bank of the Tapti river, about 64 km (40 miles) south-west from Khandwa and 3·2 km (2 miles) from Lalbagh railway station, Burhanpur was once a place of considerable importance, but is now a shadow of its former self.

The district is covered with ruins of Muslim buildings which attest to its former significance. Founded about 1400 by Nasir Khan, the first of the Faruqi princes of Khandesh, the town was repeatedly sacked until its annexation by Akbar in 1596. The **Badshahi Qila** or citadel has a couple of ruined minarets from this period.

The **Jami Masjid** (1588), a handsome building, was erected by the twelfth prince, Ali Khan. It is a simple structure, with fifteen pointed arches to the façade flanked by two tall minarets, similar to some of the later mosques of Gujarat.

The **Bibi-ki-Masjid** or Mosque of the Lady is a vigorous composition with a large central archway. The minarets are ornamented with oriel windows and projecting balconies. Each is crowned by a spherical cupola.

Shah Jahan's wife, for whom the Taj was built, died near here at Zainabad in 1629. In 1635 the capital transferred to Aurangabad, but between 1720 and 1728 the Nizam Asaf Jah made this his capital. In 1731 the town was fortified and strengthened with a brick wall crossed by nine gateways. Wellesley occupied the town in 1803, but it was returned to

Scindia, with whom it remained until 1860, when again it was transferred to the British.

The **Lal Qila** or Red Fort was built by Akbar and still contains some remnants of its original Imperial splendour. Other historic buildings include an old aqueduct, which is still in use, the Imad Shahi Palace and the **Tomb of Shah Nawaz Khan** (17th century). The latter is interesting because it combines elements from various sources, including Gujarat, the Tughluq buildings of Delhi, Bijapur and the Lodi tombs, in an accomplished design.

The town has a traditional local industry of textiles and silks embellished with gold and silver thread.

CHANDERI

Chanderi, 34 km (21 miles) west of Lalitpur, was once a town of considerable strategic importance, picturesquely sited in a great bay of sandstone hills pierced by narrow passes. It was the northern capital of Malwa, an independent Muslim sultanate. In the early 16th century it was conferred on Medini Rao and then it was seized by Babur in 1528.

The Ghuri and Khalji sultans of Mandu left a number of interesting architectural monuments. The widespread use of recycled temple columns, a trabeated style and the small, domed kiosks found on a number of the buildings are also indicative of an early example of Rajput style.

The **Fortress** lies on a low, flat-topped hill overlooking the valley of the Betwa. It is irregular in shape and commands fine views of the city and lake. Only three of the original five city gates survive, the most interesting being that on the south side, the **Khuni Darwaza** or Gate of Blood, so called because criminals were executed here by being hurled

from above. The main entrance is now via the **Fakir Darwaza**, a simple yellow stone edifice enriched with a carved sunk panel. The third gate, the **Delhi Darwaza**, is also built in stone, with a similar carved panel based on the shardula motif, taken from the North Gate of the Purana Qila in Delhi. A serpentine passage leads from the city to the fortress, which is now in ruins; the three original bastions can only just be discerned. The fort was captured by Sir Hugh Rose after stubborn resistance during his central Indian campaign of 1858. Two palaces within the fort were built by the Bundela Rajputs.

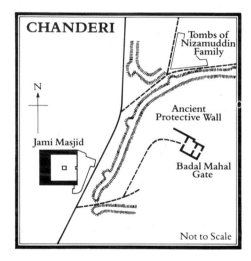

The **Badal Mahal Darwaza** (c. 1460) below the fort is a beautiful, freestanding triumphal gateway with massive tapering turrets to the entrance. The central portion has two arches, one above the other, the upper retaining four original decorative stone screens. The bizarre style represents a fusion of elements culled from numerous existing styles, from Delhi, Malwa, Rajasthan and even Gujarat, a reflection of the diverse origins of the workmen employed at Chanderi.

The earliest monument at Chanderi is the **Kushk Mahal**, in the suburb of Fathabad, the remains of a seven-storey structure built by Mahmud Shah I of

Malwa in 1445. Only four storeys survive, but they demonstrate the vitality of the Malwa style at its most vigorous, with elegant ogee-shaped arches to tall arched passageways.

The **Jami Masjid** (c. 1450) has interesting, convoluted eaves' brackets taken from local temple architecture. They are rather incongruous on a mosque which otherwise stands firmly in the local Malwa tradition.

Two other monuments are worth close inspection: the **Madrasa** and the **Shahzadi-Ka-Rauza** (c. 1450), similar in architectural form and conception to the mosque. The latter stands outside the city in a desolate area, a square mass of grey sandstone with a single chamber. Each frontage has a series of five blind arches carried on pillars, crowned by projecting eaves carried on serpentine brackets similar to those at the Jami Masjid.

The Madrasa lies in the forest, 3·2 km (2 miles) from the city, with a central chamber surrounded by a verandah; the huge crowning dome has disappeared.

Architecturally, the monuments at Chanderi are interesting because, although still well within the Rajput tradition, stylistically they lie between the vigorous, robust forms of the early Rajput period and later Gujarati refinements.

CHUNAR

Situated on a commanding site by the Ganges, Chunar was once a town of considerable strategic importance. The **Fort**, built on a spur of the Vindhyan range, stands 53·3 m (175 ft) above the surrounding countryside and was built with materials obtained from earlier Hindu buildings in the area. Stone towers and bastions line the ridge. The town lies immediately north of the Fort.

The Mughal emperor Humayun seized the Fort in 1537, but it was stormed by

the Afghans, who held the town until 1575, when Akbar recovered it. In 1750 the Fort was given over to the Nawabs of Oudh. It was attacked by the British in 1764 after the decisive Battle of Buxar. Warren Hastings retired here after Chait Singh's rebellion in 1781. Beneath the Fort is a notable British cemetery.

The **Mausoleum of Shah Kasim Suleimani** containing his cap and turban, stands behind a stonework screen in a walled enclosure.

DATIA

Datia, former capital of the principality of the same name, in 24 km (15 miles) from Jhansi. The main interest of the town lies in the palace and cenotaphs of its former ruling family. The palaces at Datia and Orchha are the best surviving examples of a style of architecture which arose in the late 16th and early 17th centuries in the Bundelkhand area of central India under the Bundela Rajputs.

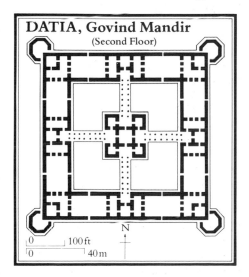

DATIA, Govind Mandir
(Second Floor)

The palace at Datia was built by Raja Bir Singh Deo circa 1620. It is widely regarded as one of the finest domestic buildings in India. Situated on an outcrop of rock, the multi-storey palace is known as **Nrising Dev Palace** (Govind Mandir). It is square in plan, with four corner towers and string courses of stone lattice work defining the five storeys. The south elevation overlooks a large lake, the Karna Sagar. The extraordinary pile has large suites of underground rooms hewn from solid bedrock on a series of different levels to provide hot-weather accommodation. In the central courtyard is a five-storey structure containing royal apartments, which are connected by flying bridge corridors to the middle of each side. The façades are enriched with bracketed balconies, kiosks, arcades and wide eaves, affording delightful vistas dappled by patterns of light and shade. From a distance the palace comprises a powerful array of domes, cupolas and serrated parapets, but it was never actually occupied and it remains a deserted monument to a bygone age of architectural accomplishment.

West of the old palace lies **Rajgarh**, built by Subhakaran, which accommodates government offices. A number of 17th- and 18th-century temples survive on surrounding hills but they are of very limited interest. At the village of **Sirol**, 8 km (5 miles) from Datia, is a small building resembling in outline Raja Bir Singh Deo's palace at Datia, possibly constructed from leftover material. It has two storeys with an open court and four ribbed domed towers at the corners, three of which are in ruins. The village also retains an early-17th-century step-well.

Originally, Dhar was the stronghold of the powerful Hindu dynasty of the Paramaras, who were patrons of literature rather than architecture. With the arrival of Muslim invaders in the 15th century, the local Ghuri dynasty looked to Delhi for inspiration and for trained workmen rather than to nearby Gujarat, with which relations were strained, and the result was the development of a pronounced hybrid style at Dhar and Mandu, characterized by polychrome ornament. In about 1405 the capital moved to the more secure site of Mandu.

The principal edifices at Dhar were built from masonry taken from earlier dismantled Hindu temples. The **Kamal Maula Masjid** (c. 1400) is the earliest, followed by the **Lat-ki-Masjid** (c. 1405). Outside is a lat or pillar of wrought iron, believed to have been a pillar of victory, a broken remnant of which, about 6 m (20 ft) high, is buried in the ground.

Both mosques have an obvious hybrid character. They comprise low arcaded ranges which betray the Hindu origin of many of the constituent parts, crowned by shallow domes which have a minimal impact on the overall composition.

The **Fort** at Dhar, also in red stone, stands outside the town on a shallow eminence. It is surrounded by ramparts embellished with twenty-four round and two square towers, on the larger of which stand the remains of an old palace. The west face has an octagonal tower protecting the entrance gate. In 1857 the Fort was the scene of military operations under General Stewart.

DHAR

53 km (33 miles) west of Mhow is Dhar, the ancient capital of the former state of that name. Together with Mandu, it was important as the centre of a provincial style of Indo-Islamic architecture in Malwa.

ETAWAH

106 km (66 miles) from Gwalior and 116 km (72 miles) from Agra, Etawah lies among rugged ravines on the left bank of the Jumna. The town is divided into two parts by a wide ravine running from north-west to south-east.

In the new town **Hume Ganj Square** is the major centre containing the principal public buildings. It is named after the local collector and so-called Father of the Indian National Congress, A. O. Hume, CB. The marketplace, mission, courts and police station are grouped here. Hume's High School is a handsome range. Adjoining the square is a sarai marked by a fine well and arched gateway. The Civil Station lies about 800 m (½ mile) to the north of the town.

The **Jami Masjid** (*c.* 1460), built from old Hindu masonry, stands on rising ground near the river. It is closely affiliated in its design to the mosques of Jaunpur and shares with them the typical arched pylon in the centre of the façade, which is 39·5 m (130 ft) long but only 6·1 m (20 ft) wide. Below the ruined fort are bathing ghats lined with handsome shrines. The building with a tall white spire is a Jain temple.

The town was probably founded by a Chauhan chief. In 1193 the area was seized by Qutb-ud-Din Aybak, but the Chauhans regained control until 1392, when Muhammad bin Firuz destroyed the fort and sacked the town. After 1432 Etawah passed under the Sharqi kings of Jaunpur, who built the brick fort on the Jumna and the Jami Masjid. The town was of some significance under the Mughal emperors before it entered a period of inexorable decline, control passing through the Marathas, the Rohillas and the Nawab of Oudh to the East India Company in 1801.

FATEHGARH

Fatehgarh is the cantonment area of the city of Farrukhabad, which lies 4·8 km (3 miles) away to the east. The cantonment was founded as early as 1777, although the area did not pass to the British until 1802. In 1804 Holkar attacked the fort, but was defeated and forced to flee by the intervention of Lord Lake. However, it is

the melancholy events of the Mutiny which are associated with the town.

The fort was besieged for over a week in July 1857. The Europeans were forced to abandon the position and escape to the boats. On the way down river they were assailed by rebels from both banks. One boat reached Bithur, where it was seized and the prisoners transferred to Kanpur (Cawnpore), where they were massacred. Those who were caught and returned to Fatehgarh were shot or sabred on the parade ground. As at Kanpur, their remains were cast into a well, over which there is a **memorial cross** with a **memorial church** nearby.

FATEHPUR

Fatehpur is a town of considerable antiquity which lies about 80 km (50 miles) south-east of Kanpur. Of the Islamic monuments, the **Tomb of Nawab Bakar Ali Khan** (late 18th century), minister of the Nawabs of Oudh, forms the principal adornment of the main street. The **Jami Masjid** and **Mosque of Hakim Abdul Hasan of Kara** are also noteworthy.

In 1798 Fatehpur was agricultural wasteland, but the new land revenue settlements of 1814 created an era of prosperity. Nevertheless, the town was the centre of a mutinous insurrection on 8 June 1857, during which the judge, Mr R. T. Tucker, was slaughtered, fighting to the end. This incident is commemorated by four huge stone pillars on the Grand Trunk Road. Inscriptions in Urdu and Hindi are taken from the Ten Commandments and the Gospel of St John.

FATEHPUR SIKRI *Map overleaf*

Fatehpur Sikri is one of the architectural marvels of India. It should not be missed. Now deserted, this royal city, 37 km (23 miles) south-west of Agra, was once the

211

capital of a mighty empire and its pink sandstone palaces bask in the refulgent glow of its magnificent past.

Fatehpur Sikri was begun by Jala-ud-Din Akbar, the third Mughal ruler of India, in 1571. The buildings of Fatehpur Sikri and the various works of art that were created there between 1571 and 1585 reflect the emperor's vision of the world. The city was founded here to celebrate a prophesy made by the Chishti saint, Shaikh Salim, of the birth of Akbar's son and heir, Prince Salim, later Emperor Jahangir. When, on 30 August 1569, the child was born at the residence of an elderly Sufi mystic outside the little town of Sikri, Akbar resolved 'to give outward splendour to this spot which possessed spiritual grandeur'. The result was the transformation of the barren hillside above Sikri into a magnificent new city. The birth is depicted in a famous miniature of the time.

Akbar's adoption of Persian state ceremonial was paralleled in his architectural ambitions. The entire city was planned on Persian principles but built and executed in the Indian manner, resulting in wonderfully inventive decorative forms. Its period of glory was brief, for by 1600 the water supply became incapable of sustaining the large population. Akbar was involved elsewhere and the city was abandoned in favour of Agra.

The conservation of the surviving buildings and monuments was begun by the British in 1876. Early works were rather excessive and involved several ill-considered clearances of vernacular buildings, but under Lord Curzon (1899–1905) the proper restoration of the buildings began.

The city lies on two rocky outcrops of the Upper Vindyhan range along the crest of a ridge. It is about 11·2 km (7 miles) in circuit, surrounded on three sides by high battlemented walls, pierced by more gateways. The fourth side was formed by a large artificial lake over 32 km (20 miles) in circumference, long

since dry. The principal buildings run in sequence along the spine of the ridge.

The outer walls comprise rough concrete and stone debris, faced in stone with loopholes and a wide internal path to permit bowmen and soldiers to pass.

The nine gateways are known as the Delhi Gate, then, from north to south on the eastern side, the Lal (red), the Akbarabad (Agra), Suraj (Sun), the Chandar (Moon) and Gwalior. Beyond, to the west, are the Tehra (Crooked) and Ajmeri Darwazas, with a postern gate between the last two at the summit of the ridge. Each gateway has semicircular bastions to each side, with tiered loopholes based on Sher Shah's fort, the Purana Qila, at Delhi.

Visitors enter via the **Agra Gate**. Off to the right are the road to Bharatpur and the tombs of Shaikh Musa and Shaikh Ibrahim rising over the fields. Inside the gate immediately to the right is an **old caravansarai** containing ruined cloisters.

Beyond, the road passes through the old garden quarter. On the ridge to the right are the ruins of nobles' houses, including **Tansen's Baradari**, a fine sandstone pavilion, that has no connection with the famous minstrel. It passes through the inner gateway, the **Naubat Khana** or Music House, where drums were beaten to mark the royal approach. The original name of this building was the Chahar Suq or marketplace. The two triple arches over the road are splendid.

On the right is a large ruined building called the **Mint** or taksal, but it was more probably workshops or karkhanas, of which the mint was just part. The brick domes of this building are of interest as they have radiating rather than horizontal courses.

Close to the Karkhana, behind the car park, are the remains of the old Imperial kitchens, adjacent to the walls of the Diwan-i-Am, and a small tank. Between the north wall of the Diwan-i-Am and the western wall of the Karkhana are the ruins of the **House of Muhammad**

212

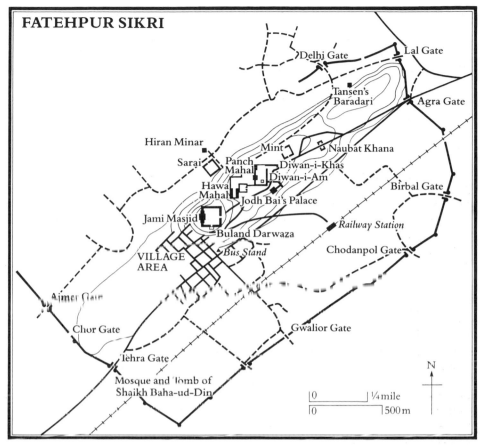

FATEHPUR SIKRI

Delhi Gate · Lal Gate · Tansen's Baradari · Agra Gate · Hiran Minar · Mint · Naubat Khana · Sarai · Panch Mahal · Diwan-i-Khas · Diwan-i-Am · Hawa Mahal · Jodh Bai's Palace · Birbal Gate · Jami Masjid · Railway Station · Buland Darwaza · VILLAGE AREA · Bus Stand · Chodanpol Gate · Ajmer Gate · Chor Gate · Gwalior Gate · Tehra Gate · Mosque and Tomb of Shaikh Baha-ud-Din · N · 0 ¼ mile · 0 500 m

Baqur, the Superintendent of the Imperial Table, who waited upon the emperor at mealtimes. Inside the principal room is some finely chased stucco detail.

Across the road from the Karkhana is a small sandstone building called the Treasury. More probably it was the residence of an important noble, possibly the philosopher-scientist Fathullah of Shiraz.

In a depression to the south-west lie the **Hakims' Quarters**, perhaps the residence of three brothers who were favourites of Akbar and influential in fostering conciliatory policies.

The road leads through a lofty doorway to the **Diwan-i-Am** or Hall of Public Audience, a spacious rectangular courtyard surrounded by colonnades. Towards the western end is the emperor's platform, a projecting building with a pitched stone roof with five equal openings. The platform is divided into three parts; the emperor sat in the centre on gorgeous cushions and carpets. On each side are fine geometric stone screens carved with six-pointed stars. From here the emperor could move straight into the Daulat Khana or private apartments. Note the huge stone ring at the foot of the colonnade opposite the pavilion. Reputedly the state elephant that crushed to death the condemned was tethered here.

West of the Diwan-i-Am is the Daulat Khana or Abode of Fortune, the main Imperial Palace. This comprises a series of rooms and buildings of exceptional beauty with characteristic architectural features, including elaborate supporting brackets, broad oversailing eaves and richly carved bell-shaped pedestals to the columns, with the capitals treated as elephants' heads. The finely carved pierced stone screens are one of the breathtaking delights of the city.

The **Diwan-i-Khas** or Hall of Private Audience is a plain square building with a fine interior. In the centre is a magnificent carved column with a huge bracket capital supporting a circular stone platform; from this four railed bridges radiate to meet the first floor gallery at the four corners. The Hall was clearly devised for Akbar's personal use, so he could sit enthroned on the central platform and listen to arguments from the different religious communities on an equal basis, symbolizing his 'dominion over the Four Quarters'. An alternative theory holds that the building is a symbolic interpretation of Hindu mythology, with the central pillar and lotus capital signifying the seat of Brahma; another holds that it was a jewel house.

The **Khwabagah** or House of Dreams is a beautiful sleeping-chamber on the first floor where the emperor received the ladies of the harem and retired on hot afternoons to be entertained by his favourite courtiers. Over the internal walls are faded verses in Persian script.

The **Anup Talao** or Peerless Pool is a pretty tank north-east of the Diwan-i-Khas, completed in 1575 but altered in the early 1840s. At the north-east angle is the **Anup Talao Pavilion**, with a fine portico, almost as high as the main chamber, carried on square piers with octagonal corner shafts. It is known as the Turkish Sultana's House, and was possibly a hammam or bath, but more likely it was a pleasure pavilion. Architecturally, it is elaborately carved in the style of the woodcarvers of Kashmir. The elaborate dado comprises eight carved panels depicting forests, animals and other scenes.

The **Abdar Khana**, wrongly called the Girls' School, was a water store, probably for the emperor's own use. It is raised on rough stone piers with panelled arched screens.

The Daulat Khana is separated from the other buildings to the north by the **Pachisi Court**. In the centre is a small raised platform and on each side the pavement is blocked out like a gigantic game board. It is alleged that the emperor sat on the platform and played pachisi, a form of chess, with slave girls as living pieces. Large courtyards of this nature were a Persian concept.

The **Ankh Michauli** lies at the northern end of the courtyard. It was one of the Imperial treasuries for gold and silver coins, but literally its name means 'hide and seek'. Here, it is reputed, the emperor amused himself playing the game with ladies of the harem. Within are some unusual stone struts or torana brackets, each shaped into the head of a monster, guardians of the royal treasure. Two staircases on the east side lead to the roof.

In the south-west corner is a small kiosk, 3 m (10 ft) square, enriched with extravagantly carved stone brackets. Known as the **Astrologer's Seat**, the ornament is of Jain origin and it may have been where Akbar's guru sat to instruct him, but more likely it was a simple kiosk which, when strewn with cushions, would have offered a retreat from where the emperor could watch his coins being counted.

North-east across the courtyard lies the Diwan-i-Khas. Emerging from here towards the north-east corner are some old ruined cloisters. Originally, an opening in the south wall of the Diwan-i-Khas led to the Daftar Khana. Today it is necessary to use the road to reach it.

The **Daftar Khana** (1574–5) was built later than the other principal buildings. It stands on a platform of piers and arches, with an elegant façade to the north of paired columns with bracketed capitals and overhanging stone eaves. The bases of the columns are chiselled in the pattern of a double peacock's tail.

Of the historic **Ibadat Khana** or House of Worship little remains; even the original site is uncertain. It was the first of the great religious buildings of the city. The remains lie to the right of the sandstone and rubble building as the visitor approaches the eastern gate of the great mosque, the Badshahi Darwaza.

The **Haram Sara** or Imperial Harem is a huge complex of apartments and chambers for the women of the court. The emperor allowed wives of eminent nobles to reside in the court as a mark of distinction and favour, similar to ladies-in-waiting at an English court. The largest building is called **Jodh Bai's Palace**, an exotic mingling of Hindu and Mughal styles. On the north side is an arcaded viaduct and a splendid balcony, the Hawa Mahal. The viaduct once provided private access for the emperor to every part of the Haram Sara. The palace is massive and austere in character, but the upper rooms in the north and south wings have a ribbed roof covered with bright-blue glazed tiles from Multan, a pure point of dazzling colour which gives a semblance of how the city must have looked.

Legend asserts that the palace was a special residence for a princess of Jodhpur, hence the appellation, but it was more probably Akbar's sleeping-chambers.

The **Hawa Mahal** or Palace of Breezes is an architectural gem attached to the north wall. The first storey, carried on square columns in double rows, is open; the second is enclosed by elaborately carved stone lattice screens. A viaduct, from which there are splendid views, leads past the zenana garden to the Hathi Pol, where in the fifth and final pavilion is the only surviving arabesque screen in the city.

The **Panch Mahal** or Tower of the Winds can best be viewed from the court, south-east of the Jewel House or Diwan-i-Khas. Probably used originally by the ladies of the court, this five-storey palace diminishes in stages to a small

kiosk at the top. There are eighty-four columns to the ground storey (an auspicious number, derived from the seven known planets multiplied by the twelve zodiac signs). Once some of the sides were enclosed by pierced stone screens, since removed, and the open areas were covered by wet cane tatties, still in common use. Note that no two columns are alike.

The **Sunahra Makan** or Golden House is also known as Mariam's House, and was used by Akbar's mother, Mariam Makani, not to be confused with his wife, the mother of Jahangir, Mariam Zamani. The house was richly decorated with gold and paintings.

To the north-west is a garden, once enclosed by rubble walls, but these have since been demolished. Back towards the Hawa Mahal a screened arch leads to the **Nagina Masjid**, a small private mosque used by the ladies of the harem. Near the west wall of the Treasury building is the **Ladies' Guest-House** or Hospital, used to accommodate passing high-born female guests. En route from the guest-house to the courtyard before the Golden House is a plain, red sandstone building with carved walls unequalled in the city. The walls are curiously built in sections and carved with a herringbone pattern embellished with rosettes, diamonds and other devices.

The **Bhirbal Bhavan** is alleged to have been built for Akbar's favourite courtier. It wasn't. It was part of the Imperial harem and probably accommodated Akbar's senior queens. To Victor Hugo it was a very large jewellery box, a two-storey building with two domed upper rooms set on octagonal bases providing separate accommodation for each queen. Marvel at the spectacular carved detail.

Behind the main Haram Sara Palace and south of the Bhirbal Bhavan are enormous quarters, popularly thought to be stables for either camels, horses or elephants, a view reinforced by the stone rings in the front of some bays. It is more likely they were used as servants' quarters for the harem. The **Tosha Khana**, a vast pillared store house, is wrongly called a camel stable.

The rough, steep road to the Hathi Pol is flanked by ruins of several substantial buildings, probably guard-houses.

The **Karbutar Khana** or Pigeon House is a massive plastered building with sloping walls. Opposite is the **Fil Khana** or Elephant House, which was in fact used as guards' quarters.

The **Hathi Pol** has a four-centred arch dressed in red sandstone with guard recesses to each side. Two huge elephants act as silent stone sentinels. The **Sangin Burj** was the principal music gallery, where the imperial drums were beaten to mark the time or passage of the emperor.

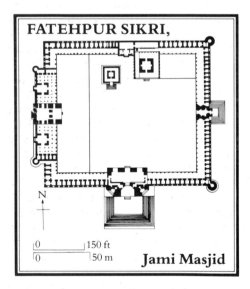

FATEHPUR SIKRI,

N

0   150 ft
0   50 m   **Jami Masjid**

Turning back, high on the topmost point of the ridge is the **Jami Masjid** or Dargah Mosque, Akbar's chef d'oeuvre. It took five years to build, was completed in 1572 and dedicated to Shaikh Salim Chishti, who died as it was nearing completion.

The usual entrance is via the eastern gateway, the **Badshahi Darwaza** or royal door. This provided access from

the palace. It projects in the form of a half-hexagonal porch with splayed sides pierced by arches. Beyond lies the huge expanse of the courtyard. To the left is the rear of the famous Buland Darwaza, with its great façade and domed kiosks.

The small well in the south-east corner of the courtyard is in fact a rainwater tank. In the centre stands a much larger masonry tank, shaded by a large tree.

The Jami Masjid is entered via a majestic central arch alleged to be modelled on that at Mecca. Inside is a vast painted dome. In each of the seven bays there are three mihrabs or recesses; the central one is pentagonal and covered by a dome. From the central chamber the way to the north and south aisles is marked by three arches. The side halls have pillars in a Hindu idiom. The entire city is planned at an angle to the north-east to south-west alignment of the ridge to accord with the fixed orientation of the mosque.

The **Tomb of Shaikh Salim Chishti** is an architectural masterpiece, one of the most exquisite examples of marble work in India. Completed in 1581, the tomb was originally only partly faced in marble. The verandah and dome were of red sandstone, but marble screens and other embellishments were added later. The dome was encased as late as 1806. The remarkable serpentine brackets supporting the eaves are modelled on those in the Stone-Cutters' Mosque. The carved lattice screens are simply miraculous examples of the mason's art and some of the finest in the world. Over the doorway are carved the names of God, the Prophet and the four Caliphs. Above the cenotaph is a remarkable catafalque of veneered ebony covered with mother of pearl and bound in brass. Barren women pray to the saint for fertility.

To the east is a red sandstone tomb with perforated stone screens, crowned by a dome surrounded by thirty-six small domed kiosks. This is the **Tomb of Islam Khan**, although other noble remains also lie here, including those of

216

Shaikh Hajji Husain (d. 1592), a follower of Shaikh Salim. An elegant arched gateway capped by three kiosks and flanked by turrets leads to the **Zenana Rauza** or Women's Tomb, the northern cloister of the mosque and the oldest part.

The crowning glory of the mosque is the **Buland Darwaza** or Gate of Victory, set in the south wall, the greatest monument of Akbar's glorious reign and one of the finest Mughal buildings. It is 53·6 m (176 ft) high, the effect of which is enhanced by a great flight of steps on the outside. It may commemorate his victorious campaign in the Deccan, but is more likely earlier, relating to his conquest of Gujarat in 1573. It is a spectacular mass of masonry which dominates the entire city, pierced by a huge central arch and crowned by a romantic array of domed kiosks.

In the archway are two inscriptions. On the right-hand side going out one reads:

Jesus Son of Mary (on whom be peace) said: The world is a bridge, pass over it, but build no houses on it. He who hopes for an hour may hope for eternity. The world endures but an hour. Spend it in prayer, for the rest is unseen.

The great door is covered with horseshoes placed there by believers for divine intercession. There is a gate at either end of the courtyard façade which provides access to the top. Near to the steps on the outside is the Jhalra, a rainwater reservoir into which local divers leap to amuse the tourists.

The imposing hammam of Nawab Islam Khan faces the Buland Darwaza. Outside the north wall of the Dargah are some well-preserved early Mughal domestic buildings with interesting decorative features. Reputedly these are the houses of Ab-ul-Fazl and Faizi, Akbar's favourites. The pairs of tall columns in the façade of the red sandstone house have pedestals carved with a peacock's tail, while the engrailed arches opening into the corner rooms mark an important stage in the development of Mughal architecture.

At the back of the mosque is a small enclosure, ostensibly the **Tomb of Bale Miyan**, son of Shaikh Salim Chishti, whose marble tomb stands in the courtyard. It is alleged he offered his own life so that Prince Salim (later Jahangir) could survive.

To the west lies the **Stone-Cutters' Mosque**, built by quarrymen in 1565 for use by Shaikh Salim to the south of his cell. The central arch is cusped; behind it is a richly ornamented mihrab and a mimbar or pulpit with five, rather than the usual three, steps. After the Shaikh's death, his cell was incorporated into the mosque. Note the serpentine brackets, prototypes for those on the Shaikh's tomb.

Opposite the north-west corner of the mosque is a door leading to the Shaikh's house, now rebuilt and still occupied by his descendants. From here a tortuous path leads to the **Rang Mahal** (1569), built by Akbar for one of his favourite wives, the mother of Prince Salim, later Jahangir. It is now used as a weaving factory. Only part can be visited. Much of the unique carved and moulded plaster detail is damaged, but there are fine views of the Buland Darwaza.

Perched on the edge of the main ridge is the **Mosque of Shaikh Ibrahim** with a huge basement. It is unusual in that the mosque is not aligned with the qibla. To the north-east is a porch in the Hindu style and there is some interesting ancient graffiti on the walls.

To the north and west of the palace beyond the Hathi Pol are a number of other interesting buildings. The **Waterworks** comprise a single deep well or baoli flanked by two chambers in which treadmills were used to raise the water, which was then distributed by several channels and reservoirs across the city.

Beneath the Hathi Pol is the famous **Hiran Minar** or Deer Minaret, a circular tower 21·3m (70 ft) high, studded with protruding elephant tusks of stone. Tradition alleges that this was built over the grave of Akbar's favourite elephant, but it was probably a lamp tower and city milestone from which distances were calculated.

From the top can be seen the **Water Palaces**, an hour's return visit by foot.

The octagonal pavilion is the **Hada Mahal**, a royal pleasure pavilion crowned by a kiosk with slender columns. To the east is a red sandstone octagon. It is surrounded by a ruined colonnade with heavy parapets fitted to gush cascades of water on the occupants within. Note the elegant, carved foliated capitals.

The **Caravansarai** outside the Hathi Pol is a large courtyard surrounded by merchants' hostels and vaulted rooms behind a masonry arcade. In Darogha's House, on the western end of the upper range, are traces of painted ornament. To the west is a slope studded with ruins, including the **Samosa Mahal**, set around a triangular courtyard.

The **Emperor's Baths** are in a simple plastered building east of the Anup Talao pavilion. Traces of red, yellow and green decoration on a white background survive around the dados.

In the rocky ravines to the south of the Daftar Khana are **Hakim's Baths**, once containing some of the finest plaster ornament in India and now in a ruined condition, Not far off is Shah Quli's Baoli, a deep octagonal well. The Sukh Tal is the largest tank in Fatehpur, opposite the principal Court Baths.

In the broken expanse between the modern town and distant city walls, there were once fine mansions, pavilions and gardens, but now only one building survives intact. This is **Todar Mal's Baradari**, an octagonal pavilion.

Just outside the Terha Dawaza, by the road to Bayana, is the **Mosque and Tomb of Baha-ud-Din** (1611). This is one of the prettiest corners of the city, shaded by ancient tamarind trees. A low battlemented wall encloses both build-

ings, which are faced in red sandstone. The dome on the tomb resembles that on Shaikh Salim Chishti's tomb, but the double perforated screens and elegant eastern wall are extremely fine.

On the Bharatpur road by the Terah Mori barrage, built by Akbar, is the red sandstone **Tomb of Shaikh Musa**, brother of Shaikh Salim, which has a fine segmented domed ceiling. Splendid views of the city can be obtained from here at sunset. In the village of Rasulpur, about 1·6 km (1 mile) away, is the domed **Tomb of Shaikh Ibrahim** (1591), a former Governor of Agra.

FYZABAD (FAIZABAD)

Fyzabad, once the capital of Oudh, is a decayed town situated on the left bank of the River Gogra, 125·5 km (78 miles) east of Lucknow. Adjoining it to the west is Ayodhya, which lies on the site of an ancient city of the same name.

Fyzabad is a comparatively modern settlement. The third Nawab of Oudh, Shuja-ud-Daula (1754–75) resided here. After his defeat at the hands of Sir Hector Munro at Buxar in 1764, the Nawab fell back on the town and built **Fort Calcutta**, with enormous clay ramparts. Following his death in 1775 his widow, Bahu Begum, remained here, while the new Nawab, Asaf-ud-Daula, moved to Lucknow.

The **Mausoleum of Bahu Begum** (c. 1816), described as 'the finest building of the kind in Oudh', is in marble but without inscription. Bahu Begum was alleged to have suffered ill-treatment at the hands of Asaf-ud-Daula and his British advisers in an attempt to disclose the whereabouts of the state funds, an incident for which Warren Hastings was later indicted. Afterwards the Begum adopted a conciliatory attitude to the East India Company and wrote condolences to Warren Hastings. Her tomb is a huge sepulchre over 42·5 m (140 ft) high.

The **Gulab Bari** or **Mausoleum of Shuja-ud-Daula** ($c.$ 1775) lies about 2·4 km (1½ miles) away. In form and outline it resembles that of the Begum, but with three simple tombstones on the ground storey, that in the centre being the tomb of the Nawab. His mother lies to the west, his father to the east. The mosque on the edge of the compound and the imambara to the south are both of similar date.

The **Museum** (1871) lies in Guptar Park, where there is a temple marking the spot from where Rama is supposed to have disappeared. To the north-west is the cantonment, which, with the civil station, is well laid out with woods and trees.

GARHKUNDAR

Garhkundar is one of a cluster of fortified strongholds which lie scattered across Bundelkhand. It is about 48 km (30 miles) east of Jhansi in a wild and forbidding tract of broken country renowned for dacoity. Situated on a scorched outcrop of black granite, it dominates the surrounding countryside.

It was founded, probably in the late 12th century, by Khub Singh of the Khangar clan, a ferocious tribe of warlike Rajputs who established themselves in the rough country of Bundelkhand. In the 14th century they were annihilated by Tughluq forces from Delhi, and at the siege of Garkhundar the entire garrison of women and children committed voluntary self-immolation. Suttee pillars still dot the surrounding fields.

The citadel is square in plan, three storeys high, with octagonal bastions and lofty corner towers. The main entrance gate is a huge square bastion with arcaded storeys. The real delight is the marvellous view across the surrounding plains which can be had from the parapet walls.

GHAZIPUR

Ghazipur lies about 64 km (40 miles) north-east of Varanasi and was once a centre of the opium trade. The principal site of interest is the **Mausoleum of Marquess Cornwallis**, Governor-General, who died here on 5 October 1805. The monument (1806) comprises a domed, quasi-Grecian building, reminiscent of Hawksmoor's famous tempietto at Castle Howard in Yorkshire, with a marble statue by John Flaxman.

The cenotaph at Ghazipur was not erected to the original designs of the architect, Thomas Fraser, but to simpler, alternative proposals using a Doric order.

In the cemetery are some unusual table-shaped monuments as well as the more characteristic obelisks and pyramids of the early 19th century.

Also of interest are the **Chahal Situn**, the old palace, and numerous masonry ghats on the river frontage, which is dominated by a mud fort. The tank and tomb of Pahar Khan, Governor in 1580, and the garden, tank and tomb of Abdullah, an 18th-century governor, are also noteworthy.

GWALIOR *Map overleaf*

Gwalior, once the capital of the influential state of that name, remains an important administrative centre of the new state of Madhya Pradesh. Situated 312 km (194 miles) from Delhi, it is renowned for its huge hillfort, which dominates the entire area. (For its temples, rock sculptures and the museum see Volume I.)

The **Old City** lies to the north and north-east of the hillfort. Just to the north is an old Pathan archway, a remnant of an ancient tomb and cemetery. The **Jami Masjid** (1661) stands outside the gateway of the fort. Built in red and white sandstone by Mutamad Khan, it has lofty minarets and gilt pinnacled domes, a fine example of the later Mughal style.

Situated near the Delhi Gate, the Mosque of Khandola Khan, his tomb, and that of his son Naziri Khan, together

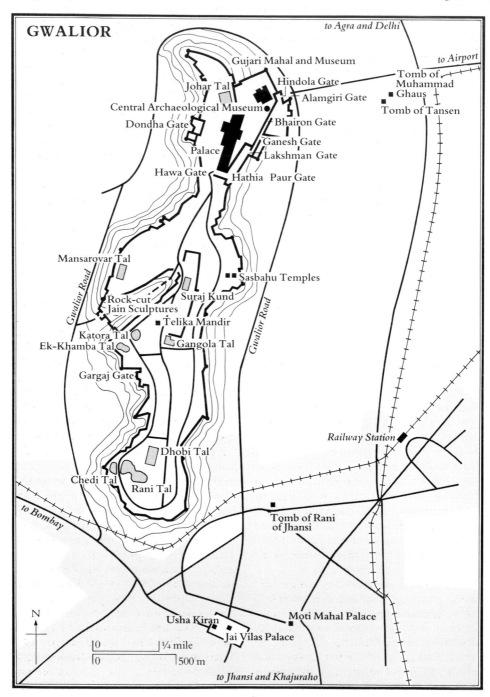

with several other tombs, exhibit some fine carved stonework and pierced screens.

On the east side of the old city lies the **Tomb of Muhammad Ghaus** (late 16th century), a Muslim saint who assisted Babur's acquisition of the fort. It is square with hexagonal corner towers crowned by small domes. The body of the building is enclosed on all sides by delicate carved stone lattices, over which rises a large dome once inlaid with blue glazed tiles. It is a distinctive example of early Mughal architecture.

Close by, to the south-west, is the **Tomb of Tansen** (early 17th century), the famous musician of Akbar's court. It is a rectangular pavilion standing on an elevated platform and carried on pillars which surround the tomb-stone, over which rises a carved dome. A festival to which musicians from all over the country come is held here annually. The leaves of the adjacent tamarind trees are alleged to confer exceptional clarity on the voice.

The **Great Fortress** of Gwalior stands on a long, narrow, rocky hill of sandstone which rises abruptly, 91·4 m (300 ft) above the surrounding countryside. The Fort has imprinted itself indelibly on the imagination of generations of poets and is known as the 'pearl in the necklace of the castles of Hind'. The hill is about 2·8 km (1¾ miles) long and varies in width from 183 m (600 ft) to 853 m (2,800 ft). In places the cliff overhangs; elsewhere the sides are steeply scarped. The walls are from 9·1 m (30 ft) to 10·6 m (35 ft) high above a lower glacis of crumbling basalt. Seen from the north the view is impressive, a long line of battlements broken by formidable bastions and fretted domes. On the west side of the hill are a deep gorge, the Urwahi valley, and two winding entrances flanked by loopholed bastions.

The foundation of the Fort is shrouded in the mists of time. An inscription within records that a Temple of the Sun

was erected in 510, but local legend asserts that it was constructed by Suraj Sen, who was cured of his leprosy by an ascetic called Gwalipa. In 950 Gwalior was part of the kingdom of Kanauj, which was captured by the Kachhawahas. They ruled Gwalior for over 200 years and built many temples in the Fort and surrounding area. They were succeeded by the Pratiharas, who retained it until 1232 when Iltutmish besieged and reduced the Fort. Gwalior remained in the possession of the Muslim kings of Delhi until the invasion of Timur in 1398, when it was seized by the Tomara Rajputs, who ruled for over 100 years. It was recaptured by Ibrahim Lodi in 1516, and later passed on to the Mughals.

In 1755 the Mughals conquered the Fort, but in the confusion following the Battle of Panipat in 1761, it was seized by the Jats, who lost it again eight years later. The British stormed the Fort in 1780, 1804 and again, after the Battle of Maharajpur, in 1844. At the time of the Mutiny it was vested in the hands of Scindia, who remained loyal although his troops mutinied. In May and June 1858 Gwalior was the centre of fierce fighting between the British under Sir Hugh Rose and a large force of die-hard mutineers led by Tantia Topi and the Rani of Jhansi. In 1886 Gwalior was ceded to Scindia by the British in exchange for Jhansi.

There are three main entrances to the **Fort**, one in the east and two in the west. The eastern side is the main approach, the chanelled steps having been replaced by a continuous sloping ramp. On the eastern approach there are six gates.

The **Alamgiri Gate** was constructed by Mutamad Khan in 1660 and called after Aurangzeb. It is plainly detailed, with a small courtyard and open hall.

The **Badalgarh** or **Hindola Gate** is a fine example of Hindu architecture in the ornate style of the Man Mandir, attributed to the 15th century but restored in 1648. A swing or hindol once existed outside. The gate takes its name from Badal Singh, uncle of the famous Raja Man Singh. It is flanked by round towers on either side and reinforced by double-leaved doors.

Close by the gate to the right is the **Gujari Palace** (*c.* 1510), built by Raja Man Singh for his favourite wife, Mrigangaya. This fine two-storey masonry building now contains the **Archaeological Museum**, which has an outstanding collection of Brahman and Jain sculpture, inscriptions and paintings. It is set around a spacious courtyard surrounded by small rooms with carved brackets and door openings. Externally, the building is relieved by domes, curved eaves, brackets and bands of moulded ornament. Just outside is the old **European Cemetery**, which contains the graves of Europeans who died in the Fort.

The **Bhairon Gate** is now demolished. Beyond, the **Ganesh Gate**, built by Dongar Singh in the mid-15th century, is a plain Hindu doorway. Nearby is the **Kabutar Khana** or Pigeon House, containing a tank called Nur Sagar. Just beyond the gate stood a shrine to Gwalipa, which was replaced by a mosque in 1664 at the behest of Mutamad Khan. The present shrine beside the mosque is a later structure, using earlier masonry from the original shrine. Note the inverted faces on some of the sculptures.

Before the **Lakshman Gate** is the Chatarbhujmandir Temple (876). Opposite the tank is the Tomb of Taj Nizam (1518), a noble of Ibrahim Lodi's court who was killed in an assault. A flight of steps leads to the north-east group of Jain statues.

The **Hathia Paur Gate** (1486–1516) concludes the series. It forms part of the palace of Man Singh, the inner Hawa Gate having now been removed.

The secondary western approach is guarded by two gates, the Urwahi Gate forming part of the outer defences built by Iltutmish in the 13th century.

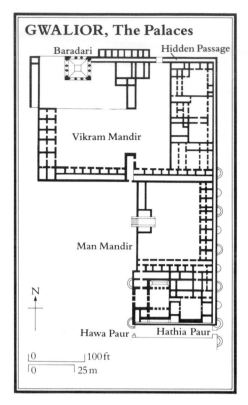

GWALIOR, The Palaces

The Fort possessed numerous tanks, rock-cut cisterns and wells. Many were originally quarried to provide stone for the defences. From north to south, the earliest tank is Suraj Kund, with the Temple of Surya on its western bank. Johar Tal is named after the self-immolation performed by the Rajputs on the fall of Gwalior to Iltutmish in 1232.

Mansarover, Rani Tal and Chedi Tal were built by Raja Man Singh, the Rani Tal being used as a swimming-pool for ladies. The Assi Khamba is a large, circular step-well protected by a wall and arched doorways at the south-west corner of Raja Man Singh's palace. The Rani Tal and Chedi Tal are connected by an underground passage excavated *circa* 1500.

The Katora Tal behind the Teli Mandir is bowl-shaped. Close by, to the west, is the deep Ek-Khamba Tal, with a stone pillar in the middle. Many other smaller tanks lie scattered across the hilltop.

There are numerous monuments within the Fort, including six palaces, four of which are Hindu and two Muslim.

On reaching the Hathia Paur on the eastern approach, there are five palaces to the right; the ramped approach passes beneath them.

The first is the **Man Mandir** (1486–1516; restored 1881), the most spectacular monument in the Fort and described as the most remarkable and interesting example of a Hindu palace of an early age in India. It has two storeys above and two below ground level in the eastern part, overhanging the cliff. Here, in the underground chambers, royal prisoners were tortured and killed. The last Sultan of Ahmadnagar died here in 1600, as did Aurangzeb's brother Murad in 1659. The gigantic east face comprises a sheer wall of sandstone rock, punctuated by five massive round towers, crowned by domed cupolas and linked by delicately carved parapets. The whole façade is enriched with brilliant blue tiles.

The southern façade is more diverse and picturesque, with three round towers connected by latticework battlements. The face is enriched with carved ornament, including bands of crocodiles holding lotus flower stalks between their heads with intertwined tails forming vases, interspersed with beautiful emerald-green panels. Other courses carry figures of men, elephants, tigers, peacocks and trees in enamelled tiles and mosaics in blue, green and gold. The interior of the building is much more ornate, with two open courtyards surrounded by suites of rooms with elaborately decorated ceilings.

Many of the small square rooms in the Man Mandir were used as sleeping-apartments. The multiple iron rings in the ceilings, doors and windows were used for swinging cots as well as hanging screens and ceremonial drapery.

The Man Mandir has an inexhaustible variety of roofs, cupolas, paintings, ornamental friezes, balconies, cornices and details which prove an irresistible fascination for visitors and repay careful inspection.

The **Vikram Mandir** (1516) lies between the Man Mandir and Karan Mandir and is connected to them by narrow secret passages, hidden in the depth of the walls. Inside is an open hall or baradari with a domed roof.

The **Karan Mandir** or Kirti Mandir (1454–79) lies at the northern end of the Fort opposite the Dhonda Gate. It is a long, double-storey building with one large room measuring 13 m (43 ft) by 9 m (28 ft) and a roof carried on two rows of pillars. There are smaller rooms on either side, with fine ornamental plaster work on the domed ceilings. Adjacent to the south is a hall (1516) with a Hindu dome on eight carved ribs which once carried a pavilion.

The two Muslim palaces at the north end – the Jahangiri and Shah Jahan, built of rubble and plaster – are of no great interest.

The south portion of the Fort contains various buildings which are used as a residential school.

The **New City** or **Lashkar** lies 3 km (2 miles) to the south of the hill fortress. It was founded by Daulat Rao Scindia in 1810 as a military camp or lashkar, from which its name is derived. By 1829 it was laid out as a town, with wide streets and stone houses.

Beyond the station lies the Phool Bagh, a vast walled enclosure which contains palaces, a museum, a zoo and other buildings, including Gandhi Park, formerly King George Park, which was opened in 1922. The park was designed to have 3,500 jets for waterfalls, with ornamental tanks laid out in terraces. The large statue under a marble canopy is of Maharani Sakhya Raja. A Hindu temple, a Muslim mosque, a Sikh gurudwara and a Theosophical Lodge were built to symbolize the royal tradition of tolerance.

The **Jai Vilas Palace** (1872–4) was

designed by Lieutenant-Colonel Sir Michael Filose in a mixed style of architecture along the lines of an Italian palazzo. Part is now open as a museum, although the Maharaja still lives there. The ground floor is Tuscan, the first floor Italianate and the second floor Corinthian, executed in sandstone painted brilliant white to simulate marble. The main entrances are via covered porticos east and west of the centre of the south façade.

Internally, a crystal staircase leads to the Durbar Hall, a spectacularly decorated chamber with a magnificent arched roof carrying two of the world's largest chandeliers, each weighing over three tons, as well as the largest carpet in Asia (made in the Gwalior Jail) and furniture and ornaments made from solid crystal. Elsewhere is a room of erotica and the famous model railway which circulated brandy and cigars around the table after dinner.

The **Moti Mahal Palace** is now used as offices, but it retains suites of rooms enriched with coloured glass and mural paintings of scenes from Hindu mythology.

The **Kampoo Kothi** is an old residential palace, now used as a school. It has remarkable paintings on its ceilings and walls. Nearby is the **Imam Bada**, built for use during the Muharram festival.

The Jayaji Chowk is the biggest square in Lashkar. It is surrounded by the vegetable market, government press, post office and state bank of India. At the centre, beneath a high pointed spire, is a statue of Maharaja Jayaji Rao.

Other noteworthy buildings are the Jayaji Rao Hospital and the Victoria College, which was built to commemorate the Golden Jubilee in 1887. It has some excellent stone lattice work.

There is a Memorial Family Chapel to the Filose family at Lashkar which contains graves from 1840 to 1925, including that of Lieutenant-Colonel Sir Michael Filose, designer of the Jai Vilas Palace.

The Chatri Bazaar contains the chatris of the Scindias of Gwalior. The most elegant and charming is that to Jayaji Rao. It is a massive oblong structure of sandstone carved with mythological devices and surrounded by a cupola.

In Patankar Bazaar the High Court is an accomplished essay in Ionic style, formerly known as the Jinsi building. En route to the railway station, passing through Jayandraganj and Shinde-Ki-Chhaoni, a little to the west of Park Hotel, is the **Memorial of Rani Lakshmi Bai of Jhansi**; a platform marks the spot where she was cremated by her loyal followers.

Further out, towards Morar, is the old racecourse. Morar was founded in 1844 as a cantonment for the Gwalior Contingent and it is still used by the army. There are three large European cemeteries in the station.

INDORE

Indore is the former capital of the Holkar dynasty. It is about 189 km (117 miles) from Bhopal by road and is situated at an altitude of 550 m (1,805 ft) on the banks of the Sarasvati and Khan rivers. Of no great age, it was established from a small village in the 1760s by Ahalya Bai, the second chief of the dynasty. Today it is one of the largest commercial centres in Madhya Pradesh. It is a pleasant, affluent town, with the older areas on the western side, the newer to the east.

The **Juna Rajawada** or **Old Palace**, built by Maharaja Malhar Rao Holkar II (1811–34), is a splendid range of buildings with a lofty, seven-storey gateway with canted bays on either side of a central archway. To the right, the Gopal temple (1832) has a large central hall with granite pillars supporting an elaborately decorated roof. It faces the main square. Within the palace is a temple of Malhari Martand, the family deity. Opposite, across the square, is the **Anna Chatra** or

224

alms-house for the poor. To the north is the New Palace (1894) and garden, built in a classical manner with a French style pavilion roof by Gopal Rao, a local engineer.

There are some excellent examples of local vernacular buildings with deep recessed verandahs and carved corbels and columns. Near the bridge over the Khan is a statue of Sir Robert Hamilton (1802–87), the local agent of the Governor-General prior to the Mutiny.

On the riverside are the **Chatris** of the ruling family. In the Chatri Bagh, a large

enclosure surrounded by a crenellated wall, are various cenotaphs; one to Malhar Rao Holkar I (1766) with ornamental sculpture and low relief work, a slightly smaller one to Ahalya Bai (1795) and another, a twelve-sided pavilion on a low plinth, to her son Male Rao Holkar (1766). There is another similar enclosure beyond containing the Chatri of Maharaja Hari Rao Holkar IV (1843). Others of note in the city are at the Krishnapura Ghat on the River Khan and a beautiful monument with a towering dome on the right bank of the Khan commemorating

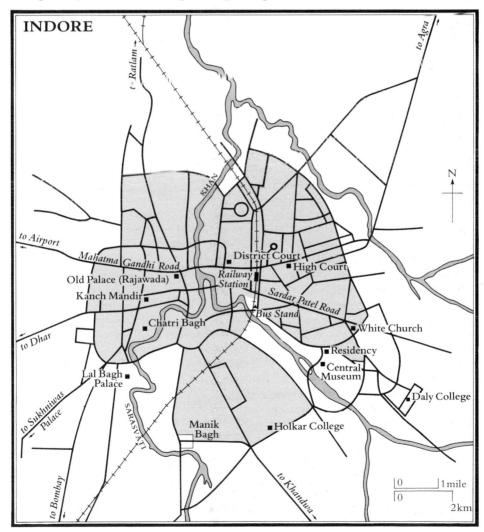

Sardar Chimnaja Rao Appa Sahab Bolia (1858).

The former **King Edward Hall**, opened in 1905 by the future King George V and now **Mahatma Gandhi Hall**, is known popularly as the Clocktower. It is a splendid example of Indo-Saracenic architecture, designed by Charles Frederick Stevens of Bombay. Faced in white Seoni and red Patan stone, it has a central domed clocktower and two-storey wings terminated by domed towers. The ground floor is arcaded with a porte-cochère.

Inside is a spacious hall for over 2,000 people above which are a terraced roof, minarets and cupolas in Rajput style. Nearby the **Courts of Justice** (1910) are also very handsome, with four central domes designed in an Indo-Saracenic style.

The **Central Museum** has a good reference library and sections on archaeology, natural history, ethnography, etc. (For details see Volume I.)

Outside the town are numerous palaces. To the south-west the **Lal Bagh Palace** (c. 1890) is a quaint three-storey range set in a luxuriant garden built by Maharaja Shivaji Rao Holkar. Architecturally, it is similar to the New Palace and was designed by Triggs of Calcutta.

The **Hawa Bungalow** (1894) is a charming classical building of considerable refinement in an Italianate style. On the edge of the Bhameri Tank, 11.2 km (7 miles) from Indore, is the **Sukhniwas Palace** (1883), the summer retreat of the family. The vast **Duryao Mahal** at Burhawa was the residence of Shivaji Rao Holkar from 1903, a huge pile of a building along the river front in white and yellow stucco linked by classical balustrades. The **Nurbada Mahal** is in the same vein as the Hawa Bungalow.

Other buildings of note around the city include the **Durbar Offices** (c. 1890), a plain, classical range built by the local engineer Ramchandra Bullal Mulye, the old Officers' Club (1901) and **Holkar College** to the south of the town, an Italianate composition also by Mulye.

To the east of the city is the former British Residency and treaty area, which retroceded in 1931.

The **Residency** is a handsome stone bungalow (early 19th century) set in a fine park, through which the Khan flows. It has a pedimented entrance and semicircular verandahs to the wings. This district also contains the old European buildings: the Anglican and Roman Catholic Churches, post office, King Edward Hospital and **Daly College**, an exclusive school in a fine marble building with a series of portraits by Herbert Olivier.

There are a number of interesting temples which fall outside the scope of this volume, including the **Kanch Mandir**, a Jain temple near the Cloth Market, with walls, roof and floor decorated with glass depicting sinners being tortured in the afterlife.

IRICH

This ancient town, lying 67.5 km (42 miles) north-east of Jhansi on the right bank of Betwa river, is now in ruins. It was once a town of considerable importance under the Mughal Empire and the remains of mosques and tombs scattered among the suburbs attest to its former prosperity. In 1804 it was the focus of British operations against Amir Khan, who had made it his headquarters for expeditions against Kunch and Kalpi. In 1817 the Marquess of Hastings camped here en route to Gwalior.

The **Jami Masjid** (1412) lies within the walls of the ancient fort on the west side of the town. It is of interest as it embodies the transition in style between the Tughluqs and the succeeding Lodi dynasty. Built in brick with stone dressings, the design and execution of the arches and the central mihrab show typical Hindu details.

JABALPUR (JUBBULPORE)

Jabalpur has no ancient history. Its importance can be traced first to the formation of a civil and military station here in 1819 and then to the junction of the Great Indian Peninsular and East India Railways in 1870, which enhanced

its role as a regional route centre. (For the Jain temple and the Museum see Volume I.) Situated on the banks of the Narmada river at a height of 402 m (1,318 ft), it is a pleasant, spaciously laid out town and is well maintained. The principal buildings are the **Victoria Town Hall**, the Protestant and Catholic churches, six high schools, three main colleges and the

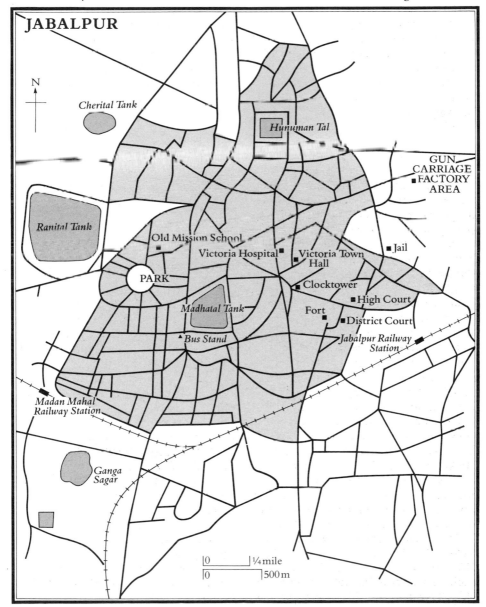

District Court. The **High Court** is in Gothic style and is clearly based on Gilbert Scott's University Hall in Bombay, with curved corner towers crowned by slender turrets carrying spiral staircases with arcaded wings to each side, complete with buttresses, turrets and crocketed finials.

To the north-east of the railway station is the Government Gun Carriage Factory. The 'School of Industry', now a Reform School for Boys, was established in 1836 by Captain Low for families of Thug informers. It was at Jabalpur that many were confined as part of Colonel Sleeman's work to suppress 'thuggee' throughout the region. The **Man Mandir** is a splendid and rare example of 15th-century Hindu palace architecture. The **Jai Vilas Palace** (19th century) is now used as a museum and the **Gujri Mahal** is the archaeological museum. The **Tomb of Tansen** (late 16th-century) is an alleged alternative site to Gwalior for the last resting-place of the fabled musician from Akbar's court.

Jabalpur is an excellent base for a visit to Marble Rocks, 21 km (13 miles) away. The route passes an ancient Gond fortress, the **Madan Mahal**, before reaching the limestone gorge and waterfalls. Near the ghat, where boats can be hired, is a **memorial** to a British engineer officer who drowned while escaping from a swarm of wild bees.

JALALI

This small town, 21 km (13 miles) east of Aligarh, may have been founded by Jalal-ud-Din Khalji in the reign of Ghiyath-ud-Din Balban. There is evidence to indicate that it existed in 1244.

The **Jami Masjid** (1266–7) sometimes called Balban's Mosque, is the principal building of interest. It is a noble edifice of brick and plaster with a prayer chamber measuring 14·6 m (48 ft) by 4·6 m (15 ft),

covered by three domes crowned with gilt pinnacles. The façade is flanked by tall, square minarets surmounted by cupolas with gilt finials. There are three arched entrances to the sanctuary, the central one emphasized by small minarets, capped by cupolas.

JAORA

Jaora is the capital of a small, former Muslim state situated 32 km (20 miles) north of Ratlam. The town was laid out by the British to the designs of Colonel Borthwick, with regular streets on a classic grid pattern within a perimeter wall. There is a fine stone bridge over the River Piria, built by Borthwick. The palace of the former ruler is called the Machhi Bhavan.

JAUNPUR

Jaunpur, 58 km (36 miles) from Varanasi, is an ancient city, the former capital of a substantial Muslim kingdom which flourished between 1397 and 1476 under the Sharqi dynasty. The short trip from Varanasi is extremely rewarding and a visit is thoroughly recommended. The city was the centre of a provincial manifestation of Indo-Islamic architecture of considerable distinction. The most notable characteristics of this particular style are the use of the arched pylon in the centre of the façades, two-storey arcades, huge gateways and the unifying use of the depressed four-centred arch with a fringe of ornament.

Jaunpur was a vital dependency guarding the eastern flank of the Delhi Empire, its governor being honoured by the Tughluq rulers with the title Malik-ush-Sharq or King of the East, after which the Jaunpur dynasty is named. The Sharqi dynasty lasted less than a century before it fell to Sikander Lodi of Delhi, resulting in the ruthless destruction of many fine buildings. Only the mosques survived the onslaught. No trace remains of the once-fine secular buildings.

The origins of the Jaunpur style may well be found in the village of Zafarabad, 6·5 km (4 miles) outside the city. Here the **Mosque of Shaikh Barha** (1311) is an early, rather crude, improvisation using materials taken from Jain temples

in the vicinity. The hypostyle hall has a roof carried by a veritable forest of over sixty columns, but the massive front displays the rudimentary pylon form, which was to become one of the hallmarks of the architecture of the Sharqi dynasty.

From Zafarabad the road into Jaunpur leads over the River Gumti via the massive **Akbari Bridge** (1564–8) built by Munim Khan, the local governor under

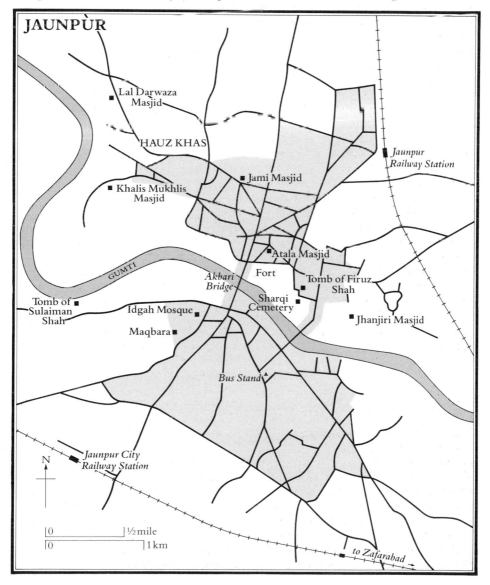

JAUNPUR

Akbar. The Afghan architect, Afzal Ali, created a splendid structure 200 m (654 ft) long with fifteen arches, the central four being larger than the outer spans. It was damaged by floods in 1773 and 1871. The pavilions crowning the piers were restored in 1887. Further damage occurred during an earthquake in 1934. At the south end of the bridge a large **stone lion**, depicted seizing an elephant, was the provincial milestone from which distances were calculated.

The **Fort** (1360) of Firuz Shah is an irregular quadrangle overlooking the north of the Gumti. It comprises a stone wall around an earth mound which utilizes earlier masonry inscribed with Hindu motifs. Most of the towers were blown up after the 1857 Mutiny but the entrance gate constructed by Munim Khan survives. Remnants of its original cladding of blue and yellow glazed brick are still visible.

About 62 m (200 ft) beyond the entrance gate is a large reservoir with a low **mosque** beyond, built in 1376 by Ibrahim Naib Barbak, brother of Firuz Shah Tughluq. Note the minar, which is reputed to survive in its original state. Between the mosque and the river wall, which stands 46 m (150 ft) above the surrounding countryside, is a round magazine tower with the **Hammam** or baths of Ibrahim on the left (c. 1420).

The **Atala Masjid** (1408) lies about 366 m (1,190 ft) north of the Akbari Bridge. Built by Sultan Ibrahim Sharqi (1402–40) on the site of the old Hindu temple at Atala Devi, the mosque incorporates a great deal of temple masonry.

It comprises a square courtyard, 54·5 m (177 ft) in diameter, with three cloistered ranges, the fourth side being the sanctuary. The cloisters are 13·1 m (43 ft) across, with five aisles rising to two storeys, two aisles of the lower storey forming cells with a pillared verandah facing the street. These provided external accommodation for travellers or merchants. In the centre of each range is a

gateway. However, the most impressive element is the sanctuary on the western side. It has an elegant, original façade, dominated by a central pylon over 22·9 m (75 ft) high, with a huge arched marble mihrab or recess containing the entrance to the nave and arcaded window openings. To either side are similar, smaller structures, providing a symmetrical frame. The courtyard is paved to resemble a prayer carpet.

Immediately behind the central pylon is the dome, which is ribbed internally and carried on an arcaded triforium. Notice the way in which the nave comprises three distinct stages, cleverly unified by the manipulation of arches and arcades. The transepts extending each side of the nave are long pillared halls, which open into an octagonal bay or side chapel crowned by a smaller dome.

Externally, the juxtaposition of the dome and the pylon is somewhat incongruous, but the mosque is a remarkably vigorous development of provincial style, using many elements derived from the architecture of the Tughluqs at Delhi – in particular, the sloping sides of the pylons and the fringe ornamentation of the central arch. It is probable that many of the workmen trained in Delhi under Firuz Shah Tughluq were pressed into service by the Sharqi rulers. Quite who was responsible for directing the great works at Jaunpur in such a wholly inventive way is not known, but the resulting architectural synthesis is beautiful.

Two further mosques were built about 1430: the **Khalis Mukhlis Masjid** and the **Jhanjiri Masjid**. The former, a plain, austere edifice modelled on the Atala Masjid, was built by two governors of the city, who gave it their names. It has a domed hall and two wings masked by a low façade and lies on the site of the Hindu temple of Vijaya Chandra. The Jhanjiri Masjid lies about 400 m (⅓ mile) from the city, but only a fragment survives: the central portion of the façade, the screen-like appearance of which has given the building its name, Jhanjiri.

To the west of the city is the **Lal Darwaza Masjid** or Red Door Mosque, the smallest of the Jaunpur mosques, built in about 1450 as part of a wider palace complex planned by Bibi Raja, queen of Sultan Mahmud (1440–57) and later destroyed by Sikander Lodi. It appears to have been a sort of private chapel, approached through a 'high gate painted with vermilion', hence the name. Architecturally, it is a simplified version of the Atala Masjid, but with the notable variation that the screened chamber for the zenana is located centrally, adjoining the nave, doubtless a result of the royal ladies' demanding better provision for their sex. The design is attributed to a Hindu named Kamau, but this is unsubstantiated and, in the absence of any published indigenous influences, unlikely. The central pylon or gateway is 14·6 m (48 ft) high, the towers containing staircases which lead to a mezzanine floor adjoining the dome.

The largest and most ambitious of the Jaunpur mosques is the **Jami Masjid**, which lies about 800 m (½ mile) northwest of the Atala Masjid. Built largely by Sultan Hasain Sharqi (1458–79), the last of the Sharqi kings, it is the final example of the dynastic style. It has much in common with the Atala Masjid, but stands on a raised platform, approached by steep flights of steps. Here the two-storey cloisters are only two aisles wide. The entrances to each range have handsome domes, but the crowning centrepiece is the huge five-storey central pylon, over 26 m (85 ft) tall and 23·4 m (77 ft) wide at its base, which dominates the entire composition. Flanking the pylon are arcaded wings to the side aisles which screen the interior transepts.

Many Hindu stones can be seen embedded in the cloisters and walls. At the South Gate is an inverted inscription in 8th-century Sanskrit on one of the outer voussoirs of the arch.

North of the mosque is the **Burial-**ground of the Sharqi dynasty. In the quadrangle is the tomb of Ghulam Ali. In the centre is the alleged tomb of Sultan Ibrahim Shah (1440). The adjacent tomb is reputed to be that of his grandson Sultan Hasain Shah (*c.* 1479).

There are three other mosques of interest: the **Mosque of Nawab Muhsin Khan** (*c.* 1560), built by Muhsin Khan, one of Akbar's governors, on the site of an earlier temple; the **Mosque of Shah Kabir**, built in 1567 by Baba Beg Jalair; and the **Idgah Mosque**, built by Sultan Hasain Shah (*c.* 1470) and later repaired by Munim Khan in Akbar's reign. It was restored in 1802.

The civil station lies south of the Gumti. There are a church, jail, small court building and old cantonments, now used as police lines.

JAWAD

Jawad is a small town 426 m (1,400 ft) above sea-level, 19 km (12 miles) north of Nimach. The town is surrounded by a stone wall with fifty-two bastions. It was stormed by the British in 1818 and subsequently made over to Daulat Rao Scindia.

JHANSI

Jhansi, 98 km (61 miles) south of Gwalior, is notable for its fine fort and its historical associations with the famous Lakshmi Bai, Rani of Jhansi, a leading figure in the 1857 Mutiny. Today it is used as a convenient point from which to visit the erotic temples at Khajuraho (see Volume I).

The town lies in the once-turbulent area of Bundelkhand, which had a reputation for lawlessness and dacoity. Orchha state once exercised a vague suzerainty over the area and under the rule of Bir Singh Deo (1605–27) a powerful fort was built at Jhansi. Bir Singh Deo was closely involved in the dynastic squabbles of the Mughal emperors, and his fortunes rose and fell accordingly. In 1602 he escaped the wrath of Akbar for his part in the murder of Abu-al-Fazl, Akbar's chief minister and biographer, an act performed at the behest of Prince Salim, later Emperor Jahangir. On the accession of Jahangir in 1605 Bir Singh Deo became a powerful figure and he remained so until he revolted against Shah Jahan in 1627 and was defeated by the young Aurangzeb. After this Jhansi was torn between rival Muslim and Bundela factions.

Jhansi remained a small village until 1742, when it came under the control of a Maratha general, Naru Shankar, who developed the fort and built the great stronghold (Shankar Fort), an extension of the older building. The area remained under the control of the Peshwas until 1805, when the East India Company acquired certain rights. With the death of the Raja Gangadhar Rao in 1853, the territory lapsed to the British. The civil station and cantonment (known as Jhansi Nauabad) date from this time.

In 1857 a few men of the 12th Bengal Infantry mutinied, shot their European officers and seized the fort. Later, the remaining British contingent was massacred in spite of assurances of safe conduct. The dispossessed Rani of Jhansi, Lakshmi Bai, tried to seize control, but she was hampered by local quarrels. The town was recaptured in 1858 by Sir Hugh Rose with a small British force after bitter hand-to-hand fighting. A large table taken from the palace was used subsequently by the Army Council. After numerous escapades the Rani fell, on 18 June 1858, at Kotah-Ki-Sarai outside Gwalior, using her sword with both hands and holding the reins of her horse in her mouth. She is now revered as a Joan of Arc figure, an early heroine of Indian independence.

The **Fort** has been modernized but it remains an impressive sight, with concentric tiers of loopholed walls crowning a large granite outcrop. The fortified walls vary between 5·5 m (18 ft) and 9·1 m (30 ft) in height and are built of solid masonry. The Radak-Bijli or lightning cannon, with its nozzle carved like a lion's mouth, can be seen on the ramparts with other pieces of ordnance used in the Mutiny.

The city extends beyond the old wall, which has ten gates: Khanderao, Datia, Unao, Orchha, Baragaon, Lakshmi, Sagar, Sainyar, Bhander and Jhirna. The first eight have wooden doors. Between Sainyar and Jhirna gates is the breach made by Sir Hugh Rose during the assault of 1858.

Retribution Hill, to the north-east of the railway station, marks the last stand of the mutineers in 1858.

KALINJAR

Kalinjar is one of the most ancient sites in Bundelkhand, a high place sanctified by superstition and fortified by both nature and man. It is a classic example of a venerated hill shrine converted into a hill fortress and occupied by successive generations of invaders. It boasts one of the oldest forts in India, referred to by Ptolemy as Kanagora.

Situated 53 km (33 miles) south of Banda, the fort crowns the last spur of the Vindhya mountains above the Gangetic plains, a plateau 375 m (1,230 ft) high with a perpendicular scarp on all sides. According to Ferishta, the city at the foot of the hill was founded by Kedah Nath in the 7th century. In 1023 Mahmud of Ghazni encircled the fort, but eventually came to terms. In 1202 Qutb-ud-Din Aybak took the fort and destroyed the temples, but Muslim power over the area remained unconsolidated until the rise of the Mughal Empire.

Emperor Humayun besieged the fort intermittently for fifteen years, from 1530 to 1545. In 1545 Sher Shah marched against the stronghold, only to die of terrible burns when a live shell ignited gunpowder supplies, causing a great fire in the battery where he stood. His son Jalal pressed home the attack and succeeded where others had failed.

In 1812 Colonel Martindell attacked the fort and obtained the surrender of the contumacious Daryan Singh. During the Mutiny a small British garrison, entirely isolated from outside assistance, retained possession throughout. The fortifications were dismantled in 1866, but interesting ruins survive.

The only approach is from the north, which is defended by a loopholed wall and seven gateways. The first, with strong wooden doors, is known as the

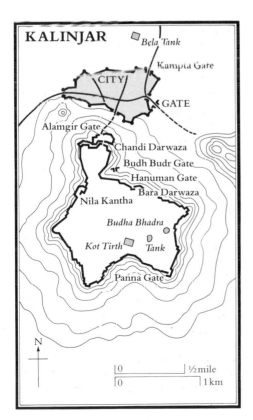

Alam Darwaza, after Alamgir or Aurangzeb, to whom there is a Persian inscription. The rough path to the Ganesh Gate is called Kafir Ghat. The third gate, Chandi Darwaza, is a double one. A stone to the right carries a Sanskrit inscription. The fourth, Budh Budr Gate, is approached by a flight of steps. A break in the wall beyond permits an ascent to the Bhairan Kund, a large tank hewn from solid rock, above which is a gigantic carved figure of Bhairan. Below is a water-filled cave, used as a hot-weather retreat, in which can be found inscriptions dating from the Chandel–Chauhan wars of 1193.

The fifth gate, the Hanuman gate, lies surrounded by numerous sculptures and inscriptions. The sixth gate is called Lal Darwaza and the seventh, the Bara Darwaza, or main gate, is flanked by two iron cannon on stone barbettes.

Beyond the gate is a drop of about 3·6 m (12 ft) leading to Sita Sej, a stone couch in a chamber hewn from the rock. The inscription over the door is 4th century. Beyond is a passage to Patalganga, a cave receding 12·2 m. (40 ft) into the hillside. To the north-east is the Pandu Kund, where Martindell breached the defences in 1812. Fragments of architectural ornament can be seen in the shattered walls. Next comes a large tank called the Budha Badra. Continuing the circuit of the fort the Panna Gate is reached on the angle of the hill. To the east lies the Mrigdhara, so called for the seven deer cut into the rock. The two chambers are crowned by a domed and a pyramidal roof respectively, and within one there is a cistern of clear water.

Kot Tirth, at the centre of the fort, is a large tank, 91 m (300 ft) long, once surrounded by sculptures and the linga and yoni forms of Shiva and Parvati.

Throughout the fort are many Muslim tombs, as well as relics of the Bundelas and Chaubes. The British, not to be outdone, left their mark. At the highest point is a fine monument to Andrew

233

Wauchope, an energetic Scot and the first Commissioner of Bundelkhand.

The town of Kalinjar below retains three gates but is of little interest.

KALPI

Kalpi was once a place of far greater importance than it is today. It lies about 148 km (92 miles) from Jhansi, on the right bank of the Jumna among rugged ravines. Allegedly founded in the period 370–400 by Basedo or Vasudeva, who ruled at Kamba, it fell to the Muslims in 1196.

In 1400 the country around was conferred on Mahmud Khan. Ibrahim Shah of Jaunpur besieged Kalpi in the early 15th century, and in 1435 it was captured by the King of Malwa. It remained a bone of contention until Husain of Jaunpur was defeated in a great battle here in 1477. Under the Mughals Kalpi played an important role and later it became the Maratha headquarters. In 1806 the territory was acquired by the British. During the Mutiny it was a strategic route centre. Here, on 23 May 1858, Sir Hugh Rose defeated a large rebel force of 12,000 men led by the Rani of Jhansi, Rao Sahib and the Nawab of Banda.

Outside the town to the west is the tomb called the **Chaurasi Gumbaz** or **Eighty-four Domes**, together with twelve other mausolea. The Gumbaz contains several tombs, including that of Mahud Shah Lodi. Its name is a misnomer as it never had eighty-four domes. It is more likely a reference to the former groin-vaulted cloisters. In each corner is a typical Lodi tapering bastion with a domed chatri. In the centre of each side are square chatris with sloping roofs.

A ruined fort overhangs the ghat. There is little of interest in the town other than a huge cylindrical tower built in 1895 by a local lawyer who was convinced he was an incarnation of the Ravana, who is depicted on the monument. The 80 m (263 ft) bridge across the Jumna, a splendid example of Victorian engineering (1888), has ten spans on piers sunk 30·5 m (100 ft) beneath the water level.

KANAUJ

Kanauj, 51·5 km (32 miles) from Fatehgarh, is an ancient city which was the capital of a great Aryan kingdom which reached its apogee in about the 6th century. In 1018 it was sacked by Mahmud of Ghazni. Later, in 1540, it was the scene of Humayun's crushing defeat by Sher Shah, after which he left India.

The surviving ruins form an arc 7 km (4 miles) in diameter. In most cases only the foundations survive. However, the **Shrine of Raja Ajaipal** dates from 1021. The **Jami Masjid** is an ancient structure with florid Hindu sculpture which still bears the name 'Sita's Kitchen'. It was converted to its present use around 1400 by Ibrahim Shah of Jaunpur. Northwest of the town are the Muslim tombs of Bala Pir and his son Shaikh Mehndi (1650).

The town is of little interest. There is an old gateway at the eastern end, built in the reign of Shah Jahan and once part of a large sarai, of which only a few fragmentary chambers remain.

(For details of the museums see Volume I.)

KANPUR (CAWNPORE)

79 km (49 miles) south-west of Lucknow lies Kanpur, now an important rail centre and industrial city. Its main interest is historical: in particular, the lamentable events which occurred here in 1857 – the siege of Wheeler's entrenchment, the massacre at the Sati Chaura Ghat and the ferocious reprisals exacted by the British when they retook the city.

234

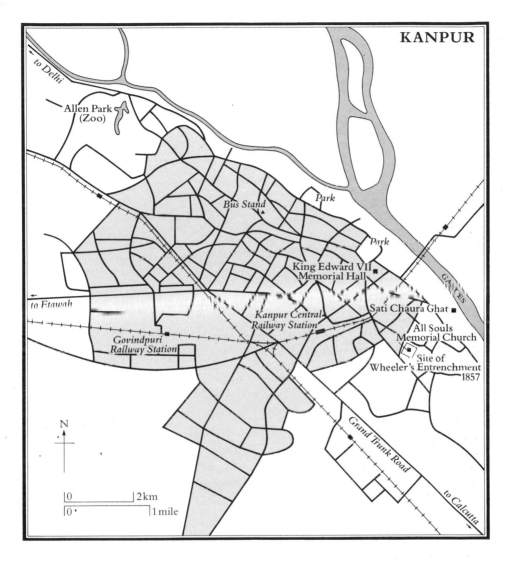

KANPUR

The principal British monuments are concentrated at the site of Wheeler's entrenchment, which lies in the old cantonment area about 2·5 km (1½ miles) from the centre of the city. Once revered, these sites are now rarely visited, but for those interested in British India they are a must.

The lines of the old entrenchment are marked with inscribed stone posts. In the centre stands **All Souls' Memorial Church**, designed by Walter Granville, architect to the East Bengal Railway and later consulting architect to the government of India. Commenced in 1862, it was not completed until 1875, the design being simplified during the course of its erection. It is a handsome building in a Lombardic-Gothic style, faced in red brick with polychrome dressings, dominated by a tall campanile and spire. The interior is surprisingly cool and spacious, a welcome refuge from the unremitting heat and glare. There is a fine stained-glass rose window over the west door. The apsidal east end carries fourteen marble memorial tablets to the fallen. Numerous other poignant memorials line the walls. In the vestry is a plan of the entrenchment and a brief account of the siege.

Outside are a number of interesting monuments, notably a blue and white tiled pavement enclosed by iron railings marking the graves of over seventy officers and men captured and executed on 1 July 1857, four days after the massacre at the Sati Chaura Ghat. Nearby is the capped well-head where so many died during the siege in vain attempts to draw water.

In a separate enclosure to the east of the church is the **Memorial Garden**, approached through two gateways over which are inscribed the moving words: 'These are they who come out of great tribulation.' A short path leads to Baron Carlo Marochetti's famous mournful seraph, set in front of a pierced Gothic screen designed by Sir Henry Yule. Originally, the statue and screen stood in the Municipal Gardens in the centre of the city, over the site of the Bibighar well, where the dismembered remains of European women and children were discovered by Havelock's relieving troops, but the memorials were relocated here after independence in 1948.

The **Sati Chaura Ghat**, where the massacre at the boats took place, is little changed since 1857. Situated about 1·2 km (¾ mile) north-east of the church, a dry, dusty track winds down below high banks to the river frontage, where the little hexagonal temple of Shiva survives. A small plaque inlaid in a wall at the head of the track in 1930 is all there is to mark the spot.

The **Military Cemetery** on the edge of the cantonment contains a number of interesting graves from the late 19th century. Within the city the **King Edward VII Memorial Hall** is noteworthy and **Christ Church** (1840), close to the municipal gardens, is worth a visit. The interior contains monuments to the Mutiny, including several memorial tablets.

KARA

Kara, a small town on the right bank of the Ganges, 67·5 km (42 miles) north-west of Allahabad, was once the capital of a native fief and a town of considerable importance. It is famous as the site of the murder of Firuz Shah Khalji II by Ala-ud-Din, his nephew, in 1296. In 1338 Nizam Ma-in attempted a revolt at Kara. He was flayed alive in retaliation. When Akbar moved the seat of government to Allahabad in the 16th century, Kara declined.

A ruined fort and numerous Muslim tombs bear witness to its former glories. On the opposite side of the river are a large number of ruined Mughal tombs. Most of the finest buildings were dismantled by Asaf-ud-Daula for use as building materials at Lucknow.

KHAJUHA

Khajuha lies 34 km (21 miles) from Fatehpur. Once it was a centre of considerable commercial importance. It was here that Aurangzeb deposed his brother Shuja in 1658 and in commemoration of his victory he built the **Badshahi Bagh**, a large, enclosed 7·3 hectares (18 acres) garden with a baradari at the eastern end. Other architectural ruins of note include the gateway and walls of an old sarai, through which ran the Mughal road to Agra and Etawah, and a fine Hindu temple dedicated to Shiva.

LUCKNOW *Map on p. 238*

The buildings and places of interest are described in the order in which they appear along a continuous route commencing at Dilkusha Palace in the east of the city, proceeding north-west to the Jami Masjid, then returning via Victoria Park, the Chowk, Kaisarbagh and Aminabad to Hazratganj, the hub of Lucknow. (For details of the collections in the State Museum see Volume I.)

The **Dilkusha** or Heart's Delight was built by Saadat Ali Khan (1798–1814) as a hunting-box in the centre of a large wooded park once stocked with deer and game. Built in a classical European style with square corner towers, it is now a ruin set among flower gardens. During the Mutiny it was the scene of fierce fighting and was taken by Sir Colin Campbell on 25 September 1857. Major-General Sir Henry Havelock died here on 24 November 1857, just after the evacuation of the garrison. His body lies at the Alambagh. Several Mutiny graves lie in the gardens, including that of Lieutenant 'Charlie' Dashwood, who endured the entire siege only to lose both legs while sketching later in the Residency gardens.

To the east lies the **Wilaiti Bagh**, laid out as a zenana garden by Nasir-ud-Din Haidar (1827–37). Little remains other than a few pillared retreats around the enclosing wall and more British graves from the Mutiny.

About 1·6 km (1 mile) south-west of Dilkusha, the **Bibiapur Kothi** is a two-storey classical building reputedly designed by Claude Martin. Originally, it was a guest-house for the incoming Resident before presentation to the Court. It is now the Government Dairy Farm.

To the north-west of Dilkusha stands **La Martinière Boys' School**, formerly Constantia, one of the most fascinating buildings in the city, on no account to be missed. Access is not always easy, but pupils are usually eager to guide the inquisitive visitor. It was designed as a palace-tomb by the charismatic Major-General Claude Martin (1735–1800). Artist, man of science, banker, engineer, political agent and benefactor, Martin

was an extraordinary, mysterious figure, an eccentric dilettante who acted as an intermediary between the court and the British Resident. Born and educated in Lyons, he served with Lally until his capture at Pondicherry in 1761, after which he formed a company of Chasseurs and served with the East India Company.

Constantia was his country retreat, a colossal, disturbing building of the most peculiar hybrid design. Situated on an immense podium, it comprises a symmetrical block with curved semicircular wings added in 1840. The first storey has corner pavilions and statuary in full silhouette on the skyline. Vast heraldic lions based on the Company's arms enrich the façade. The building faces a large lake, from which rises a fluted column designed by J. P. Parker and added thirty years later. Unfortunately, recent flood-precaution measures have severed the lake from the house.

To the front is a large bronze cannon, 'The Lord Cornwallis', cast by Martin in 1786. On the steps beneath are carved the initials of generations of past Martinière pupils. The central room on the ground floor has a bust of Martin. Beneath this lies the crypt, with Martin's tomb in a sarcophagus. Originally four life-size figures of French grenadiers stood with arms reversed at each corner of the tomb, but these were destroyed in the Mutiny. The **Library** and **Chapel** were the original reception rooms, lavishly enriched with Italian plasterwork and hundreds of real Wedgwood plaques. Great hollow pillars carrying air shafts run from top to bottom throughout the building, allowing cool air to circulate, while the principal rooms have purdah galleries half-way up the walls.

In the park near the road is a mausoleum to Martin's wife. Close by is a small enclosure, in which lie the graves of the famous Major William Raikes Hodson and others killed in the final assault on Lucknow in March 1858. 274 m (900 ft)

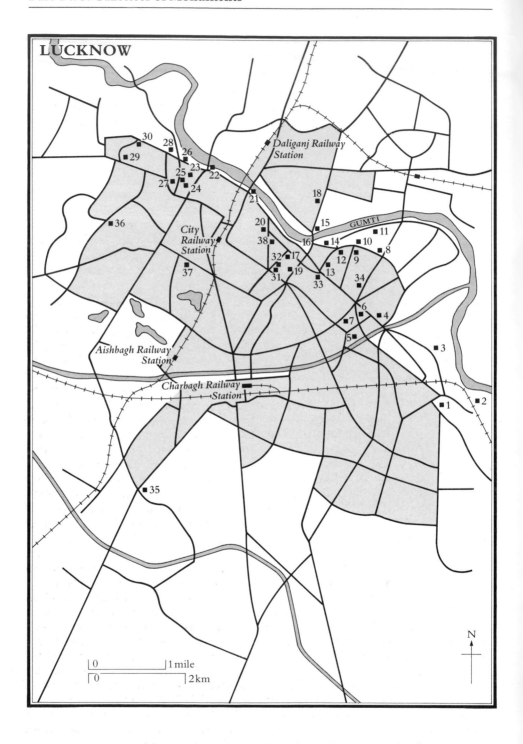

KEY

1 Dilkusha
2 Wilaiti Bagh
3 La Martinière Boys' School
4 Wingfield Park
5 Government House
6 Christ Church
7 Legislative Council
8 Sikandarbagh
9 Carlton Hotel
10 Shah Najaf
11 Kadam Rasul
12 Khurshid Manzil

13 Tara Wali Kothi
14 Moti Mahal
15 Bruce's Bridge
16 Chattar Manzil
17 Court
18 College
19 State Museum
20 The Residency
21 Iron Bridge
22 Hardinge Bridge
23 Machhi Bhavan
24 Hospital and College
25 Great Imambara

26 Rumi Darwaza
27 Victoria Park
28 Clocktower
29 Jami Masjid
30 Husainabad Imambara
31 Kaisarbagh Palace
32 Tombs
33 Nur Bakhsh Kothi
34 Lawrence Terrace
35 Alam Bagh
36 Dargah of Hazrat Abbas
37 Badam Mahal
38 Tomb of Saadat Ali Khan

west lies another small grave enclosure. The school area was fortified by the rebels but cleared by Sir Colin Campbell on 14 November 1857. The pupils provided sterling service as the Martinière Contingent during the defence of the Residency.

Wingfield Park was laid out as a memorial to Sir Charles Wingfield, Chief Commissioner of Oudh (1859–66). The marble pavilion and statues once adorned the Kaisarbagh Palace and form the centrepiece of the Park. Nearby stands **Christ Church** (1860), at the junction of Park and Abbot roads. The Church was designed by General Hutchinson as a memorial to the Mutiny dead and was enlarged and improved in 1904. It contains many fascinating memorial tablets and brasses. The cross on the spire was twisted by an earthquake in 1933.

Close to the junction of Outram Road and Banks Road is the **Legislative Council Chamber** (1928), a huge exercise in Baroque civic grandeur by Lanchester and Rodeck.

To the south lies **Government House** or Raj Bhavan, most of which dates from 1907, when the ballroom and guest suites were added to an earlier house, known as Banks' House, which was the residence of the Commissioner of Lucknow.

Reputedly haunted by Major Hodson, who was carried here to die in March 1858, ironically the house occupies the site of the Hayat Bakhsh Kothi (literally Life-giving Palace), built by Saadat Ali Khan (1798–1814).

The **Sikandarbagh** was built by Wajid Ali Shah (1847–56) as a pleasure garden. The gateway still stands adjoining the Horticultural Gardens. Intense fighting occurred here during Campbell's advance, on 16 November 1859. A tablet on the east wall marks where it was breached, together with a regimental memorial. Almost opposite, due east of the entrance, is an obelisk to the British fallen.

In the gardens, opposite the elegant **Carlton Hotel**, stands the ruined redbrick **Kadam Rasul** (1830s.) Beyond lies **Shah Najaf**, tomb of Ghazi-ud-Din Haidar (1814–27), an impressive building crowned by a white dome and glittering gold pinnacle set in a pleasant garden compound. The musty interior is richly ornamented with crystal chandeliers and portraits, and contains the silver tomb of the Nawab flanked by two of his wives. The building is illuminated during Muharram and on the anniversary of the death of his favourite wife.

The **Khurshid Manzil** or House of

239

the Sun, now La Martinière Girls' School, was built between 1800 and 1810 by Saadat Ali Khan and completed by his son. Designed in a hybrid European style, it has six irregular towers and four entrances, which were originally drawbridges over a deep, revetted moat. The outside had a distinctive frieze of carved suns. Inside the gateway to the left a small pillar marks the historic spot where Generals Outram, Havelock and Campbell met on 17 November 1857 in the final relief of the Residency. The western turret of the house is the one where Lieutenant (later Field Marshal Lord) Roberts planted the flag during the relief operations in an attack commanded by his future rival, Captain (later Field Marshal Lord) Wolseley.

South of the house the **Tara Wali Kothi** (1820s) (later the Imperial Bank) is a low classical-style bungalow used as an observatory by Nasir-ud-Din Haidar's own Astronomer Royal, Colonel Wilcox.

North-west of Shah Najaf, along Clyde Road, is the **Moti Mahal** or Pearl Palace, so called from the resemblance of its original dome, now destroyed, to the shape of a pearl. It is a two-storey building painted pale turquoise and crowned by a gold finial. Originally, it comprised three distinct buildings: the Moti Mahal on the north side, built by Saadat Ali Khan, and the Mubarak Manzil and Shah Manzil, built by his son on the river frontage. The Italian wrought-iron entrance gates were installed in 1923 after an earlier gateway had collapsed. The royal fish badge of the Nawabs of Oudh can be seen to advantage here.

A number of tablets commemorate the events of 1857. One on the garden path marks the reuniting of the two wings of the 90th Perthshire Light Infantry during the intense fighting. Another by Clyde Road commemorates the gap through which Outram and Havelock passed to reach Campbell on 17 November 1857.

Bruce's Bridge (1866), east of the Chattar Manzil palaces, leads to **Badshah Bagh**, once a royal garden. It was laid out by Nasir-ud-Din Haidar with a fine open pavilion for cockfights and was surrounded by pleasant walks. From here came the shell which killed Sir Henry Lawrence. Today it is the centre of the **Lucknow University**. Little remains of the old buildings. The **Isabella Thoburn College** (1923), a traditional exercise in colonial classicism, is part of the university complex. Many of the principal buildings were designed by Sir Samuel Swinton Jacob in a successful Indo-Saracenic style. They are a far more accomplished commingling of European and native architectural styles than the grander palaces of the kings of Oudh.

Close to Bruce's Bridge are the **Chattar Manzil** or Umbrella Palaces (1820s), so named for their distinctive, triple umbrella pavilions or chatris which ornament the domes. The larger or Greater Chattar Manzil has three storeys with tykhanas or suites of underground rooms. It is used as the United Services Club. The Lesser Chattar Manzil comprises government offices. Both are impressive if ill-disciplined architectural hybrids. To the south-east is the Darshan Bilas (literally Pleasure to the Sight), with four different façades, each modelled on different local buildings, and to the south-west, the Gulistan-i-Eran (literally Heavenly Garden). The complex embraces the Farhad Bakhsh (literally Giver of Delight), formerly Claude Martin's town residence, where he died. Once it extended up to the Baillie Guard gate of the Residency. It accommodated the king's wives and family. Here, in 1837, Nasir-ud-Din Haidar was poisoned by a cup of sherbet laced with powdered glass.

Between the Chattar Manzil and High Court (the latter well worth a visit to see the cumbersome Indian legal system in action) is the **Lal Baradari** or Kasr-i-Sultan, a red sandstone edifice now accommodating the State Museum (1863) and formerly the throne room of

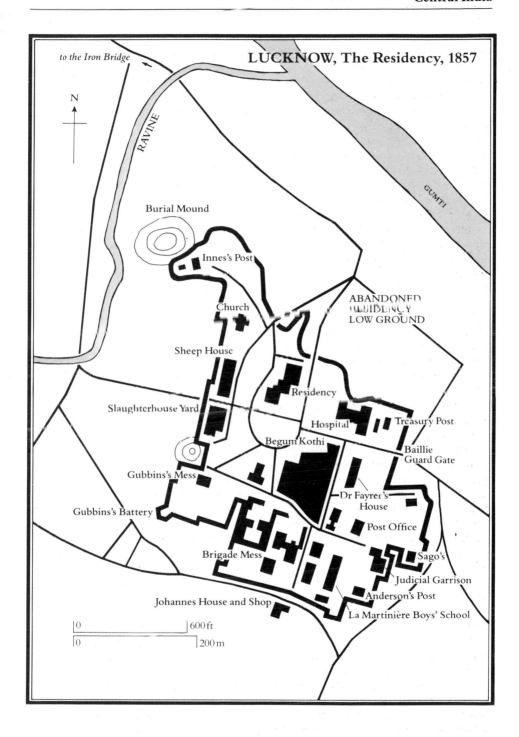

LUCKNOW, The Residency, 1857

to the Iron Bridge

N

RAVINE

GUMTI

Burial Mound

Innes's Post

Church

ABANDONED RESIDENCY LOW GROUND

Sheep House

Residency

Slaughterhouse Yard

Hospital

Treasury Post

Begum Kothi

Baillie Guard Gate

Gubbins's Mess

Dr Fayrer's House

Gubbins's Battery

Post Office

Brigade Mess

Sago's

Judicial Garrison

Johannes House and Shop

Anderson's Post

La Martinière Boys' School

0 — 600 ft
0 — 200 m

the kings of Oudh. The Museum has a fine collection of archaeological artefacts, including Buddhist and Jain sculptures and a notable coin collection.

Nearby is the **Post and Telegraph Office** (1931–2), designed by Henry Lanchester and capped by a lofty clock-tower. To the north lies the **Sher Darwaza** or Tiger Gateway, from the top of which was fired the shot which killed Brigadier-General Neill in the square below on 25 September 1857. A masonry pillar marks the spot where he fell.

Beyond lies the **Residency Complex**, one of the most hallowed sites in British India and scene of the epic siege and relief in 1857. The map on page 241 showing the entire entrenched position and the location of all the defensive posts, provides an easy route through the site.

The site is now a national monument. The rubble has been landscaped to provide a delightful setting for the surviving ruins, which still convey the classical grandeur of the original structures. Enter via a shallow incline through the **Baillie Guard** gateway. To the right is the **Treasury**, the long central room used as an arsenal in 1857. Adjacent to the west is the **Banqueting Hall**, once a sumptuous council chamber and used during the siege as a hospital. **Dr Fayrer's House** is to the south, an extensive single-storey building with tykhanas which were allotted to the women and children during the fighting. A tablet marks the spot where Sir Henry Lawrence died. On the lawn is a large Memorial Cross to Lawrence. The peculiar skyline of the **Begum Kothi** is still a distinctive landmark and was once the house of Mrs Walters, who was married to the King of Oudh.

The **Residency** stands on the north-east side of the enclosure with its famous battered tower. This once-elegant building was erected in 1800 by Saadat Ali Khan. Beneath, in the tykhanas, the women and children sought refuge in appalling conditions for the duration of the siege, and the cool, dank atmosphere is very evocative. The ground floor houses a small museum, which has a model showing the entire position in 1857. In the back room is a poignant plaque to Susanna Palmer, killed by a cannon ball on 1 July 1857.

The **Cemetery** contains the graves of many notable figures, of which the simple graves of Sir Henry Lawrence ('Here lies Sir Henry Lawrence, who tried to do his duty') and Brigadier-General J. S. Neill are the most famous. To the west stood **St Mary's Church** (1810), of which only the low foundations remain.

The entire compound contains many obelisks, tablets and memorials, together with guns and other memorabilia of this British Thermopylae, which occupies a unique place in the annals of British arms in India.

North-west of the Residency is the **Iron Bridge** (1798), designed by Sir John Rennie, based on the design of a similar bridge over the Witham at Boston in Lincolnshire, and cast only twenty years after the first iron bridge in England. It lay in packing-cases by the river for over forty years before it was assembled and mounted by Colonel Fraser for Amjad Ali Shah (1842–7).

To the north-west again, on the site of part of the old Machhi Bhavan Fort, are **King George's and Queen Mary's Medical Hospital and College** (1912), by Sir Samuel Swinton Jacob in Indo-Saracenic style. Nearby is the **Hardinge Bridge** (1914), which replaced an earlier structure erected in 1780 by Asaf-ud-Daula, and also the Mosque of Aurangzeb.

The **Great Imambara** (1780s) is a colossal edifice, one of the largest vaulted halls in the world, over 49·6 m (163 ft) long and 14·9 m (49 ft) high.

An imambara is the general term for a building in which the festival of Muharram is celebrated, and sometimes, as here, used for a mausoleum. In contrast to a masjid, which is unornamented to avoid distraction from the spiritual to the material, an imambara is usually decorated and dedicated to the three imams: Ali, Hassan and Hussein.

It was designed by Kifayat-ullah for

Asaf-ud-Daula in 1784 as a famine-relief measure. It should not be missed for, without doubt, it is one of the most impressive buildings in India, dominating the north-west corner of the city.

It is approached through a square gateway crowned by an octagonal pavilion, from which two courtyards rise one above the other, linked by wide flights of steps. A lofty mosque with two minarets encloses the west side. Over the main chamber a staircase leads to a series of rooms and passages designed as a maze, above which is a flat roof from which magnificent views of the city can be obtained. Inside the main hall lie Asaf-ud-Daula and his architect.

Outside the Great Imambara and straddling the road is the **Rumi Darwaza** or Turkish Gate (1784), erroneously supposed to be a facsimile of the Porte Sublime in Constantinople. This vigorous edifice is half a vast dome cut perpendicularly and lavishly encrusted with exotic ornament. It harmonizes with the adjacent Great Imambara to produce a wonderful complex of Oriental forms, 'recalling Kublai Khan's fabled Xanadu', to quote W. H. Russell, *The Times* correspondent of 1857.

Just beyond the Rumi Darwaza are a number of neglected British tombs adjoining **Victoria Park** (1890). South of the park, through an old gateway, the Gol Darwaza, is the **Chowk**, the principal bazaar area, which runs south to the Akbari Darwaza.

Continuing north-westward beyond Victoria Park is the **Husainabad Clocktower** (1881) an ambitious essay in Victorian Gothic by Roskell Bayne, over 67 m (220 ft) high, carrying the largest clock in India. Contiguous is the Husainabad Tank, built by Ali Shah (1837–42). The **Taluqdar's Hall**, now the offices of the Husainabad Trust (*c.* 1840), containing portraits of the kings of Oudh, is a terracotta-coloured building with iron pillars and a terrace facing the tank. On the opposite side of the lake is the **Satk-**

handa (1840), or seven-storey tower, built by Ali Shah, from the top of which the king could survey the progress of his building schemes from a couch. Only four storeys were completed. The **Daulat Khana**, north of the clocktower, is an irregular group of houses, once occupied by Asaf-ud-Daula, principal among which is the Asafi Kothi.

The **Husainabad Imambara** or Palace of Lights (1837) has a fairy-tale appearance when illuminated. It stands in a large quadrangle and is well-detailed if somewhat tawdry to Western eyes. Erected by Muhammad Ali Shah (1837–42), the hall contains a silver throne and divan, flanked to the west by a crude copy of the Taj and on the east by a mosque. The dummy gate opposite the main entrance is where music was played to honour the dead.

Further west is the **Jami Masjid** (*c.* 1845), on a high platform with two lofty minarets and three cupolas. The mosque is surrounded by ruins.

On rising ground to the right is the 'Yellow House', where British troops were ambushed on 25 September 1859. Two miles to the north-west is the **Musa Bagh**, named after Moses, designed by Claude Martin and built by Saadat Ali Khan (1798–1814). Wild beast fights were staged here for royal amusement. In the garden lies the solitary tomb of Captain Wales, killed on 21 March 1858.

In order to complete the tour, head back to the **Kaisarbagh Palace** (1848–50) via Victoria Park. The palace was intended to be the eighth wonder of the world by its founder, Wajid Ali Shah. Larger than the Tuileries and Louvre combined, the effect is confused and decadent, an incoherent jumble of hybrid Indo-European façades grouped around an open space with a central pavilion. In the open space in front of the north-east gate is a small memorial to two separate parties of Europeans massacred after incarceration in the palace during the Mutiny. Outside the west gateway and behind the Kaisarbagh is the **Roshan-ud-Daula Kothi**. Close by is the **Kaisar Pasand**.

North-east of old Canning College in the Kaisarbagh is the **Maqbara (Tomb) of Saadat Ali Khan** (1814). There are two virtually identical tombs with fine silhouettes, the larger being the king's, the smaller that of his wife, Khursid Zadi. The king's tomb is paved in black and white marble, beneath which lies the vault, which can be reached by a narrow, dark stair.

From the roof of the **Nur Bakhsh Kothi** (literally Light-giving Palace) Havelock planned his attack on the Residency. The **Maqbara of Amjad Ali Shah** (1847) is a plain enclosure of little interest, but the **Begum Kothi** (1844), residence of his queen, Malka Ahad, is the place where Major Hodson was mortally wounded. It should not be confused with the building of the same name in the Residency. **Lawrence Terrace** (c. 1805), now the Gymkhana Club, with its cruciform plan, was once the king's stables.

Outside of the main centre of the city are some noteworthy sites. 3·2 km (2 miles) south-west of **Charbagh Railway Station** is the **Alam Bagh**, once a sylvan glade, now a dilapidated enclosure containing the grave of General Havelock, with an obelisk to his memory. The mango tree over his grave was carved with the letter 'H'.

To the west of the Chowk are two Dargahs or shrines. The **Dargah of Hazrat Abbas**, near Sarai Mali Khan Road, is surrounded by pillared porticos and contains part of a banner carried at the Battle of Kerbala. Muharram banners are displayed on the fifth day of the festival.

In a nearby garden enclosure on Nadan Mahal Road is the **Badam Mahal** (c. 1600), tomb of Shaikh Abdur Rahim Khan, Governor of Oudh under Akbar. It is a fine building in the Mughal style, faced in red sandstone from Agra with vigorous carved detail and vestiges of

original tile work. Adjacent, to the east, is the **Sola Khamba**, which contains fine tombs with carved elephant ornament to the corner pillars.

The **Tomb of Ibrahim Chishti** (c. 1545), father of Abdur Rahim Khan, lies to the east.

About ten minutes' drive to the north-east of the city from the Chattar Manzil palaces is an old disused European cemetery in a district called **Lat Kalai-ki-Lat**. Here are a number of interesting sepulchral monuments, including the tombs of Colonel John Collins, British Resident in 1806–7, and Colonel Wilcox, Astronomer Royal to the Court.

Between the third and fourth milestones on the Sitapur Road an obelisk marks the site of the old cantonment of Mariaon. Elsewhere in the city St Mungo's Church of Scotland (1909), All Saints' (New Garrison) Church (1913) and the Railway Church (1915) at Charbagh are straightforward British churches.

MAHABAN

Mahaban, on the left bank of the Jumna, lies 9·5 km (6 miles) south-east of Mathura. This ancient town is still a place of pilgrimage for Hindus. When sacked by Mahmud of Ghazni in 1017, the Hindu Raja is alleged to have killed his wife and children before committing suicide. In 1234 the army of Shams-ud-Din gathered here before the attack against Kalinjar, but it is chiefly remembered for its ancient legends and mythical associations with Krishna. There are large numbers of Buddhist and Hindu remains, but the most significant Muslim building is the **Palace of Nanda**.

The Palace comprises a covered court which was re-erected as a mosque by the Muslims under Aurangzeb. It has four aisles, formed by five rows of sixteen pillars, eighty in all, from which it takes its popular name of Assi Khamba or the

244

Eighty Pillars. The reuse of ancient Buddhist and Hindu materials provides a fascinating additional dimension. Four of the columns are alleged to represent the ages of the world. The first, the Sataya Yug or Golden Age, is exquisitely carved. The Durapar Yug or Second Age is carved in a similar fashion. The Treta Yug or Third Age is less profusely decorated, while the Kali Yug, representing the Fourth Age or present Iron Age of the world, is depicted by a crude unsculptured pillar.

Within the Palace are scenes from Krishna's infancy. There are numerous memorabilia, which account for the thousands of Vishnu worshippers who visit annually to commemorate the infancy of the child-god.

MAHARAJPUR

This small village lying 24 km (15 miles) north-west of Gwalior was the scene of a resounding British victory over Maratha forces by Sir Hugh Gough on 29 December 1843. The Marathas were routed and retreated to their fort at Gwalior, losing fifty-six guns and all their ammunition wagons.

A monument designed by Colonel W. H. Goodwyn and made from the guns captured in the battle stands opposite the Water Gate of Fort William in Calcutta.

MAHOBA

The ancient town of Mahoba lies 51·5 km (32 miles) south-west of Banda, overlooking the Madan Sagar Lake. It was constructed by the Chandel Rajas and comprises three distinct portions: the Old Fort, lying north of the central hill, the Inner Fort on the summit of the hill and Dariba to the south.

The hillfort at Charkhari is surrounded on three sides by water. The landward approach is through a huge gateway with doors studded with elephant spikes. The gate has three domes with sun and moon finials over windows filled with pierced screens of jali work. Abandoned cannon can be found on every bastion. Within there is a baoli or step-well and a temple containing two 17th-century images of the goddess Kali. Later, the ruins accommodated an Edwardian summer palace.

A large number of architectural antiquities remain throughout the area, mostly relating to the Chandel past. In 1195 the town fell into the hands of Qutb-ud-Din. A number of Muslim remains survive. The **Tomb of Jalhan Khan** is constructed from the remnants of a Shivaite temple. According to a Persian inscription, the **mosque** was founded in 1322, during the reign of Ghiyath-ud-Din Tughluq.

MANDASOR

Mandasor lies on the bank of the Seuna river, 462 m (1,516 ft) above sea level, about 48·2 km (30 miles) from Nimach.

Formerly known as Doshapura, it is a place of considerable antiquity, with extensive archaeological remains. A local inscription refers to a Temple of the Sun erected in 437, but today the town is entirely Muslim, though numerous Jain and Hindu remains can be seen.

On the east side of the town is the **Fort**, founded by Ala-ud-Din Khalji in the 14th century and later enlarged by Hoshang Shah (1405–35) of Malwa.

Near a large tank outside the town, Humayun defeated Bahadur Shah in 1535 and drove him from Malwa. When Malwa was taken by Akbar in 1562, Mandasor became a centre of major importance. In the 18th century it fell to Scindia, in whose possession it remained.

In 1857 an uprising by local Rohillas was suppressed. Later severe fighting took place here between the rebels and

British troops marching to relieve Nimach.

MANDLA

Mandla, the principal town of a district of the same name, lies on the banks of the Narbada river, about 42 km (26 miles) north-east of Nainpur. Its principal interest resides in its ancient connections as the capital of the Garha-Mandla Gond.

In 1564 the Mughal viceroy Asaf Khan invaded the Gondwana kingdom at the head of a considerable force. At the time, the kingdom was under the enlightened regency of Rani Durgavati, who, after sustaining an initial defeat at Singaurgarh, retired to Mandla and took up a position in a narrow defile. After a ferocious engagement Asaf Khan routed the Gondwana forces and the Rani took her life. A later Bundela invasion led to further loss of territory. Hirde Shah built himself an extensive palace at Ramnagar in the mid-17th century, at a commanding site overlooking the river, but this is now in ruins. Mandla fort was reinforced and strengthened a few years later but, with the exception of a few towers, most of the masonry has been dismantled for use elsewhere.

At the conclusion of the last Maratha War in 1818, Mandla was transferred to the British, but the Maratha garrison refused to surrender. As a result it was assaulted by the British under General Marshall on 24 March 1818.

MANDU

Mandu is situated about 40 km (25 miles) south of Dhar on an outcrop of the Vindhyas at a height of 592 m (1,944 ft). It is best visited from Indore, which is 98 km (61 miles) away, and a full day should be allowed. The hillfort is separated from the surrounding plateau by a deep ravine, the Kakra Khoh, which encircles it on its west, north and east sides. The ruins occupy about 21 sq. km (8 square miles), surrounded by luxuriant undergrowth, lakes and ponds, and for this reason it was known by its Muslim rulers as Shadiabad or City of Joy. It has a fine architectural heritage of buildings designed in a distinctive provincial style and a notable school of Malwa painting and manuscripts.

The crown of the hill was fortified as early as the 6th century, but Mandu gained prominence at the end of the 10th century, when the Paramaras formed an independent kingdom based initially at Ujjain and then at Dhar under Raja Bhoj and his successors. It was conquered by the Muslim Khaljis of Delhi in 1304 and the Hindu kingdom of Malwa became part of the Delhi Sultanate under Muslim governors. With the Mongol invasion of Delhi in 1401, Malwa seized independence under its Afghan governor and entered a golden age of prosperity, which persisted long after the Mughal invasion until control was eventually lost to the Marathas in 1732.

After Dilawar Khan, the Afghan governor, asserted his independence from Delhi, the capital remained at Dhar until his death in 1405, when his son Hoshang Shah moved permanently to Mandu. Under him a steady period of expansion took place and some outstanding monuments were erected, including the Jami Masjid, the Delhi Gate and his own tomb – some of the finest buildings in the East.

Muhammad Shah ruled a single year, before being poisoned by Mahmud Khan. The first king of the new dynasty, Mahmud Shah I Khalji, was an exceptional soldier-sultan, under whom the kingdom was taken to its widest limits, with a continental reputation and status. A number of great buildings were erected at this time, including his own tomb, the madrasa and a seven-storey Victory

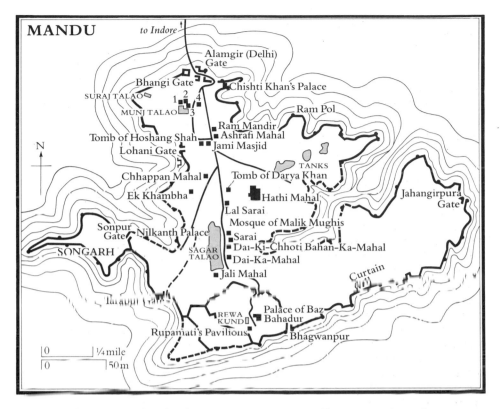

MANDU

Tower, of which only the base now survives. From 1469 his son Ghiyath-ud-Din presided over a long peaceful period, before being poisoned by his son at the age of eighty. It is reputed that he had over 15,000 women in his seraglio, 1,000 of whom were personal guards. Nasir-ud-Din enjoyed a troubled reign and was said to have died of guilt ten years later. In turn, his son was vacillating and dominated by his advisers. In 1526 Bahadur Shah of Gujarat conquered Mandu, and in 1534 Humayun seized control. Under Baz Bahadur, Mandu enjoyed a brief resurgence, but in 1561 he fled from Akbar's troops, who seized control of the fort, and Mandu faded from the pages of history.

Architecturally, Mandu is important as one of the two great centres of a provincial style of Islamic architecture (the other is at Dhar). Most of the extant buildings were erected between 1401 and 1526, initially using salvaged masonry from local Hindu temples. The early mosques of Dilawar Khan and Malik Mughis are from this first period. Most of the other buildings belong to the second phase, of which the best examples are the Jami Masjid and Tomb of Hoshang Shah. Stylistically, this provincial expression of Islamic architecture eschewed elaborate ornament, in favour of simplicity, mass and power. Battered or buttressed walls, bold but austere masonry and the prominent use of colour, of which only vestiges now remain, are the hallmarks of the style. Traces of glazed patterns, tiles and inlay work of semi-precious stones remain. The potters of Mandu were renowned for the brilliant colours of their work.

Originally, the **Fortifications** extended 59·5 km (37 miles) in circumference around the plateau, built from rubble and stone boulders. The Kakra Khoh, or deep ravine, is crossed by a causeway with ascending and descending steps providing ample scope for defence. Within the perimeter walls are two fortified enclosures where the royal palaces are located: the great Royal Enclave and another near the Rewa Kund, protecting the palace of Baz Bahadur. In addition there is the impregnable citadel of **Songarh**, separated from the main hill by a narrow neck of land.

The main approach is from the north, the shallowest side. Accordingly the serpentine path has been reinforced by formidable bastions: the Alamgiri Gate, Bhangi Gate and Kamani Gate. After the Bhangi Gate the road branches off to the Delhi Gate and Gadi Gate.

The **Delhi Gate** (1405–7), the main entrance to the fort, bears testimony to the violence of past sieges. The steep path bends sharply into a long gateway with low steps for elephants. Beyond the gates are guardrooms. The vaulted passage has long since collapsed.

The **Ram Pol** is earlier, dating, as can be seen from its jambs, from the Paramara period.

The fortifications are thrown across the great ravine to the north-east and carried along the southern side. At the eastern end is **Jahangirpura Gate**, with a double enclosed entrance, now marooned in thick jungle. Although the hill is steep on the south side, the fort was attacked from this direction more frequently. It has a continuous wall and a gate, the **Bhagwanpur**, down in the valley below, a double arched entrance with massive walls. The passage from this gate leads to the Rewa Kund complex of palaces.

The outer curtain wall runs south-west to the **Tarapur Gate** (1406–7), a robust structure with three right-angle turns and steep ramps between the outer and inner doorways. The wall continues to the junction with the narrow neck of land leading to Songarh, the last redoubt in an emergency. An arched gateway, reconstructed by the Marathas in the 19th century, commands the entrance. Songarh is

covered with jungle and contains the ruins of Maratha works of the 18th and 19th centuries.

The fort is littered with many early Hindu remains and fragments of masonry, much of which was used in the construction of the later buildings of Mandu. The walls of the Hindola Mahal, for instance, show that their core is composed of huge quantities of early remains.

The buildings of Mandu can be divided into six distinct groups: commencing at the Delhi Gate, these are the Royal Enclave, the group around the village, the Sagar Talao group, the Rewa Kund group, the group between the Sagar Talao and the village, and finally, a group of miscellaneous monuments.

Royal Enclave

The **Mosque of Dilawar Khan** (1405) is the earliest Islamic building at Mandu, comprising a central court enclosed by a colonnade, which is four aisles deep on the western side. The Hindu elements in the main entrance, columns and ceiling are obvious, with their richly ornate detail.

At the south end of the square, which lies to the east, are the ruins of a balcony, the **Nahar Jharoka** or Tiger Balcony, so called because the figure of a tiger once supported it. It is Mughal in origin and was used for public audience.

The **Hathi Pol** is the main entrance to the palace enclosure, with two elephants flanking the gateway. There are side bastions and guardrooms between the outer and inner arches in the conventional manner. The gun bastions suggest a late date, probably from the time of Jahangir (1605–27). Nearby are two wells, one of which has arcades and landings, the other a domed centrepiece.

Gada Shah's Shop and **House** (c. 1520) are popular names given to a very impressive range of buildings, probably once used by Medini Ray, a Rajput chief who was the *éminence grise* behind Mahmud II. Now in ruins, the enormous masonry arches suggest a person of substance rather than the beggar chief that the name implies. In the centre of the hall was a fountain. In the south-west corner are two paintings of a chief and his lady.

The **Hindola Mahal** or Swinging Palace (1425) acquired its name from its battered, or sloping, side walls and its austere simplicity. On both sides are windows filled with delicate stone tracery. 'T'-shaped in plan, it is probably late 15th century in date and was designed as a hall of audience under Ghiyath-ud-Din. A copy of this curious building exists at Warangal.

Running along the north side of Munj-Talao are a jumble of ruins which were once the opulent retreats of the Sultans of Malwa. Within the ruins is the **Champa Baoli**, an underground well with a labyrinth of underground rooms for use in hot weather, and a cunning ventilation system for the palace complex. A **hammam** or hot bath lies close by. The **Water Pavilion**, with vestiges of coloured ornament, is at the western end of the tank.

The **Jahaz Mahal** or Ship's Palace (late 15th century) embodies the romance of India, for it is situated between two lakes and was once staffed entirely by women. From a distance it resembles a ship, but in reality it is an elegant range with an arcaded ground storey and a wide flight of steps leading to a roof terrace, punctuated with kiosks and pavilions. Inside there are three large halls, with a bath at the north end, surrounded by a colonnade. Architecturally, it comes at the end of Mandu's classical period, by which time the style was imbued with qualities of lightness and grace, enriched with dazzling coloured glazes.

The **Kapur Tank** in front of the Jahaz Mahal is lined with masonry, in the middle of which is a ruined pavilion once connected to the west side by a causeway. Remains of an aqueduct from which water cascaded into the tank survive in the front of the Jahaz Mahal.

The **Taveli Mahal** was once stables and a guardhouse. From the terrace there is a wonderful panorama of the ruins of Mandu and the surrounding countryside.

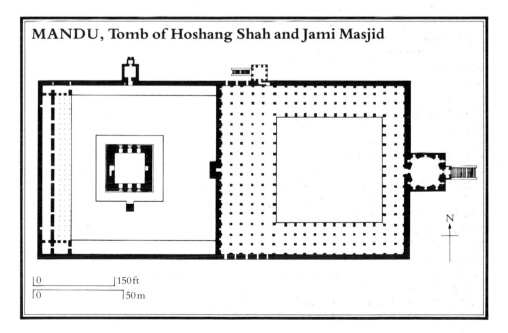

MANDU, Tomb of Hoshang Shah and Jami Masjid

Around the Village

This sector begins with the **Tomb of Hoshang Shah** ($c.$ 1440), which stands in a square enclosure contiguous with the west wall of the Jami Masjid. The entrance is a square portico with arched openings carrying the flattened marble dome above. It stands on a broad plinth and is crowned by a central dome and crescent finial with corner cupolas. It is 26·2 m (86 ft) square and 9·1 m (30 ft) high. Elephant tusk brackets carry the overhanging chajja or cornice, which is treated as a band of miniature arches. Built in marble, it is one of the earliest tombs of its type in India. The decoration on the south doorway carries rosettes in relief and lotus flowers with blue enamel stars. Perforated screens of geometric designs enclose both sides. The sarcophagus is in the form of a casket with a mihrab at the top. An inscription to the right of the door records Shah Jahan's visit in 1659.

West of the tomb is a colonnade with three aisles, behind which is a narrow hall intended for pilgrims and a barrel-vaulted ceiling in Islamic style, in sharp contrast with the Hindu decoration of the aisles outside.

The **Jami Masjid** (1454), begun by Hoshang Shah and completed by Mahmud I, is the most majestic building in Mandu. Reputedly modelled on the Great Mosque at Damascus, it is conceived in a monumental manner with a huge domed porch projecting from the eastern façade.

Flanking the porch the façade of the plinth forms a deep verandah with arched openings for cells. The doorway of the porch is beautifully ornamented with carved jali screens and bands of blue enamel tiles in the form of stars and lozenges. Beyond the west door is the Great Courtyard, faced on all sides by colonnades, that to the west, the qibla wall, being the prayer hall, with fifty-eight small and three large domes. It is a well-disciplined, simple composition of considerable power. On the qibla wall there are seventeen niches with crenellations, the central one with Quranic inscriptions. Along the north side are two subsidiary entrances, one for the priests, the other for the zenana.

Facing the Jami Masjid is the **Ashrafi Mahal**, built in the early years of the reign of Mahmud I (1436–69) and now a ruin. Originally a religious college or madrasa, it was extended by Mahmud Shah to become his tomb. Although the tomb collapsed some time later the vestiges suggest an enormous, brilliantly coloured domed structure, which, had it survived, might have been one of the glories of Muslim funerary architecture. The seven-storey Tower of Victory ($c.$ 1443), erected by Mahmud Shah to commemorate his conquest of the Rana of Chitorgarh, stood here, on the north-east angle. Only the base remains. Originally, the two great domes of the Jami Masjid and the marble dome of Hoshang's tomb aligned with the tomb built by Mahmud Shah on the madrasa, a unified architectural composition of outstanding grandeur.

The Sagar Talao

The most important monument in this group is the **Mosque of Malik Mughis** (1432), a structure similar to that of Dilawar Khan, with a colonnaded central courtyard, a high plinth and widespread use of Hindu masonry. The plinth is arcaded with basement rooms; the central porch projects from the front with small corner pavilions. The dome over the porch has gone. The western colonnade of the courtyard has three small domes with flat or star-shaped compartments between. The west wall has mihrabs with blue tiles and bands of foliated patterns.

To the front of the mosque is a **caravansarai**, an open court flanked by a pair of vaulted halls used for storage. South of

250

the sarai is the **Dai-Ki-Chhoti Bahan-Ka-Mahal** or Gumbad, a great domed octagon with arched openings set in some lovely scenery. The **Dai-Ka-Mahal** stands on a high plinth with arched openings and traces of circular towers at the south-east and north-east corners on which beautiful pavilions once stood. Along the western edge of the tomb are the ruins of a mosque with vaulted ceilings and remnants of tile work. Note the attenuated octagonal neck of the dome surrounded by an ornamental parapet with miniature kiosks at each corner of the octagon. This is a rare device in Mandu but one that is common elsewhere in the Deccan.

Beyond the echo point on the road (give it a try) south of the Sagar Talao, the road leads over to the **Jali Mahal**, the square, stately tomb of a noble with carved screens.

Rewa Kund

This group is about 3·2 km (2 miles) south of the monuments around the village.

The **Rewa Kund** is a masonry-lined tank of sacred water adjoined by some ruined arches. Up on the hill above is the **Palace of Baz Bahadur** (1509), once supplied with water from the Kund by a water-lift. The Palace complex is an eccentric mixture of local and Mughal styles, built before Baz Bahadur came to power, but occupied by him. The main part of the Palace is a spacious open court with halls and rooms on all four sides, with a delightful cistern as the focus. On the north side beyond the colonnade is a projecting octagonal pavilion with arches overlooking an old garden. On the terrace at the south end are two beautiful baradaris commanding fine views across the countryside.

At the edge of the fort, south beyond the palace, are **Rupamati's Pavilions** (probably early 15th century, with later extensions), built in three different stages and associated with Baz Bahadur's beloved mistress. The first stage, seen clearly from the east, was a massive low hall with two rooms at each end and a thick sloping plinth. Subsequently, the building was extended westward alongside the plinth, but it is the latest addition, the pavilions, which have imparted distinction to the building. They are square in plan surmounted by hemispherical domes. The view from here at sunset or by moonlight across to the Narbada valley 305 m (1,000 ft) below is an experience of a lifetime.

Between the Sagar Talao and Village

The **Hathi Mahal** or Elephant Palace stands to the east of the road. Its stumpy massive pillars account for its nickname, but it was probably a baradari or pleasure pavilion, later converted into a tomb. There are three arches to each side. A high octagonal base with banded mouldings carries the dome. Traces of old tile work can still be seen. A double-hall mosque divided into ten bays stands adjacent.

The **Tomb of Darya Khan** (c. 1526) is a red masonry mausoleum, once embellished with intricate enamel patterns. Situated on a raised platform with a conventional dome, it has four small corner domes, like the Tomb of Hoshang Shah. The interior is square, with corner arches which carry the dome above, enriched with delicate trellis work.

A number of ruins lie nearby in overgrown gardens.

Miscellaneous Monuments

On the eastern edge of Mandu is the **Lal Mahal** or Ruby Palace, once used as a royal summer retreat. In front of the central bay is a large enclosure with a ruined baradari. The western section retains a colonnade with double halls at the end, the eastern comprises three halls and end rooms.

Chishti Khan's Palace stands on the edge of a projecting spur to its east. Now in ruins, a central court enclosed by a number of halls and rooms can still be discerned. The south wing is better preserved. One room at the eastern end still retains coloured enamels and paintings. It was probably used as a retreat in the rainy season.

The **Chhappan Mahal** (early 16th century) is a nobleman's tomb, placed on a high plinth on a wide terrace. It is a graceful, well-proportioned building blending Hindu traditions of decoration with Muslim concepts of composition and mass. Note the Hindu-style brackets and mouldings supporting the chajja.

Internally, it is enriched with niches inset with blue tiles with a fringe of intricate carving around the edge of the dome.

Finally comes the **Nilkanth Palace**, built on the site of a Shivaite shrine, with magnificent views over the valleys below. Situated at the end of one of the great ravines along the fort, the palace lies perched on the edge of the cliff and is reached by a flight of steps down the ravine. The Mughals used this as a water palace, with a cascade running through the middle. The rooms to the east and west have semi-domical roofs. On the walls of one of the outer rooms are inscriptions recording Akbar's expeditions to the Deccan and prophetic verses about the impermanence of worldly power.

This completes the tour of the city. Travellers may wish to visit the Bagh Caves, 48 km (30 miles) west of Mandu.

MANIKPUR

Manikpur is a picturesque ruined city situated 58 km (36 miles) from Allahabad and is the principal town in the district of that name. On the overthrow of the Kanauj dynasty in 1193–4, it became a permanent part of the Muslim conquests, though owing to its strategic position it was the scene of bitter internecine warfare until Akbar finally established Mughal suzerainty over the area.

Under the next three Mughal emperors, Manikpur was at the height of its prosperity, being the residence and court of a succession of highly placed Imperial nobles. During the decline of the Mughal Empire, the town suffered severely from raids by the Rohillas in 1751, and the Marathas from 1760 to 1761. With the defeat of the Marathas, Manikpur became part of the territory of the Nawabs of Oudh.

The ruins are still notable, with many acres of old tombs, vestiges of old mosques and other public buildings. Much of the masonry has been dismantled for use elsewhere, most significantly some splendid carvings by Akbar's governor, Nawab Abdul Samad Khan, which were incorporated in the construction of the Great Imambara at Lucknow.

MATHURA (MUTTRA)

Mathura (or Muttra, as it is sometimes called) lies about 77 km (48 miles) north of Agra. It is one of the holiest Hindu cities owing to its legendary associations with Krishna. (For details of temples, archaeological remains and the Government Museum see Volume I.)

When Mahmud of Ghazni sacked the city in 1017, most traces of Buddhism had disappeared already. He completed the process by carrying off vast amounts of gold and silver idols. In 1500 further damage was done when Sikander Lodi attacked the city. Later, Aurangzeb utilized a local revolt as a pretext for demolishing all the main temples, and with the decline of the Mughal Empire Mathura became a focus for local rivalries.

Following Lord Lake's campaign of

252

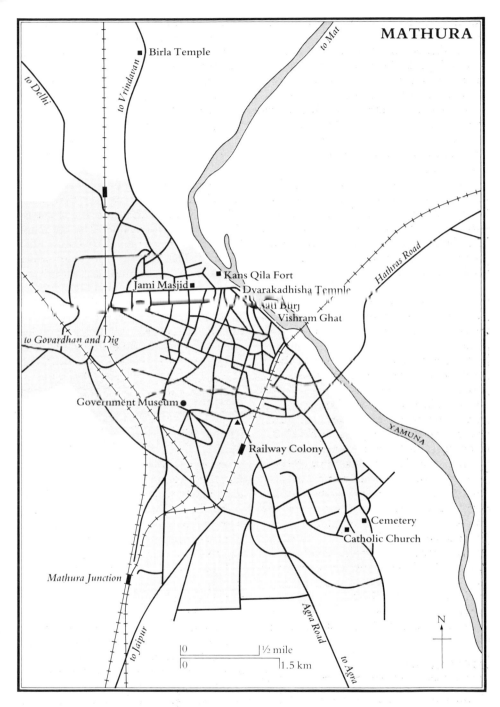

MATHURA

- Birla Temple
- to Mat
- to Vrindavan
- to Delhi
- Hathras Road
- Kans Qila Fort
- Jami Masjid
- Dvarakadhisha Temple
- Sati Burj
- Vishram Ghat
- to Govardhan and Dig
- Government Museum
- YAMUNA
- Railway Colony
- Cemetery
- Catholic Church
- Mathura Junction
- to Jaipur
- Agra Road
- to Agra
- N
- 0 ½ mile
- 0 1.5 km

1803–5, the city came under British control.

The River Jumna flows through the centre of the city and is lined by bathing ghats and ornamental pavilions. The city is entered through the Hardinge or Holi

Gate. The main Islamic monument is the **Jami Masjid** (1660–61) built by Abd–un–Nabi, Aurangzeb's governor, and once covered with brightly enamelled encaustic tiles. The courtyard is raised above street level. Over the façade are the ninety-nine names of God and to either side Persian inscriptions. On each side are outer pavilions roofed in a Hindu style. The four minarets are each 40 m (132 ft) high.

About 400 m (¼ mile) beyond is the **Katra**, a large enclosure within which stands another large **mosque** of red stone, built by Aurangzeb and used as a shrine. This stands over the ruins of the famous Kesava Deo Temple, which was destroyed by the emperor, although traces of the foundations can be seen at the rear of the mosque.

The old **Kans Qila** fort on the riverbank was built by Raja Man Singh of Amber. It was rebuilt by Akbar, but only the foundations now remain. No traces survive of Jai Singh's famous observatory, which was built here.

The **Sati Burj** is a square tower of red sandstone with a later plastered dome, 16·8 m (55 ft) high, alleged to have been built after 1574 to commemorate the suttee of a wife of Raja Bhar Mal of Amber.

Within the town the fine carved stonework of the façades of many of the houses is worth close inspection.

The **Government (formerly Curzon) Museum of Archaeology** in Dampier Park was opened in 1933. It has an interesting collection of ancient artefacts.

The **Cantonments** lie to the south of the city. There are a number of European monuments of importance here. The Anglican Church has some interesting memorial tablets. The **Roman Catholic Church of the Sacred Heart** (1870) was designed in a highly unusual style, combining Eastern and Western architecture. It is by F. S. Growse, the local Collector and exponent of native architecture, who did much to foster a revival of local craftsmanship.

The **Cemetery** contains a monument to those who fell at the Battle of Deeg in 1804. Nearby is the tomb of Lieutenant C. H. C. Burlton, who was shot by his men during the Mutiny of 1857.

MEHIDPUR

This small town on the right bank of the Sipra river, located 38 km (24 miles) from Ujjain, was the scene of a resounding British victory in 1817 by Sir Thomas Hislop over the Marathas under Holkar. The British troops advanced across the river by means of a ford just above the town and routed the enemy at bayonet point, seizing the camp, sixty-three guns and large quantities of ammunition. The British had 174 men killed and 604 wounded; the Marathas lost over 3,000 men.

MHOW

Mhow lies 22 km (13½ miles) from Indore. Under the terms of the Treaty of Mandasor (1818) with Malhar Rao Holkar II, it became an important British cantonment. It is a typical example of colonial planning, built on a grid pattern with a church, three chapels, a large library, arsenal and theatre.

MORADABAD

29 km (17 miles) north-west from Rampur lies the large town of Moradabad, the administrative headquarters of a district situated on the banks of the Ramganga river. The town was founded in 1625 by Rustam Khan, a famous Mughal general, in honour of Prince Murad Bakhsh, son of Emperor Shah Jahan. It lies on a ridge that forms the right bank of the river and has several notable buildings.

The **Jami Masjid** (1634) lies north of the ruins of the **Fort** of Rustam Khan, which overhangs the river. The **Tomb of Nawab Azmat-ulla Khan**, once governor of the city, is also of interest. To the north-west is the civil station, situated among luxuriant trees, extending from the racecourse to the Meerut Road. About 800 m (½ mile) north of the railway station, which lies to the south of the cantonments and civil station, is the **American Church** (mid-19th century).

35 km (22 miles) to the south, at **Sambhal**, there is a mosque (1526) which bears an inscription stating it was built by Emperor Babur, but this is unsubstantiated and unlikely, although Babur's son, Humayun, was governor of the place. It is an interesting example of Islamic architecture and is venerated also by Hindus as a shrine of Vishnu.

NIMACH

This town, on the borders between the old territories of Gwalior and Malwa, has a cantonment bought from Daulat Rao Scindia in 1817 under the Treaty of Gwalior. A small fort was constructed to provide a safe haven for families in times of emergency. The cantonment area lies close to the town walls.

NOWGONG

Nowgong, which should not be confused with a district of the same name in Assam, is a small town situated about 30·5 km (19 miles) from Harpalpur station. It is an old military cantonment which was once of some significance. The cantonment, which is fairly typical, is the site of **Kitchener College**, founded in 1930, with a statue of the famous Field Marshal outside. It is now used as a training centre for non-commissioned officers.

ORCHHA

Orchha lies 11 km (7 miles) south of Jhansi and although now little more than a village, it was once the old capital of Orchha state. The site, chosen by Raja Rudra Pratap (1501–31) on an island of rock protected by a loop of the Betwa river, is unequalled in central India. It is approached via an arched bridge set in a landscape of great beauty. Pratap's successor, Raja Bharti Chand, completed the city walls and citadel and built the first of three palaces, a magnificent complex, which are of considerable interest in that their overall plan and massing are conceived symmetrically.

The **Ramji Mandir** is the prototype of Bundela Rajput architecture. It is based on the Koshak Mahal at Chanderi. It has a central rectangular courtyard and apartments rising in receding planes. The outer walls coruscate with rich blue tilework. The second palace, the **Raj Mandir**, was built between 1554 and 1591 by Madkukar Shah. It comprises a solid single block crowned by pavilions. The third, and by far the most accomplished, palace is the **Jahangir Mandir**, built by Raja Bir Singh Deo (1605–26.) This is a wonderful vertiginous mass of masonry which is crowned by eight elegant domes with rounded angle bastions, capped by open pavilions. A doorway in the southern façade leads through a hall into an open quadrangle, containing a central fountain, around which are disposed apartments and terraces in three-storey ranges. Lateral communication between the suites of rooms is obtained along hanging balconies, protected by wide eaves which run along the outer walls. Windows enriched with delicate Jali work overlook the Betwa river, on the banks of which lie the memorial chatris of the Orchha kings.

The Jahangir Mandir is an architectural conception of unusual vigour and intricate sophistication, built at the height of the dynastic power of the Bundela

Rajputs, and, together with the old palace at Datia, it is one of the best examples of mediaeval fortification in India.

PANNA

Panna lies about 100 km (62 miles) south of Banda in a wild and hilly area of Bundelkhand, once renowned for the lawlessness of its inhabitants, who preyed on the rich towns of the Ganges valley to the north and on passing travellers. Dacoity and banditry were endemic and it was to here that the last rebels from the Mutiny retreated in 1858. The wild, remote hills of the Upper Vindhyas still have a reputation for fierce self-reliance.

Panna is situated 350 m (1,147 ft) above sea level. It is a clean, well-laid-out city built from local stone, with several late-19th-century temples. The prosperity of the area was based on diamonds, discovered here in the late 18th century, which provided the wealth of the ruling dynasty.

The **Palace** (1886) was built by Rudra Pratap Singh to the designs of an English architect, who had already designed the Balram Temple in the town on the model of St Paul's Cathedral, London. The main western range has a colonnaded façade on a monumental scale, with lotus leaf capitals in lieu of the acanthus leaves of the Corinthian order. It is French in style in the Beaux Arts tradition of the late 19th century, a well-ordered composition of considerable sophistication. Behind the façade are the principal public rooms, but in the courtyard at the rear lie the rooms of the old palace and the zenana, a rambling series of classical buildings set behind an ornamental tank.

PANNIAR

Panniar, a small town 19 km (12 miles) south-west of Gwalior fort, was the scene of an engagement on 29 December 1843 between British and Maratha forces. A force under Major-General Grey was attacked by a large Maratha army of 12,000. The British formed a defensive position here and in a series of attacks drove the enemy from his positions and captured his artillery. The Marathas were repulsed severely for the small British loss of thirty-five killed and 182 wounded.

PHILIBHIT

This town and district headquarters lies about 48 km (30 miles) north-east of Bareilly on the left bank of the Deoha river. In 1740 the Rohilla leader Hafiz Rahmat Khan established his capital here. On his death in 1774 at the Battle of Miranka Katra against the Nawabs of Oudh and a small European force despatched by Warren Hastings, it was occupied by the Nawab until 1801, when it passed to the British. In 1857 the population rose in revolt and expelled the British authorities.

It is a long, straggling town with two large markets. The most interesting area is on the western outskirts, where there are the remains of the old Rohilla chief's palace, a large mosque built in imitation of the Jami Masjid in Delhi (1770s), a school and a dispensary.

RAE BARELI

77 km (48 miles) south-east of Lucknow, Rae Bareli is an old town and administrative headquarters founded by the Bhars (hence the name). After the expulsion of the Bhars by Ibrahim Sharqi of Jaunpur (1402–40) in the early 15th century, the town became a Muslim centre.

The **Fort**, erected by Ibrahim Sharqi, is constructed from peculiar bricks 60 cm (2 ft) by 30 cm (1 ft) thick and 45 cm (1½ ft) wide, probably taken from earlier strongholds of the Bhars. In the centre of the fort is an enormous **well**, 98·5 m (320 ft) in circumference, lined in brick, with galleries and chambers at water level. Beside the gate is the tomb of a Muslim saint (early 15th century). Other notable buildings include the **Tomb of Nawab Jahan Khan** (mid-17th century) and four handsome mosques, one comprising three large halls without domes and said to be a copy of the Ka'aba in Mecca.

The bridge over the Sai river was erected in the late 1870s.

RAIPUR

290 km (180 miles) east of Nagpur, Raipur is an old town with a number of fine tanks. The modern town was laid out from 1830 by Colonel Agnew with a wide central street flanked by houses with elaborately carved pillars and balconies.

Nothing remains of the Fort built by Raja Bhubaneswar Singh in 1460. The **Burha Tank** (1460) still survives, although once it covered nearly 1·5 sq. km (1 square mile). There are public gardens on the east side. The **Maharaj-bandh Tank** was built by a Maratha revenue-farmer, who created a beautiful tank from a fever-ridden swamp. The Temple of Ramchandra (1775) was built by the Raja. The **Amba Tank** (*c*. 1680), which has massive stone terraces, was built by a Teli merchant. In the centre of the town is the **Kankali Tank** (late 17th century), with a small temple dedicated to Mahadeo in the centre.

3·2 km (2 miles) from the centre is the **Rajkumar College**, an exclusive school.

(For the Museum see Volume I.)

RAMPUR

Rampur lies about 29 km (18 miles) east of Moradabad. It was founded in the late 17th century by two Afghan Rohillas, Shah Alam and Husain Khan, who came to seek service under the Mughal Empire and were given free rein to pacify the area which came to be known as Rohilkhand. However, by 1750 the emergent martial Rohilla state attracted the attention of the Nawabs of Oudh and the expanding East India Company. In the Rohilla War of 1773–4 most of the Rohilla chiefs fled or were slain and Rampur became the sole refuge of Rohilla power. Sayyad Faiz-ulla Khan built an enormous defensive bamboo hedge around the entire per-imeter of the state. It is 16 km (10 miles) in circumference and can still be seen today.

In return for his loyalty in 1857 and for his support during the Second Afghan War, the Nawab was rewarded with territory and titles by the British. By the late 19th century Rampur was a centre for Rohilla culture. Under Hamid Ali Khan, who ascended to the throne in 1896, a whole series of improvements took place which laid the foundations for a modern policy. All building works were supervised or designed by Mr W. C. Wright, the chief engineer.

The entire Fort and palace complex in the north-west of the town was remodelled by Wright: the Ranj Mahal, the Machchi Bhavan, the Imambara and the old Benazir and Badri-Muni palaces.

Wright built the **Khas Bagh**, a huge palace, on the foundations of the old fort. It has an enormous, rambling stucco façade, with a centrepiece crowned by a high French pavilion roof, flanked by long arcuated ranges in a variety of clas-sical styles. The palace contains an art gallery, zenana, mardana (a male zenana), hospitality suites and a fine music room. Lord Reading, the Viceroy, stayed here in 1923. Among the collec-tion of furniture is an elegant early gramophone crowned by an Islamic moon and star.

Other buildings of note include the Jami Masjid (18th century) located in the

Safdarganj Square and the Tomb of Faiz-ulla Khan (late 18th century) located to the north of the town on a raised masonry terrace.

RATANPUR

Ratanpur, 24 km (15 miles) north of Bilaspur, is the old capital of the Haihai-Bansi kings of Chhatisgarh. Since 1787 the town has been steadily decaying, but the dilapidated ruins of the old fort, the crumbling walls of the old palace and the old dry moat testify to the former grandeur of the place. Interspersed with the numerous tanks and temples are great blocks of masonry, commemorating many long-forgotten suttees. One of the largest blocks, near the old fort, dates from the mid-17th century.

RATLAM

Ratlam is the capital of the former state of that name and is situated 125 km (78 miles) equidistant from Mhow and Mandu. The state was granted by Emperor Shah Jahan to Ratan Singh, a heroic figure who died at the Battle of Fatehbad in 1658 at the head of the Rajput armies, opposing the combined strength of Aurangzeb and Murad.

The town is a significant district centre. Within the walls stands the **Ranjit Bilas Palace** (late 19th century) and a chowk or market square, built by Munshi Shahamat Ali. The Chandni Chowk leads to the main Tripulia Gate and a large tank.

REWA

Rewa, renowned for its white tigers, lies 211 km (131 miles) south-west of Allahabad and is the capital of the former state of Rewa in a wild tract of country known as Baghelkhand (after the immigrant Rajput marauders or Baghelas). Tansen,

the famous singer to the court of Akbar, hailed from Rewa, and it was his talent which drew Mughal attention to the remote state.

After Akbar seized control, the area was fragmented into smaller states, of which Rewa was the chief.

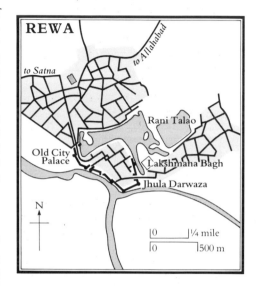

The **Old City Palace** is a remarkable example of organic growth over time. The core dates from the 16th century, but it has been added to many times since its foundation. Situated next to a wide stretch of water, its romantic silhouette is striking: a rambling range of ghats, temples, courtyards and a vast Durbar Hall. The entrance to the City Palace is flanked by panels of lamp niches with a gatehouse above.

The **Govindgarh Palace** (late 19th century) lies 24 km (15 miles) from the city and was built in an eclectic Rajput style on a lake surrounded by mango groves and jungle as a hunting-retreat for Raghuraj Singh of Rewa. Five rare white tigers patrol the courtyard. In an adjacent compound is a sacred arch on a huge platform carved in the shape of a lotus.

(For the reconstructed 11th-century stone gateway and sculptures see Volume I.)

SAGAR

Sagar, the principal town of the district, can be reached on the branch line from Bina Junction, 76 km (47 miles) away. It stands at a height of 600 m (1,940 ft) above sea level on the edge of a fine, ancient man-made lake nearly 1·6 km (1 mile) wide. The town was founded by the Bundela Raja Udaussa, who built a small fort on the site of the present structure in 1660.

The **Fort** was completed in about 1780 by the Marathas. Comprising twenty round towers connected by thick defensive walls, it dominates the area from a hill to the north-west of the lake. In 1829 it was used as a prison for the suppression of thuggee; today it is used as a Police Training School.

About 1·6 km (1 mile) east of the lake is an old Mint (1820). Nearby is a large, castellated jail, which was opened in 1846.

Rahatgarh Fort, 39 km (24 miles) west of Sagar, was the scene of an engagement between Sir Hugh Rose and the Nawab of Garhi Amastani in February 1858.

(For the University Museum see Volume I.)

SAMTHAR

Samthar, 40 km (25 miles) north-east of Jhansi, was India's only Gujar state. It has a huge triple-walled fort similar in design to that built by the Sikhs at Patiala.

The rulers of Samthar belong to the Bar-Gujar clan, an illustrious ancient royal line. By the late 18th century Madan Singh joined forces with the Marathas, invaded Datia and formed a breakaway state. In 1817 a separate treaty was drawn up with the British which afforded protection and recognition.

The **Fort**, built in the late 18th century, is surrounded by a wide moat, behind which rise three tiers of crenellated walls, interspersed with austere semicircular bastions. The entrance is via huge iron elephant gates.

During the Mutiny the fort provided sanctuary for British residents fleeing the communal riots. After this a series of buildings was erected on European lines, designed by an Italian called 'Tonton Sahib', who also built the seven-storey fort palace, an extraordinary pile which dwarfs the entire complex. A depleted menagerie still survives from the great days of the late 19th century, and the fort is still lived in by the Samthar family.

The entrance to the fort palace passes the **Raj Mandir**, an elaborate monumental gateway which houses the family deities.

SHAHJAHANPUR

This is an important district centre, 27 km (17 miles) from Shahabad on the Lucknow Road, lying on the left bank of the River Deoha or Garra, just above its confluence with the Khanaut, where there is an old fort overhanging the river and a large masonry bridge, built by Makim Mehndi Ali.

The city was founded in 1647 under Emperor Shah Jahan, after whom it is named, by a local Pathan leader called Nawab Bahadur Khan. The monuments here – an English church, a few schools and some undistinguished mosques – are of no great note.

On 31 March 1857 the local Europeans were attacked at morning service. They defended themselves in the church and, with the aid of loyal sepoys, fell back to Muhamdi, 32 km (20 miles) to the east, where they were unfortunately murdered.

The city is still a centre for silk cloth manufacture.

UJJAIN

Ujjain, one of the seven sacred cities of the Hindus, lies 37 km (23 miles) north-west of Dewas at a height of 512 m (1,679 ft). The ancient ruins and archaeological remains are of great interest. Ujjain, being in the centre of the country, was the place where scientific mathematical astronomy was first evolved, and the meridian was fixed here for the purposes of astronomical calculations. (For the sacred associations of the town and principal temples see Volume I.)

In addition to the ruins of antiquity a number of later interesting monuments remain.

The **Jaisingh Observatory** (*c.* 1725) was built by Raja Jaisingh of Jaipur when he was Governor of Malwa under the Mughal emperor Muhammad Shah. As early as the time of Ashoka, Ujjain was the leading astronomical centre, and, owing to the efforts of Jaisingh, its importance was underscored.

The Observatory lies to the south-east of the town and consists of five monuments. The Samrata Yantra is 6·7 m (22 ft) high and was used for calculating the time. The inclination of the staircase to the horizon is 23° 10′. On both quadrants the hours and minutes are marked to indicate time, from sunrise to noon on the west quadrant and from noon to sunset on the east.

The Nadi Walaya Yantra is a circular dial lying to the south, comprising a cylinder 2·28 m (7½ ft) long by 1 m (3 ft 7½ in) in diameter. An iron peg fixed on the northern face gives the time when the sun is in the northern hemisphere, the one on the south face is for the southern hemisphere. This Yantra helps to calculate the equinoctial days of the year.

The Digansha Yantra lies to the east of the Samrata Yantra. It comprises an outer circular wall 10·05 m (32 ft 10 in) in diameter and 2·53 m (8 ft 4 in) in height. Concentric with this is another wall, 6·1 m (20 ft) in diameter and of the same

height. In the centre is an iron rod 1·2 m (4 ft high). Wire attached to the rod stretched in the direction of a particular star or planet enabled its position to be fixed.

The Dakshinottara Bhitti or Bhitti Yantra is a meridian instrument: a wall lying in the plane of the meridian and constructed north and south. It is 6·7 m (22 ft) high and long and 2·13 m (7 ft) thick. On the eastern surface are double quadrants marked with degrees, to enable the declination of the sun and zenith distance to be calculated.

The **Chowis Khamba Darwaza** (probably 11th century) is a massive ancient gateway which may once have led to the Temple of Mahakal. The pillars are of carved black stone.

The **Bina Niva-Ki-Masjid** is located in Anantpeth. Formerly a Jain temple, this was converted to a mosque by Dilawar Khan Ghuri in 1397.

The **Kaliyadeh Mahal** is a central hall with galleries on all four sides. Akbar stayed here in 1601 and left behind a long, low building on the banks of the river. It is different from the main building in style and is called Astabel or stable, as it was once used by Pindaris for horses.

VARANASI (BENARES)

Varanasi is one of the seven sacred cities of the Hindus. Some claim that it is the oldest city in the world. Situated on a great bend of the holy Ganges, it rises steeply over the water in a continuous series of ghats, temples and civic buildings. Traditionally known as Kashi, the City of Light, it is the supremely sacred place of Hinduism and has been the focus of pilgrimages for over 2,500 years.

The city is mentioned in both the Mahabharata and Ramayana and, justifiably, it may be regarded as the religious capital of India. It was to Varanasi that the Buddha (563 BC–483 BC) came to

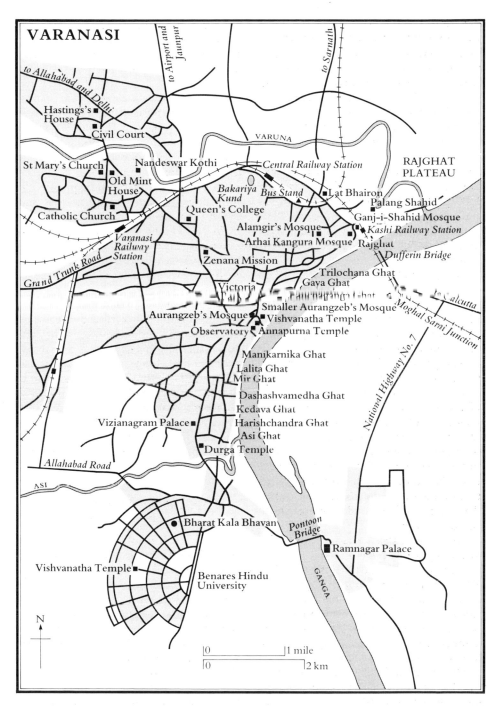

VARANASI

establish his religion. Almost 900 years later, in 399, the Chinese traveller Fa-Hien visited the city. When Hiuen Tsang arrived in 629–45 he recorded over 100 temples and a thriving centre of spiritual philosophy.

The Muslim influence can be traced back to the early raids of Mahmud of Ghazni in 1033. In 1194 the Hindu Raja of Benares was defeated by Ala-ud-Din Khalji, who destroyed the temples and built mosques. Since this date the city has been under continuous Muslim control. As a consequence, few temples date from before the time of Akbar, in the late 16th century.

In 1775 the city was ceded by the Nawabs of Oudh to the British, and in 1787 the East India Company took over the revenue settlement. A British Resident, Jonathan Duncan, was installed. In 1857 the garrison mutinied, but the Raja remained loyal.

The principal European buildings are concentrated in the **Cantonment** area, which lies about 4·8 km (4 miles) from the river, to the north-west of the city.

St Mary's Church (*c.* 1820) is a typical cantonment church of Upper India with a low tower and spire and projecting portico, now partly infilled. Note the louvred doors to the sides, in lieu of windows, and the hooded ventilation slots beneath the cornice.

The **Churchyard** is a pleasant, shaded compound containing a number of tombs and memorials removed from the old city cemetery at Chaitganj. The large column, crowned by an urn, commemorates officers massacred at Sewaleh on 16 August 1781. A pavilion marks the remains of twelve bodies and was removed here by James Prinsep in 1829.

North, across the River Barna, is the **Civil Station** of Sikraul. The District Courts, Club and residential bungalows are here. Beyond the Civil Courts is **Hastings's House**, outside which is a stone sundial erected in 1784 by Lieutenant James Ewart by order of Warren Hastings. The bridge over the river was designed by Colonel John Garstin in the late 18th century.

Raja Bazaar leads southward past the church to the **Nandeswar Kothi** (late 18th century). This fine house belongs to the Maharaja of Benares, but it is now mouldering away in a state of romantic decay. King George V and Queen Mary stayed here in 1906, as Prince and Princess of Wales. Little has changed since that date, although the once fine garden compound is now being built upon. It was in this house that Samuel Davis, the magistrate, defended himself and his family from the followers of Wazir Ali, the deposed Nawab of Oudh, in January 1799. After securing his family on the roof he defended the staircase with a spear until he was rescued by cavalry from the old cantonment at Bitabur.

Opposite is the former **Mint Master's House**, designed by James Prinsep and built in 1820–21. It is a fine building of the period. Prinsep lived here as Mint Master until 1830. The grand external staircase leading to the former banqueting hall and drawing-room was added in 1926. It is now a carpet showroom and offices.

The Grand Trunk Road loops north of the city. After 2·4 km (1½ miles) the **Bakariya Kund** is reached. On the right-hand side is a large tank surrounded by Muslim monuments, mosques and ruins, mostly converted from Hindu buildings and constructed from salvaged Hindu masonry. The Battis Khamba was once a shrine. It is now a Muslim tomb.

The **Lat Bhairon** lies between the two great railway lines at the entrance to a small idgah. It was damaged by riots in 1809. It is of Buddhist origin and may be one of Ashoka's Lats.

On the south side of the open space opposite Kashi railway station a flight of steps leads to the **Ganj-i-Shahid Mosque**. This is a converted Buddhist temple commemorating the Muslims who fell in the early captures of the city.

Nearby is the **Arhai Kangura Mosque**. This carries a Hindu inscription of 1190 but dates from the early Muslim conquest. The pillars are of Hindu origin and were taken from an older temple.

262

Behind the station is the site of the old Raj Ghat fort, now dismantled. Within the confines of the fort on the south corner of the plateau is the **Tomb of Lal Khan**, the minister of a former raja, which is enriched with tiles and mosaics. It is one of the few original Muslim buildings of any great beauty in the city. To the north-west is the **Palang Shahid**, a small Muslim cemetery.

The Malaviya (1887) or Dufferin Bridge is 1,071 m (3,517 ft) long. It carries the Grand Trunk Road over the river in a series of seven spans.

Across the river the National Highway No. 7 crosses the Grand Trunk Road and leads to the **Ramnagar Palace** and fort of the Maharaja of Benares. The outer ramparts date from the 17th century. The approach from the river front is very impressive. A series of massive bastions, overhung by a bracketed balcony and punctuated with pavilions, guards a vast flight of steps, which leads to a pointed archway. A series of courtyards leads to the white tower of the main palace within the fort. The private apartments lie on one side of the tower, the Durbar Hall and reception rooms on the other.

The Durbar Hall and reception rooms are sumptuously furnished. The throne is of sandalwood. Locally made gold and silver brocades, tiger skins, inlaid ivory, carpets and crystal chandeliers create a vision of great opulence. The main carpet was the gift of Lord Curzon, the smaller came from the Shah of Iran. Outside the Durbar Hall is a splendid marble balcony and verandah, from which there are fine views across the river.

From Nandeswar Tank Raja Bazaar Road leads under the railway to Talia Bagh Road. To the south is the London Mission. South of Pensioner's Lane is the Pisach Mochan Tank, which reputedly contains the head of a demon or pisach.

The road leads to **Queen's College**, designed by Major Kittoe in 1847–52. It is one of the earliest secular buildings in a scholarly Gothic style in India. Designed in a Perpendicular style, it is built of Chunar stone with a lofty central tower and corner towers joined by open arcades. Inside the main entrance in the south-east corridor is a plaque recording the foundation of the original Sanskrit College by Jonathan Duncan in 1791.

At the Bagh the road splits. One fork, Chaitganj Road, leads to the river via Victoria Park and the old cemetery.

To the south, near Anandbagh, is the Central Hindu College and the Maharaja of Vizianagram's Palace.

The other fork runs east past the Zenana Mission, the Ishwari Memorial Hospital and King Edward VII General Hospital. At the Municipal Gardens is the **Town Hall**, built by the Maharaja of Vizianagram, who died here in 1845, and the Kotwali or Police Station, which resembles a fort.

One of the principal attractions of the city is the line of bathing ghats which run down to the water's edge, and from which pilgrims and holy men engage in their daily ritual cleansing. There are two cremation ghats. (For these and other sacred Hindu and Buddhist sites within the city see Volume I.)

The Muslim monuments are interspersed among the ghats and temples.

Adjacent to Man Mandir Ghat is the Observatory. Most of the ghat is later work from the end of the late 19th century, but the stone balcony high up on the north-east corner is original and was erected by Raja Man Singh of Amber in 1600.

The **Observatory** was built by Raja Sawai Jai Singh in the early 18th century, one of five, the others being at Delhi, Jaipur, Mathura and Ujjain. The instruments are made of masonry.

The first instrument is the Bhitti Yantra, or mural quadrant. This comprises a 3·35 m (11 ft) high wall, 2·8 m (9 ft 1½ in) wide, in the plane of the meridian. It is used to calculate zenith distance, solar altitude and thereby the latitude. Next are two large circles and a stone

263

square, probably used to mark the shadow of the gnomon and degrees of azimuth.

The Samrat Yantra is another wall, 10·9 m (36 ft) long and 1·3 m (4½ ft) wide, also set in the plane of the meridian. This resembles a ramp 1·92 m (6 ft 4¼ in) high at its lowest point and 6·8 m (22 ft 3½ in) at its highest, pointing to the North Pole. This is used to ascertain distance from the meridian and the position of the heavenly bodies. There is a double mural quadrant, a circle of stone for ascertaining the equinox, and another ramped Samrat Yantra. The Chakra Yantra lies between two walls and is used for finding the declination of planets and stars. The adjacent Digansa Yantra measures the degrees of azimuth of a planet or star.

Mir Ghat on the nearby river front is also used by Muslims.

Down river behind Panchaganga Ghat rises the **Smaller Mosque of Aurangzeb**, also called the Madho Rai Ki Masjid or Minarets. The mosque occupies the site of an earlier temple of Vishnu, which accounts for its mixture of Hindu and Muslim details. The minarets were dismantled and reconstructed by James Prinsep in the early 19th century. There is a magnificent view of the entire city from the top. The Buddhist stupas at Sarnath can be seen in the distance.

The **Great Mosque of Aurangzeb** (late 17th century) is situated on the north-west side of the famous Gyan Kup or Well of Knowledge. It has two colossal octagonal minarets towering 70·7 m (232 ft) above the river, and was built on the site of one of the most sacred temples in Varanasi by the emperor Aurangzeb. It is a remarkable piece of masonry construction. The columns in the front of the mosque were taken from the old temple, the remains of which can still be discerned at the rear.

One of the greatest delights of Varanasi is the tortuous complex of lanes and alleys, known as the Pukka Mahals, which link the ghats to the remainder of the city. Some excellent examples of local vernacular architecture can be found here. The narrow streets are lined with picturesque domestic buildings which overhang the carriageway in the manner of the mediaeval cities of Europe.

Alamgir's Mosque (late 17th century) lies in a back lane, about 91 m (296 ft) south of the Briddhkal temple, northeast of the Municipal Gardens. The columns are of Buddhist origin.

Benares Hindu University lies on a large campus to the south of the city. It has a number of interesting secular buildings, erected since its foundation at the turn of the century. The Bharat Kala Bhavan has a splendid collection of miniature paintings and sculptures of national importance.

EASTERN INDIA

TEN

EASTERN INDIA

Bihar, Orissa, West Bengal, Sikkim, Assam, Arunachal Pradesh, Tripura and North East Frontier

Introduction

Geographically, this vast area of eastern India is a coherent region bounded on the north by the Himalayas, on the south by the Bay of Bengal and on the east by the dense jungles of Assam and Burma. Historically, the life of the region has revolved around its two great river systems, the Brahmaputra and the Ganges, which combine in the plains of Bengal to create a huge delta of rich alluvial soil and marshland that is one of the most fertile regions of the world. This unique location, with its shifting river channels, dense forests, heavy rainfall and recurrent floods, shaped the destiny of the people and had a profound impact on the art and architecture of the country.

Although isolated from the centre of Islamic civilization, the Bengal delta contains one of the greatest concentrations of Muslims in the world. It is remarkable that a territory as remote as Bengal should have been invaded and retained so early in the Islamic conquest of India, but the relentless zeal with which the faith was spread should not be underestimated.

When a renegade Turkish officer displaced the Raja of the last Hindu dynasty of Bengal in 1204, a period of continuous Muslim occupation commenced which lasted until political power was supplanted by the East India Company in the 18th century. The area had been settled and cultivated for hundreds of years, probably since the 6th century BC.

Gradually, between the 5th and 12th centuries, Brahmin communities and Buddhist monastic groups advanced from the west, promoting the intense cultivation of the lands of West Bengal.

From 1204 to 1338, when Bengal was under the sway of the Delhi Sultanate, Muslim power was centred at Lakhnauti (later **Gaur**). Eastern Bengal remained an underdeveloped frontier zone of aboriginal peoples less affected by Brahmanical society. However, the process by which Islam spread had profound consequences for the entire region.

The early chronicles are full of stories of warrior-priests (ghazis), such as Shah Jalal (d. 1346), who conquered the area and then permitted their followers to settle on the land as local leaders and cultivators. So the actual expansion of Islam was closely associated with the formation of energetic new agrarian communities led by a Muslim elite, many of whom organized the local people in land clearance and rice cultivation. Changes in the course of the river system in the Bengal delta between the 12th and 16th centuries actually helped to reinforce the Muslim position, fostering the growth of wet-rice agriculture and, with it, Islam.

Between the 15th and 17th centuries Islam was consolidated throughout the region. This was aided by two factors. From 1338 to 1576 a new dynasty of

Muslim kings asserted their independence from Delhi. Under the restored Ilyas Shah dynasty (1437–87) and the Husain Shah dynasty (1494–1539) Muslim culture flourished. The second factor was the grass-roots activity of Bengali poets and scholars, who invested the romantic tales of the Islamic tradition with the local religious symbolism of the ancient Hindu epics.

When the Muslims arrived in Bengal they brought with them a highly developed tradition and architectural vocabulary of their own. The dome, arch, minaret and other distinctive elements were already established.

The earliest Muslim monuments, built before 1410, such as the Adina Mosque at Pandua or the Victory Tower at Chota Pandua, seem to have a distinctly alien character, foreign impositions on a native culture. Conversely, many of the later monuments lacking minarets and with low domes, low façades and curved chala roofs, modelled on the thatched bamboo bungalow, exhibit an interpenetration of architectural styles and forms more suited to the peasant society of Bengal.

The heavy Bengal rains dictated the form of the early mosques in the region. They do not have open courts, the liwans, ablution tank and attached minar common elsewhere. Generally, the Bengal mosque is a compact building with a simple prayer chamber and grassy courtyard with a large tank to one side. The later Mughal mosques are fundamentally different, with either one or three domes. The most interesting feature of the Bengal style is the way in which foreign Muslim elements were transformed to the demands of local tradition, culture and climate.

This fusion of the Muslim and local vernacular traditions contributed to the evolution of a distinctive indigenous style. The local do-chala and char-chala roofs, made of thatch or bamboo, were taken by the Muslim masons and translated into effective brick or stone build-ings. The characteristic curved cornice and parapet became common from the early 15th century until they were superseded by the Imperial Mughal style.

With the break-up of the great building centre of Bengal in the late 16th century, many craftsmen emigrated to the emergent Mughal court and on to Rajasthan, bringing with their skills the distinctive characteristics of Bengali architecture. Later, these architectural features were taken up and carried right across India to **Agra, Delhi, Fatehpur Sikri** and **Udaipur**.

Locally available brick and terracotta were employed universally as building materials. Although stone was sometimes used for structural support, and occasionally for the facing of brick structures, terracotta was employed for surface decoration and ornament. The ready availability of fine alluvial clay, coupled with a long historical tradition of terracotta decoration, created an art form which occupies a unique position in the history of Islamic culture.

The Mughal conquest re-established regional links with north India. Akbar conquered Bengal in 1576, but it was over thirty years before local resistance movements were crushed and the region became a Mughal province. With the advent of Mughal rule, Bengal was brought into the mainstream of Indian political and artistic life. As a result, much of its distinct regional character was eroded. With the eastward movement of the Bengal delta and the silting up of the old river channels, the once-great cities of **Gaur** and **Pandua** declined. They were replaced by new centres of power, such as Dhaka, for instance. A new wave of Muslim nobles or ashraf moved in – soldiers, administrators and merchants reinforcing Mughal rule and the doctrines of Islam – but as an urban-based ruling class rather than as rural cultivators.

The Islamic architectural history of the region, then, can be broken into five distinct phases. The first period, from the conquest in 1204 to the transfer of the capital from **Gaur** to **Pandua** in 1340, can be seen in the surviving monuments at **Tribeni** and **Pandua**. The second stage, from 1340 to 1430, covers the period from the establishment of **Pandua** to the building of the Eklakhi tomb. The stately Adina Mosque at **Pandua**, with its innovative use of the drop arch, is from this time. The third stage, from 1442 to the Mughal conquest of 1576, represents the development of a native provincial style in which features dictated by local circumstances, such as the need for curved roofs to throw off the heavy rainfall, were adopted and then adapted as part of the Islamic architectural vocabulary. The Eklakhi tomb at **Pandua** (*c.* 1425) is an evolutionary landmark and prototype in the development of this style. The Dakhil Darwaza or triumphal arch at **Gaur** displays some of the finest surviving brickwork of the period. Although the best examples of the style are confined to Bengal, it was forceful enough to spread east into Assam. At Dimapur, for example, there is an arched gateway identical to the façades of the mosques at **Gaur** and **Pandua**. The fourth or Mughal period bequeathed a legacy of monuments that were Imperial in style but secular in nature, while the fifth, in the late 18th and 19th centuries, witnessed the spread of European influence and architecture into both religious and secular buildings. Some of the 19th-century mosques of **Calcutta**, for instance, show a strong classical European character derived from colonial architecture.

With the conquest of Bengal and the expansion of British power across the region, European forms of architecture began to make a significant impact on local styles. At **Murshidabad** the Palace of the Nawab (1835) was designed on classical lines by a British army engineer, as was the adjacent imambara, built ten years later.

With the establishment of British supremacy after the Battle of Plassey (1757), the old European trading factories of the Dutch at **Chinsura** and the French at **Chandernagore** declined in importance, replaced by the powerful new capital of British India at **Calcutta**.

Founded on the mud-flats at the mouth of the Hooghly river in 1690 by an English merchant adventurer, **Calcutta** grew steadily until in 1756 it was sacked by the Nawab of Murshidabad. With the assumption of British control, between 1780 and 1840, Calcutta grew into a magnificent 'city of palaces', the capital of British India. Mud and thatch gave way to pukka buildings of brick and stucco, designed in a variety of classical styles. Each was set in its own compound but all shared common architectural characteristics and a classical vocabulary. With greater security huge forts, such as Fort William, were superseded by spacious cantonments on the outskirts of the city, at **Barrackpore** and **Dum Dum**, for example.

Later, Bengal became a powder-keg of nationalist aspirations. To a large degree, this arose from the growth of a more conservative Islamic tradition, nurtured by contacts with Arabia and the consequent desire to liberate Bengali Islam from local Hindu and, indeed, British Imperial influence. After the defeat of the Japanese attack on India at **Kohima** and **Imphal** in the Second World War, the British withdrew and the Muslims of Bengal formed their own separate nation outside the state of India.

Above The Tomb of Fateh Khan at Gaur

Below Tomb of Sher Shah Sur, Sasaram

Above The Gola, Patna

Below The Temple of Fame at Barrackpore

Right Tomb of Job Charnock, Calcutta

Above La Martinière School, Calcutta

Below St John's Church, Calcutta

Right Park Street Cemetery, Calcutta

Left The Victoria Memorial, Calcutta

Below The Ochterlony Memorial or Shahid Minar, Calcutta

Right St Paul's Cathedral, Calcutta

Left The Law Courts, Calcutta

Above The Old Silver Mint, Calcutta

Below View of Darjeeling

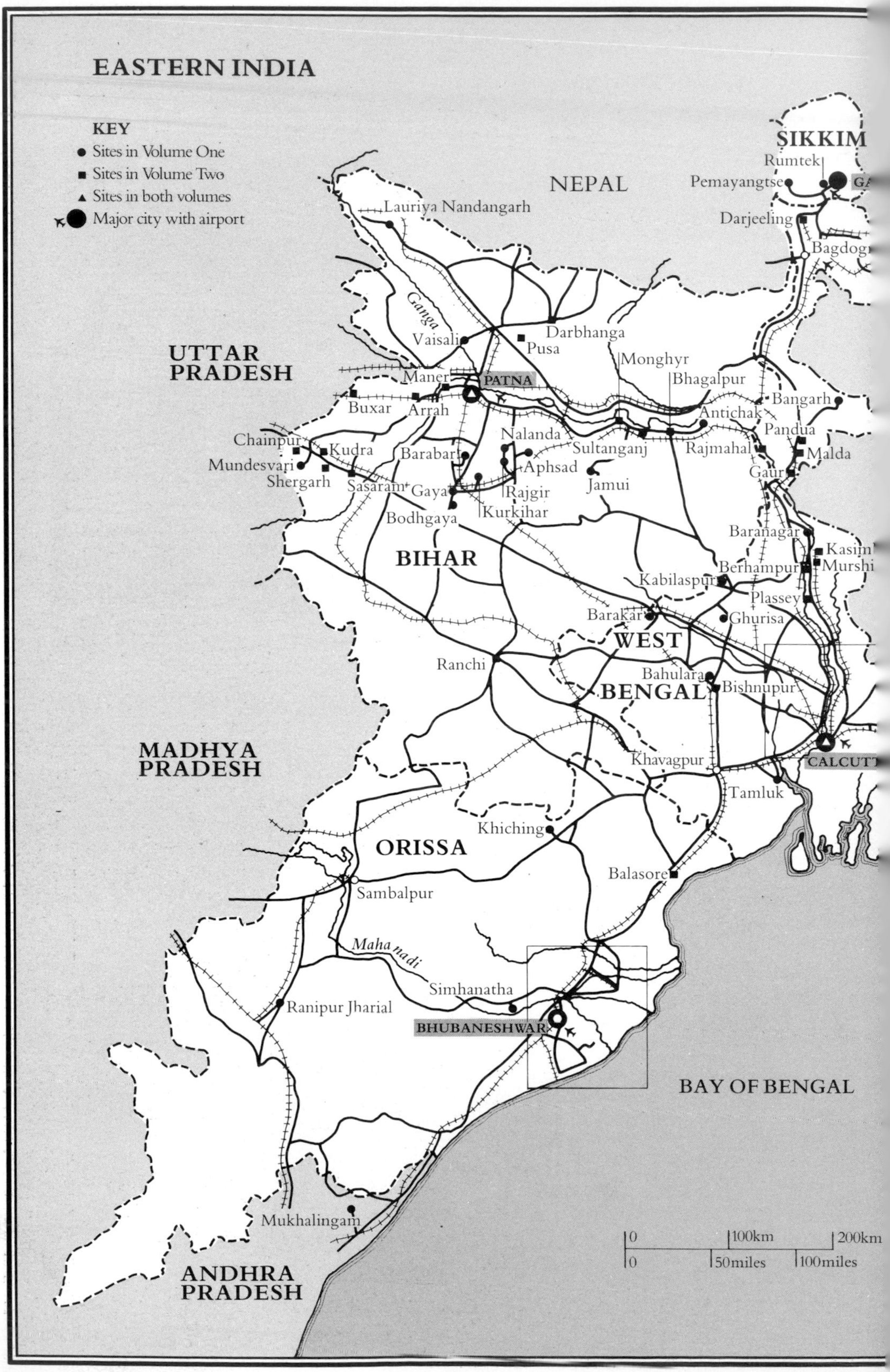

EASTERN INDIA

KEY
- Sites in Volume One
- Sites in Volume Two
- Sites in both volumes
- Major city with airport

NEPAL

SIKKIM

Rumtek
Pemayangtse
Darjeeling
GA
Bagdog

Lauriya Nandangarh

Ganga

UTTAR
PRADESH

Vaisali
Darbhanga
Pusa
Monghyr
Bhagalpur
Bangarh

Maner
PATNA

Buxar
Arrah

Antichak
Pandua

Chainpur
Kudra
Barabar
Nalanda
Sultanganj
Rajmahal
Malda

Mundesvari
Aphsad
Jamui
Gaur

Shergarh
Sasaram
Gaya
Rajgir
Kurkihar

Bodhgaya

BIHAR

Baranagar
Kasim
Murshi

Kabilaspur
Berhampur

Barakar
Plassey
Ghurisa

WEST

Ranchi

Bahulara
Bishnupur

BENGAL

MADHYA
PRADESH

Khavagpur
CALCUTT

Tamluk

Khiching

ORISSA

Balasore

Sambalpur

Maha nadi

Simhanatha

Ranipur Jharial

BHUBANESHWAR

BAY OF BENGAL

Mukhalingam

| 0 | 100km | 200km |
| 0 | 50miles | 100miles |

ANDHRA
PRADESH

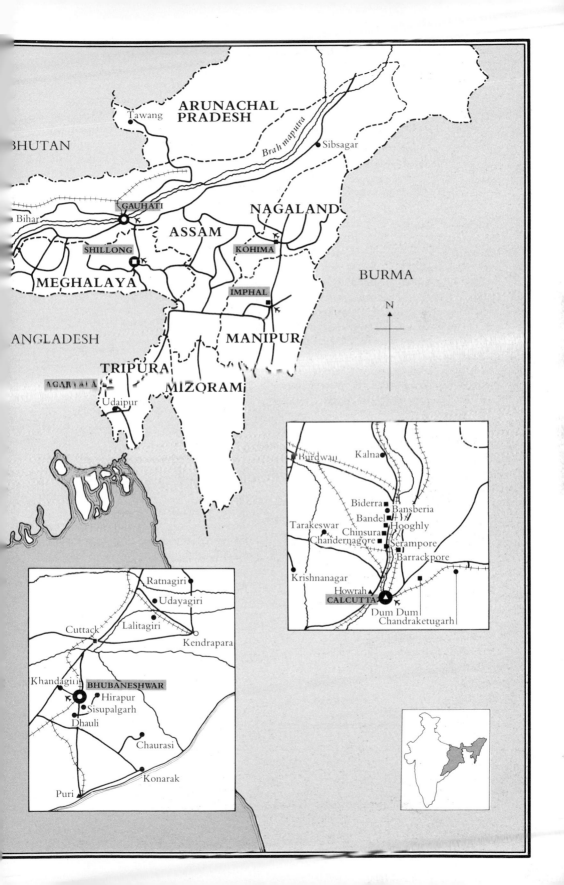

AGARTALA

Old Agartala was the residence of the local Rajas until 1844, when the capital moved to the new town of Agartala, 6·4 km (4 miles) away, now the capital of the state of Tripura, on the remote eastern border with Bangladesh and Burma.

The ruins of the old palace still stand, surrounded by decaying monuments to the ruling dynasty, but in places later buildings have been erected on the foundations of the old.

The **Ujjayanta Palace** (early 20th century) was designed by Sir Alexander Martin and Sir R. N. Mukherji in a mixed European and Mughal style after the old palace was damaged by an earthquake. Situated in a large 28-hectare (70 acres) park landscaped on Mughal lines, the palace is approached via a broad stone staircase above which a huge domed centrepiece rises from an octagonal drum. Inside are a whole series of reception rooms, durbar halls and banqueting suites. The palace was built as a museum to house the fine collection of paintings and manuscripts acquired by the family.

In 1932 the Maharaja Bir Bikram Singh Kishore built the **Neer Mahal Summer Palace**, a romantic series of walkways and kiosks in the centre of Lake Sonamura, for his wife, who was missing her home in Udaipur. It was abandoned in 1944 when the water level of the lake dropped. The **Kunjaban Palace**, on a hilltop to the north of the town, was a favourite retreat of the Bengali poet Rabindranath Tagore.

ARRAH

Situated close to the confluence of the Ganges and Son rivers, Arrah was the scene of heroic exploits during the fighting in 1857.

The historical associations focus on the famous **Little House at Arrah**, which is now an historical monument in the grounds of the Judge's House. It is a simple square, two-storey building with an arcaded verandah to three sides, but from 27 July to 3 August 1857 it was held by twelve Englishmen and fifty Sikhs for over a week against 2,000 sepoys from Dinapore and a large body of local rioters. The stoical British resistance stirred the imaginations and hearts of many contemporaries and secured a unique place in British military history.

In the church there are two memorials to the Mutiny. Look for the one which commemorates Captain the Hon. Edward Plantagenet Robinhood Hastings (d. 17 October 1857).

East of the Treasury and Rauna Road is a memorial to the officers, non-commissioned officers and men of HM 35th Regiment who fell in action in the Shahabad district on 23 April 1858.

BALASORE

Balasore (literally Bal-eswara or the Young Lord, i.e. Krishna) lies 231 km (144 miles) south of Calcutta on the route to Madras. Once a place of considerable commercial importance, it was one of the earliest English settlements in India.

In 1636 Mr Gabriel Broughton, surgeon of the ship *Hopewell*, cured the emperor's daughter, whose clothes had caught fire, and later in 1640 successfully treated one of the ladies of the zenana. He obtained as a reward the right for the English to establish a maritime station in Bengal. In 1634 the first factory was established at Pippli (Philip's City) but in 1642 it transferred to Balasore, to be joined by rival Dutch, Danish and French factories. Later, the port silted up and was superseded by Calcutta.

In a small compound near the town are some fine early Dutch tombs, built in 1683 in the form of three-sided pyramids 6 m (20 ft) high.

BANDEL

1·6 km (1 mile) north of Hooghly is Bandel, a railway junction renowned for the spectacular Jubilee Bridge, a cantilevered structure 370 m (1,213 ft) long, built by the engineer Bradford Leslie in 1887.

Bandel is an early European settlement containing what is alleged to be the oldest Christian church in Bengal. A Portuguese monastery and church were built here by Augustinian friars in 1599, but the original church was demolished in 1640 by the emperor Shah Jahan and it was not reinstated until 1660, by John Gomez de Soto. The **Church of Our Lady of the Rosary** incorporates an original keystone dated 1599 and lies on a north-south axis, with the altar at the north end. At the west corner of the south end is a low tower, south of which is a niche, beneath which stands a statue of the Virgin and Child, Our Lady of Happy Voyages, to which miraculous powers are attributed. Beneath is a model of a fully rigged ship. On the south side are some fine cloisters. To the east is a priory and St Augustine's Hall, added in 1820.

Outside, in a small enclosure at the south end of the church, stands the mast of an old Portuguese Indiaman, reputedly erected by a grateful sea captain in 1655 as a thanks' offering for deliverance from a storm.

The **Circuit House**, once the residence of the Dacoity Commissioner, is also of interest.

BARRACKPORE *Map overleaf*

Barrackpore, once the summer residence of the British Governors-General, lies 24 km (15 miles) to the north of Calcutta, on the banks of the Hooghly river opposite the former Danish colony of Seram-

pore. It was founded as a cantonment in 1775 and rapidly became one of the most important in India. The layout is typical, with broad avenues of detached bungalows, each set in its own garden compound. Some of the bungalows are original and there are a variety of attractive neo-classical styles. Marquess Wellesley (elder brother of the Duke of Wellington) began to build a summer retreat here, but it was never completed. The long avenue of mature trees lining the road from Calcutta is the only vestige of Wellesley's original grandiose vision of a continuous processional route from the city. There are a number of interesting buildings and monuments, but access is restricted.

Government House was designed by Captain Thomas Anbury in 1813. The main north façade is enriched with an octastyle Tuscan entrance portico and shallow pediment. Colonnaded verandahs enclose the other three sides. The house was never spacious. Guests were accommodated in a series of bungalows dispersed around the park. It is now a police hospital and the large first-floor drawing-room is a typhoid ward. Once the greatest delight was its setting by the Hooghly river, but the beautifully landscaped gardens are now sadly overgrown and the building is dilapidated. An exotic menagerie was established here in the 1820s, but no trace now remains of the neo-classical pavilions and Gothic aviaries which Bishop Heber encountered. The marble fountain and basin situated close to the house once formed part of the Mughal baths at Agra and were imported by Lord Hastings. A number of other interesting monuments remain.

The **Temple of Fame** (1813), by Captain George Rodney Blane, stands between the main house and Commander-in-Chief's bungalow. It resembles an elegant Greek temple, embellished with hexastyle Corinthian porticos at each end and colonnades to the flanks. It was built by the Earl of Minto to commemorate the

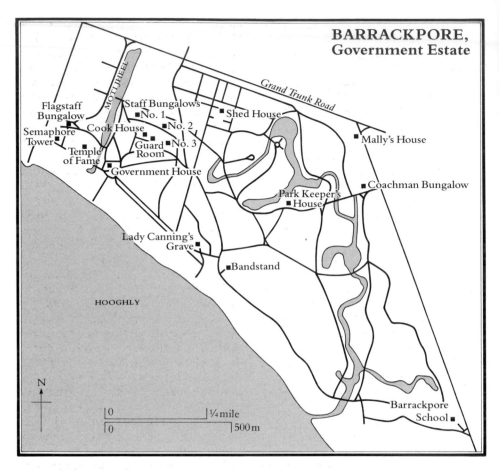

soldiers who fell in the conquest of Java and Mauritius between 1810 and 1811. The memorial chamber is a simple barrel vault with four black commemorative plaques and an inscription over the entrance: 'To the Memory of the Brave'. A later tablet erected in 1843 commemorates the Gwalior Campaign. Around the building are discarded statues of King George V, Peel, Minto, Mayo, Lansdowne, Roberts, Woodburn and Napier of Magdala, relocated here by the Calcutta authorities.

Lady Canning's Grave should be seen. Lady Charlotte Canning died of fever at Barrackpore on 18 November 1861. She was interred beside the River Hooghly in the gardens she did so much to enhance. Her grave lies in a small enclosure, with ironwork designed from the intertwined initials of her name, C. C. The distinctive memorial, crowned by the Cross of St Andrew, is a replica; the original, by George Gilbert Scott, was relocated to the north portico of St John's Church, Calcutta. In a touching gesture the equestrian statue of her husband, Lord Canning, was moved here from Calcutta after independence and placed beside her grave.

Nearby is the famous banyan tree from which the first sepoy mutineer, Mangal Pande, was hanged in March 1857.

Semaphore Tower (*c.* 1820) is immediately adjacent to the former Flagstaff Bungalow. It is a local landmark, an old circular semaphore tower, crowned by a small ball, one of a chain of signal stations once used for communicating rapidly up river before the advent of the electric telegraph.

Several **Staff Bungalows** were built in 1863. To the west of Government House lies Flagstaff Bungalow, originally occupied by the Private Secretary and later by the Commander-in-Chief. To the north are three other bungalows of a similar date and style, which replaced some earlier 'Swiss Cottages'. In the grounds of the bungalow once occupied by Lord Kitchener is a garden memorial to the horse Myall King, three times winner of the Calcutta Cup, who died dramatically on the Calcutta racecourse in 1893.

The **Parade Ground** at Barrackpore is famous as the first scene in the terrible chapter of events of 1857. The mutinous 19th Regiment were disbanded here and ten days later, on 29 March, the rebellious Mangal Pande ran amok.

Close to the Parade Ground is **St Bartholomew's Church**, opened in 1831, consecrated in 1847 and altered in 1868, when the tower, chancel, verandahs and western porch were added in a crude classical style reminiscent of Soane's primitivist order. The font in the transept was the gift of Lord Ellenborough.

There are some interesting monuments, including one to Major Arthur William Fitzroy Somerset, who died in the Sikh War of 1845, and another to Frederick Sherwood Taylor, who was 'overwhelmed' by the dreadful landslip at Naini Tal in 1880. The **Old Cemetery** has many military graves.

BERHAMPUR

As one of the earliest English cantonments in India, Berhampur is of considerable interest. Located 8 km (5 miles) from the old city of Murshidabad, the town was selected for the site of a military barracks as early as October 1757, just after the Battle of Plassey, in order to guard against any future rebellion by the Nawab. By the early 19th century it had grown into a large brigade station of significance. In 1857 it witnessed the first act of overt mutiny when incensed sepoys of the 19th Native Infantry rose in rebellion against their British officers, but the situation was defused by the tactful intervention of their commanding officer.

The cantonment layout repays careful study. The old British camp lies between two Indian villages and the whole area is characterized by a grid pattern of streets and ditches interspersed with large tanks, which were designed to serve a defensive purpose. The focus of the cantonment is a large regular barrack square around which are disposed quarters for officers and soldiers in a symmetrical form. On the far side of the Lal Digee, the largest tank, lies the Catholic Chapel, beyond which are more tanks and the racecourse. Large old European residencies for civilians lie towards the Indian village. The former European hospital is close to the river.

The layout demonstrates the strict segregation of officers and men, not just with separate quarters but even with their own cemeteries. The troops were finally withdrawn by Lord Kitchener in 1906.

Within the town the principal buildings are the Town Hall, Jubilee Hospital and Kalikot College. The **Old Cemetery** has some interesting memorials.

BHAGALPUR

Chief town, cantonment and headquarters of the district which bears its name, Bhagalpur is a small town about 3·2 km (2 miles) long on the south bank of the Ganges, 426 km (265 miles) by rail from Calcutta.

Akbar's troops passed through here in 1573 and 1575. The town and district are littered with Muslim monuments and ruins. Within the town are two **Monuments to Augustus Cleveland**, the local Collector who organized the Bhagalpur Hill Rangers, an auxiliary force which pacified the entire area of the Santal Parganas in the 1780s. The massive brick monument was raised by grateful local landowners; the stone monument, by the Court of Directors of the East India Company, as a mark of their recognition of his services.

BIDERRA

This small town, between the old Dutch settlement at Chinsura and the French colony at Chandernagore, was the scene of a decisive British victory over the Dutch on 25 November 1759. Although technically not at war, Clive wrote a memorable letter instructing Colonel Forde to fight first and to worry about the order afterwards.

BURDWAN

Burdwan is an interesting old town in Bengal, located 107 km (67 miles) from Calcutta. It is the chief town of the district and the residence of the Maharajas of Burdwan, a leading Bengali family which held high office in the Bengal Executive Council in the 1920s.

Thara Palace (19th century; altered) is a fine edifice with extensive gardens and an excellent collection of pictures, including works by Chinnery, Tilly Kettle and the Daniells. Many of the rooms are furnished and treated in European style.

At the entrance to the town is the **Star of India Arch**, built to mark Lord Curzon's visit in the early 1900s.

The **Dargah of Pir Bahram** (1606) is designed in typical regional style, with engaged octagonal corner turrets, a curved cornice and a single dome. The

Jami Masjid (1699) has seven simple arches to the east façade, which is crowned by three central domes and two char-chala vaults at each end. Small arched doors on the west side of the verandah lead to an austere prayer chamber.

The **Tomb Complex of Khwaja Anwar-i-Shahid** (*c*. 1698) is highly picturesque. The tomb stands in a large compound entered through a gateway in the south wall. On either side it is flanked by rectangular wings, one a mosque and the other a madrasa, each with a steeply pitched do-chala roof. The façade of the tomb is enriched with incised stucco patterns and cusped recessed niches.

BUXAR

A place of Hindu pilgrimage located on the Ganges about 117 km (73 miles) up river from Patna, Buxar was the scene of a great victory won by Sir Hector Munro against the combined forces of Shah Alam, Shuja-ud-Daula and Mir Qasim on 23 October 1764. The battle consolidated English supremacy in Bengal, after Clive's earlier victory at Plassey in 1757. Munro turned an impending defeat into a brilliant tactical victory, capturing the entire enemy camp and over 160 guns, but with severe loss to his own minute forces. Over 816 British were killed or wounded.

CALCUTTA

Calcutta was founded on insalubrious mud flats beside the River Hooghly by the English merchant Job Charnock in 1690. From this initial toe-hold, the settlement grew to become the capital of British India and, after London, the second city of the Empire.

In its heyday it was called the city of palaces, and it still retains a fine heritage of 18th- and 19th-century buildings,

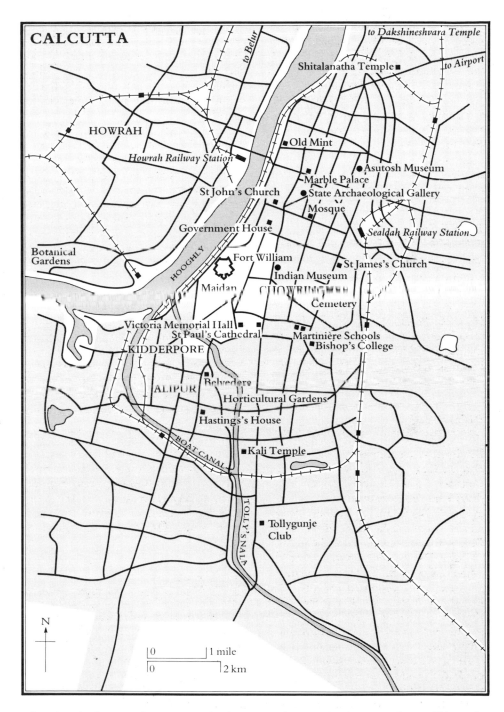

CALCUTTA

often in a bad state of repair. By the late 19th century darker associations of urban squalor began to predominate, popular-ized in Kipling's *City of Dreadful Night*. However, although Calcutta has become a byword for social deprivation and overcrowding, it is something of a surprise for the visitor to discover the fascinating legacy of colonial architecture which survives to give the city its distinctly British mould.

The original settlement was centred on Old Fort William, which lay to the north of its present site, roughly between the current General Post Office Building and the river. After the sack of Calcutta and the notorious incident of the Black Hole in 1756, when Clive recaptured the city, a new fort was laid out at enormous cost. The entire area around the fortifications was cleared to create an open field of fire, and this vast open space or Maidan became the focus for the subsequent development of the city.

Northern Section

Many of the principal historic buildings and monuments are to be found in the northern section of the city, between Eden Gardens and Howrah Bridge. All can be visited easily on foot at a leisurely pace.

The suggested route may be varied at will but begins at the junction of Council House Street and Hastings Street at **St John's Church** (1787). Modelled on the design of St Martin-in-the-Fields, London, St John's was formerly the cathedral church. It was designed by Lieutenant James Agg. The stone steeple has a dumpy, compressed appearance, the entire fourth tier having been omitted, owing to the weight of stone on the treacherous foundations. Originally at the east end, the main entrance was moved to the west front in 1797, when a carriage porch was added. Further alterations were carried out in 1811, including the addition of colonnaded verandahs to the north and south sides to reduce glare and of Corinthian capitals to the Doric columns in the nave. The original galleries were removed in 1901.

Inside are a number of fine memorials, including a marble tablet by John Bacon Jr, to Major James Achilles Kirkpatrick, the Resident at Hyderabad (1789–1805). Other distinguished examples include those to Major George Cruttenden and John Adam by Richard Westmacott. Bishop Middleton, first Bishop of Calcutta, is interred at the east end of the nave. The former altar piece, a picture of the Last Supper by Johann Zoffany (1733–1810), depicts famous Calcutta residents in the guise of the Apostles. It is now in the south aisle. Under the north portico lies Lady Canning's original tomb, by George Gilbert Scott (1861), relocated from Barrackpore, where a replica now stands.

The **Churchyard** is well worth close inspection as there are numerous fine historical monuments here.

Especially noteworthy is the **Rohilla Monument** (1817), a domed cenotaph based on Sir William Chambers's Temple of Aeolus at Kew. It has twelve Doric columns carrying a frieze enriched with triglyphs, shields and bucrania (rams' skulls). It commemorates the dead of the Rohilla War of 1794.

The **Tomb of Job Charnock** (c.1695) is one of the earliest surviving British monuments in India, surrounded by over thirty early tombstones. It comprises an octagonal pavilion crowned by a serrated parapet and kiosk. The tomb is built of gneiss from Pallavaram near Madras, decorated with horizontal ribs. Inside are four raised tombstones. One is dedicated to **Surgeon William Hamilton** (1717), who cured the Mughal emperor Farrukhsiyar of venereal disease and as a result won extensive trading rights for the East India Company in Bengal.

Nearby is **Admiral Watson's Tomb** (c. 1757), crowned by a large obelisk, which was relocated within the churchyard in 1983. There is a monument to his memory in Westminster Abbey. A white domed classical pavilion covers the **Tomb of Begum Johnson** (1812), matriarch of Calcutta society. In the western corner lies a marble **monument** (1902) to the Black Hole of Calcutta which originally stood at the western end of Writers' Building in Dalhousie Square. It replaced an earlier structure erected in 1782, but was removed here on independence. The **Grave of Lord Brabourne** (d. 1939) lies nearby.

Immediately to the north of the churchyard, in Hare Street, is the **Small Causes Court** (1878), by William H. White in a French Palladian style. It has unusual locally carved Ionic capitals, which more closely resemble intertwined dolphins and serpents

At the junction of Hare Street and Strand Road stands **Metcalfe Hall** (1840–44), now partially obscured by a high wall. The west front is based on the Tower of the Winds in Athens. It was designed in handsome Greek Revival style by C. K. Robison, the City Magistrate, for the Agricultural and Horticultural Society and Calcutta Public Library.

A short walk south to Esplanade Row West leads to the **High Court** (1872), by Walter Granville (1819–74). It is the most important Gothic building in the city. Based on George Gilbert Scott's designs for the Hamburg Rathaus and inspired by the great mediaeval Cloth Hall at Ypres, the High Court is an impressive arcaded structure set around a central courtyard. The ground floor arcade is faced in Barakur sandstone with elaborate carved capitals of Caen stone. The central tower was modified owing to subsidence, but the whole complex, linked by high-level, arcaded Gothic bridges, is delightful.

In the main entrance beneath the tower is Chantrey's statue of Sir Edward Hyde East, who was Chief Justice from 1813 to 1822.

East of the High Court lies the **Town Hall** (1813), by Colonel John Garstin, recently threatened with demolition but now reprieved. A handsome Tuscan-Doric portico faces the street and a similar portico on the north side acts as a carriage entrance. It is one of the most accomplished classical buildings of the period.

Beyond is **Government House** (1799–1802), residence of the British Governors-General and Viceroys until 1911, now renamed Raj Bhavan and the official residence of the Governor of Bengal. It stands at the north end of the Maidan, and it was the focus of the entire development of Calcutta.

The design, by Captain Charles Wyatt (1758–1819), is based on Kedleston Hall, Derbyshire, built by Robert Adam between 1759 and 1770. The house, set in a large garden compound, is well adapted to the climate. The entrances, enriched with four monumental, neo-classical gateways, crowned with sphinxes and lions, set the fashion for British government houses and residencies throughout India. Access is restricted, but externally the main features can be seen from the surrounding roads. It comprises a central block with quadrant corridors linked to four corner wings. There is a domed bow to the garden frontage and a pedimented portico to the north. The dome was added in 1814. Numerous martial trophies lie in the grounds, including a huge iron gun mounted on a winged dragon, captured from Nanking, and two brass cannon from Afghanistan.

The interior is striking for there is no grand central staircase. The north front gives access to the Breakfast or Tiffin Room, which has a screen of columns at either end. This is linked to the Throne Room on the south front by the spectacular Marble Hall. Above this lies the Ballroom, with later coffered ceilings by H. H. Locke (1865) and a splendid series of lustres and chandeliers from Claude Martin's mausoleum-palace at Constantia, Lucknow. The Viceroy's private

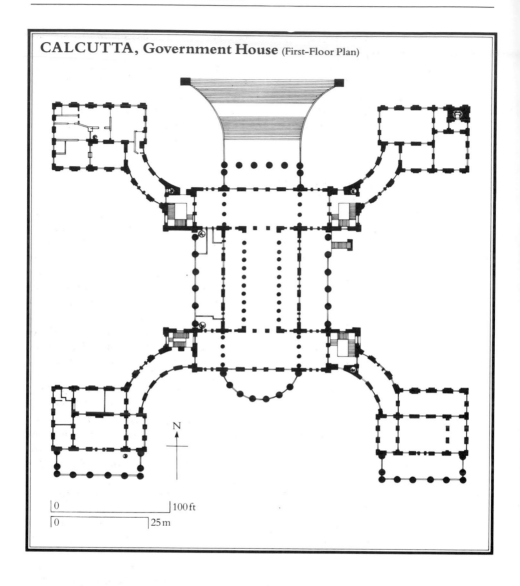

CALCUTTA, Government House (First-Floor Plan)

0 — 100 ft
0 — 25 m

apartments were in the southern wings.

On the east side of Government House, Old Court House Street leads north past the Great Eastern Hotel towards Dalhousie Square, which has a large central tank constructed in 1712. Closing the vista down Old Court House Street is **St Andrew's Kirk** (1818), built by Messrs Burn, Currie & Co. Like St John's, which it was designed to upstage, it is based on James Gibbs's St Martin-in-the-Fields in London, but it is more

successful. It is a good example of how new civic buildings were planned and located for maximum visual effect, a reflection of growing Imperial and civic pride.

East of the square in Mission Row lies the **Old Mission Church** or Lal Girja (1770), which was founded by the Swedish missionary Johann Zachariah Kiernander. Inside are a window presented by his grandson and many interesting mural tablets. Mission Row is one of the oldest surviving streets in Calcutta. Several houses carry memorial plaques to former occupants, including Sir John Clavering and Colonel Monson, members of Warren Hastings's council.

Dalhousie Square lies in the heart of the area once covered by the original Fort William before the new fort was erected to the south between 1757 and 1770.

The entire north side of the square is occupied by **Writers' Building**. This enormous edifice was refaced in 1880 with terracotta dressings, reflecting Victorian Imperial and civic pride, but the refacing conceals a much earlier structure, built by Thomas Lyon in 1780 as the mercantile headquarters of the East India Company, where the Company's writers were housed.

Holwell's original memorial to the Black Hole and Curzon's later replacement (now in St John's Churchyard) once stood immediately to the west. A small obelisk on the pavement commemorates Coleworthy Grant, founder of the Calcutta Society for the Prevention of Cruelty to Animals in 1881.

On the west side of the square is the **General Post Office** (1864–8). This monumental building stands on the actual site of the Black Hole. Huge rusticated pylons are linked by Corinthian colonnades to a curved, colonnaded corner bay crowned by an impressive dome. It is Walter Granville's best classical composition.

Netaji Subhas Road in the north-west corner of the square leads north, past the **East Indian Railway Offices** (late 19th century), a colossal Italianate structure occupying an entire street block and designed by R. Roskell Bayne. The principal cornice is copied from the Palazzo Farnese in Rome. The two corner pavilions are decorated with Italian sgraffito work. Four mural panels depict Architecture, Sculpture, Music and Commerce. The iron floor trusses and columns are made from worn-out rails. The main floors have tesselated marble pavements – a highly inventive and unusual building.

Nearby is the **Royal Exchange** (1916), by T. S. Gregson, an eloquent composition resembling a London bank, with paired Corinthian columns in antis and a crisply detailed attic storey, unfortunately impaired by an advertising hoarding.

Other notable commercial buildings include Gillander House, by H. S. Goodhart Rendel, the Chartered Bank and the National Bank of India.

In Armenian Street, close to the Howrah Bridge, is the oldest church in Calcutta. The **Armenian Church of Holy Nazareth** (1724) has a tombstone from 1630 in the churchyard. The Church was designed by an Armenian from Persia named Gawand. In 1790 Catchick Arrakiel built the adjoining clergyhouse and added a clock to the steeple. Slightly to the east is the **Roman Catholic Cathedral** (1797), the Portuguese Church of our Lady of the Rosary.

Continuing northward, Strand Road North leads beyond Howrah Bridge to the old **Silver Mint** (1824–31). This splendid Greek Revival complex of buildings is now sadly dilapidated. Designed by Major W. N. Forbes (1796–1855), it stands on a high platform with a pedimented central portico copied in half-size from the Temple of Athena in Athens. Opposite is the **Mint Master's House** (1820s), a delightful bungalow also in Greek Revival style.

Beyond the Mint in Strand Road North is the **Mayo Hospital** (1874), designed by T. A. Osmond and built by Mackintosh, Burn & Co.

Howrah Bridge, a civic landmark, is the only connection across the river. It was designed by Hubert Shirley-Smith and erected in 1943 to replace an earlier pontoon bridge constructed by Sir Bradford Leslie in 1874. The vast, single, cantilever span is over 457 m (1,500 ft) long and it dwarfs the entire area. The bridge leads to **Howrah Station** (1900–08). This enormous railway terminus

291

was designed by the gifted English Arts and Crafts architect Halsey Ricardo (1854–1928). Eight square towers articulate the red brick frontage, which has Oriental and Romanesque nuances.

From here a tonga or horse-drawn landau can be obtained for the journey back to the centre in true Victorian style.

A short detour can be made on the return journey along Mahatma Gandhi Road past the **Nakhoda Mosque** (1942). Modelled on the tomb of Akbar at Sikandra near Agra, this massive red sandstone and marble mosque is crowned by two minarets, 46 m (150 ft) high, and a huge onion-shaped dome. The choice of a Mughal style was probably an expression of rising Muslim nationalism.

In a narrow congested lane to the north of the mosque, off Chittaranjan Avenue, is the extraordinary **Marble Palace** (1835), a decaying treasure-house of paintings, sculpture and *objets d'art*, including pictures by Rubens and Sir Joshua Reynolds. To locate it, a guide is essential. It was built by Raja Rajendra Mullick Bahadur and has remained in the Mullick family ever since, an enormous repository of porcelain, lustres, gewgaws and antiques chaotically displayed in mouldering profusion.

Central Section

This comprises the Maidan, Fort William and the area immediately to the east, known as Chowringhee. The resemblance of the Maidan to Hyde Park in London is still striking, 160 years after Bishop Heber first remarked on the similarities when approaching this 'city of palaces' in 1823.

Fort William is one of the most impressive examples of European fortification in the East. Roughly octagonal in shape, with six principal gates, it was designed by Captain John Brohier in 1757. It took thirteen years to complete at a staggering cost of over £2 million. It

replaced old Fort William, which lay slightly to the north. Modelled on Vauban's 17th-century defensive concepts, the work was finished by Archibald Campbell after Brohier was charged with fraud and absconded from custody. The construction of the Fort altered the whole plan of Calcutta and generated a wave of rebuilding. A huge open space, the

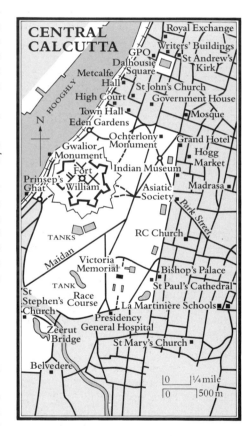

Maidan, was cleared to give an unrestricted field of fire. Excellent views of the outer ramparts and the fosse may be obtained from the Maidan, which, with its numerous tanks, offers a pleasant retreat with shaded walks and distant vistas of Government House and the Victoria Memorial.

292

The Fort is occupied by the army. Access is restricted but it can be arranged by appointment. **St Peter's Church** (1826) forms a picturesque centrepiece to the Fort. It is now a library. The barrack buildings are typical of the period: long, three-storey blocks, plainly detailed in a classical style and faced in chunam. The **Outram Institute** (late 18th century), formerly the Fort House, is notable as one of the former residences of the Governor-General prior to the erection of Government House in 1803, after which it was used by state guests and the commanding officer.

Outside the Fort on the river frontage is **Prinsep's Ghat**, an Ionic pavilion erected to commemorate James Prinsep, the antiquarian and Orientalist. To the south is the war memorial of the Indian Lascars of Bengal and Assam. To the north, opposite the Water Gate, is the **Gwalior Monument** (1847), designed by Colonel Goodwyn. Faced in Jaipur marble and crowned by a cupola made from the bronze of enemy guns, it is a two-storey, octagonal affair raised by Lord Ellenborough. The inner sarcophagus is inscribed with names of the fallen. Further north, beyond Outram's Ghat, is **Babu's Ghat**, a handsome Doric colonnade erected by Raj Chandra Das. Beyond that lies Chandpal Ghat, once the official landing-place of the Governor-General, Commander-in-Chief and Supreme Court Judges.

East of Strand Road, between Babu's Ghat and Chandpal Ghat, lies **Eden Gardens**, bequeathed by Emily and Fanny Eden, daughters of Lord Auckland. Part of the area is occupied by the Calcutta Stadium, home of Test cricket. In the garden area is a small lake, beside which lies the **Burmese Pagoda**, seized during the First Burmese War, dismantled and re-erected in 1854 as an exotic war memorial.

Eden Gardens Road curves northward towards Government House compound, where glimpses of the south front may be caught between the mature perimeter foliage. To the east lies the **Ochterlony Monument** or Sahid Minar (1828), designed by C. K. Robison and completed by J. P. Parker. The monument, commemorating General Sir David Ochterlony, victor of the Nepal War (1814–16), is an extraordinary fluted Greek Doric column, 46·3 m (152 ft) high, standing on an Egyptian-style plinth and crowned by a metal cupola of Turkish origin. At the top are two narrow viewing platforms from which spectacular views of the city can be obtained. Access is not usually possible. **Curzon Gardens**, immediately to the north, were laid out by Lord Curzon on the plan of the Union Jack.

Beyond Curzon Gardens, in Chowringhee Square, lies one of the four Islamic monuments of Calcutta. It is one of three mosques built by descendants of the great Tipu Sultan of Mysore. All three buildings share an unusual combination of European, classical and traditional Islamic styles.

Tipu Sultan's Mosque (1842) is the third in the series, built by his son Muhammad. It is based on a slightly earlier prototype, the mosque of Ghulam Muhammad in the suburb of Tollygunge (1835–43). The interior has a strong European flavour, with Tuscan colonnettes and classical rather than Islamic details. Externally, semicircular window openings and fan-shaped motifs, derived from Robert Adam's neo-classical works, recur. The corner turrets, inlaid with shallow niches, soar high over the multi-domed roof.

Chowringhee Road, running southward from the square, forms the eastern boundary of the Maidan. The elegant interior of the **Grand Hotel**, one of the most fashionable in the city, facing the Ochterlony Monument, is hidden behind an understated classical façade. At the rear, in Surendraneth Banerjee Road, are the Municipal Offices, designed by W. Banks Gwyther.

Behind the Grand Hotel, in Lindsay Street, lies **Hogg Market** named after

Sir Stuart Hogg. It is a ramshackle market building with a Gothic clocktower, corrugated iron roofs and fretwork timber valances, resembling a provincial English railway station. Unwelcome redevelopment threatens. Beyond, in Wellesley Street, stand the **Calcutta Madrasa**, a Muslim college founded in 1780 by Warren Hastings and, in Wellesley Square, the **Scottish Church**.

Back in Chowringhee Road is the **Indian Museum**, opposite the Monohar Das Tank, excavated in 1793. The Museum, on the corner of Sudder Street, is one of the best in India, with an enormous collection of geological, archaeological and zoological artefacts. The building was designed in 1875 by Walter Granville around a central quadrangle enclosed by galleries of Ionic columns. (For more specific details of the collections, and in particular of the fine Graeco–Buddhist sculptures from Gandhara, and the temples in the city see Volume I).

At the corner of Park Street is the **Royal Asiatic Society of Bengal**, in a partially demolished building. Founded by Sir William ('Oriental') Jones, linguist, classicist, judge and polymath, in January 1784, it was the forerunner of a series of learned societies which became a notable feature of the British presence in Asia. It predates the Royal Asiatic Society of London (1834) by fifty years. The library has over 15,000 volumes, including Arabic and Persian manuscripts from the library of Tipu Sultan, as well as Burmese, Sanskrit, Tibetan and other rare documents. The house was designed by Captain Lock in 1805 and completed in 1806 by the French builder Jean–Jacques Picher.

Park Street leads south-east to the Lower Circular Road. On the south side, in Middleton Row, are a number of well-preserved Calcutta town houses of the late 18th and early 19th century, of a type which gave the city its soubriquet 'City of Palaces'. The **Convent of Our Lady of**

Loretto was once the home of Henry Vansittart, Governor of Bengal (1760–64), and also of Sir Elijah Impey, first Chief Justice of the Supreme Court (1774–82). St Thomas's Roman Catholic Church (1841) stands close by. The **Royal Calcutta Turf Club** (1820) was formerly the home of the Apcar family, shipping magnates. Such houses demonstrate the first stage in the adaptation of European classical styles to an Indian context, with pedimented verandahs, portes-cochères and exaggerated intercolumniation. Once common in Chowringhee, Alipur and other areas, many have been demolished or are submerged beneath the sprawl of the central business district, but here and there ornamental gateways, boundary walls and peeling stucco façades reveal vestiges of original fabric.

At the eastern end of Park Street lies the **Cemetery**, an essential part of any itinerary. For a true understanding of life in the days of the East India Company, the surviving Georgian houses in Chowringhee and nearby Park Street Cemetery are a must. Recently restored under the aegis of the British Association for Cemeteries in South Asia, Park Street resembles an Imperial city of the dead. Pyramids, catafalques, pavilions and obelisks, some of colossal scale, lie thickly concentrated behind the perimeter walls in one of the finest repositories of neo-classical funerary sculpture outside Europe. With restoration, some of the air of melancholic desolation has now vanished. Action was essential but it came too late to save many sepulchral monuments. Noteworthy tombs include the huge pyramid **Tomb of Elizabeth Barwell**, the neo-classical **Pavilion to Major-General John Garstin**, architect of the Town Hall, Calcutta, and the Gola, Patna, and the famous spiral **Monument to Rose Aylmer**, carrying a later inscription by the poet Walter Savage Landor. For many in 18th-century Calcutta, life was just two monsoons.

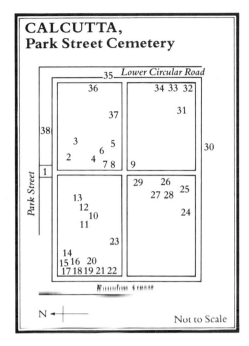

CALCUTTA, Park Street Cemetery

Lower Circular Road

N ← Not to Scale

KEY

1 Entrance Porch
2 Tomb of Charles Short (1785)
3 Tomb of Lieutenant-Colonel James Lillyman (1774)
4 Tomb of Mary Bowers (1781)
5 The Remfry Mausoleum
6 Tomb of B. Crisp (1811)
7 Tomb of Captain Edward Cooke, RN (1799)
8 Tomb of Captain W. Mackay (1804)
9 Tomb of Rose Aylmer (1800)

10 Tomb of Lieutenant-Colonel Charles Russell Deare (1790)
11 Tomb of Richard Becher (1782)
12 Tomb of Colonel Thomas Deane Pearce (1789)
13 Tomb of Rev. Dr John Christian Diemer (1792)
14 Tomb of Major-General John Garstin (1820)
15 Tomb of Lucia Palk (1772)
16 Tomb of Charlotte Hickey (1783)
17 Tomb of Lieutenant-Colonel George Monson (1776)
18 Tomb of Lady Anne Monson (1775)
19 Tomb of Thomas Fitzmaurice Chambers (1782)
20 Tomb of Lieutenant-General Sir John Clavering (1777)
21 Tomb of Edward Wheeler (1784)
22 Tomb of Elizabeth Jane Barwell (1779)
23 Tomb of Augustus Cleveland (1784)
24 Tomb of Sir John Hyde (1796)
25 Tomb of Sarah Pearson (1768)
26 Tomb of George Bogle (1781)
27 Tomb of Catherine Sykes (1768)
29 Tomb of Major William Baillie (1799)
30 Tomb of Chidley Coote (1807)
31 Tomb of Josephine Skinner (1850)
32 Tomb of Sir John Royds (1817)
33 Tomb of Sir John Hadley D'Oyly (1818)
34 Tomb of James Siddons (1818)
35 Tomb of M. Dennison (1806)
36 Tomb of Thomas Boileau (1806)
37 Tomb of Charles Weston (1809)
38 Tomb of Charles Waring (1813)

Slightly to the north is **Lower Circular Road Cemetery**, opened in 1840, which contains a number of interesting graves. Close to the Gothic-style entrance range lies Sir William Hay Macnaughten, the British envoy to Kabul, who was assassinated there on 23 December 1841. Nearby is the grave of Sir William Casement (1844).

Approximately 800 m (½ mile) north, on the Lower Circular Road, lies **St James's Church** (1864), by C. G. Wray and Walter Granville in an Early English style with Norman detailing. The interior is spacious and handsome, with a groined vault over the crossing and elaborate geometric carved roof trusses. Two lofty towers, 39 m (128 ft) high, adorn the west end. About 1·6 km (1 mile) northward lies **Sealdah Station**, the terminus for railways running to northern and eastern Bengal and Assam. The original train shed, now demolished, was designed by Brunel.

At the south end of the Lower Circular Road is **Bishop Middleton's College** (1823), comprising a chapel, planned as a small basilica, the principal's and professors' house, library and lecture rooms. Opposite lie the **La Martinière Schools** (1833). The girls' school was designed around a remodelled 18th-century house with an elephant porch. The boys' school was erected to the designs of R. H. Rattray and Captain Hutchinson, a military engineer, in 1835 and built by J. P. Parker. Ionic porticos on the north and south façades provide access to a central chapel. The circular roof pavilion once carried a dome.

In the gardens to the north of the school is a bust of Claude Martin. Behind these gardens are a fine group of mid-19th-century classical town houses with Ionic details.

Lower Circular Road meets Chowringhee Road south of St Paul's Cathedral. From here a tour of the third or southern section of the city may be commenced.

Southern Section

The southern section can be combined easily with either of the other two sections, but adequate time is essential to permit a proper appreciation of St Paul's Cathedral and the Victoria Memorial. The southern route may be extended considerably by visits to the outlying areas of Garden Reach and Tollygunge, but transport is required if this is envisaged.

St Paul's Cathedral lies in the south-eastern corner of the Maidan, close to Chowringhee Road, and is visible from some way off, soaring high above the trees. An earthquake destroyed the original steeple in 1897. It was reinstated, but after another earthquake in 1934, the main tower was recast to the design of Bell Harry Tower at Canterbury.

Commenced in 1839 to the designs of Major W. N. Forbes, architect of the Silver Mint, it is 75·3 m (247 ft) long and 24·6 m (81 ft) wide, widening to 34·7 m (114 ft) at the transepts. The style is distinctly conservative, a pretty, whimsical exercise in an Indo-Gothic style, owing more to 18th-century ecclesiastical architecture than to the robust, vigorous forms of the Victorian Gothic Revival. The interior is spanned by an iron trussed roof adorned with Gothic tracery and, when built, it was one of the widest spans in existence. The absence of a traditional nave and side aisles was due to the lack of bearing in the poor subsoil. There are several obvious adaptations to local site conditions and to the climate, including the extension of the lancet windows to plinth level to improve ventilation.

The original east window, presented by the Dean and Chapter of Windsor, was destroyed in a cyclone in 1864. The present glass, by Clayton and Bell, is exceptionally good, but the magnificent west window, designed by Sir Edward Burne-Jones in 1880 as a memorial to Lord Mayo, the Viceroy, who was assassinated in the Andaman Islands, is a Pre-Raphaelite masterpiece and, without doubt, the finest piece of stained glass in India.

Other notable fittings include the reredos, in alabaster inlaid with panels of Florentine mosaic depicting the Annunciation, the Adoration of the Magi and the Flight into Egypt, designed by Sir Arthur Blomfield, and the Willis organ, installed in 1881, and one of the best produced. The choir stalls lining the flanks of the church carry the arms of the cities of India, while the cassocks bear regimental insignia. In the tower the Great Bell is inscribed: 'Its sound is gone out into all lands.'

Of the many monuments, there is a

bust of the architect Forbes and one of Bishop Daniel Wilson, close to the library over the porch. A statue of Bishop Heber, second Bishop of Calcutta, in pure white marble by Chantrey (1835), stands in the transept, while the vestibule is ornamented with many tablets and monuments to British figures. A black marble tablet on the left side of the vestibule represents the destruction of the Kashmir Gate, Delhi, during the Mutiny. Other fine examples include those to Sir William Hay Macnaughten, the Hon. John Paxton Norman, Sir Henry Lawrence and the Earl of Elgin and Kincardine.

An extended visit to the Cathedral is recommended. It is refreshingly cool inside and a clear impression of the ceremonial splendour of British India can be gained.

Immediately to the east of the Cathedral, on Chowringhee Road, is the **Bishop's Palace**, embellished with a hexastyle portico on a pierced, rusticated plinth. It is a good example of an early-19th-century Calcutta house, once the property of the Hon. Wilberforce Bird and purchased by Bishop Wilson in 1849, at which time alterations were carried out. Note the bronze Chinese bell (c. 1720) in the front area.

To the west of the Cathedral lies the most potent symbol of British supremacy in India, the **Victoria Memorial** (1921), by Sir William Emerson, president of the Royal Institute of British Architects. Soaring high over the southern end of the Maidan, the Memorial dominates the centre of the city. Superbly sited behind two large ornamental tanks, the main entrance is from Queen's Way. Outside is a rond-point of statuary with fine bronze allegorical figures. In the centre of the pathway leading to the entrance is a statue of Queen Victoria by Sir George Frampton with excellent Art Nouveau details. Note the British lion beneath the Imperial sun on the reverse of the bronze throne. The

gates and surrounding details were designed by Vincent Esch and the bronze panels flanking the bridge on which the statue stands are by Sir William Goscombe John.

Externally, the Victoria Memorial owes a lot to contemporary British civic classicism and not a little to Belfast City Hall, as well as earlier Indian works by Emerson. Faced in Makrana marble from Jodhpur, the entire composition is crowned by a revolving bronze figure of Victory, 4·8 m (16 ft) high and weighing three tons. The corner domes are faintly Mughal in origin, but the statuary over the entrances is Italian. The sides are linked by open colonnades and the south entrance, approached through a triumphal archway commemorating Edward VII (by Mackennal), has a statue of Lord Curzon, who conceived this Imperial Valhalla.

Inside the main entrance hall are bronze busts and marble statues of royal figures; those of King George V (by Mackennal) and Queen Mary (by Frampton) were presented by the Aga Khan. The Queen's Hall is the most impressive internal space. At the centre stands a charming statue by Sir Thomas Brock of the young Victoria on her accession to the throne. High on the walls above the gallery are murals depicting scenes from her life and inscriptions of Imperial virtues.

The interior comprises a succession of rooms and galleries containing important collections of paintings, artefacts, sculpture, books and manuscripts. In the Royal Gallery are paintings and memorabilia recalling episodes from Victoria's life and also a huge picture of the entry of the Prince of Wales into Jaipur. The Portrait Gallery (left of the entrance hall) has pictures of the Nawab of Arcot and Lord Clive, and also Major-General Stringer Lawrence, plus statues of Wellesley and Dalhousie. In the Prince's Hall is a replica of Clive's statue in King William Street, London, and in the Durbar Hall the black stone throne or musnud of the Nawabs Nazim of Bengal, Bihar and Orissa, on which Clive sat in 1765 when he proclaimed the civil administration of the East India Company.

In the picture galleries are a superb collection of the paintings of Thomas and William Daniell, who did so much to convey Indian scenes to the English public. Other notable paintings include Zoffany's famous picture of 'Claude Martin and his Friends', 'Sir Elijah Impey' by Tilly Kettle and 'Rudyard Kipling' by Burne-Jones. One room contains a series of prints of early Calcutta, from which a clear impression of the 18th-century city may be obtained, together with a model of Fort William.

Opposite the south entrance of the Memorial in Lower Circular Road is the **Presidency General Hospital** (1768), with a memorial arch on the road frontage. To the west of the Victoria Memorial is the large expanse of the **Royal Calcutta Turf Club Racecourse**, a splendid monument to British social and cultural life right in the heart of the city and reputedly the finest track in the East.

Zeerut Bridge leads south over Tolly's Nullah to the district of Alipur. Down a short incline the road bifurcates. Between the two arms lies **Belvedere**. Once the property of the Lieutenant-Governor of Bengal, it was used by numerous viceroys on visits from New Delhi, before being given over to the National Library. The centre section is the only original 18th-century portion. A neo-classical mausoleum lies close to the west gate, a short distance from which the famous duel between Warren Hastings and Philip Francis took place on 17 August 1780.

The **Agri-Horticultural Gardens** (1872) lie south of Belvedere and the **Zoological Gardens**, opened by the Prince of Wales in 1876, lie beyond. Close to Judge's Court Road stands **Hastings House** (1777), typical of the opulent town houses of the period and set in

its own garden compound. Originally, it was a simple square block with living-quarters at ground-floor level, 'a perfect bijou' built for Warren Hastings, the first Governor-General. It was later extended. Hastings spent many happy hours here and laid out his estate at Daylesford in England in the image of its gardens. It is reputed to be haunted. Several well-authenticated incidents have occurred. Today it is a women's college.

The route back to the centre via Diamond Harbour Road passes **St Stephen's Church** (1846; consecrated 1870), with its pretty, graceful spire. There are a number of interesting memorials, including one to Commander James Henry Johnson, who fought at Trafalgar and took the first steamship to Calcutta in 1825. The fine Gothic pulpit was reinstated in 1901, after lying in an undertaker's shop for fifty years. The memorial east window recalls Mrs Colquhoun Grant. A gateway to the south of the entrance to the church leads to Kidderpore House, once the home of Richard Barwell, Hastings's associate, and now used as a Military Orphan Asylum.

Nearby, in Bridge Road, a duel was fought between Richard Barwell and General Clavering in May 1775. Hastings Bridge, close by the river frontage, leads over Tolly's Nullah to **Garden Reach**, formerly one of the most fashionable areas but now run-down and commercialized, with the once-fine Palladian mansions lining the river approach to Calcutta in grandiloquent decay.

The southern suburb of Tollygunge has the famous **Royal Calcutta Golf Club**, another well-preserved late-18th-century house in beautiful surroundings. Here also is the **Mosque of Ghulam Muhammad** (1835–43), a double-aisled rectangular mosque with an unusually inventive commingling of European and Islamic details. Its form is derived from the British bungalow style, with round arched window openings enriched with fan-shaped motifs and other neo-classical devices. It was built by Prince Ghulam Muhammad, son of Tipu Sultan, who lived in England for a long period, which may account for the hybrid style. The skyline of domes and minarets is exotically Oriental, with Persian and Quranic inscriptions on the stucco exterior. It was the first of three built in Calcutta by the descendants of Tipu, Tiger of Mysore.

Nearby is the second in the series, the **Mosque of Shahbani Begum** (1840–41), another double-aisled, multi-domed structure – unusual in Bengal, where a tradition of single-aisled mosques developed. Externally, the lower parts are wholly European in inspiration, with stylised Ionic columns and Venetian arches crowned by a classical cornice and entablature, oversailed by an array of Islamic domes and corner minarets. Shahbani Begum was the granddaughter of Tipu Sultan.

The west bank of the river has relatively little of interest. However, the **Botanical Gardens**, opposite Garden Reach, laid out in 1786 by Colonel Kyd, have made a valuable contribution to scientific research ever since. The gardens, which are huge (109 hectares: 270 acres), can be reached by river or by road and enjoy a frontage to the river enhanced by long palm avenues. The Great Banyan tree covers an area over 381 m (1,250 ft) in circumference, although the original central trunk has been removed.

The road from Howrah to the gardens passes **St Thomas's Church** (1831; consecrated 1833), a handsome, if rather meanly proportioned, pile. The font commemorates the hospitality of John Stalkart of Ghoosery. The two conspicuous towers nearby mark the **Roman Catholic Church of Our Lady of a Prosperous Voyage**. The **Government Engineering College** was formerly part of an ambitious scheme for a Theological College for India com-

menced by Bishop Middleton along the lines of a Cambridge college.

CHAINPUR

11·2 km (7 miles) west of Bhabua town lies the residence of the Chainpur Rajas, who were expelled by the Pathans in the 1650s. An old fort surrounded by a ditch and protected by a stone rampart and flanking bastions bears testimony to the former importance of the town. Within the fort are a 17th-century mosque, built as a tomb for Fateh Khan, wells and numerous ancillary buildings.

CHANDERNAGORE

As one of the French enclaves in India, Chandernagore is something of an historical curiosity. It was first settled in 1673, but it was not occupied on a permanent basis until 1688. Until the time of Dupleix (1697–1764), when it became a considerable trading centre, it was of little importance. There is a bust of Dupleix in the little town square.

Just 32 km (20 miles) from Calcutta, Chandernagore was once a centre for opium smuggling. In 1757 it was bombarded by Admiral Watson and captured by Clive. It was restored to the French in 1763, retaken in 1794, restored by the Peace of Amiens of 1802, only to be retaken yet again and held by the British until 1816, when it was finally given to France. In 1951, after a referendum of its inhabitants, it became part of India. French influence is still discernible.

There is a church (1726), built by Italian missionaries, a school and a convent. The Collège Dupleix, founded in 1882, is now an English school. The ditch separating French Chandernagore from Dutch Chinsura was a provision of the Treaty of Versailles of 1783. In the cemetery are some interesting French tombs.

CHINSURA

1·6 km (1 mile) south of Hooghly lies the former Dutch enclave of Chinsura. Established in the early 17th century, it was held until 1825, when it was ceded in part exchange for English possessions in Sumatra and a cash payment of £100,000. On acquisition by the British it became a major military centre for the East India Company and a reception area for troops newly arrived from England. In 1871 the military station was given up, but large blocks of early-19th-century barracks and quarters remain.

The **Old Dutch Church** and former **Government House** lie to the north on the river. The octagonal Church is alleged to have been built as early as 1678 by the Dutch Governor, but most of the existing fabric was built by Sir G. L. Vernet in 1767. Vernet was a former page of Louis XV. The steeple and chime clock were the gift of Mr Sichterman and were erected in 1774. In 1824 the interior was adapted to suit the Anglican liturgy. It is now used as a biology laboratory attached to the local college. To the west lies the old cemetery, which contains a number of early Dutch tombs enriched with crests and armorial devices, the oldest from 1662.

The **Armenian Church of St John the Baptist** (1695) is also worth a visit. It was founded by Margar Johannes in 1695 and completed two years later. The early tombs in the churchyard, which date from 1697, include that of the father of the builder. The prominent steeple was added in the early 19th century.

South of the former Dutch Church is **Hooghly College** (1804), established by a private benefactor in 1836 in a house built by General Perron, the French general who surrendered to Lord Lake in the war with Scindia of 1803. The

house is a fine example of Anglo-Indian Palladian architecture and the town, a good example of an early-19th-century military cantonment.

COOCH BEHAR

Cooch Behar is one of the most isolated areas of India, situated by the Brahmaputra river in the narrow neck of land which connects the main body of the country to Assam. It is surrounded by a tangle of international boundaries. Nepal, Sikkim, Bhutan and Bangladesh all lie nearby, but it is rarely visited by tourists. The dynasty arose from the Koch tribe, who established paramountcy in the 16th century. Later the state acted as a buffer between Bengal and the tribal kingdoms of Assam. In 1863 the British reorganized state administration and trained a series of model rulers, as a result of which the state became an exemplar of social progression. This is expressed in the principal buildings and institutions, which are disposed around the main square: two schools, a court house, a jail, a state archive and printing office.

The **New Palace** (c. 1875) is built in an Italian renaissance style with arcaded inner courtyards and a large central dome modelled on St Peter's, Rome. It is by a Western architect and is a creditable composition, if somewhat lacking in cohesion. The Durbar Hall has decorations in the manner of Raphael. The principal rooms are also European in conception, with Chippendale-style mirrors, painted and gilded ceilings, and elaborate French furnishings.

CUTTACK

Once the old capital of the state of Orissa, Cuttack lies about 32 km (20

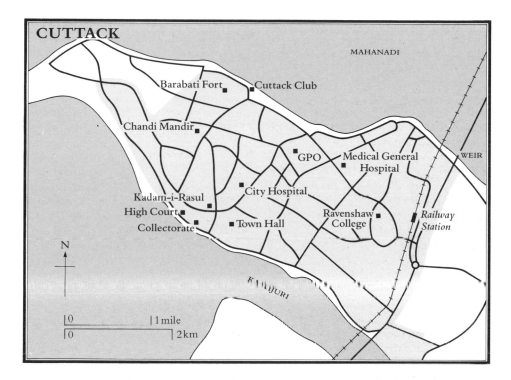

miles) north of the new capital, Bhubaneshwar. The town was founded by Nripati (920) of the Lion dynasty. It has long been of military and commercial significance.

The stone revetment on the Kathjuri river dates from the 11th century. The principal feature of interest is **Fort Barabati**, which is largely ruined, with the exception of the fine arched Lion gateway. The date of its original construction is uncertain, probably 14th century, but in 1750 a large round bastion and gateway were erected by the Muslim governor. Only parts of the citadel survive: principally, the gateway and a mosque dedicated to Fateh Khan Rahim. The area of the fortress is now a mass of mounds and pits. Little survives to convey the original grandeur which so impressed M. la Motte that, when he passed here in 1767, he drew parallels with Windsor Castle. The fort was taken from the Bhonsla Raja of Nagpur by the British in 1803.

The **Kadam-i-Rasul** is a complex of three mosques, each crowned by a fine dome. There is a **Naubhat Khana** or Music Gallery and a shrine with a huge dome, the largest in Orissa. The footprints of the Prophet are engraved on a circular stone inside the building, which is venerated by both Hindus and Muslims.

North of the town, along the Taldanda Canal, is a complex of weirs. The Mahanadi Weir is over 1,950 m (6,400 ft) long and was built between 1863 and 1870 as a flood-precaution measure.

Ravenshaw College, the School of Engineering and the Museum are noteworthy buildings.

DARBHANGA

Darbhanga, 38·6 km (24 miles) north of Samastipur, is the principal town of the district and one of the largest towns in

301

Bihar. It has been the residence of the Maharajas since 1762. The family, who trace their origins from Mahesh Thakur, a priest under the ancient Rajas of Tirhut, hold the title Maharajadhiraja and, until recently, they were the leading landlords in this part of India. The title of Raja was bestowed as early as 1710 by Ali Vardi Khan.

At Rajnagar there is a large palace, damaged by an earthquake in 1934. The Amandbagh Palace at Darbhanga is also a very fine building of considerable distinction, complete with an aviary and menagerie.

DARJEELING

Darjeeling is one of the most famous hill stations in India, renowned for the sublime grandeur of its scenery and the stunning views of the snow-clad eastern Himalayas. Darjeeling (literally Place of the Thunderbolt) was once the summer headquarters of the government of Bengal. It lies on a narrow ridge running from north to south, varying in width between 1,981 m (6,500 ft) and 2,133 m (7,000 ft).

The centre or **Chowrasta** (literally four roads) is a large, open space marked by an ornamental bandstand, the Charing Cross of Darjeeling. Leading from north-east to the north-west is the Mall, the main promenade of the station, which encircles Observatory Hill, a bracing and rewarding walk. From the top of the hill twelve peaks can be seen, all over 6,100 m (20,000 ft), including Kanchenjunga, 72 km (45 miles) away. Beneath are picturesque, wooded foothills.

St Andrew's Church is situated on a knoll to the left of Observatory Hill, close to the **Gymkhana Club**. The original church was designed by Captain Bishop in 1843, but this collapsed in 1867. It was reconstructed in 1873. Later, a large clocktower, porches and the north and south transepts were added. Inside are numerous interesting memorial tablets.

St Columba's Kirk (1894), near the Railway Station, has good stained glass to the family of Peterson Lennox Blackwood. There is a **Union Chapel** (1869). The **Roman Catholic Church** (1893)

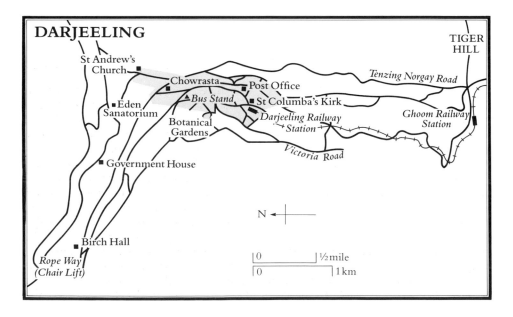

below the Mall is part of the Loretto convent.

About 800 m (½ mile) beyond St Andrew's is **Government House**, on a fine site with grounds resembling an English park. The original house, 'The Shrubbery', built in 1879, collapsed in an earthquake in 1934 and the palatial new building has a bright-blue dome. The **Town Hall** (1921) is a handsome colonial Gothic edifice at the junction of Mackenzie Road and Auckland Road. Nearby is the **Post and Telegraph Building**. Beneath Chowrasta is the **Eden Sanatorium**. Below Victoria Pleasance Park (1902) is the **Museum** (1902), with a fine collection of butterflies and insects. Birch Hall houses the Himalayan Mountaineering Institute, run, until his recent death, by Tenzing Norgay of Everest fame. The **Bazaar** lies in the centre of town, near the Jami Masjid, erected by Nasir Ali Khan between 1851 and 1862.

The surrounding hills offer many enjoyable walks and are studded with private residences in a variety of European styles.

DUM DUM

Now the site of Calcutta airport, 11 km (7 miles) outside the city, Dum Dum was once the headquarters of the gallant Bengal Artillery, from 1783 to 1858, after which it transferred to Meerut. It is also the birthplace of the dreaded soft-nosed bullet.

St Stephen's Church (1822), consecrated by Bishop Heber, is the old garrison church, studded with monuments to officers of the Bengal Artillery. In the churchyard is a tall column to Colonel Thomas Deane Pearse, a friend of Warren Hastings and founder of the regiment, who died in 1769.

The **Cantonments** are now dilapidated. The centre of Barrack Square is marked by a large gun. Close to the south wall of the Small Arms Factory is a column erected in 1844 to commemorate the officers and men of the Bengal Horse Artillery killed in the retreat from Kabul during the First Afghan War of 1841–2. It was restored in 1980. There are also numerous military graves in the **Old Cemetery**.

The **Outram Institute** (formerly the Old Bengal Artillery Officers' Mess) is a fine late-18th-century classical bungalow with paired Tuscan columns and balustraded parapets. The ground-floor columns are distinctly less refined than those of the first storey. A bust of Sir James Outram stands on the verandah.

Lord Clive had a country retreat here. His house was described by Bishop Heber as 'built on an artificial mound of considerable height' with 'a venerable appearance . . . of some antiquity'. **Fairley Hall**, near the Church, was the residence of Henry Lawrence, the hero of Lucknow, in his early days in India.

Dum Dum enjoyed an insalubrious reputation until the late 19th century. One house was given the sobriquet 'Cholera Hall' on account of its notorious reputation.

GAUR *Map overleaf*

The deserted city of Gaur lies about 8 km (5 miles) south-west of English Bazaar, on an old channel of the Ganges. It was once the capital of the last Hindu dynasty of Bengal. Later, it became the capital of the first Muslim rulers, from the mid-15th to mid-16th centuries. The name is of considerable antiquity, but its known history commenced in about 1200, when it was conquered by Bakhtiyar Khalji, whose dynasty ruled for 300 years. In 1338 Fakhr-ud-Din founded an independent Afghan kingdom at Pandua and Gaur lost much of its building stone at this time, but in 1500 it became the

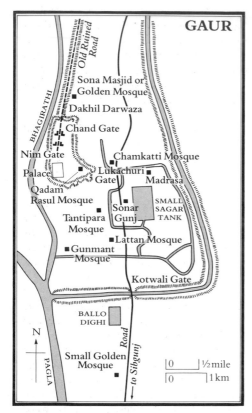

GAUR

receded many miles. On the north a 9·6 km (6 miles) fortification curves across the countryside over 30·4 m (100 ft) wide at its base.

Of the **Fort** within the city the Dakhil Darwaza and Lukachuri gates still exist. The former, to the north, is built of small red bricks with carved detail on the corner towers and a monumental central entrance. In the south-east corner was the old palace, enclosed by a brick wall 20·1 m (66 ft) high, enriched with an ornamental cornice. It was known as the **Bais Gaji** or Twenty-two Yards Wall.

The only remnants of original Hindu settlement are the tanks scattered throughout the city, the most important being the **Sagar Dighi**, a huge reservoir of water 1,463 m (4,754 ft) by 731 m (2,375 ft) and built in 1126. On its bank lies the **Tomb of Shaikh Akhi Suraj-ud-Din** and the small, six-domed **Jhanjhaniya Mosque** (1535), erected in the reign of Mahmud Shah. At Sadullapur is a burning ghat.

At the south-east corner of the fort are two mosques. The **Qadam Rasul** (1530) was built by Nusrat Shah (1519–32) to house a representation of the Prophet's footprint. The north and south walls have rows of recessed panels and the arched entrances are carried on massive octagonal piers. To the north-east and south sides is a vaulted verandah. Nearby is the **Tomb of Fateh Khan** (17th century), with a curved Bengali roof, the south-east gateway to the fort.

800 m (½ mile) to the north of the east wall is the **Firuz Minar** (c. 1487) or Pir Asa Minar. It is a brick Victory Tower, 25·6 m (84 ft) high, with three polygonal stages carrying two top circular storeys. There is a single arched opening at each level and a chajja divides the lower from the upper stages.

800 m (½ mile) to the north-west is the **Sona Masjid** (1526), the Golden Mosque or Baradarwazi, the largest building still standing in Gaur. It lies on the western

capital again. Humayun considered the city so beautiful he renamed it Jinnatabad: 'Abode of Paradise'. In 1537 it was sacked by Sher Shah Sur and in 1576 it was absorbed into Akbar's empire, after the city had been devastated by plague a year earlier.

The old city covers an extensive area, over 51·7 sq km (20 square miles), now mostly cultivated. Most surviving ruins are from the later period, with some Mughal remains. The Kotwali Darwaza, in the southern sector of the city, is now the border with Bangladesh. The dimensions of the city can be traced via the old embankments, which are 12·8 km (7½ miles) from north to south and 1·6 km (1 mile) to 3·2 km (2 miles) from west to east. On the east a double line of huge embankments protected the city from erosion by the Ganges, which has now

304

side of a raised quadrangle with eleven arched openings facing the restored entrance gateway. The interior was covered with forty-four small domes supported on stone pillars, but only those which form a verandah to the front of the building survive, with the three aisles beyond. Built by Nusrat Shah, it is faced in plain stone. Traces of a raised platform or takht for the ladies can be seen in the north-west corner.

800 m (½ mile) east of the Qadam Rasul is the ruined **Tantipara Mosque** (c. 1480), with some of the finest embossed brick detail in Bengal. There is an octagonal turret to each corner. The five entrance arches correspond with the mihrabs on the qibla wall.

800 m (½ mile) to the south is the **Lattan Mosque** or Painted Mosque (late 15th century), whose attribution is due to the bricks being enamelled in bright banded colours, of which traces remain. The single dome, carried on brick pendentives, is enriched with multi-coloured tiles. To the north is the Piasbari Tank, with an insalubrious reputation for disease. In the south wall of the city the **Kotwali Darwaza** (late 15th century) marks the border with Bangladesh. Once it had a monumental pointed entrance arch flanked by semicircular bastions, but it is now in ruins. 1·6 km (1 mile) to the south, in the suburb of Firuzpur, is the **Chota Sona Mosque** or Lesser Golden Mosque, known as the Gem of Gaur .(c. 1493–1519), with carved stone panels of intricate design in black basalt. The central corridor has typical Bengali charchala vaulting.

Within the fort ramparts near the Qadam Rasul are the **Lukachuri** or East Gate (mid-17th century), a two-storey building with guardrooms to each side built of brick and stone with traces of plaster. The **Chika Building** was probably a jail or office and may date from the early 15th century. It is a plainly detailed structure with a large brick dome. It

resembles the Eklakhi Tomb at Pandua. Directly opposite is the **Gumpti Darwaza** (possibly 1512), the eastern entrance to the old Imperial citadel. It is a small square structure with engaged corner turrets and a single dome. Fluted turrets flank the main entrance.

East of the Lukachuri is the **Chamkatti Mosque** (possibly 1478), a small dilapidated building with a single dome and a vaulted verandah to the east. Vestiges of a glazed tile and terracotta relief remain.

Between the Kotwali gate and Mahadipur lies the ruined **Gunmant Mosque** (late 15th/early 16th century), a multiaisled mosque with a central, barrelvaulted corridor influenced by the earlier Adina Mosque at Pandua. In a mango grove to the north-west is the ruined façade of an old Mughal mosque of the 17th century. Nothing now remains of the darashari or Lecture Hall, a building similar to the Baradarwazi which lay between Mahadipur and Firuzpur. The **Dhunichak Mosque** (late 15th/early 16th century) lies in the southern suburbs. Only the west and north walls remain. Nearby is the **Rajbibi Mosque** (late 15th/early 16th century), now restored. It is a rectangular structure with a domed square prayer chamber and triple-domed verandah.

Also in the southern suburbs is the ruined **Darasbari Mosque** (late 15th century), comprising a central corridor flanked by aisles. The roof structures have long since fallen, but the design is unique.

The **Mosque and Tomb of Shah Nimat Allah** (17th century) lie in Firuzpur, 800 m (½ mile) north-west of the Chota Sona Mosque. The mosque is attributed to Shah Shuja, Governor of Bengal. It is Mughal period, an early example of the Imperial Mughal mausolea of Bengal. The sarcophagus lies in a square, central chamber surrounded by a domed, vaulted verandah.

HOOGHLY

40·2 km (25 miles) north of Calcutta, Hooghly lies adjacent to the old Dutch settlement of Chinsura.

This historic settlement was founded in 1537 by the Portuguese when Satgaon, the old royal port of Bengal, began to silt up. Traces of the Portuguese fort can be seen on the river bed. The town was sacked by Emperor Shah Jahan in 1633 with considerable loss of life, the Portuguese survivors being taken to Agra and forcibly converted to Islam. The Portuguese returned, but by 1640 the English had established a factory. In 1686 the English retreated after a confrontation with the Nawab and from then on Calcutta grew in importance. In 1742 the Marathas sacked the town and in 1757 Clive took it in a river assault.

The **Imambara** (1836) was built by Karamat Ali, the local superintendent between 1837 and 1876. It is a huge building with a central gateway flanked by two minarets, 34·7 m (114 ft) high, with a central quadrangle surrounded by rooms and chambers, including a hall paved in marble with a silver pulpit. The pulpit is inscribed with verses from the Quran. There is a fine library. Opposite is the **Old Imambara** (1776–7). In the west corner, near a white marble slab, lie the remains of Karamat Ali.

IMPHAL

Imphal is the capital of the remote eastern state of Manipur. It lies in a beautiful valley, over 96·5 km (60 miles) long, at a height of 792 m (2,600 ft) above sea level.

Its early history is unknown before 1714, but it has been subject to frequent Burmese invasions. Under the terms of the Treaty of Yandalo (1826) it was annexed by India.

Today Imphal is best known for the heroic battle fought by the British and Indian armies against the Japanese in April 1944 which stemmed the flood of Japanese success and turned the tide in Asia.

There is a large **war cemetery** managed by the Commonwealth War Graves Commission.

KASIMBAZAR (COSSIMBAZAR)

This decayed town on an island site about 8 km (5 miles) from Murshidabad was once the main trading centre of the entire area. Its name is derived from its legendary founder, Kasim Khan. It was an early centre of English influence.

An English agent was appointed as early as 1658. By 1700 it was the leading commercial agency in Bengal. Job Charnock, founder of Calcutta, was Chief here in 1681, when the town was alleged to have been so full of lofty buildings that the sun never penetrated to street level. Its importance was due to its proximity to the Muslim capital at Murshidabad, but local climatic changes in the early 19th century gave rise to alterations in cultivation patterns and a change in the course of the river.

Few buildings of any consequence now survive. A fragment of the fortifications of the original factory can be seen. The ruins of buildings and huge mounds hint at its former splendour.

The **Maharaja's Palace**, occupied by the family of Warren Hastings's diwan, Kantu Babu, is a fine building of carved stone, modelled on the palace of Chait Singh at Varanasi.

The **Old Dutch Cemetery** lies down river and contains a few early tombs. (See Murshidabad.)

KOHIMA

Kohima stands at a height of 1,432 m (4,700 ft), at the summit of a broad pass or saddle flanked by much higher mountains. An important route centre, it achieved immortal fame in April 1944 when the Royal West Kents and a scratch force of 1,500 British and Indian troops held at bay virtually an entire Japanese division for over a fortnight. The battle, the Stalingrad of the Burmese campaign, marked the zenith of Japanese expansion and the start of the Allied counter-offensive which drove the Japanese from Burma.

There is a fine **war cemetery** around the old District Commissioner's bungalow, beautifully maintained by the Commonwealth War Graves Commission.

KUDRA

26 km (16 miles) south of Kudra is the hillfort of Shergarh, situated on a plateau 244 m (800 ft) high. The summit was fortified by Sher Shah Sur and the palace that he constructed is still well preserved.

MALDA or OLD MALDA

Malda or Old Malda, 6·4 km (4 miles) from English Bazaar, is a small town at the confluence of the Kalindri and Mahananda rivers which once prospered as the port of Pandua. During the 18th century it thrived as a cotton and silk market, with English, Dutch and French factories, but with the transfer of the English factory to English Bazaar in 1771, Malda lost its prosperity and it declined throughout the 19th century.

The old English factory at Malda, founded in 1656, has virtually disappeared, the site being marked by the Court House and public buildings. A **column** erected in 1771 by Thomas Henchman stands in the courthouse compound. Most of the houses are built with masonry taken from the nearby ruins of Gaur and Pandua.

The principal building of interest is the **Jami Masjid**, built in carved brick and stone by Musum Saudagar in 1596. It has a barrel-vaulted corridor based on Bengali and north Indian forms. The central bay of the façade sweeps high above the flanking bays and the pillars at the entrance are handsomely carved.

The **Shrine of Shah Gada** (probably c. 1505) is reputed to contain the remains of a parrot which learned to recite prayers from the Quran. The **Phuti Masjid** (1495) is now entirely ruined and overgrown by jungle. The **Nawab's Mosque** is attributed to the munificence of the Nawab of Murshidabad.

Across the river is the **Nim Serai Minar** (late 16th century), a curious tower 16·7m (55 ft) tall and 7·4 m (18 ft) in diameter. It is studded with projecting stones resembling elephants' tusks and was probably a watch tower or hunting-tower, used to display the heads of thieves. The top can be reached via a winding staircase. It is comparable to the Hiran Mahal at Fatehpur Sikri.

Within the town is the **Katra** (late 16th century), originally a warehouse and later a fortified sarai for travellers. Only traces of the arched gateways remain.

MANER

This small village lies 27·8 km (17 miles) west of Patna on the road to Arrah. An ancient strategic point, it may well have been the extreme western gate to Pataliputra in Mauryan times. It was here at Maner that Islam first made an impact in Bihar, in 1198.

There are two fine Muslim tombs. The **Choti Dargah** or Tomb of Shah Daulat (1616), built by Ibrahim Khan, is the finest Mughal monument in eastern India, with delicate carving and surface ornament. It is situated on a raised platform with slender corner towers and crowned by a huge dome. Internally, the ceiling is covered with Quranic inscriptions. Within the compound is a mosque built by Ibrahim Khan in 1619. The gateway to the north (1603–4) is also distinguished.

The **Bari Dargah** or Tomb of Yahia Maneri is located in a mosque to the east of a large tank with porticos and ghats extending into it. The tank is connected to the old course of the Son river by a 122 m (400 ft) tunnel. The tomb lies in an old tree-lined enclosure. To the north is a three-domed mosque, to the west, quaint cloisters built by Ibrahim Khan in 1605–6. Although architecturally far less remarkable than the Choti Dargah, the **Bari Dargah** has been a place of pilgrimage for centuries. Emperor Babur came here in 1529.

The **Tomb of Tingur Kuli Khan** (1575), on the bank of a tank, is in a ruined state. A stone inscription remains.

MONGHYR

Monghyr was a place of considerable importance from the earliest days of English settlement in Bengal. It lies on the south bank of the Ganges, about 9·6 km (6 miles) from Jamalpur junction, and was one of the principal centres of Muslim administration. Prince Danyal, son of Husain Shah, the Afghan King of Gaur, repaired the fortification in 1497 and built a vault over the tomb of Shah Nafah, the town's patron. Under Akbar the town was again repaired and used as the headquarters of his general, Todar Mal. Later Mir Qasim moved here from Murshidabad to prepare his moves against the English in 1762.

The **Fort** is an impressive structure, in spite of damage sustained in the earthquake of 1934. It contains numerous houses and public offices and projects some distance into the river. A deep ditch protects the landward approach. The main entrance is through the Lal Dar-

waza or Red Gate. The main road passes two tanks, behind one of which is the Karna Chaura house. The Collector's office, once the palace of Shah Sahib, stands on a low hill behind the other, with a former residence of Shah Shuja beyond that.

Near the north gate of the fort is an old European cemetery, which has fine 18th-century tombs in the form of pillars and pyramids raised from 1769 onwards.

MURSHIDABAD

The history of Murshidabad is synonymous with the history of Bengal during the 18th century. In 1704 the great Nawab Murshid Quli Khan transferred the seat of government here from Dacca, but it rapidly lost importance with the rise of English supremacy in Bengal after Plassey in 1757. In 1772 Warren Hastings removed the courts from the city to Calcutta and in 1790 Lord Cornwallis transferred the entire revenue and judicial staff to the emergent new capital of the East India Company. Nevertheless, as the residence of the Nawabs Nazim of Bengal it remained a vital centre of native power in Bengal at a crucial period of English expansion.

Situated 196 km (122 miles) from Calcutta, today it is a small town with a fine heritage of historical monuments from its days of greatness in the mid-18th century.

The **Palace of the Nawab** or Aina Mahal (1837), designed by General Duncan Macleod (1780–1856) of the Bengal Engineers, is loosely based on Government House, Calcutta. It stands in a large compound, together with numerous other buildings, enclosed by a wall. The palace, which is Italian in style, is an imposing edifice intended to convey the power and importance of the Nawab at a time when, in reality, that power was little more than nominal. It is a splendid building over 129·5 m (425 ft) long, with a banqueting hall 88·5 m (290 ft) long with sliding doors faced with mirrors, at the west end of which is a painting of Sir John Moore by Marshall. The centre-piece is a dome from which hangs a fine chandelier of 150 branches, presented by Queen Victoria, over an ivory throne with painted and gilded flowers. There is a fine circular Durbar room, an armoury and a library containing rare manu-scripts.

The zenana is situated to the right of the main entrance at the rear of the palace.

The **Imambara** stands within the same enclosure and carries the inscription 'the Grove of Karbala'. Built in 1847 in a similar European style to the palace, it is an enormous structure, the largest in east India. It replaces an earlier structure reputedly built by Nawab Suraj-ud-Daula and was erected under the instruc-tion of Nawab Feredun Jah. The façade is of two storeys, with a semi-circular cen-tral entrance arch with cusped surround flanked by Tuscan columns. Beyond is a high, plain dome.

The **Medina** (mid-18th century) is a free-standing pavilion situated between the palace and the Imambara. It is alleged to have foundations containing earth from the Karbala at Mecca and is the only surviving remnant of Suraj-ud-Daula's original Imambara. It is square in plan with a verandah, central dome and corner minarets.

Also within the palace compound are two small 18th-century mosques. The **Safid Mosque** is in painted stucco with basalt dressings. The **Zarad Mosque** is raised on a low platform and has a large central dome flanked by two smaller outer domes.

On the outskirts of the city is the **Katra Mosque** (1724–5), completed two years before the death of the great Murshid Quli Khan, whose tomb lies here under the entrance of the courtyard. Now in ruins, it is an interesting building with rectangular ornamental panels decorating the outside. Two of the orig-inal four corner octagonal minarets sur-vive and may be derived from Mughal precedents, such as the Badshahi Mosque in Lahore, built in 1674.

Just off the road nearby is the **Great Gun** (1637), measuring 5·33 m (17½ ft) long, 1·52m (5 ft) round at the breech, with a 15 cm (6 in) calibre. It is one of a pair, the other being in Dacca, and it is supported high above the ground on a pipal tree which has grown up beneath it.

3·2 km (2 miles) south of the city is the **Moti Jhil** or Pearl Lake, probably formed from excavations for brick earth. It is a beautiful spot, but little survives of the famous palace of Suraj-ud-Daula, where Clive held the first revenue collec-tion after Plassey and where Warren Has-tings and Sir John Shore later resided. East of the Moti Jhil is the **Mubarak Manzil** or Old Court House of the East India Company.

Opposite the lake is the **Khushbagh** or Garden of Delight, the old cemetery of the Nawabs. It comprises three separ-ate enclosures. The outer one is entered from the east, past an old ruined ghat. The river wall is fortified and loopholed. In the outer enclosure are eighteen tombs. The central enclosure contains the **Tombs of Alivardi Khan** and **Suraj-ud-Daula**, his son-in-law. Ali-vardi's tomb (1756) is a square, flat-roofed structure with a central chamber surrounded by an arcaded verandah, European in influence. The third enclo-sure contains a tank.

On the right bank of the river, oppo-site the main palace, is the **Roshnibagh** or Garden of Light. Here is the **Tomb** (1738–9) and **Mosque** (1743–4) of **Nawab Shuja-al-Din**. The tomb is a heavily restored, squat, flat-roofed struc-ture set in a walled enclosure. To the north of the tomb is a small mosque built by Alivardi Khan, with engaged corner turrets and a central dome flanked by smaller vaults.

The **Nizamat College**, once reserved for the Nawab's family, is now open to all. About 1·6 km (1 mile) north of the palace is the **Jaffarganj Cemetery**, which contains the graves of all the Nawabs Nazim from 1765 to 1838. Directly to the west of the cemetery is the **Mosque of Shah Nisar Ali** (1778–9), a plain, three-domed, rectangular affair. The **Jaffarganj Deorhi** was the residence of Mir Jafar before he became Nawab.

The city has a number of other notable buildings. The **Chowk Mosque** (1767) stands in the centre of the town and cannot be missed. It is a large, seven-bay building with five graduated domes and two outer char-chala vaults flanked by slender minarets. The exterior is richly ornamented, with moulded stucco niches and arabesques. The **Chowk Sarai Mosque** (1801) is a small part of a wider complex intended as a sarai for travellers. Architecturally, it is based on the nearby **Mian Holal Mosque** (1801), a fine affair with fluted, bulbous domes and elaborate stucco ornament. Close to the Chowk Mosque is the **Mosque of Nusari Banu**, wife of Murshid Quli Khan, reputedly built in 1735 though most of the building appears to date from 1881. Her tomb lies under the steps leading to the mosque.

The **Pil Khana Mosque** resembles the Chowk Mosque and was probably built in the late 18th century. About 800 m (½ mile) to the south is a small, three-domed mosque, also of 18th-century date, with shallow, rounded domes and rectangular panel decoration. Other mosques of note include the **Mosque of Saif Allah** (1748), the **Mosque of Abd Allah** (1780), the **Mosque of Farhat Ali Khan** (1748), the **Gulab Bagh Mosque** (late 18th century), a picturesque ruin situated 274 m (890 ft) west of the Pil Khana, and the **Qadam Sherif** (1780).

The ruins of the **Mosque** and **Tomb of Azim Al-Nisa Begum** (1734), daughter of the great Murshid Quli Khan, and the **Mosque** and **Tomb of** **Badr Nisa Begum** (1840) are also of interest.

The **Old Dutch Cemetery** at Kalkapur has tombs dating from 1721. In the Old Residency Burialground is the tomb of Mary Hastings, the first wife of Warren Hastings, and her daughter (1759). The tomb was restored in 1863.

PANDUA

Pandua, 11·2 km (7 miles) north-east of Old Malda, straddles the main road. Together with Gaur, it was one of the ancient capitals of Bengal.

A brick-paved road 3·65 m (12 ft) wide ran through the town, which stretches for about 9·65 km (6 miles) in length. The town was the capital of Bengal from about 1338 to 1500, after which it was progressively deserted in favour of Gaur and abandoned to the jungle. Most of the surviving ruins lie close to the Dinajpur Road.

Approaching from the south a series of shrines can be seen. These are mostly 17th century, the most important being those of Makhdum Shah Jalal and Qutb Alam Shah. To the north stands the **Qutb Shahi Mosque** or Golden Mosque (1585), built by Makhdum Shah and close to his tomb. It is faced in stone with five entrance arches. Originally, the crowns of the minarets were glazed yellow and the roof was covered with ten small domes.

Beyond the mosque is the **Eklakhi Tomb** (early 15th century). Alleged to be the burial place of Sultan Jalal-al-Din, it is one of the first square brick tombs in Bengal. It is a massive structure, crowned by a plain dome and carved with brick ornament. Inside, the chamber is octagonal in shape, crowned by a ribbed dome carried on eight squinches. There are three tombs. 1·6 km (1 mile) beyond is an old bridge with a carved figure of Ganesh, the elephant god.

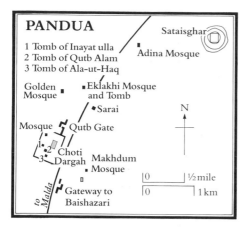

PANDUA
1 Tomb of Inayat ulla
2 Tomb of Qutb Alam
3 Tomb of Ala-ut-Haq
Golden Mosque
Eklakhi Mosque and Tomb
Sarai
Mosque
Qutb Gate
Choti Dargah
Makhdum Mosque
Gateway to Baishazari
Sataisghar
Adina Mosque
N
0   ½ mile
0   1 km
to Malda

1·6 km (1 mile) past the bridge is the **Adina Mosque** (1374–5). Built by Sikander Shah, it is one of the best surviving examples of early Indo-Islamic architecture in India, with a plan and dimensions similar to the great mosque at Damascus. It was once the largest mosque in the subcontinent and it incorporates earlier Hindu and Buddhist masonry probably taken from Gaur. Although ruined, enough remains to discern its original form.

The walls enclose a space 152·4 m (500 ft) long from north to south, and 91·4 m (300 ft) wide from east to west. The north, east and south sides had windows, the west led to a chamber containing the tomb of Sikander Shah. Inside and following the outer walls was a series of cloisters enclosing an open quadrangle. The mosque proper lay on the western side of the quadrangle. The surviving portions are the outer walls, the royal platform with its domes, the pulpit and part of the outer chamber. The qibla and mimbar exhibit fine carved stone detail.

The west wall of the nave and the royal platform are faced in polished black stone inscribed with texts from the Quran. In the outer chamber is an inscription to Sikander (1374). The barrel-vaulted central bay of the prayer chamber was unique in India at this time. Usually this was domed, but the precedent was copied later elsewhere in Bengal, at Rajmahal and Old Malda, for instance, and it allowed an unimpeded view of the central mihrab.

Adjoining the north bay of the mosque is a small square chamber or takht approached by a ramp. The doors are built of reused Hindu masonry. It is reputed to be the tomb of Sikander Shah.

The **Choti Dargah** (early 15th century; altered) contains the grave of Nur Qutb Alam (d. 1415), a local Muslim saint.

About 1·6 km (1 mile) to the east of the Adina Mosque is the **Sataisghar** or old palace of Sikander. Only two small ruins survive, used as bath houses.

PATNA *Map overleaf*

Patna, the ancient Pataliputra, is the capital of the state of Bihar. Situated on the southern bank of the Ganges, it lies close to the confluence with the River Gandak, 544 km (338 miles) from Calcutta on the main line of the Eastern Railway.

The city is very extensive, running from east to west parallel to the river. It is one of the most ancient cities in India, the capital of the Maurya dynasty of the 4th and 3rd centuries BC. The excavated remains of the original settlement of Pataliputra lie between Patna and Dinapore. (For details see Volume I.)

After lapsing into obscurity for centuries the city revived under Sher Shah Sur, who constructed the fort in 1541. Under the Mughals it was a provincial capital until 1765. With the creation of Bihar and Orissa in 1912, Patna was restored as the capital of Bihar.

The Western Sector: New Patna

New Patna lies 3·2 km (2 miles) west of Bankipore and is the headquarters of the government of Bihar. The layout of the new city, which is virtually contemporaneous with New Delhi, is a typical

311

exercise in Imperial town planning, with long, wide avenues flanked by government buildings and vistas terminating in impressive façades. Architecturally, it is an Indian rendition of the style of classical architecture popularized by the Wem-

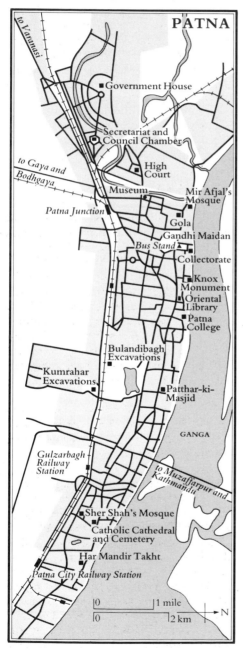

bley Exhibition of 1923, executed in brick and plaster rather than stone.

The new capital was laid out by the architect J. F. Munnings, a partner in Power, Adam & Munnings of Sydney, Australia. The main axis is King George's Avenue, which links the Secretariat with Government House in the grand manner, over 1·6 km (1 mile) long, 60·8 m (200 ft) wide and lined with trees. The secondary roads are 45·7 m (150 ft) wide.

Government House or Raj Bhavan was designed by Munnings. It stands at the western end of the capital, a three-storey building on a north–south axis, situated in a large landscaped garden of over 44·5 hectares (110 acres). Internally, the ground floor is given over to reception rooms, including the main dining- and drawing-rooms. The Durbar Hall and ballroom lie on the west side of the main block and rise through two storeys, overlooked by the colonnaded balconies of the first floor. It is the official residence of the Governor of Bihar.

The **Secretariat** (1929) lies at the end of King George's Avenue, a huge building with a prominent clocktower, originally 54·25 m (178 ft) high although the tower partly collapsed following the earthquake of 1934. During the Second World War the balconies and corridors were converted into improvised rooms and this has badly impaired the character of the building. A fine view can be obtained from the balcony at the top of the clocktower.

The **Council Chambers** (1920), designed in Free Renaissance style by A. N. Millwood, are situated to the east of the Secretariat. The chambers measure 18·2m (60 ft) by 15·2 m (50 ft) and extend through both floors, with an upper gallery for the public and press.

About 228 m (740 ft) east of the eastern gate of the Secretariat is the **Martyrs' Memorial**, bronze statuary in a heroic manner commemorating seven nationalist students who died on 9 August 1942 after being shot by police while trying to hoist the national flag on the Secretariat.

Between the Secretariat and railway station is **Hardinge Park**, which commemorates the visit to Patna in 1913 of the Viceroy Lord Hardinge of Penshurst, architect of the province of Bihar and Orissa. A bronze statue of Hardinge, by Herbert Hampton, which once stood in the park, a bust of Lady Hardinge and two plates depicting justice between men and sympathy to suffering humanity, were moved to the Patna Museum in 1967.

Off Bayley Road is the **High Court** (1916), a fine exercise in civic Baroque, closely modelled on the High Court at Allahabad by Frank Lishman. Internally, there is a fine marble staircase behind the pedimented entrance portico.

On the Patna–Dinapore road is the **Sadakat Ashram**, which guided the freedom movement in Bihar. Gandhi, Rajendra Prasad and Maulana Mazarul Haque were frequent visitors.

The **Patna Museum** (1929), on Buddha Marg, is an elegant range in Indo-Saracenic style with square corner towers capped by domes. It has a fine collection of stone sculpture, bronzes, terracotta figures, prehistoric implements, copper plates, pottery and other ancient artefacts.

The Central Sector

This sector lies east of the Buddha Marg on the edge of Patna University campus. The road from the railway station to the Maidan passes a number of interesting houses. Opposite and beyond the jail is an early-19th-century bungalow with crenellated parapets. Further on is a fine Art Deco house of the 1920s. The **Gandhi Maidan** covers 25·8 hectares (64 acres) and is well laid out with trees and footpaths. To the north-east is the Anglican Christ Church (1857).

The **Gola** or **Golghar** is one of the most extraordinary buildings in India and cannot be missed. It stands by a small park on the west edge of the Maidan and resembles a huge beehive towering over the trees. It was built by Colonel John Garstin in 1786 as a famine-relief measure but was never used. Over 27·4 m (90 ft) high, there is an external staircase to the top, where the grain was unloaded. The flat platforms adjoining the stairs were resting places. It has a theoretical capacity of 137,000 tons and a spectacular internal echo. 137 m (426 ft) round at the base and about 33·2 m (109 ft) in diameter, it is a local landmark. The view from the top across the Ganges is stunning. It is alleged that Sir Jang Bahadur of Nepal once rode a pony to the summit. Note the plaque commemorating Garstin at the base.

The **Randfurlie Knox Monument** (c. 1765) lies close to the river in the compound of the Judge's Court. This tall obelisk recalls the gallant Knox, who marched from Burdwan to relieve the siege of Patna by Shah Alam in 1760.

About 800 m (½ mile) to the east the **Khuda Bakhsh Oriental Public Library**, founded in 1900 by Maulavi Khuda Bakhsh Khan Bahadur, is a famous repository of ancient and rare Arabic and Persian manuscripts. Among the collection are the only surviving volumes from the sack of the university at Cordoba in Spain.

Patna College lies close to the Oriental Public Library. The administrative block, close to the river, is a fine Dutch colonial building of the 18th century. The lower range has a Doric order, the upper Corinthian, and although altered and extended in the 19th century, it is a fine example of the period. The elegant **Lecture Theatre** was erected in 1927.

On the north-west corner of the Maidan is the **Gandhi Museum**. On the river front is **Gandhighat**, a pleasant garden and pavilion commemorating the Mahatma, whose ashes were dispersed at the confluence of the Ganges and Gandak on 30 January 1948. Close by is the **Bihar College of Engineering**, in a

313

simple Indo-Saracenic style. Other buildings near the river bank include the Collectorate, National College, Prince of Wales Medical College and Hospital, University Senate House and Law College.

The Eastern Sector

This sector completes the tour and extends from Gandhighat to the eastern limit of the city.

About 4·8 km (3 miles) east of Patna College is **Gulzarbagh**, the old opium quarter, which traded until 1911, when it was closed by the government. The old buildings are now occupied by the Government Press but can be recognized by the high wall around the compound on the river bank. The site is that of the original English factory. The **Duchess of Teck Hospital** (1893–5) lies on higher ground about 1·2 km (¾ mile) to the west.

East of Gulzarbagh is the west gate of Patna city. Near the Chowk is the **Har Mandir Takht**, a Sikh temple which marks the birthplace of the tenth Guru, Govind Singh (1660). It is one of the four holy temples of the Sikhs. There are Jain and Hindu shrines of note, including that of Moti Brahma, a contemporary of Ashoka, who lies buried at the Brahmasthan.

800 m (½ mile) to the west of the Har Mandir at Padri-Ki-Haveli is the **Roman Catholic Cathedral of the Blessed Virgin Mary**. Built between 1772 and 1779, it was probably designed by Edward Tiretta and was built by Capuchin Father Joseph of Rovato. It is a distinguished church with a lofty dome and a fine pedimented Ionic portico. Internally, the order is Corinthian. The bell was donated in 1782 by Bahadur Shah, son of the Maharaja of Nepal.

Opposite the Cathedral is the **Old Cemetery**. Close to the City Dispensary is an **obelisk** on the site of the well where the bodies of sixty English captives were thrown by Samru (Walter Reinhardt) on

the orders of Mir Qasim on 6 and 11 October 1763. In November the massacre was avenged by Major Adams, who stormed the city. The nearby **Mangal Talao Tank** was built to commemorate Mr Ross Mangles, VC, the local Collector and one of the heroes of the siege of the house at Arrah in 1857.

There are three Muslim buildings of note. **Sher Shah's Mosque** in Haziganj was built between 1541 and 1545 in a bold Afghan style. The citadel was in the north-east corner. The **Patthar-Ki-Kasjid**, a rather inelegant stone mosque in Sultanganj, was built in 1626 by Mahabat Khan. **Mir Afjal's Mosque**, which lies behind the Bihar College of Engineering, is a little gem where the Emperor Farrukhsiyar worshipped.

PLASSEY

Little remains of the actual site of the most famous European battleground in India owing to the erosion of the site by the meandering Bhagirathi river. The scene of Clive's memorable victory of 23 June 1757 is marked by a number of monuments, one of which was erected at the instigation of Lord Curzon.

The position of the British forces is indicated by a mound near the river bank and by various memorials. The battle was a fairly small affair. Only twenty-eight British were killed and fifty wounded out of a total force of 3,000. The Nawab lost about 200. In comparison with later British military exploits, Plassey was little more than a skirmish, but it had massive political repercussions.

As early as 1801 the river had eaten away the battlefield, and by 1900 the entire Mango Tope had disappeared.

PURI

Puri, once the summer headquarters of the government of Orissa, lies 498 km

(310 miles) from Calcutta. It is a sacred town of great antiquity, with the colossal Temple of Jagannatha dominating the entire area. (For a full account of the Hindu temples and monuments see Volume I.)

PUSA

Pusa, a small town close to Muzaffarpur, lies on the Gandak river. Its principal interest is the former Imperial Agricultural Research Institute, designed in Free Renaissance style by James Ransome, consulting architect to the Government of India.

This important group of buildings was damaged severely in an earthquake in 1934. Only a fragment of the original range survives, faced in red brick with Mirzapur stone dressings.

RAJMAHAL

This small town on the right bank of the Ganges, about 38·5 km (24 miles) from English Bazaar, has extensive ruins of an old Muslim city buried in the jungle, about 6·4 km (4 miles) west of the modern town.

Man Singh, Akbar's famous Rajput general, chose Rajmahal as the capital of Bengal in 1592 owing to its strategic location. The seat of government was moved to Dacca in 1607, but it returned here again under Sultan Shuja in 1639. After the move of the capital to Murshidabad in 1707 the town fell into decay.

The chief monuments are the **Jami Masjid of Man Singh** (late 16th century) and the **Tomb of Miran** (c. 1760), the son of Mir Jafar, who killed Suraj-ud-Daula and was himself struck by lightning.

The ruins of the old palace of Sultan Shuja, son of Shah Jahan and local gover-

nor, can be seen. The **Sangi Dalan** or Hall of Stone (mid-17th century) is the largest surviving fragment. Close to the **Maina Tank** is a massive brick edifice with Arabic inscriptions. 92 m (300 ft) to the south is the **Akbari Mosque** (mid-17th century), once used as a British dispensary.

The road to the **Hadaf**, 6·4 km (4 miles) to the north-west, passes the Tanksal or Mint. The entrance to the Hadaf is by the eastern gateway. The mosque has a façade 60·8 m (200 ft) long with seven arches 6·7 m (22 ft) high. In the centre of the quadrangle is a tank.

On the road from Sahibganj to Rajmahal, close to the Jami Mosque, is a Mughal period bridge in brick and stone still in use today. It has fine, massive diamond-shaped piers carrying six arches with two circular bastions at each end.

Other notable structures include the Choti Mosque (1701–2) a rectangular, three-bay structure with a single dome; an old ruined hammam near the Akbari Mosque; a fine octagonal 17th-century tomb at Begampur; and the well-preserved Jumma Mosque (17th century), which has a fine carved slab of black basalt in the threshold of the central bay.

RANCHI

Ranchi is the old summer capital of the government of Bihar. It lies at a height of 651 m (2,138 ft) above sea level and is a typical hill station, with the usual club, library, courthouse and church, but it is now overshadowed by a large industrial suburb for the iron and steel industry.

There is a strong Christian presence in the town. The SPG (the Society for the Propagation of the Gospel) have a number of schools here and a handsome church. Other than the religious missions, schools and convents there are no buildings of any great consequence.

Ranchi is a useful centre for excursions in the Chota–Nagpur area.

SASARAM

Sasaram, 98 km (61 miles) south of Arrah, is famous for its mausolea. The name is reputed to be derived from a chief with a thousand arms.

The magnificent five-storey **Tomb of**

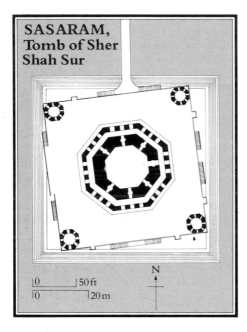

SASARAM, Tomb of Sher Shah Sur

0 — 50 ft
0 — 20 m
N

Sher Shah Sur (1540-45), on the west edge of the town, is built of red stone. Constructed by him to the designs of his architect, Aliwal Khan, it stands on a stepped square plinth on a terrace approached through a gateway via a bridge placed across a large lake. An error in orientating the tomb on the main axis was corrected only after the lower platform had been built, creating a curious skewed relationship between the upper and lower levels.

The tomb, an immense pyramidal pile of masonry ordered in five distinct stages, rises over 46 m (150 ft) and is a sophisticated development of earlier Lodi prototypes in Delhi. The dome has a 22 m (72 ft) span. It comprises an octagonal chamber surrounded by an arcade, which forms a gallery. The domed canopies in each corner of the platform, the ubiquitous kiosks and delicate merlons, and the octagonal drum coalesce to form a highly accomplished design and a remarkably powerful silhouette.

Within the town is the **Tomb of Hasan Sur Khan** (early 16th century), the father of Sher Shah Sur, who was killed at Kalinjar. The **Tomb of Salim Shah** (mid-16th century), who was the son of Sher Shah Sur, lies about 1·6 km (1 mile) to the north-west, but it is incomplete.

On a high hill east of the town is the remarkable **Mosque of Chandan Shahid**. In a small cave near the summit of the hill is an early Ashokan inscription from 232 BC.

At Koraich, about 1·6 km (1 mile) to the north, is a small British cemetery from the time of the Mutiny.

SERAMPORE

Serampore, situated 21 km (13 miles) north of Calcutta, was the former Danish settlement of Fredricksnagar. Established in 1755 by the Danish East India Company, the town was captured by the British in 1801 but then restored to the Danes by the Treaty of Amiens on 27 March 1802. In 1808 it was captured once more, then returned again in 1815, at which time it had begun to silt up and ceased to have much maritime use. In 1845 the Danes sold their Indian possessions – Tranquebar, Fredricksnagar and some land at Balasore – to the British for £125,000.

Later Serampore became renowned for the work of the three Baptist missionaries – William Carey, William Ward and Joshua Marshman – who resided in the

Danish port to avoid the hostility of the English authorities in Calcutta.

Serampore College (1821) faces Barrackpore Park across the river. It was built by Major B. Wickede in the Ionic style and recalls the palace of the Nawab of Murshidabad. It comprises a central range, with a projecting apse on the south face flanked by two wings. The centre of the main building is occupied by two halls set behind an Ionic entrance portico with a rich moulded entablature. The façades of the wings are less elaborate. Internally there are two iron staircases, which were cast in Birmingham, as were the entrance gates and fanlights.

The College contains numerous portraits, including Marshman by Zoffany and Fredrik VI of Denmark, King Christian and his queen, Louisa August of Augustenberg. The latter portrait has been mistaken for Madame Grand, the object of Sir Philip Francis's passions and later the wife of Talleyrand.

The fine classical mansion next to the Chapel is owned by the India Jute Mill. From here J. C. Marshman, son of the missionary, edited the *Friend of India*, progenitor of the Calcutta *Statesman*. In the grounds of the College is the house where Carey died in 1834. The central avenue, fringed with casuarina trees, is laid out attractively. **St Olav's Church** (1805; completed 1821) stands to one side. The design was based on a drawing prepared by an English engineer, Lieutenant Alexander Armstrong (1782–1817), but it was adapted during the course of its construction by Major Wickede. It is based on the usual Gibbs's prototype of St Martin-in-the-Fields, London, and more particularly on the early Indian example of St John's, Calcutta, but the broken pediment over the portico is distinctly Danish in character. The church was financed partly through the efforts of the Danish governor Ole Bie and partly by a gift of 10,000 rupees from the Marquess of Wellesley, who wished to enhance the view from Bar-

rackpore opposite with a steeple. The church contains a memorial to Dr Carey and his associates, who are buried in the Baptist Cemetery.

The former Manager's House or **Government House** retains a fine entrance gateway (1814), which was once enriched with the monogram of Fredrik VI set in a triangular pediment carried on paired Ionic pilasters, but much of this Baroque detail has been eroded.

Nearby is the **Roman Catholic Church** (1776), endowed by the Baretto family, with a fine Doric order carrying an enormous segmental pediment.

A number of early-19th-century classical bungalows survive, but the reputation of the town as a refuge for adventurers, debtors and radicals has long since faded. It is now a quiet, backwater suburb of Calcutta, but none the less it is worth an excursion from the city.

SHILLONG

Shillong, a pleasant hill station, is now the capital of Meghalaya, a state created in 1971 as a home for the Khasia, Jantia and Garo tribespeople. It is known as the Scotland of the East, as much for its incredibly high rainfall (23 m [75 ft] in one record year!) as for the Highland appearance of the landscape.

The entire town was razed by an earthquake in 1897, so there are few buildings of any interest. There are a church, a Welsh Presbyterian Mission, Roman Catholic College and Schools, as well as the Pasteur Institute. The local Khasis are interesting in that they are matrilineal and trace their language and culture to Cambodian roots.

Government House, close to Ward Lake, is worth a look.

Little is known of the region prior to the arrival of the British. Today it offers enchanting scenery, a cool invigorating

317

climate and an opportunity to visit the famous tea plantations of Assam and Meghalaya, where a strong British influence remains.

TRIBENI

Tribeni, a small riverside village in Hooghly district, was one of the earliest Muslim settlements in Bengal. From their base here the Muslims pressed inland and established control over a wide area between Hooghly and Burdwan.

There are two interesting early remains. The **Mosque of Zafar Khan Ghazi** bears the Arabic chronogram 1298, but several later inscriptions can also be found which suggest that the mosque was remodelled over time, although the simple rectangular plan is probably original. The east façade has five large basalt-faced arched entrances crowned by domes. The interior is split into two aisles by huge piers with pre-Islamic characteristics. Zafar Khan was a 13th-century military agent of the Sultans of Delhi.

The **Tomb of Zafar Khan Ghazi** (1313) is the oldest surviving mausoleum in eastern India. The date 1313 is inscribed on two basalt slabs cemented into the sarcophagus. The tomb was probably used as a madrasa and it may stand on the site of an earlier temple. The doorways are reused from a temple and sculpted panels bearing Vaishnavite subjects can be seen embedded in the plinth.

WESTERN INDIA

ELEVEN

WESTERN INDIA

Gujarat, Rajasthan

Introduction

Western India comprises the states of Rajasthan and Gujarat, both of which have a distinctive regional flavour. Rajasthan, the land of princes, is one of the most romantic regions of India, an evocative blend of exuberant people, arid deserts and beautiful lakes and forests studded with spectacular fortresses and luxurious palaces. To the south-west is Gujarat, a great contrast. It is a fertile land of wheat, cotton and banana plantations irrigated by a complex of rivers, including the Sabarmati, Mali, Tapi and Narmada. The southern borders of the state run into the high, rolling hills of the Western Ghats.

The myriad small kingdoms and principalities which once comprised the Rajput states now form the state of Rajasthan. In the south-east lie the rugged ranges of the Aravalli Hills. To the north-west is the burning, inhospitable plain of the Great Thar Desert, where exotic camel trains can be seen trailing serenely across a blistered landscape.

The Rajputs, fierce martial clans who claim descent from the early Aryan warriors, boast a legendary lineage. The Solar Rajputs, or Suryavansh, include the Sisodas of Mewar, Rathores of Marwar and Bikaner and the Kachhawahs of Amber and Jaipur. These claim descent from Lord Rama. The Lunar Rajputs or Chandravansh, such as the Bhattis of Jaisalmer, claim descent from Lord Krishna. The Fire-born Race or Agnicula

are considered the greatest, having been born from sacred fire rather than woman. These include the Chauhans of Delhi and Ajmer, the Harachauhans of Bundi and Kota and the Deoras of Siroli, created by the Brahmin sage Vashista from the sacred pit of fire or agnikunda on Mount Abu.

These Rajput clans were bound by strict codes of honour. They were a formidable force who never acknowledged defeat, but unlike the Marathas they were never united. They fought as much among themselves as against outsiders. When faced with overwhelming odds, the women and children would commit ritual johar, mass immolation in the sacred flames, to escape the indignity of capture or surrender, while the men sallied forth to certain death.

Chitorgarh was conquered three times by Muslim invaders and three times there was mass slaughter. In the second great johar of 1535 over 13,000 women followed their princess into the sacred fire and 32,000 warriors fell fighting to the last. This proud and chivalrous warrior race was also immensely gifted and their martial history is interwoven with fine music, poetry, painting and architecture.

Much of the early architecture of the region was destroyed by the recurrent waves of Muslim invasions. At **Ajmer** the Arhai-din-Ka-Jhonpra Mosque, a major religious centre for the Sufi Chish-

Overleaf The romantic desert skyline of Jaisalmer

tia order, is a rare survival from the 12th century, but the most attractive feature of Rajasthan is its unparalleled heritage of fortified cities and palaces. Even small towns and villages are defended by formidable bastions and protective ramparts, a product of the warlike history of the region.

Generally, most palaces were built as inner citadels, surrounded by the city and enclosed by a fortified wall, although this was not always the case. At **Jodhpur** and **Alwar** huge forts were built on the summits of adjacent hills, while at **Amber** and **Bundi** the palace is perched on the hillside with the fort above and the ramparts below. At **Kumbhalgarh, Chitorgarh** and the exotic desert city of **Jaisalmer** impregnable fortifications encircle the entire settlement, reinforced with bastions and watchtowers. Often the palaces of Rajasthan, such as those at **Bundi** and **Udaipur**, were the product of incremental additions, each generation adding further extensions and refinements, but with care and thought given to maintaining a well-integrated, harmonious whole. The City Palace of the Maharanas of **Udaipur** is a classic example of this, a sequence of individual palaces connected by labyrinthine corridors constructed over a period of 300 years.

In contrast to the perfect symmetry and relentless logic of Mughal architecture, these Rajput palaces are complex compositions. Their planning and spatial arrangements are designed to tease and mislead the observer; their character is both elusive and mysterious.

Some forts, such as those at **Bharatpur** and **Deeg**, were protected by wide moats. As in most desert regions, water plays a vital role in the culture of the people. Many of the finest palaces at **Amber** and **Bundi** are enhanced by the conscious use of water in the landscape, and where it was insufficient, as at **Udaipur**, entire artificial lakes were created, overlooked by luxurious gardens and terraces punctuated with pavilions, kiosks, ghats and temples.

The Rajputs were great patrons of the arts. Under their enlightened tutelage, a unique architectural style was developed that originally owed little to alien external influences. Only with the establishment of Mughal pre-eminence from the late 16th century was a synthesis of Rajput and Mughal forms achieved. The Rajasthani school of miniature painting is an interesting example of this cultural exchange.

From the middle of the 18th century mural painting became increasingly popular and elaborate, the most splendid being added to the palaces at **Bundi, Kota** and **Jodhpur**. It also flourished, however, in the smaller states such as Kishangarh, where it offered a means of embellishing otherwise pedestrian buildings.

With the decline of the Mughal Empire, many Rajput princes reasserted their independence. At **Jaipur** its enlightened ruler indulged his love of astronomy, architecture, art and beauty in the creation of the city of **Jaipur**, a unique planned settlement arranged according to traditional Hindu canons and European principles on a grid plan, with wide tree-lined streets and a sumptuous palace at its heart.

Under British paramountcy, most states remained under native rule, so the most significant European buildings are confined to the old British residencies or to the work of British architects employed by the native princes. Among these the Indo-Saracenic buildings built by Sir Samuel Swinton Jacob in **Jaipur, Ajmer** and elsewhere are notable.

Gujarat comprises a fertile arc of territory which can be split into three areas: the mainland region, with the great cities of **Ahmadabad** and **Vadodara** (Baroda) and the coastal port of **Surat**; the Kathiawar peninsula, known as Saurashtra, an area never absorbed into British India but fragmented into over 200 petty states;

and across the Gulf of Kutch, the isolated salt marshlands of Kutch.

There is archaeological evidence of settlements in the Narmada valley as early as 3000 BC. Lothal was a centre of the Harappan or Indus Valley civilization over 4000 years ago, and the area has been settled continuously ever since. Early Muslim influence can be traced to the raids of Mahmud of Ghazni in the 11th century, but the first architectural impact must be attributed to the governors appointed by the Khalji sultans of Delhi, who established themselves in the coastal towns of the western seaboard early in the 14th century.

The regional style of architecture which developed in Gujarat was the largest and most important provincial expression of Indo-Islamic architecture. It flourished for over 250 years, until the last half of the 16th century, when the country was absorbed by the Mughal Empire. Stylistically, it may be divided into three distinct periods.

In the early 14th century there was the familiar process of demolition and reconversion of Jain and Hindu temples into mosques, and the evolution of a transitionary style which had not yet attained a distinctive character. The Jami Masjid at **Cambay** (1325) is a good example of this, but other buildings, such as Hilal Khan Qazi's Mosque at **Dholka**, the ruins of the Adina Masjid at **Patan** and the Jami Masjid at **Broach** (1300), bear witness to this early period.

By the second half of the fifteenth century the style had become more refined and assured. A specific architectural expression had been developed, but it was one which was still tentative and exploratory. The best examples are the Ahmad Shahi buildings at **Ahmadabad** and, in particular, the Jami Masjid (1424), the finest architectural achievement of the period. The consummation of the style is achieved in the third period under the power and patronage of Mahmud Begada (1458–1511) and his successors.

For a period of about ninety years, until 1550, the provincial style of Gujarat was at its apogee, with a splendid series of buildings at **Ahmadabad** and **Champaner**.

Water has played an important part in the architectural heritage of western India from the earliest times. One of the most characteristic features of the early Harappan towns was the presence of a sophisticated system of drains, wells and tanks, indicating a controlled use of water. The practice of making wells into an art form was begun by the Hindus but it developed under Muslim rule.

The vavs or baolis of Gujarat consist of two parts: a vertical shaft from which water is drawn and the surrounding inclined subterranean passageways, chambers and steps which provide access to the well. Some of these are spectacular creations, the most notable being Bai Hai's vav at **Ahmadabad**, built in 1499. The galleries and chambers surrounding these wells, often carved profusely with elaborate detail, became cool, quiet retreats during the hot weather.

In addition to the distinctive Islamic style which developed in Gujarat, with its intricate stone lattice screens and pointed minarets, there is a rich legacy of vernacular architecture in towns such as **Bhuj**, Dwarka and **Ahmadabad**. In the old quarters of many towns and villages fine, intricately carved timber houses may be found oversailing the narrow alleys and streets. The reputation of the region for architectural exuberance can be traced right through the 19th century in the remarkable mausolea of the rulers of **Junagadh**, a city with a fascinating array of buildings which combine local, European and Gothic forms in a riotous mixture of styles.

Some of the distinctive regional character of Gujarat can be attributed to its long maritime tradition. The proximity of the sea and the development of strong business and trading links across the Arabian Sea created an enterprising mercantile spirit and fostered early links with the European trading companies. **Surat**, on the old trade route for silks and spices in the Gulf of Cambay, was the site of the first English factory to be established, followed by the Dutch and Portuguese. At **Daman** and **Diu** the Portuguese seized local control in the 16th century, but, after a brief period of prosperity, these coastal towns declined into colonial backwaters. Today they are imbued with a charming Mediterranean-style atmosphere. Throughout Gujarat there is a fascinating legacy of early European funerary architecture in the form of sepulchres, tombs and cemeteries, the most notable being the Oxinden mausoleum and the adjacent Dutch tombs at **Surat**.

For the duration of the Raj, much of the area was ruled indirectly through the native princes, so that, as in Rajasthan, the principal British influence was confined to local residencies and later to the work of British architects in the native states. The buildings of Major Charles Mant (1840–81) at **Bhavnagar, Surat** and **Vadodara** (Baroda) pioneered the development of Indo-Saracenic styles of architecture. This was taken further by Robert Fellowes Chisholm (1840–1915), the Madras-based architect who took over Mant's work in **Vadodara** and built the spectacular Laxhmi Vilas Palace and other fine civic buildings for the Gaekwar. Similarly, the exotic palaces of the native rulers at **Dungarpur, Morvi, Porbandar** and **Wankaner** demonstrate the extent to which the Indian ruling classes were influenced by European culture and design at the height of the Raj.

The Arhai-din-ka-Jhonpra Mosque at Ajmer

Above Qutb Shah's Mosque, Ahmadabad

Left Gateway to the Palace, Bundi

Right The Tower of Victory or Jaya Stambh, Chitorgarh

Right above Step well or baoli at Bundi

Right below The Great Walls of the City Palace at Udaipur

Left The mighty fortifications of Kumbhalgarh

Below Meherangarh Fort, Jodhpur

Above right The Sawan Bhavan, Deeg

Below right The Hawa Mahal, Jaipur

The Chandra Mahal in the Palace at Jaipur

Above right Laxhmi Vilas Palace at Vadodara

Below right The Umaid Bhavan Palace, Jodhpur

Ranjit Vilas Palace, Wankaner

The Maqbara of Baha-ud-Din Bhar at Junagadh

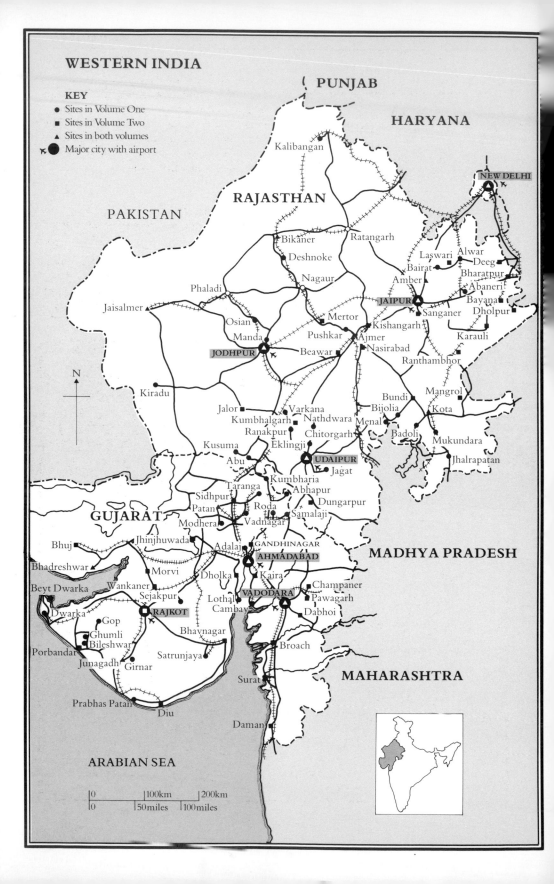

WESTERN INDIA

KEY
● Sites in Volume One
■ Sites in Volume Two
▲ Sites in both volumes
✈● Major city with airport

ABU

Abu, the Mount Olympus of India, is situated on a rocky plateau which rises 1,165 m (3,822 ft) above sea level. It comprises a hill station of exceptional natural beauty, but is more renowned for the magnificent complex of Jain temples at Dilwara, which is a place of widespread pilgrimage (see Volume I).

This celebrated sacred mountain was visited by Lieutenant-Colonel James Tod early in the 19th century and the hill station was formed shortly after. It has an English church, club, barracks, hospital and a Police Training School, formerly the Lawrence School. Honoria Law-rence, wife of Sir Henry Lawrence, the hero of Lucknow, died here in 1854 and is buried in the cemetery. Two rocky crags near the station are called 'The Nun' and 'The Toad' for their curious resemblance to a veiled woman and an immense crouching toad.

AHMADABAD (AHMEDABAD)

Ahmadabad, situated on the banks of the Sabarmati river, is known as the Manchester of western India. It is a large industrial centre and the principal city of Gujarat, the new capital of which, Gandhinagar, lies 19 km (12 miles) to the north.

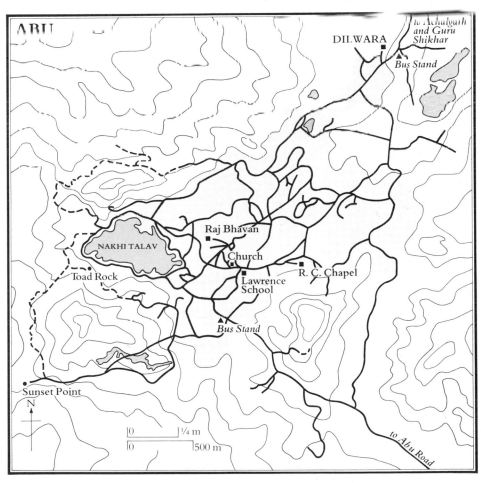

335

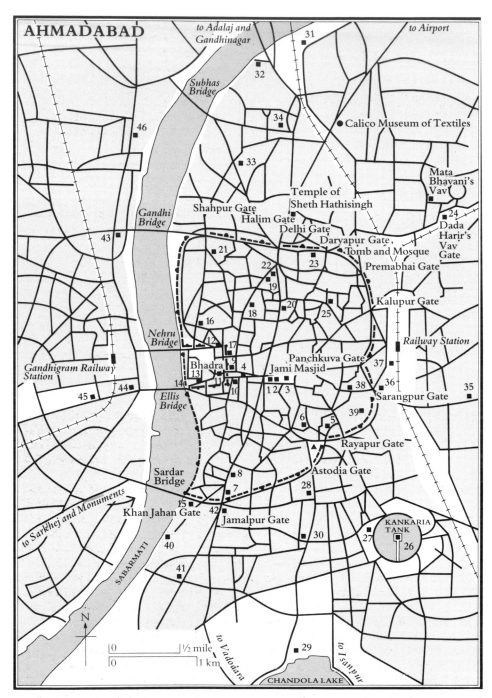

KEY
1. Jami Masjid
2. Tomb of Ahmad Shah
3. Tomb of Ahmad Shah's Queens
4. Tin Darwaza
5. Rani Sipri's Mosque

6. Mosque of Dastur Khan
7. Mosque of Haibat Khan
8. Nawab Sardar Khan's Mosque and Tomb
9. Mosque of Malik Shaban
10. Mosque of Shah Khub Sayyid
11. Palace of Azam Khan
12. Mosque of Sidi Sayyid
13. Ahmad Shah's Mosque
14. Manik Burj
15. Khan Jahan's Mosque
16. Mosque of Sayyid Alam
17. Mosque, Tomb and Madrasa of Shujaat Khan
18. Rani Rupavatis Mosque and Tomb
19. Christ Church
20. Mosque of Muhafiz Khan
21. Mosque of Shaikh Hasan Muhammad Chishti
22. Mosque of Qutb Shah
23. Futi Masjid
24. Mata Bhawani Well and Dada Hari Well, Tomb and Mosque

25. Sakar Khan's Mosque
26. Hauz-i-Qutb and Kankaria Tank
27. Dutch Tombs
28. Mosque of Ibrahim Sayyid
29. Rauza of Shah Alam
31. Shahi Bagh Palace
32. Mosque of Miyan Khan Chishti
33. Achyut Bibi's Mosque and Tomb
34. Tomb of Darya Khan
35. Bibi-Ki-Masjid, Rajpur
36. Sidi Bashir's Minars
37. Minars at the Railway Station
38. Queen's Mosque and Tomb Sarangpur
39. Mosque of Muhammad Ghauth Gwaliyari
40. Baba Lului's Mosque
41. Tomb of Abu Turab
42. Old English Cemetery
43. High Court
44. Town Hall
45. Gujarat College
46. Mosque and Rauza of Sayyid Uthman, Usmanpur

(For the Calico Museum of Textiles see Volume I.)

The old city lies on the left bank of the river, but in recent years it has sprawled across to the right bank, to which it is connected by a series of robust bridges capable of withstanding the seasonal floods. In the 17th Century it was renowned as the greatest city of Hindustan, comparable in size and wealth to London, and in spite of the vicissitudes of fortune, it remains a prosperous and influential city, famous for its historic buildings and associations with Gandhi's social work. It was from here that Gandhi commenced his famous march against the Salt Law. Although it is not usually visited by tourists, the narrow streets, vernacular buildings and historic monuments make this a rewarding experience, but the noise, pollution and dust can be wearing.

Ahmad Shah I waged incessant wars against his tough Rajput neighbours and as a result of ceaseless punitive expeditions, the Ahmad Shahi dynasty secured a local hegemony which lasted over 150 years.

The original settlement was the old Hindu town of Asaval, where Ahmad Shah had resided as heir-apparent. He presumably found the place agreeable to him, for in 1411 he founded the new city of Ahmadabad, which eventually subsumed Asaval. The foundations of the city and the precise location were vested with deep sanctity and chosen on the advice of his spiritual preceptor.

The oldest part of the city, the Bhadra towers, massive square bastions in the royal citadel, were erected in 1411, but the remaining fortifications were erected over a long period of time. The historian Ferishta records that they were largely completed by 1486. Originally, the city walls comprised twelve gates, 139 towers

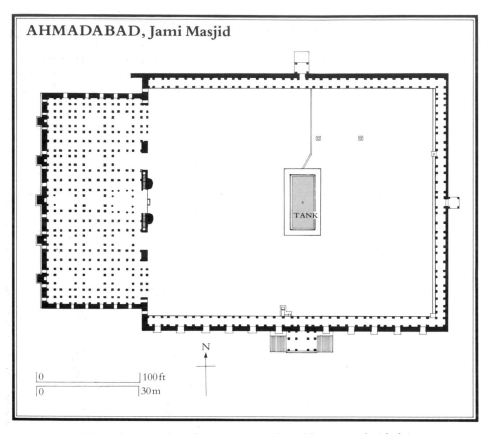

AHMADABAD, Jami Masjid

and over 6,000 battlements, but these are now nearly all demolished, although a few of the old gates remain. The city is the centre of the northern Jains.

Architecturally, the buildings of Ahmadabad are important as they include some of the most interesting examples of the provincial style which flourished in Gujarat from the mid-15th century. The monuments in and around the city fall broadly into two main periods: the period of Ahmad Shah I, from the first half of the 15th century, and the period of Mahmud Begada, from the second half of the 15th century and later. The name Begada means 'two forts', commemorating his capture of Champaner and Junagadh. The city has an excellent heritage of vernacular buildings, with fine carved timber houses in Gujarati style.

The old city is divided into separate quarters or pols. The monuments should be visited in sequence, and the best starting-point is the Jami Masjid in Gandhi Road, a short distance beyond the Tripolia Gate or **Tin Darwaza**. This triple-arched gateway bisects the main street running east from the Bhadra Citadel. It is from the earlier part of Ahmad Shah's reign and carries a later datestone (1814) recording a municipal order. This gateway once led to the outer court of the Bhadra or royal citadel. In 1638 records show it was surrounded by palm trees and tamarinds. Opposite the Bhadra gate is a public garden. To the west is the Hemabhai Institute and beyond that the Government Telegraph Office.

The **Jami Masjid** or Friday Mosque lies at the centre of the city. It was completed in 1424 and is entered from the north by a flight of steps. The vast courtyard is surrounded by an arcaded cloister. The qibla wall lies to the west. Close to the main arch is a large black slab, which is the inverted base of a buried Jain idol on which the faithful tread. Immediately to the east a white marble crescent marks the spot where the imam leads prayers.

The interior is carried on 260 columns

divided into fifteen bays, corresponding to three rows of five domes in the roof and five mihrabs. The centre cupola is higher. The central nave rises to three storeys. At each stage of the central gallery are balconies overlooking pillared loggias enclosed by perforated screens. The five mihrabs are all of decorated coloured marble. Originally, there were two lofty minarets, but these were reduced to half their height by an earth-

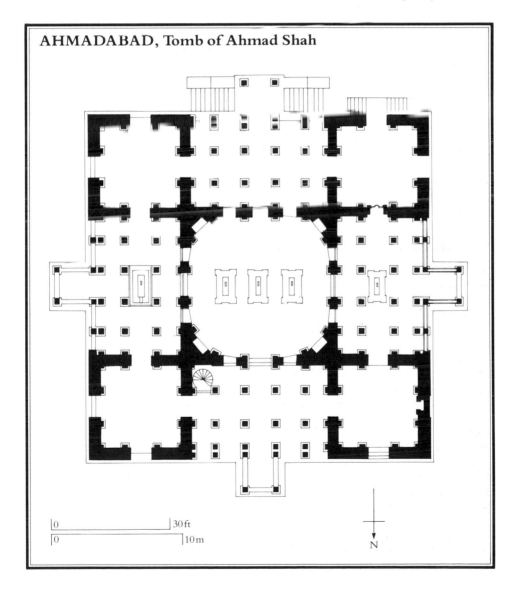

AHMADABAD, Tomb of Ahmad Shah

0 — 30 ft
0 — 10 m

N

quake in 1819 and the 'shaking minarets', as they were known, were finally demolished by an earth tremor in 1957.

In the enclosure immediately to the east of the mosque, in the Manek Chowk, is the magnificent **Tomb of Ahmad Shah I**. He died in 1442, but the tomb was probably commenced in his lifetime. It was restored in 1587. It is a square structure crowned by a dome, with projecting porticos on each side, that to the south providing the main entrance. Enclosed verandahs connect the porticos to small square corner chambers capped by small domes. Perforated stone screens allow light to come into the interior. The central chamber, over which rises the main dome, is paved with multi-coloured marble. The centre tomb is that of Ahmad Shah I (1442), that to the left Muhammad Shah, his son (1451), and that to the east, Qutb Shah, his grandson (1458).

Just beyond the tombs, across the street, are the **Tombs of the Queens of Ahmad Shah** or the Rani-Ka-Hujra. Similar in style to Ahmad Shah's mausoleum, eight marble tombs stand on a platform within an arcaded and screened outer cloister. The façade has thirteen highly ornamental carved recesses. The centre tomb is probably that of Bibi Mughali, wife of Muhammad Shah II and mother of Sultan Mahmud Begada (1458–1511). Adjacent is another tomb, of black stone once inlaid with mother of pearl, possibly the grave of Murki Bib, sister of Bibi Mughali and first wife of Shah Alam, the saint. The tomb is in poor repair, enclosed by houses and used as a market.

Close to the Astodiya Gate, south-east of the centre of the city, is **Rani Sipri's Mosque**, also known as the Masjid-e-Nagira or Jewel of a Mosque on account of its elegant design. Built in 1514 it is a small structure only two bays deep with a row of paired columns to the front. It has been called 'one of the most exquisite buildings in the world'. It is strongly

Hindu in character, in the style of the early 16th century, with an open façade and crenellated parapet over the cornice. The slender corner minarets are in four sections and the windows are elaborately embellished with stone tracery.

The **Rauza** or Tomb lies in front of the mosque, square in plan with twenty columns enclosing the central chamber. The upper sections have perforated stone screens, now restored. The queen's grave was originally marble but is now plaster. Only the inner tomb is raised up beneath the central dome; the lower storey is articulated by carved merlons to the parapet, punctuated by four small corner domes.

On the west side of the street, about 500 m (1,625 ft) from the Astodiya Gate, is the **Mosque of Dastur Khan** (1486), built by one of Mahmud Begada's ministers. It has an unusual and irregular plan, surrounded by a cloister with double cloisters on the western side forming the sanctuary. The entrance porch is on the east side. Finely perforated jali screens enclose the outer walls of the cloister, which has a domed roof carried on pillars. To the south-east is a large tank linked to a vaulted reservoir. The grave of Dastur Khan lies in the open courtyard near the south doorway. Just to the east of the mosque is Asa Bhil's Mound, the ancient site of a Bhil chieftain's grave, after whom the original settlement of Asaval was named.

The **Mosque of Haibat Khan** (c. 1425) lies north-east of the Jamalpur Gate, in the south sector of the city. It is similar in appearance to the Ahmad Shah Mosque but more plainly detailed, utilizing Hindu masonry. The entrance, through an ornate outer porch, leads to the sanctuary, which is pierced by three pointed archways, the central one higher than the outer two. The minarets are small, unadorned shafts rising from the roof. The central dome is richly carved with a wealth of Hindu details. The pillars come from various Hindu temples and boast a wide variety of carved detail. Remnants of Hindu and Jain temples have obviously been salvaged and reused, but it is also possible that the mosque is built over and incorporates an earlier native temple. Haibat Khan was a leading nobleman at the court of Ahmad Shah.

About 366 m (1,190 ft) away to the east of Jamalpur Road is **Nawab Sardar Khan's Mosque** and **Tomb**. The enclosure is entered by a high gateway and is very dilapidated. The mosque has three pointed arches to the façade and solid four-storey minarets, octagonal at the lower level and circular above. The roof has three onion-style domes crowned by crescents. The Rauza or tomb stands close by in a separate court. It has eight smaller domes around a large central dome.

Close to the Government Telegraph Office, near the Khas Bazaar and the jail, is the **Mosque of Malik Sha'ban** (1452), with a peculiar plan reminiscent of a Hindu mandapa. It is a Hindu structure converted into a mosque. Seven smaller domes surround a larger central one, the inner ceilings covered in Hindu-style coffers. The central hall is carried on twelve pillars. Trelliswork windows at either end provide light to the interior.

To the south of Karanj, in Khas Bazaar, is the **Mosque of Shah Khub Sayyid** (1538), one of the last to be erected in Ahmadabad under the sultanate. The roof carried three rows of seven equal-sized domes. The building is hemmed in on all sides by shops. To the north is the tomb of Khub Sayyid Muhammad Chishti.

The **Bhadra** or **Bhadar** is the ancient royal citadel, built by Ahmad Shah in 1411. It is the oldest part of the city. It takes its name from the goddess Bhadra, an incarnation of Kali, and is now used as government offices. On the east side, facing the Tin Darwaza, is the **Palace of Azam Khan** (1635–42), nicknamed 'the white ant' for his love of building. It is

now used as a post office. Over the gateway is the date 1636. The north entrance to the Bhadra is through an archway and opens out into a large octagonal hall, containing an arched gallery in the upper level, enclosed by a low wall of pierced stone. Each gallery is crowned by a cupola. Beneath the hall is a lofty vaulted chamber with a fountain and tank to the centre.

The **Mosque of Sidi Sayyid** (1572–3) stands in the north-east corner of the citadel and once formed part of the city walls. It has been attributed to a slave of Ahmad Shah I, but the architectural style, form and composition suggest a much later date and it is now accredited to a distinguished noble of the time of Sultan Muzaffar III (1561–72). It is famous for its ten carved, semicircular windows enclosed with exquisite tracery in the form of tree stems and branches. Those on the western wall are considered to be the finest examples of carved stone tracery in India, surpassing even those in Agra and Delhi. Internally, eight pillars divide the space into fifteen bays, crowned by domes of differing styles.

In the south-west corner of the Bhadra is **Ahmad Shah's Mosque** (1414), once used as the sultan's private place of worship. As one of the oldest mosques in the city, it is of interest as it is a Muslim composition with internal features of Hindu and Jain origin. The façade is plain, with incomplete minarets. The hall is three bays wide, with four other arched openings besides the central entrance. Eight perforated stone windows light the interior. To the north-west is the zenana enclosure, distinguished by twenty-five richly carved pillars. The entrance porch leading to it may be a remnant of an earlier temple on the site. Note the central mihrab on the west wall, with its fine black and white marble casing. On the platform opposite the sultan recited his prayers.

Close to the Khan Jahan Gate in the south-west corner of the citadel is **Khan**

Jahan's Mosque (early 16th century), with an open pillared façade and low ceiling. At each end are thin minarets. In front of the mosque is a single pavilion, believed to be the grave of Khan Jahan.

The Ganj-i-Shahid immediately to the left of the entrance is the martyrs' burial ground.

To the north is the **Manik Burj** or Ruby Bastion, incorporating the foundation stone of the city. The small circular tomb next to the Collector's Office is alleged to be that of the Persian warrior Ibrahim Quli Khan.

The **Tomb of Shah Wajih-ud-Din** (c. 1609) is a fine Muslim sepulchre, worthy of note, built by Saiyad Murtaza Khan Bokhari, the 11th viceroy.

The **Mosque of Sayyid Alam** (1412) was built by Abubakr Husaini and is one of the first to have been erected in the city. Architecturally, it comes at the earliest stage of the provincial style, with rich Hindu decoration and motifs, three arched entrances of equal height, a higher central wing and multi-storey balconied minars.

The **Mosque, Tomb and Madrasa of Shujaat Khan** (1695) stand close to the Lal Gate of the Bhadra. The Marble or Ivory Mosque has two thin minarets, with a frontage of five bays divided by piers. The inscription over the qibla is the date. The walls are lined to dado level with marble. The brick tomb is badly damaged.

Rani Rupavati's Mosque is situated in the Mirzapur district, north-west of the Delhi Gate near the Grand Hotel. Like most local mosques, it incorporates elements of Hindu and Islamic design in a mixture of arcuated and trabeated elements. It is now believed to date from the reign of Muzaffar Shah II (1511–26). It has a high central arch flanked by low minarets, truncated by the earthquake of 1819, and two other arched openings. The roof carries three domes, corresponding to the entrances in the façade. The central section is raised a storey

above the flanks, providing a clerestory which admits light to the interior. The gallery has richly carved parapets. Note the finely worked mihrabs in the sanctuary.

The Rauza or **Tomb of Rani Rupavati** lies to the north-east of the mosque. Beneath the main dome are two white marble graves, the central one that of Rupavati (1430–40). Both are enriched with the typical chain and censer device. Architecturally, the building looks later and it could be contemporary with the mosque, that is, early 16th century.

East of Rani Rupavati's Mosque is the **Mosque of Muhafiz Khan** (1465), near the Delhi Gate. It was built by Jamail-ud-Din Muhafiz Khan, governor of the city under Mahmud Begada in 1471, and is an exquisite expression of elegance and symmetry. The façade is pierced by three high arched doors and the roof is carried on eight columns, dividing the sanctuary five rows long and three deep. At each end of the façade are beautifully carved minars, which contain staircases.

To the north-west is the **Rauza** or tomb of its founder, standing on a low plinth and carried on sixteen pillars. To the south-east is the large Swami Narayan Temple (1850). Close by is a Jain Asylum for Animals, beyond which is the **Nau Gaz Pir**, a group of nine tombs called the 'Nine Yard Saints'.

In the Shahpur district, close to the Shahpur Gate and the river, is the **Mosque of Shaikh Hasan Muhammad Chishti** (1565), which has large ornate but incomplete minarets. Over the central arch of the façade is a tiny balcony projecting on carved brackets.

The **Mosque of Qutb Shah** (1449) or Pattharwali Masjid lies in a crowded district about 274 m (890 ft) from the Delhi Gate. The central dome rises one storey above the general roof and is supported on eight pillars in an eight-point-star plan. The sanctuary walls are pierced by twelve traceried stone windows. At the north-west corner is a

rauza or tomb with thirty-two columns.

Between Daryapur Gate and Delhi Gate is the **Fath Masjid** (*c.* 1450–1500), probably built by Darya Khan. It has a central ornate mihrab. The façade is terminated by two slender minarets. In the courtyard opposite is an elaborate Hindu pavilion marking a grave.

Many of the remaining monuments are scattered across the city and its outskirts. Gujarat is famous for its baolis or step-wells and some fine examples can be discovered around Ahmadabad.

At Asarva, about 800 m (½ mile) north-east of the Daryapur Gate, are the **Wells of Dada Hari** and **Mata Bhavani**. Dada Hari (1499) is a peculiar place. A portico provides access to three tiers of platforms linked by spiral staircases that terminate deep underground in an octagonal well, which carries Sanskrit and Arabic inscriptions. It is a chill, eerie place, overlooked by galleries. About 46 m (150 ft) to the west is the **Mosque of Dada Hari**, with sinuous traceried windows, similar to those in Sidi Saiyid's Mosque, and two minarets damaged in 1819. To the north is the **Rauza of Dada Hari**. A finely carved door leads to a plain interior.

About 91 m (296 ft) to the north is the **Mata Bhavani**, reputedly dating from the time of Kayna Solanki (1063–93). From the platform, fifty-two steps lead to the water, which is overlooked by pillared galleries. The canopies, niches and friezes exhibit examples of premediaeval Hindu carving.

12·8 km (8 miles) north of Ahmadabad at Adalaj is a famous well, a model of which is in the Bodleian Library at Oxford.

Near the Kalupur Gate of the city is **Sakar Khan's Mosque** (late 15th century), a rather crude affair with an open hall and five domes.

1·2 km (¾ mile) south-east of the Rajpur Gate is the **Hauz-i-Qutb** or Kankariya Lake. It is a regular thirty-four-sided polygon over 1·6 km (1 mile) in circuit. Built by Sultan Qutb-ud-Din in 1451, it had sloping ramps to the sides and tiers of stone steps. On the east side is a beautifully carved inlet sluice. At each end of the triple-arched opening is a buttress similar in form to a low minar. The inlet is decorated with traceried sluice screens, a magnificently refined composition combining rare engineering skill with architectural grace. There is a zoo and children's park by the lake. On the island in the centre is an aquarium in the Ghattamandal pavilion.

On the east bank of the lake on the high ground are some fine **Dutch and Armenian Tombs** dating from 1615 to 1700, a fascinating group of obelisks, pyramids and pavilions. The Armenian tombs belonged to brokers in the Dutch factory. The tomb of Aldworth is notable. He established the East India Company's factory at Ahmadabad and died here in 1615.

North-west of the tank on the route from the Astodiya Gate is the Mosque of Ibrahim Sayyid (1540), a virtual copy of the Mosque of Shah Khub Sayyid in Khas Bazaar.

The journey may be continued to Batura, 8 km (5 miles) south of the Rajpur Gate. It is here that the saint Burhan-ud-Din Qutb-ul-Alam is buried. He exercised great influence over the court of Ahmad Shah I and died at Batura in 1452.

His mausoleum has arched and vaulted aisles and a central dome raised high on a second tier of arches, but parts have collapsed and it is in a ruined condition.

The **Rauza of Shah Alam**, the son of the saint, lies 3·2 km (2 miles) south-east of the city, on the road to Batura, in the village of Dani Limda. The road passes two plain gateways and a third with a music gallery or Nakkar Khana above. This leads to a huge courtyard. To the west stands the mosque, to the east the Rauza, protected by metal screens. To the south is the Assembly Hall (*c.* 1565), partly destroyed by the British under

General Goddard in 1780.

Shah Alam was the spiritual preceptor of Mahmud Begada. According to a chronogram on the tomb, it was built in 1485 by Taj Khan Nariali, a nobleman at Begada's court.

The Dargah of Shah Alam occupies the centre of the complex and took ten years to build. It is designed on a 'casket' pattern, with an outer hall enclosed by trellis screens, divided by twenty-eight pillars. The inner sanctum is crowned by a dome which rises over the grave. The main entrance is from the west. Each outer aisle has seven smaller domes to each face, while the main tomb chamber has finely perforated marble jali screens. The inside of the dome is enriched with mother of pearl and semi-precious stones provided by Asaf Khan, brother of Empress Nur Jahan. The brass doors to the tomb show signs of inferior restoration. Outside the outer north wall is the grave of Shaikh Kabir, a Muslim scholar, who died in 1618.

The **Jamaat Khana** or Assembly Hall (*c.* 1447) lies to the north-east of the mosque and faces south. It was restored by Muzaffar Shah III (1561–72) and then on several later occasions. The ancillary buildings are used by pilgrims.

The **Mosque** built by Muhammad Salih Badakhshi has later galleried minarets of seven storeys which were damaged in the earthquake of 1819 and restored. There are three large domes on the roof and eighteen smaller domes along the periphery. In front of the mosque is a large underground reservoir approached by a flight of steps in the north-east corner.

South of the mosque is a tomb similar to the main mausoleum, where the family of Shah Alam are buried.

About 1·6 km (1 mile) south of the city, near to the village of Dani Limda and near Shah Alam's complex, is the **Mosque of Malik Alam**, reputedly built in 1422 although no inscription survives. The central entrance is flanked by two robustly detailed low minars and parapets capped with merlons.

The **Shahi Bagh Palace** lies close to the railway bridge over the Sabarmati river. This royal garden palace was built in 1622 by Shah Jahan, who was then the Viceroy of Ahmadabad, as a famine-relief measure. Later, additions were made by Mr Williams, a British civil servant, in 1835, and since 1960 it has been used as the Raj Bhavan of the Governor of Gujarat. An underground passage is alleged to connect Chhata Shahi Bagh with the main house.

About 500 m (1,625 ft) southward, near the river, is the **Mosque of Miyan Khan Chishti** (1465), a fine commingling of Hindu and Muslim features built by Malik Maksud Wazir. The screened façade has three arches, with elaborately carved minarets in the centre. The sanctuary is also in three compartments, that to the centre forming the nave and raised a further storey in height, crowned by three domes. In 1574 much of the back wall was replaced when the adjacent area was made into a house.

800 m (½ mile) to the south-west is **Achyut Bibi's Mosque and Tomb**, built in 1469 by Imad al Mulk, one of Mahmud Begada's chief ministers, for his wife Bibi Achyut Kuki, whose tomb lies close by. It is a fine amalgamation of Hindu and Muslim elements. Note the arches supporting the ends of the gallery in the front aisle – an unusual device in Gujarat – and the beautifully decorated mihrab and inner surfaces of the central dome. The tomb is located to the north-east of the enclosure. It has a central dome, surrounded by eight smaller domes and some good jali screens inside.

About 1·2 km (¾ mile) north of the Delhi Gate towards Shahi Bagh is the **Tomb of Darya Khan** (1453), one of the few surviving brick tombs in the area. The structure is similar to the Khan Masjid and is by the same builder, but it has suffered from neglect and alteration. Each face is pierced by five arched entrances, above which rises a large imposing dome 2·7 m (9 ft) thick and the largest in Gujarat. To the south-east is the large Hathi Singh Jain Temple (1853).

At Rajpur, about 1·2 km (¾ mile) south-east of the Sarangpur Gate, is the **Bibi-ki-Masjid**, an immense mosque built in 1454, perhaps by Budhan bin Sayyid Yaqut in memory of his wife. It is a vast, ponderous building with a triple arched façade and robust minar buttresses, one taller than the other. Internally, the five mihrabs are richly decorated with rosettes and chain and censer details. At the north end is a royal gallery, over the landing to which is a remarkable carved dome with a spiral pendentive in the centre.

About 1·6 km (1 mile) south of the railway station, opposite the Sarangpur Gate, are **Sidi Bashir's Minars**, two lofty minarets with a connecting bridge, which once formed the principal entrance archway to the original mosque, destroyed by the Marathas in 1753. A modern mosque occupies the site. Each minar has three elegant bracketed balconies. They are the finest examples of the 'shaking minarets' common in Gujarat, a phenomenon caused by the use of flexible sandstone in the foundations.

Near the railway station are two other splendid brick minars (early 16th century) similar in style to Sidi Bashir's.

Not far from the Sarangpur Gate is the **Queen's Mosque and Tomb**, not to be confused with Rani Rupavati's Mosque. It was built by Malik Quivam ul Mulk Sarang, one of the distinguished nobles at the court of Mahmud Begada. He was a Rajput who converted to Islam and he became governor of the city in 1521.

The **Mosque** (later 15th century) has five large domes above a series of fine arched gateways, the central one being larger and higher than those to each side. The two elaborate minars are truncated at roof level and resemble those at the Bibi-ki-Masjid.

The **Tomb**, which is in poor condi-

tion, lies in front of the mosque. The inner sanctum carries an upper projection and long gallery around the central high dome. Two tombs lie inside.

Also in the Sarangpur quarter is the **Mosque of Muhammad Ghauth Gwaliyari** (c. 1565), known as the Ek-Toda or Turreted Mosque. Situated on Daulat Khan Street, a little to the south of Malik Sarang's mosque, it was built by the saint Shaikh Muhammad Ghauthu'l Alam of Gwalior. It is a bizarre structure, ruggedly conceived in an alien style and altered by bad restoration. The minar to the northern wing is solid, the other octagonal and plainly treated, terminating at roof level. Internally, groined arches with carved pendentives support the flat domes of the roof.

At Sarkhej, about 9·5 km (6 miles) south-west of Ahmadabad, there is a great complex of tombs, gardens and palaces.

The road to Sarkhej crosses the Sabarmati river on the Ellis Bridge, a massive iron structure of fourteen spans. On the east bank is Victoria Garden, with a statue of Queen Victoria by G. A. Mhatre. To the south of the Ellis Bridge are the ruins of an older structure, destroyed in the floods of 1875. At the west end of the bridge is Gujarat University and, near by, the Science Institute, built by the late Sirdar Sir C. M. Ranchhodlal.

After 4·5 km (2¾ miles), in the village of Vasana, is the **Mausoleum of Azam and Mu'azzam** (1457), reputed to be the grave of the two brothers who designed the monuments at Sarkhej. It is a massive brick mausoleum raised on a platform, similar to that of Darya Khan, with corner bastions which provide access at the drum level to double corridors which lead to the dome.

On the outskirts of Sarkhej are two brick towers 9·1 m (30 ft) high, so severely undercut that they balance precariously. The road passes two arches and opens into the courtyard at Sarkhej.

On entering the complex the **Mausoleum of Mahmud Begada** (1511) lies to the left. It is connected by a fine portico to the tomb of Queen Rajabai, wife of Muzaffar Shah III (1590). Mahmud's tomb has a balcony window overlooking the adjacent tank and a central dome over the tombs, which are contained on raised platforms.

Immediately to the right is the **Tomb of the Saint**. Shaikh Ahmad Khatri Ganj Bakhsh, known as the Maghrabi, was the spiritual guide of Sultan Ahmad I, who retired to Sarkhej and died there at the venerable age of 111 in 1445. The tomb is the largest of its kind in Gujarat, roofed by a vast central dome and several smaller ones. A Persian inscription over the door records the date 1473. The interior is richly ornamented with finely chased brass lattice screens, coloured marble and lavish gilding to the inside of the dome.

The adjacent **Mosque** (1446–58) is enormous but simply treated, without an arched façade or minars, in a distinctly Hindu style. This is characteristic of most of the Sarkhej monuments. It has ten cupolas carried on eighteen carved pillars, with bracket capitals of Hindu design. To the south is the tomb of his disciple Shaikh Salah-ud-Din.

The **Tank** was created by Mahmud Begada and is fed by a channel to the west of the Mosque. It is surrounded by flights of stone steps, and in the southwest corner is the old palace and harem. Note the richly decorated supply sluice.

To the south of the lake is the **Tomb of Baba Ali Sher**, a Muslim saint. Nearby are the remains of the Garden of Victory, laid out by Mirza Khan Khanan (1584) after the defeat of the last of the Ahmadabad sultans, Muzaffar III.

South of the river, near the village of Kochrab, is the **Rani's Masjid** or Bawa Ali Shah's Mosque (*c.* 1500–1515). Three neatly carved domes crown the roof. The four pillars in the façade have projecting capitals, which support the eaves.

At Isanpur between Vatva and Rasulabad is a **Mosque** known as Blessed on All Sides (early 16th century). It stands at the west end of an oblong court, surrounded by a corridor, with the Tomb of Malik Isan symmetrically opposite. The entire court has outer gate porches to the east and north. The mosque has trabeated wings carrying domes flanking and equal in size to the main dome on the raised central section, which has a triple arched entrance. Being a private chapel, it has no minars.

The **Mosque and Rauza of Sayyid Uthman** (1460) at Isanpur is one of the first groups of monuments falling within the period of Mahmud Begada. The mosque is the first local example of a façade with minarets terminating the ends.

The Rauza is square in plan with a central chamber set in the centre of a double aisle of pillars and covered by a dome. It is a notable local shrine vested with miraculous powers of healing.

At Vatva is the **Tomb of Qutb al Alam** and at Sojali near Mahmudabad, the **Tomb of Sayyid Mubarak**. Stylistically, both are similar but lesser versions of the great tomb of Mahmud Begada.

About 1·6 km (1 mile) south-west of the city, on the banks of the Sabarmati river, is the **Mosque of Baba Lului** (1560). He is reputed to have been one of the twelve saints who participated in the consecration of Ahmadabad, but it is more likely that he lived later, an elder contemporary of Shaikh Hasan Chishti. The mosque is partly undermined by the river. It has a nine-arched open façade and trabeated interior with a large central dome raised to a higher storey. The frontage is terminated by massive low minar buttresses.

A little to the south-east at the village of Berhampur is the **Tomb of Abu Turab** (1597), a Persian saint. It has a hemispherical dome and an outer enclosure of twenty pillars. Much of the orig-

346

inal perforated stonework has gone. The mosque which once stood nearby is now in ruins.

The **Cantonment** area lies 5·6 km (3½ miles) to the north-east of the city from the Delhi Gate. There are an Anglican Church and several public buildings. **Christ Church** is 457 m (1,485 ft) south of the Delhi Gate in the old Idaria quarter. The old **English Cemetery** lies close to the Jamalpur Gate.

Gandhinagar, 19·3 km (12 miles) north of the city, was commenced in 1965 and named after Mahatma Gandhi. After Chandigarh, it is India's second modern planned city, laid out in numbered sectors. Now the new administrative capital, the city boasts several impressive buildings designed by famous architects of the International Modern Movement, including Le Corbusier.

AJMER

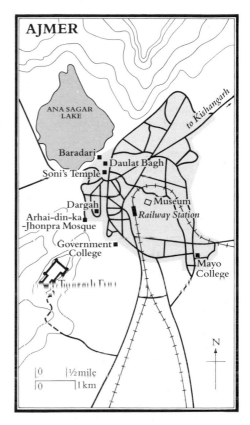

Ajmer, the celebrated capital of the Chauhan Rajputs and the key to Rajasthan, lies at the foot of Taragarh Hill, 870 m (2,855 ft) above sea level, about 367 km (228 miles) west of Agra. Ajayameru or 'invisible hill' became Ajmer.

The city is reputed to have been founded by Raja Ajaipal in 145 and, after numerous dynastic changes, it was sacked by Mahmud of Ghazni in 1024, and again by Muhammad Ghuri in 1193. Later it fell to Rana Khumbha of Mewar and was held by the rulers of Malwa from 1470 to 1531, when it passed to Jodhpur. Akbar annexed the city in 1556 and made it his royal residence. Owing to its strategic location, both Jahangir and Shah Jahan lived here for long periods, and it was at Ajmer that Sir Thomas Roe, the English ambassador from James I, was received in 1615–16. With the disintegration of the Mughal Empire, the city fell again to Jodhpur and later to the encroaching Marathas. In

1818 it was annexed by the British as part of the treaty with Daulat Rao Scindia. It was one of the few places in the region controlled by the British rather than the princely states.

The former British Residency stands on a hill overlooking the **Ana Sagar Lake**, built by Raja Anaji between 1135 and 1150. The embankment or bund has a row of elegant, polished marble pavilions, built by Shah Jahan and restored in 1899 by Lord Curzon. Emperor Jahangir laid out the gardens in front of the lake. A walk along the bund at sunset is an unforgettable experience. The water supply comes from **Foy Sagar**, 4·8 km (3 miles) away, which was formed as a famine-relief measure in 1891–2 by damming the local river.

Taragarh Fort or Star Fort crowns the summit of the hill. It is a rectangular fortress with walls over 4·5 m (15 ft) thick and large corner bastions, believed to have been built by Ajairaj in the 12th century. The path to the top is rough, but the views are worth the effort. Nearby is a small graveyard of Muslim martyrs who died storming the fort.

In the south-west corner of the city the most important building is the **Dargah of Khwaja Muin-ud-Din Chishti** (1143–1235), the tomb of a Sufi saint of the first rank, known as the 'Sun of the Realm of India', who came to Ajmer in 1192. It was commenced by Iltutmish of Delhi and finished by Emperor Humayun, and remains an important place of pilgrimage for Hindus and Muslims alike. So great was the pilgrim traffic from Agra and Fatehpur Sikri that Akbar erected Kos-minars or milestones along the route.

The entrance is via a high gateway painted white with blue dressings. Shoes must be removed. In the first courtyard are two huge copper cauldrons, the great and little deg. Rich pilgrims offer a deg feast whereby a large mixture of rice, ghi, almonds and other ingredients is cooked in the cauldron and given to local families. To the right is the **Akbar Masjid** (*c.* 1570), a white marble mosque with drums and candlesticks presented by Akbar in 1576. To the left is an Assembly Hall for the poor. In the inner courtyard is **Shah Jahan's Masjid** (mid-17th century), a white marble mosque 30·5 m (100 ft) long with a Persian inscription under the eaves, surrounded on three sides by a carved balustrade.

In the centre of the second court is the **Dargah**, a square white marble tomb with a domed roof and two entrances, one with a silver arch. The ceiling is gold-embossed velvet. Silver rails and gates enclose the grave, which pilgrims sprinkle with rose petals and votive offerings. Akbar is reputed to have walked barefoot from Agra to the shrine in thanksgiving for his son and heir, Salim, later Emperor Jahangir. Nearby is

a small compound with marble lattice-work, the **Mazar** or tomb of Bibi Hafiz Jamal, daughter of the saint, and west of it is that of Chimni Begum, daughter of Shah Jahan. The Jhalra is the deep tank at the south end of the Dargah.

Akbar's Palace lies in the heart of the city, near the east wall. It is now the Ajmer Museum. It is a massive rectangular building with a fine entrance gate. The Museum contains some early Hindu sculptures from the 6th and 7th centuries, a fine portrayal of Kali in black marble and a few examples of Rajput paintings and weaponry. (See Volume I.)

The **Arhai-din-ka-Jhonpra Mosque** or the Hut of the Two and a Half Days, now ruined, lies just outside the Dargah. It is a very important example of early Indo-Islamic architecture, commenced around 1200 by Qutb-ud-Din Aybak and allegedly built in two and a half days; more probably its name is due to the site of a fair here which lasted for this period. Its design has been attributed to Abu Bakr of Herat.

The building is composed of large amounts of reused Hindu and Jain masonry taken from local temples. The pillars in the main chamber are extraordinary, as three separate pillars have been placed one above the other to form single columns in order to gain extra height over the sanctuary. The roof of the prayer hall comprises a series of ten shallow corbelled domes carried on square bays. The impressive carved arched screen or liwan was added by Iltutmish in about 1230. This is an elegant work of art, with a raised central arch flanked by six smaller side arches, four of which are multifoil and derived from Arab sources. Note the small rectangular panels on the spandrels of each arch, a survival of a system of lighting from the ancient mosques of Arabia, reappearing in India centuries later as a blind decorative motif.

Of the British buildings the **Mayo College** (1875) is a distinguished example of the work of Sir Samuel Swinton Jacob, the state engineer of Jaipur. The white marble college stands as the centre-piece of a large park to the south-east of the city. To the front is a statue of Lord Mayo. The college was one of a number founded to provide a liberal English education for young Indian princes.

The King Edward Memorial Rest-house (early 20th century) is also worth a quick look.

Seven miles west of Ajmer is the sacred lake of **Pushkar**, the most revered in India and the object of a huge cattle fair and festival in October and November, attended by over 100,000 pilgrims. There are fine modern buildings by the lake, which is very evocative and full of sacred crocodiles! The caves of Snake Moun tain, between Ajmer and Pushkar, were an ancient resort of Hindu hermits and sages. (See Volume I.)

ALWAR *Map overleaf*

This impressive town, founded by Rao Pratap Singhji of Macheri in 1771, is the capital of the former state of Alwar. It is protected on all sides by a rampart and moat, except where the hills crowned by the fort secure it from attack. There are five gates to the city, within which lie the chief buildings.

The **City Palace**, commenced in 1793 by Raja Bakhtawar Singh, consists of a varied group of buildings of different styles facing a large ornamental tank. The interior is notable for the Mirror Room, which overlooks the tank, the Library, which contains a fine collection of Oriental manuscripts, including a copy of a beautifully illustrated 'Gulistan' manuscript from 1848, and the Arm-oury, with a rich collection of bejewelled sabres, swords and weapons. The New Court dates from *circa* 1850.

On the south side of the tank or sagar lies the **Cenotaph of Maharaja Bakh-**

tawar Singh (1781–1815), in marble enriched with Bengali arches on a red sandstone podium. The monument is surrounded by hundreds of peacocks and colourful birds. To the right of the main entrance of the palace is the house of the elephant carriage, which contains a two-storey processional car built to carry over fifty people drawn by four elephants.

The **Tomb of Fateh Jang** (1647) is a local landmark, with a huge dome and internal plasterwork ornament in low relief. The **Tomb of Tarang Sultan** (mid-17th century), the brother of Emperor Firuz Shah, is called the Tri-polia.

308 m (1,000 ft) above the Tripolia stands the **Fort**, in which lie the remains of a palace and other buildings erected for the first rulers of Alwar. There are six gates. To the west is Chand Pol, east is Suraj Pol and south Lakshman Pol. The fourth and fifth gates are known as Jai Pol and Kishan Pol, while the sixth, in the north, is Andheri Pol. Within the fort lie the ruins of the Nikumbh Mahal, ten pools and the remains of fifteen temples.

The most impressive aspect is the spectacular view of the city and the lake-studded countryside below. The fortifi-cations extend 3·2 km (2 miles) along the hilltop, beneath which lie two outworks, the **Chitanki** and **Kabul Khurd**. At Siliserh, 14·5 km (9 miles) to the west, runs an aqueduct which supplies the city.

About 1·6 km (1 mile) outside the city lies the **Vinai Vilas Palace**, now the Rajrisai College, built by Maharao Raja Vinai Singhji (1815–57). Beyond is the former British Residency.

AMBER *Map overleaf*

Amber (pronounced Ambair), the ancient capital of the Kachhawaha Raj-puts, lies 11 km (7 miles) north of Jaipur. Now in ruins, this once beautiful town was the Rajput capital from 1037 until

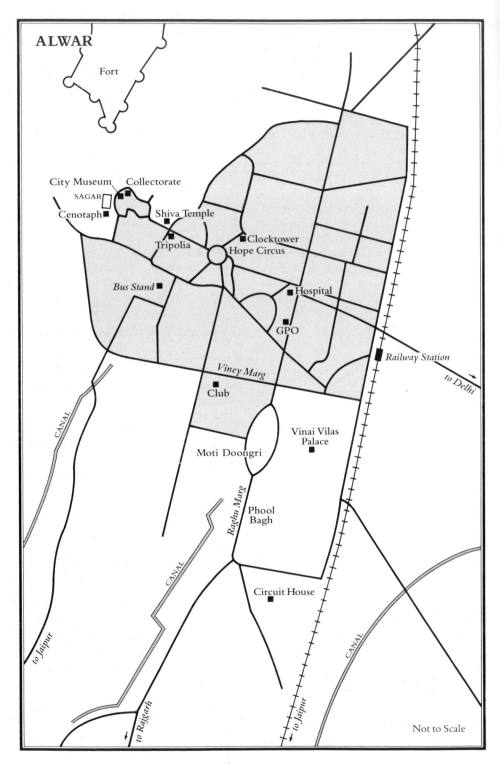

ALWAR

1728, when Sawai Jai Singh II moved to Jaipur. Situated at the head of a rocky mountain gorge and lake, its picturesque charm has been admired for centuries.

The entrance of the valley is via the Ghati Darwaza, an arched gate on the crest of the ridge. On the eastern side of the road to Delhi in the centre of the lake is the **Jal Mahal**, built by Man Singh I, Akbar's celebrated general, and later added to by his successors. On the western side of the road are numerous temples and gardens. The road enters the valley via the Ghati Gate (1914). The old gate stands close by.

Maota Lake provides the setting for Amber. The dam is laid out as the **Dil-i-Aram** garden on Mughal lines, with two pretty red pavilions and an Archaeological Museum. (For the Museum and temples see Volume I.)

In the middle of the lake is **Mohan Bari**, a picturesque garden connected to Jaigarh Fort. Opposite is the shrine of Mahatma Dadu, who spent eighteen years here.

The ascent to the fort is best made by elephants, which provide a shuttle service throughout the day from the village beneath the fort.

Jaigarh Fort (*c.* 1600) stands at the summit of the hill, dominating the palace which lies beneath it. It is an awesome sight: huge, high towers with crenellated walls pierced by arrow slits and loops command the whole area and rise sheer from the natural bedrock. The ramparts run across the hill down the incline and up to the opposite range in the northeast. The fort, built by Man Singh I (1592–1615) on the ruins of an earlier stronghold, remains the personal property of the Maharaja. Inside the fort is the shrine of Madho Singh, younger brother of Man Singh.

The **Old Palace** or Raj Mahal overlooks Maota Lake. Built by Man Singh I from 1600 onwards, later additions were made by his successors. It is approached by a paved, sinuous path passing five

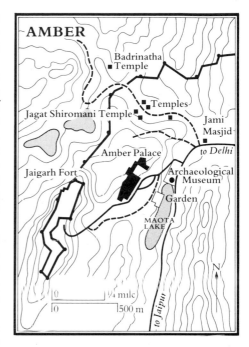

gates at intervals with a strong wall to either side. A footpath from Dil-i-Aram joins the road near the gateway. On the lakeside are elephant stables. At the upper junction one path leads to the fort, the other to the palace gate, **Sivaji Pol** or Sun Gate, an arched gateway leading to Jaleb Chowk.

Jaleb Chowk is the courtyard beyond, surrounded by administrative buildings. On the west side, opposite Suraj Pol is **Chand Pol** or Moon Gate, a great barbican with guardrooms either side. To the south-west a broad flight of steps leads to **Singh Pol** or Lion Gate and the upper court. It is a double gate with a right-angled turn, enriched with faded frescoes. There are guardrooms on all sides.

To the right is **Shree Shila Devi Temple**; the idol was brought here from Bengal by Man Singh I in 1604. The first court beyond the **Diwan-i-Am** or Hall of Public Audience was built by Mirza Raja Jai Singh I in 1639. It is raised on a podium and approached by a double flight of steps. Originally open on all sides, the eastern façade was enclosed by a room added by Sawai Ram Singh II. The inner hall is rectangular, with a vaulted roof carried on grey marble columns in the Mughal style. The portico has a double row of red sandstone pillars

AMBER Palace
(Sketch Plan)

Chand Pol

Jaleb Chowk

Suraj Pol

Singh Pol

Diwan-i-Am

Temple of Sila Devi

Ganesh Pol

Sukh Niwas

Sheesh Mahal and Jess Mandir

Servants' Quarters

N

Zenana Mahal

Not to Scale

with carved elephants. The roof is flat, with panels of intricate latticework.

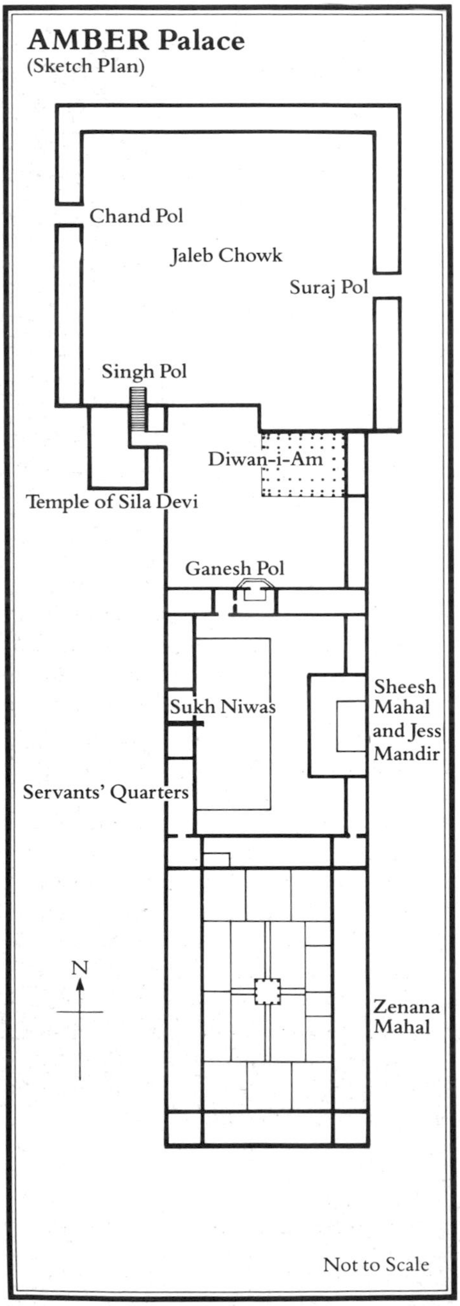

On the southern side is **Ganesh Pol**, probably built between 1699 and 1725, but possibly as early as 1639. It is a beautiful structure, covered in mosaic and painted in delicate colours, with projecting oriels filled with the finest carved lattice screens. Held to be one of the finest gateways in the world, it leads into an open courtyard, where the royal apartments are grouped around a fine garden.

The **Jai Mandir**, the Diwan-i-Khas, comprises a central hall surrounded by a deep verandah. The sides have oblong chambers and the back wall, facing the lake, has windows which promote a cool flow of air and from which there are stunning views across the lake. The main hall is white marble with square columns and floral ceilings in elegant relief of alabaster and glass inlay and other devices. The **Sheesh Mahal** is faced in mirrors with coloured ornament of fabulous intricacy. The carpets which once furnished this exquisite room are in the Albert Hall of the Jaipur Museum.

Near the Jai Mandir, in a wing of Ganesh Pol, is the hammam, a white marble bath.

To the west is the **Sukh Mandir**, a pleasure room with a cool marble cascade enclosed in a marble framework pierced with foliated decoration. The doors are inlaid with ivory and sandalwood. The **Bhojan Shala** is in the west wing of Ganesh Pol. Once a dining-room, its walls are adorned with paintings of Delhi, Agra and other holy cities.

The upper part of Ganesh Pol, the Sohag Mandir, comprises a beautifully coloured rectangular chamber with octagonal rooms to each side, which break out as oriels over the entrance.

On the roof of the Jai Mandir are further wonders in the **Jas Mahal** (1635–40), luminescent with exquisite mosaics, spangled mirrors and brilliant colours, a cool summer retreat for hot nights. The carved marble screen faces across the lake and attracts refreshing breezes.

The **Palace of Man Singh I** is the oldest part of the complex and comprises numerous apartments disposed around a large courtyard. A high wall separates the palace of Jai Singh I. One passage leads to the Jai Mandir, another to Sukh Niwas. The focus of the huge courtyard is a baradari with marble mahals on the northern side and Mughal-style pillars; the remainder is of Hindu origin. The four corners are punctuated by high towers. At the rear there are latrines and baths.

The **Old Palace** lies at the base of Jaigarh Fort and the palace of Man Singh I. A stone path from Chand Pol leads to the ruins. The buildings were commenced by Rajdeo in 1216. Only the Sal of Bala Bai is worthy of note. Bala Bai was responsible for the conversion of the Raja to the Vaishnavite cult, and two idols are associated with her. In the courtyard of the Narsingha shrine is a marble swing or jhoola (1645). The Jagat Shiromani Temple and Laxhmi Narain Temple lie close together, on the north west side. The Ambakeshawar Mahadeo Temple lies to the north-west of the old palace. An ancient sun temple (945) lies on an isolated outcrop.

Panna Mian's Tank (early 18th century) is square in shape, with octagonal corner kiosks and a double-storey verandah.

On the left of the road to Delhi is the **Jami Masjid**, built for Akbar by the architect Bharmall in 1569. Following extensive subsequent alterations, it retains few original features.

Around the valley runs the outer curtain wall, the Sahar-Panaha, fortified with bastions and towers. There are only five main gates but several entrances. The Birhi Darwaza is the most impressive, a large double gateway with a temple to Birhi Mala between the two entrances.

To the right of the Delhi road lie the **Chatris** of the ruling dynasty. None carry inscriptions.

Sagar Tank, with octagonal bastions and huge dams, lies north-west of Jaigarh. A chatri stands on the upper dam.

BAYANA

76 km (47 miles) from Fatehpur Sikri, Bayana was once a famous city lying on the banks of the Gambhir river. Close by Babur defeated Sangram Singh of Chitorgarh, on 16 March 1527, and it was after this victory that Sikri received its name of Fatehpur.

In 1601 Akbar planted a fine garden here. A handsome gateway to the enclosure still survives, together with many other Muslim remains.

The **Ukha Masjid** is an extension of an older mosque, now converted to a temple and known as the Ukha Mandir. It was probably built by Baha al-Din Tughral, the first Muslim governor of the region and one of the leading commanders of the Ghurid Sultans in the last decade of the 12th century. It is contemporaneous with the mosque of Quwwat-al-Islam, then under construction in Delhi. The Ukha Masjid was added to the south side of the complex in 1320–21 by Kafur al-Sultani, the Governor of Bayana under Sultan Mubarak Shah Khalji of Delhi. It is a provincial manifestation of the Khalji style, probably built by local workmen under the supervision of an overseer from the capital.

There is also an incomplete minaret built in 1519–20 by Nizam Khan, the Governor under Ibrahim Shah Lodi. Its construction was abandoned beneath the level of the first balcony at the time of Babur's invasion of Delhi.

BEAWAR

This interesting little town owes its existence to Colonel C. G. Dixon, former Superintendent of Merwara from 1836 to 1848. The town has a regularly drawn plan, with allotted sites for traders, shops and other uses in a typical colonial pattern. The streets are wide and tree-lined and the town is enclosed by a stone wall.

The **Tomb of Colonel Charles George Dixon** (1857) takes the form of a local shrine, which is worshipped by the Mers. The tomb provides the origin of Kipling's story *The Tomb of His Ancestors*.

BHADRESHWAR

This ancient town and seaport, 32 km (20 miles) from Kandla in Kutch, is of considerable historical significance as it was the site of a very early Muslim community. (For details of the temple see Volume I.)

There are two mosques, both of which date from the mid-12th century. The most important is the **Solah Khambi Masjid**. This is the only known surviving Muslim structure from the period prior to the Muslim conquest which retains almost all its original features intact.

BHARATPUR

Situated at the confluence of the Ruparel and Banganga rivers, today Bharatpur is renowned internationally for its splendid bird sanctuary. Less well known are its notable fort and interesting palace, the principal architectural adornments of the former Jat state. The ruling family are descended from a Jat freebooter who harassed Aurangzeb's army at a time when Mughal rule was at a low ebb. Although the Jat bands were scattered in retaliation, they re-formed under Badan Singh and soon controlled a swathe of territory between Delhi and Agra. In

1763 the high point was reached under Suraj Mal, who seized Agra and marched on Delhi, before he was killed in battle near Agra.

In 1803 Lord Lake was repulsed from here with severe losses – over 3,000 men, the most disastrous setback in his illustrious career. In 1825 Lord Combermere attacked the fort from the north-east side and successfully captured the position after a month's siege.

The **Fort**, built by Suraj Mal, appears impregnable, with massive double ramparts of mud and rubble surrounded by a wide moat 46 m (150 ft) wide and 18 m (59 ft) deep, with a secondary inner moat around the central palace. The outer ramparts are now largely demolished. On the inner ramparts are several gates. The Jawarhar Burj, from which there is a fine view, was built to mark Suraj Mal's victory over the Mughals. Fateh Burj commemorates the defeat of the British in 1703. The gateway over the moat has huge round bastions with war elephants painted on the stone portals.

From east to west across the fort are three palaces: the Raja's Palace, the Old Palace, built by Badan Singh in 1733, and the Kamra Palace, north of which lies the Court of Justice and Jewel Office.

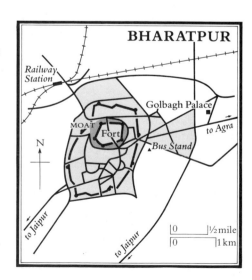

354

The **Victoria Park Gardens** contain a memorial pavilion (1928) to General James Willcocks.

The **Palace** of the Maharaja is at Golbagh, 1·6 km (1 mile) outside the city. Built around 1905, Golbagh is a beautiful piece of Edwardian eclecticism executed in local sandstone. Much of the detail is cribbed from the fortress at Deeg, but the combination of balconies, pavilions and ornamental jali screens, linked by powerful horizontal bracketed chajjas, is wholly delightful. The surrounding lakes, which once witnessed exclusive viceregal duck shoots, have now been made over to the bird sanctuary.

BHAVNAGAR

Bhavnagar is now an important coastal town and modern seaport, situated on a tidal creek in the Gulf of Cambay, opposite Broach (Bharuch). It was founded in 1723 by the Rajput Bhavsinhji Gohil, after whom it is named, in an attempt to generate wealth from the maritime trade in the area.

The principal attraction is Gaurishankar Lake, a popular picnic spot, but there are a number of interesting monuments.

The **Old Palace** (Darbargadh) lies in the heart of the city and is now used as bank offices. The Town Hall (1932) is an imposing civic building. The main mosques are the Nagina Masjid, near the Khar Gate, and the Jami Masjid, in Amba Chowk.

The **Takhtsinhji General Hospital** (1879–83), a two-storey range with a long arcaded frontage terminated by domed pavilions and a large central dome over the staircase, was designed by Sir William Emerson, President of the Royal Institute of British Architects. He also designed a vast new palace for the Maharaja between 1894 and 1895.

The **Barton Museum** (1895) has a good collection of arms, armour and coins. In the same building the Gandhi Smitri is a library, museum, gallery and memorial to the Mahatma.

BHUJ

Bhuj, the principal town of Kutch, is an old walled city situated at the base of a fortified hill, curving in an arc around the lake. Considerable lengths of the city wall survive and within lies a maze of alleyways and streets retaining fine examples of Gujarati vernacular architecture, with carved timber façades and oversailing balconies.

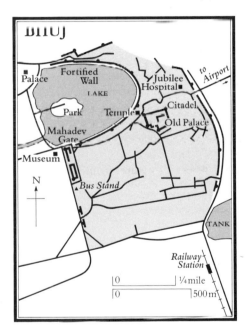

The Old Palace lies in the heart of the citadel, near which is the Swaminaryan Temple. The Maharao's Palace is on the north-west side of the lake. Although there are few outstanding individual buildings, Bhuj is an unforgettable experience, retaining the atmosphere and character of an unspoilt Indian city. The mausolea of the Raos of Kutch are within the town.

BIKANER

Bikaner is the capital of an old Rajput state of the same name, a side branch of the principality of Marwar, its princes coming from the house of Jodha. Bikaner, the fourth largest city in Rajasthan, was founded in 1488 by Bhika. He was the sixth son of Rao Jodha, the founder of Jodhpur and one of a leading Rajput family of the Rathor clan. The old state is bounded by Jaipur to the east and Jodhpur and Jaisalmer to the south and south-west.

In 1459 Bhika left his father's capital at Jodhpur. For almost thirty years he led a band of marauding freebooters through Rajasthan, carving out a kingdom for himself and his devoted followers. The city lies in a vast arid wasteland of desert and scrub, out of which rises the spectacular ramparts of the outer walls.

Situated on rising ground, the approach to Bikaner is magnificent. The city is encircled by a 5·6 km-long (3½ miles) crenellated stone wall in rich pink sandstone. There are five gates and three sally-ports, the walls varying in height between 4·6 m (15 ft) and 9·2 m (30 ft).

Junagarh Fort, opposite the public park, was built between 1588 and 1593 by Raja Rai Singh (1571–1611), one of Akbar's generals. The outer walls are 986 m (3,205 ft) in circuit, reinforced with thirty-seven pavilions silhouetted against the skyline. Lines of windows and balconies impart a harmonious domestic character and fragment the austere strength of the structure. The main entrance is via the **Suraj Pol** or Sun Gate (1593), in front of which in the courtyard is the Joramal Temple. Royal weddings and births were celebrated in the Har Mandir chapel. On the nearby walls can be seen two groups of suttee hands. Two great warriors, Jaimal and Patta, mounted on painted stone elephants, guard the gateway.

Within the walls are a series of palaces built by successive rulers. The fort and palaces are beautifully preserved and well maintained. Each palace contains particular treasures.

In the second courtyard lies **Karan Mahal** (1631–9), built by Karan Singh, which leads to **Durgar Niwas**. This is a beautiful enclosure with painted walls and a white marble tank, filled with coloured water during the festival of Holi. **Lal Niwas**, with its richly painted floral motifs, is the oldest apartment (1595).

The **Gaj Mandir**, over the Karan Mahal, was built between 1745 and 1787 as a suite of royal apartments. The **Chatra Niwas** is a small pavilion on the roof of the Gaj Mandir, built by Maharaja Dungar Singh (1872-87) and decorated with English plates embedded in the plasterwork which depict scenes from a series of English prints of 'Oriental Field Sports'.

Chandra Mahal or Moon Palace, built together with the Phul Mahal and Gaj Mandir by Gaj Singh (1746–87), is beautifully painted. The Phul Mahal or Flower Palace has elaborate inlaid mirror work. This contains Bhika's bed, a tiny resting-place. It is reputed that Bhika's grandfather was murdered after being tied to his bed by a treacherous courtesan. Determined to avoid a similar fate, Bhika slept with his feet beyond the end of the bed so he could stand up complete with his bed and defend himself if history should be repeated.

Anup Mahal, built between 1669 and 1698 and decorated later by Maharaja Gaj Singh, is an exquisite building with a stunning Coronation Hall in red and gold. The Raj Tilak Hall, as it is known, is enriched with ornamental lacquer work and opaque glass inlay. One antechamber is vivid aquamarine blue inlaid with gilt. Another room contains the famous hindola or swing, a rare specimen. The Anup Mahal is the epitome of all the gorgeous exoticism of the East, the fabulous treasure-house of a desert prince.

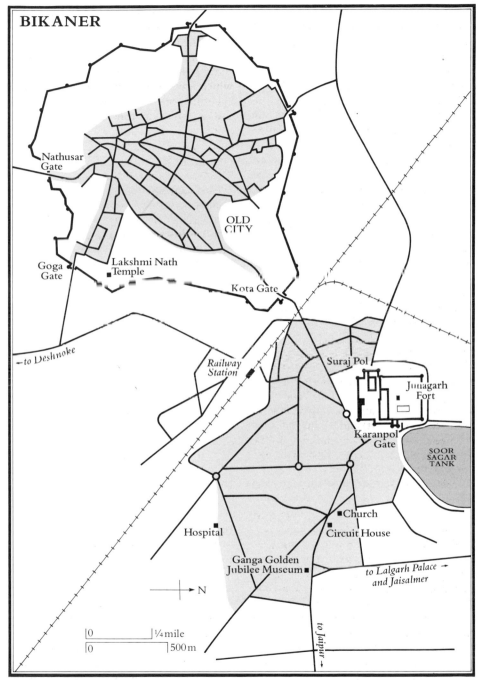

Map labels: BIKANER, Nathusar Gate, Goga Gate, Lakshmi Nath Temple, OLD CITY, Kota Gate, to Deshnoke, Railway Station, Suraj Pol, Junagarh Fort, Karanpol Gate, SOOR SAGAR TANK, Church, Circuit House, Hospital, Ganga Golden Jubilee Museum, to Lalgarh Palace and Jaisalmer, to Jaipur, N, 0 ¼ mile, 0 500 m

Other palaces include the **Chetar Mahal** and **Chini Burj** of Dungar Singh (1872–87). The Ganga Niwas, with its fine carved sandstone façade and beauti-ful audience hall, was added in the late 19th century by Ganga Singh (1887–1943).

The Fort has an excellent library of

Persian manuscripts and ancient Sanskrit books and an impressive armoury. Nearby is a well over 137 m (450 ft) deep.

The **Lalgarh Palace**, now a luxury hotel, lies outside the city in beautiful landscaped gardens. It should not be missed. Built by Ganga Singh, it was designed by Sir Samuel Swinton Jacob, one of the most accomplished British architects ever to work in India and an authority on the Rajput style of architecture. At Lalgarh he developed and extended the Rajput style, bringing it into the 20th century, enlarging and stretching the vernacular styles of the past through the filter of his own extensive studies. Lalgarh is a wonderful palace in rich red sandstone, a wealth of carved screens, pavilions, exotic ornament and arcaded balconies. The cloistered courtyard of Lakshmi Vilas, the old guest wing, is a magnificent tribute to Jacob's genius. Notwithstanding his scholarly approach, Jacob's masterpiece is clearly influenced by European ideas of form and composition, particularly the interiors.

Lalgarh was built with profits from Ganga Singh's enlightened policy of modernization. He developed the railway system to exploit local coal deposits, and it was he who formed the legendary Bikaner Camel Corps, one of the great auxiliary forces of the Empire which fought with such courage in Egypt and Somaliland. Lalgarh bears eloquent testimony to the close relationship between the princely states and the Raj.

Other buildings of note within the suburbs include the Dungar Memorial College and the Walter Noble Schools. Near the Circuit House the **Ganga Golden Jubilee Museum** has a fine collection of pottery, paintings and weapons. (For the Museum and temples see Volume I.)

The great irrigation system centred on the Bikaner Gang Canal, a tribute to British engineering expertise, was opened in 1927 by Lord Irwin.

The old Fort built by Bhika, lying outside the southern city wall, is now a shrine containing cenotaphs of the ruling family. The cremation tank of Bikaner lies 4·8 km (3 miles) east of the city among the cenotaphs of the previous rulers. Many of these are fine domed pavilions in red sandstone and marble.

BROACH (BHARUCH)

Broach is one of the oldest ports in western India. Situated about 48 km (30 miles) from the mouth of the Narbada river, it flourished in the 1st century as one of the chief trading centres of Gujarat, with trade links to western Asia and beyond. In the 17th century its ships traded with Java and Sumatra. In 1614 an English factory was established here, followed three years later by the Dutch. By order of Emperor Aurangzeb the fortifications were partly demolished in 1660, leaving the city open to Maratha attacks in 1675 and 1686, after which the walls were rebuilt. In 1771 the British attempted but failed to take the town, although a year later they succeeded.

The river frontage has a massive stone wall at the water's edge, above which the town rises in a picturesque fashion. The southern city wall is intact, with five gateways, and the city proper lies on a narrow spit of land 4 km (2½ miles) long by 1·2 km (¾ mile) broad. 91 m (296 ft) above the river stands the **Fort**. Within the fort are the Collector's Office, Civil Courts, the old Dutch factory, the English Church, public offices, Victoria Clocktower and other civic buildings.

The city has quaint, tortuous, narrow streets rising up the hill. About 182 m (592 ft) from the bastion at the northwest corner of the fort is the **Tomb of Brigadier David Wedderburn**, killed during the storming of the city on 14 November 1772.

At the eastern base of the fort is the **Jami Masjid** (early 14th century), built from the materials of an old Jain temple. Although constructed from recycled masonry, it was planned and built according to conventional mosque design, comprising a courtyard with gateways on three sides and an open pillared sanctuary at its western end. The interior has three compartments based on three temple mandapas, removed and reassembled in their present position. The three mihrabs in the western wall are clearly indigenous in design and are copies of temple niches, but with pointed Islamic arches. The roof of the sanctuary has three large domes and ten smaller ones. The ceilings are enriched with cusped and geometrical patterns. Another mosque in the south-west corner of the fort may be as early as 1037.

3·2 km (2 miles) west of the fort is an interesting complex of early Dutch tombs. Two of them are over 4·9 m (16 ft) high. They lie about 91 m (296 ft) off the road and are worth a visit. Opposite the tombs are fine Parsee **Towers of Silence**, one of which is still used.

1·6 km (1 mile) to the north-west of the city is the **Tomb of Bawa Rahan**. Near the east gate is the Temple of Bhrigu Rishi.

BUNDI

This delightful town is completely unspoilt, being situated well off the usual tourist route. It is the chief town of the old state of Bundi. To the north lie the former states of Jaipur and Tonk, to the east and south, Kota, and to the west, Udaipur. The town is about 48 km (30 miles) south-east of Deoli and is recommended for those who don't mind basic facilities. Kipling wrote *The Last Suttee* here in 1889 and the place is still imbued with all the romance of old India.

The history of Bundi state is that of its ruling family, the Hara Chauhan clan of Rajputs, who were held in high esteem in

the princely hierarchy. It is still an isolated, introverted place where time has stood still and where the 20th century has made little impression.

The town lies on the side of a steep hill. The palace dominates the foreground, with its pinnacled terraces and pavilions rising one above the other. At the summit of the hill is **Taragarh Fort**. Taragarh or Star Fort was built in 1342. It is square in plan with large corner bastions. In the middle of the west wall is a fine gateway and in the middle of the east wall, a postern. The ramparts are crenellated, with high parapets.

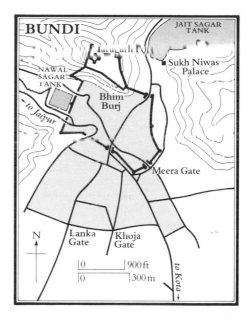

The main gate to the west is flanked by octagonal towers defended by a strong barbican. The approach is difficult, always commanded by the towers above. The main entrance has vaulted guardrooms. The fort is dominated by a huge masonry tower, the **Bhim Burj**, which provided a gun platform for a vast cannon, the Garbh Ganjam, now lost. A deep adjacent pit provided shelter for the artillerymen when firing. The steep ramp provided access for the cannon. The Sabirna-Dha-Ka-Kund is a square, stepped water tank of a great depth. Built in 1654, it is a marvellous exercise in three-dimensional geometry.

With increasing security the Hara Rajputs built outside the fort. The **City Palace** was begun in 1580 by Balwant Singh. It is a distinguished piece of Rajput architecture, running from the Raniwal or women's quarters half-way up the hill. The **Chatar Mahal** palace was built in 1660 by Chatar Sal, a loyal servant of Emperor Shah Jahan. It is the largest and most impressive of the jumble of palaces that cascade down the hillside. Built in a green serpentine rock, it is an exercise in Rajput architecture unadulterated by Mughal influences. Characteristic motifs such as lotus-flower spandrels and elephant symbols recur throughout, amid a profusion of arcuated roofs, kiosks and pavilions. A steep carriageway provides access. The first gate is Hazari Pol or Gate of the Thousand, where the garrison lived. The palace quarters are entered via the Hathi Pol (1607–31), an enormous stone gateway spanned by ornamental elephants and decorated in red, yellow, blue, white and silver. Within the porch is an old water clock, supervised by an elderly retainer. In the Diwan-i-Am or Hall of Public Audience there is a canopied balcony where the ruler made his appearance.

The **Chitra Mahal**, an open courtyard with a gallery running around a garden of fountains, has a fine collection of Rajput miniatures in the local Bundi style depicting scenes from Raslila, the Radha-Krishna story. The colour scheme in blue, green, white and turquoise is exquisite. The murals on the walls of the cloister of the Chitra Shali (mid-18th century) are some of the finest in Rajput art.

It is alleged that the area beneath the fort and palace is honeycombed with subterranean passages leading to the Chatar Mahal. Deep in these underground caverns the state treasure is supposed to be stored. Each ruler was permitted a single visit, but when the last surviving guide died in the 1940s, the secret of its precise location was lost, a tantalizing enigma buried in the haunted ruins of Bundi's past.

Sukh Niwas is a summer palace on the Jait Sagar tank with a beautiful formal garden, the scene of festival processions. The square, artificial lake of **Nawal Sagar** is visible from the fort, in the centre of which is a half-submerged temple to the Anjan god of water, Varuna. The surface of the lake reflects the entire city and palace, providing a further dimension to its attractions.

To the west of the Nawal Sagar lake is the **Phool Sagar** or Flower Palace, a relatively modern complex commenced by Maharaja Bahadur Singh in 1945 around a large artificial lake. It is still unfinished. The cenotaphs of the ruling family are at Khshar Bagh.

CAMBAY

84 km (52 miles) from Ahmadabad at the mouth of the Mali river on the Gulf of Cambay, this small town is an ancient port which once served the great city up-river. In 1304 Ala-ud-Din Khalji plundered the city and destroyed most of the buildings. It was well known to Arab travellers and until 1400 it was governed by the kings of Anhilwara. At this time it was renowned as the first city of Hind.

So great was Cambay's reputation that the first ambassadors from the court of Queen Elizabeth bore letters to Akbar addressing him as the king of Cambay. By 1600 it had reached its height. An English factory was established in 1613, but with the rise of Surat it declined in importance and fell prey to the Marathas. The silting up of the harbour completed its eclipse.

The **Jami Masjid** (1325) is built from the ruined fragments of Jain and Hindu temples. Architecturally, it is a very

360

important building, probably constructed by local artisans under the supervision of craftsmen from Delhi. The enclosed arcuated façade to the sanctuary is in the manner of the Quwwat-ul-Islam mosque at Delhi, and it is clear that the design of the Cambay mosque provided a blueprint for the subsequent development of the provincial Gujarati style. The town is still a major centre of Jainism, with a fine library of ancient texts. It contains the tomb of Imran Ahmed Kajarani. The **Nawab's Kothi** was the old English factory. Portions of the old city walls survive in poor repair.

Cambay is the centre of trade in carnelian, onyx, agate and other semi-precious stones.

CHAMPANER

The ruined city of Champaner lies 125.5 km (78 miles) south-east from Ahmadabad and 43.5 km (27 miles) north-east from Vadodara. It was the ancient

stronghold of local Rajput kings until, in 1484, Mahmud Begada, enraged by provocative raids from Champaner,

besieged and took the city. It was Mahmud who founded the new city and made it his capital. It is recorded that it took twenty-three years to build and, after a brief occupation, that it was deserted and left to the jungle. In 1535 Emperor Humayun himself led a small party which scaled the outer defences by means of iron spikes driven into the bare rock and threw open the main gate. With the collapse of the Mughal Empire, Champaner fell to the Marathas. In 1802 it was held for a short period by the British before reverting to Scindia. In 1861 it was finally ceded to the British.

The **Fort of Pavagadh** stands at the crown of an isolated rock 820 m (2,700 ft) high and is visible from a great distance. The fortifications enclose a large space within which are two forts, the upper and lower. Both are difficult to assail. The former has a temple to Kali and the latter, ancient Hindu monuments. The ascent is steep and passes several interesting ruins, including the Medi and Medi Talao, the Champavati, the Champa Ranina Mahal (a three-storey summer pavilion) and the Buria Darwaza. The temple on the summit is crowned by the shrine of Sadan Shah, a Muslim saint, the original temple spire having been removed to accommodate it, a deliberate and overt representation of Muslim victory over the Hindu Rajput kings.

Within the town many of the buildings are ruins, set in grass-lined streets, but the citadel walls and bastions and one or two civic buildings, such as the Mandir or Custom House and guardrooms, still survive. Most of the intact structures are mosques or tombs, the most important of which is the **Jami Masjid** (1523).

The Jami Masjid is a large, well-articulated symmetrical structure of considerable architectural significance. A notable feature is the rich ornamental treatment of the exterior, with traceried openings and fine entrance pavilions of unusual sophistication. Inside, the sanc-

361

tuary façade contains five pointed archways with two slender minarets flanking the central opening, enriched with prominent oriel windows, a typical Gujarati vernacular device. It is modelled on the Jami Masjid at Ahmadabad, built over seventy-five years before, but with numerous subtle refinements. Around the upper balconies are stone seats for peaceful meditation, set above and apart from the worshippers in the main hall beneath.

The architecture of the surviving buildings at Champaner has particular local characteristics not found elsewhere in Gujarat. This can be attributed to its isolated location. Other mosques of note include the beautiful Nagina Masjid (mid-16th century), a similar variation on the theme of the Jami Masjid, and the Borah Masjid (mid-16th century). The numerous tombs are also noteworthy, with domed central chambers surrounded by arcades crowned with smaller domes. Access is usually provided via a portico on one side, but the real delight of these funerary monuments is the use of the carved arch, which imparts exceptional vigour and elegance.

CHITORGARH

110 km (69 miles) from Udaipur, Chitorgarh is imbued with all the romance of Rajput history. It is an awe-inspiring hillfort crowning a rocky ridge running north-south, parallel to the Gambheri river.

Chitor was founded around 728 by Bappu Rawal. His lineage continues unbroken, so that today the hillfort is still vested in the Rajput rulers of Mewar. The fort is remembered for the three bloody sieges which dominate the annals of Rajput history. (For the temples see Volume I.)

The first sack of Chitorgarh occurred in 1303, when Ala-ud-Din Khalji, Sultan of Delhi, claimed the hand of Padmini, the wife of Rana Bhim Singh. Rather than disgrace the Rajput code, all the women of the garrison gathered in a procession to a huge underground cavern and there immolated themselves in the sacred fire, Padmini entering last. Having witnessed this astonishing act of mass self-sacrifice, the fierce Rajput warriors sallied forth on to the plains in ceremonial dress and chose death on the battlefield rather than dishonour. Over 50,000 were killed in this terrific battle alone.

Over 130 years later, in 1535, Sultan Bahadur Shah of Gujarat attacked Rana Bikramjit Singh. History repeated itself when over 13,000 women and children died in the sacred johar in a last desperate act of defiance. The saffron-clad warriors, led by Baga Singh of Deolia, launched a fierce, last-ditch attack on the Gujarati armies. Every Rajput clan lost its leader and over 32,000 were slain.

The third and final sack of Chitor occurred in 1567, when Emperor Akbar stormed the fort. The defence rested on two young chieftains, Jaimal of Bednore and Patta of Kelwa, about whose deeds Rajput ballads are still sung. Akbar himself killed Jaimal, and when Jaimal fell alongside his mother and bride, a third and terrible johar was ordained. This time several thousand women and children were consumed in the flames, including five princesses and nine ranis. Over 8,000 Rajput soldiers burst out of the open gates and fell, fighting to the end. When Akbar entered the fort, it resembled a city of the dead and he ordered the destruction of the buildings. In 1615 Chitor was restored to the Rajputs by Jahangir, by which time the capital of Mewar had been transferred to Udaipur.

The **Fort** stands on a rocky hill 152 m (500 ft) above the plain, approached through thick jungle. Within the fort is a large palace, built in 1930 by Maharana Sir Fateh Singh.

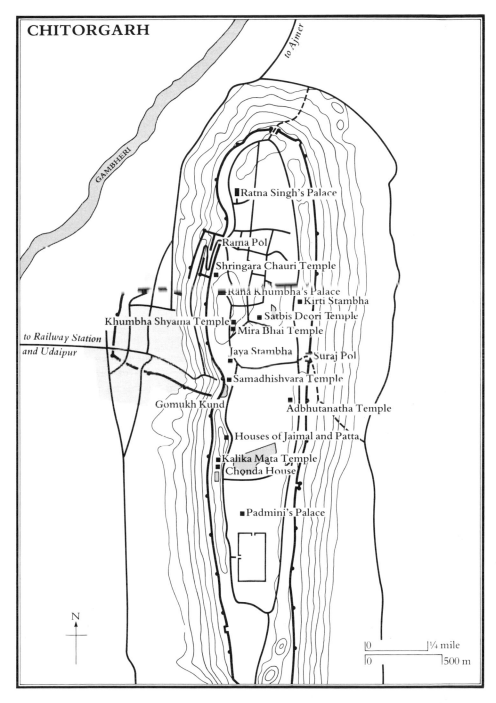

CHITORGARH

to Ajmer

GAMBHERI

Ratna Singh's Palace

Ratna Pol

Shringara Chauri Temple

Rana Khumbha's Palace

Kirti Stambha

Satbis Deori Temple

Khumbha Shyama Temple

Mira Bhai Temple

to Railway Station and Udaipur

Jaya Stambha

Suraj Pol

Samadhishvara Temple

Gomukh Kund

Adbhutanatha Temple

Houses of Jaimal and Patta

Kalika Mata Temple

Chonda House

Padmini's Palace

N

0 — 1/4 mile

0 — 500 m

Access is across an old limestone bridge over the Gambheri river. The Bridge is carried on ten arches, nine pointed and one which, curiously, is semicircular. A winding ascent is defended at intervals by seven splendid

363

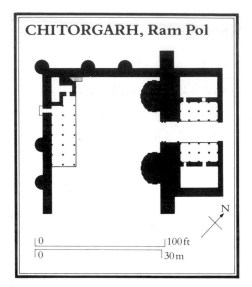

CHITORGARH, Ram Pol

gateways. The Padal Pol is where Bagh Singh fell in 1535 during the second siege of Chitor. Beyond is Bhairon Pol, where Jaimal was killed by Akbar in 1567; chatris mark the spot. Hanuman Pol is followed by Ganesh Pol, then the Jorla or Joined Gate, attached by its upper arch to the base of Lakhsman Pol. Ram Pol (1459) is the main gate, surmounted by a Hindu horizontal arch with deep corbelling. Inside on each side is a hall carried on square-shaped tapered pillars crowned by chatris.

The gateways of Chitor are of considerable architectural interest. They demonstrate the transition in form and style from the elaborate ornamental portals of Gujarat to the pointed-arched gateways of northern India. To prevent flanking movements, a cross-wall connects the gateways to the main curtain wall, so that the ascent is always commanded for its entire length.

The main curtain wall surrounding the summit has massive crenellated parapets punctuated by merlons and loopholes. The loopholes and embrasures provide wide fields of fire.

Within the fort stands the oldest palace at Chitor, the ruined **Palace of Rana** **Khumbha** (1433–68), built of dressed stone and originally covered with stucco, of which traces remain. It is approached from the east by two gateways, the Badi Pol and the Tripolia, which lead to a large, open area on the south side of the palace. On the east end of the south façade is the Darikhana or Sabha, once a council chamber. Beneath the courtyard is an underground entrance reputed to lead to the chamber where Padmini and her followers committed johar. The north front boasts a wonderful array of cantilevered, canopied balconies and a stepped outer wall, a distinctive feature of Chitor.

Facing the palace is a beautiful three-storey building with two wings, the **Pade ka Mahal** or Kanwar (c. 1450), the palace of the heir apparent. This is designed in the Hindu tradition but embraces certain stylistic nuances, such as the vaulted substructure and ogee arch, which were to develop into the Rajput style. **Padmini's Palace** is also of note. A compact three-storey structure, it lies mid-way towards the south end in a tank of water. The bronze gates which stood here were carried off by Akbar to Agra as plunder.

Chronologically, the next palace to be built was that of Rana Ratna Simha II (1527–32); it is in a similar style to that of Rana Khumbha but with more widespread use of the ogee arch. Note the arched gateway leading to the compound to the south of the palace; this contrasts with the flat lintels used in Rana Khumbha's palace.

The fort is dominated by two extraordinary towers: the Tower of Fame or Kirtti Stambh and the Tower of Victory or Jaya Stambh. The **Tower of Fame** is the older of the two, probably 12th century, and is reputed to have been dedicated to Adinath. It is a Jain monument 22·8 m (75 ft) high. The seven storeys are carved with elegant figures and mouldings for the entire height. A narrow staircase leads to the top storey, which is

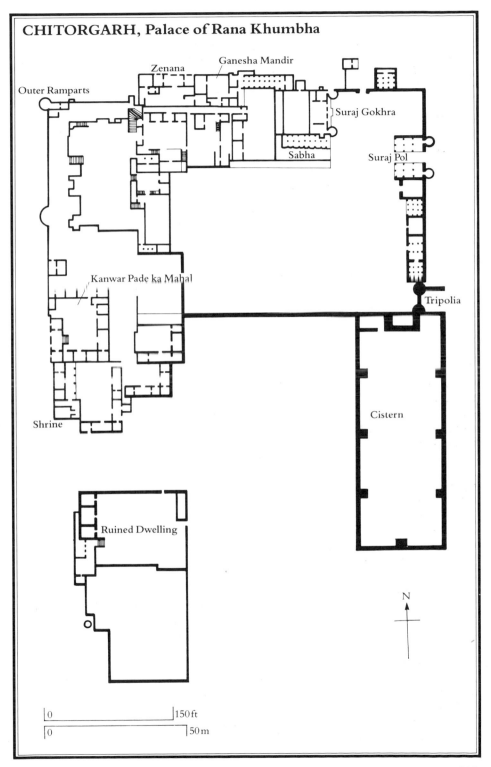

CHITORGARH, Palace of Rana Khumbha

Zenana
Ganesha Mandir
Outer Ramparts
Suraj Gokhra
Sabha
Suraj Pol
Kanwar Pade ka Mahal
Tripolia
Shrine
Cistern
Ruined Dwelling

N

0 ____ 150 ft
0 ____ 50 m

open. The **Tower of Victory** (1457–68) is a masterpiece of 15th-century revivalist Jain architecture, built by Khumbha, one of the most powerful kings of Mewar. It was designed by an architect called Jaita to commemorate the victory over Mahmud Khalji of Malwa in 1440. It has nine storeys rising to 37·2 m (122 ft) above ground level and is an extraordinary sight, visible for miles. Although subsequently restored, the upper stages retain good examples of original carved panels depicting Hindu deities.

Between the Towers of Fame and Victory is **Suraj Pol** or Sun Gate, which allows access from the east. Beyond is Adhbuthnath, a 15th-century temple. An even older Sun Temple in the fort, the Kalika Mata, dates from the 8th century.

800 m (½ mile) to the south of Rana Khumbha's palace are the houses of Jaimal and Patta, the heroes of the siege of 1567. South of Patta's house is the Chonda house (c. 1400), an early structure with a three-storey tower, now in ruins.

South-west of the Tower of Victory is the Mahasati, a small terrace where the Ranas were cremated, surrounded by many suttee stones. Below are springs, tanks and reservoirs. South-west again is an ancient temple embellished with the head of Vishnu.

North of the Tower of Victory is the **Temple of Vriji**, built by Rana Khumbha in 1450, with a large shikhara or tower. Nearby is another to his wife, Mira Bai. Between the Tower and Ram Pol are a magazine and treasury connected by a small Jain temple. There is little at the south end of the fort. The circuit can be truncated at the Padmini Palace to save tired legs.

DABHOI

Dabhoi, 24 km (15 miles) south-east of Vadodara, was fortified by the Solanki Rajputs from about 1100. The fine 13th-century fort is said to have been built by the Vaghela king of Patan, or Anhilvada. It is a notable example of Rajput military architecture, famous for the design of its four 13th-century gateways, which boast brackets carved with musicians, dancers, warriors and mythical beasts framed by miniature pilasters decorated with lotus ornament.

The **Baroda Gate** is over 9·1 m (30 ft) high, with carved pilasters depicting the incarnation of Vishnu with nymphs and crocodiles. Close by are colonnades which sheltered the garrison.

The **Nandod Gate** to the south is 8·8 m (29 ft) high and over 4·8 m (16 ft) wide, with trees growing from the masonry structure. The **Hira Gate** or Diamond Gate is the subject of local legends, with a carved relief of a man and woman flanking a tree, reminiscent of Adam and Eve. To the left is the devil and nearby, a carved elephant beneath which, it is alleged, the builder is buried. Outside the gate is a shrine.

To the north of the town is the old palace, beside which is the **Mori Gate**. On the left is the Kalika Mata Temple (1225), a wonderful carved building with exquisitely detailed friezes of miniature figures, animals and birds, and stylized lotus motifs, now badly eroded by the passage of time.

DAMAN

161 km (100 miles) north of Bombay lies one of the former Portuguese Indian enclaves, Daman, situated at the mouth of the Gulf of Cambay. It was not incorporated into India until 1961, when the Indian government seized control after negotiations to secure its retrocession had failed.

Daman occupies an area of 385 sq. km (149 square miles) and has three distinct parts: Damão, Dadra and Nagar Haveli.

It was taken by the Portuguese by 1531, then restored shortly after, but in 1558 it was seized again and retained as a permanent settlement.

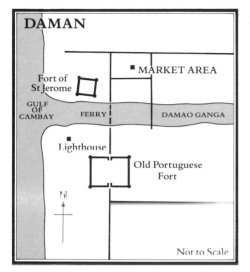

The town was conquered by Don Constantino de Braganza in 1559 and, until the decline of Portuguese power in the East, it was a great trading centre for East Africa. Between 1817 and 1837 it operated a profitable opium trade with China, until it was halted by the British after their conquest of Sind, thus depriving the town of its principal source of wealth.

The settlement has two stone **Forts** situated on either side of the River Damaoganga. The former is square in shape and contains the ruins of old monastic establishments, the Governor's Palace, barracks, hospital and other public buildings, including two churches. The landward side is protected by a ditch and drawbridge. The northwest bastion commands the harbour entrance. The smaller fort of St Jerome, with high stone walls, comprises an irregular quadrilateral enclosing a church, parochial house and cemetery. A few cannon and gun carriages remain on the outer walls.

The **Church of Bom Jesus** is a massive structure, built in 1606. The main altar, which is carved and gilded, is embellished with the statues of six saints and a centrepiece of Our Lady of the Rosary.

The **Church of Our Lady of Remedies** (1607) has five altars. The main altar is carved, gilded wood with 17th-century engravings. Near the fort, the **Church of Our Lady of the Sea** (1901) has a fine classical façade of twelve columns crowned by a cross. It was renovated in 1966.

DEEG (DIG) *Map overleaf*

38·5 km (24 miles) west of Mathura and about 40 km (25 miles) from Bharatpur, the fortress and pleasure palaces of Deeg are of major architectural importance. The town lays claim to great antiquity, but it came to prominence in the late 18th century when it was saved from the Jats by Najaf Khan in 1776, after whose death it reverted to the Raja of Bharatpur. On 13 November 1804 a British force under General Fraser defeated Holkar's army here and a month later the fort was carried by storm, after which the fortifications were dismantled.

It was Badan Singh (1722–56), a Sinsini Jat, who began the development of Deeg as the capital of his newly founded Jat kingdom, but the strong central citadel was built by Suraj Mal, his son, in 1730.

The **Fort** is square in plan, excluding the north barbican. The walls are of coursed rubble and mud reinforced by a dozen bastions, the largest, Lakha Burj, in the north-west corner. A shallow, wide moat encircles the fort. There is a bridge on the north approach. The walls are about 8 km (5 miles) in circumference, pierced by ten gateways and studded with seventy-two bastions.

However, the main interest of Deeg is

367

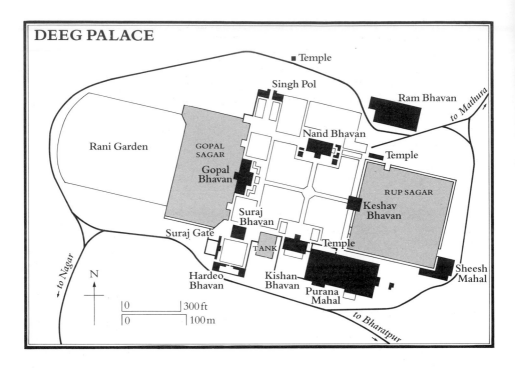

DEEG PALACE

the splendid group of palaces begun by Suraj Mal of Bharatpur. The palaces lie along the edge of a central garden flanked by two large reservoirs: the Rup Sagar and the Gopal Sagar. A secondary garden, separated from the main one by a causeway, lies to the north.

The main entrance is through the Singh Pol or Lion Gate. This is an unfinished entrance with a huge archway enriched with lions and other carved ornament. The Suraj Gate and Nanga Gate on the north-east and south-west sides are later. The main pavilion is the **Gopal Bhavan** (1763), the largest and best of the palaces, an oblong with a projecting central range, a central hall and side chambers. Two smaller, detached pavilions, the Sawan and Bhadon (*c.* 1760), flank the main range, which is faced with an arch for a hindola or swing, brought from Delhi as part of Suraj Mal's spoils of war, and two marble thrones.

The **Suraj Bhavan** (*c.* 1760) is to the south, a single-storey marble edifice treated like a pavilion. The **Hardeo**

Bhavan lies immediately behind a garden court surrounded by a quadrangle. East again of these is the **Kishan Bhavan**, on the southern edge of the complex, with five central arches and fountains playing on the terrace. Inside is an apsidal balcony with a carved front. Flowers, plants and peacocks provide a decorative unity to the interior. Above the southern room is a pavilion on arches, built by Balwant Singh (1826–53).

The **Keshav Bhavan** is a baradari or single-storey garden pavilion facing the Rup Sagar tank to the east and a garden on the other side. The **Nand Bhavan** (*c.* 1760) is a fine hall 45·7 m (150 ft) by 24·3 m (80 ft) by 6·1 m (20 ft) raised on a terrace and enclosed by an arcade of seven arches oversailed by deep projecting eaves. West lies the Singh Pol gate.

The **Purana Mahal** or Old Palace (1722 onwards) lies to the south of the Rup Sagar. Built by Raja Badan Singh, it has a curved roof embellished with chatris and contains two separate inner

368

courts lined with rooms. It is now used for government offices.

Architecturally, the most distinctive characteristic of the palace complex is the double cornice detail which recurs on a number of the buildings: the lower cornice acts as a sloping entablature; the upper is horizontal, virtually an extension of the flat roof out on to the face of the building. The effect of these projecting cornices on the appearance of the building is striking, creating a crisp balance of light and shade.

In the south-east corner of the Rup Sagar is the **Sheesh Mahal** (1725), with a curved bangaldar dome to the roof pavilion.

DHOLKA

Dholka, 35·5 km (22 miles) south-west of Ahmadabad, has an important heritage of Muslim buildings, built when it was the residence of the Governor of Delhi.

The **Masjid of Hilal Khan Qazi** (1333) is a simple structure dating from the earliest period of the Gujarati provincial style. Its façade is distinguished by a pair of tall ornamental turrets flanking the central archway. The design of the turrets is indigenous, with no trace of Islamic influence, a local stab at designing minarets without any detailed knowledge of their form or purpose.

The **Tanka Masjid** (1361) has an open sanctuary with over 100 richly carved pillars of Hindu design, a clear indication of the influence of temples on mosque architecture at this time.

The ruined **Mosque of Alif Khan** (1453) was built under Qutb-ud-Din Ahmad Shah II and was contemporaneous with the Darya Khan at Ahmadabad. Unlike other Gujarati mosques, it is built in brick with arches and solid brick piers. It is probably a manifestation of south Persian architecture executed by foreign workmen who were imported via the coastal trading ports.

DHOLPUR

Dholpur, 55 km (34 miles) south of Agra and 59·5 km (37 miles) north-west of Gwalior, is the capital of the former Jat state of Dholpur, which was created out of territory ceded by Scindia in 1805 at the behest of the Governor-General.

The original town is reputed to have been built in the early 11th century by Raja Dholan Deo. In 1658 Aurangzeb defeated his brother 4·8 km (3 miles) east of the town at Ran-Ka-Chabutra and in 1707 his sons fought for the right to succeed him at the village of Bareta.

Rana Kirat Singh built the **Palace** (early 19th century), which is a fine building in red sandstone. The old Mausoleum of Sadik Muhammad (1597) is now used as a school.

Within the old state are a number of other historic buildings. **Shergarh Fort** is supposed to be over 3,000 years old. In 1540 it was restored by Sher Shah Sur and was last used in the early 19th century. It is now in ruins. Near Bari there are three sites: the **Fort**, built in 1286 by Firuz Shah; the **Khanpur Mahal**, which lies 4·8 km (3 miles) to the south of Bari and is a series of inter-connected pavilions built for Shah Jahan by Safi Khan Aziz Khan; and **Mach Kund**, an ancient tank surrounded by a series of temples of different dates.

DIU *Map overleaf*

The island of Diu is only 11·2 km (7 miles) long and 3·2 km (2 miles) wide, situated just off the southern tip of the Kathiawad peninsula, from which it is separated by a narrow channel. It is fascinating on account of its Portuguese colonial past.

The town of Diu and the fort, built in 1535 by the Portuguese, lie at the eastern end of the island. Once this was a booming, prosperous settlement, the 'Gibraltar of the East', which reached its heyday in the 17th century, after which it declined into a remote colonial backwater.

Owing to its natural position and the great advantages afforded for trade with Arabia and the Persian Gulf, Diu was an early centre of Portuguese ambition. In 1535 they formed a defensive alliance with the Sultan of Gujarat against the Mughals and, in return, received permission to fortify the island. In 1538 the fort was besieged by Mahmud Ahmad Shah III, but the garrison foiled the attack. In 1545 it was invested again, but Dom João de Castro routed the Gujarati forces in a pitched battle, raised the siege and annexed the entire island. In 1670 Arabs from Muscat plundered the fort. In 1961 the Indian government invaded the island and expelled the Portuguese. During the attack a number of historic buildings, including the old fort church, were bombed.

The north coast is flat salt marsh, but the south coast is rocky. The entire island is pitted with quarries used for building stone.

The **Fort** is well worth the effort of travelling to the island. It is considered to be one of the most important Portuguese forts in Asia and commands a magnificent view of the sea and surrounding area. The approach is across a bridge and via a gateway flanked by two pointed pillars carrying a Portuguese inscription and defended by a bastion called St George. Cannon and cannon balls can still be seen throughout, many in an excellent state of preservation, which is more than can be said for the fort, which is crumbling into decay.

Other noteworthy buildings are the College of the Jesuits (1601), now the Se Matriz Cathedral. The old convent of St Dominic is in ruins, that of St John of God is a cemetery and that of St Francis a hospital. The town is compressed between the massive fort and a city wall to the west. One gateway is embellished with carved reliefs of lions and an angel.

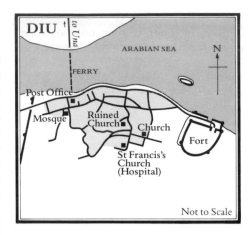

Inside it there is a small chapel built in 1702. **St Paul's Church** (founded 1610) is located near the Office of the Civil Administrator. Dedicated to Our Lady of Immaculate Conception, it has an impressive Gothic façade, rebuilt in 1807.

The town has a distinctly Portuguese atmosphere with its brightly coloured buildings ornamented with balconies and verandahs.

Elsewhere on the island, there is an old, derelict church – Our Lady of Remedies (16th century), with an old carved altar – at Fudam. Vanakbana, on the western extremity, has the Church of Our Lady of Mercy, a small fort and a lighthouse.

The **Fortress of Panikhot** faces the town of Diu and is situated on an island at the mouth of a creek. It is a massive rectangular stone fort containing a lighthouse and a small chapel dedicated to Our Lady of the Sea.

DUNGARPUR

About 224 km (139 miles) from Nimach on the road to Deesa, Dungarpur lies at the base of a hill 213 m (700 ft) high, on the edge of a cool, refreshing lake.

The ruling dynasty claim descent from the house of Mewar, the premier Rajput clan, and in spite of the vicissitudes of fortune, they managed to hold a small territory of rough country until afforded protection by the East India Company in 1818.

The **Juna Mahal Palace** (*c.* 1500 onwards) is an ancient, rambling mass of cream stucco, a chaotic jumble of terraces, pavilions and oversailing balconies, rising up the hill. Its form is dictated by its defensive functions, with narrow internal passages and corridors only wide enough for a single person. The principal rooms are ornamented lavishly with Rajput miniatures, mirror and lacquer work and polished coloured chunam decorated by craftsmen from Udaipur. Deserted for over 200 years, the interior is remarkably well preserved.

The **Udai Vilas Palace** is later designed in the late 18th century by Adit Ram Silawat but not completed until the late 19th century, which accounts for the European references in some of the details. It stands beside the lake and is approached by a long drive through the jungle. It is faced in local grey-green stone in a mixed Rajput-Mughal style. Within the central courtyard, which was once a pool, rises an extraordinary ornate pavilion. It is a riot of cusped arches, massive columns and elaborate balconies carried on sinuous, serpentine brackets. Inside, the walls are inlaid with semi-precious stones similar to the Great Taj at Agra. The whole is crowned by a canopied pavilion in exotic Rajput Style.

The modern wing was built in 1943. In the formal garden adjacent is a stone arch brought from a nearby temple, originally part of an elaborate weighing machine used to balance the Maharaja against his weight in gold. The resulting treasure was distributed to the poor.

GANDHINAGAR

Situated 19 km (12 miles) north of the old city of Ahmadabad, Gandhinagar is a new administrative capital, laid out from 1960 onwards under the aegis of Le Corbusier. When the old state of Bombay was divided between Maharashtra and Gujarat, a new state capital was planned for Gujarat named after its most illustrious son, Mahatma Gandhi.

Like Chandigarh, which was also supervised by Le Corbusier, it is an interesting centre of international modern-style architecture. Laid out in numbered zones, it embodies all the aspects of European planned cities, both good and bad. The Secretariat was built in 1970.

JAIPUR *Map overleaf*

Jaipur, the fabled pink city of Rajasthan, lies 241 km (150 miles) from Agra at a height of 431 m (1,414 ft) above sea level and is the state capital. Founded in November 1727 by Sawai Jai Singh II (1699–1744), it is one of the most spacious and picturesque cities in India and is of outstanding architectural and historical interest. Jai Singh had supported the son of Prince Azam Shah in the dynastic struggles for control of the Mughal Empire after Aurangzeb's death, and he drove the Mughals from the region. With the waning of Mughal power, Jai Singh advanced from his hill fortress at Amber and founded the city.

The title Sawai means one and a quarter, a reference to a remark made by Aurangzeb. He saw Jai Singh when the boy was only seven and was so impressed that he predicted that Jai Singh would be one and a quarter times greater than his great-grandfather.

The first thing to note about Jaipur is the town plan, which is unique in India. Unlike other Indian cities, which developed on more organic lines, similar to the mediaeval cities of Europe, with a winding road network and tortuous alleys capable of defence in times of emergency, Jaipur has a strict geometric grid plan. This represents a unique fusion of

371

Western and Eastern ideas of town planning. It is known that Jai Singh had close contact with European sources on astronomical works and, almost certainly, his great library held volumes on European cities. Evidently his ideas were complemented by the Shilpa-Shahstras, an ancient Hindu treatise which laid down abstract rules for city planning. The design and layout of the city can be attributed to a Bengali, Vidyahar Bhattacharya, who collaborated with the Maharaja in his historical and astronomical research. There is no truth in the assertion that the plan was that of Constantinople or, indeed, that of the Chandni Chowk in Delhi.

The distinctive pink wash, which is the hallmark of the city, is relatively recent. Originally, the buildings were painted a variety of colours, including grey with white borders, but in 1883 the buildings were repainted pink, the traditional colour of welcome, to harmonize with the sandstone used on some of the original buildings.

(For details of the museum and temples see Volume I.)

The city is surrounded by rocky hills to the north and east which are crowned with fortifications. To the north-west, overlooking the city, is the **Tiger Fort** (1734). A huge, battlemented wall, the **Sahar Panaha**, encloses the city to a height of 6·1 m (20 ft) and a width of 2·7 m (9 ft), with bastions and towers at regular intervals, loopholed for musketry. There are seven fortified gateways; to the south, the Kishan Pol or Ajmeri Darwaza, the Ram Pol or Sanganer Darwaza, and the Shiva Pol or Ghat Darwaza; to the west, the Chand Pol Darwaza; to the east, the Suraj Pol Darwaza; and to the north, the Ganga Pol Darwaza and the Dhurwa Pol or Amber Gate.

The city is divided into nine sections, of which the palace and its grounds occupy two and the city the remaining seven. The main streets are 34 m (111 ft)

wide and paved. The distance from Chand Pol to Suraj Pol is 3·6 km (2¼ miles). At the intersection of the principal streets is a spacious landscaped chopar. The central chopar is **Manak Chowk**, the western is **Amber-Ki-Chopar** and the eastern is **Ghat Darwaza Chopar**.

The Sawai Man Singh Highway (Chaura Rasta) is a later development. It formerly stopped at the city wall, where once there were cages for tigers and panthers.

The centre of the walled city is occupied by the **City Palace** or Sarhad, a spectacular synthesis of Rajput and Mughal architecture of supreme assurance with exquisite details, set in a garden adorned with fountains, trees and flowering bushes. This covers the entire central northern sector of the city. The Maharaja still lives here, but most of the apartments are now a museum.

From the Sireha Deorhi Bazaar, the first entrance to the palace is through the Sireha Deorhi Gate, built by Jai Singh II. In the first courtyard lies a building which housed an elephant chariot. Next is the Nobat Khane-Ka-Darwaza, a splendid portal built by Madho Singh II, which leads on to the **Jaleb Chowk**, a spacious open courtyard surrounded on all sides by rooms intended for personal attendants. These were repaired and extended by Sawai Ram Singh II, who added verandahs in the mid-19th century for use as courts and offices.

Sireha Deorhi (also called Udai Pol) is the main gate of the palace; then, in succession, come the Vijai Pol, Jai Pol and Ganpati Pol. To the right of Vijai Pol is a courtyard containing the Treasury and Accounts Offices. The Naya Naka gateway leads to the Jai Niwas Garden, another to the temple of Shree Ramchandra. Ganpati Pol leads to a large courtyard and the Diwan-i-Am. The last gate, the Amba Pol, connects this with the Diwan-i-Khas.

From the Tripolia Bazaar, the palace

372

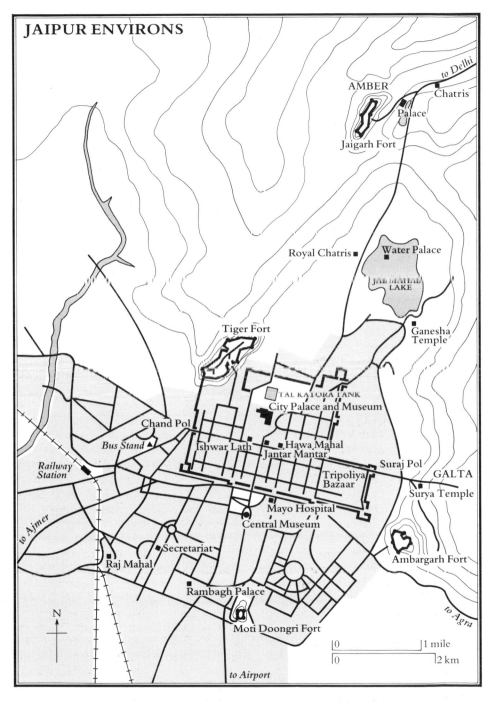

JAIPUR ENVIRONS

entrance is through a fine gateway. Usually, it is used only by the royal family for ceremonial occasions. Normally, it is not open to the public. In the north, this gate opens on to a square called Chandni Chowk. The Singha Pol opens into the courtyard containing the Mubarak Mahal (1900), in delicate carved marble in the manner of Fatehpur Sikri. In the south is Rajendra Pol or Deorhi Moalla (1880), the finest gate in the palace, with gigantic brass doors leading to the Diwan-i-Khas.

The **Chandra Mahal** or the Moon Palace (*c.* 1727–34) forms the centre of the complex, a seven-storey building with a spacious verandah overlooking the Jai Niwas Garden. The verandah is painted with frescoes by an Italian artist, including full-size portraits of some of the rulers of Amber and Jaipur. To the south the building opens on to the **Pritam Mahal** (literally Abode of the Beloved), which has a long, wide verandah decorated with fine doors and chandeliers by Man Singh II. At first-floor level, the **Sukh Niwas** (literally Abode of Pleasure), decorated with floral patterns, opens on to a terrace. At second-floor level the **Rang Mahal** is ornamented with mirrors, similar in style to the Sheesh Mahal at Amber. The upper chambers are the Sobha Niwas, Chub Niwas and Shee Niwas. At the top is the **Mukut Mahal**, from which a magnificent view of the city can be obtained, including the hilltop fortress of Nahargarh, the Tiger Fort.

Today, the ground and first floor of the Chandra Mahal form part of the Maharaja Sawai Man Singh II Museum, established in 1952. The upper storey of the Pritam Mahal contains an armoury with an excellent collection of match-locks, swords, daggers and spears. To the west of this courtyard is the shrine of Raj-Rajeshwar Mahadeo. The **Mubarak Mahal**, now part of the Museum, was built in 1890 with the assistance of Sir Samuel Swinton Jacob.

To the west of Chandra Mahal beyond a small courtyard is **Madho Niwas**, built by Madho Singh I and extended by his successor. On the north side this opens into the Jai Niwas Garden. There is a red sandstone gateway known as Gajendra Pol.

The **Diwan-i-Khas** or Hall of Private Audience (*c.* 1730) was built by Jai Singh II, partly of white marble. It stands on a raised podium, square in plan and open on all sides. The four corners are enclosed. It has double columns of marble pillars carrying the arches with a beautiful roof pavilion.

The **Diwan-i-Am**, or Hall of Public Audience, built by Madho Singh I (*c.* 1760), stands on a high plinth and comprises a large hall surrounded by a verandah, open on three sides. At the south end upper galleries permitted VIPs to watch the proceedings below. The decoration of floral designs in gold and bright colours is recent. Today, the building houses a picture gallery with a fine collection of Persian and Indian miniatures, an extensive library of rare books and valuable Persian and Afghan carpets. In the south-east corner of the courtyard is the Clocktower (late 19th century).

The **Jai Niwas Garden** was laid out in 1727 by Jai Singh II. Further improvements were made by his successors in the late 18th century. It is a beautiful enclosure criss-crossed with shallow channels and ponds. Fountains play among the trees and flowering shrubs. The garden is enclosed by high walls to east and west. Opposite a large, enclosed swimming pool is the former Billiards Room, now remodelled with Italian marble pillars and high arches as a banqueting hall.

At the northern end of the garden is the Badal Mahal, north-west of which is a portal leading to the Cenotaph of Sawas Ishwari Singh, a simple chatri (*c.* 1751). Ishwari Singh committed suicide in December 1751. Three of his wives took poison with him, one became suttee and over twenty-seven maids and servants entered the funeral pyre.

The **Town Hall** (late 19th century) once housed the State Council. It faces west over Sireha Deorhi Bazaar and has a large terrace and verandah. The **Hawa Mahal** or Palace of the Winds (1799) is

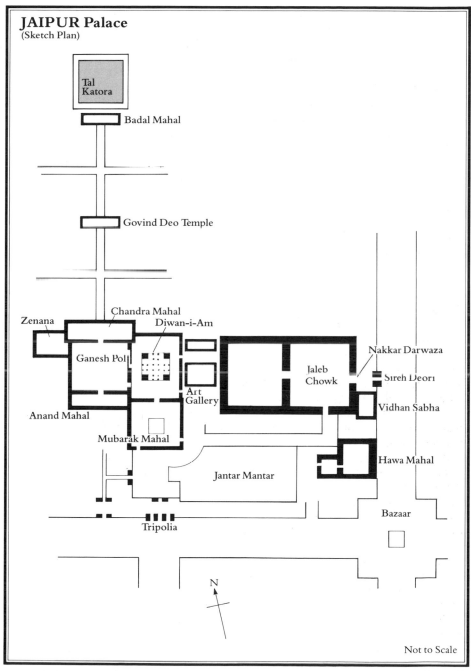

JAIPUR Palace
(Sketch Plan)

Tal Katora

Badal Mahal

Govind Deo Temple

Chandra Mahal
Diwan-i-Am

Zenana

Ganesh Pol

Nakkar Darwaza

Jaleb Chowk

Sireh Deori

Art Gallery

Vidhan Sabha

Anand Mahal

Mubarak Mahal

Hawa Mahal

Jantar Mantar

Bazaar

Tripolia

N

Not to Scale

one of the most famous buildings in Jaipur. Built for the ladies of the harem by Sawai Pratap Singh and designed by Lalchand Usta, it is a remarkable architectural composition, standing on a high podium with an arched entrance from the west. The five-storey symmetrical façade overlooking the Sireha Deorhi Bazaar is composed of 953 small casements in a huge curve, each with a projecting balcony and crowning curved arch. The windows provide a constant flow of cool air into the apartments and permit a view down into the town below. The corresponding view from the bazaar, with camels passing by, is one of the most picturesque sights in India.

Close to the Chandra Mahal is the famous **Jantar Mantar** (1718–34), the largest of the five Observatories built by Jai Singh II in the early 18th century (the others are at Delhi, Mathura, Ujjain, and Varanasi). It was restored in the late 19th century. The instruments are made of masonry and lie in a group in the courtyard. To the west are two circular Ram Yantras for reading azimuths and altitudes, with twelve radiating stone sectors around a central vertical pole. East of these are twelve Rashivalayas for determining celestial latitudes and longitudes, then the great gnomon, or Samrat Vantra, 27·4 m (90 ft) high, lying between two calibrated quadrants with sextants placed in an outer chamber. The shadow of the Samrat Yantra touches the west quadrant at 6.00 a.m. and descends at a rate of 3·9 m (13 ft) per hour until midday, when it ascends the eastern quadrant. The Dakshina Bhitti Yantra lies to the north. This is a meridianal wall adjoining which is Jai Singh's seat, a raised platform. Other brass circles and instruments are disposed around the main masonry devices.

Adjoining the Tripolia Gate, southwest of the Observatory, are the Stables or Atash. Nearby is the **Ishwar Lath**, a tower of victory erected by Ishwari Singh in 1749 to commemorate his defeat of his stepbrother Madho Singh. It is a beautiful octagonal minaret of seven storeys crowned by a canopy, with balconies on alternate levels. It is known locally as Swarga Suli (literally a dart piercing Heaven).

The **Zenana Deorhi** lies in the west, adjoining the Mardana Palace, a vast building capable of accommodating thousands. An outer portal leads to an open courtyard at the end of which an arched gateway leads to a long, oblong area with chambers on either side.

This completes the tour of the City Palace. However, within the walled city but outside the palace complex are numerous other sites of interest. The **School of Arts and Crafts** was opened in 1866 and is accommodated within the Haveli of Pandit Sheodin, half-way along the east side of Kishan Pol Bazaar. Opposite is the Temple of Harash Bihari, outside which the British Resident was murdered in 1835.

In the south-west corner of Amber-Ki-Chopar is the **Natani-Ki-Haveli**, once a banker's mansion, now a girls' school and police station. At the end of the Gangauri Bazaar is a gateway of the same name which leads to the Chaugan or Maidan. Here crowds gather for local festivals. In the north-west corner is the **Khiri-Ki-Buraj**, with beautiful blue tiles, then Moti Buraj and, to the north, Shyan Buraj. Elephant fights used to take place on the Chaugan and elephant stalls abut the palace walls. The **Tal Katora Tank** lies below the Badal Mahal of the palace, a small lake once surrounded by dense forest.

The **Madho Bilas** is a palace built by Madho Singh I. Now used as a hospital, it retains a number of good chambers, including a pavilion in the first apartment. The Maharaja's College lies opposite the Hawa Mahal; the Public Library is at the junction of Chaura Rasta and Tripolia Bazaar.

Outside the walls the city has expanded to the south and west.

The Ram Niwas Garden lies just outside the walls and was laid out in 1868 by Surgeon-Major F. W. de Fabeck for Ram Singh II. Here there are cricket and football grounds, a zoo and the **Albert Hall and Museum** (1876–87), designed by Sir Samuel Swinton Jacob, the State Engineer. Jacob, a scholar-architect with a great understanding of local styles, was the most accomplished practitioner of the

Indo-Saracenic style. The Albert Hall is one of the finest buildings, many of which are concentrated in and around Jaipur. The Hall contains a Durbar Hall for lectures and a Museum of Art and Antiquities.

The **Mayo Hospital** (now the Judicial Courts) (1870–75), also by Jacob, lies outside the Sanganer Gate in the eastern sector of the Ram Niwas Garden. Built in rough-hewn white stone, it has a high clocktower. The King Edward VII Memorial Building (1912), outside the Ajmer Gate, is now a medical hostel.

St Xavier's School and Hostel is an imposing building on the Bhagwan Dass Road. The Sawai Man Singh Hospital and adjacent Medical College were built in 1954, the Zenana Hospital, outside Chand Pol Gate, in 1932 and the Military Hospital in 1891.

The **Jaipur Club** is on Jacob Road, opposite the Public Works Department (PWD) Offices. **Rambagh Palace** (c. 1920), 3·2 km (2 miles) south of the town, was built as a successor to the City Palace by Ram Singh; it is now a hotel. It was altered to designs prepared by Sir Samuel Swinton Jacob. There is a Chinese room with exotic red and gold tapestries and Chinese furniture, now used as a bar, and a huge private swimming pool in a separate outbuilding.

At **Raj Mahal** (1729) viceroys and visiting royalty were accommodated. In 1958 the Maharaja remodelled it as his private residence.

Raj Bhavan, originally two conjoined bungalows, was altered and extended for the Governor in 1969. The **Government Secretariat** (1936) is an impressive range, once used by the Maharaja's private guards.

About 2·4 km (1½ miles) south of the city, on the University Road, is a small palace-fortress, an outer defence post for Jaipur built by Madho Singh I, known as **Moti Doongri** and resembling a Scottish castle.

The Anglican Church lies near the main hotels on the road to the railway station. The Roman Catholic Church is at Ghat Darwaza.

At Gaitor (Gethur), outside the northeast city wall on the Amber Road, lie the royal cenotaphs or chatris, set in a landscaped garden. The **Chatri of Jai Singh II** is beautifully composed, a white marble dome carried on twenty carved pillars rising from a square platform lavishly enriched with scenes from Hindu mythology. South-east is the **Chatri of Madho Singh I**, second son of Jai Singh II, also in white marble: a dome over an octogon with carved peacock ornament. West is the **Chatri of Pertab Singh**, his son, a peculiar composition in marble with a dome carried on pendentives and square pillars. The **Chatri of Ram Singh II** lies to the north of Jai Singh's and is similar in form and detail; the **Chatri of Madho Singh II** is in white and pink stone. Opposite the cenotaphs is the **Jal Mahal Water Palace** (1735), in the middle of a lake filled with water hyacinths.

Excursions can be made from Jaipur to Amber (see separate entry); Galta; Tiger Fort; Gaitor; the Sisodia Rani Palace and gardens (early 18th century), located on the Agra Road, with fine murals of hunting scenes on the outer walls; Sanganer, with its Jain temples and two Tripolia gateways; and Vidyadhar's Garden, which is set in a narrow valley and which commemorates Jai Singh's accomplished architect-planner, who created the glories of Jaipur.

JAISALMER *Map overleaf*

Far out into the Thar Desert, about 287 km (178 miles) from Jodhpur, Jaisalmer rises like a mirage from the sands, a huge fortified city in the middle of nowhere. The journey across the hot, barren desert to Jaisalmer, one of the remotest places in India, is rewarded by views of the spectacular fortress which dominates its hilltop site and which contains a fascinating heritage of merchants' houses.

The Thar Desert (literally Abode of Death) is an unremitting, arid wasteland 800 km (500 miles) long by 320 km (200 miles) wide. For centuries it acted as a natural barrier between the Indus valley and the fertile plains of northern India. The town was founded by Prince Jaisal in 1156 and was the capital of the Bhatti Rajputs. It grew to be a major trade centre for camel trains, linking the routes from India to Egypt, Arabia, Persia, Africa and Europe and controlling the way into northern India across the desert.

Architecturally, the city has a wonderful legacy of old buildings, united by the common use of local yellow-brown stone and beautifully preserved because of the isolated location. Stylistically, they are a blend of Rajput and Islamic influences, untouched by any European nuances.

The **Fort** stands on Tricuta Hill, 76 m (250 ft) high and enclosed by an imposing crenellated sandstone wall 9·1 m (30 ft) high, reinforced with ninety-nine bastions, of which ninety-two were built between 1633 and 1647 for use as gun platforms. Wells within the fort provide a regular source of water. The fortifications have grown organically over the centuries.

Between 1577 and 1623 the Suraj Pol, Ganesh Pol and Hawa Pol were erected. The **Suraj Pol** (1594) is enriched with a large sun–roundel, denoting that it is the first to receive the rays of the rising sun. To its right is a large tower crowned by a kiosk with delicate carved balconies – the **Tazia Tower**, five storeys of ornately carved detail with drooping Bengali-style roofs. It is part of the Badal Mahal, where the former ruler and his family still live. Beyond a spiked entrance gate, on a sharp turn in the path, is Ganesh Pol, which leads to Rang Pol. The outer defences are reinforced by a second ram-

part, which runs parallel to and higher than the first.

The town at the base of the citadel was enclosed by a fortified wall in 1750 by Maharawal Mulraj. There are four important gateways to the city wall: Gadhisar Pol, leading to the Gadhisar Tank, which has a fine gateway adjacent to it which was reputedly erected by a prostitute; Amarsagar Pol; Baron-Ki-Pol; and Malka Pol. There are also two gateways to the south, later sealed.

Some of the glories of Jaisalmer are the mansions, called **havelis**, of the Rajput nobles and merchants. These beautiful town houses built of honey-coloured sandstone are enriched with delicately carved façades and balconies of the finest jali work oversailing the narrow streets. Behind these intricate stone screens the women withdrew in purdah.

Salim Singh-Ki-Haveli was the residence of the influential Mohta family and is still occupied. Built *circa* 1815, possibly on the core of an earlier building of the late 17th century, it has a beautiful arched roof and exquisitely carved details, with brackets in the form of peacocks. The entrance is guarded by a large stone elephant. The upper portion of the house oversails boldly like a ship's prow and, as a result, is often called Jahazmahal or Ship's Palace. The top two storeys – the Kanchanmahal and Rangamahal – once were adorned with glass mosaics and bright colours.

Patwon-Ki-Haveli (*c.* 1805) is the largest and most elaborate of all. It stands in a narrow alley and has beautiful murals, one of a group of five built for the five Patua brothers. The entire front is carved with elaborate detail.

Nathumal's Haveli was built for the prime minister as late as 1885. The entrance is flanked by stone elephants and the entire façade is carved with a riot of ornamental detail – soldiers, horses, elephants, flowers and birds. The building was designed and built by two craftsmen-architects Hathi and Lulu.

378

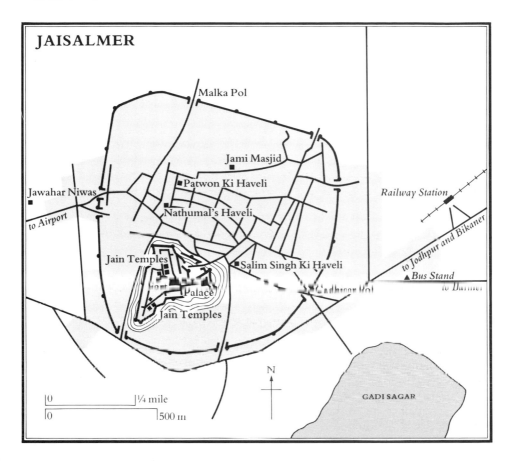

JAISALMER

Malka Pol
Jami Masjid
Patwon Ki Haveli
Jawahar Niwas
to Airport
Nathumal's Haveli
Railway Station
to Jodhpur and Bikaner
Jain Temples
Salim Singh Ki Haveli
Fort Palace
Bus Stand
to Barmer
Jain Temples
N
GADISAGAR
0 ¼ mile
0 500 m

One carved the left side, the other the right, but the overall impact is one of complete harmony. Extraordinarily, the house is built of rock and not dressed stone. In the main room at first-floor level the entire front wall is a huge, single rock carved into a bay. The inner walls are counterpointed with beautiful miniatures.

The **Royal Apartments** at Jaisalmer are equally splendid. Inside the fort are a maze of interconnecting palaces and chambers, the oldest part of which, the **Juna Mahal**, dates from about 1500, with ancient jali screens on the south front.

Rang Mahal, situated above Hawa Pol, was built by Mulraj II (1762–1820) and has richly detailed murals. **Sarvottam Vilas**, probably the most distin-

guished, was built by Akhai Singh (1722–62). It is ornamented with blue tiles and glass mosaics.

Adjacent is the **Gaj Vilas**, built in 1884. It stands on a high plinth, its eastern elevation facing the square or chauhata. The plain base is oversailed by a honeycomb of projecting pavilions, pillars and balconies.

Moti Mahal lies across a narrow, winding lane. It was built in 1813 by Mulraj II. The front is treated with floral patterns. The carved doors are very fine. The second storey is decorated with mirrors and inlay work. The first floor, the former audience chamber, is now a school.

Zenana Mahal (16th and 17th centuries) is run-down but can be recognized by its arch decoration.

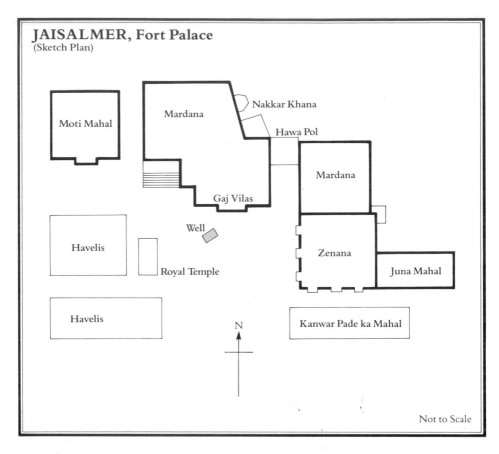

JAISALMER, Fort Palace
(Sketch Plan)

Moti Mahal — Mardana — Nakkar Khana — Hawa Pol — Mardana — Gaj Vilas — Well — Havelis — Royal Temple — Zenana — Juna Mahal — Havelis — Kanwar Pade ka Mahal — N — Not to Scale

Also within the fort walls is an interesting group of Jain temples dating from the 12th to 15th centuries. The oldest is Parshwanath. They are all impressive and add a further dimension to the secular buildings of the city. (For details of the temple see Volume I.)

Outside the town lies **Jawahar Niwas** (*c.* 1900), an opulent palace built as a guest-house for private visitors. On the banks of the Amar Sagar, a few miles west of Jaisalmer, is the pleasure palace of Amar Singh (1661–1703), built around a courtyard with an extensive formal garden.

To the north at Bada Bagh is the old royal cremation ground. The **Royal Chatris**, set in gardens, have fine carved ceilings.

Today the town owes its resurgence to the military presence here and to growing tourist traffic. Jaisalmer is a good centre for camel trips into the surrounding desert.

JALOR

Jalor, situated on the southern edge of the vast sandy plain of Marwar in Rajasthan, retains an impressive fort which commands the town from a rocky outcrop 366 m (1,200 ft) high. The main approach is from the north, up a steep, slippery road through three lines of fortification to a single rampart wall 6·1 m (20 ft) high.

The **Fort Mosque** and **Topkhana Masjid** (late 16th century) are noteworthy as they demonstrate the widespread influence of the architectural decoration associated with Gujarati styles of this period. The former recalls the architecture of Ahmadabad, while the latter has arcades of perforated stone screens, which were a distinctive hallmark of the Gujarati style.

JHINJHUWADA

Jhinjhuwada is situated about 50 km (31 miles) from Viramgam on the edge of the Little Rann of Kutch.

Set into the massive walls of the ancient fort are some impressive original 12th-century stone gateways with intricately carved brackets similar to those on the gateways at Dabhoi and comparable to carvings on contemporary temples. Large stone guardians are set into niches either side of the gateways.

There is a 12th-century well, an elaborate construction with carved balcony slabs, columns and brackets.

JODHPUR *Map overleaf*

Jodhpur, once the capital of the old princely state of Marwar (literally Land of Death), is the largest city in Rajasthan after Jaipur, about 386 km (240 miles) away. Situated at a height of 235 m (771 ft) on a range of sandstone hills, the fort dominates the city and can be seen for miles across the bare desert plain. After the defeat of the Rathors of Kanauj in 1211, Rao Siha came to Rajasthan and founded a settlement here. Later the Rajputs established themselves in Marwar with Mandor as the capital. Jodhpur was founded by Rao Jodha in 1459, after he had been expelled from Mandor, which was too vulnerable. The site chosen was impregnable, dominating the Thar Desert.

The old city is surrounded by a huge wall with 101 bastions, nearly 9·5 km (6 miles) long, with seven gateways outside of which the new city has expanded.

Within the old city are some fine examples of local vernacular architecture and temples set in an inextricable confusion of picturesque streets and alleyways. (For the Sardar Museum see Volume I.)

The **Meherangarh Fort**, 122 m (400 ft) above the plain, stands on a steep escarpment with a sheer drop of over 36·5 m (120 ft) at the south end, enclosed by a high wall with bastions. The summit is divided into three areas: the palace to the north-west, the strongly fortified area to the south edge of the cliff and a long, wide terrace to the east of the palace.

The approach, via a steep zigzag path up the west side of the hill and through seven separate gateways of enormous dimensions, is arduous. En route, to the right, is the Jaswant Thada, the cremation ground of the rulers of Jodhpur, dotted with cenotaphs. The white marble memorial (1899) is to Jaswant Singh II.

Fateh Gate has a barbican, pockmarked by cannon balls, with a wing wall and heavy spiked gates. After a short turn, the second gate is reached. It has pointed arches, ogee heads and the ubiquitous armoured spiked gates. The third is similar, with capacious guardrooms; the fourth is demolished; but the fifth is an unusual composite affair standing over a turn in the path with loopholed battlements. In the north-east corner of the palace lies the sixth gate, with a long passage defended on either side by guardrooms. On the last gate, Loha Pol or Lion Gate, are the handprints of fifteen royal suttees, wives of the Maharajas.

Within the fort are two small tanks: the Rani Talao or Queen's Lake and the Gulab Sagar or Rose-Water Sea, to the south.

The **Old Palaces** are a series of interconnecting courtyards surrounded by ranges of buildings with intricate carved stonework and beautiful filigree sandstone windows. Commenced in 1499, the surviving apartments generally date from 1640 onwards.

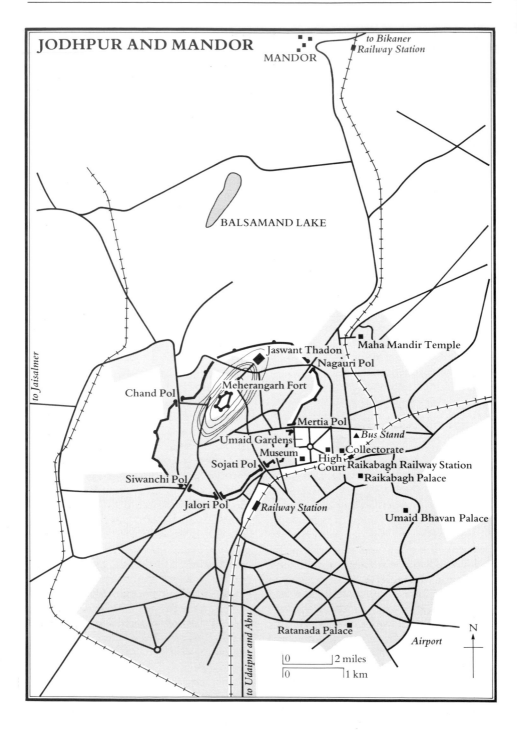

JODHPUR AND MANDOR

The **Moti Mahal** or Pearl Palace, possibly built by Sur Singh (1581–95), and the **Phool Mahal** or Flower Palace, built by Abhai Singh (1730–50) but decorated

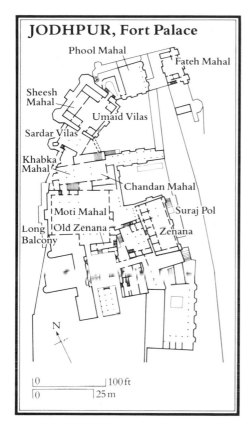

JODHPUR, Fort Palace

Phool Mahal
Fateh Mahal
Sheesh Mahal
Umaid Vilas
Sardar Vilas
Khabka Mahal
Chandan Mahal
Moti Mahal
Suraj Pol
Long Balcony
Old Zenana
Zenana
N
0 — 100 ft
0 — 25 m

murals depict dancing girls and other traditional themes.

Along the battlements of this majestic fort are ancient cannon commanding magnificent views of the old city beneath and the arid desert beyond.

Within the **Old City** the colourful Sadar Bazaar, running from the Sojati Gate, has an ornate Clocktower (late 19th century). The red standstone buildings of the bazaar area repay close inspection in between the silver, textiles and other attractions. The **Tulahti Mahal**, now a women's hospital, was built by Jaswant Singh I (1638–81). The Kunjebehari Temple, dedicated to Krishna, and the garden palace of Raj Mahal are located on the banks of the Gulab Sagar.

The **New City** is also of interest. The **Umaid Gardens and Museum** on High Court Road have a positively Victorian exhibition of stuffed animals and other eccentric bric-a-brac. Further out, overlooking the Umaid Sagar, is the **Umaid Bhavan Palace**, now a hotel, built between 1929 and 1944 as a famine-relief exercise. It was designed by Henry Lanchester (1863–1953), an architect with a keen interest in Baroque civic classicism. This vast monolithic pile is conceived in the classical grand manner, but on an Indian plan. It contains 347 rooms, including eight dining-halls. The nuances and details are Hindu and the materials, red sandstone and marble. The Raikabagh Palace lies south-east of the city. The Ratnada Palace is given over to military use. Close to the former are **Jubilee Buildings**, the public offices, designed by Sir Samuel Swinton Jacob in Indo-Saracenic style. The **Judicial Court** (1893–6), now the Collectorate, is a splendid essay in a hybrid Anglo-Rajput style.

The Mahamandir is a huge temple set in a separate enclave of 800 houses about 2·1 km (1½ miles) north-east of the city. The old British Residency is a fortified complex set in the hills. Balsamand Lake is surrounded by beautiful gardens laid

between 1873 and 1895, have exquisite painted ceilings and walls. The north, east and south ranges of the former comprise the **Moti Vilas** (1638–78), with beautiful intricate jali screens so minutely detailed that they resemble the finest lace. Adjacent, to the south, is a zenana court (1640), also with fine carved stonework.

The Sheesh Mahal (1707–24) and Rang Mahal are also noteworthy, with fine decoration enriched with inlay work and mirrors. In the **Sileh Khana** is the armoury, with ornamented swords, shields, maces and antique guns. The Man Mahal was built by Man Singh in 1819. The splendid **Takhat Vilas**, with its exotic interior, was built over a thirty-year period from 1843 to 1873. The

383

out in 1936. The pleasure pavilion on the bund is late 19th century, with an internal layout which is purely European in concept.

JUNAGADH

This fascinating old town is rarely visited by tourists, but it is a rewarding centre of considerable interest, close to the temples on Girnar Hill and near the border with Pakistan.

The town is surrounded by an old fort wall, part of which has now been demolished to facilitate growth. The fort was expanded in 1472 by Mahmud Begada, and enlarged later again in 1683 and 1880.

The old citadel, **Uparkot**, lies to the north-east of the town. It is an ancient stronghold of the Maurya and Gupta empires. It is alleged that for over 300 years, between the 7th and 10th centuries, the fort was abandoned to the jungle, but after rediscovery it was reused and strengthened. Over its long history since 976 it has endured no less than sixteen sieges. The approach is through solid rock and via three gateways with massive walls. Over the entrance is carved an inscription of 1450. The top of the old fort is flat and crossed by pathways linking the principal sites.

Within the fort is the **Jami Masjid**, built from the remains of a former Hindu temple. The **Tomb of Nuri Shah** lies close to the mosque and may be recognized by the fluted cupolas and ornate carving over the door. The **Adi Chadi Vav** (15th century) is a huge step-well with over 172 steps, named after two slave girls. The **Navghan Kuva**, a similar well, was completed in about 1060. It is over 52 m (170 ft) deep, reached by a splendid circular staircase. Nearby are a number of ancient Buddhist caves, over 1,500 years old, cut into the soft rock of the hillside. Some of the caves are from the time of Ashoka.

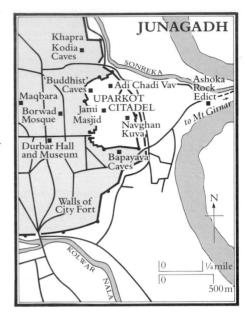

On the western wall are two colossal guns. The larger of the two, the Nilam, cast in Egypt in 1531, is over 5·2 m (17 ft) long, with a bore of 25 cm (9½ in). The smaller, the Chudanal, is 3·8 m (12 ft 8 in) long. They were left at Diu by Sulaiman Pasha, the Turkish Admiral, to help the Sultan against the Portuguese in 1538 and were later brought here by the Fouzdar of Junagadh. South-west of the fort the Jami Masjid (late 19th century) is a vigorous, robust mosque with onion domes and minarets.

The mausolea of the rulers of Junagadh are some of the most interesting and unusual buildings in Gujarat. Situated close to a main intersection, the **Maqbara** are richly ornamented sepulchres of an exuberant design. From the north gate the first tomb is that of Nawab Bahadur Khan II (1840), which lies to the left. Adjacent is the Tomb of Nawab Hamid Khan II (1851) and to its left, that of Laddibu Bibi. Beside these is the tomb of Mahabat Khan I (1774), in Saracenic style with fine carved detail. The spectacular tomb of Vizir Sahib Baha-ud-Din Bhar has minarets with spiral stairs curling round in a fantastic display of architectural ebullience.

The city has a remarkable heritage of buildings which combine European Gothic with exotic local forms in a riotous mixture of styles bordering on the decadent.

The **Reay Gate** is a large, arcaded, two-storey crescent with a central clocktower and an engrailed entrance arch, capped by domes and minarets. Within the town are numerous fine local buildings. The **New Bazaar** is an elegant classical terrace leading to huge Gothic gateways. The **Nawab's Old Palace** (c. 1870), which contains the Rasaul Khanji Museum (1925), is opposite the Haveli and Durbar Kacheri Hall. The Aiyena Mahal or Palace of Mirrors lies to the east, with a fine Gothic range to one side of the entrance.

The Moti Bagh, Lal Bagh, Rajibagh and Sakar Bagh gardens all confer a verdant character on the city and provide pleasant parks in and around it. The Sakar Bagh includes the Zoo.

East of the town is the **Willingdon Dam** (1936), a large barrage 13·4 m (44 ft) high and 259 m (850 ft) long. The surrounding hills, gardens and lake coalesce to form a beautiful view.

(For a full description of the ancient temples on Mount Girnar and the Ashoka rock edicts see Volume I.)

KAIRA

Kaira, 32 km (20 miles) south-west of Ahmadabad, is an ancient settlement reputed to date from 1400 BC. Certainly, copper-plate grants verify its existence in the 5th century. Early in the 18th century it was acquired by the Babi family, but in 1736 it was taken by the Marathas before passing to the British in 1803. Until 1830 it retained a significant military garrison and this accounts for the large **Church**, designed by Captain Thomas Ramon and

consecrated in 1822 by Bishop Heber. The bell has been removed to St Paul's, Pune (Poona).

In the centre of the town the **Town Hall** is designed in a handsome Greek Revival style – a building of some distinction. The clocktower and library are conventional civic adornments.

KARAULI

Once the capital of a small state of the same name, Karauli is about 120 km (75 miles) equidistant from Agra, Gwalior, Jaipur and Mathura.

It was founded in 1348 by Raja Arjun Pol and was called Kalyanpuri after a local temple. The town and palace have a striking appearance. The town is encircled by a wall of red sandstone and protected to the north and east by a series of ravines. A moat, outer wall and ditch, reinforced by bastions, provide a formidable defensive perimeter. There are six gates and eleven posterns.

The **Palace** is about 182 m (591 ft) from the eastern wall of the town. It was built by Arjun Pol. Little of the original structure remains. The present building is mid-18th century, by Raja Gopal Singh in the Delhi style of architecture. The entire palace is surrounded by a lofty bastioned wall with two fine gates.

KISHANGARH

Kishangarh was a tiny principality surrounded by powerful neighbours – Amber, Marwar and Mewar – and its reputation for artistic and cultural genius was out of all proportion to its size.

Founded in 1597 by Kishan Singh, son of the Raja of Jodhpur, the state served the Mughals loyally and later accepted British protection.

The **Fort**, reflected in the still waters of Lake Gandalan, contains a wealth of fine miniatures depicting religious epics and Hindu deities. The main entrance gate has a huge pointed central arch flanked by painted murals of elephants and guards. Today it lingers on in ramshackle splendour, a marvellous decaying palace of overgrown courtyards, abandoned balconies and forlorn roof pavilions.

KOTA

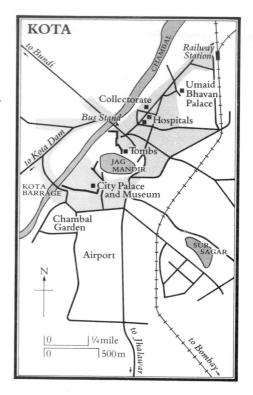

39 km (24 miles) from Bundi, Kota is the capital of the former state of that name, which was created in 1579. The town lies on the east bank of the Chambal river, below a deep gorge straddling one of the main lateral trade routes from the plains of Delhi to the fertile lowlands of Gujarat. It is now a fast-growing industrial centre with an atomic power station and a river barrage, which provides hydroelectricity to the entire area.

Kota relied on astute diplomacy to preserve its integrity in the face of rapacious neighbours and its history alternated between periods of expansion and contraction, depending on wider political circumstances. In the early 19th century, under the enlightened tutelage of Zalim Singh, Kota weathered the worst political storms and emerged a prosperous and flourishing state. On his death this stability was lost. It was not recovered until 1894, when British intervention reunited the territory.

The **City Palace** reflects the turbulent history of the state in that it evolved over a long period, growing in times of stability and stagnating in adversity. Built from about 1625 onwards, there is no ordered plan other than a large Durbar Hall, the Bhim Mahal (early 18th century), which is covered with Rajput miniatures depicting the history and legends of Kota. There is some fine ivory and ebony inlay work and a profusion of surface ornament. The Elephant Gate (1625–48) is flanked by later murals showing a royal wedding procession and bracketed elephants, whose trunks form a triumphal gesture over the central arch. The exterior of the palace is a mixture of robust fortification and delicate ornamental stonework.

The **Akhade Ka Mahal** was added to the west of the inner court between 1723 and 1756, and was later enlarged and recast between 1888 and 1940. The prominent **Hawa Mahal**, added next to the entrance to the fort in 1864, is based loosely on the famous façade at Jaipur.

The cenotaphs of the ruling family lie nearby.

The **Umaid Bhavan** or New Palace was built for Umed Singh II in 1904 to the designs of Sir Samuel Swinton Jacob. It is faced in buff-coloured stone with stucco dressings and incorporates a great deal of scholarly Rajput detail, but the overall composition and much of the interior is European and Edwardian in

386

conception. There is a fine drawing-room and banqueting hall and a beautiful garden, renowned for its spectacular herbaceous borders.

Other buildings of note include the General Hospital, Hospital for Women, the Crosthwaite Institute, the Curzon Wyllie Memorial, the Herbert High School and the Girls' School. (For details of the collections in the Museum see Volume I.)

KUMBHALGARH

Kumbhalgarh is a spectacular Rajput hill-fort situated at a height of 1,087 m (3,568 ft) above sea level and 213 m (700 ft) above the plain which it commands. The fort lies near the village of Kailwara, on the site of a more ancient fortress, possibly built by Sumprit, a Jain prince of the 2nd century. After Chitorgarh, it was the most important fort of Mewar. It lies on the topmost ridge of the mountain, surrounded by thirteen other peaks.

The approach is impressive, across deep ravines and through thick jungle. Seven massive gates guard the approaches, while seven ramparts, one within the other, reinforced by rounded bastions and huge watchtowers, render the position impregnable.

The first gate is Arait Pol, from which mirror signals could be flashed to the fort in times of emergency. Hulla Pol, the Gate of Disturbance, is next, named after the point reached by invading Mughal armies in 1567, where the mark of cannon shot can still be seen on the walls. The third gate, Hanuman Pol, contains a shrine and temple. The Bhairava Pol has a tablet ordering the exile of a treacherous prime minister in the 19th century. The fifth gate, the Stirrup or Paghra Pol, is where the cavalry gathered prior to battle. The Star watchtower nearby is an early structure with walls 8 m (26 ft) wide. The Cannon Gate or Top-Khana Pol is reputed to have an underground

passage leading to a secret escape tunnel. The last gate is Nimboo Pol or the Gate of Lemon Trees, near which is the temple of Chamundi, one of 365 temples within the fort, before which stands a shrine of the founding Mer ruler. The infant Udai Singh, future founder of Udaipur, was saved from murder at his uncles' hands after being hidden in the chambers close to the Nimboo Pol.

The outer wall embraces an area of several square miles. The tiers of inner ramparts rise to the summit, which is crowned by the Badal Mahal or Cloud Palace of the Ranas. The palace has several sets of rooms furnished in pastel colours in a 19th-century style.

East of the old Jain temples are two royal chhatris and a temple dedicated to Kali. One is that of Rani Khumbha, who was murdered here, the other of Prithviraj, a grandson.

The views from the Cloud Palace across the deserts of Marwar are matchless. Long sinuous lines of walls with loopholed, crenellated parapets stretch as far as the eye can see along the crown of the hill. The stronghold is one of the finest examples of defensive fortification in Rajasthan.

LASWARI

This small village lying 32 km (20 miles) south-east of Alwar in Rajasthan is famous as the site of a great battle fought on November 1803, when Lord Lake crushed the French-trained troops of Daulat Rao Scindia's army. The engagement was a ferocious affair. After a march of 104 km (65 miles) in forty-eight hours, the small British force attacked a well-entrenched Maratha army, which defended its position with the utmost valour. Over half of the Maratha force were left on the battlefield killed or wounded. The British captured the entire Maratha camp and over seventy guns.

Laswari was one of four pitched battles fought by Lord Lake over a two-month period in 1803, resulting in the complete destruction of Scindia's armies and the deliverance of the Mughal emperor.

There is no monument, but the mounds under which the dead were buried may still be seen.

MANDOR

8 km (5 miles) north of Jodhpur is Mandor, the old capital of Marwar, set on a plateau over the Mandor Gardens. The gardens are a delightful mass of trees, shrubs and fountains, enlivened by strutting peacocks and gambolling monkeys set around the former cremation ground of the Rathor rulers. The sites of the funeral pyres are marked by individual devals. A number of accomplished sandstone chatris can be seen, the largest to Ajit Singh (*c.* 1724) and Jaswant Singh (1681), the former considerably more assured, in close-grained freestone. (See Volume I.)

Maharaja Ajit Singh built a pleasure palace at Mandor. It comprises a zenana, a small formal garden and the curious **Ek Thamba Mahal** (1707–24), approached via the Ajit Pol. Note the pseudo-Ionic capitals.

The **Shrine of the 300 Million Gods**, a large pillared hall containing gigantic figures of heroes and gods, is the pantheon of the Rathors.

At Osian, about 67 km (42 miles) from Jodhpur, is a complex of Jain and Brahmanical temples from the 8th to 11th centuries. The main Sachiyamata Temple was built in 1178.

MANGROL

This small town, situated about 74 km (46 miles) east of Kota, lies on the old trade route to Gwalior. It was the site of a battle fought on 1 October 1821 between the ruler of Kota, Maharao Kishur Singh, and forces loyal to the Prime Minister, Zalim Singh, assisted by a detachment of British troops. Kishur Singh was defeated. A memorial to two British officers who were killed in the engagement – Lieutenants Clarke and Read of the 4th Bengal Light Cavalry – lies outside the town.

MERTA

122 km (76 miles) north-east of Jodhpur, Merta is a small town situated on high ground with a striking appearance created by its walls, which are partly mud and partly masonry. On the plain before the town a great battle took place in 1754, when the Marathas under Scindia defeated Vijaya Singh of Jodhpur. The battle led to the acquisition of Ajmer by the Marathas, under the Frenchman de Boigne, and their permanent hold on Rajput territory.

MORVI

The peninsula of Kathiawad may be a remote, self-contained part of north-west India but it has played an important role in the historical development of the country. By the early 19th century the area was fragmented into a complex mass of over 220 petty states, all of which were confirmed by the British in a treaty of 1807, some no larger than 600 sq m (¼ square mile). Dominating access to the entire peninsula was the state of Morvi, strategically commanding the entrance to this introverted cul-de-sac. Riven by internecine strife and infanticide in surrounding territories, Morvi remained under constant threat until the mid-19th century, when stability was secured and the state evolved into a prosperous entity. Under Thakur Sahib Waghaji, who ruled continuously from 1879 to 1948, the little city state modernized its roads and ports. A railway and tramway were introduced.

The **Dubargadh Waghaji Palace** (*c.* 1880) is approached via a suspension bridge (1882). Designed in a Venetian Gothic style, embellished with classical balustrades and a few Oriental conceits, the internal courtyards are even more eclectic, with Rajput cusped arches, Gothic windows and Saracenic domes.

The **New Palace** (1931–44) is an extraordinary exercise in late Art Deco, a low two-storey affair with banded horizontal fenestration and curves and bays resembling the London underground stations of Charles Holden. Faced in local granite, it is a remarkable example of its genre, furnished and decorated throughout in Art Deco style. There are three drawing-rooms, six dining-rooms and fourteen bedrooms, including an exotic subterranean bedroom reached by lifts, decorated with erotic murals, and a bathroom made from seashells.

NASIRABAD

Nasirabad is the military cantonment for Ajmer, from which it is 1·6 km (1 mile) distant. About 1·6 km (1 mile) in length, it is of interest only in that it was laid out by General Sir David Ochterlony in 1818 to accommodate an artillery battery, infantry and cavalry. For this reason it is a typical example of an early-19th-century military cantonment.

PATAN

Patan or Jhalra Patan, once the ancient town of Anhilvada, capital of the Hindu kings of Gujarat, lies at the foot of a low range of hills close to a large artificial lake. It was the chief town of the native state of Jhalawar.

The old town lay a little to the south of the present site on the banks of the Chandrabagha river. The name may be derived from 'City of Bells'; Originally there were 108 temples with bells, but all that survives from the early period is the temple of Sat Saheli or Seven Damsels.

The present city was founded by Zalim Singh in 1796. The **Maharaja's Palace**, enclosed by a high masonry wall with corner bastions, lies in the Chhaoni, a cantonment about 6·4 km (4 miles) outside the city, together with the principal public offices. The main entrance is on the east side.

(For the 11th-century monuments at Anhilvada see Volume I.)

PAWAGARH

Pawagarh or Quarri-hill, about 45 km (28 miles) east of Vadodara, is an isolated hill on a wide plain, from which it rises to a height of 853 m (2,800 ft) above sea level. The lower slopes are clad with stunted timber, but the upper slopes are bare and rocky on three sides.

At the east end of the hill are some Jain remains and to the west, some 17th-century granaries erected by the Muslims overlooking a deep precipice. The fortifications comprise a lower fort with strong bastions across the eastern spur. The **Atak Gate** provides access through, but the outer gate is now in ruins. The path winds upwards through a series of gates, each commanding the one below. Massive walls link these gates to the fortifications which crown the crest. The **Mohoti Gate** is followed by the **Sadan Shah Gate**, which is cut through solid rock, commanded by towering walls and crossed by a double Hindu gateway.

It is an ancient site, first mentioned in the 11th century. In 1300 it was seized by Chauhan Rajputs. Later, the Muslim kings of Ahmadabad tried to capture it repeatedly. In 1484 it was reduced by Sultan Mahmud Begada, after a siege lasting two years. He strengthened the defences and made it his citadel. In 1535 it fell by treachery to Humayun and in

1573 it was captured by Akbar. In the 18th century Krishnaji made it his headquarters for raids into Gujarat, and in 1761 Scindia took and held it, until 1803, when the British under Colonel Woodington wrested control.

PORBANDAR

Porbandar is the capital of a former state of that name. It lies in a remote corner of the Kathiawad peninsula, an ancient settlement which has been identified with Sudamapuri, mentioned in the *Bhagavadgita*, and it has maintained a continuous trading contact with Africa and Arabia for centuries. The town is renowned as the birthplace of Gandhi and also for the quality of its local building stone, which was exported to Bombay and Karachi for the great municipal buildings of the late 19th century.

By the late 18th century the Rajput clan to which the ruling dynasty belonged was so hemmed in by rapacious rivals that in 1807 it accepted the overlordship of the East India Company, under which the town flourished as a prosperous port.

The principal buildings are the two main palaces. The **Daria Rajmahal** was built in the late 19th century by Maharaja Bhavsinhji to designs prepared by the state engineer, Phulchand Parekh. Built in creamy local stone, it stands on the edge of the Arabian Sea and, in its plan and layout, shows distinct Arab influences. However, the façades are Italianate in style, with an interesting blend of Renaissance and Gothic detail conceived by a man of knowledge and taste. Internally, the palace has all the usual princely trappings – chandeliers, painted murals and European furniture. The Town Hall, Library and most other public buildings were all built under the watchful eye of the Maharaja.

The **Anut Nivas Khambala** was built in 1927 by Maharaja Natwarsinhji, a progressive figure. It is a large, two-storey building along straightforward classical lines in a delightful position bordering the sea. The interior is lavish but not ostentatious. The Rajput Room is a museum of Kathiawad's past.

The **Kirti Mandir**, the birthplace of Mahatma Gandhi in 1869, is a simple, cloistered building which is a shrine to his memory. A 24-m (79 ft) shikhara stands in the grounds.

RAJKOT

Rajkot is the capital of the small but once influential second-class state of the same name. It lies 38·5 km (24 miles) from Gondal in the Kathiawad peninsula. Until 1947 it was the headquarters of the local British Resident for the Western India States. Today it is an important industrial centre.

The **Kaisar-i-Hind Bridge** (*c.* 1910) over the Aji was designed by R. B. Booth, who was responsible for most of the public buildings in the state. It was financed by the Maharaja of Bhavnagar.

The **Rajkumar College** (1870) was founded by Colonel R. H. Keatinge, VC, for the education of the sons of the local princes and other gentlemen, a sort of Indian Eton. The ground-floor hall is fine. There is a rectangular tower over the east entrance and two circular towers over the west. West of the quadrangle are the houses of the Principal and Vice-Principal.

The **Alfred High School** (1875) was donated by the Nawab of Junagadh and has an impressive main hall. Gandhi was educated here and there is a statue to him outside.

The **Jubilee Gardens and Memorial Institute** lie in the civic station.

The **Watson Museum** (1888) has an interesting collection of local paintings, weapons and products.

The Victoria Jubilee Waterworks and Lalpuri Irrigation Works lie to the north-west of the city.

390

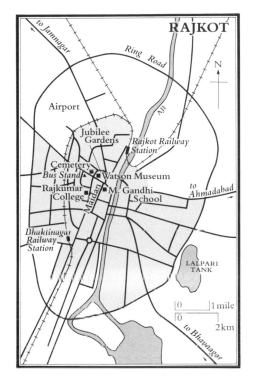

The main approach is via a serpentine route of steep ramps barred by four powerful gateways. The first gateway is protected by a barbican with a zigzag turn and guardrooms. The door is armoured with ferocious-looking elephant spikes and a huge iron chain. The second gateway has similar defences. The third lies on a sharp loop of the path. Outside is a huge monolithic head. The gateway is embellished with a pointed arch and trefoils. The fourth gateway is a formidable bastion, close to the summit. Situated at the head of a steep flight of steps, it is reinforced by a turret and huge doors with elephant spikes. The inner passage is flanked by a raised platform, beyond which a long vaulted tunnel leads to the fort.

The curtain wall follows the summit of the hill and has semicircular bastions. In some places there is a sheer drop of over 61 m (200 ft). The interior is largely bare but for two small temples occupied by monkeys, a few ruins and the Rani's Tank. The old Temple of Lord Ganesha (8th century) is a place of pilgrimage in September.

RANTHAMBHOR

Situated on an isolated rock 213 m (700 ft) high in the middle of dense forest, the ruins of Ranthambhor Fort lie 19·2 km (12 miles) north-east of Sawai Madhopur game reserve. The fort was built in 944 by a Chauhan ruler, Sapaldksh. It was captured in 1194 by Qutb-ud-Din Aybak, who later surrendered possession to Rajput forces. In 1301 it was besieged by Ala-ud-Din Khalji, who sacked the fort and destroyed the Chauhan temples. Ranthambhor was the scene of perpetual strife until 1569, when Akbar wrested control, after which it passed to the ruler of Jaipur.

The only approach is from the west, along a valley and through a narrow fortified defile. At a second defile there was a further fortified gateway, now demolished. Most of the surviving walls and bastions are 13th century.

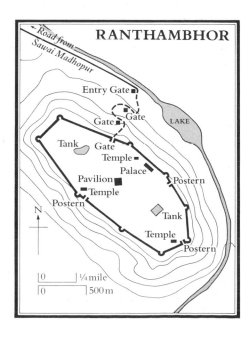

SANGANER

11·2 km (7 miles) south-west of Jaipur, Sanganer is a picturesque spot with a complex of Jain temples reputed to be over 1,000 years old. The road into the town passes through two ruined Tripolias or triple gateways of three storeys about 20 m (66 ft) high. On each, the second stage has an open verandah carried on four pillars. To the right is a handsome door leading to a small temple sacred to Krishna. Opposite is an interesting temple of Sitaram. Beyond, to the left, are the ruins of the Old Palace.

The fortifications around the town are now in ruins. Four gateways remain: the Dausa Darwaza, Malpura Darwaza, Amber Darwaza and Chaksu Darwaza.

SURAT

Situated on the banks of the River Tapti, Surat has a long history of commercial intercourse with Europe. It may have been the Pulipula mentioned by Ptolemy in 150. In 1373 Firuz Shah Tughluq III built a fort at Surat to guard against the Bhils, but the foundations of the modern city can be traced only to the early 16th century, when a rich Hindu trader called Gopi settled here. The Portuguese assailed and burnt the town in 1512, 1530 and 1531. In 1572 it fell to Akbar, and under Mughal rule it became one of the premier mercantile cities of India and the centre of early European influence.

In 1612 the Mughal emperor sent a firman allowing the English to trade at Surat. Three years later a small English fleet routed a large Portuguese naval force in the Swally estuary off 'Bloody Point', thereby ending Portuguese colonial aspirations. The Dutch opened a factory in 1616 and the French in 1668. In 1664 Shivaji sacked the city, but left the well-defended English factory intact. English defiance of the Maratha leader earned the respect of Aurangzeb and boosted English prestige. In spite of Maratha depredations, the prosperity of the port grew. In 1759 the English gained overall control. In 1837 two events occurred which dealt a major blow to its pre-eminence. A huge fire destroyed the entire centre of the city and, in the same year, the river burst its banks and devastated the city and surrounding countryside. Many Hindu and Parsee merchants left for Bombay, hastening the decline of the port. Today it is no longer a port of any consequence, but a major centre of the textile industry.

The **Castle** (1546), a low brick structure, lies beside the Tapti Bridge. Although it is of no great interest, it does provide a good vantage point. To the east is the **Victoria Garden** and **Anglican Church**, consecrated by Bishop Heber in 1825.

The remains of the old European factories are difficult to find but lie near the Mission High School. The **English Factory** is midway from the Castle to the Kataragana Gate out of the old city. It is marked by a plaque, but it is doubtful if the site is accurate. Nearby is the **Portuguese Factory**, which retains some early records. The old church site is marked by a wooden cross. Close by are the sites of the French Lodge (abandoned in 1725) and the Persian factory.

The **Clocktower** on the Delhi Road was erected in 1871 at the expense of Khan Bahadur Barorji Merwanji Frazer.

The most interesting historical monuments are the old cemeteries.

The **English Cemetery** lies just beyond the Kataragana Gate, on the right-hand side on the Broach Road. On entering, the enormous **Mausoleum of Sir George Oxinden** may be seen on the right. Oxinden was President of Surat and Bombay and it was he who defended the English factory against Shivaji. The tomb holds him and his brother, Christopher, who died in 1659. Sir George is styled '*Anglorum in India, Persia, Arabia, Praeses Insulae Bombayensis*

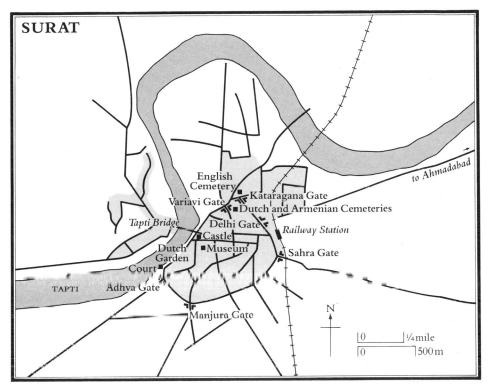

SURAT

Labels on map: English Cemetery, Kataragana Gate, Variavi Gate, Dutch and Armenian Cemeteries, Tapti Bridge, Delhi Gate, Railway Station, Castle, Dutch Garden, Museum, Sahra Gate, Court, Adhya Gate, TAPTI, Manjura Gate, to Ahmadabad, N, 0 ¼ mile, 0 500 m

Gubernator'. It is really two tombs, one enclosing the other, crowned by an open-cross cupola denoting a Christian tomb. Close by is the alleged **Tomb of Gerald Aungier** (1677), Oxinden's successor. There are over 400 tombs in the cemetery in a poor condition, the earliest being that of Francis Breton (1649).

The **Dutch Cemetery** also contains a number of splendid sepulchral monuments. It can be reached en route back to the city about 460 m (1,500 ft) to the left, off the main road. The **Tomb of Baron Adriaan van Reede** (1691) comprises an enormous double cupola with a gallery above and below carried on fine columns. Once it was decorated with frescoes and wood carvings, but these have disappeared. Note that 'Souratta' and 'Cochin' merit capital letters in the inscription, but not 'bombai', which is lower case. Adjacent is the **Armenian Cemetery**, which also has some good stones and inscriptions.

Of the Islamic monuments four mosques are worth a visit. The **Nau Saiyid Mosque** stands on the west bank of the Gopi Lake. Beside the mosque are nine warriors' tombs. The **Saiyid Idrus Mosque** (1639) has a tall minaret, which is a local landmark, and was built in honour of the ruling dynasty. The **Mirza Sami Mosque** (1540) was erected by Khudawand Khan, who also built the castle. It has some excellent carving and tracery. **Khwaja Diwan Sahib's Mosque** (1530) is reputed to be dedicated to a Bokhara traveller who lived to the age of 116.

The **Tombs of the Bohras** are also of interest, as are the two **Parsee Fire Temples**, built in 1823. The Hindu **Swami Narayan** temple is crowned by three white domes and is visible from all parts of the city. Large numbers of Jain temples may also be visited.

At Randar, 4·8 km (3 miles) from the city, the **Jami Masjid** stands over the site of an ancient Jain temple and incorporates some early fragments of masonry. In another nearby mosque are wooden columns and domes taken from a Jain temple which are unique in India.

At Swally, the old seaport of Surat, 19·3 km (12 miles) to the west of the town, is another cemetery of historical interest. Here it is alleged that Thomas Coryat is buried. Known as 'the English fakir', he walked from England to India living as a beggar before he died at Surat in 1617. His grave is reputed to lie beneath a Muslim monument at the village of Rajgari near Swally, but there is no evidence to support this. Adjacent is the **Vaux Tomb** (1697), a fine domed sepulchre containing the remains of the former Deputy-Governor of Bombay and his wife, who drowned in the river.

UDAIPUR

Udaipur, the celestial 'City of Sunrise', is the residence of the highest of the Rajput rulers and chief of the 'Solar' Rajput clan. Situated about 259 km (161 miles) from Jodhpur at a height of 577 m (1,893 ft) above sea level, it is one of the most romantic and evocative cities in India, surrounded by incandescent blue lakes with fairy-tale palaces of outstanding beauty.

The fourth and last capital of the state of Mewar, Udaipur was founded by Maharana Udai Singh after the third and final sack of Chitorgarh in 1567. The title Maharana means great warrior.

Located in a fertile valley between the great hill fortresses of Kumbhalgarh and Chitorgarh, the city is planned around three lakes: the Pichola, Fateh Sagar and the Umaid Sagar.

The **Old City** is built on undulating ground surrounded by 17th-century fortifications strengthened by huge bastions. There are five main gates: the Hathi Pol or Elephant Gate to the north,

Kishan Gate to the south, Delhi Gate to the north-east, Chand Pol or Moon Gate to the west and Suraj Pol or Sun Gate to the east. The streets and alleyways of the old city are charming and picturesque, studded with shrines to Hanuman, Kali and other deities.

The main street leads from Hathi Pol to the Maharana's Palace. En route are the Clocktower and Lansdowne Hospital. The **Jagdish Temple** (1640) is an imposing building about 400 m (¼ mile) from the City Palace. (For the temples and museum see Volume I.)

The **City Palace of the Maharanas** (1567 onwards) stands astride a low ridge along the shore of Pichola Lake, an impressive complex of buildings in granite and marble flanked by octagonal corner towers surmounted by cupolas. A blend of Rajput and Mughal styles, the City Palace is a colossal series of buildings which, beyond the edge of the natural bedrock, are carried on huge stone arches and are a continuation of the city walls. The whole exterior is faced in white plaster.

The entrance is via the **Bari Pol** or Great Gate (1600), which contains the royal drums, and on to the Tripolia Gate (1725). Between the two are eight carved **Toranas**, arches under which the rulers were weighed against gold and silver, which was then distributed to the poor. In the court beyond Tripolia elephant fights were staged. The Ganesh Deori Gate leads to the Rai Angan or royal courtyard (1571), on the east side of which is the Jewel Room. The central pavilion, the **Choti Chitra Shali**, is enriched with brilliant blue mosaics.

These exotic palaces are wonderfully decorated. The **Sheesh Mahal** has inlaid mirrors, the **Krishna Vilas**, painted miniatures, installed by Raja Bhim Singh in 1805, after his daughter Krishna Kumari chose suicide rather than marriage to a rival prince. The **Manak Mahal** or Ruby Palace has glass and porcelain, the **Moti Mahal** or Pearl

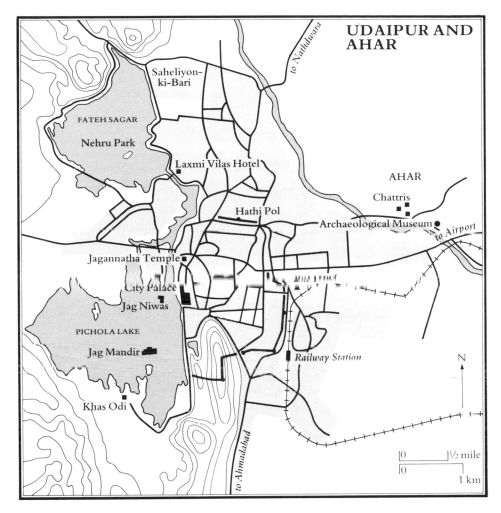

UDAIPUR AND AHAR

Palace, mirrors, the **Chini-Ki-Chitra Mahal** (1711–34) has lovely Dutch and Chinese tiles counterpointed with inlaid mirror work, the **Bari Mahal** (1699–1711), a delightful garden as a centrepiece. To the west of Tripolia are the Karan Vilas (1620–28) and Khush Mahal, the latter an extraordinary mid-19th-century pleasure palace built for European guests, with a grotesque mixture of European, Rajput and Mughal detailing, now used as a honeymoon suite. To the south is Shambhu Niwas Palace, to which the Shiv Niwas was added. The latter is now a hotel. One room has a suite of crystal furniture. The interiors, with mosaic and mirror, tile and glass, enamel and inlaid stones, are a glorious celebration of the power and opulence of the premier Rajput dynasty.

The **Museum** includes the Mor Chowk, with its beautiful late-19th-century peacock mosaics, above which are a splendid series of figures in mid-19th-century inlaid glasswork on the outer walls of the Surya Prakash. The Museum contains the armour worn by Pratap Singh in his fight against Akbar. The view across the lake from the terraces and pavilions on the roof of the city palace is breathtaking.

Lake Pichola was formed in the 14th

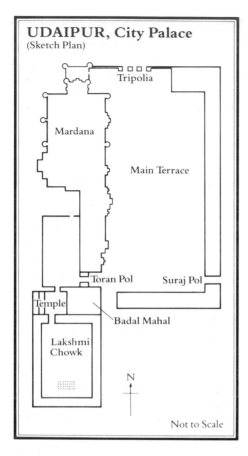

UDAIPUR, City Palace
(Sketch Plan)

Tripolia

Mardana

Main Terrace

Toran Pol   Suraj Pol

Temple

Badal Mahal

Lakshmi Chowk

N

Not to Scale

pavilion or Gul Mahal, which is its greatest landmark, was commenced by Karan Singh (1621–8). It is one of the few examples of Mughal-style architecture in the state. In 1623 Prince Khurram, the future Emperor Shah Jahan, lived here when in revolt against his father, Jahangir, and it is maintained that the pietra dura work on the interior later inspired the detailing of the Taj Mahal. European refugees fleeing the Mutiny were given sanctuary in this palace in 1857. Most of the buildings are of 18th-century origin. Sometimes it is called Jagannath, the Lord of the World, after the temple within the walls of this water-garden palace.

A number of the smaller islands contain pavilions and small palaces. The **Mohan Mandir**, in the north-east corner of the lake, was built by Jagat Singh between 1628 and 1652.

The road along the east side of the lake leads to **Khas Odi**, built by Sir Sajjan Singh between 1874 and 1884 as a shooting-box. The lake palaces and Khas Odi can be visited by boat. The boat trip should not be missed, for the view from the south end of the lake is outstandingly beautiful.

North of the Shambhu Niwas is **Minto Hall**, a large Durbar Hall erected in the late 19th century and named after the Viceroy. North of the Pichola Lake a canal leads to **Fateh Sagar**, built in 1678 with an embankment added by Fateh Singh in 1889. The road along its shores is very picturesque. Beneath the dam is the **Saheliyon-Ki-Bari** or Garden of Ladies, laid out with lush green lawns, kiosks, trees and fountains by Sangram Singh II (1710–34). The former **British Residency**, now a Circuit House, also has lovely gardens. The island garden is called Nehru Park and has a restaurant at its centre.

West of the city **Sajjangarh Hill** 335 m (1,100 ft) over Fateh Sagar Lake, is crowned by the **Monsoon Palace**, which commands a panoramic view of

century. Fringed with green hills and studded with ghats and gardens, the lake provides a transcendental beauty to Udaipur which is accentuated by the two island palaces – the Jag Niwas or Lake Palace, now a hotel, and the Jag Mandir.

The **Lake Palace Hotel** (mostly 1754, with recent additions) is simply one of the most beautiful hotel-palaces in the world, like a serene ocean liner perpetually moored in the centre of the lake. The hotel is really a complex of palaces, built from the mid-17th century onwards, interspersed with courts, fountains, trees and gardens. Once the summer residence of the Ranas of Mewar, the former royal banquet rooms are now used as reception suites and bars.

The **Jag Mandir**, on the southern island, was built in 1551. The domed

396

the lakes and palaces of the city below. Moti Magri, overlooking the lake, has an equestrian statue of Maharana Pratap, the Rajput hero.

3·2 km (2 miles) east of the city at Ahar is the site of an ancient capital of Mewar, the residence of the Guhilot rulers, ancestors of the present Ranas. Here is the **Royal Cremation Ground**, with the elegant cenotaphs of the ranas interspersed among the trees. The **Chatri of Rana Amar Singh I** (1621) has a four-faced statue in the centre and panels of bas-reliefs of ranis who chose suttee. There is a small local museum with some excellent exhibits of 10th-century sculpture. (See Volume I.)

56 km (35 miles) to the north **Rajsamand Lake** at Kankroli has a massive masonry bund or embankment over 335 m (1,100 ft) long and 12·2 m (40 ft) high, with ornamental arches and pavilions built in 1660 by Raj Singh, who inflicted several defeats on Aurangzeb.

51·6 km (32 miles) south-east of Udaipur, Jaisamand Lake, built by Jai Singh in the late 17th century, has a similar dam. It is the second largest artificial lake in Asia, surrounded by the summer palaces of the queens of Udaipur.

VADODARA (BARODA)
Map overleaf

Vadodara, formerly known as Baroda, was once the capital of the Gaekwad state. Situated in Gujarat, 393 km (244 miles) from Bombay, it is prosperous, neat and well maintained, with broad tree-lined avenues, extensive parks and numerous buildings of considerable distinction, including various exceptional museums and art galleries. (See Volume I.)

The state arose as part of the expansion of Maratha power in the 18th century and the family name 'Gaekwad' means literally 'Protector of Cows', a title of religious merit.

The select residential areas lie to the west of the railway station. East is the old city. The **Museum and Art Gallery** (1894) are contained in the Victoria Diamond Jubilee Institute in the Sayaji Bagh, a pleasant riverside park, at the entrance to which is a large bronze equestrian statue of HH Maharaja Sayaji Rao III. The Museum pavilion, designed by the Madras architect Robert Fellowes Chisholm (1840–1915), contains a section on Industrial Arts. The Art Gallery has a collection of Mughal miniatures and European masters. A modern planetarium stands nearby. Within the park, which is a relaxing retreat, are a zoo, miniature railway and an equestrian statue of Shivaji, the Maratha warrior-prince. Between the park and the Kirti Mandir is a bridge (16th century), one of four over the Vishvamitri river.

The **Kirti Mandir** or Temple of Fame (early 20th century) is the Gaekwad family burial ground, containing the cenotaphs of previous rulers. The vault is decorated by the Indian artist Nandial Bose. Opposite is the Shri Sayaji General Hospital (1876), designed by Major Mant (1840–81), a pioneer of Indo-Saracenic architecture. To the west lies the **Kothi Building** (late 19th century), housing the Secretariat. This resembles an English college, with mullioned and transomed windows and a central hall with traceried windows crowned by a flèche spire. Adjoining the Sursagar Tank is the **Nyaya Mandir** (1896), the High Court, an interesting commingling of Mughal and Gothic styles. The **City Library** (1876) is also by Major Mant.

The centre of the old city is a marketplace marked by the **Mandvi**, a square Muslim pavilion (1736) and clocktower. Adjacent lies the **Nazar Bagh Palace** (1721; altered), a three-storey pile with arcaded verandahs in Corinthian style, with a cresting of 'pie-crust' parapets. A solid gold and solid silver gun are kept here, the former weighing over 127 kg (280 lb), drawn on ceremonial occasions by a team of white bullocks.

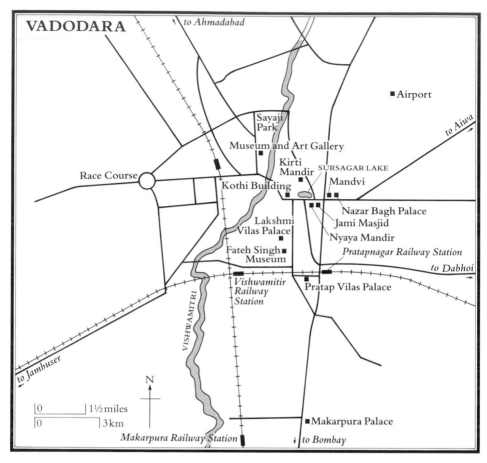

To the south is **Lakshmi Vilas Palace** (1880–90), which should not be missed. It is reputedly the most expensive building constructed by a private individual in the 19th century. It was designed initially by Major Mant, but was completed by Robert Fellowes Chisholm after Mant died insane. Judging by the febrile eclecticism of the design, it is hardly surprising. The building is a romantic confection of Rajput and Mughal forms, Jain domes, Gothic and classical sources and Hindu martial architecture. It has a spectacular silhouette of enormous power with a central cupola and tall tower. The skyline is a riot of ornamental forms and detail. The entrance to the park is through a handsome gateway, which whets the appetite for the archi-

tectural feast to follow. The palace is faced in red sandstone from Agra, with dressings of blue trapstone from Pune and marble from Rajasthan.

The interior is equally spectacular. The huge Durbar Hall has a floor of Venetian mosaic, with Italian marble employed throughout. The stained glass is by Dix of London, the staircase figures by an Italian sculptor and the gardens by an expert from Kew. The rooms are appointed in a sumptuous manner with beautiful fittings, Old Masters, armour and 18th-century furniture.

Immediately to the south of the palace (off Nehru Road) is the **Maharaja Fateh Singh Museum**, which contains some of the state collection of European art, including works by Murillo, Titian and

398

Raphael, as well as Chinese, Japanese and Indian exhibits.

South of the railway is the **Pratap Vilas Palace** (*c.* 1910), now the Railway Staff College, an elegant classical range of two storeys with a rusticated base, corner quoins and semicircular bays flanking the entrance. The corner towers are capped by shallow domes with circular windows in a faintly Arts and Crafts style.

Beyond the military parade grounds 6·5 km (4 miles) south of the city is **Makarpura Palace** (late 19th century), built in an Italian Renaissance style. It has a main façade of three storeys, each arcaded with semicircular arches, crowned by a balustraded parapet and shallow urns. Only the full-blooded Bengali-style curved roof over the side entrance porch and the shallow dome over the tower betray the Oriental context. The gardens are stunning. There is a splendid summerhouse of painted trellis work embellished with domes and covered in creepers, plants and shrubs.

The **Kalabahavan Technical Institute** (1922) is a fine Indo-Saracenic pile with a high central tower and dome in polychromatic stonework, continuing a tradition established by Mant and Chisholm over forty years earlier.

To the north of the city are the **Cantonment** and **Residency**. The Anglican Church was consecrated by Bishop Heber in 1825, but was rebuilt thirteen years later. 19 km (12 miles) outside the city is Ajura Lake, the local reservoir.

About 45 m (150 ft) north of the Makarpura Palace is the **Naulakhi Well**, a well-preserved structure of the baoli type containing galleried apartments, a development unique to Gujarat.

WANKANER

Wankaner, 38·5 km (24 miles) north-north-east of Rajkot in Kathiawad, is the capital of a former state of that name,

renowned locally both for its textiles and for the residence here of Mahatma Gandhi during part of his childhood. His father was diwan to the Maharaja.

The ruling dynasty belong to the Jhala Rajputs. Their possession was guaranteed by the East India Company in 1807, when many of the small Kathiawad states came to terms with the Company in exchange for protection and recognition.

The state was turned into a model example of self-reforming enterprise by Maharaja Amarsinhji (1881–1948). The **Ranjit Vilas Palace** (1907–14) was designed by the Maharaja in a synthesis of architectural styles. Victorian Gothic, Italianate and Mughal can all be discerned, but it is an effective symmetrical composition executed by the State Engineer in warm-brown stone and dominated by a huge central clocktower capped by an onion dome. It is visible for miles across the baked, flat landscape of Kathiawad. Today it is a hotel and resort, with a collection of vintage cars on display. Internally, the *tour de force* is a double marble spiral staircase, so that those ascending are screened from those descending. It is ornamented with engrailed arches, classical balustrades and Grecian urns.

In the grounds (101 hectares: 250 acres) are numerous outbuildings.

The Purna Chandra Bhavan, or Full Moon House (*c.* 1920), is the state guesthouse, a fairly conventional two-storey block in cream and white stucco, enriched with Corinthian pilasters.

Wankaner and Kathiawad generally are renowned for pallias, tombstone monuments which commemorate a death or act of bravery. The symbolism is fascinating. An image of an arm or hand records a suttee or act of self-immolation. Many carry a mounted bard brandishing a spear. These peripatetic poets were used by nobles as surety for a loan, in default of which the bard committed suicide. Many pallias can be seen in the area.

THE DECCAN

TWELVE

THE DECCAN

Maharashtra, northern Andhra Pradesh, northern Karnataka, Goa

Introduction

The Deccan plateau is bordered by rolling ranges of hills which run parallel to the coast on both the east and west sides. The Western Ghats are bordered by a wide coastal strip and are higher than the Eastern Ghats. The great rivers, the Godavari and Krishna, rise on the eastern slope of the Western Ghats, cross the dry tableland of the Deccan and discharge into the Bay of Bengal.

This vast area, comprising the present states of Maharashtra, Goa and the northern areas of Andhra Pradesh and Karnataka, is littered with extensive remains of human occupation dating from the 2nd century BC onwards. The adoption of rock-cut techniques by ancient Buddhist communities has left evidence in the form of cave temples at Ajanta and other sites. By the 7th century sacred architecture was well established in the region. The temples of the Early Chalukya period at sites such as Aihole, Badami and Satyavolu, described in Volume I, comprise one of the most extensive early groups of standing Hindu shrines in the region. So, by the 14th century, and the beginning of the Muslim incursions, there was a well-established tradition of monumental art and architecture represented in a large number of standing temples.

In 1328 Hoysala power in the region was destroyed by the predatory raids of Muhammad Tughluq Shah II and the united opposition of other Hindu king-doms. Ten years later, Muhammad Tughluq resolved to move his capital from **Delhi** to **Daulatabad**. The venture was a failure. The forced expulsion and wholesale emigration of the Muslim population from Delhi into the Deccan was defeated by famine and the population returned.

Nevertheless, as a result of this mass movement of people, the roots of Muslim culture and architecture were planted in the Deccan. However, neither of the two major monuments of the period exhibits the distinctive architectural style of the Tughluq dynasty. The Jami Masjid at **Daulatabad** was built from local temple masonry and the Deval Mosque at Bodhan was basically a converted Jain temple.

Architecturally, the Muslim buildings of the Deccan are of particular interest. Unlike other areas of India, a unique building style developed here, based more on the development of overseas ideas than the evolution and adaptation of local architectural traditions to Islamic needs. There were numerous reasons for this.

By the 14th and 15th centuries, links across the Arabian Sea were well established as a result of trade, commerce and the pilgrim traffic to Mecca. There was a steady stream of talented immigrants from Persia, Turkey and Arabia seeking service with the increasingly powerful Muslim kings of the Deccan. Artisans,

Overleaf The exotic Dargah of Hazrat Gesu Nawaz at Gulbarga

artists, master craftsmen and builders, all trained in the Islamic tradition, were eager to impart their ideas to the energetic new Muslim overlords of the Deccan. Moreover, the great new fortress cities of the region – **Bidar, Bijapur, Golconda** and **Gulbarga** – were not built around existing centres of Hindu culture. As such they tended not to use salvaged temple masonry buildings, with all the structural and artistic compromises which this entailed. A vigorous architectural style and an alien new culture were injected into the conservative heartland of Hindu India.

Generally, the course of Muslim architecture in the region revolved around the particular capital city from which the country was administered. During the first period, from 1347 to 1422, it was centred on Gulbarga where the foundations of a distinct architectural style were laid. The second period began in 1425 with the transfer of the capital to **Bidar**. This marked a period of consolidation and experiment under the Barid Shahi kings. Later, in 1512, power transferred to the Qutb Shahi kings of **Golconda**, where the style reached its zenith before the Mughal conquest of 1687. For much of this period, from 1336 until its collapse in 1565, the great Hindu kingdom of **Vijayanagara**, based at Hampi, acted as a bulwark against Muslim expansion further south.

Gulbarga was the first capital of the Bahmani kingdom of the Deccan. The Bahmanis dominated regional affairs until, in 1489, the kingdom split into five independent dynasties: at **Ahmadnagar,** Berar, **Bidar, Bijapur** and **Golconda**.

In 1347 Ala-ud-Din Bahman threw off his allegiance to Delhi and established his capital at **Gulbarga**, which he surrounded with impressive fortifications. The Jami Masjid, with its covered hall in place of the courtyard, was highly original and virtually unique in India. The bold, plain surface and harmonious treatment of the entire structure influenced

Deccani architecture throughout the region, as did the finest of the royal tombs.

In 1425 Ahmad Shah Wali Bahmani shifted the capital to **Bidar**. This gave a renewed impetus to the building arts. The chief monuments here were the fortress and its palaces, two mosques, a madrasa and the royal tombs. The sober solemnity of the Solah Khamba mosque stands in vivid contrast to the colourful secular buildings. As there was no tradition for the palace buildings, Persian forms and styles were borrowed but modified to the needs of the Indian court. Colour played a vital role in the overall effect. Glazed tiles, mosaics and arabesques were imported from Kashan in northern Persia.

The development of tomb architecture in the Deccan continued under the Barid Shahi dynasty, which prevailed from 1489 to 1619. Their tombs comprise a simple cubic chamber beneath a distinctive dome. Bands of coloured tiles carrying sacred inscriptions enrich the exterior. Stylistically, the domes developed an inward curve at the base, a form evolved as much from the Safavid domes of Persia as from the indigenous lotus domes of the Buddhist tradition.

With the demise of **Gulbarga** and **Bidar** as centres of Muslim power, the appointed governors at **Golconda** and **Bijapur** established their own independent dynasties.

At **Golconda** the Qutb Shahi kingdom flourished from 1512 to 1687. Today this ruined and deserted city retains impressive fortifications. The most eloquent examples of the Qutb Shahi style are the royal tombs outside the city. These are a development of those at **Gulbarga** and **Bidar**, with ornamental decoration added to the established structural form. The Qutb Shahi tombs have bulbous domes, rising from a petalled calyx and moulded stucco enrichment, including battlements. Some have outer verandahs.

403

The culmination of the Golconda style of architecture can be found in **Hyderabad** in the famous Char Minar. This is both dignified and inventive, but it borders on ostentation and the downward path towards decadence.

Unlike the Qutb Shahi kings of **Golconda**, who directed their patronage into a variety of channels, at **Bijapur** the ruling Adil Shahi dynasty concentrated their energies on architecture. As a result, although both shared a similar building art, at **Bijapur** the architecture developed structurally and aesthetically into the most important manifestation of Islamic style in the Deccan region, in spite of the rather unfortunate preponderance of local brown basalt. Here the Jami Masjid, the largest mosque in the region, was the most successful example of the Bijapuri style in its most restrained form. The Ibrahim Rauza, the tomb of Ibrahim Adil Shah II (1580–1627), within its attractive garden enclosure, is important for its extraordinary hanging ceiling, a monument to the sophisticated structural skills of the architect.

The desire for architectural impact and originality was taken to great lengths. The Mehtar Mahal, for instance, was elaborately carved with ornamental detail, but the crowning glory, the Mausoleum of Sultan Muhammad Adil Shah, was an attempt to build a monument to outclass even the Ibrahim Rauza. The result, the famous Gol Gumbaz, is a vast building with the second largest dome in the world after St Peter's, Rome, spanning the largest area of uninterrupted floorspace anywhere. While this may be regarded as one of the finest structural triumphs of the Indian masterbuilder, a building of awesome size and bulk, the mausoleum lacks the elegance and refinement of later Mughal funerary architecture, although ironically the most notable Mughal tomb complex in the region, at **Aurangabad**, is merely a pale imitation of the Taj.

The Gol Gumbaz marks the zenith of Deccani architecture. Its construction seems to have exhausted the creative energies of the entire kingdom. Thirty years after the death of Muhammad Adil Shah, harassed by the persistent attacks of the Marathas, **Bijapur** fell to the Mughal forces of Aurangzeb. In 1724 it was ceded to the Maratha Peshwa and its magnificent architectural heritage was looted to provide building materials.

The extension of the Mughal empire into the Deccan was a sporadic affair. Akbar was forced to subdue the Rajputs at **Ajmer** and **Chitorgarh** in 1567, before he could annex Gujarat, **Ahmadnagar** and Berar. It was not until 1686 that Aurangzeb swept away the Muslim kingdoms at **Bijapur** and **Golconda**. Two years later, at the high-water mark of Mughal power, he captured **Gingee** from the Marathas. With the death of Aurangzeb in 1707, the Mughal Empire entered a period of gradual but inexorable decline.

Some of the greatest fortifications in the Deccan are the Maratha forts perched high up in the Western Ghats. Under their legendary hero Shivaji (1627–80), the Hindu Marathas fought incessantly against the Muslim kingdoms, the Mughals and, later, the expanding European powers. Shivaji alone built over 100 forts. These colossal defensive strongholds built by 'the mountain rat' dominated the military strategy of the entire region. **Partabgarh, Purandhar, Raigarh, Shivner** and **Sinhagarh** all bear witness to the ferocity with which war was waged between the competing kingdoms of the Deccan. The Marathas also realized the importance of naval power. It was they who built **Janjira** and kept in check the Portuguese, who had captured **Goa** in 1510.

After dominating the trade routes to Europe, in the early 17th century the Portuguese lost their maritime supremacy to the English and **Goa** declined into a somnolent colonial backwater. Here an attractive and unique colonial architectural style developed. This can still be seen in **Old Goa, Panaji** and other towns and villages in the enclave, an evocative mixture of the Mediterranean and Indian traditions.

The English were latecomers to the Deccan. In the early years the centre of their commercial activities was on the east coast at Madras and Calcutta. **Bombay**, which had been acquired in 1665 as part of the marriage dowry of Catherine of Braganza to Charles II, was a backwater. Only with the elimination of Maratha power in 1817 was the last constraint lifted on European trade and communications across the Deccan.

The burgeoning economic prosperity of the city can be seen in the early-19th-century Town Hall and the Mint, which exude the rising power and confidence of the East India Company. Similarly at Hyderabad, where the Nizam had formed an autonomous kingdom on the decline of the Mughal Empire, the British supplanted the French and built a superb new Residency – a monument to the way in which architecture was used for conscious political ends, to overawe the native states with the wealth and power of the East India Company.

In the 1860s the combination of enlightened patronage by leading Parsee and Jewish philanthropists, an energetic reforming government and a cotton boom fuelled the transformation of **Bombay** into one of the great cities of the world with an unequalled heritage of tropical Gothic architecture: '*Urbs Prima in Indis*'. The great buildings – the Law Courts, Secretariat, University and railway stations – are spectacular monuments to Victorian civic and Imperial pride. With the establishment of security in the interior and the rise of Bombay, new resorts and hill stations were created at **Mahabaleshwar**, for instance, while the old Maratha capital of **Pune** was developed into a garrison town and summer retreat.

The Indo-Saracenic buildings of the late 19th century at **Bombay, Hyderabad, Kolhapur** and elsewhere reflect not only a greater awareness of local historical tradition and culture but also the need to convey the Imperial mission in a more subtle way.

The Ibrahim Rauza, Bijapur

Above The famous Gol Gumbaz at Bijapur

Below Bahmani Tomb, Gulbarga

Right Qutb Shahi Tombs, Golconda

Right The Chor Gumbad, Gulbarga

Below Tombs of Ahmad I and Ala-ud-Din Ahmad II, Bidar

The Fort, Bidar

Char Minar, Hyderabad

Above The Bibi ka Maqbara at Aurangabad

Below The former British Residency at Hyderabad

Left Church of St Francis of Assisi,
Old Goa

Above Churchgate Railway Station,
Bombay

Below Victorian civic pride –
Municipal Buildings, Bombay

Left The Rajabai Clocktower, University, Bombay

Below The New Palace, Kolhapur

Right Tropical Gothic – Victoria Terminus, Bombay

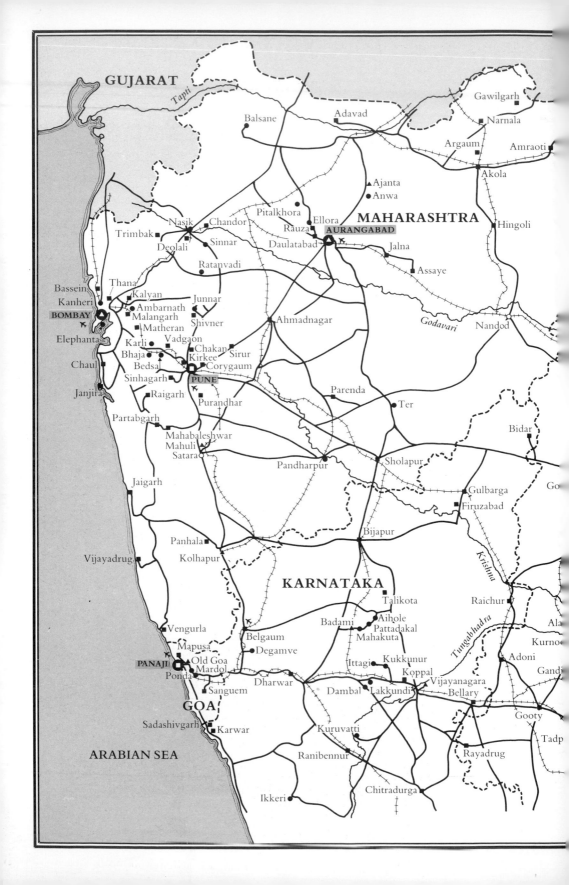

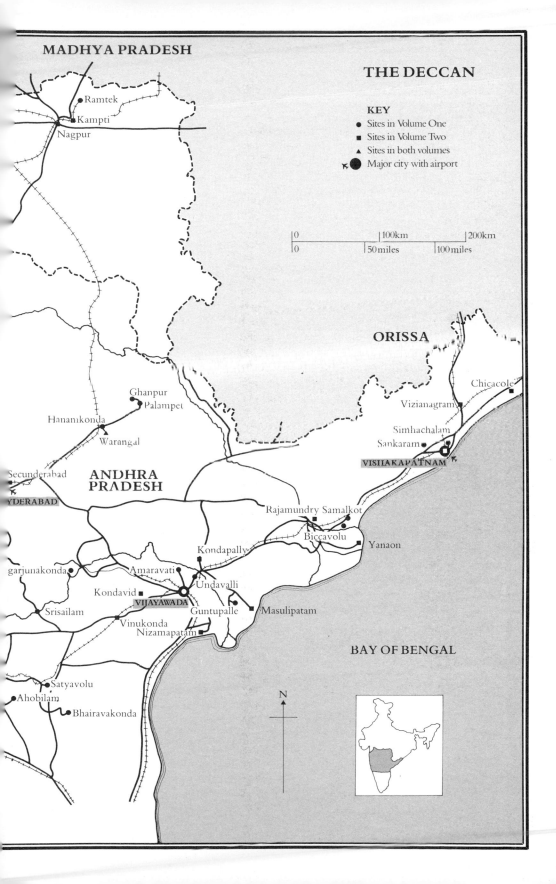

THE DECCAN

KEY
- Sites in Volume One
- Sites in Volume Two
- Sites in both volumes
- Major city with airport

MADHYA PRADESH

Ramtek
Kampti
Nagpur

ORISSA

Chicacole
Vizianagram
Ghanpur
Palampet
Hanamkonda
Simhachalam
Sankaram
Warangal
VISHAKAPATNAM

Secunderabad
ANDHRA PRADESH
HYDERABAD

Rajamundry Samalkot
Biccavolu
Yanaon
Kondapally
garjunakonda
Amaravati
Kondavid
Undavalli
VIJAYAWADA
Srisailam
Guntupalle
Masulipatam
Vinukonda
Nizamapatam

BAY OF BENGAL

Satyavolu
Ahobilam
Bhairavakonda

N

ADAVAD

This small town, 19·2 km (12 miles) east of Chopda, contains a fine old step-well, 9 m (30 ft) by 3·7 m (12 ft), in a ruined enclosure known as the Lal Bagh. To the north of the town is a mosque built in 1678. 4·8 km (3 miles) to the north-west are the Unabdev hot springs, celebrated for their salubrious qualities.

ADONI

Once the capital of an important frontier tract, Adoni played a conspicuous part in the Deccan Wars. Alleged to have been founded by Chandra Sen in 1200 BC, it was subsequently absorbed by the Vijayanagara Rajas, who held it until defeated by the Muslims in 1564. Then it became the stronghold of the Muslim kings of the Adil Shahi dynasty of Bijapur and Golconda, who built its lower forts and outer walls.

The **Fort**, now in ruins, stands on five rocky granite hills to the north-west of the town. In 1690 it was taken by Aurangzeb's generals. In 1778 Haidar Ali twice attacked the fortress without success, but eight years later, after a month's siege, Tipu took the fort and razed its battlements. It was ceded to the British in 1799.

AHMADNAGAR

Situated on the flood-plain of the River Sina, the town was founded by Ahmad Nizam Shah in 1494 on the site of an earlier settlement. Ahmadnagar became the centre of a powerful state under the Nizam Shahi dynasty. It was the only state on the west coast of India to maintain control in the face of Portuguese piracy.

The **Fort**, built by Husain Nizam Shah in 1559, lies 800 m (½ mile) to the east of the city. The main entrance is protected by a powerful circular bastion. In plan the fort is more or less circular in shape, 164 m (533 ft) in circumference. Built of dressed ashlar up to the level of the wall-walk, the outer wall is crenellated with embrasures 18·3 m (60 ft) high with a glacis to the outer ditch. Twenty-two circular bastions, including one which is three-lobed, reinforce the defences.

In 1599 it was seized by Akbar. Later it was taken from the Nizam by the Marathas. In 1797 the fort was assigned to Daulat Rao Scindia, from whom it was captured by Wellesley on 12 August 1803.

The town is famous as the residence of the historian Ferishta (1570–1611) and as the last resting-place of Emperor Aurangzeb, who died here on 3 March 1707. **Alamgir's Dargah**, a small enclosure near the cantonment, marks his final resting-place before his burial at Aurangabad.

The city has an interesting heritage of Islamic monuments. The **Qasim Mosque** (1500–1508) is one of the best. Small and plainly detailed, it is built of dressed stone with two aisles on either side of the nave.

The **Husaini Mosque** was built by a Persian Shiite who settled here and established a madrasa. The dome of the mosque is spherical and resembles early Persian style, with a broad span carried on a high drum. The mosque in the Kothla enclosures was constructed in 1536–7 as part of a Shia university under royal patronage. It is a classic example of the flat-roofed technique, built in dressed stone with a heavy eaves cornice over the façade.

The **Farhad Khani Mosque** (1560) has ornamental crestings over the main entrance. A multifoil arch with minarets surrounds the entrance of the courtyard, which has arched chambers and projecting corbelled eaves.

Rumi Khan, a Turkish officer of artillery under Ahmad Nizam Shah, was famous for casting the Malik-i-Maidan cannon (literally Lord of the Battle Plain) at Ahmadnagar. It stands on the Lion Bastion at Bijapur. He also constructed the **Mecca Mosque** at some time between 1505 and 1525 in trap and limestone masonry. The façade has four unusual polished stone pillars resembling black marble, reputedly brought from Mecca.

Gradually, flat-roofed structures with taller minarets emerged as a distinct style in the reign of Burhan Nizam Shah. The Mosque of Ghulam Ali, near the Gandhi Maidan, is typical of this, with sleek minarets.

The **Damadi Mosque**, 800 m (½ mile) east of the fort, was constructed between 1567 and 1568. It is a small mosque with beautifully carved details and corner piers which carry highly ornamented minarets. The parapet is battlemented with indentures. The carved stonework is superb.

Outside the Zenda Gate is the Kari Mosque or Aghi Behizad, with a stilted dome and four high corner minarets.

2·4 km (1½ miles) north-east of the fort is **Jamal Khan's Mosque** at Darga Daira. It has a disproportionately large dome.

The **Tomb of Nizam Shah**, one of the finest and best-preserved buildings in the city, is situated in a large enclosure on the left bank of the River Sina. Inside, enough of the original ornamental stucco work survives for the overall effect to be gauged, including geometric designs and Quranic texts, once highlighted in gold. The tomb is enclosed by a 3-m-high (10 ft) wall with four gates on each side. The façade over the main entrance is decorated with beautifully chased stucco work. Adjacent is a canopy alleged to cover the grave of a redoubtable elephant which rendered invaluable assistance at the Battle of Talikota in 1565 against the Vijayanagara Raja.

A number of other Islamic tombs can also be seen, including those of Abdur Rahman Chishti and Rumi Khan. The latter has a stilted dome with a band of petals around the base and a trefoil battlement.

The **Farah Bakhsh Palace** was started in 1508, completed in 1574 and rebuilt in 1583. It is now in ruins, as are the buildings around the Niamat Khani, which were erected between 1576 and 1578.

9·6 km (6 miles) east of the city at the summit of a hill lies the **Tomb of Salabat Khan** or the Chand Bibi, an octagonal tomb of three storeys without any inscription.

AJANTA

Ajanta is renowned for its world-famous Buddhist cave temples, which make it one of the most remarkable ancient sites in India. The sacred temples and monasteries date from about 200 BC (they are described fully in Volume I).

The old town of Ajanta lies 8 km (5 miles) south of the caves. It is surrounded by a strong fortified wall and moat constructed by the Nizam in 1727. General Wellesley halted here after his victory at the Battle of Assaye on 23 September 1803. The roof of the nearby baradari, which was used as a hospital by British troops, offers fine views of the surrounding countryside.

AKOLA

253 km (157 miles) from Nagpur, Akola is a district headquarters. Its old brick fort and stone-faced walls attest to its former importance. A battle between the Marathas and the forces of the Nizam was fought under its walls. Later the Pindari Ghazi Khan was defeated here in

1790 by the Bhonsla's general. Wellesley camped here in 1803 before the Battle of Argaum.

There is a church, a town hall and a hospital.

AMRAOTI

9·5 km (6 miles) from Badnera, off the main railway line, Amraoti is an old town surrounded by a strong stone wall. There are five gates and four wickets. The wall was built in 1807 by the Nizam to protect the local traders from raids by the Pindaris. The Khunari (Bloody) Wicket derives its name from the death of over 700 people in a skirmish nearby in 1818.

There are a number of old temples, the principal of which is the Temple of Bhavani (c. 9th century), together with the usual public buildings associated with a local headquarters: a courthouse, library, hospital and government offices.

ARGAUM

Argaum (literally City of Wells) lies 51 km (32 miles) north of Akola and is a small town famous for the great victory of General Wellesley over the Nagpur army of Venkaji (the Bhonsla's brother) on 28 November 1803. The battle on the broad plains before Argaum, together with the capture of Gawilgarh on 15 December, led to the Treaty of Deogaon, whereby the Bhonsla ceded all territory west of the Wardha river.

ASSAYE

Situated about 48 km (30 miles) from Jalna is the battlefield of Assaye, where British troops under General Wellesley

(the future Duke of Wellington) inflicted a crushing defeat on the French-trained Marathas under Scindia of Gwalior on 23 September 1803. It was the most brilliant tactical victory of Wellesley's career, a ferocious contest with heavy losses on both sides.

A fine view of the field can be obtained from the tower of Assaye fort. The two fortified villages of Pipalgaon and Warur, which provided Wellesley with the key to victory, can still be seen. The battlefield is surrounded by a low wall marked with a plaque to the Highland Light Infantry.

The burial ground lies about 400 m (¼ mile) to the west of the village. In the centre is a large banyan tree beneath which is an uninscribed grave, often bedecked with marigolds and other fresh flowers. This is the tomb of Colonel Patrick Maxwell, who is believed by villagers to protect the village.

AURANGABAD

Once known as Khadke, Aurangabad lies on the Khan river in the Dudhana valley between the Lakenvara Hills to the north and the Sathara range to the south. It is an historic city in its own right, of very considerable interest, but nowadays it is more often used by travellers as a base for visiting the renowned Aurangabad Caves, which date from the 6th and 7th centuries. (For a full description of these caves see Volume I.)

The Muslim architecture of Aurangabad lies firmly in the Deccan tradition. The oldest structures belong to the early 14th century, but later the architecture developed its own peculiar local characteristics. Although part of the same stylistic movement as the buildings of Bidar, Bijapur, Golconda and Gulbarga, at Aurangabad the rich styles and varied forms of the Jains of Gujarat were borrowed and adapted for Islamic ends. The

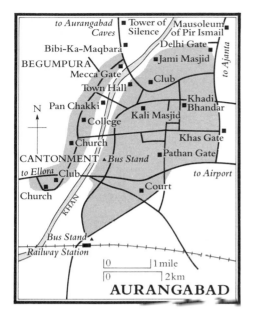

AURANGABAD

result is a fascinating commingling of architectural styles.

The **City Walls**, built by Aurangzeb in 1682, are impressive and were designed to repulse Maratha attacks. They are about 4·5 m (15 ft) high, with crenellated parapets, loopholed for musketry, and machicolated merlons over the gateways. The flanking angles have semicircular bastions capped by towers. These recur at regular intervals along the walls, which run for over 9·5 km (6 miles), much of which sadly is in ruins. The four principal gates were the Delhi Gate on the north, Jalna on the east, Pathan on the south and Mecca on the west, but there were nine other secondary gates. From the walls the fortress of Daulatabad can be seen in the far distance.

Naukonda Palace (1616) is now in ruins. It was built by Malik Ambar and later added to by Asaf Jah I. The interior contained five zenanas, a Diwan-i-Am and Diwan-i-Khas, a mosque and a kacheri, as well as a hammam or hot bath, which still survives.

The **Killa Arrak** (1692) was built by Aurangzeb. This vast complex with battlemented walls and gateways once covered the entire area between the Mecca and Delhi gates of the city. A high terrace to the right of the entrance still survives, with an extensive garden and ruined tanks. Only the Am Khas, or Durbar Hall, and the Jami Masjid remain intact. An inscription dated 1659 can be seen over the enclosure close to the mosque.

Close to the Delhi Gate is the **Damri Mahal**, which has a projecting arcaded verandah of five scalloped arches, behind which lie ten rooms. Nearby is the **Baradari of Ivaz Khan**, above which runs an aqueduct which once showered water into the oblong cistern below.

The **Jami Masjid** lies over the Killa Arrak. It has fifty polygonal pillars arranged in five rows, connected by a series of arches which create twenty-seven equal compartments, each covered by a domed vault. There are nine pointed arches to the front, five of which were erected by Malik Ambar in 1612, the remainder by Aurangzeb. The cornice is bracketed and the parapet above perforated. The corner angles have octagonal shafts ornamented with discs carrying little domes. The quadrangle has accommodation for travellers on three sides and a cistern at the centre.

In Juna Bazaar is **Kali Masjid** (1600), a six-pillared stone mosque on a high plinth also built by Malik Ambar.

In the great market square is the large **Shah Ganj Masjid** (*c.* 1720), on a raised platform with shops on three outer sides, the fourth being open, with a flight of steps leading to an open arcade of five arches in Indo-Islamic style. The interior has twenty-four pillars and the main chamber is crowned by a graceful bulbous dome and spire, with a base of carved lotus leaves. The east and west wings form arcaded chambers or Kham Khas, with corner minarets echoing those on the main building. The courtyard, which is approached through a

421

pointed arch and two minarets, has two cisterns.

The **Chauk Masjid** (1665) was built by Shayista Khan, uncle of Aurangzeb. It has a front of five pointed arches by two deep, carrying five onion domes, the central dome being lofty with a metallic spire. Like the Shah Ganj Mosque, there are shops at the base of the raised platform and a gateway with two minarets. The **Lal Masjid** (1655) is in red-painted basalt enriched with stucco.

The **Chila Khana** (early 17th century) was later used as a jail. It is a circular building around a central courtyard, now the Town Hall.

Outside the Delhi Gate on the Harsul Road is the **Mausoleum of Pir Ismail** (late 17th century), a combination of Mughal and Pathan themes, commemorating a former tutor of Aurangzeb. The entrance gate has a high pointed archway. Each corner of the terrace has a tower capped by an onion dome and finial.

The **Dargah of Baba Shah Muzaffar** lies to the right of the road from the cantonment to the Begumpura Bridge. He was the spiritual guide of Aurangzeb. The Dargah has a mosque, a madrasa, a kacheri, sarai and zenanas. The tomb is a plain edifice of red porphyry surrounded by a screen of cusped arches. The outbuildings are designed in similar style, with projecting kiosks crowned by Bengali roofs. There are numerous fountains and tanks supplied by a water mill.

The **Pan Chakki** or water mill is surrounded by other buildings erected in 1695, and an oblong reservoir added in about 1715 by Jamil Beg Khan. The water mill is fed by an underground conduit via the Pan Chakki reservoir. The cistern in front of the mosque forms the roof of a large hall beneath, carried on massive pillars. In the south-west corner of the mosque is the **Tomb** of a saint in beautiful chaste marble.

The most famous building in Aurangabad is the **Bibi-Ka-Maqbara**

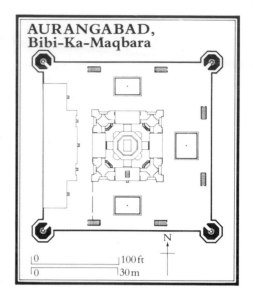

AURANGABAD, Bibi-Ka-Maqbara

N

0 .... 100 ft
0 .... 30 m

(1678). It lies a short distance from Begumpura off the Daulatabad Road and is a local landmark for miles around. Designed by the architect Ata Aula, it was intended to rival the Taj Mahal at Agra, but, although stunning, it is inferior to its rival in every respect, lacking the transcendental mastery of the Taj. It was built by Prince Azam Shah in memory of Begum Rabia Durani, wife of Aurangzeb. The mausoleum stands in an enclosure 457 m (1,485 ft) by 274 m (890 ft), surrounded by a high crenellated wall with bastions set at intervals and little minarets.

The southern wall has a handsome gateway with brass-inlaid doors, near to which is a tiny carved bird. The doors are inscribed with the name of the architect. The enclosure has open pavilions to the other three sides, connected by broad tessellated pavements. The tomb lies at the centre, a square block with a huge pointed arch to each front crowned by a magnificent marble dome with four corner minarets. A screen of perforated marble surrounds the grave.

The south-east angle has fine running inlaid patterns of foliated decoration over a scalloped arch. The entrance leads to an inner gallery overlooking the tomb. The delicate marble trelliswork and inlaid panels are a mere echo of those at Agra. White marble is used throughout, interspersed with stone and brick, but there is no inlay of semi-precious stones as at Agra; instead, delicately moulded stucco plaster is used in a variety of graceful designs. To the west of the platform there is a mosque with fine cusped arches and corner minarets. Little recesses, rosettes and arabesques embellish the façade.

Although the structure and form may lack the spiritual conviction and brilliance of the Taj, much of the applied surface ornament is distinguished, a testament to the continuing skill of the craftsmen after the spirit of the art had passed its climax.

To the west and south of the city lies the Cantonment, which was once stationed by the British. It has a fine racecourse and wide avenues laid out on conventional lines.

BADAMI

For over 200 years under the early Chalukyas Badami was the ancient capital of the Deccan. Today it is better known for its Hindu and Jain cave temples, which are of considerable interest. (Details of these can be found in Volume I.)

Situated 211 km (131 miles) from Bijapur, Badami is located between two rocky hills which lie on its north and south sides. A dam to the east forms a large artificial lake between them.

The fortifications at Badami comprise a lower fort enclosing the town, commanded by two strong forts on the hills above, the northern one being called Fifty-two Rocks Fort and the southern one, Battlefield Fort. They are barely 274 m (890 ft) apart and were largely dismantled in 1845.

The **North Fort** is the stronger of the

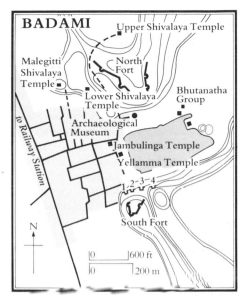

two, perched on steep outcrops of bedrock cut by deep chasms. Bastions and loopholed masonry walls command the approaches. Access to the fort was from the inner town via stone steps, narrow gateways and a slow, winding ascent.

The **South Fort** crowns the summit of a rocky crag, which is separated from the main body of the hill by a deep defile. There are two lines of works, defended by bastions.

In 1818 the forts were taken from the Marathas by Colonel Thomas Munro. A fort was depicted on his coat of arms.

BASSEIN

45 km (28 miles) north of Bombay, situated just across the Ulhas river, which separates Bombay island from the mainland, lies Bassein, an old fortified Portuguese city which flourished from 1534 to 1739. The old city lies about 11 km (7 miles) from Bassein Road station.

In 1534 the Portuguese seized Daman and forced Sultan Bahadur of Gujarat to cede Bassein in perpetuity. For the next

423

200 years Bassein enjoyed a reputation for opulence and prosperity. This was expressed in the architecture. At its height Bassein was adorned with five convents, thirteen churches and an orphanage. Only the Portuguese nobles, the hidalgos, were allowed to reside within the city walls, in elegant two-storey houses adorned with balconies and oyster-shell glazing. In spite of a severe plague in 1695 which killed a third of the population, Bassein remained prosperous until 1739, when Chimnaji Appa, the Maratha general, besieged the town. It eventually capitulated, with great loss of life. The Marathas were expelled by the British in December 1780 after a heavy bombardment of the city which caused much damage. Later, in 1802, the Treaty of Bassein was signed here with the Peshwa Baji Rao II. In 1818 the city and district were absorbed into the Thana district of the Bombay Presidency.

Old Bassein is an evocative ruin. The walls and ramparts survive in a state of crumbling ruination, often completely invested with undergrowth. Within the walls, the ruins of the Cathedral of the Dominican convent, the Jesuit church of St Paul and St Anthony's Church (1537) can still be traced.

BELGAUM

Belgaum, 75·5 km (47 miles) from Dharwar, lies on a level plain 762 m (2,500 ft) above sea level. Once the regional capital, it contains a number of historic buildings.

The **Fort**, which lies to the east of the town, is an irregular ellipse about 914 m (2,970 ft) long by 640 m (2,080 ft) wide, surrounded by a deep ditch. Khwaja Mahmud Gawan of the Bahmani dynasty seized control in 1473. In 1818 Sir Thomas Munro captured the fort after a siege of twenty-one days.

About 110 m (358 ft) from the fort lie the ruins of an old music gallery, the **Nakkar Khana**. To the east lies the Masjid-i-Sata, a mosque built in 1519 by the Governor, Azad Khan. Further south is a Jain temple.

BELLARY

Situated on a spur of the Sandur range, Bellary was once an important military station on the trunk road between Madras and Bombay. It lies 55 km (34 miles) from the hill fortress of Rayadrug on a dry, arid plain at the foot of a great granite outcrop on which lies the fort.

The **Fort** has two lines of impressive fortifications, the upper and lower forts. The upper fort, which is virtually impregnable, contains the citadel and several ancient tanks. The lower fort, containing the arsenal, guards the eastern base. Beneath the wall at the eastern gate is an old Muslim-style tomb (1769), reputed to contain the remains of the luckless French engineer who was employed by Haidar Ali to fortify the site and then hanged for his efforts when it was realized that the fort could be commanded from a neighbouring rock.

Bellary was ceded to the East India Company in 1800 in lieu of payment for the British Subsidiary Force maintained at Hyderabad. After a rising of Moplahs in 1921, rebel prisoners were confined in the fort.

BIDAR

Bidar, once the capital of the Bahmani kings and later of the Barid Shahi dynasty, lies 116 km (72 miles) north-east of Gulbarga and about 130 km (80 miles) north-west of Hyderabad, at the head of a promontory overlooking the surrounding plain. The fort, which is one

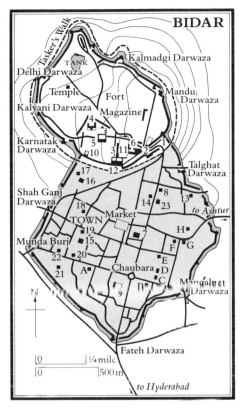

BIDAR

5 Diwan-i-Am

6 Rangeen Mahal

7 Madrasa of Khwaja Mahmud Gawan

8 Takht-i-Kirmani

9 Jami Masjid

10 Naubat Khana

11 Lal Bagh

12 Gagan Mahal

13 Kali Masjid

14 Manhiyar Talim

15 Ali Bagh

16 Tomb of Multani Padshah

17 Tomb of Shaikh Ibrahim

18 Khan Jahan Mosque

19 Chita Kana

20 Khas Mahal

21 Talim of Siddiq Shah

22 Tomb of Siddiq Shah

23 Haveli of Afdal-ud-Daula

A Khanqah of Hazrat Nur-Sammani

B Khanqah of Shah Abul Faid

C Khanqah of Shah Wali-Ullah-al-Husaini

D Khanqah of Shah Ali Husain Qutb II

E Khanqah of Mahbub Subhani

F Choti Khanqah

G Khanqah of Makhdum Qadiri

H Khanqah of Hazrah Minnat-Ullah-Bi

KEY

1 Sharza Darwaza

2 Gumbad Darwaza

3 Solah Khamba Mosque

4 Takht Mahal

of the most formidable in the Deccan, stands on the headland and the town stretches south beyond. Although rarely visited, Bidar is a fascinating mediaeval town.

Legend associates Bidar with Vidarba, but this has not been substantiated. In 1347 it was annexed by the Bahmani kingdom, but it did not become the capital until 1424, when Sultan Ahmad Shah Wali Bahmani (1422–36) transferred here from Gulbarga for its strategic location and fine climate. With the demise of the Bahmanis came the Barid Shahi dynasty (1487–1619), the tombs of whose rulers lie about 1·6 km (1 mile) to

the west of the town. For thirty years the town was the focus of local political rivalry, until Aurangzeb captured it in 1656 and renamed it Zafarabad. It remained under Mughal suzerainty until Nizam-ul-Mulk Asaf Jah of Hyderabad established control in 1724.

The **Fort** is an impressive bulwark built of local laterite and trapstone. 9·5 km (6 miles) in circumference, it was built between 1426 and 1432 by Ahmad Shah Wali Bahmani. To the north and east the fort is protected by the steep hillside; to the south and west, the walls are defended by a triple moat, the intervening ridges hewn from solid rock. The fortifications are enormously strong, with thirty-seven bastions, some of which still carry heavy ordnance. There are seven gateways in addition to the main entrance from the city. These are the Mandu Darwaza, Kalmadgi Darwaza, a postern and side gate, the Delhi Darwaza, Kalyan Darwaza and Karnatak Darwaza. Huge projecting bastions punctuate the outer walls, the largest being the Munda Burj (16th century), which in reality is a gun platform. Three pedestals – the Black, Red and Long Gun bastions – were built behind the walls to carry heavy artillery.

The eastern gateways are approached through long serpentine tunnels. The citadel, now largely in ruins, stood at the highest point in the north angle with its own postern. The main entrance from the town is through a triple gate and zigzag passage. The outer gate was defended by a moat, now filled in, and sealed by two successive doors, the outer studded with spikes. Between the gates are guardrooms. The second gate has engraved tigers in low relief, above which is an old music gallery. A long fortified gallery leads to the third gate, which differs from the other two. It has an octagonal passage with guard recesses and a lofty dome enriched with bright painted colours.

The walls between the fort and the town are designed as separate compositions to enable the fort to be isolated from the town in times of emergency. The fort contained extensive chambers for storage of powder, food and oil, as well as its own water supply.

Within the fort, many of the principal buildings are ruined. The **Takht Mahal** or Throne Palace, possibly the palace of Shihab-ud-Din Ahmad I, had two side pavilions with elegant arches and exquisite surface ornament. Coronations of a number of Bahmani and Barid Shahi kings took place here. The large gateway on the western side of the court preserves portions of its original ceramic tilework,

including emblems of the tiger and the sun.

The **Tarkash Mahal** is reputed to have been built for a Turkish wife of the sultan and was extended by the Barid Shahi rulers, who had large harems.

Rangeen Mahal or the Coloured Palace is the best-preserved example of palace architecture in Bidar. The thick black stone walls were once embellished with brightly coloured tiles; elaborately carved brackets and beams inlaid with mother of pearl can still be seen. To the west is the **Shahi Matbakh** or Royal Kitchen, originally a royal residence. The Royal Bath or **hammam** is adjacent and near it is the **Lal Bagh** or Red Garden.

The **Gagan Mahal** or Heavenly Palace was built by the Bahmani kings and later altered by the Barid Shahi dynasty. There are two courts. The main building was used by the sultan and his harem.

The **Diwan-i-Am** or Hall of Public Audience is also called Jali Mahal. It lies west of the zenana and has two entrances, one from the east and one from the west. Behind the main hall are three chambers; the one in the centre was the sultan's. Traces of tilework can still be discerned.

Solah Khamba Mosque (1327), to the west of Lal Bagh, has sixteen central pillars. It was an important mosque and the centre of religious devotion. Built in a sober and unaffected style, it is one of the earliest mosques in the Deccan, but was rebuilt extensively later. Over the large bay in front of the mihrab is a high dome raised on a circular drum ornamented with a frieze of trefoil merlons.

Old Naubat Khana was the residence of the commander of the fort. It has a large hall with a room to the west and a platform outside. At the rear are delightful windows, which afford an excellent view of the city wall and buildings.

The **Town** has five gateways. The Mangalpet and Fateh gates are relatively modern. The former was rebuilt in 1850, but the latter is a formidable affair, with a

426

moat, once crossed by a drawbridge, and a barbican standing proud of two enormous towers which guard the winding approach. The passage is commanded by oversailing machicolations and the gates are plated and spiked with iron. The **Talghat Gate**, the most picturesque, was repaired in 1671 and carries a flowing tribute in Persian.

The **Shah Ganj Darwaza**, close to the Munda Burj, comprises two arches, the outer being closed by massive plated and strapped doors. The **Dulhan Darwaza** is also a recent rebuild.

At the intersection of the two main roads in the town is the **Chaubara**, a tall round tower rising from a 10·5-m-diameter (33 ft) plinth tapering towards the top. Built as a watchtower, the lower outer concentric ring has a series of arched niches. A winding staircase leads to the top.

The **Madrasa of Khwaja Mahmud Gawan** is a distinguished example of

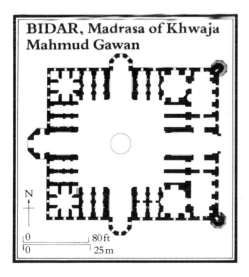

BIDAR, Madrasa of Khwaja Mahmud Gawan

Bahmani architecture, built in 1472 by Mahmud Gawan, the minister of Muhammad Shah III (1463–82), 'the Cardinal Wolsey of the Deccan'. The madrasa is an extraordinary building in Persian style and although damaged, its character can still be discerned. It com-

prises a conventional quadrangle with halls and chambers on all sides. On three sides there are semi-octagonal projections crowned by bulbous Central Asian domes, on the fourth is the main entrance, flanked by two stately three-stage minars. The façade is adorned with multi-coloured tiles in green, yellow and white in a variety of designs, arabesques and inscriptions. It was built by imported Persian craftsmen, an exotic impression of the Persian style in central India. Within the enclosure is a large pillar 39·5 m (130 ft) long. The madrasa was struck by lightning in 1696. Later it was used as a cavalry barracks and powder magazine, the explosion of which severely damaged the towers and entrance.

The **Jami Masjid** (1430), like the Solah Khamba, is in the same sedate and unpretentious style as the covered mosque at Gulbarga. The prayer hall is divided into seven arches, with an impressive façade facing the courtyard. The arches rest on massive low columns. The mihrab, projecting from the hall, has a pentagonal base. The external arches are capped by angled eaves carried on brackets and a parapet of trefoil merlons. The distinctive chain and pendant motif of the Barid Shahi dynasty, a Hindu device, can be seen here to advantage.

Kali Masjid lies about 1·2 km (¾ mile) from Bidar railway station. Called the Black Masjid on account of its trap-stone, the dome is raised on a high square base with an open arch on each side. The main hall has two minars with octagonal towers and crisply detailed bandcourses. The vaulted ceilings are decorated with elaborate plasterwork. A Persian inscription of 1694 attributes the building to an architect called Abdul Rahman Rahim in the reign of Aurangzeb.

South of the madrasa a small dome marks the Mint. **Takht-i-Kirmani** (c. 1430) lies between the madrasa and the fort. It contains the couch associated with the Muslim saint Khalil-ullah-Kirmani. A large arch enriches the main gateway, flanked by four smaller arches arranged in two rows, one above the other. The edge of the arch is treated with beadwork engraving. In the centre of the main hall is a couch set on a gilded platform which is widely revered. The bands and roundels of foliated and arabesque designs are among the best examples of Bahmani plasterwork.

The **Manhiyar Talim** is the remains of one of four physical training schools which taught wrestling, fencing and martial arts.

Bidar is well known for its monasteries or khanqahs. The **Khanqah of Hazrat Nur-Sammani** has a large hall and mosque. The **Khanqah of Hazrat Shah Abu'l-Faid** is a large enclosure approached through an arched gateway embellished with polished black stones. The **Khanqah of Shah Wali-Allah-al-Husaini** has a spacious hall with three arched openings carried on masonry columns. To the east is a small dome approached through a large arch. Nearby is the monastery of Shah Ali Husain Qutb II, built of trapstone with an arched gateway.

The great **Khanqah of Mahbub Subhani** has a mosque at the centre of the complex; the parapet has overlapping arches and the prayer hall, three arched openings. A smaller monastery, the **Choti Khanqah**, is dedicated to the same saint. The **Khanqah of Makhdum Qadiri** is close to that of Mahbub Subhani and has several buildings within an enclosure; the main block has a double hall and fine arched openings. His tomb lies on the road to Chidri. Nearby is the **Khanqah of Hazrah Minnat-Ullah Bi**, renovated, according to an epigraph, by Min-Allah Shah in 1696.

The **Royal Necropolis of the Twelve Bahmani Rulers** lies in the village of Ashtur, to the north-east of the town, and includes the tomb of Humayun the Cruel (1458–61). The tombs are significant because they express the rational development of the Bahmani

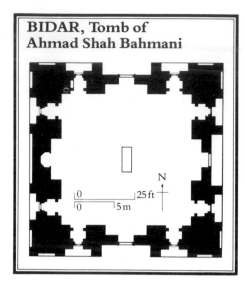

BIDAR, Tomb of Ahmad Shah Bahmani

style as it became increasingly influenced by Persian forms and features.

Generally, the tombs have taller and more bulbous domes than those at Gulbarga and none have sloping walls. All are similar, a development of the earlier examples of Gulbarga. Each tomb comprises a large square building with tiers of arched arcades around the walls, battlemented parapets and corner turrets. Usually this carries an octagonal drum, above which rises a huge dome, which in form and shape is a refinement of domes at Gulbarga. Early traces of the development of a bulbous 'Tartar' form of dome, which was later adopted almost universally, can be seen here. Although the form and style are based on the funerary architecture of Gulbarga, the superb tile work and use of colour show strong Persian influence, particularly on the tomb of Ala-ud-Din Bahman (1458).

West of Bidar are the great **Tombs of the Barid Dynasty**, which were once surrounded by beautiful gardens. Their architectural form and massing were intended as a backdrop for brightly coloured tilework and surface ornament containing eulogies and sacred inscriptions. These monuments portray a further evolution of the Bahmani style. Typical features include the use of four-centred arched recesses and openings, outlined masonry bands, and elaborate parapets and foliated bands to the bases of the domes, which are fully-formed with a slightly bulbous profile.

The first tomb is that of Qasim Barid (d. 1504) and it develops the older Bahmani style. It is set on a platform with a tapering dome divided into eight facets. The tomb of Amir Barid (d. 1542), an imposing pile on a raised platform with a roofless hall, is incomplete. Ali Barid (d. 1579) built his own tomb, which is a sophisticated refinement of Bahmani style, having a large dome with a circular base decorated with niches and mouldings. A mosque and cistern are attached to the tomb, which lies in the middle of a four-square garden or chahar bagh.

The **Tomb of Ibrahim Barid** (d. 1586) resembles that of his father, Ali Barid, and contains three graves. The sepulchre of Qasim Barid II (d. 1589) faces that of Ibrahim, the walls on each side pierced with lofty arches. The tomb of his wife lies beside him.

Khan Jahan has a well-detailed tomb, approached by flights of steps on all sides, with a dome carried on a circular drum. The tomb of Abdullah Maghribi is that of a saint of the Barid period. It is in similar style, capped by a splendid dome and set in its own enclosure.

Barber's Tomb is an elegant structure in the shape of a pavilion.

Close to the Farah Bagh Mosque is the Jharani Narasimha Cave Temple. The water spring of Nanak Jhira Sahib lies outside Bidar and is a famous place of pilgrimage to Guru Nanak (1469–1539), the first of a series of ten Sikh gurus, who performed a miracle here. It is also associated with the Muslim saint Sayyid Muhammad Harif, whose venerated tomb lies among those of the Barid kings.

Bidar is a fast-growing town and a large educational centre. It is famous for its Bidri-ware handicrafts.

BIJAPUR *Map overleaf*

Bijapur, once the capital of the Adil Shahi dynasty, is one of the great cities of India, 'the Palmyra of the Deccan'. Situated about 386 km (240 miles) south-east from Bombay, it lies on the north slope of a desolate ridge that forms the watershed between the Krishna and Bhima rivers. The approach to the city from all directions is strikingly evocative – an array of fortifications, domes, minarets and noble buildings dominated by the huge dome of the Gol Gumbaz.

Tradition maintains that the dynasty was founded by Yusuf Khan, younger brother of Muhammad, Sultan of Turkey, who was sent as a child to Alexandria to spare his life during the succession as it was the custom to kill the younger sons. He arrived in India in 1459 and later became Governor of Bijapur, proclaiming independence and founding the Adil Shahi dynasty in 1490. At the height of its power Bijapur ruled a huge tract of central India, extending to Goa and the west coast.

The **Walls** of Bijapur (or Vijayapura, literally City of Victory) are about 10 km (6¼ miles) in circumference and enclose the city in an irregular ellipse of which the major axis from the Mecca Gate to the Alipur Gate is 4·5 km (2¾ miles) long. A deep moat, 12·2 m (40 ft) to 15·2 m (50 ft) wide, runs around the walls. There are ninety-six principal bastions and five main gates. What is now actually the city is only the core of a much larger settlement over 48 km (30 miles) in circuit, of which the present city was merely the central fort. The walls have a broad platform protected by a battlemented parapet and regular bastions which carried guns, some of which remain. The holes for the gun pivots can still be seen. Originally, there was no protection for the gunners, but later a

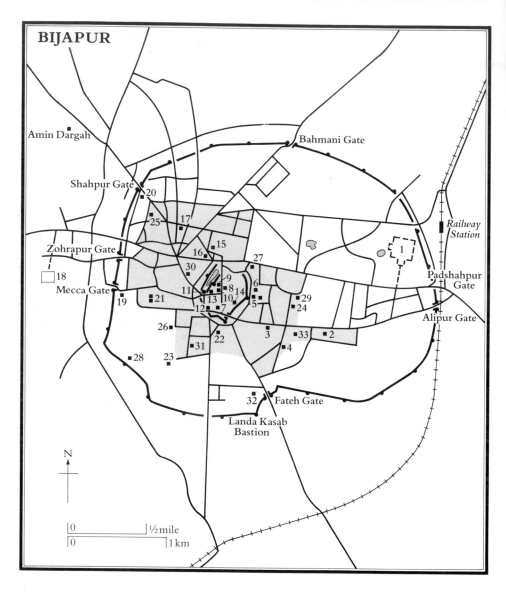

BIJAPUR

KEY

1 Gol Gumbaz
2 Jami Masjid
3 Mehtar Mahal
4 Mosque of Ali Shahid Pir
5 Asar Mahal
6 Jahaz Mahal
7 Old Mosque
8 Anand Mahal
9 Gagan Mahal

10 Station Church
11 Sat Manzili
12 Chini Mahal
13 Jal Mandir
14 Mecca Masjid
15 Unfinished Tomb of Ali Adil Shah II
16 Bukhara Masjid
17 Tomb of Sikander Ali Shah
18 Ibrahim Rauza
19 Taj Bauri

20 Chand Bauri	27 Mosque and Tomb of Yaqut Dabuli
21 Jor Gumbad (Two Sisters)	28 Tomb of Qadiri Brothers
22 Andu Masjid	29 Nau Gumbaz
23 Tomb of Ali Adil Shah I	30 Malika Jahan's Mosque
24 Mustafa Khan's Mosque and Palace	31 Ibrahim's Old Jami Masjid
25 Idgah	32 Ikhlas Khan's Mosque
26 Begum Sahib's Tomb	33 Yusuf's Old Jami Masjid

low shelter wall was erected around each bastion, with embrasures large enough to fire through.

There are five principal gates, all protected by bastions and covered approaches. In plan they are much the same: two massive circular towers with a doorway between, reinforced with spikes and studs. The **Mecca Gate** to the west has figures of lions trampling on an elephant. It is now a school. The **Shah pur Gate**, with long anti-elephant spikes, is to the north-west, and the **Bahmani Gate** to the north. The **Alipur Gate** or High Gate leads to the east. The **Fateh Gate** or Mongoli Gate, to the south-west, is where Aurangzeb entered in 1686. There are several other smaller gates – principally the **Zohrapur Gate** and the **Padshahpur Gate** – as well as numerous diddis or posterns.

The **Arquila** or **Citadel** walls have a circuit of 160 m (520 ft), but long sections have been demolished. The curtain walls, strengthened by bastions, a rampart and ditch, have earlier Hindu temple masonry embedded in the structure. The main entrance was via the Arquila Gate, now in ruins. It is approached from the south, past a covering wall and bartizan carrying an inscription and date (1544). Between the inner and outer gates are arcades and guardrooms. High on the right-hand bastion are two inscriptions. Only the skeletal form of the inner gateway remains.

On the outer city walls the **Burj-i-Sherza** or Lion Bastion lies 274 m (890 ft) north of the Zohrapur Gate. It is embellished with two lions' heads and, according to an inscription, was built in

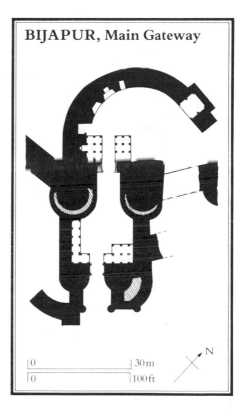
BIJAPUR, Main Gateway

just five months in 1671. Above on the bastion is the **Malik-i-Maidan** or Lord of the Battle Plain, a huge gun cast at Ahmadnagar from bell metal and located here in 1632 after wreaking havoc at the Battle of Talikota in 1565. The original pivot and carriage have gone. The muzzle is cast with a figure of a monster swallowing an elephant. It is 4·2 m (14 ft) long with a bore of 70 cm (2 ft 4 in). Around the touch hole is the inscription of its maker, Muhammad Bin Husain Rumi. Another flowing verse surrounds the muzzle. About 137 m (445 ft) east of

131

the Burj-i-Sherza is the **Upari Burj**, Upper Bastion or Haidar Burj. It comprises an 18·6 m (61 ft) oval tower with an outer staircase which carries a Persian inscription recording its construction in 1583. Above are two guns strapped together by iron bands. The larger is called the Lamcharri or Far-flier.

On the south wall the **Landa Kasab** bastion carries the largest gun in Bijapur. It measures 6·55 m (21 ft 7 in) long and weighs 47 tons.

The **Waterworks** of Bijapur are fascinating. The water supply to the city bears testimony to the sophistication of the Muslim engineers. Underground ducts bring water from Towreh, 8 km (5 miles) to the west, and from the Begam Tank, 4·8 km (3 miles) to the south. Towers line the route of the pipes. These were built to relieve pressure in the system. The profusion of baths, cisterns, channels and tanks demonstrates the importance attached to the restorative qualities of the water in the unremitting climate of the Deccan.

Many of the stone water channels were cut into zigzag ridges to produce a sparkling, rippling effect. In the south-east corner of the town **Mubarak Khan's Mahal** is a three-storey pavilion built as a display of waterworks on all levels, with a shower bath on the roof. Within the city the Taj Bauri and Chand Bauri are the largest tanks.

The **Gol Gumbaz** or Mausoleum of Muhammad Adil Shah II (1627–57) is the largest and most conspicuous building in Bijapur and one of the most celebrated in India. Built in 1659, at the architectural zenith of the Adil Shahi dynasty, probably by a masterbuilder, Yaqut of Dabul, it is a masterpiece of Muslim architecture, designed to eclipse the spectacular tomb of his father, Ibrahim Adil Shah II.

Situated on a 183-m-square (600 ft) podium, the tomb resembles a giant cube crowned by a hemispherical dome with a seven-storey octagonal tower at each of its four corners, capped by smaller domes. The great dome is the second largest in the world, 37·9 m (124 ft 5 in) in diameter, compared with 42·4 m (139 ft) at St Peter's in Rome, and 32·9 m (108 ft) at St Paul's, London. The space it encloses is the largest in the world covered by a single dome: 1682·35 sq m (18,109 sq. ft) compared with the Pantheon in Rome at 1470·8 sq. m (15,833 sq. ft).

The most ingenious aspect of its construction is the use of groined compartments or pendentives, which counteract the outer thrust of the dome, a spectacular example of the sophistication and confidence of the architecture of the period. Externally, it is faced in plaster. The façades have a large central arch, above which is a cornice of grey basalt and a row of small arches carrying a second line of plain work crowned by a balustrade 1·8 m (6 ft) high.

The corner towers are entered from winding staircases in the walls of the main building. Each storey has seven arched windows. At the eighth storey is a broad gallery around the dome which has remarkable acoustic properties: a tenfold echo can be obtained. From the base of the dome there is a fine view across the city.

Over the south doorway are three inscriptions giving the date of Muhammad Adil Shah's death: 1657. Below the dome in the centre of the chamber is the tomb of Muhammad. To the east are the graves of his youngest wife and his son Ali Adil Shah II; on the west are those of his favourite Hindu mistress, a dancing girl called Rambha, his daughter and eldest wife.

A small annex to the north side was intended as a resting-place for his mother, but it is a later, unfinished addition. To the west is a well-proportioned mosque of considerable elegance. On the south side is the **Nakkar Khana** or Music Gallery, also unfinished as the minars were never extended above the roofline. It is now a museum.

432

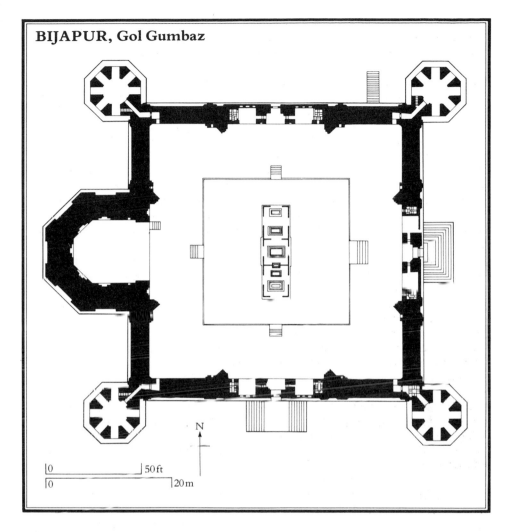

BIJAPUR, Gol Gumbaz

N

0 — 50 ft
0 — 20 m

The **Jami Masjid** (late 16th century onwards) lies 800 m (½ mile) to the south-west of the Gol Gumbaz, on the south side of the road leading from Alipur to the citadel. It is a finely proportioned building with arcaded sides and a large inner courtyard containing fountains and a reservoir. The mosque proper lies across the west end of the court, with a façade of nine bays crowned by a huge dome, probably the best proportioned in the city. It was commenced by Ali Adil Shah (1558–80) but was not completed until 1686. The pavement is divided into rectangular compartments resembling prayer rugs, one for each worshipper. The subdivision was ordered by Aurangzeb. There are 2,250 spaces. The mihrab, gilded and inscribed with Persian verses, is from the time of Muhammad Adil Shah.

The **Tomb of Shah Karim Muhammad Qadri** (1741) and that of **Sayyid Abdul Rahman Qadri** lie near the south-east corner of the Jami Masjid. Both boast ceilings alleged to be coated in pulverized mother of pearl, the latter with some pretty stucco work and iron bosses on the doors.

The **Mehtar Mahal** (*c.* 1620) is a little

433

gem, an ornamental gateway leading to the Mehtar Mosque, south of the road between the Jami Masjid and the citadel. It is a small but elegant gateway covered with ornamental detail and surmounted by two slender minarets. It is one of the finest buildings in the city.

In the fields to the south of the Mehtar Mahal is a small but peculiar mosque with an unusual wagon-vaulted roof which covers the entire structure. This is **Ali Shahid Pir's Mosque** (*c.* 1560), with a finely modelled façade enriched with receding lines of moulding around the arches, which convey a deep-set appearance. The spandrels are enriched with beautiful stucco medallions. Short, thin minarets terminate each end of the façade. Traces of the original encaustic tiles and enamel can be seen on the decorated mihrab, which, unusually, has a door inserted in it, providing access from outside. Above is a dome breaking the roof line. Adjoining the mosque is the tomb of Hazrat Sayyid Ali Shahid, after whom the mosque is named.

The **Asar Mahal** (1646), on the edge of the citadel moat, faces east. It was built as a Hall of Justice and was later used to house two hairs from the Prophet's beard. The east side is open. Four huge teak pillars carry the ceiling and form a portico which faces a large tank. The ceiling is coffered and painted. A staircase leads to a large hall, where carpets and brocades are displayed. To the right is an upper verandah which looks down on the portico. The three doors leading from the gallery are ribbed and inlaid with geometric patterns. Inside, the walls and ceilings are painted with figures and leaves, the room off the south side of the gilded hall being notable. At the base of the southern staircase is the Kitabkhana or library. From the balcony there is a beautiful view of the eastern part of the town. A bridge once linked the Asar Mahal to the citadel. The remains of other buildings, the Jehaz Mahal complex, lie to the north.

The only remaining entrance to the citadel lies to the south, facing east. Just inside, to the north-west of the gate and not far from the Chini Mahal, is the **Old Mosque**, constructed from an earlier Jain temple. The mandapa acts as a porch, but the inner doorway, with perforated screens, is Muslim. The body of the mosque is built from Jain and Hindu pillars of various patterns and heights, an extraordinary collection of salvaged masonry. The upper part has an inscription which states that Malik Karim-ud-Din built this section in 1320 and Revoy was the carpenter. Other inscriptions in Sanskrit and Kanarese survive.

The **Anand Mahal** or Palace of Delight was built by Ibrahim Adil Shah II in 1589, but it remained unfinished and is now impaired by later additions. It is the most prominent of the palaces in the citadel, with a fine open hall. It probably contained the private apartments and zenana.

The **Gagan Mahal** or Heavenly Palace (1561) was built by Ali Adil Shah I. It lies on the west of the citadel, close to the moat, facing north. It was the Durbar Hall and is easily identified by the huge central arch flanked by two tall narrow arches which form its façade. The span of the central arch is 18·6 m (61 ft), the height of all three 15·2 m (50 ft). It is alleged that Aurangzeb accepted the submission of the king and nobles here in 1686.

The station **Church** lies in an old gateway to the south-east. The wrought-iron screen comes from the Chini Mahal.

North-east of the Gagan Mahal is an old mosque built from Jain masonry with ten rows of pillars, seven deep. To the east lies the **Adalat Mahal** or Hall of Justice, later the Collector's residence. It has been extensively rebuilt, with a small mosque on the north side and a pretty pavilion or pleasure house to the east. To the north are the **Tomb and Mosque of Yakut Dabuli**. The square tomb is enriched with lattice screens. Yakut Dabuli

434

decorated the mihrab in the Jami Masjid. Over his tomb runs the inscription: 'One atom of divine grace is better than to be chief of 1,000 villages.'

The **Arash Mahal**, to the east of the Adalat Mahal, is also a converted building, now used as the Civil Surgeon's residence. It has some fine masonry detail.

At the western end of the citadel is the **Sat Manzili** or Seven Storeys (1583), of which only five remain. Situated to the south-west of the Gagan Mahal, this palace lies at the corner of a range of buildings wrongly called the Granary. It is a distinctive building with a large number of water pipes and cisterns, probably intended as a pleasure house. Traces of figures can be seen on the walls. From the top of the palace there is an excellent view of the citadel.

At the south end of the Granary is the public palace of the kings, where audiences were held. This is the **Chini Mahal**, probably so called because of the tiling which once decorated the building. Inside is a fine hall, 39 m (128 ft) long, rising to the roof and flanked by suites of rooms. To the front is a lofty open verandah. Around the arcaded quadrangle troops were billeted. Today it is the Judge's Court.

In front of the Sat Manzili is the **Jal Mandir**, a delightful water pavilion which once stood in the middle of a reservoir and is now in the centre of the road. From here the road crosses the moat, which on average is 45·5 m (150 ft) wide. At the end of the causeway is the **Jhanjiri Mosque**, attributed to Ibrahim Adil Shah II (c. 1600) in honour of his daughter Malika Jehan. It is a compact, well-proportioned building with a rich façade. The central arch is cusped, the cornice and brackets finely chased, the outer edge of the former cut into scallops resembling lacework. Traceried windows, chatris and perforated parapets enhance the delicacy of the composition.

North-east of the gateway is the

Mecca Masjid (c. 1669), a lovely little mosque enclosed by high walls with crisply carved details. The massive minarets constructed from rough material are the only remnants of an earlier mosque on the site. The principal façade of five bays is two bays deep and crowned by a dome. The great walls are curious. Given the presence of the four large arched openings on the south face, it is evident that they were not intended for defence.

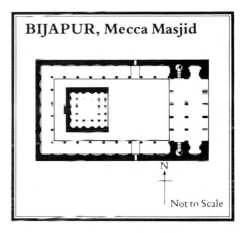

BIJAPUR, Mecca Masjid

N

Not to Scale

At the west end of the enclosure is an area known as the **Hathi Khana**, probably used as elephant stables. It is possible that the high walls were intended to keep the animals sheltered from the sun. Adjacent to the south is the Bijjanhalli Tower, an old water tower from an earlier village on the site, probably used later for grain storage. Perched on a bastion close to the east wall of the citadel is the **Chinch Diddi Mosque**, which overlooks the Asar Mahal. It is a plainly detailed building with some rather undistinguished wall paintings within.

West of the dak bungalow, just to the north of the citadel, is the **Unfinished Tomb of Ali Adil Shah II** (1650s), intended to have surpassed every other monument in the city. The base is 65·5 m square (215 ft), compared with 48 m (158 ft) on the Gol Gumbaz. The centrepiece was to have been a large dome over the central enclosure, but only the outer arcade of curious-looking Gothic arches remains. The masonry has been left undressed, ready for plastering. On a raised platform in the inner enclosure is the tomb of Ali Adil Shah; to the south-west corner, a small platform for a female, reputed to be the tomb of Khurshe Khanam, mother of Sikander. There are thirteen other graves here.

South-west is the **Bukhara Masjid**, once occupied as the Post and Telegraph Office. The brackets to the cornice and the internal stucco ornaments are notable. Just to the north are the **Tomb and Mosque of Malik Sandal**, the great architect of Bijapur. It is a beautiful but modest edifice. Within the enclosed courtyard is a small canopy beneath which is a woman's tomb, possibly that of his mother. One of the open-air tombs is that of the architect himself. In one corner is a primitive mosque. The other buildings contain arcades and tombs. Just to the north, the small canopied tomb with a ribbed dome is called the Kamrak-i-Gumbaz.

Close beside this group of buildings is the **Zamrud Masjid**, a miniature mosque, 3·6 m square (12 ft), the smallest in the city. The mural carries inscriptions from the Quran in Persian. To the west, towards the Haidar Burj bastion, is the **Sikander Rauza**, a large plain tomb of the last of the Bijapur sultans (1672–86).

365m (1,186 ft) from the Mecca Gate, to the west of the city, is the **Ibrahim Rauza** (1626), a splendid group of buildings which includes the tombs of Ibrahim Adil Shah II and his Queen, Taj Sultana. It was designed by Malik Sandal and is enclosed by a high wall pierced by a tall gateway with corner minarets. Within, set on a raised plinth, are two large buildings facing each other. To the east is the **Tomb of Ibrahim Adil Shah II**, his Queen, Taj Sultana, and four members of his family. In sequence, from east to west, lie Taj Sultana, his mother, Haji Bada Sahiba, then Ibrahim himself, his

BIJAPUR, Ibrahim Rauza

daughter Zohra Sultana, then his son Darvesh Padshah and another son, Sultan Salaman.

The tombs lie north to south in a single sepulchral chamber. To each of the four sides is a doorway flanked by an exquisite ornamental window with interlaced Arabic script, but the most remarkable feature is the hanging ceiling, which defies all the rules of architectural and structural logic. It is composed of stone slabs with no apparent means of support, the secret lying in the exceptional tenacity of the mortar. Above is another chamber in the dome, reached by a narrow staircase. Over the north door is a Persian inscription, including a chronogram of 1626. Over the south door is the date 1633, with an inscription praising Ibrahim and another commemorating the architect.

Around the tomb is a colonnaded verandah with a beautifully carved and decorated ceiling divided into compartments and inlaid with arabesques and wreaths of flowers. Traces of the gilt and azure colours remain. It is one of the finest examples of Islamic ornamental decoration in India. Outside, the double arcade is crowned by a fine cornice with

436

corner minarets and eight smaller ones between them.

To the west, within the enclosure, is a building in similar style. This is the **Mosque**, with five elegant arches beneath a finely detailed cornice enriched with stone chains carved from single blocks of stone. Four slender minarets with onion domes crown the four corners.

The **Taj Bauri** (probably *c*. 1620), the largest tank in Bijapur, lies on the west of the city near the Mecca Gate. To the east and west are long arcaded ranges which once provided accommodation for travellers. Broad flights of steps lead to the water's edge. Around the high enclosing wall is a terrace with a low parapet wall. In the centre of each side are sets of rooms which overlook the tank.

The Chand Bauri, 137 m (445 ft) south of the Shahapur Gate, is named after the famous Chand Bibi, wife of Ali Adil Shah I. It is smaller, earlier (1579) and similar to the Taj Bauri.

Near to the Mecca Gate are two domed tombs known as the **Jor Gumbaz** or Two Sisters. The octagonal one is the **Tomb of Khan Muhammad** and of his son, Khawas Khan, Wazir to Sikander. Khan Muhammad was assassinated for his treachery in the field. The tomb has a high dome which springs from a foliated band of ornament. Within is a fine chamber. The plain square tomb is the **Mausoleum of Abdul Razzak Qadir**, the religious tutor of Khawas Khan and a man much revered. To the west is a third tomb, said to be that of Siddi Rahan, a minister under Muhammad.

En route from here to the citadel one passes the old execution tree in the grounds of the Judge's Bungalow.

In the south-west quarter of the city is the **Andu Masjid** (1608), which stands on the east side of the road running south from the citadel to the Landa Kasab bastion. It is a two-storey building with a mosque on the second storey and a rest-house beneath. It was built in 1608 by It'bar Khan, one of the ministers of Ibrahim Adil Shah II. The façade has three bays with four small minarets. The masonry is exceptionally fine and the whole affair is crowned by a ribbed melon-shaped dome, a pattern which is repeated on the domes to the minars. A lace-like fringe adorns the dome and crest of the building.

West from here is a road which leads to the **Tomb of the Begum Sahiba**, wife of Aurangzeb. Another road to the west, 274 m (890 ft) to the south of the mosque, leads to the **Jami Masjid of Ibrahim I** (1551), which lies out in the fields. This is an old-fashioned mosque with brick and mortar minarets over the corners and central piers. Only the brackets of the cornice remain. Inside, it is plain. 228 m (741 ft) to the south-west is the **Tomb of Ali Adil Shah I** (*c*. 1580), a plain edifice, rectangular in plan, surrounded by a corridor and containing four tombs. At the south-eastern corner is a high platform with a beautiful dark-green tombstone in the centre. It is not known who lies in this grave, but clearly it is a person of rank.

Out in the fields, about 457 m (1,485 ft) east of the citadel, are **Mustafa Khan's Mosque and Palace**. The façade has three tall arches, that to the centre being wider than the outer two. A deep cornice oversails the front, and octagonal buttresses, which were intended to carry the minarets, flank the façade. The central bay masses up by pendentives into a fourteen-sided figure and from this rises the dome. Behind the mosque lie the remains of Mustafa Khan's Palace. He was one of the principal architects of the alliance between Ahmadnagar, Bidar, Bijapur and Golconda which led to the destruction of Vijayanagara at the Battle of Talikota. A short distance to the south is the **Bari Kaman**, a great archway which appears to have been the entrance to the palace grounds.

On the highest ground within the

walls of Bijapur is the **Dekhani Idgah** (*c.* 1590), a rather clumsy, ancient building, possibly designed by Malik Sandal. 228 m (741 ft) to the east is the **Chota Asar**, a small mosque with rich stucco work which covers the walls, ceiling and façade.

About 3·2 m (2 miles) beyond the Shahapur Gate is the **Amin Dargah**, its prominent white dome forming a local landmark. The road to it passes an old sarai (1640), which was once the jail. Although there is nothing remarkable about the Dargah, the view from the hilltop across the surrounding country-side, which is dotted with mosques, tombs and ruins, is worthwhile. It con-tains a collection of old pictures.

1·6 km (1 mile) to the south-west, in the village of Afzalpur, is the tomb of Chindgi Shah and 800 m (½ mile) to the west again are the **Cenotaph, Mosque and Palace of Afzul Khan**. Afzul Khan was the unfortunate victim of the fatal encounter with Shivaji at Partabgarh, where he was treacherously murdered by the Maratha leader, disembowelled with a waghnakh or 'Tiger's claws' (steel claws attached to the fingers) under a flag of truce. During his life he began his own tomb and attendant mosque beside his palace. The mosque was completed in 1653, but the tomb was never finished. His body remained on the slopes of Partabgarh. Before he set off to fight, he had a premonition of his own death. He personally put the date 1658 on his own cenotaph and also, it is said, drowned his sixty-four wives in anticipation of his own demise. Beside the tomb is the mosque, a two-storey affair, the upper level reserved for the women of the zenana. To the south lie the ruins of his palace.

Some way south-west of this, in a grove of trees, is a platform with a large tank: the Muhammad Sarovar. On the platform are eleven rows of identical tombs, sixty-three in all, reputed to con-tain the remains of the drowned wives.

One is alleged to have escaped. 228 m (741 ft) to the east is the Surang Bauri, from where the great tunnel which brought water into the city starts.

In 1599 Ibrahim Adil Shah II resolved to found a new city of unparalleled splen-dour, centred on the village of Torweh or Nauraspur. The walls extended 4·8 km (3 miles) from the west gate of the fort. Over 20,000 masons and artisans were summoned from all over the king-dom and placed under Nawab Shavaz Khan. Many fine buildings were erected, but the new town was sacked by Nizam Shah of Ahmadnagar in 1624 and, later, astrologers predicted dire consequences if the capital changed. The ruins of the incomplete great wall remain. Around the village of Torweh are the ruins of the Sangat Mahal and Nari Mahal. Beyond are the Tagani Mahal and other mosques, tombs and ruins.

Other outlying sites of interest are the **Begum Tank** (1651), 3·2 km (2 miles) south of Bijapur, built by Muhammad Adil Shah II to supplement the water supply, the **Ibrahimpur Mosque** (1526), 1·6 km (1 mile) away in the village of the same name, and two tombs. The **Tomb of Ain-ul-Mulk** (1565) lies 3·2 km (2 miles) to the east of the city, a massive square building with an elegant dome and some pendant stuccowork. Adjacent is the mosque. The **Tomb of Jehan Begum** is similar in size and design to the Gol Gumbaz, with similar corner towers, but it is unfinished. It is uncertain precisely whose tomb this is; possibly the third wife of Muhammad Adil Shah II or his mother.

16 km (10 miles) east of Bijapur, in the village of Kumatgi, lies an old pleasure resort studded with pavilions and tanks. On the walls of one are some fine fres-coes. Above one archway is a representa-tion of the game of polo, over another there is a hunting scene, on a third there are European envoys to the court of Bijapur. The walls are badly eroded and

scratched. The remains of the old road leading to the lake and pleasure pavilions can still be seen, together with some interesting stone cisterns, fountains and bath houses.

BOMBAY *Map overleaf*

In 1661 Bombay was ceded to England as part of the marriage dowry of Catherine of Braganza, but it was not transferred to the East India Company until 1668. It was probably named after the goddess Mumbai, who still has a temple in the city.

In the early years its climate was notoriously unhealthy. Of the 800 white residents, only 100 survived the seasonal rains of 1692. The two months which followed the monsoon, September and October, were usually fatal. The settlement was consolidated by Gerald Aungier, but it did not displace Surat as the headquarters of the Company on the west coast until 1708. The town was centred on Bombay Castle, which lay on the site of the present dockyard, and from the earliest days it became a haven for oppressed minorities, particularly the Parsees, who arrived in 1670.

The town was refortified in the middle of the 18th century, but, isolated from the east coast, it remained a backwater until the early 19th century, when the defeat of the Marathas and the abolition of the Company's trade monopoly fostered sustained growth. With the sudden loss of cotton supplies from the United States during the American Civil War, Bombay boomed as an alternative source of supply. The impetus was maintained by an energetic local government, so that by 1890 the city had become '*Urbs prima in Indis*', with an unrivalled heritage of Victorian Gothic buildings made from local stone.

The most appropriate starting-point for any tour of the city is the **Gateway of India** (1927) at Apollo Bunder, overlooking the Arabian Sea. This symbolic national landmark, the Marble Arch of India, was designed by George Wittet to commemorate the visit of George V and Queen Mary in 1911, en route to the Delhi Durbar. In 1948 it was the point of exit for the 1st Battalion Somerset Light Infantry, the last British regiment to leave India. Architecturally it is Indo-Saracenic in style, modelled on 16th-century Gujarati work and constructed in honey-coloured basalt, with side chambers and halls to accommodate civic receptions. In recent years the surrounding area has been landscaped as part of a welcome civic improvement scheme. In the gardens stands an equestrian statue of Shivaji, erected in 1961.

Behind the statue is the former **Yacht Club** (1898), by J. Adams, now the offices of the Indian Atomic Energy Commission, an evocative mixture of half-timbered gables and corner towers in yellow sandstone with stucco dressings. Unfortunately, this excellent building is dominated by the massive pile of the modern annex of the Taj Hotel, a vulgar if unusual modern Moorish skyscraper.

Fortunately, the original **Taj Hotel** (1903), by Chambers, is a powerful enough composition to be able to predominate, with its atmosphere of self-assured Edwardian solidity. One of the great hotels of the East, it was built by the millionaire industrialist J. N. Tata and it still retains its social cachet. It is best viewed from out at sea; its prominent red dome, belvedere and curved corner towers, capped by Moorish domes, form a metropolitan landmark.

Before venturing into the heart of the city an extensive but worthwhile detour can be made to the Colaba peninsula, which comprises one of the two horns which enclose Back Bay. Colaba Causeway is studded with small domestic buildings set in garden compounds.

Beyond Sassoon Dock, the first wet

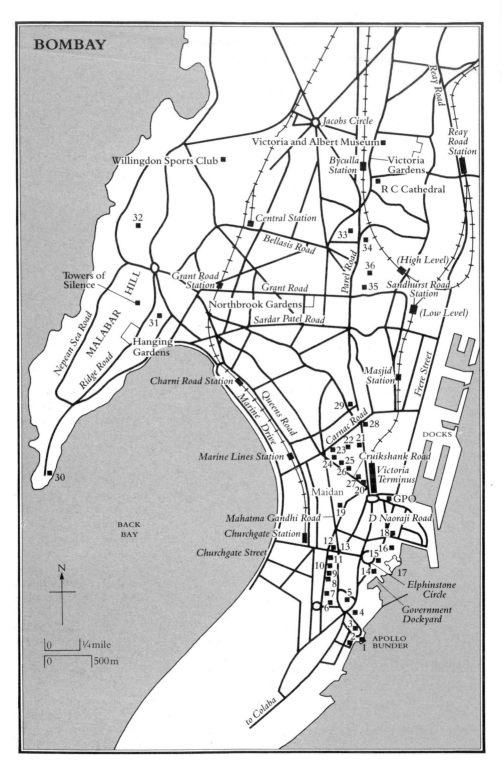

BOMBAY

KEY

1 Gateway of India
2 Taj Mahal Hotel
3 Yacht Club
4 Council Hall
5 Prince of Wales Museum
6 Institute of Science
7 Secretariat
8 University Hall
9 Library and Clocktower
10 High Court

11 Public Works Office
12 Telegraph Office
13 Flora Fountain
14 Custom House
15 Town Hall
16 Mint
17 Castle
18 Port Trust Office
19 Bombay Gymkhana
20 Municipal Offices
21 School of Art
22 Gokaldas Tejpal Hospital
23 St Xavier's School

24 Elphinstone School
25 St Xavier's College
26 Cama Albless Hospital
27 Police Court
28 Crawford Market
29 Jami Masjid
30 Raj Bhavan
31 Balbulnath Temple
32 Parsee Hospital
33 Christ Church
34 J J Hospital
35 J J Hospital
36 Grant Medical College

dock in India, lies the **Afghan Memorial Church of St John the Baptist** (1847–58), designed by the town engineer Henry Conybeare and completed by Captain Tremenheere. The bell chamber and modified steeple were designed by Lieutenant (later General) James Augustus Fuller. The Church is important as it was the first in India to be designed using the new principles of Gothic architecture advanced by Pugin and the English Ecclesiological Society. It is Early English in style with a tall tower and spire, 58 m (189 ft) high, which form a landmark from a considerable distance at sea. The walls are made of rubble faced in buff-coloured basalt from Coorla, with Porbandar stone piers, arches and dressings. Internally, the narrow lancet windows have some of the finest stained glass made by William Wailes; in particular, the great west window, the central panel of which depicts the Crucifixion and Christ seated in majesty. At the west end of the north aisle is a triple window of stained glass to General David Barr. In the west end of the south aisle is a fine Holditch organ. The chancel is paved with English encaustic tiles and between

the lancet windows are the memorial marbles to the fallen of the Sind Campaigns and First Afghan War, 1835–43, in white, red, yellow and blue stone. The ornamental illuminated screen is a later addition, designed by William Butterfield. Many of the fittings were made by the Bombay School of Art.

In the church compound is a fine banyan tree and also a marble **memorial cross**, raised by the officers and soldiers of HM's 45th Regiment to commemorate the NCOs, men, women and children who died in Nimach and Colaba between March 1865 and January 1866.

Beyond the church at the extreme tip of Colaba lie the observatory and old **European Cemetery**. A large square tomb marks the spot where 184 persons were buried from the wreck of the *Castlereagh*. Beyond are the **Old Lighthouse** (1771) and the **New Lighthouse** (1874).

To return to the city visitors can either retrace their route along Colaba Causeway or take the left fork, skirting the harbour, to Back Bay along Cuffe Parade, once a small resort but now overtaken by land reclamation and

441

redevelopment, continuing along Wodehouse Road to the **Wellington Fountain** (1865), built to commemorate the two visits by the illustrious Duke in 1801 and 1804. Until 1928 the area to the right of Wodehouse Road was the old Cotton Green.

At the junction with the circus stands the Majestic Hotel, behind which are the new Roman Catholic Church of the Holy Name and the official residence of the Roman Catholic Archbishop of Bombay.

Around the circus at the junction of Mahatma Gandhi Road and Apollo Bunder Road lie a number of notable buildings.

On the south-east corner the **Council Hall** (former Royal Alfred Sailors' Home) is the first major work of the outstanding architect of Victorian Bombay, F. W. Stevens, under the supervision of Colonel (later General) James Augustus Fuller. Commenced in 1870 and completed in 1876, it superseded earlier designs for a cast-iron structure by the English architect J. Macvicar Anderson. It is a large Indo-Gothic structure, 82 m (270 ft) long, with two wings and a central entrance hall and staircase faced in blue basalt with dressings of Porbandar, Coorla and Hemnager stone. The sculpture on the front gable by Bolton of Cheltenham depicts Neptune with nymphs and seahorses. Full details of its construction can be found on a memorial tablet in the Hall. In 1928 the home was taken over by the government and a new Council Chamber for the Bombay Legislature was added at the rear.

On the island site opposite at the south end of Mahatma Gandhi Road, set among verdant gardens, is the huge **Prince of Wales Museum of Western India**. A bronze statue of George V stands outside. An equestrian statue of Edward VII, by Boehm, presented by Sir Albert Sassoon, stands on the other frontage. The Museum, designed by George Wittet and commenced in 1905, is dominated by a huge tiled concrete dome and, at present, comprises two out of the three planned ranges disposed around a central courtyard. The central range (1914) and one wing (1937) are complete. This vast complex, based on local Gujarati architecture of the 15th and 16th centuries and built in local stone, is typical of Wittet's accomplished Indo-Saracenic style.

The Museum has three main sections: Art, Archaeology and Natural History. The Art section contains an excellent collection of arms, the Sir Ratan Tata bequest of pictures, including works by Lawrence, Gainsborough, Poussin and Titian, and fine examples of Indian silver and brass, jade and tapestries. The Archaeological exhibition has three main sections: Brahmanical; Jain, Prehistoric and Foreign collections; and Buddhist. (For details see Volume I.) The Natural History section is based on the collections of the Bombay Natural History Society, founded in 1833.

Just behind the Museum, in Marine Street, is **St Andrew's Kirk** (1819), a simple neo-classical church in the manner of James Gibbs. The steeple was demolished by lightning in 1826 and rebuilt a year later by John Caldecott, FRS, Astronomer of Trivandrum University. On the site next door a circular ice house was constructed in the 1840s to preserve imported American ice, a luxury until ice was made locally in the 1880s. The structure has now gone.

On the west side of the circus, at the south end of Mahatma Gandhi Road, is the **Institute of Science**, by George Wittet, commenced in 1911. This huge range of buildings includes the College of Science in a three-storey block facing Mayo Road, a science library, public hall and other buildings, unified by the common use of local yellow basalt and a discernible Renaissance style. The Institute owes its foundation, like many public buildings and institutions in the city, to the munificence of private Parsee and Jewish benefactors.

442

Beyond, in Mayo Road, follow a magnificent group of High Victorian Gothic buildings which coalesce to form a romantic, evocative skyline. This self-confident series of public buildings is imbued with all the vigorous attributes of the age in which it was built.

The former **Secretariat** of the government of Bombay (1874) was designed by Captain (later Colonel) Henry St Clair Wilkins in Venetian Gothic style. It is 143 m (470 ft) long, with wings terminated by three sides of an octagon. The façade is made up of arcaded verandahs enriched with structural polychromy, with a central axis accentuated by a huge gable which breaks forward beneath the 52 m (170 ft) tower. The gable, carrying the great staircase window in a single 27·5 m (90 ft) arch, in the central feature of the composition. It is faced in buff-coloured Porbandar stone, enriched with blue and red basalt and details carved by native artists in white Hemnagar stone.

Next comes the **University Convocation Hall**, designed by Sir George Gilbert Scott (1874), supervised by Fuller, in the Decorated French style of the 15th century. It was financed by the great Parsee benefactor Sir Cowasjee Jehangir Readymoney, to whom there is a statue by Thomas Woolner in the Gardens. The south end is apsidal and separated from the body of the hall by a grand arch. A handsome carved timber gallery carried on enriched cast-iron brackets encloses three sides. Open spiral staircases, recalling those of the great French châteaux at Blois and Chambord, provide external access to the side verandahs.

Adjacent lie the **University Library and Rajabai Clocktower**, to designs sent from England by Sir George Gilbert Scott. Built between 1869 and 1878, it is one of his best but least-known schemes, a sophisticated amalgam of 14th-century French and Italian Gothic. The library comprises a two-storey structure with arcaded galleries, pierced parapets and delicately carved stonework. In each corner are open spiral staircases rising full height, capped by stone spires. The cool interior is lit by traceried windows filled with stained glass.

At the western end is the colossal **Rajabai Tower** 79·2 m (260 ft) high and based on Giotto's campanile in Florence. It takes its name from the mother of its benefactor, Mr Premchand Roychand. Around the octagonal lantern are sculpted figures 2·4 m (8 ft) high representing the castes of western India. Above these, forming crocketed finials, are another set of figures, twenty-four in all, modelled by the Assistant Engineer, Rao Bahadur Makund Ramchendra. Under the clock dials on each face are four small machicolated balconies. From the top of the tower a magnificent view of the city can be obtained, but access is not always possible. Sadly the clock chimes of 'Home Sweet Home' and 'God Save the Queen' are now rarely heard.

Adjacent is the **High Court** (1871–9), another exotic extravaganza of tropical English Gothic designed and built by Colonel (later General) James Augustus Fuller, 'the leading constructional engineer of his day'. This enormous pile is 171 m (562 ft) long and 60 m (195 ft) broad, dominated by a large central tower 57·3 m (186 ft) high, on either side of which are lower octagonal spire-capped towers crowned by figures of Justice and Mercy. These contain private staircases for judges, the main staircase on the eastern side being approached by a groin-vaulted corridor in Porbandar stone with a floor of Minton tiles. The gaunt exterior is roughly dressed in blue basalt enriched with dressings of stucco, Porbandar, Coorla and Sewri stones, surmounted by steeply pitched roofs clad in Taylor's patent red tiles.

Next in line is the **Public Works Office** (1869–72), 88 m (288 ft) long and another magnificent essay in Venetian Gothic, by Colonel Henry St Clair Wilkins. It is similar in conception to the

Secretariat but with a curious centrepiece, a deep staircase tower with twin pyramidal roofs. The wings are terminated by end bays with arcaded storeys enriched with structural polychromy, but much of its impact is now reduced by the mature trees on the forecourt.

The old **General Post Office** (1869–72), now called the **Telegraph Office**, was designed by James Trubshawe in mediaeval Italian style with wide bracketed eaves. The building stands opposite the Public Works Office, with its main façade to Vir Nariman Road (formerly Churchgate Street). It is punctuated by two towers with steeply pitched roofs, between which projects a cavernous porte-cochère. The upper part was once used as an outdoor dining-room for clerks. Unsightly modern aerials impair the roofline.

Adjacent to the north is the original **Telegraph Office**, built like the Post Office under the supervision of Colonel James Augustus Fuller, but designed entirely by W. Paris, who had collaborated with Trubshawe on the design of the Post Office. Both buildings are faced in honey-coloured sandstone from Coorla, with columns and dressings of blue basalt.

To the west, along Vir Nariman Road, lies **Churchgate Station** (1894–6), by F. W. Stevens for the Bombay, Baroda and Central India Railway. Part was damaged by fire in 1905 and reinstated by his son, C. F. Stevens. The terminus has a Byzantine character, with facings of rough-hewn basalt inlaid with bands of red Bassein sandstone and white stone dressings. Each façade has a gabled centrepiece and projecting wings enriched with Oriental domes. The main tower reduces in stages to a crowning cupola, with the central hall beneath lit by the huge west window. A statue of Engineering on the west gable, carved by Roscoe Mullins, holds a locomotive and wheel, symbols of Western progress.

Returning along Vir Nariman Road

past the Maidan, the **Flora (Frere) Fountain** (1869) is reached. The figure of Flora stands above a confused jumble of dolphins, shells and beasts. The fountain was designed by a committee, and it shows, even though the eminent Richard Norman Shaw had a hand in it. The sculptor was James Forsyth. Painted in garish colours, it lies marooned in a sea of traffic. Commanding the fork of Mahatma Gandhi Road and Dadabhoi Naoroji Road lie buildings once occupied by the citadels of commerce and trade. On the left, the Khadi building was once Whiteaway and Laidlaw, military suppliers and tailors, and it still retains its period ambience. The domed building next door formerly housed Macmillan, the publishers. Beyond, to the right, stands the former **Fort House**, now Handloom House, once the mid-19th-century residence of the great Parsee Sir Jamsetjee Jeejeebhoy, and nearby lies his eponymous Institute (1871), built in a Gothic style.

Heading south down Mahatma Gandhi Road back to the Wellington Fountain lie a group of buildings of considerable interest, recalling Oxford rather than the Orient. First on the right is the old **Watson's Building** (1867), once a hotel, with cast-iron pillars and tiers of external galleries. It was the first iron-framed building in Bombay and caused a sensation when it was built on the former Esplanade. The sedate classical building next door was the former Army and Navy Stores (1870), onetime purveyor of provisions to the denizens of the Raj. Beyond is the delightful **Mechanics' Institute** (David Sassoon Library), designed by Colonel James Augustus Fuller in 1870. The Institute provides a library, lecture facilities and a small museum, with an octagonal lecture theatre set behind its arcaded frontage. In the entrance hall is a statue of Sassoon by Woolner.

Beyond is the elegant Romanesque range of **Elphinstone College** (1890) in honey-coloured stone. The school, dedicated to Mountstuart Elphinstone, Governor of Bombay, was endowed by Sir Cowasjee Jehangir, after whom the main hall is named. The library has a portrait of Elphinstone by Lawrence. The wings contain the **State Record Office**, with a fine collection of documents of the East India Company, including Wellesley's letter announcing his victory at Assaye.

The route leads back past the Institute of Science and the Wellington Fountain into Apollo Street. This district stands at the core of the old fort area, which was swept away in 1860 for municipal expansion. A number of fascinating early buildings survive and the area retains much of its 18th-century character even though it is now dilapidated. At the junction of Apollo Street and Marine Street lies the old **Writers' Building**, an early-19th-century bow-fronted house. Next is an extensively altered 18th-century house, the second Governor's House between 1757 and 1829, submerged beneath later accretions but once an elegant building set in its own garden compound. An unobtrusive plaque on the outside wall records the history of the house. Jonathan Duncan, the Governor, died here on 11 August 1811.

At the lower end of Marine Street, just beyond St Andrew's Kirk and the site of the former Ice House, lies a late-18th-century house. Originally occupied by Governor Hornby between 1771 and 1784, it later became Admiralty House, the High Court and finally the Great Western Hotel. The core of the building is original but the verandah has been demolished. Note the bollards in Marine Street and the old Fort area, many of which are inverted 19th-century cannon.

Marine Street leads to Elphinstone or Horniman Circle. On the right-hand side, south of the Town Hall, lie a number of early buildings within the former Fort area, now the Government Dock-

yard. Access and photography are prohibited.

The **Custom House** is an ancient structure, parts of which may incorporate a Portuguese barrack block of 1665. Over the entrance portico are the arms of the East India Company and the inscription 'Hon. W. Ainslabie, 1714'. Vestiges of the original Portuguese fortifications survive, including, incredibly, parts of the original **Manor House** (c. 1560), built by Garcia da Orta. These are embedded in the old Arsenal or Pattern Room. Nearby are a sundial and coat of arms of similar age. Over the gate in the bastion wall is a cartouche of Portuguese soldiers. Fragments of the old Fort walls can be discerned, but the most complete stretch lies within the restricted Naval Dockyard complex.

The Dockyard was begun by the famous Wadia family, who transferred here from Surat in 1736. Generations of East Indiamen were built here. It was alleged that a teak-built man-of-war lasted five times as long as a ship of English oak. A flagstaff and clocktower with a time signal ball remain between the Custom House and Mint.

The **Mint** stands close to the Town Hall with a tank before it. It is a restrained, rectangular building with an Ionic portico, built by Major John Hawkins on the Fort rubbish dump between 1824 and 1829. Hawkins was sent to England to study minting techniques in the office of Boulton & Watt with Major Forbes, architect of the Calcutta Mint.

On the south-west edge of the old Fort area is **Forbes's House**, the late-18th-century house of John Forbes, a Scots trader and leading businessman. The house survives in a state of precarious dilapidation.

The **Town Hall** (1820–23), on the east side of Elphinstone Circle, is the finest neo-classical building in India, a sophisticated, assured essay in the Greek Revival style. It was designed by Colonel Thomas Cowper and completed after his death in 1825 by others, principally Charles Waddington, although a certain Augustine of Portuguese origin is reputed to have played an important subordinate role. The façade is raised high on an arcaded basement approached by a massive flight of steps. Projecting jhilmils or window hoods are part of the original design and demonstrate the successful adaptation of Greek Doric architecture to an Indian context. Note the Greek palmettes on the pelmets to the jhilmils. The Doric columns were shipped from England but were considered so monumental on arrival that the original idea of paired columns was dropped, the leftovers being diverted for use at Christ Church, Bycullah, then in the course of erection.

Internally, the order is generally Corinthian, but the Medical Board rooms on the ground floor have four splendid Ionic columns, modelled from a Greek temple on the banks of the Ilyssus. There are good statues of Mountstuart Elphinstone, Sir Charles Forbes and Sir John Malcolm, all by Chantrey, and others of Elphinstone by Foley, Sir Bartle Frere by Woolner and Sir Jamsetjee Jeejeebhoy by Marochetti. The interior is occupied by Assembly Rooms, the Bombay Asiatic Society and other learned institutions – the Burlington House of Bombay. The Library contains over 100,000 volumes in desperate need of effective conservation.

Elphinstone or **Horniman Circle** lies on the site of Bombay Green and was laid out from about 1860 under the instructions of Charles Forjett, the Municipal Commissioner, to a scheme prepared by George Clerk, predecessor of Sir Bartle Frere. The buildings were designed with unified Italian façades enriched with cast-ironwork from England. On the western edge of the Circle by Vir Nariman Road is **Elphinstone Buildings** (1870), a splendid Venetian Gothic palazzo in warm-brown sandstone with interlacing arches and arcaded storeys, one of the most accomplished Victorian Gothic buildings in Bombay. The central gardens, enclosed with Victorian iron railings, provide a pleasant resting-place.

Immediately to the west is the **Cathedral Church of St Thomas**, commenced in 1672 by Gerald Aungier and opened in 1718. The See was established in 1833, at which date the old belfry was replaced by the present tower. The interior is capacious, with a simple plan and plain Tuscan detail. The chancel (1865), by James Trubshawe, is a curious remnant of a much larger reconstruction scheme which failed with the financial collapse of 1865.

The principal interest of the cathedral lies in its splendid heritage of monuments. The best is Bacon's monument to Governor Jonathan Duncan, depicting him receiving the blessings of Hindus, commemorating his energetic suppression of infanticide in Varanasi (Benares) and Kathiawar through his agent Colonel Walker. Duncan is buried under a pavement in the nave. The monument to Katharine Kirkpatrick (1766), mother of Major-General William Kirkpatrick and Major James Achilles Kirkpatrick, who as Residents at Hyderabad established English supremacy in central India, is a fine marble medallion by Bacon. Note the eloquent inscription.

Other noteworthy monuments are Chantrey's figure of Stephen Babington, who revised the Judicial Code; and those to Captain Hardinge, RN, who seized the French cruiser *Piedmontese* in an audacious attack in 1808; to Colonel Burr, who commanded at the Battle of Kirkee on 5 November 1817 against the Peshwa; to Colonel John Campbell, heroic defender of Mangalore against Tipu Sultan in 1787; to Major Eldred Pottinger, the hero of Herat, by Bacon; to Admiral Maitland, who conveyed Napoleon to St Helena; and many others which mark the passage of the British in India.

In the chancel on the left-hand side is

446

the tomb of General Carnac, Clive's second-in-command at Plassey. Nearby is a simple plaque to Henry Robertson Bowers, 'noble Birdie Bowers', who died with Scott of the Antarctic in 1912. A large chalice and cover (1675) presented by Governor Gerald Aungier are still preserved.

Outside the west door in the churchyard is a small Gothic fountain presented by Sir Cowasjee Jehangir Readymoney to the designs of George Gilbert Scott.

North of Elphinstone (Horniman) Circle the road leads past the **Offices of the Port Trust** to Frere Road and the dock areas. Immediately to the west, behind Victoria Terminus, is **St George's Hospital**, the boundary wall of which accommodates some of the old bastions of the fort. To the west in Fort Street is the **General Post Office** (1909), a vast Indo-Saracenic block based on the architecture of Bijapur, designed by John Begg and supervised by George Wittet.

To the east lies the huge frontage of **Victoria Terminus** (1878–87), by F. W. Stevens, the finest Victorian Gothic building in India and a riot of polychromatic stone, decorative ironwork, marble and tile. The frontage is symmetrical, with projecting wings and a colossal dome, 'the first applied to a Gothic building on scientific principles'. Beneath the dome is a majestic staircase. The booking-hall is arcaded and ornamented in High Victorian Gothic style, with stained glass, glazed tile and stencilled patterns. It is a highly original work, inspired by Gilbert Scott's St Pancras Station but wholly different in conception. The dome is crowned by a huge statue of Progress, 4·2 m (14 ft) high, executed by Thomas Earp, who designed the stone medallions of Imperial figures which enrich the façade, as well as the Imperial lion and Indian tiger which crown the monumental gate piers. Most of the architectural ornament was carved locally by the Bombay School of Art.

Immediately to the west of the ter-minus, at the apex of Cruikshank Road (Mahapalika Marg) and Dadabhai Naoraji Road, are the **Municipal Buildings** (1893), also by F. W. Stevens. This colossal edifice has a tower 77·7 m (255 ft) high, capped by a bulbous dome, an ebullient expression of Indo-Saracenic architecture symbolizing Victorian civic and Imperial pride. The statue crowning the gable is '*Urbs Prima in Indis*'. It is a fine building by the most accomplished practitioner of Indo-Gothic architecture. The statue outside is of Sir Pherozeshah Mehta, by Derwent Wood.

Wardby Road runs south-east, skirting the Maidan and **Bombay Gymkhana Club**. The area is studded with interesting buildings, notably the Capital Theatre, the Davis Kirk, the Tady Ratan Tata Palace and the Alexandra School for Girls.

To the north Dadabhai Naoraji Road runs parallel to the railway. To the left lie the **Times of India Office**, the **Anjuman-i Islam School** (1893), by James Willcocks, and the **Sir Jamsetjee Jeejeebhoy School of Art** (1877), where John Lockwood Kipling was once Principal. At the junction with Carnac Road are the **Crawford Markets** (1865–71), founded by Arthur Crawford, Municipal Commissioner from 1865 to 1871, and designed by William Emerson in 12th-century-French-Gothic with cast-ironwork by Mr Russel-Aitken. There is a large central hall and drinking fountain to Emerson's design (simplified by Kipling), crowned by a 39-m (128 ft) clocktower. One wing is the fruit market, the other is for vegetables. Beyond lie markets for fish, mutton and poultry, the whole complex in a state of perpetual pandemonium. Over the entrance are fine bas-reliefs carved by John Lockwood Kipling. The paving-stones are from Caithness.

Across Carnac Road is Abdul Rahman Street and the Indian part of the city, which is rewarding to explore. The narrow, packed streets are flanked by many old vernacular buildings of considerable interest. The **Jami Masjid** lies in Princess Street.

In Carnac Road the **Gokaldas Tejpal Hospital** (1877) owes its foundation to Parsee benefactors and its Early English Gothic designs to the redoubtable Colonel James Augustus Fuller. On the south-east and south-west faces are medallions by Lockwood Kipling. The iron staircases are by Macfarlane's of Glasgow. Next is **St Xavier's School**, founded in 1867, a huge range with a high octagonal tower. Opposite is the **Court of Small Causes**.

Elphinstone High School, at the junction with Cruikshank Road, is the government public school. Designed in 1872 by G. M. Molecey, the assistant of James Trubshawe, and endowed by Sir Albert Sassoon, it stands on a high platform screened by trees, but it is firmly in the Indo-Gothic tradition, robustly decorated with polychrome detail and elaborate ironwork. Next is **St Xavier's College**, an attractive complex of Gothic buildings, followed by the **Cama Albless Obstetric Hospital**, which has Gothic windows shaded by conical iron hoods. The **Police Courts** (1888), by John Adams, complete the group, with their slender flèche spire and vigorous carved Gothic details.

Between the Police Courts and the flank of Municipal Buildings is an excellent piece of modern infill, sympathetic to the Gothic surroundings and disciplined by its context. Opposite lies the broad open sweep of the Maidan.

There are other points of interest in outlying districts. Close to the junction of Grant (Maulana Shakat Ali) Road and Parel (Dr Babasaheb Ambedkar) Road is the **Jamsetjee Jeejeebhoy Hospital**, built in 1845 and endowed partly by the Jeejeebhoy family and partly by the East India Company. The overall complex includes several later affiliated hospitals erected in 1889 and 1890.

Immediately to the north is the **Grant Medical College** (1845): crenellated stucco in a pretty Regency Gothick style commemorating Sir Robert Grant, Governor of Bombay between 1835 and 1838. Attached is an interesting Museum. Northbrook Gardens (1874) lie nearby.

To the south-east of the hospital in Jail Road is the **Boys' Remand Home**, housed in a late-18th-century structure with massive masonry walls that was once the jail, built on the site of Fig Tree Creek.

Further north, in Parel Road, **Christ Church, Bycullah** (1835), has a Greek Doric portico using spare columns imported for use on the Town Hall. The stained-glass window (1870) commemorates Mr Spencer Compton. A fine monument to Sir Robert Grant and other tombs and brasses of interest can be seen.

Beyond are the **Victoria and Albert Museum** and **Victoria Gardens**. The Museum (1871) is a two-storey range in a Palladian style, unusual in Bombay, where Gothic usually prevailed. Founded by Sir George Birdwood, it was designed in 1862 by William Tracey. The foundation stone was laid by Sir Bartle Frere and, when opened nine years later, it was eulogized as 'one of the greatest boons which England could have conferred on India'. The Museum houses an interesting collection depicting the history of Bombay.

In front of the Museum is an Italianate **Clocktower** (1865), the gift of David Sassoon to the designs of Scott, McClelland & Co., in Porbandar stone with panels of Minton tiles and dressings of Blashfield's terracotta from Lincolnshire. The four faces portray morning, evening, noon and night. At the base is a drinking-fountain.

In the garden immediately behind the building are some salvaged artefacts and civic statuary, including an excellent but sadly defaced marble statue of Queen Victoria (1872), by Noble, which once stood at the junction of Mayo Road and

448

the Esplanade, and a splendid bracketed cast-iron lamp column and drinking-fountain formerly on the Esplanade.

The adjacent entrance to **Victoria Gardens** (14 hectares: 34 acres) is through a classical screen enriched with medallions of the then Prince and Princess of Wales by James Forsyth. The capitals are copied from the Temple of Jupiter Status in Rome.

Within the gardens are a statue of Prince Albert, by Noble, and a rotunda with a bust of Lady Frere designed by Tracey and modelled on the Choragic Monument of Lysicrates in Athens. On the east side are Zoological Gardens. The wonderful tropical planthouse with its curvilinear cast-iron frame covered with dark-green latticework is reminiscent of Decimus Burton's Palm House at Kew. The gardens provide a welcome oasis for the teeming city and are well worth a visit.

Opposite the gardens and next to the railway is a Gothic range with a lofty central tower and projecting canopied balcony (1871), by James Trubshawe. Originally Elphinstone College, it was endowed by Sir Cowasjee Jehangir Readymoney and later housed the Victoria Technical Institute. It is now a hospital.

The whole area to the north of Grant Road, known as Kamatipura, is the notorious red-light district of Bombay, a sprawling slum of human degradation.

Parel Road continues for a considerable distance to **Old Government House** (now the Haffkine Institute). The original Portuguese Franciscan friary (1673) was taken over by Governor Boone in 1719 as a country residence. From 1771, when Hornby first resided here, it was preferred to Government House in the Fort. The house was enlarged by Mountstuart Elphinstone in 1819 with two side wings. The banqueting hall and ballroom are housed in the shell of the original vaulted chapel. After the death of Lady Fergusson from

cholera here in 1882, Malabar was preferred. In 1899 W. M. Haffkine opened the Plague Research Laboratory. Since 1925 it has been the Haffkine Institute and the original grounds now contain a number of medical institutions.

At Flagstaff Hill, Sewri, is the **European Cemetery** (1867), once a Botanical Garden. The remaining district of interest is **Malabar Hill**, 54·8 m (180 ft) high, which forms a peninsula enclosing Back Bay to the north. The drive along Marine Drive (Netaji Subash Road) and up to the hill is a pleasant one, passing a Parsee Fire Temple and Wilson College, founded by the Scots missionary and scholar Rev. Dr J. Wilson.

Government House (Raj Bhavan) (early 19th century) stands in a large private compound at the summit of the hill. The house has a rustic character, with a pitched roof and timber verandahs. It was enlarged by Mountstuart Elphinstone in 1819 and again in 1828, by Sir John Malcolm. The dining-hall, billiard room, porch and verandah were added in 1868. Since 1885 it has been the Governor's official residence.

The Hindu temple of Walkeswar stands on the west side of the hill. The Pherozeshah Mehta or **Hanging Gardens** are worth a visit for the views of the city which can be obtained. Nearby is **All Saints' Church** (1882).

The famous **Five Parsee Towers of Silence**, where the Parsees lay out their dead, are surrounded by gardens designed to foster contemplation and spiritual repose. The veneration of the elements of fire, water and earth dictate a unique form of disposal of the dead by their exposure to vultures and other birds of prey. The outer enclosure may be visited, but permission is required to proceed further.

Near the steps leading to the Towers is the distinctive profile of the **Babulnath Temple** (1900). The **Parsee Dharmsala** (1812) in Gamdevi Road is for poor Persian Parsees.

449

Malabar Hill and the area towards Breach Candy retain a few surviving colonial bungalows, as well as numerous examples of modern Indian domestic architecture.

CHAKAN

Chakan is a small market village, 29 km (18 miles) north of Pune. The **Fort** is nearly square, with bastions and corner towers. Part of the outworks are reputed to be the remains of fortifications made by an Abyssinian chief in 1295. In 1595 it was given to Shivaji's grandfather. In 1662 it was seized by a Mughal general but was restored to Shivaji five years later. The fort was taken from the Marathas by Lieutenant-Colonel Deacon in 1818.

CHANDOR

The old fort of Chandor lies 64 km (40 miles) north-east of Nasik and is virtually inaccessible, perched on a high, flat summit commanding the road from Khandesh to Bombay. The fort was captured by the Mughals in 1635 and then passed to the Marathas. Aurangzeb seized it in 1665. Later it was enlarged extensively by Holkar of Indore (1763), whose family became hereditary castellans. It was stormed by the British under Colonel Wallace in 1804, and again in 1818.

CHAUL

Lying 48 km (30 miles) south of Bombay, Chaul is a port of great antiquity. It is probably the location of Symulla, mentioned by Ptolemy in 150, but its more recent past is associated with the Portuguese, who arrived in 1505 and established a factory in 1516. In 1594 they scored a brilliant victory here over troops from Ahmadnagar.

On the north side of the river lies the old city fort of Chaul, now overgrown by vegetation and studded with a few ruined monuments. The town was lost to the Marathas in 1739, and in 1818 passed to the British. At the nearby village of Korlai is the Church of our Lady of Mount Carmel, which contains some interesting bas-reliefs.

CHICACOLE

Chicacole retains a handsome mosque (1641) built using materials from a demolished Hindu temple by Sher Muhammad Khan, the first military governor under the Qutb Shahi dynasty of Golconda. The town was an important military station until it was hit by a furious cyclone in 1876.

CHITRADURGA (CHITALDRUG)

203 km (126 miles) north-west of Bangalore on the Hampi Road, Chitradurga stands at the base of a cluster of hills covered with extensive fortifications. Inscriptions of the Chalukya, Ballala and Vijayanagara dynasties have been discovered, but the fortifications were built by the Naik Pallegars in the 17th century. Eventually they clashed with Haidar Ali, who in 1779 captured the fort and dispersed the population.

The remains of the old mud fort and palace of the Naiks can be seen. The stone fortress erected by Haidar Ali, within which Tipu built a palace, was later used as a court house. Within the city immense pits were dug for storing food and oil. Inside the fort are the remains of fourteen old temples.

CORYGAUM (KOREGAON)

24 km (15 miles) north-east of Pune, a 22 m (70 ft) stone obelisk in a square enclosure on the right bank of the River Bhima marks the site of the last of the three great battles which led to the collapse of Maratha power in western India. On 1 January 1818 a battle was fought at Corygaum between a small British contingent of about 800 men under Captain Francis Staunton and an entire Maratha army of 25,000 men under Baji Rao Peshwa.

After a series of fierce attacks launched across the river, the Maratha forces were checked and repulsed in some confusion. The British force, composed almost entirely of native levies, lost a third of its strength in casualties. On a small rise near the river is a simple round tomb which marks the grave of the English artillerymen.

DAULATABAD (DEOGIRI)

Daulatabad, close to the famous Ellora caves, is renowned for its formidable hillfort. Deogiri was the celebrated capital of the Yadava dynasty after the demise of the Western Chalukyan kingdom. The fort was captured by Ala-ud-Din Khalji in 1296, marking the first Muslim invasion of the Deccan. Though the fort was restored to the Raja, subsequent occupations occurred in 1307, 1310 and 1318, at which date the last Raja, Harpad, was flayed alive. It became an important centre for Muslim operations and Ghiyath-ud-Din Muhammed Shah II sought to make it his capital, by transferring the entire population of Delhi and changing the name from Deogiri to Daulatabad. It was in the possession of the Bahmanis until 1526, when it was captured by the Nizam Shahis, only to be wrested from them by Shah Jahan. It

remained in Mughal control until Aurangzeb's death, when it passed to the Nizam of Hyderabad.

The spectacular **Fortress** stands on a huge conical granite outcrop which rises 183 m (600 ft), the lower 46 m (150 ft) comprising a perpendicular scarp. There are three concentric lines of fortification between the outer wall and the citadel. The outer walls, which are entered via three gateways, enclose the original town of Deogiri, of which little remains.

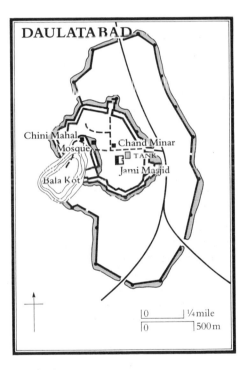

The **Jami Masjid** (1318) was built in the time of Qutb-ud-Din Khalji and comprises a large enclosed square with a pillared prayer hall on the west side, whose 106 pillars form twenty-five aisles, each five bays deep, supporting a flat roof. Four external columns carry a corbelled dome over the mihrab. The columns were reused from local Hindu and Jain temples. There is an entrance gate in the middle of each side, that to the

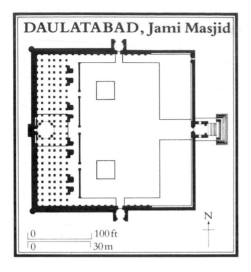

DAULATABAD, Jami Masjid

east carrying a tall stilted dome, probably a later Bahmani alteration.

Opposite is the **Chand Minar** (1435), an elegant pillar of victory of four well-balanced circular storeys, with a central

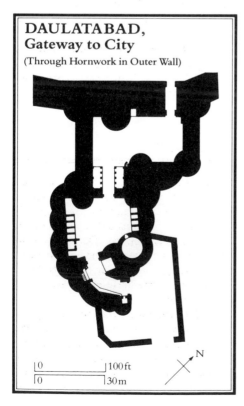

DAULATABAD, Gateway to City

(Through Hornwork in Outer Wall)

fluted section erected by Ala-ud-Din Bahmani to mark his conquest of the fort. The base of this well-preserved minaret contains twenty-four small chambers and a rather mean small mosque. Originally, the entire edifice was clad in glazed Persian tiles. The carved brackets to the balcony are of Hindu origin.

Beyond the outer moat another triple gateway marks the entrance to the inner defences. To the right of the gateway is a huge bastion protecting the gate and drawbridge. The gate is studded with iron spikes to prevent battering by elephants. This second line of defence comprises two sets of walls 18·2 m (60 ft) apart, each with a protective moat. Two more gateways in fortified walls must be crossed before the base of the citadel or Balakot is reached. 12 m (40 ft) to the right of the third gate is the **Chini Mahal** or China Palace, where the last of the kings of Golconda was imprisoned for thirteen years by Aurangzeb in 1687. On a nearby bastion is the **Kila Shikan** or Fort-breaker, a huge piece of heavy ordnance 6·6 m (21 ft 10 in) long.

The moat around the citadel is crossed by a stone bridge, the level of water in the moat being controlled by dams which could render the bridge inaccessible during siege. The way into the citadel is past a defensive tower and through a series of underground chambers and passages hewn from solid rock. The monumental doorway to the tunnel is Hindu in form, resembling the doorway of the Kailasa Temple at nearby Ellora. Enemy advance through the tunnel could be impeded by a stone barrier drawn from a socket by iron rings on one side of the passage.

At the head of the tunnel is a ribbed iron door, 6 m (20 ft) long and 2·5 cm (1 in) thick, which was heated red-hot from a small adjacent chamber in times of emergency, with the resulting air currents causing smoke to circulate up the tunnel and suffocate the enemy. At the

452

end of the tunnel is a wide flight of steps past the **Shrine of Fakir Sukh Sultan** to the **Hindu Pavilion**, with a verandah above a 30 m deep (100 ft) chasm. It is reputed to have been the residence of the Yadavi Rani of Deogiri and was later occupied by Shah Jahan.

The citadel lies above, approached by a further zigzag flight of steps and defended by two more gateways. At the summit in the west corner is a single 17·5 cm (7 in) gun, 6 m (19 ft 6 in) long. On an adjacent bastion is another large cannon, known as Creator of Storms and inscribed in Gujarati, reputedly raised to its platform by a European gunner in the service of the Mughals.

The impregnable defences of Daulatabad and other fortified cities of the Bah mani kingdom show pronounced similarities with contemporary castles in the Levant and there is little doubt that the Bahmani builders were acquainted with Western methods of fortification.

DEOLALI

This is an old cantonment lying 6·5 km (4 miles) south-east of Nasik off the Pune Road. The town is also a resort for Parsees and others from Bombay on account of its healthy position and good views of the distant hills.

The cantonment is a large area of military barracks, which were used as a clearing centre for troops arriving from Europe during both World Wars. The slang word 'doolally' is a corruption of its name, popularized by the thousands of Allied troops who were based here.

DHARWAR

Dharwar is the principal town of the district of the same name, lying on the railway about midway between Bangalore and Pune. It lies on one of the last spurs of the Western Ghats, at a height of 727 m (2,384 ft), and was a cantonment until this was abandoned in 1884 and taken over as Police Lines.

The remains of the **Fort** lie to the north, but not much can be seen, the site having been given to the Civil Hospital. Local legend asserts that the fort was founded in 1403 by Dhar Rao, an officer in the service of the king of Anigundi. It was seized by Muhammad Ali Adil Shah I of Bijapur in 1568. In 1685 the Mughals captured it and in 1753 it capitulated to the Marathas, who in turn lost control to Haidar Ali in 1778. In 1791 a British force wrested control.

The town is a straggling affair, but it has prospered in recent years as the site of the University of Karnataka. The only monument of any historical significance is an **obelisk** to the memory of St John Thackeray, an uncle of the writer, and J. C. Munro, who were killed in a rebellion at Kittur in 1824.

2·4 km (1½ miles) south of Dharwar is the hill of Mailargad, which is crowned by a small square Jain temple with massive carved stone beams.

FIRUZABAD

Firuzabad is an old ruined town situated on a bend of the Bhima river, about 25 km (15½ miles) south of Gulbarga. It was probably established as a Bahmani capital by Taj-ud-Din Firuz Shah in about 1400 and abandoned in the mid-15th century, but at present little is known about the circumstances of its foundation or decline.

Massive stone fortifications with part-circular bastions embrace the former city on the east, north and south sides. In the centre of each side are vaulted gateways and barbican walls. Within this enormous enclosed area are a series of mounds of rubble and collapsed buildings which were once elegant gateways, mosques, houses, palaces and other structures.

West of the centre is the largest single monument, the Jami Masjid. This comprises a rectangular courtyard entered on the east through a domed gateway. Behind lay the former palace area, a series of courts enclosed by high walls, in which lie the ruins of many old buildings. Elsewhere in the city isolated structures still stand, including vaulted chambers, bath houses and another small mosque.

About 2 km (1¼ miles) north of the city is the **Tomb Complex of Khalifatur Rahman**. This takes the form of a tomb, tank and mosque and is still in a reasonable state of repair.

The ruined buildings of Firuzabad exhibit the typical features of the Bahmani style of the late 15th century: tapering walls, bulbous finials, flattish domes and stilted arches. What is interesting is that Firuzabad was built as a royal city in one single effort and never again built upon. It exhibits influences from Central Asia as much as from local Hindu cities like Vijayanagara.

GANDIKOT

This famous ancient fortress, 'The Fort of the Gorge', lies in the Cuddapah district in the Yerramalai mountains, 509 m (1,670 ft) above sea level.

Built in 1589 it was captured by Golconda and later absorbed by the Pathan Nawab of Cuddapah. The fort was strengthened by Haidar Ali, but was captured by the British under Captain Little from Tipu Sultan in 1791. Strategically, the fort commanded the Pennar valley and its remains are perched on a scarped rock overhanging the river.

GAWILGARH

This hill fortress lies on the watershed between the Purna and Tapti rivers, north of Ellichpur, at a height of 1,096 m (3,595 ft) above sea level.

The **Fort** was built in the 1420s by Ahmad Shah I of the Bahmani dynasty. It was acquired by Ahmadnagar in 1574 and was later held by the Nizam and the Marathas, before it was captured by the British under Colonel Arthur Wellesley on 15 December 1803, during the Second Maratha War. The fort was breached by batteries and taken by a manoeuvre of General Stevenson, described by Wellesley as one of the most difficult, and successful, operations he had witnessed. Today the fort is in ruins, but two mosques remain. In its heyday the walls were fortified with towers and bastions. There was an inner fort facing the steepest part of the mountain, covered by an outer fort, defending the approaches from the north and north-west.

GOA

Portuguese India has a character and ambience quite unlike the rest of the country, a product of the melding of European and Indian cultures over many generations.

Until 1962 Goa was a Portuguese colony. It is 3,496 sq. km (1,350 square miles) in area, with a beautiful coastline over 104 km (65 miles) long, including the small island of Anjidiva near Karwar.

Goa is mentioned as early as the 3rd century BC as part of the Mauryan Empire. In 1310 it fell to the Muslims, but in 1370 it was absorbed by Vijayanagara. In 1469 it was conquered by the Bahmani Sultans of Gulbarga and later passed to the Adil Shahi Sultans of Bijapur.

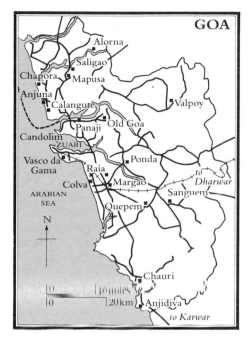

accelerated the decline of the city. In 1639 the Dutch attempted to seize Goa but failed. During the Napoleonic Wars British troops occupied Goa in 1800 and again in 1808.

Cocooned between the Western Ghats and the warm waters of the Arabian Sea, Goa became a charming colonial backwater. The towns and villages have a distinct Mediterranean atmosphere, with red-tiled roofs, narrow streets and brightly painted stucco houses, while the people bear witness to centuries of intermarriage between the Portuguese and Indians.

Panaji (Panjim or Nova Goa)
Map overleaf

Panaji (Panjim), the capital of the Union territory of Goa, Daman and Diu, is situated on the southern bank of the Mandovi river. The earliest reference to the town is in an inscription of a Kadamba king in 1170. Under Muslim rule the town was notable for its castle, built by Yusuf Adil Shah, and it was from here that the Bijapur forces offered such vigorous resistance to Albuquerque in 1510.

During the first century of Portuguese rule, Panaji was the temporary residence of the Viceroys and Governors on their arrival from Portugal, but in 1759 the Viceroys moved there permanently from Old Goa to escape the recurrent epidemics which plagued the old capital. By 1811 many of the administrative and state offices had also moved, including the Custom House, High Court and Chancery. In 1843 it was formally declared the capital of Portuguese India.

Panaji, with a population of about 40,000, is one of the smallest but most atmospheric of all the state capitals of India. It is laid out on a typical grid pattern, centred on a church set in a civic square. The river front extends from Gaspar Dias to the Mandovi Bridge in a

The Portuguese enclave was carved out by Affonso D'Albuquerque. Born in 1453, he was a veteran naval commander well over fifty years old by the time he attacked Goa. In November 1509 he became Governor of the Eastern Possessions and four months later, on 1 March 1510, he launched a successful attack on the fortress at Panaji. He was soon dislodged by the Adil Shahi forces of Bijapur, but on 25 November 1510 he returned, stormed the city and fortress and ordered a general massacre of Muslims. Over 6,000 men, women and children perished.

Albuquerque died on 15 December 1515, en route from Ormuz to Goa. His body was transferred to Lisbon, where it rests in the Church of Nossa Senhora da Graca. By the early 17th century Portuguese naval supremacy had been displaced by the English and their commercial pre-eminence was challenged by the English, French and Dutch. The activities of the Inquisition and the devastating epidemic of 1635

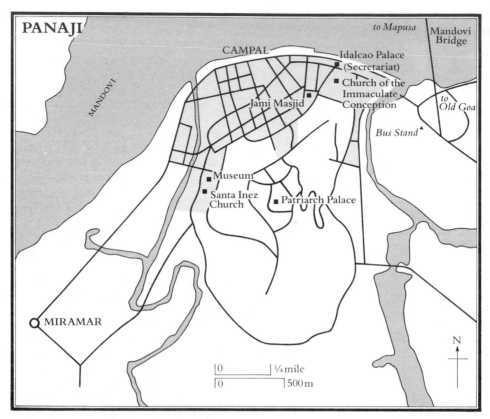

succession of open spaces, pretty vernacular houses with stucco walls and tiled roofs, and administrative buildings. The estuary is commanded by the picturesque forts of Aguada and Reis Magos.

Largo da Igreja or Church Square is the heart of the town. The **Church of the Immaculate Conception** (1541) is here, with a grand balustraded staircase and tall, twin towers, a local landmark for sailors. Designed in Portuguese Baroque style, it was modelled on the Church at Reis Magos. Originally a small chapel, it was renovated in 1619. The image of Our Lady of Fatima can be found on one of the altars. There are two major feasts at the church each year: on 13 May and 8 December. The bell in the tower is the second largest in Goa.

The **Shrine of Our Lady of Fatima**, in the compound of Don Basco's High School, was built in 1970.

The **Jami Masjid** lies near Church Square. It has no dome but can be identified by the star over the front entrance and the minarets. Built in the mid-18th century by Sulaiman Shet and Aba Shet, it was renovated in 1935.

The **Idalcao (Adil Shahi) Palace** or Secretariat faces the river, part of a sequence of handsome buildings. Once the castle of the Adil Shahi Sultans of Bijapur, it was rebuilt in 1615 by the Portuguese Viceroy Jeronimo de Azevedo. Until 1759 it was used as a residence by the Viceroy and in 1843 it became the Secretariat. To the southwest is the Palace of the Archbishop.

Much of the charm of Panaji lies in its narrow, cobbled streets lined by vernacular buildings with tiled roofs, overhanging eaves and intricate ironwork balconies, some of which date from the 17th century. The eastern part of the town is a middle-class residential area. A walk around the Christian area of **Fontainhas** is a pleasant, relaxing way to spend an afternoon.

The **Campal** or riverside boulevard is one of the most picturesque parts of the town, with delightful views across the river and glimpses of Aguada Fort in the distance.

At Cabo on the western tip of Panaji district is **Raj Niwas**, the official residence of the Lieutenant-Governor of the Union Territory of Goa, Daman and Diu. In 1594 a Franciscan convent was built here. In the 17th century it was selected as the temporary residence of the Archbishop of Goa owing to its salubrious position and panoramic view. Further changes were carried out by the Count of Rio Parde (1816–21) and, with the abolition of some of the religious orders in Goa, it was converted into a summer palace for the Governors.

British troops were garrisoned here between 1779 and 1813 to defend Goa from the French. The Raj Niwas is a large building of mud and laterite set in landscaped gardens.

Old Goa (Goa Velha)

The 8-km (5 mile) journey from the new to the old capital is a pleasant drive. The road from Panaji to Old Goa passes the Fountain of Banguinim, which once supplied water to the old capital. (For the sacred Hindu buildings see Volume I.)

Old Goa, once the 'Rome of the East', a fabulous city where East and West met, is now little more than a village. Once it rivalled Lisbon in size and splendour. Even before the arrival of the Portuguese, it was a thriving city, the second capital of the Adil Shahi Sultans of Bijapur, a vast complex of mosques, temples and fortifications. Today only a small fragment of the old gateway to the Sultan's palace survives; the rest dates from the Portuguese occupation.

The town lies on the banks of the River Mandovi. Once it was the first Christian colony in the Indies, with a population of 200,000 in 1565, but its site was afflicted by recurrent epidemics. It is now a city of ruins. Here, set picturesquely among groves of coconut palms,

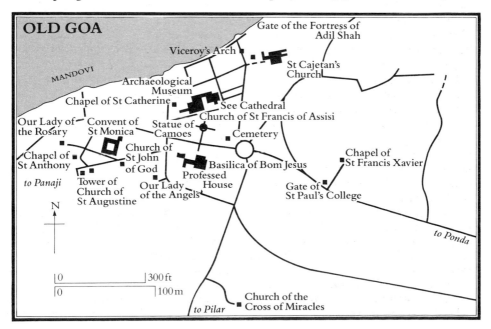

457

are some outstanding Portuguese buildings. It is difficult to visualize the ancient maritime splendour of Old Goa as so many of the most important buildings have disappeared.

The city was protected by a continuous fortified wall. Enclosed within lay a rich and prosperous city. West of the present Chapel of St Catherine was Ribeira Grande or the Great Embankment, which housed the mint, gun foundry, arsenal and workshops, together with the Archbishop's Prison, Aljube, Chapel of St Martin, College of St Bonventure and the Royal Hospital. To the right of St Catherine's Quay was Ribeira das Gales, where great galleys were built. Next was the Terreiro Grande, the commercial and administrative centre, including the Viceroy's Palace and Custom House. East was the great market and to the south, the town of Goa, approached through the Viceroy's Arch.

The **Viceroy's Arch** lies a short way from the modern jetty, which was the principal landing-place of Old Goa. It was built in black stone as a Centennial Memorial to Vasco da Gama, to commemorate his discovery of the sea route to India, under the orders of his grandson, the Governor Francisco da Gama (1597–1600). It was designed as a triumphal arch and was decorated on the occasion of the entry of every new Viceroy. On the right-hand side is an inscription, 1656, the date of Portuguese emancipation from Spanish domain. In the niche at the top of the arch is a statue of Vasco da Gama; behind is a statue of the *Argonaut*. The arch was restored in 1954.

To the left of the Viceroy's Arch is the **Gate of the Fortress of Adil Shah**. Also constructed in black stone, it comprises a lintel carried on moulded pillars, flanked by the remains of perforated stone screens. Situated on a low plinth, it is purely Hindu in form and style and was probably built by Sabaji, the Hindu ruler of Goa before the Muslim conquest of 1471. The palace, demolished in 1920,

was occupied by the Adil Shahi Sultans of Bijapur prior to the acquisition of Goa by the Portuguese in 1510.

From 1554 to 1695 the Palacio de Fortaleza or Palace of the Fortress was the residence of the Portuguese Viceroys. It faced a large square surrounded by beautiful houses and was the most conspicuous building in the city. It is reputed that the walls of the palace were decorated with paintings of Portuguese ships that had sailed to India since the time of Vasco da Gama. In front of the palace stood the High Court, flanked by the Chief Jail or Tronco and, to the left, the royal magazines.

The **See Cathedral** or Cathedral of St Catherine is the biggest of the churches in Old Goa and the largest Christian church in Asia. Commenced in 1562, the main body of the building was completed by 1619, but it was not until 1652 that the altars were finished. The cathedral was built for the Dominicans from the proceeds of a sale of Crown property. It is 76 m (250 ft) long, 54·8 m (180 ft) wide and the façade is 35·3 m (116 ft) high.

The Cathedral is a magnificent exercise in European Renaissance architecture. The principal façade faces east. There are three porticos and three naves. In the centre of the middle portico is an inscribed memorial slab carrying the papal insignia. Externally, it is designed in a Tuscan Ionic style; internally, it is Corinthian. Originally, there were two towers, but the southern tower collapsed in 1776. The remaining tower houses the Golden Bell, cast at Cuncolim in 1652.

The interior is stunning. It is divided by two rows of massive pillars into a nave and two large side aisles. The ceiling is vaulted. To the right of the entrance is an octagonal baptismal font made of a single block of granite. Here St Francis Xavier is reported to have baptized hundreds of followers in 1542. To the left is a large painting of St Christopher carrying the Infant Jesus.

Turning right there are four chapels: to St Anthony, St Bernard, the Cross of Miracles and the Holy Spirit. The cross in the third chapel is alleged to grow in size.

On the left are four more chapels: to Nossa Senhora de Necessidades, St Sebastian, the Blessed Sacrament and Nossa Senhora de Boa Vida. The Chapel of the Blessed Sacrament has a beautiful decorated altar.

Beyond, in the transept, are six altars. In the vestry are pictures of St Catherine and the Twelve Apostles. The High Altar terminates the vista down the nave with an elaborately carved and gilded altarpiece, richly adorned with pillars, pilasters and engravings. It has three niches in the centre, with alcoves the vilin t containing images of St Catherine, Nossa Senhora d'Assumpçao and Christ Cruci-fied. On either side of the altarpiece are images of St Peter and St Paul and four engravings depicting the martyrdom of St Catherine.

South-east of the Cathedral stood the **Palace of the Inquisition**, a fearful complex of dungeons and prisons. From the terraced roof of the Cathedral, the most dreadful sights could be seen when the great cathedral bell tolled the cel-ebration of an auto-da-fé. Once a splen-did edifice with a magnificent hall and vaulted front, nothing now remains. Between 1561 and 1774 over 16,172 cases were tried here by the Inquisition.

West of the See Cathedral lies the former Palace of the Archbishop, which links with the **Convent of St Francis of Assisi**, built by Franciscan friars in 1517 and restored in 1762 and 1765. The entrance portico is a fine example of Portuguese Gothic or Manueline archi-tecture. The Convent is now an Archaeological Museum, which houses portraits of former Viceroys and sundry other artefacts.

The **Church of St Francis of Assisi** is attached to the Convent. It is one of the most interesting buildings in Goa. A church was built here in 1521. It is a marvellous repository of ecclesiastical art of the period. Externally, it is Tuscan in style. In a niche on the façade is a statue of St Michael. The church faces west, with a central nave and three altars or chapels on each side and a choir and two altars in the transept beside the High Altar. The nave is rib-vaulted. The inter-nal walls separating the chapels have frescoes of elaborate floral patterns in Indian style.

Over the tabernacle in the High Altar is a large statue of St Francis of Assisi and another of Christ Crucified. Flanking the altar are paintings on wood depicting scenes from the life of St Francis. The floor is paved with carved tombstones.

A short distance from the Cathedral is the huge **Basilica of Bom Jesus**, facing a large central square, more popularly known as the Church of St Francis Xavier. The Basilica of Bom Jesus (lit-erally Good Jesus) is a spectacular build-ing. Erected in 1594 and consecrated in 1605, its principal façade faces west. It is a Renaissance Baroque building combin-ing Ionic, Doric, Corinthian and compo-site styles in an imaginative and original manner. Crowning the stone façade are the letters IHS: '*Iaeus Hominum Salvator*'.

The church is cruciform in plan, sup-ported by three buttresses on the north-ern side. Built of laterite, the exterior is divided into four stages. The lowest has three elegant entrances, above which are three large windows, then three circular windows culminating in a richly carved central gable with arabesques. The bell tower is at the rear.

The interior of the church is plainly detailed in a Corinthian style. On each side are three bays of windows rising above each other. Note the plaques on the columns supporting the choir; they record the construction of the church in Latin and Portuguese.

In the centre of the nave is the ceno-taph of the benefactor of the church, Don Jeronimo Mascarenhas, who died in

1593. It is a splendidly elaborate affair in richly gilded bronze, carried on two lions.

The wooden pulpit is also lavishly carved with figures of Jesus, the Evangelists and the four doctors of the church. Around the base are seven figures. In the transept on the north side is the chapel of the Blessed Sacrament.

The **Chapel and Tomb of St Francis Xavier** lie on the south side of the transept.

St Francis Xavier was born on 7 April 1506 in Navarre in Spain. A former pupil of St Ignatius Loyola, founder of the Jesuit order, he was ordained in 1537 and came to Goa in 1542. He spent the next few years nursing the sick and spreading the gospel in south India. On hearing of the baptized but uninstructed Christians of Malacca, he went east, where he taught and preached. After a brief return to Goa in 1547, he left once more for Malacca and from there sailed on to Japan. In September 1551 he was appointed Provincial of all the Jesuits east of the Cape of Good Hope. A year later he left Goa once more for the east, but at Sancian Island, off the coast of China, he fell sick and died in September 1552 at the age of forty-six. His body was interred at Sancian, but later moved to Malacca and then to Goa. In 1613 it was transferred to the Professed House. After canonization it was removed to the Basilica.

The **Tomb of St Francis Xavier** was the gift of Grand Duke Cosmos III of Tuscany. Carved by the sculptor Givonni Batista Foggini, it took ten years to complete and was erected in 1698. It consists of three tiers of sarcophagi in jasper and marble, the base, the mausoleum and the casket. On the middle section are bronze plaques depicting scenes from his life and work. There are two cherubs of Carrara alabaster in each corner.

The silver casket, a magnificent specimen of Italian and Indian art, is a reliquary containing the sacred remains of the saint. The casket is divided on each side into seven panels. There is a cross on top with two angels. In front of the casket is a fine silver statue of the saint.

The interior of the chapel is richly ornamented with carved detail and paintings illustrating scenes from the life of St Francis. One of the paintings in the top row shows his death at Sancian. The corridor from the chapel to the sacristy is decorated with nine beautiful paintings. The entrance to the vaulted sacristy is via a splendid door carved in relief with the figures of four saints.

Every ten years the holy relics are displayed to the public on the anniversary of the saint's death. The next exposition is in 1994. There is a modern art gallery next to the church.

The **Professed House of the Jesuits** (1589) is a handsome, two-storey laterite building covered in plaster and connected to the Basilica. From here devoted Jesuit missionaries travelled throughout the East. It was damaged by fire in 1663 and extensively reconstructed in 1783. Today it is used as priests' quarters.

The **Chapel of St Catherine**, situated to the west of the Church of St Francis of Assisi and near the gate of the old Muslim city wall, was built in 1510 by Albuquerque to celebrate his conquest of Goa. In 1550 it was enlarged by Jorge Cabral, the Governor. The façade, in Renaissance style, carries a statue of Our Lady. There is a statue of Our Lady of Piety over the altar.

The **Royal Hospital** lay beside the Chapel, facing north. It was established in 1510 by Albuquerque for the care and benefit of his soldiers, but later it was handed over to the Holy House of Mercy. The hospital was a fine two-storey building bearing the royal arms, which are now in the Museum. Nothing now remains of the structure.

To the west lay the **Arsenal**. This was demolished in 1869. Some of the cannon manufactured here can still be found in

460

the fortresses of Goa, Daman and Diu.

On the east side of the road leading to the Gomanteshwar Temple in the city square is the **Old Pillory**, a single shaft of basalt which had iron rings affixed to it.

Opposite the See Cathedral are the **Convent** and **Church of St Cajetan**, dedicated to Our Lady of Divine Providence. They were built by Italian friars of the Theatine Order, who were sent to India by Pope Urban III to preach Christianity in the kingdom of Golconda. The Convent was built in 1649 and the Church in 1651.

Architecturally, the church is designed in the style of St Peter's, Rome, with a Corinthian order externally and internally. It is crowned by a dome and two low towers. Faced in plastered laterite, the church is vaulted and designed on the plan of a Greek Cross. The nave terminates in an apse and aisles marked by four massive piers faced with Corinthian pilasters which carry the base of the drum of the dome. On the threshold is inscribed in bold letters '*Domus mea Domus Orationis*': 'My House is a House of Prayer.'

Inside are three chapels to the left and three to the right. The main altar in the sanctuary is profusely carved and gilded. The altars in the chapels are treated in a similar manner. Note the elaborate pulpit with the carved figures of a bull, an eagle, an angel and a lion. In the crossing is a square platform beneath which is a well.

To the south of this church, on the main road leading to Ponda, is the **Gate of the College and Church of St Paul**. The College was founded in 1541 to instruct converts in arts and sciences and to train them as preachers in their own languages. It possessed a vast library and in 1556 boasted the only printing-press in the East. Later it was abandoned in favour of a less pestilential location. Only the Doric façade of the church remains.

In the grounds of the College is the **Chapel of St Francis Xavier**, founded in 1545. The present chapel, in a Doric style, was built in 1884.

On the hill opposite the Basilica of Bom Jesus, en route to the Church of Our Lady of the Rosary, is a vast three-storey building of laterite, square in plan but with a large inner courtyard surrounded by a cloister, cells and halls. There is a vaulted ceiling and painted ornament illustrating scenes from the Bible.

The **Church and Convent of St Monica** is the oldest and biggest in eastern Asia. It was completed in 1627 as a retreat for cloistered nuns. Externally, it is designed in a free combination of Tuscan, Corinthian and composite styles. Inside it is Doric and composite. Over the entrance to the convent is a coat of arms.

Immediately to the right is the **Convent of St John of God** (1685), founded by the Order of Hospitallers of St John of God to care for the sick. The church was commenced in 1691 and completed in 1721. The Convent was rebuilt in 1953.

The **Church of the Cross of Miracles** lay on the southern perimeter of Old Goa. It was built by the Carmelites in 1619 and rebuilt in 1674. Only the façade remains.

On the Holy Hill, west of Bom Jesus, is the tower of the **Church of St Augustine**, now in ruins. The church and former convent were erected in 1512 and reconstructed in 1597 and 1602. Designed in a Gothic style, the church once boasted eight richly adorned chapels and two high towers. The vault collapsed in 1842, burying a colossal image of St Augustine. In 1931 the façade and main tower fell.

Nearby is the **Chapel of St Anthony**, the national saint of Portugal. Built in 1543, it has a vaulted chancel with four frescoes on the walls. It closed in 1835, reopened in 1894 and was restored by the Portuguese government in 1961.

The **Chapel of Our Lady of the Rosary** commands a panoramic view from the summit of Holy Hill. From here Albuquerque directed the battle against the Adil Shahi troops in 1510. The chapel was built in 1526 and belongs to the earliest Manueline period of church architecture in Goa. Built of laterite and faced in Ionic plasterwork, it has a two-storey portico, a single tower and cylindrical turrets each side of the façade. Note the Bijapur-style carved designs in the stonework of the tomb to the right of the main altar.

The remaining villages and towns in Goa are dealt with alphabetically for ease of reference.

Alorna

This quiet village across the Chapora river has an interesting **Fort** to the northeast of Pernem, on the right bank of the river. The fort was seized from the Bhonsla by the Portuguese in 1746, as a result of which the Governor was made Marquis of Alorna. Today it is in a dilapidated state.

Anjidiva Island

Anjidiva Island lies about 8 km (5 miles) south-west of Karwar. It is irregular in shape, measuring 1·6 km (1 mile) by 266 m (867 ft). It is a steep, rugged island with a small harbour on the eastern side.

Anjidiva was the centre of Portuguese activity in the area before they captured Goa in 1510. After this it ceased to have any importance and declined.

The **Fort** was built in 1682 and was briefly threatened by Sambhaji in the same year. For many years it was used as a penal settlement for Goa and Diu. On 19 December 1961 a confrontation took place here between the Portuguese and Indian navies.

The **Church of Nossa Senhora das Brotas** was reconstructed with the fort in 1682.

Anjuna

This small village lies about 11·2 km (7 miles) from Mapusa. **Chapora Fort** is in one of the most beautiful and unspoilt parts of Goa. Perched on a rocky hill to the south of the River Chapora, it was commenced in 1717 by the Viceroy and completed by his successor, Francisco José de Sampaio e Castro. It was designed to defend the estuary. Although captured by the Sawant Bhonsla of Sawantwadi in 1739, it was surrendered again two years later.

Nearby palm-fringed Vagator Beach is a wonderful tropical retreat much favoured by Europeans and hippies.

Calangute

This has one of the most famous beaches in the country and was one of the principal centres of Western counter-culture in India in the 1960s and 1970s. There are no monuments of any consequence.

Candolim

The most important monument is the **Fort of Aguada**. This encloses the peninsula on the northern side of Goa Bay. Built in 1612, there is a statue of a freedom fighter outside, erected since 1961.

The fortifications skirt the seashore. At the centre is a citadel with a circular lighthouse tower which carries a huge clock and bell, taken from the Convent of St Augustine.

Within the citadel is a large cistern. There are two powder rooms, two magazines, two prisons, four barracks, a chapel and several staff quarters. Note the inscription over one of the old fountains cut from a rock in 1624.

Today the fort is used as a Civil Jail and is well maintained. Several nationalist leaders were imprisoned here by the Portuguese.

462

Colva

Colva is renowned for its world-famous beach and also for the miraculous image of the Infant Jesus in the local church.

The **Church of Our Lady of Mercies** is situated just off the Margao-Colva road and cannot be missed as it is a huge edifice. Founded in 1581, it is famous for the miraculous image of Jesus alleged to have been found by a Jesuit priest on the coast of Africa after a shipwreck. In October there is a feast, which is a popular attraction.

Mapusa

Mapusa is both a route centre in northern Goa and an important trading centre.

The **Church of Our Lady of Miracles** was built in 1594 and rebuilt in 1719. It was destroyed by fire in 1838 and rebuilt again. Over the altar is the image of Nossa Senhora de Milagres, which is venerated by Hindus as well as Christians.

Margao

Margao lies about 40·2 km (25 miles) south-east of Panaji. It is the capital of Salcete district and the biggest commercial centre in Goa, a pleasant provincial settlement raised to the rank of a town by royal decree in 1778. It has a strong Portuguese flavour.

The **Church of the Holy Spirit** is impressive. Built in 1565 on the ruins of a Hindu temple, it was sacked by Muslims in 1589 and rebuilt in 1675. The main altar is dedicated to the Holy Spirit, one of the side altars to St Roque.

Ponda

Ponda is the headquarters of a local district and a route centre. Located about 35·4 km (22 miles) south-east of Panaji, it is distinctly different in character from the Latinized coastal areas. (For the sacred Hindu buildings see Volume I.)

The **Fort**, which is now in ruins, is the main building of interest. It was founded by the Adil Shahi rulers of Bijapur, but destroyed by the Portuguese in 1549. Shivaji conquered the town in 1675 and rebuilt it, but it fell to the Portuguese in 1682–4.

Raia

Raia lies on the left bank of the River Zuari, about 51·4 km (32 miles) on the way from Panaji to Margao.

The **Fort of Rachol** lies on the left bank of the Zuari river, opposite the village of Siroda. It predates the Portuguese occupation and was attacked frequently by Bijapur and the Marathas. It was strengthened and repaired in 1604 and again eighty years later. There is an inscription of 1684 on the gate.

After the Maratha campaigns of 1740, it was repaired by the Marquis of Alorna in 1745. Most of the buildings have been demolished. Only the Church and Seminary remain.

The **Church of Nossa Senhora das Neves** (1576) was expanded and rebuilt between 1584 and 1596. There are five altars. The **Seminary and Church of Rachol** was established here in 1606 under the auspices of King Dom Sebastio, whose portrait can be seen in the main room. It was used as a Jesuit College until 1762 and boasted a printing-press, but after the expulsion of the Jesuits from Portuguese territory, it became a Diocesan Seminary. It is a large, turreted building. The Church of St Ignatius Loyola is attached to the seminary. The vestry, which is vaulted, contains some fine paintings.

Reis Magos

Reis Magos, situated opposite Panaji across the Mandovi river, is an ancient town of considerable charm.

Erected on the ruins of an older strong point, the **Fort** was built in 1551 by Don Afonso de Noronha. It was extended and altered in 1704. The underground vaulted casements were built in the late 16th century. Situated on a high hill, the fort commands a fine view of the river and sea. It still retains nine cannon and a lighthouse.

To the east is the **Church of Reis Magos**, dedicated to the three Magi, Gaspar, Balthazar and Melchior. It is reputed to have been built on the ruins of a Hindu temple in 1550 by Franciscans. The main façade is superb, with some excellent carved detail and armorial bearings. In the sanctuary is the grave of Dom Luis de Athaide, twice Viceroy of Portuguese India. The old Franciscan college is now in ruins.

Saligao

Saligao or Salgaon lies about 6·4 km (4 miles) north-east of Mapusa. A dirt road leads to the **Church of Mae de Deus** (1867), a beautiful Gothic building. In the compound wall are two statues of Our Lady of Fortune and Mae de Deus.

The **Seminary** is situated on a low hill near the village. It is a large modern building commenced in 1937 and completed in 1952.

Sanguem

This district headquarters, 75·6 km (47 miles) south-east of Panaji, is a somnolent backwater.

The **Church of Our Lady of Miracles** stands in the centre of the town. It was built in 1763 and repaired in 1857.

The **Jami Masjid** is a 19th-century mosque, renovated in 1959. It has four minarets and two elegant turrets crowned by kiosks.

Vasco da Gama

Vasco da Gama lies on the left bank of the Zuari river, close to Marmugao harbour. It is a pleasant, tree-lined town.

The village and port of Marmugao lie 8 km (5 miles) south of Panaji. They are the site of an attempt in the late 17th century to abandon Goa and concentrate the seat of government here. In 1684–5 the foundations of a new capital were laid, under the supervision of the Portuguese Viceroy, the Count of Alvor. Work stopped a year later. Over the next fifteen years orders were received repeatedly to resume work, to demolish the public buildings of Goa and to use the materials for the new capital. Under Caetano de Mello e Castro the works were pursued vigorously. Several buildings, including a palace and a hospital, were completed and the Viceroy himself resided here in 1703. By a royal edict dated 8 March 1712 work was stopped and never resumed, although during the Maratha emergency of 1739, women, children and nuns were evacuated here.

The principal buildings are now all in ruins, but a fine old church survives, together with the fort.

According to an inscription over the gate, the **Fort** was built in 1624. It covers a huge area – the walls are over 9·6 km (6 miles) in circumference – and in its heyday it was one of the most important fortresses in western India.

Today the port and harbour are the focus of economic activity in Goa.

In the heart of the town **St Andrew's Church** has a statue of the saint dating from 1570. The principal façade is in Gothic style.

GOLCONDA

Golconda was the centre of a rich and powerful state formed on the disintegration of the Bahmani kingdom in the early 16th century. It is of outstanding interest for both its fort and the royal tombs, which represent the third and final phase of the Deccan style of Islamic architecture. A full day should be

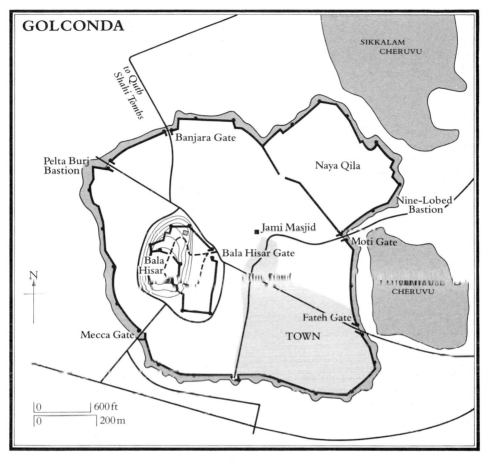

GOLCONDA

allowed to tour the monuments at a reasonable pace.

Golconda was a well-known fort and commercial centre throughout the 13th and 14th centuries. It was described as a flourishing city by Marco Polo as early as 1292, but it was not until the emergence of the Qutb Shahi Sultans in the 16th century that the town became a dynastic centre and capital.

In 1363 the Rajas of Warangal ceded Golconda to the Bahmani kings and in 1512 they in turn lost control to Sultan Quli, who assumed the title Qutb Shah and made Golconda his capital. With the fall of Vijayanagara in 1565, its importance increased and it flourished until 1687, when it fell to Aurangzeb. The city had a reputation for fabulous diamonds.

It was the centre for the cutting and polishing of gems from neighbouring mines, including the legendary Koh-i-Noor diamond, now part of the British Crown Jewels.

The kingdom reached its height under Ibrahim Qutb Shah between 1550 and 1580. In 1565 an alliance between the four Muslim sultans of the Deccan led to the final defeat and collapse of the Vijayanagara forces, but the alliance rapidly disintegrated and by 1569 there were struggles with the Adil Shahis. Ten years later the allied forces of Golconda and Ahmadnagar ravaged Bijapur. The end came in 1687, after repeated attacks from the Marathas and Mughal forces, when the last Sultan, Abul Hasan Qutb Shah, was taken prisoner to Daulatabad. After

1687 Golconda–Hyderabad became the residence of the new Mughal governor.

The **Fort** lies about 8·5 km (5 miles) west of Hyderabad on an isolated granite hill. It predates the Qutb Shahi dynasty and incorporates earlier fabric, including megalithic masonry. The outer curtain wall is 4·8 km (3 miles) in circumference, with eighty-seven bastions at the angles, some of which retain 17th-century ordnance. Roughly elliptical in shape, the plan is similar to that at Bijapur, but at Golconda there is a later extension to the north-east, built in 1724. In the north-east corner is the corrugated Nine-Lobed Bastion or Naya Qila, built in 1624.

Three formidable lines of curtain walls with crenellations and merlons invest the town, one within the other. The first surrounds the town, the second double wall encloses the base of the hill and the third incorporates boulders and other natural features of the landscape. Of the eight original gates, only the Fateh, Banjara, Mecca and Jamali gates are used.

Fateh Gate is the main entrance to the town, approached via a curved passage through a barbican and commanded by box machicolations and guardrooms. The teak entrance gates are spiked with iron as a defence against elephants and reinforced with internal bars. Over the pointed arch is a carved protective Hindu deity. Beyond the entrance is an open court, defended at either end by doors, machicolations and loopholes.

Mecca Gate lies at the south-west of the curtain wall, with an outer and inner gate at right-angles to each other and a courtyard in between. The outer gateway is approached through a barbican and the approach enfiladed from loopholes. The gates are plated with iron spikes.

The **Banjara Gate**, to the north-west, also has a barbican, but the outer and inner doors are protected by a flat, vaulted, covered passage flanked by large guard chambers covered with cupolas.

The **Bala Hisar** or citadel occupies the crown of the hill and is approached via a winding set of steps through the second and third curtain walls. Before the remarkable Bala Hisar Gate is a triumphal arch and an outer mantlet with a polyhedral centre and side wings. Over the side access are figures of animals in low relief. The gateway beyond is closed by a two-leaved door and a long passage. Many of the battlements have been adapted subsequently to permit artillery fire. Half-way to the summit is a large well and at the top of the hill are the ruins of the old royal apartments and the white-washed Hall of Justice. The buildings within the fort are arranged to reflect sound from the entrance gate to the citadel, but not in other directions, so that a shout or clap from the Fateh Gate can be heard at the summit.

The fort was besieged by Aurangzeb's army in 1686. It only fell a year later when a traitor opened one of the gates and allowed the Mughal armies to enter.

Within the fort are a number of notable buildings. Between the Fateh Gate and Musa Burj, along the wall to the north-east, are the ruins of palaces, of which the **Diwan's Palace** is best preserved. On the main street is the **Jami Masjid**, built by Quli Qutb Shah in 1518 and the site of his assassination in 1543. Constructed in a plain but robust style, the prayer hall is entered through an impressive domed entrance porch. The interior comprises five by three domed bays. The central mihrab is carved with a chain motif.

Close to and east of the entrance to the Bala Hisar are the **Habshi Kamans**, elegant arched structures which once housed the royal Abyssinian guard, and the Naubat Khana or Drum House. The adjacent terrace marks the graves of the loyal guards who died in the sack of Golconda in 1687. The **Parade Ground** lies below the eastern wall and is commanded by the ruins of a mosque, from where the king reviewed his armies and where they saluted their king, and also God, simultaneously.

466

Inside and to the right of the entrance gate to the **Bala Hisar** is the **Nagena Bagh**, a derelict garden commemorating **Abdur Razzaq Lari**, a faithful general who fell mortally wounded here in 1687.

Opposite is the old armoury or **Sileh Khana**. Beyond, to the left, are the **ruins** of the old palaces and factories, some still five or six storeys high, with huge, dark, vaulted cellars. They are of considerable architectural importance, colossal masonry structures of great sophistication and ingenuity.

On the way to the citadel and close to the well is a platform from which a deep underground passage runs into the heart of the hill. Opposite are the ruins of the Ambar Khana or Royal Treasury, inscribed 1642 but probably older. Further up the terrace is a mosque, the Ibrahim Qutb Shahi Masjid.

At the summit in one corner of the ruined palace is a large, sealed, circular opening, reputed to be the entrance to a secret passage emerging at Gosha Mahal, 8 km (5 miles) away. To the west a stone staircase leads to the flat roof of the courtyard. At the southern end is the Bala Hisar, on the roof of which is a throne. Here the sultans spent leisurely hours being serenaded by the ladies of the harem from the baradaris of Taramati and Pemamati, built on two distant hillocks.

At the entrance of the Bala Hisar to the north of the Habshis Kamans is the **Safa Mosque**. To the front of the mosque are the ruins of **Ashurkhana**. Elephants were kept in the adjoining **Feelkhana**.

On the road to the west is the Fateh Rabbar Top or Guide to Victory cannon, a huge piece of artillery used by Aurangzeb against Golconda in 1686–7.

The **Katora Hauz** (1560) is reputed to be the largest masonry tank in the world. Built by Ibrahim Qutb Shah, it is fed by underground pipes and lies between the Banjara Gate and the royal tombs.

North-west of the main fort is the **Naya Qila** or New Fort, built on a rocky outcrop by Abdullah Qutb Shah in 1724 to deny its occupation to the Mughal armies. Within the fort is a baradari at the centre of a complex of tanks and fountains, a beautiful resort much frequented by Asaf Jah II.

The **Royal Tombs** of Golconda lie about 549 m (1,784 ft) to the north-west of the fort. They contain the entire dynasty with the exception of two who died in exile. Located on a low plateau, they form a fascinating collection of Islamic funerary architecture. The dynastic necropolis is in the same tradition as that at Bidar. All share a common form: an onion dome carried on a cube surrounded by an arcade with rich ornamental details. Corner minarets with the guldasta motif enrich the corners of the upper and lower cubes carrying the domes. The construction of each tomb was supervised and inspected by each sultan during his lifetime.

The tombs are built of local granite and plaster. Originally, they were faced in decorative glazed colours and inscribed with verses from the Quran. The external facings have almost disappeared but traces remain on the eastern wall of Ibrahim Qutb Shah's tomb, for instance. Green and turquoise prevailed. The complex was restored by Sir Salar Jung I, who built a wall enclosing most of the mausolea.

The tour begins at the **Badshahi Hammam**, a mortuary bath and the oldest monument in the complex. The body of the deceased king was placed on the central platform and washed before burial. The twelve small tanks symbolize the twelve imams of the Shia sect.

Immediately to the west of the Hammam is the **Tomb of Sultan Quli Qutb Shah** (1512–43), the founder of the Qutb Shahi dynasty, murdered by his son Jamshid at the age of ninety. His black tombstone is engraved in the finest Naskh style of Persian calligraphy, including his popular title, Bade Malik, the Older Lord. The tombs of his sons lie

467

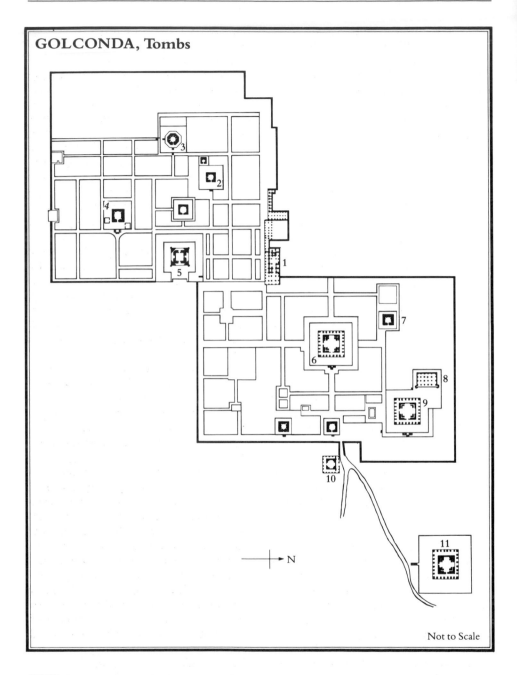

GOLCONDA, Tombs

Not to Scale

KEY

1 Badshahi Hammam, Mortuary Bath

2 Tomb of Sultan Quli Qutb Shah (1512–43)

3 Tomb of Jamshid Quli Qutb Shah (1543–50)

4 Tomb of Ibrahim Qutb Shah (1550–80)

5 Tomb of Muhammad Quli Qutb Shah (1580–1612)

6 Tomb of Muhammad Qutb Shah (1612–26)

7 Tomb of Pemamati (mistress of Abdullah Qutb Shah, died 1662)

8 Mosque (1667)

9 Tomb of Hayat Bakhsh Begum (1667)

10 Tomb of Abul Hasan Tana Qutb Shah (1672–87)

11 Tomb of Abdullah Qutb Shah (1626–72)

on the terrace of the mausoleum, which is 51 m (168 ft) high.

Next in succession is the **Tomb of Jamshid Quli Qutb Shah** (1550), who ruled from 1543 to 1550. This mausoleum lies south of his father's, a two-storey building with a single high roof but no inscription and a plain tombstone.

South-east is the **Tomb of Ibrahim Qutb Shah** (1580), whose reign spanned thirty years from 1550 to 1580. Between the two royal tombs are numerous smaller monuments. The tomb retains traces of its original colour scheme in enamel and hornblende with black basalt doorways. Only one of the four corner base pillars remains. On the terrace are the tombs of Muhammad Amin (1596) and his wife. A square, open pavilion contains the remains of Ibrahim's chamberlain, with an inscription recording a firman of the last of the Qutb Shahis, Abul Hasan Tana Shah.

The octagonal mausoleum north of Ibrahim Qutb Shah's is that of **Kulsum Begum** (1608), granddaughter of Muhammad Quli Qutb Shah. It is a plain, refined edifice with three tombstones for herself, husband and daughter.

The fifth ruler of Golconda, the poet-king Muhammad Quli Qutb Shah, founder of Hyderabad city, has the most spectacular **Tomb** of all (1612). It is 54·8 m (180 ft) high with a 18·2 m (60 ft) dome and robust granite pillars. An idgah forms an extensive enclosure next to the tomb.

The **Tomb of Muhammad Qutb Shah** (1626) lies north-east of his prede-

cessors, near the entrance to the compound. Traces of the original coloured enamel ornament can be seen here to advantage. It is in granite with vast pillars and arches hewn from two single stones. The mausoleum contains the tomb of Chand Bibi, daughter of Ibrahim Adil Shah of Bijapur, and other scions of the royal house. The tombs of Taramati and Pemamati (1663), paramours of Abdullah Qutb Shah, lie close by. The latter's tombstone carries the Persian inscription: 'From eternity was Pemamati a rose in the garden of paradise 1073.'

The **Tomb of Abdullah Qutb Shah** (1672) lies outside the enclosure built by Sir Salar Jung. It is a magnificent structure with richly ornamented domic and sinuous, convoluted merlons. The terrace has an arcade of seven arches to each side and corner minarets, on which vestiges of enamel remain.

The road to Hyderabad passes through a barren landscape with rocks weathered into extraordinary shapes.

At Karwar, on the road between Golconda and Purana Pul, is **Jham Singh's Temple of Balaji**. Over the main gate is a beautiful gopura.

The **Toli Masjid** (1671) is set on a raised platform approached by flights of steps, with an outer hall of five arched openings and an inner sanctum of three. The mosque built by Musa Khan, the chamberlain of Abdullah Qutb Shah, can be identified by its two elegant minarets.

Close to the Purana Pul is the **Mian Mishk Masjid** (1678), one of the most interesting mosques in the region. It stands at the end of a large courtyard lined with chambers which provided accommodation for travellers. It is called after its builder, an Abyssinian slave of Abul Hasan Tana Shah. The inscriptions over the east and west gates demonstrate the styles of calligraphy of different periods. It is a fine example of the Qutb Shahi style.

The **Kulsumpura Masjid** (early 17th

century) is situated near Mustaidpura in the district of Kulsumpura. It is a graceful building of considerable beauty, aptly named after the princess of the Qutb Shahi family whose tomb lies at Golconda.

The **Purana Pul** or Old Bridge was the first link across the Musi river between Golconda and the city of Hyderabad, lying to the south. Allegedly built in 1578 by Ibrahim Qutb Shah, it is over 183 m (600 ft) long with twenty-three arches leading to a gateway on the city side. In 1820 it was repaired by Sikander Jah. It was repaired again after the disastrous floods of 1908, when the ancient structure held fast.

GOOTY

51·5 km (32 miles) from Anantapur, the fort of Gooty lies 3·2 km (2 miles) from the railway station. Built between 1509 and 1530 on an immense outcrop of rock, the fort, which is 301 m (989 ft) above the plain, is approached by a tortuous path defended from the south-west by a single fortified gateway.

Once it was the stronghold of Murari Rao, the great Maratha guerrilla leader who joined Clive at Arcot in 1751. In 1776 it was besieged by Haidar Ali and was forced to capitulate after nine months. Later, during the Mysore campaign of 1799, the British captured the rock.

On one of the bastions overlooking a 91·4 m (300 ft) precipice is a small pavilion, Murari's seat, where the Maratha chief watched the spectacle of prisoners being hurled to their deaths on the rocks far beneath.

At the base of the hill is the **English Cemetery**, where Sir Thomas Munro was buried until 1831, when his body was removed to St Mary's Church, Madras. There is a **memorial well** (mid-19th century) to his memory and several interesting European tombs.

GULBARGA

Gulbarga lies 568 km (353 miles) from Bangalore and is a rapidly growing town of major historical importance.

Gulbarga was the first capital of the Bahmani kingdom of the Deccan (1347–1527), but in 1424 it was abandoned by Sultan Ahmad Shah Bahmani in favour of Bidar. The dynasty was founded by Hasan Gangu, who took the name of Bahman, and it dominated the affairs of the central Deccan for almost 200 years, before the kingdom disintegrated into five fragments: Ahmadnagar, Berar, Bidar, Bijapur and Golconda. In 1504 the city was occupied by Bijapur troops and, though recovered by Amir Barid ten years later, it was reconquered and held by the Adil Shahi kings until the Mughals invaded the Deccan.

The city lies on an undulating plain of rich black soil. Brooding over the landscape to the north-west is the **Fort**, which was originally built by Raja Gulchand and later strengthened by Ala-ud-Din Hasan Bahman Shah. It has fifteen towers but the double outer walls are in a poor state, although the main Citadel or **Bala Hisar** is well preserved. This is a formidable structure in the centre of the fort, with semicircular turrets on the sides and corners. The entrance is high up on the north wall, approached by a ruined flight of steps. On the citadel is a huge old cannon, 7·9 m (26 ft) long, with twenty pairs of iron rings attached.

There are two main entrances to the fort, in the middle of the east and west walls respectively. The outer barbican of the east gateway has disappeared and the old drawbridge has been replaced by a motor road over the moat. The **West Gate** is a massive structure, once protected by outworks. These project out as a hornwork beyond the fort and comprise four successive courts and doors. The outer door, with its twisted spikes, remains.

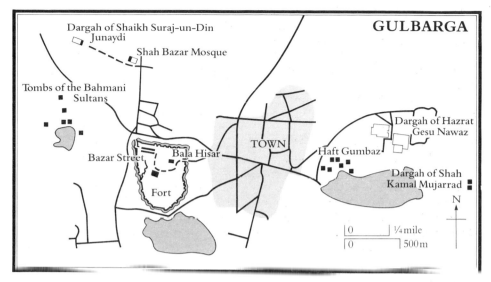

The **Jami Masjid** (1367), south of the Bala Hisar, resembles the Great Mosque at Cordoba in its form and dimensions. According to an inscription near the north entrance, the mosque was built by Rafi, son of Shams, the son of Mansur of Qazvin, but the scale of the building and much of the ornament suggest that it may have been completed during the reign of Firuz Shah, in the early 15th century. It measures 66 m (216 ft) by 53·6 m (176 ft) and is unique in India, as the whole area is covered by a large dome over the mihrab, by four corner domes and by seventy-five smaller ones. Great arches pierce the flanks on three sides.

Two groups of **Royal Tombs** are found in the city, one west of the fort, the other to the east of the city. These are of two types: single tombs, comprising simple square chambers with crenellations and corner turrets covered by a single dome; and double tombs, which are grander developments of the same style. All are about 30·5 m (100 ft) high. The tombs are robustly built but roughly finished, although some carry delicate tracery.

The tombs west of the fort stand in the fields a short distance beyond the west gate of the citadel. Those of Ala-ud-Din Hasan Bahman Shah (1358), Muhammad I (1375) and Muhammad II (1397) are typical of the series, with square domed chambers, sloping walls, low flattish domes and corner finials derived from Tughluq models.

Several of the sultans were buried east of the city in a complex known as the **Haft Gumbad** or Seven Domes. The tombs of the first two, Ala-ud-Din Mujahid (1378) and Dawud I, are similar to earlier Bahmani tombs, although the latter has two domed chambers linked to

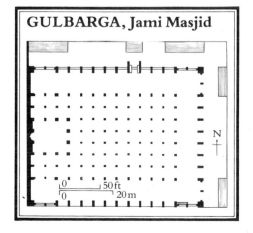

471

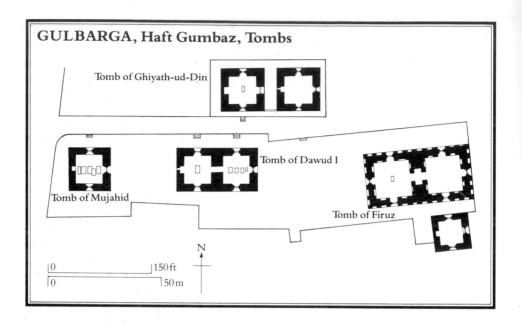

GULBARGA, Haft Gumbaz, Tombs

Tomb of Ghiyath-ud-Din

Tomb of Dawud I

Tomb of Mujahid

Tomb of Firuz

N

0   150 ft
0   50 m

form a double mausoleum. The **Tomb of Taj-ud-Din Firuz** (1422) is the masterpiece of the series. Monumentally conceived and elaborately ornamented, it is a thoroughly developed composition with geometric patterns in pierced masonry, bands of lotus decoration and arabesques and temple-like brackets supporting the angled eaves.

Set apart from the main tombs is the **Dargah of Hazrat Gesu Nawaz** (1321–1422) a saint of the Chishti family, venerated by both Hindus and Muslims, who came to Gulbarga in 1413. It is a large complex of tombs, mosques, madrasas, courtyards and gateways which conveys the influence of this Chishti saint on the history of south India. The buildings exhibit a range of styles over a period of two centuries. The tomb has two storeys divided into arched recesses, with an enriched parapet and a frieze of indented squares. Note the elaborate painted dome. The mother of pearl canopy over the grave is a later addition. In the south court is a small mosque built in the style of the Adil Shahi period, erected by Afzal Khan. The huge arch flanked by two

high towers is 17th century. Note the stucco medallions depicting heraldic animals carried on fish-like brackets.

South-east of this complex is the **Dargar of Shah Kamal Mujarrad**, another saint who lived at Gulbarga. This comprises a small, unadorned tomb in late-14th-century style, a mosque and two other structures. The mosque boasts the most elaborate stucco ornament to be found in Gulbarga, with multi-lobed bands of enriched plaster and roundels. The other buildings were probably sarais or rest-houses.

The **Langar ki Masjid** lies north of Gulbarga. It is a fine mosque and tomb, dating from the early 15th century and has an unusual pointed, ribbed vault over the prayer chamber and fine stucco ornament.

North-west of the fort close to the tombs of the earliest rulers, is the **Dargah of Shaikh Suraj-ud-Din Junaydi**, the spiritual preceptor of the first Bahmani sultans. There is a simple tomb in 14th-century style and a small plain mosque. The most interesting feature is the monumental gateway added by Yusuf Adil Khan, the founder of the Bijapur kingdom. It is framed by two tall minarets and has a long, arcaded frontage.

On rising ground to the west of the city is the Chor Gumbad, a tomb built in 1420 with a high dome, plain façades and miniature corner towers.

The principal commercial centre of Nehru Ganj lies about 4 km (2½ miles) from the railway station.

HINGOLI

297 km (185 miles) north-west of Hyderabad and 115 km (72 miles) south of Akola, Hingoli was an artillery cantonment between 1819 and 1903 and an old station of the Hyderabad Subsidiary Force.

The town was notable as a centre of thuggee. In 1833 Captain Sleeman captured many culprits here. The British cemetery is interesting, with numerous old tombs from 1829 onwards.

HYDERABAD *Map overleaf*

Hyderabad is the fifth largest city in India. An important centre of Islamic culture, it was the seat of the legendary Nizams of Hyderabad, rulers of one of the largest native states in India, the size of England and Scotland combined, second in area only to Kashmir. For generations a small Muslim minority ruled a predominantly Hindu population with guile and skill on British advice. On independence in 1947, Hyderabad declared itself independent and only acceded to union with India when invaded by Indian government troops.

The city was founded by the fifth ruler of Golconda, Muhammad Quli Qutb Shah, in 1591, eleven years after he ascended the throne. The city plan was prepared when the stars were most auspicious and, according to Ferishta, the historian, it was to be 'a replica of paradise itself'. It is a dusty, interesting city full of fine buildings. Paradise it is not.

Allegedly, the city is named after Haidar Mahal, a mistress of Muhammad Quli, but it was founded as Baghnagar, the city of gardens. It was laid out on a grid pattern with two main roads running north–south and east–west, at the intersection of which is the Char Minar. To the north lay the River Musi, to the south the Kohi-Tur Hill, west the fortress of Golconda and east the road to the coast. The city expanded to the east and on this road is the Dargah Hazrat Brahna Shah Sahab, one of the oldest Shia graveyards. Around the Char Minar, Muhammad Quli Qutb Shah built his royal palaces, with carved sandalwood details. These were destroyed during the Mughal conquest of 1687

The city was always a cosmopolitan crossroads, with Persian and Armenian merchants vying for space with local Hindu and Muslim traders. The city walls were not erected until 1724, when the Mughal governor, Mubariz Khan, began work. Completed in 1740, the walls once had fourteen gates and four posterns. Few sections now remain. Some were demolished as the city expanded and much was destroyed in the disastrous flooding of 1908. Of the gateways, only the Dabirpura Darwaza and the Purana Pol Darwaza have survived, the latter on the road from Char Minar to Golconda.

For the purpose of the tourist, the city can be divided into five sectors, with the new city of Hyderabad, on the north bank of the Musi river, forming the fifth.

There are four bridges across the river. In the east is the **Oliphant Bridge** (1831), built by Colonel James Oliphant of the Madras Engineers. Next is the **Afzal Ganj Bridge** or Naya Pul (New Bridge), which leads to the city station. To the west is the **Musallam Bridge**

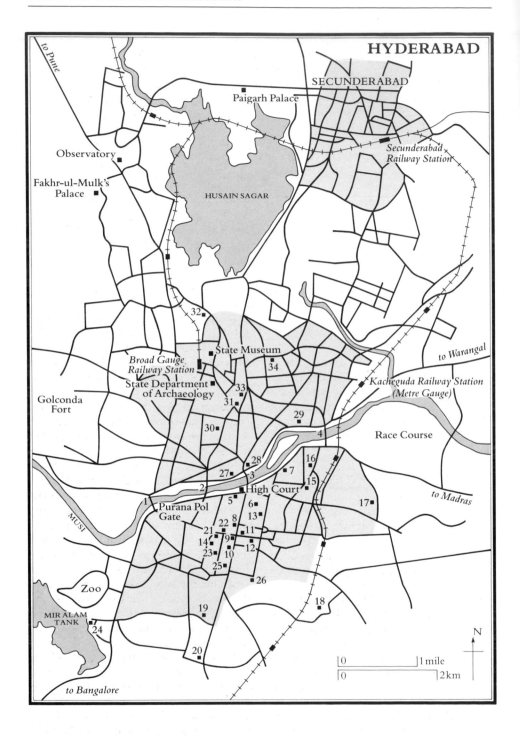

KEY

1 Old Bridge
2 Musallam Bridge
3 Afzul Bridge
4 Oliphant Bridge
5 Badshahi Ashurkhana
6 Diwan Deorhi
7 Salar Jang Museum
8 Charkaman
9 Mecca Masjid
10 Char Minar
11 Jami Masjid
12 Malwala Palace

13 Mir Alam Mandi
14 Husaini Alam Ashurkhana
15 Purana Haveli
16 Darush Shifa
17 Tomb of Michel Raymond
18 Dargah Hazrat Brahna Shah Saheb
19 Jahannuma Palace
20 Falaknuma Palace
21 Chowk Mosque and Clocktower
22 Lad Bazaar

23 Paigarh Palaces
24 New Idgah
25 Chaumhalla Palace
26 Daira Mir Momin
27 Osmania General Hospital
28 State Central Library
29 The Residency
30 Gosha Mahal
31 Moazam Jahi Market
32 Jubilee Hall
33 St George's Grammar School and Church
34 King Kothi

(1898) and then there is the **Old Bridge** (1578), close to the Purana Pol Gate.

Northern Sector (Old City)

The **High Court** (1916) stands close to the Afzal Ganj Bridge on the site of the old Champa Gate. Built in solid pink granite, it is a very impressive building in Mughal Saracenic style, enriched with panels of bas-relief decoration carved in red Agra sandstone, which is also used for the columns, arches, balustrading and chajja. The building has symmetrical convex domes finished in lapis lazuli blue glazed ware with gilded finials and a monumental central archway, 17·7 m (58 ft) high in the Mughal style, on the river frontage. It was the first of the great public buildings in the city designed by Vincent Esch (1876–1950).

Adjacent to the High Court is the former City High School for Boys (1917–18), also by Esch in a Perpendicular Mughal Saracenic style. It has an arched plinth of rough, dressed granite, the upper storeys faced in chunam.

92 m (300 ft) south of the bridge on Mahboob Shahi Road is the **Badshahi Ashurkhana** (1592–6), the royal house of mourning. It is one of the few surviving buildings from Muhammad Quli Qutb Shah's original layout and one of the oldest imambaras in India. The inner hall is in Qutb Shahi style. The outer, enriched with timber colonnades, was added by Nizam Ali Khan (1762–1802). The enamel tile mosaics (1611) in Persian style, some of the best of their kind, are comparable to those of Lahore and Multan.

The **Diwan Deorhi**, a run-down but interesting complex, was the residence of the diwans or prime ministers of the Nizams. The main buildings are the Nakkar Khana, Diwan Khana (Noor Mahal), Basanti Haveli, Aina Khana, Chini Khana, Putli Khana and Naya Makan. The first four, of which the **Diwan Khana** is the best, were built by Mir Alam. It is one of the finest examples of the Asaf Jahi style, with characteristic symmetrical indented arches, wooden pillars with carved peacocks and ceilings of delicate stone inlay, known as Khatimbandi-Lajwardi.

Mir Alam's successor, Munir-al-Mulk, made three additions: the Aina Mahal or House of Mirrors, the Chini Khana or House of Tiles and the Putli Khana or Hall of Statues. The **Chini Khana** is splendid, with mosaic walls and columns of china with inlaid ceilings. Sir Salar Jung I added the **Naya Makan**, which is in European style with semi-circular arches and high walls, and the

475

Nizam Bagh (1863), a beautiful garden with an English-style bungalow (1879).

The Salar Jung Museum is based on the collection of Salar Jung III (1899–1949). It lies in a modern building on the south bank of the river and has over 40,000 artefacts. There are fine collections of jade, jewellery, paintings, arms, ivory and carpets, including rooms of Western art with Dresden, Wedgwood, Sèvres and cut glass. The second floor accommodates an extensive collection of Persian, Arabic and other manuscripts.

Central Sector (Old City)

To the north of the Char Minar lies the **Charkaman** or Four Arches, in the centre of which is an octagonal cistern. The four arches were built in 1594 and once led to the parade ground of the royal palaces, which were destroyed in 1687. The northern arch, the Machli Kaman or First Arch, is the Qutb Shahi symbol of prosperity; the eastern, the Nakkar Khana-e-Shahi or House of Royal Drums, is known as the Black Arch. The western arch, the Daulat-Khana-e-Ali or Gateway of the Royal Residence, was once decorated with a large tapestry of gold cloth; the southern arch, facing the Char Minar, is known as the Fruit Vendors' Arch and was once the entrance to the royal mosque.

The central cistern or Gulzar Hauz is now dry and the piazza has been changed by the introduction of rows of shops in the antechambers of the old palaces.

The **Char Minar** or Four Towers (1591) is 56·7 m (186 ft) high and 30·5 m (100 ft) wide on each frontage. It is a masterpiece of the Qutb Shahi dynasty and was intended to mark the centre of the city. Each of the four façades has a familiar ogee arch of 11-m (36 ft) span, above which are diminishing arcaded storeys and richly ornamented cornices. The four corner minarets are capped by domes and finials and contain spiral staircases which lead to the upper levels. The first storey has a small mosque where a madrasa was situated. The second storey has a cistern. Designed as a ceremonial gateway leading to the original palace complex, the Char Minar was the platform from which important proclamations were read.

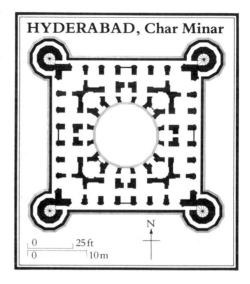

HYDERABAD, Char Minar

Immediately south-west of the Char Minar, on the road to Falaknuma Palace, is the **Mecca Masjid**. Commenced in 1614 by Muhammad Qutb Shah, it was completed by Aurangzeb eighty years later in 1693. An engraved tablet marks the date. The main entrance, built in 1692, had four minars and five arches to the front. This forms one side of a paved quadrangle laid out in 1614. To the north and south sides are two symmetrical domes over 30·5 m (100 ft) above roof level. Built in local granite, it is one of the largest mosques in India. Each column is hewn from a single stone. The small red stones in the central arch are made of earth from Mecca.

In an arched gallery at the south end of the mosque are the tombs of all the Nizams of the Asaf Jahi dynasty from 1803.

To the east of the main road a small alley leads to the **Jami Masjid** (1598), the

476

first mosque built in the city after that in the Char Minar. Ruins of a school and bath-house can still be seen. The mosque is in the Qutb Shahi style but was renovated under Asaf Jah III (1803–29).

The Malwala Palace lies 91 m (295 ft) to the east of the Char Minar. Built in 1845, it is a rather chaotic amalgamation of European and local styles with arches of lacquered wood. It was designed for Raja Shivraj Bahadur, head of a leading noble family who were hereditary Daftadars or Revenue Treasurers.

Eastern Sector (Old City)

North-east of the Charkaman is the **Mir Alam Mandi** (1804), originally an old parade ground but now a vegetable market. It retains two original gateways, a cistern and a mosque which survive from the palace complex.

The **Husaini Alam Ashurkhana** (late 16th century) houses the battle standard or alam of Imam Husain, grandson of the Prophet, who died at the Battle of Karbala. It is reputed that the standard was brought by Ali Agha from Iraq to Hyderabad, where it has been venerated ever since by Shia Muslims. The mosque adjacent was dedicated to Ali Agha and was later extended, the eastern wing in 1738 by his grandson. The west façade is original.

The **Purana Haveli** or Old Palace lies south of the Darush Shifa or Hospital. It is a group of eleven disparate buildings, once the residence of Mir Momin, the Peshwa of Muhammad Quli Qutb Shah. Most of the present fabric from the time of Nizam Mir Mahboob Ali Khan is in the European classical style. At present it is occupied by an education trust.

The **Azha Khana-e-Zahra**, between the Salar Jung and Purana Haveli roads, is an old mourning house built by Asaf Jah VII in memory of his mother.

The **Darush Shifa** was erected in 1535, a unique hospital/college of Unani medicine founded by Quli Qutb Shah.

Experienced physicians dispensed medicine and taught students in the two-storey square building. There is an interesting gateway to the north wing, adjoining which are chambers which were once outpatients' wards. In the centre of the quadrangle is a new Ashurkhana, which is supposed to contain the fetters of the fourth Shiite Imam. Just to the north-west of the main building is the **Mosque**, a perfect example from the Qutb Shahi period.

Out towards the east of the city in **Sarur Nagar** (literally Pleasure Town) 3·2 km (2 miles) east of Oliphant Bridge at Malakhpet, is the **Tomb of Michel Raymond** (1798). Raymond was the figurehead of French ambitions in central India, having risen to the position of Commandant in the Nizam's army, with a force of over 15,000. However, as a result of a treaty between the Nizam and the British Resident, Colonel James Achilles Kirkpatrick, the vastly superior French forces were disbanded and Raymond died on 25 March 1798 a disillusioned man. His tomb is of polished grey granite on an elevated masonry platform. The four sides of the obelisk are inscribed 'J. R.'; in front of it is a small flat-roofed Grecian-style building carried on columns, which is illuminated by lamps on the anniversary of his death. Nearby is the tomb of a lady named Anne Jane Elizabeth Jenkins.

Close to Raymond's Tomb is **Lord Venkateshwara's Temple**, an old reconsecrated temple. On a low mound opposite Raymond's Tomb is **Asman Garh** (late 19th century), a palace designed as a hunting-box in Regency Gothick style by a local noble and now an archaeological museum.

6·5 km (4 miles) east of the city in Edi Bazaar is a large Muslim cemetery, the Dargah Hazrat Brahna Shah Saheb, named after a follower of Sufi Sarman, He died in Hyderabad in 1663. A large tomb was erected by one of his disciples and around this a vast graveyard has grown up, an interesting repository of Muslim funerary architecture.

Southern Sector (Old City)

About 1·6 km (1 mile) south of Char Minar on Kohi-Tur Hill lies **Falaknuma Palace** (literally Mirror of the Sky), one of the spectacular palaces of the Nizams of Hyderabad.

The main palace was designed by English architects in 1872 as the private residence of a rich Muslim grandee, but in 1897 it was purchased for use as a guest-house by the Nizam. The end of the kitchen courtyard is the oldest section, built in 1830. The principal range rising over a terrace is in classical style, with a two-storey verandah carrying a central pediment. Palladian in conception, it is a curious building with reduced proportions and thick stumpy columns, Ionic to the ground floor, Corinthian to the first, approached by a wide staircase. At the rear is a rambling building in Indo-Saracenic style. This housed the zenana.

If the exterior is awkward, the interior is splendid, with a marble entrance hall and fountain, and an Italian marble staircase supporting marble figures with candelabra, lined with portraits of British Governors-General. The Reception Room is in Louis XIV style. Elsewhere there are French tapestries, beautiful inlaid furniture from Kashmir, and Victorian bric-a-brac. Hardly used since 1911, it is a curious example of the hybrid taste of the period, with Aesthetic Movement details, such as sunflowers, interspersed with Oriental references. The future King George V and Queen Mary stayed here in 1906. Electric lights were installed for the visit of the Prince of Wales in 1926. The first floor commands a fine view of the Mir Alam Tank to the south.

To the north of the entrance gate are the ruins of the **Jahannuma**, a garden laid out by Nawab Sham-ul-Umara in 1822–3. The old baradari is now in ruins. This was the former Portuguese quarter, with a chapel built *circa* 1800.

Western Sector (Old City)

West of Char Minar is the Chowk, marked by a mosque and clocktower. The mosque (1818; extended 1904) is raised on a high platform beneath which are shops. The Victorian Clocktower (1892) was built by Sir Asman Jah, the Prime Minister from 1887 to 1892. **Lad Bazaar**, which lies between the Chowk and Char Minar, is an old shopping area which has some fine examples of local vernacular architecture with carved wood and stone details. On the road to Char Minar are the old pink elephant gates and walls of the Jillukhana or Parade Ground, with canopied windows in French-Islamic style.

Immediately to the west of the Nizam's old palaces are the **Paigarh Palaces**, built for the Paigarh family, second in line to the Nizam in the court hierarchy. The Palaces of Asman Jah, Khurshid Jah and Viqar-ul-Umara were the most notable. With the exception of the last, they are now in ruins. Southwest of the Chowk is the **Deorhi Asman Jah**, one of the oldest palaces in Hyderabad, built by the Shams-ul-Umaras in Oriental style. The Khana Bagh garden was added later. The **Baradari Khurshid Jah** was designed by Khurshid Jah's grandfather, Shams-ul-Umara Amee-e-Kabir. Architecturally, it is modelled on the British Residency, in European style. In the courtyard is a star-shaped fountain, the Tara Hauz. To the West the **Ishrat Mahal** was used as a court room. It is now a girls' school. The **Viqar–ul–Umara** dates from the Asaf Jahi period and has a suite of rooms in the European style.

South-east of Lad Bazaar is the enormous enclosure of the Khilwat Mahal, a vast complex of palaces built by successive Nizams. The palaces include the Chaumahalla Palace, the Khilwat Mubarak, the Rang Mahal, Roshn Bangla, Afzal Mahal, Aftab Mahal, Tahnuja Mahal, Chandni Begum-ki-Haveli, Maijhli Begum-ki-Haveli, Bakshi Begum-ki-Haveli, Sadar Bangla, Moti Bangla, Shadi Khana, Tosha Khana, etc.

A parade ground faces Lad Bazaar. In the south-west corner is a Qutb Shahi mosque. The Nizam's fabulous wealth was housed in the Madras-i-Mubarak. The **Chaumhalla Palace** (1750) is a group of four buildings around a central quadrangle. To the north is the Durbar Hall, where state receptions were held.

In a side lane 182 m (592 ft) beyond the palace is the **Haveli of Chandu Lal**; Chandu Lal was Prime Minister from 1832 to 1843. The **Mir Alam Tank**, now part of the city zoo, lies 2·4 km (1½ miles) south-west of the Char Minar, outside the city. It was built by French engineers and named after Mir Alam, the Prime Minister from 1804 to 1808. It is a fine piece of engineering with twenty-one arches holding a lake over 20·7 sq. km (8 square miles) in area. On the east bank is the **New Idgah**, built in 1806.

The **Daira Mir Momin** is a cemetery containing a number of important tombs. Mir Momin, Prime Minister under Muhammad Quli Qutb Shah, was buried here in 1625 in a polished black basalt tomb. Mir Alam, Salar Jung I, II, III, Siraj-ul-Mulk and other high-office holders are also interred here.

The **Kali Masjid** (1702), with its three massive arches, is an interesting small mosque in the transitional style between the Qutb Shahi and Asaf Jahi styles of architecture. It was built by Rustum Dil Khan in memory of his father, Jan Supar Khan. Their tombs lie in the compound outside; that of Rustum Dil Khan is black basalt with pierced trelliswork, his father's is plain ashlar.

To the north of the Mir Alam Tank is the **Nehru Zoological Park**, opened in 1963. Outside the north wall is the Kishan Bagh Temple and Dargah, built in 1822.

New City (North of River)

The establishment of the British Residency on the north bank of the river, opposite the old walled city, provided impetus to further expansion. With local jurisdiction vested in the British Resident, the area acquired a reputation for peace and security. It became a fashionable enclave, aided by the construction in 1839 and 1857 of two bridges, and it provided a European dimension to the cosmopolitan life of the city. The arrival of the railway and the disastrous floods of 1908 added momentum to the movement of population out of the old city and across the river.

The north side of the Musi river, opposite the High Court, is dominated by the **Osmania General Hospital** (1925), a spectacular range of stone buildings dressed with chunam and designed by Vincent Esch in Indo-Saracenic style. It is 192 m (630 ft) long with wards on either side. It was one of the largest hospitals in the world when built, and its exotic silhouette forms an evocative picture when viewed from Afzal Ganj Bridge. Next door is the former Osmania Medical College. The **State Central Library** faces the Salar Jung Museum across the river. It was designed by Indian architects in the manner established by Esch, with an imposing entrance set on a high stone platform. It has an outstanding collection of Islamic manuscripts.

The **British Residency**, now occupied by the University College for Women, was designed by Lieutenant Samuel Russell, son of the artist John Russell (1744–1806), and built between 1803 and 1806. It is one of the finest Georgian houses in India and owes its inception to Colonel James Achilles Kirkpatrick, the British Resident who ousted the French and established British paramountcy in Hyderabad in 1798. Paid for by the Nizam, the house is a stylish and sophisticated example of classical architecture but flawed by a clumsiness of detail. The north front comprises a hexastyle Corinthian portico crowned by a pediment carrying the arms of the East India Company. The steps are flanked by colossal lions. Behind is the Durbar Hall, with a Greek Ionic order on two storeys with a gallery. Behind the hall is a fine neo-classical staircase in a circular well covered by a dome enriched with delicate plasterwork. Some of the furniture came from Brighton Pavilion, the gift of the Prince Regent.

The approach from the river is via a triumphal archway and past long colonnaded loggias which accentuate the axial plan. Within the compound are numerous outbuildings, including a bungalow used by the Resident's aide-de-camp, and stables. After the 1857 Mutiny, when a band of Rohillas attacked the Residency, a high fortified wall with bastions and gates was added. This provides a pleasant sense of enclosure to the beautiful landscaped gardens laid out by Kirkpatrick.

The small **Model of the Residency** (sadly damaged) now in the Begum's garden was built by Kirkpatrick for his wife, who remained in purdah in the Rang Mahal, of which no trace now remains. (For a full account of Kirkpatrick's extraordinary marriage to Khair-un-Nissa – one of the most romantic tales in the history of Anglo-India – and further details of the Residency buildings see *Splendours of the Raj* by the author.)

In the south-west corner of the compound is a **cemetery** with some interesting well-preserved tombs, including those of four Residents. Note the stirring inscription on the tomb of Lieutenant W. J. Darby (1815), the tomb of George Rumbold (1820) and that of the notorious Sir William Rumbold (1833) after whom the Rumbold's Kothi is named.

The **Gosha Mahal** (literally Secluded Palace), on the Mallakunta Road, was built in 1672 by Abul Hasan, last King of Golconda, as a pleasure garden. Only a pond and baradari surrounded by a high wall survive. It is alleged that an underground tunnel runs from here to Golconda.

The **Moazam Jahi Market** (1935) can be identified by its high domed clock-tower. Close to the Lal Bahadur Stadium are the **Nampally Public Gardens**, the largest in Asia, approached through two gateways in Early Norman style. Within the gardens are numerous notable buildings: the Jubilee Hall (1937); the Jawahar Bal Bhavan, embellished with a crest of lions; a Health Museum; the State Archaeological Museum, with a fine display of treasures, including an Egyptian mummy; the Gallery of Art, with some fine Tanjore bronzes and miniatures; and the Old Town Hall (1913), now the State Legislative Assembly.

Close to the Taj Mahal Hotel on Abid Road is **St George's Grammar School and Church**. The school was founded in 1834, a simple arcaded stucco range with a segmental pediment over the entrance. **St George's Church** (1865–7) is a conventional essay in a simple Gothic style with crenellations and a single west tower.

Opposite the Mahbubia Girls' High School in a narrow lane are the ruins of an old gun foundry set up in 1786 by Michel Raymond. Opposite Fateh Maidan on Abid Road is Nizam College. Within the Sultan Bazaar is **Pestonji Kothi**, a large building on a high platform built by famous Parsee bankers. By the roadside near the bank is the **Tomb of William Palmer** (1867), who was head of Palmer & Co., the bankers, the son of General Palmer and the Begum of Oudh. His tomb is in the Muslim style.

King Kothi, the residence of the Nizam, lies nearby, but it is not open to the public. To the south-east is **Rumbold's Kothi**, built for Sir William Rumbold in 1825. To the north a panorama of the city can be obtained from the new Hindu temple at Naubat Parhad and from Kala Palnad, overlooking the Husain Sagar Tank, on the west bank of which is Raj Bhavan, the residence of the Governor of Andhra Pradesh. The tank was formed in 1532.

Hyderabad Station (metre gauge) was built in concrete in 1914 by Vincent Esch with a central tower which houses water tanks for the station.

JAIGARH

Jaigarh or Fort Victory, 161 km (100 miles) south of Bombay, is a small seaport, now little more than a village with a good natural harbour. The fort, situated on rising ground about 61 m (200 ft) above the sea, was built by the Bijapur kings and was later the haunt of the infamous Hindu pirate the Nayaka of Sangameswar, who repulsed two combined expeditions of Bijapur and Portuguese forces sent against him in 1583 and 1585. In 1713 it was seized by the Maratha pirate Angria. It passed to the British in 1818.

JALNA

Jalna is a small town and cantonment situated 61 km (38 miles) east of Aurangabad. The military lines, laid out in 1827, were in continuous use until 1903 and were then reoccupied during the Second World War.

The only public buildings of note are the sarai, a mosque and the fort, erected in 1715 to the east of the town. In the fort is a remarkable well, the sides of which are excavated into galleries and chambers. The Muslim historian Abu-al-Fazl was exiled here by Akbar. Aurangzeb also resided here when Viceroy of the Deccan.

JANJIRA

71 km (44 miles) south of Bombay, Janjira was the principal town of a small state of the same name. The fort lies on an island at the mouth of the Rajpuri creek with 15 m high (50 ft) walls rising abruptly from the water.

Janjira, the strongest marine fort in India, was built by the Abyssinians in 1511 on an island south of Alibagh below Portuguese Bombay. The Abyssinians traded in slaves with the Adil Shahi dynasty of Bijapur and provided armed escorts for pilgrims bound for Mecca.

In 1659 Shivaji attacked the fort and later his son Shambhuji attempted to tunnel across from the mainland. Neither they nor the European powers ever captured Janjira by force.

A dhow can be hired from the old city of Murad on the coast. It is well worth the effort. Inside the fort the former palace garden is now jungle and an air of melancholic charm pervades the ruins. Rusting cannon still lie in the embrasures. Note how the joints in the outer walls are sealed with lead to prevent the ingress of sea water. By the main entrance is a carved panel depicting the lion of Abyssinia holding captive six Indian elephants.

KALYAN

Situated 53 km (33 miles) north-east of Bombay, Kalyan was once an important town and port in the district of Thana. It is an ancient settlement which rose to prominence at the end of the 2nd century. By the 6th century it was one of the chief markets of western India. Early in the 14th century the Muslims renamed Kalyan Islamabad.

The town was sacked by the Portuguese in 1536 and again in 1570. In 1674 the English founded a factory here.

When the Marathas cut off the factory's supplies in 1780 it was seized by the British and remained in their possession. The gallant defence of Kalyan by Captain Richard Campbell, and its subsequent relief in the nick of time by Colonel Hartley, were memorable feats of British arms.

Around the town are extensive ruins which attest to its former grandeur and importance.

KAMPTI

14·5 km (9 miles) north-east of Nagpur is Kampti, a large town and classic cantonment laid out in 1821 on the usual plan of a military camp, except that the cavalry lines lay on the extreme left. The town lies on the right bank of the Kanhan river, bisected by a broad central avenue. There is a large parade ground to the south-east.

The river is crossed by a fine stone bridge and also by the railway. There are an Anglican Church (1833), a Roman Catholic mission of the order of St Francis de Sales with a convent and church, five mosques and over seventy Hindu temples.

KARWAR

Once an important commercial port and now an attractive sea resort, for many years Karwar was the only safe anchorage between Bombay and Cochin. A large lighthouse 64 m (210 ft) above sea level marks the cluster of islets called Oyster Rocks, while 8 km (5 miles) to the south-east is Anjidiva Island, a former Portuguese settlement dotted with trees and houses, where many British troops died awaiting ship to Bombay (see Goa).

An English factory was established here in 1638. In 1697 the Marathas laid the town to waste. In 1715 the old fort was replaced by Sadashivgarh by the local Sonda chief. The new fort impaired the security of the factory to such an extent that it was closed in 1720. By 1801 old Karwar was in ruins. The fort and lighthouse are the only buildings of interest.

KIRKEE (KHIDKI)

Kirkee lies just under 6·5 km (4 miles) outside Pune and was once the regimental headquarters of the illustrious Bombay Engineers.

On 5 November 1817 a British force of only 2,800 under Colonel Burr defeated a huge force of over 18,000 cavalry and 8,000 foot soldiers of the Peshwa Baji Rao II on the plain to the south-east of the former Government House, Pune. It was the first of three battles which marked the end of Maratha power in western India. The Peshwa is alleged to have watched the defeat from nearby Parbati Hill, which has a fine complex of temples.

A description of the buildings of interest in Kirkee is included in the entry on Pune, of which it is now a suburb.

KOLHAPUR

Kolhapur is the interesting picturesque capital of one of the former leading Maratha states. It is situated about 232 km (144 miles) south east of Pune and is renowned for its ancient temples and fine 19th-century buildings.

It owes its existence to the division of Shivaji's kingdom on his death between two rival factions. The ruling dynasty at Kolhapur is descended from Shivaji's younger son, who forged a kingdom from the southern estates. However, the dynasty was beset by accident and misfortune, and it was not until direct British intervention in the late 19th century was that a stable line was secured. Under Shahu Chhatrapati a reforming government was established in 1894 which turned Kolhapur into a model native state.

There are a number of fine buildings which mark the reforming zeal of the dynasty in the late 19th century. The **New Palace** (1881) by Major Charles Mant, Royal Engineers, is a remarkable piece of Victorian eclecticism by a gifted young architect who died insane. Built in grey stone around a central courtyard, it is dominated by a lofty clocktower, crowned by a cupola. Superficially Indo-Saracenic in style, the building incorporates many references to local architecture. There are elements from the old palace and local temples, from the Jain temples at Ahmadabad and from the hill fortresses at Deeg and Mathura. The entire composition is an architectural tribute to Maratha resistance to Mughal domination. The interior is equally lavish and eclectic in inspiration, adorned with trophies of game tiger heads and silver. The former **British Residency** lies nearby, together with **All Saints' Church** (late 19th century),

The Palace Square in the centre of the town is entered via the **Nakkar Khana** or Music Gallery. On the right is the Rajwada or **Old Palace**, which was badly damaged by fire in 1810. It has a central stone gateway and wooden pillars. The second floor comprises the Durbar Hall, in which there is a picture of Mant's cenotaph in Florence for Maharaja Rajaram I, who died there in 1870. In the Armoury is a sword reputedly belonging to Aurangzeb and another given by Sir John Malcolm to Pratap Singh.

On the south side of the square are the **Treasury** and other government offices, behind which is the **Shrine of Amba Bai**, the tutelary deity of Kolhapur. (For details of the temple and excavations in the suburbs see Volume I.)

In the **Irwin Museum** is an inscribed bell taken from the temple. It was part of the spoils captured from the Portuguese at Bassein in 1739.

There are numerous civic buildings designed by Charles Mant which warrant close inspection, principally the Venetian Gothic **Town Hall** (1873), **General Library** (1875), the **Albert Edward Hospital** (1878) and the **High School** ($c.$ 1879). The development of his own highly individual Indo-Saracenic style can be traced clearly.

Kolhapur has many ancient shrines, including one of the goddess Mahalakshmi. In 1880 a 3rd century Buddhist crystal relic casket was discovered in a nearby stupa. To the north of the town is Brahmapuri Hill, where Brahmins are cremated. Nearby in the **Rani's Garden** is the spot where the ruling family were cremated. Beyond is a 6 m high (20 ft) stone gateway which leads to the **Cenotaphs of Raja Shambhuji** (1760), **Shivaji** (1762) and, to the left, his mother, **Tara Bai**.

The bridge across the river was built in 1878 as part of the civic improvements.

KONDAPALLY

Kondapally is an old hillfort, 16 km (10 miles) west of Bezwada. Once the capital of one of the five Northern Circars, Kondapally boasted a formidable fortress, built *circa* 1360 by the Reddis of Kondavid. The ruins of the former citadel stand high over the walled enclosure of the old city, which is now overgrown.

The fort was seized by the Bahmani king Humayun the Cruel in 1458 and it was fiercely contested for over two and a half centuries. In 1687 it surrendered to the emperor Aurangzeb. On 10 March 1766 it was stormed and taken from the

Nizam by the British under General Caillaud.

The fort is entered through three massive gates, which lie in close succession at the foot of the hill. An old English barracks and burialground are within the walls. A stone staircase marks the ascent to the summit, where the old palace lies on a crest between the two hills on either side of the pass. The summit is fortified with towers and loopholed bastions. The upper fort is entered via three successive gateways, the sides of which are single blocks of granite. Above is the Tanisha Mahal or Palace, which has a cloistered ground storey and arched roofs. Above that is the great hall. Several bathrooms have stone pipes and cisterns. The zenana quarters are approached along a terrace and enclosed by a high wall. A path leads to the great reservoir, which is of immense depth and very cold. Beyond the granary, a massive stone building with high arches and receptacles for grain, lie the magazines.

KONDAVID

Kondavid was once the capital of a province of the same name. It was constructed by the Orissa Rajas in the 12th century and has a celebrated hillfort situated on a ridge of high ground running north-east to south-west. In fact, the ruins of three forts of successive periods may be traced.

The town was the seat of the Reddi dynasty (1328–1428). It was stormed in 1516 by Krishna Raya, and later again in 1531, 1536 and then finally in 1579 by Sultan Quli Qutb Shah of Golconda. The province was acquired by the French in 1752, but it was ceded to the English in 1788.

The main fort, which stands on the ridge at a height of 320 m (1,050 ft), is a substantial structure in reasonable repair which embraces granaries, magazines, godowns and wells behind continuous ramparts. The fort has two entrances: the Kolepalli Darwaza and the Nadelle Darwaza. Within the fort is the Gopinathaswami Temple, which has some fine clustered pillars cut from a single rock. The great hall within is now a mosque.

KOPPAL

Koppal, 56 km (35 miles) from Gadag, is renowned for the two formidable hillforts which guarded an outlying district of the former dominions of the Nizam of Hyderabad.

The upper fort was regarded by Sir John Malcolm as the strongest place he had seen in India, perched at a height of 122 m (400 ft) above the plain. The lower fort is later, having been reconstructed in 1786 by French engineers for Tipu Sultan, but French ingenuity did not prevent its being taken in 1790 by joint British and Hyderabad forces and again in 1819, by Brigadier-General Pritzler.

During the Mutiny Koppal was seized by Bhim Rao, a local rebel leader, who was slain with his followers on its recapture by the British.

KURNOOL

Kurnool is the chief town of the district. It lies 55 km (34 miles) from Dhone on a rocky spit of land at the confluence of the Hindri and Tungabhadra rivers. The fort was dismantled in 1862, but four bastions and three gates survive. Within the old fort area are the ruins of the **Palace of the Nawabs**.

The most interesting building is the dome-shaped **Mausoleum of Abdul Wahab** (*c.* 1570), an imitation of one at Bijapur which commemorates the first Nawab, who converted many former temples into mosques. In 1750 the town was destroyed by de Bussy. In 1839 the last Nawab, Ghulam Rasul Khan, stock-piled enormous amounts of ammunition as a prelude to full-scale rebellion, but after firm British action and a short fight he was deposed. During the famine of 1877–8 major efforts were made to relieve the isolated town from the rail-head at Gooty, 95·5 km (60 miles) away.

There are numerous mosques and a fine ornamental fountain presented by the Maharaja of Vizianagram, who was renowned for his interest in providing free fresh drinking-water for the needy.

MAHABALESHWAR

Mahabaleshwar (literally The God of Great Power) lies 121 km (75 miles) south of Pune. It is the principal hill station for Bombay and is situated on a wooded plateau rising about 1,219 m (4,000 ft) above a level plain. The grandeur of the scenery is beyond description.

The area was first visited by Colonel Lodwick in the hot season of 1824, at considerable personal risk from the tigers, bears and cheetahs which once infested the hills in this area. No steps were taken to establish a settlement until 1828, when the Governor of Bombay, Sir John Malcolm, founded Malcolm Peth. A year later, it was declared an official sanatorium.

There are numerous local viewpoints: Connaught Point and Bombay Point for glorious sunsets, Arthur's Seat, over-looking a precipice, and Elphinstone Point and Kate's Point on the road to Panchgani.

Christ Church (1842) was enlarged and extended in 1867. There is some good stained glass depicting Christ, the four Evangelists, Moses and St John the Baptist in the chancel. 800 m (½ mile) from the Church, on the right of the Bombay Point Road, is the **Cemetery**, with a tombstone to Lieutenant Hinde,

who was hunted and gored to death by a bison.

Frere Hall (1864) resembles an English post office with its leaded lights, stone tracery and mullioned and tran-somed windows in the gimcrack Gothick style common in Indian hill stations. Designed as a library, meeting hall and theatre, it is part of the club. **Old**

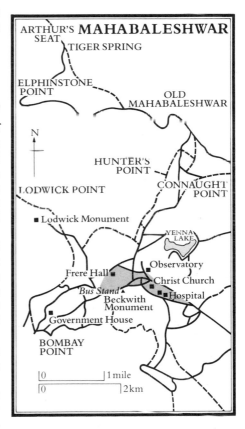

Government House (Mount Malcolm) was built in 1829, but it became a private residence in 1868. **New Government House** stands on Prospect Point and has a fine front entrance closed by railings.

The **Beckwith Monument** occupies a commanding position and lies 55 m (180 ft) west of the church. The 9 m (30 ft) obelisk commemorates Lieutenant-General Sir Sidney Beckwith, Com-mander-in-Chief, Bombay Army, who died there on 15 January 1831. Beckwith served with Cornwallis, impressed Nelson at Copenhagen and later formed the Rifle Brigade.

The **Lodwick Monument** (1874) stands 4·8 km (3 miles) north-east of Malcolm Peth and comprises a 7·6 m (25 ft) pillar crowned by an urn. At the base is a marble bust of General Lodwick in alto-rilievo. Lodwick, the first European in the hills, died in France aged ninety.

Other points of interest are Church Square, an open space below Christ Church near the Club on the road leading to Yenna Lake; Reay Gardens; the Civil Hospital, adjoining Christ Church; and the Petit Native General Library (1901). The Club was founded in 1882.

MAHULI

Mahuli, about 4·8 km (3 miles) east of Satara, is a celebrated hill fortress crowning the summit of Mahuli Hill, 858 m (2,815 ft) high. Towards the south end of the hilltop is a deep chasm, 213 m (700 ft) deep in which stand gigantic basalt pillars. A sheer precipice of black basalt 142 m (500 ft) to 183 m (600 ft) high runs all round. A smaller cleft running across the hill is alleged to have been used as a dungeon.

The approach is from the east by way of Machi village. The gateway, which stands at the head of a precipitous ravine, and the battlemented parapets are in an excellent state of preservation. The fort is probably of Mughal origin. There are three fortified summits: Palasgarh on the north, Mahuli in the centre and Bhandargarh to the south. Mahuli is the highest. The ruins of a mosque and place of prayer survive on the top.

In 1670 the fort was taken from the Mughals by the Marathas, by whom it was held until ceded to the British in 1817 under the terms of the Treaty of Poona.

Downriver from the confluence of the Krishna and Venna rivers are a number of temples. The fine bridge over the Krishna river below the confluence was built in 1915 by Mr Oddin Taylor of the Public Works Department (PWD).

MALANGARH

Malangarh or Cathedral Rock lies 16 km (10 miles) south of Kalyan. It is approached via rough country from Kalyan and an arduous climb of about 213 m (700 ft). At the base of the hill is forest-covered tableland, upon which lies the tomb of the Bawa Malang. From this plateau the ascent to the fort 91·5 m (300 ft) above is very steep, the last section by means of an almost sheer, rock-hewn staircase terminating in a formidable gateway reinforced by two large towers. This renders the entrance impregnable, even with only a small garrison.

The ascent from here to the upper fort is extremely hazardous, a perpendicular rise of 61 m (200 ft) by means of another rock-hewn staircase. It is hardly worth the climb as the upper fort comprises little more than the traces of an enclosure and a few ruined walls.

MANDOR

This small fortified village lying at the base of a high range of hills was the scene of a battle between the British under General Grey and the Marathas on 29 December 1843. The Marathas were routed, driven from their positions and lost all their ammunition and artillery.

MASULIPATAM

Masulipatam (or Machhli-patnam, literally Fish Town) lies 345 km (215 miles) north of Madras. It is the principal port of the Krishna district, one of the Northern Circars, and may have been founded in the 14th century by Arabs who rounded Ceylon on one of their ventures. In 1478 the town was captured by the Bahmani ruler Muhammad III, who lost possession to the Orissa Rajas, who in turn yielded to the Muslim Sultan of Golconda. Under the Golconda regime the commercial prosperity of the town grew.

Masulipatam was one of the earliest English settlements on the Coromandel coast. An agency was established in 1611 under Captain Hippon and eleven years later English traders, driven by the Dutch from the East Indies and from Pulicat, established a factory here. After a brief lapse of four years between 1628 and 1632, when they were expelled, the station became the centre of English trade. Although the Dutch and French also maintained factories here, by 1690 the English had obtained full right of trade by firman from the Mughal emperor. In 1753 the Nizam gave the territory to the French, but on the night of 7 April 1759 the town was stormed by Colonel Forde, who managed to capture a French force twice the size of his own and over 120 guns.

The town was once a great centre of the cotton trade but this has declined to a mere vestige of its original extent. In the 1840s it revived as a centre of the Church Missionary Society, but the real blow to its prosperity was struck in 1864, when the entire town was hit by an enormous tidal wave, which penetrated 27·5 km (17 miles) inland before receding and destroying everything in its path. Over 30,000 people were drowned. There is a monument in the fort which commemorates the incident.

The Noble College, founded in 1843, is affiliated to Madras University. In the cemetery there are some early Dutch tombs dating from 1624. The fort is now dismantled and the town largely a backwater.

MATHERAN

Situated about 48 km (30 miles) east of Bombay, Matheran is a small hill station, 750 m (2,460 ft) above sea level, renowned for the peculiar charm of its Points. These are a series of rocky promontories from which one can obtain magnificent views of the valleys over 610 m (2,000 ft) below. The six leading Points are the Hart in the north, the Chauk south of the central hill, Panorama Point at the north and Garbat at the south of the east wing, Porcupine Point at the north and Louisa at the south of the west wing. Other notable spots are known as the Artist, Sphinx and Battle Points.

The hills were explored in May 1850 by Hugh Malet of the Bombay Civil Service. Later it became a resort for Bombay, a cool, salubrious retreat during the spring and autumn months.

It is typical in form and layout of many hill stations. The chief buildings are the post and telegraph offices, the market, the library, the church and Catholic chapel and the Lord's Central Hotel. The bungalows are widely dispersed among the woods and terraces of the resort.

NAGPUR *Map overleaf*

Nagpur, 361 km (225 miles) from Jabalpur, the capital of the former Central Provinces, now lies in Maharashtra. The inhabitants of the district include a high proportion of aboriginal Gonds, many of whom worship the cholera and smallpox deities. The city is a modern route centre with no great architectural pretensions, but the view from Sitabaldi Hill, which dominates the centre of the city, is picturesque.

Although the city dates from the 18th century, the ancient history of the district is shrouded in obscurity, with traces

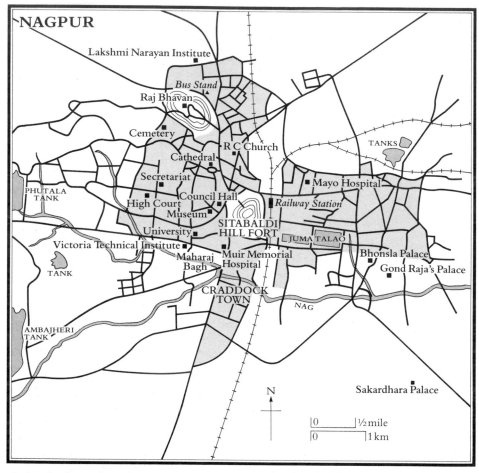

dating back to the 5th century. In 1467 Muhammad Bahmani (1463–82) conquered the area, but in the following century the local Gonds underwent a resurgence of power, which lasted until 1740, when the Bhonslas conquered the country. On 26 and 27 November 1817 Maratha troops attacked the British Resident and his bodyguard. After a lengthy struggle the British prevailed and the Bhonsla's army was disbanded. When the succession lapsed in 1853, the territory was annexed by the British and eight years later it was formed with Saugor and Narbada into the Central Provinces. In spite of a local uprising in 1857, the garrison remained loyal.

The city stands on the River Nag. It can be divided for convenience into two distinct parts: one lying east and south of Sitabaldi Fort, the other lying west and north of the railway station and civil lines.

The railway station has been rebuilt on a grand scale with an impressive façade. Outside there is a fine view of Sitabaldi Fort. The roads from here run in three directions: to Sitabaldi, Sadar and Hansapuri. Behind the railway station the road leads through the orange market towards the Jumma Talao, a large artificial lake with a beautiful garden in the centre. There are two other main tanks to the west of the city: the Ambazari Tank and the Telin Khedi. The former, built by the Bhonsla Rajas, was made into a reservoir in 1873. There is a pleasant garden area with romantic views across the lake.

In the old city, lying to the east of Sitabaldi, is the **Bhonsla Palace**. Little now remains following a fire in 1864, but the Nakkar Khana or Music Gallery can still be seen. Nearby is the Town Hall and Hislop Missionary College. The Empress Cotton Mills were built in 1877. The Mayo Hospital (1867) lies to the north and near it are the Ram Mandir Temples. The Cenotaphs of the Bhonsla Rajas lie in the Shukrawari quarter, south of the old city.

The **Fort** actually embraces two hills joined by a narrow saddle of land. There are two sets of defences, the larger embracing both hills and the smaller, much stronger set forming a central redoubt on the larger hill. The walls and ramparts are surrounded in places by sheer cliff faces and elsewhere by a moat. There are five bastions to the inner area and two to the outer defences, each with gun emplacements. Crowning the larger hill is a **monument** to those who fell in the Battle of Sitabaldi of 1817. Just before the tunnel entrance leading to the inner fort on the right-hand side are a number of British graves. Facing the city to the east is another **monument**, marking the spot where King George V and Queen Mary gave an audience to the people of Nagpur in 1911.

Between the eastern fort walls and the barracks is the Nav Gaz Ali Baba, believed to be the grave of Nawab Kadar Ali, grandson of Tipu Sultan of Mysore, who was hanged with his associates by the British for their role in the rebellion of 1857.

The Gandhi Bagh Garden commemorates the Mahatma and is beautifully laid out with creepers in the shape of arches.

The old civil station lies west of Sitabaldi Hill. The main European buildings are concentrated here. Adjacent to the Amravati–Nagpur road is the **Lakshmi Narayan Institute of Technology**.

This is a fine building, roughly semi-circular in shape, with a handsome pillared frontage and wings to each side. The clocktower is a local landmark.

Nearby the **Maharaj Bagh** is an old garden containing the zoo, laid out by the Bhonsla Rajas at the confluence of two rivers.

There are two post-independence statues of note. The Statue of Maharani Lakshmi Bai of Jhansi, cast in bronze, was erected in 1962; that of the Indian patriot Sankar was unveiled by Nehru in February of the same year.

The **Central Museum** (1863) has excellent collections divided into six separate sections: art and industry, archaeology, anthropology, geology, paintings and natural history.

The **Council Hall** (1912–13) is one of the most distinguished buildings in the city. Built by the British, it is a huge two-storey range in red brick with a distinctive central range and wings to each side. To the west lies the **Secretariat**, in modified Renaissance style.

The **Anglican Cathedral of All Saints** was designed in 1851 by Lieutenant-General Sir Richard Hieram Sankey (1829–1908) and subsequently altered in 1879 by the gifted English architect G. F. Bodley. The later alterations involved lengthening the nave, deepening the transepts and adding a chancel, two vestries and an organ chamber. Nearby is the Roman Catholic Cathedral and school.

The **High Court** (1937–42), designed by Henry Medd, is an impressive civic range in the distinctive style evolved by Lutyens at New Delhi and is very similar to Viceroy's House.

North of Sadr Bazaar is another high hill, Takli, on which stands **Government House** or Raj Bhavan. Within are some interesting drawings depicting the battle of 1817 and other paintings of local British residents.

In the south-east of the city in Sakkardara district is **Tajabad Sarif**, a square Muslim tomb with arches on all sides supported by four giant pillars crowned by minarets, over which rises a large round dome.

NARNALA

This is an old ruined hill fortress lying 16 km (10 miles) to the north of Akot. It is the highest point of the entire district, 973 m (3,161 ft) above sea level, an advanced outcrop of rock about 3·2 km (2 miles) south of the main Gawilgarh range. The upper plateau of the hill is occupied by a central fort, with two smaller forts, the Teliagarh and Jafarabad, enclosing two large spurs projecting at a lower level. The ramparts, which are in ruins, extend several miles and comprise a wall varying between 8 m (25 ft) and 12 m (40 ft) high with sixty-seven bastions, six large gates and twenty-one smaller gates embracing nineteen tanks.

The Shahnur Gate, on the north side, is a notable example of Sultanate architecture, a white sandstone gateway with projecting balconies, a rich cornice, tracery, panelling and Quranic inscriptions. Within the fort are four stone cisterns built by the Jains, the old palace, Aurangzeb's mosque, an armoury, a baradari and other buildings, all in ruins.

NIZAMAPATAM

Nizamapatam is an old sea port close to Masulipatam. It was the first port on the eastern coast of India at which the English began to trade, in 1611. It was called 'Pettipollee' by them, and a small factory was established ten years later. Later it fell into the hands of the French, but it was bestowed on the English in 1759, the grant being confirmed by Imperial firman in 1765.

The town was the scene of a massacre

of Europeans by the Malay crew of the Dutch ship *Helena*.

PANHALA

Panhala or Panhalgarh is one of the most important hillforts in the Deccan. Roughly triangular in shape, it lies about 19 km (12 miles) north-west of Kolhapur, at a height of 912 m (2,992 ft). The fort was the seat of Raja Bhoj II between 1192 and 1209. In 1489 the fort and territory passed to the Adil Shahi dynasty of Bijapur. Shivaji seized the fort in 1659, but it was retaken two years later. It was then stormed once more in 1673, and subsequently held by the Marathas, except for a short period between 1690 and 1707 when it surrendered to the Mughals. After a local rebellion in 1844 the fort was assailed and taken by the British.

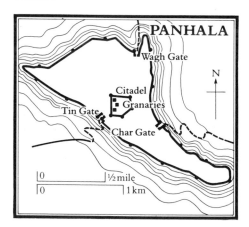

The fortifications are about 7·2 km (4½ miles) in circumference. For considerable sections they are protected by a steep scarp reinforced by a loopholed parapet wall. The remaining sections have a strong stone wall varying between 4·6 m (15 ft) and 9·1 m (30 ft) in height, strengthened by bastions. Only two of the three original gates survive.

The **Char Darwaza** or Four-doored

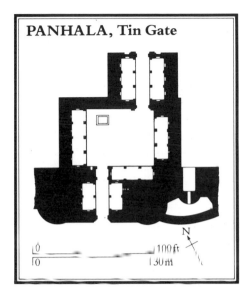

PANHALA, Tin Gate

Gate was demolished by the British in the attack of 1844. There is a temple of Maruti in the ruins. The **Tin Darwaza** or Three-doored Gate is an impressive structure with handsome sculpture approached via a steep path which is commanded by the curtain battlements. The outer entrance has a lintel and corbels set in a high pointed arch. The entrance passage leads through two doorways, past guardrooms to a courtyard, which is a killing ground for any invading troops who pierce the outer defences. The third door leads past further guardrooms. Saucer-shaped domes crown the central bays of the outer entrance passage.

The **Wagh Gate** lies in a re-entrant angle of the fort and has a long, steep approach. Part is destroyed, but the principle of guardrooms flanking the entrance is the same as elsewhere.

Within the fort are a number of ruins. Only the foundations of the old palace remain. The most interesting monuments are three huge **stone granaries** capable of supplying an entire army. The largest, the **Ganga Kothi**, covers 947·5 sq. m (10,200 sq. ft) and is 10·7 m (35 ft) high.

At the east end of the fort is **Kalava-**

tin's **Sajja** or the Courtesan's Terrace-Room. To the north is a palace of the Maharaja of Kolhapur, a two-storey mud structure. East of the palace the **Sajja Kothi** (1600) is a massive two-storey building perched on the edge of a precipice. In the south area is the **Talim-khana**, with three rooms capped by domes.

PARENDA

Parenda, located on a level plain about 29 km (18 miles) west of Barsi town, was built in the mid-15th century by one of the Bahmani kings of the Deccan.

In 1630 Shah Jahan was repulsed from here, but twenty years later Aurangzeb succeeded in capturing it during his viceroyalty of the Deccan.

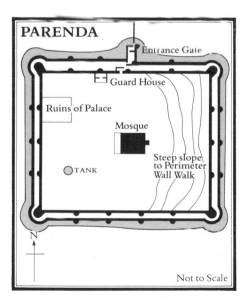

PARENDA

It is a small but interesting rectangular fort, defended by a double line of powerful curtain walls with formidable corner bastions surrounded by a wide, deep ditch. The curtain walls run parallel with each other but are separated by a wide space commanded by the inner wall, the

491

bastions of which rise high over the outer wall. The battlements of both walls are reinforced at intervals with machicolations.

The original form can be traced quite clearly as it survives largely complete. There is only one entrance to the fort, midway along the north side, with separate gateways in each wall in staggered succession. The outer gateways project into the perimeter ditch. Originally, this was approached over a drawbridge defended by a heavy iron chain, which in emergencies could be drawn across the front of the door and secured on both sides. The robust teak door was clad in iron plates and secured by a huge timber bar. The customary right-angled turn in the vaulted entrance could be commanded by guards posted to the left. Loopholes to the north and west cover the approaches and the ditch.

Note the unusual hinge adjacent to the door into the court. At the far end of the court a third gateway, reinforced with anti-elephant spikes, opens into the space between the walls.

The gateway through the second wall is protected by a barbican, bastions and a balcony projecting from the inner wall high over the barbican. The passageway is also well defended.

Inside the fort are a mosque, built after the Muslim occupation, the ruins of a palace in the north-west and a large well. To the east the ground rises sharply up to the wall-walk of the inner curtain, facilitating rapid access to the defences in times of attack.

PARTABGARH (PRATAPGAD)

This ancient hillfort lies 13 km (8 miles) to the south-west of Mahabaleshwar, crowning the summit of a hill 1,080 m (3,543 ft) above sea level. To the west and north are sheer precipices which, in places, have a vertical drop of 244 m (800 ft). To the south and east are towers and bastions about 12·2 m (40 ft) high above a steep scarp of black rock. A branch road leads to the foot of the fort and from here a steep path of 500 steps leads to the summit.

Partabgarh was the stronghold of Shivaji, founder of the Maratha empire. In 1659, it was the scene of his notorious, treacherous encounter with Afzul Khan, the Muslim general of Bijapur, who was decoyed to his death under a flag of truce. Shivaji seized the general and disembowelled him with a fearsome weapon known as a waghnakh or 'Tiger's claws' (steel claws attached to the fingers) concealed in his closed hand before routing the bewildered Bijapur troops.

The simple **Tomb of Afzul Khan** (1659) lies below the fort on the crest of the hill. It is covered by a pantiled roof.

The **Fort** comprises a double line of fortifications guarded by corner bastions. Considered to be impregnable, its massive walls, projecting towers and bastions and iron-studded spiked gates, rendered it one of the strongest hillforts in the Deccan region.

PUNE (POONA)

Pune lies 191 km (119 miles) from Bombay, at an altitude of 580 m (1,905 ft). Shivaji, the great Maratha leader, was reared here. Later it became the capital of the Peshwas, but with the eclipse of Maratha power in 1817 the British developed the town into the summer headquarters of the Government of Bombay and a major military cantonment. In recent years the town has been notorious for the Bhagwan Shree Rajneesh Ashram.

The city was first mentioned in 1599, when the districts were assigned to Malaji Bhonsla, the grandfather of Shivaji, by the kings of Ahmadnagar. In 1750 it became the Maratha capital, and

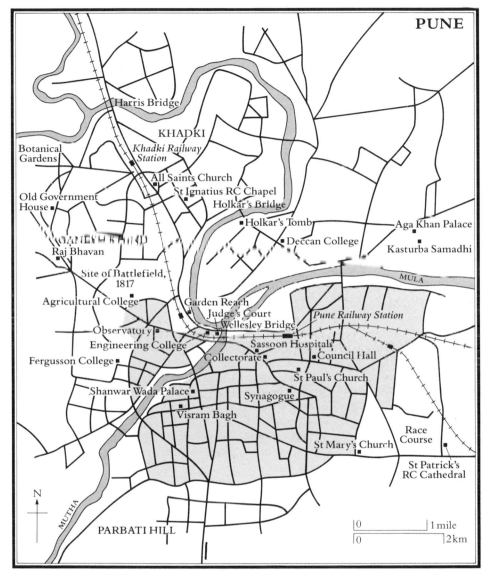

PUNE

Harris Bridge
KHADKI
Khadki Railway Station
Botanical Gardens
All Saints Church
St Ignatius RC Chapel
Holkar's Bridge
Old Government House
Holkar's Tomb
Aga Khan Palace
GANESH KHIND
Raj Bhavan
Deccan College
Kasturba Samadhi
Site of Battlefield, 1817
MULA
Agricultural College
Garden Reach
Judge's Court
Pune Railway Station
Observatory
Wellesley Bridge
Engineering College
Sassoon Hospital
Fergusson College
Collectorate
Council Hall
St Paul's Church
Shanwar Wada Palace
Synagogue
Visram Bagh
Race Course
St Mary's Church
St Patrick's RC Cathedral
N
MUTHA
PARBATI HILL
0 — 1 mile
0 — 2 km

thirteen years later it was plundered by the Nizam. In October 1802 Jaswant Rao Holkar defeated the combined armies of the Peshwa and Scindia. As a result of this defeat the Peshwa invited British assistance and Pune was occupied by troops under Wellesley in 1803. After the Battle of Kirkee in November 1817, Pune surrendered to the British.

Situated on the right bank of the Mutha river at its confluence with the Mula, Pune is widely dispersed, embracing the outer suburbs of Kirkee (Khidki). To the south is the Hill of Parbati. To the east and south-east are rolling hills. An old aqueduct, built by the Rastias, a leading Maratha family, runs from a well near Khadakwasla to a reservoir at Sadashiv Peth.

There is a cluster of civic buildings in the centre of the city. The **Council Hall**, 19·2 (63 ft) long and 6·1 m (20 ft) wide, is

493

a repository of interesting pictures, including paintings of Sir Bartle and Lady Frere, Lord Napier of Magdala, Sir Salar Jung, the Gaekwar of Baroda and several other local worthies. Opposite lies the **Record Room** or Daftar, which contains records of the Peshwas.

The **Sassoon Hospitals** (1867), designed in English Gothic style by Wilkins and Melliss and funded by Sir Jacob Sassoon, lie at the end of the Arsenal Road. In 1909 the hospitals were expanded and new buildings erected to the designs of John Begg to commemorate the visit of the Prince and Princess of Wales three years earlier. Outside the main gate is a large **war memorial**, commemorating local losses during the First World War.

Opposite are the Collector's Cutchery and Government Treasury. The large grey stone building nearby was erected in 1915 as Government offices.

St Paul's Church (1867) was consecrated by Bishop Harding. Inside are some interesting stained-glass windows. South of St Paul's is the **Jews' Synagogue**, a large red brick building with a lofty tower consecrated in September 1867. The sanctum is semicircular. The **Tomb of David Sassoon** adjoins the synagogue. It is over 8·53 m (28 ft) high, with a Hebrew inscription and the Sassoon arms.

St Mary's Church (1825) lies south of St Paul's. It is a conventional classical church with a square tower and spire. Inside it is faced in polished chunam. The baptismal font is in the south-west corner, flanked by some splendid stained-glass windows.

The **Racecourse** lies to the east of St Mary's and beyond are the **Empress Botanical Gardens**, with a fine collection of tropical trees. The **Roman Catholic Cathedral of St Patrick** lies close to the gardens, across the Nava Canal. Pune is a centre for several missions and schools. The Church of the Holy Name at Vetal Peth has a campanile

modelled on that at San Marco in Venice.

Wellesley Bridge, designed by Colonel A. U. H. Finch, was opened in 1875 to replace an earlier wooden structure built to mark Wellesley's victories in India. It is 147 m (482 ft) long.

On the west bank are the **District Courts**, designed by Major Melliss in tropical Gothic style, and Poona Engineering College (1859), a grey stone Gothic range. The Sangamvadi is a long stone range on the site of the original British Residency, which burnt in 1877.

About 274 m (900 ft) beyond the Engineering College and set behind elegant Gothic iron gates on the riverside is Sir Albert Sassoon's old house, **Garden Reach**. Built between 1862 and 1864 and designed by Colonel Sir Henry St Clair Wilkins, it is constructed of local grey stone with a corner tower capped by an iron cupola. The gardens are beautifully laid out. The rooms are paved with marble. The dining-room is connected to the house by a long open gallery with a verandah to each side. Beside this is an open room used during the Feast of the Tabernacles. Copies of Italian statues adorn the house, which is enriched with stained glass. The ceiling of the drawing-room was decorated by local artists in imitation of the ceiling at the former Government House nearby at Ganesh Khind.

The main road passes the **Institute of Tropical Meteorology and The Observatory**, transferred here from Simla in 1928. The **College of Agriculture** (1911), designed by George Wittet, can be recognized by its conspicuous white dome. South-east are Fergusson College (1884) and the Bhandarkar Oriental Research Institute.

The main road continues beside the battlefield of 1817 to Ganesh Khind and Pune University, which occupies the former **Government House** (1866), south-west of Kirkee railway station. It was designed by James Trubshawe and is dominated by a high watertower, capped by an open iron cupola. It is a rambling building in grey stone with pink granite dressings loosely inspired by Osborne House on the Isle of Wight. Inside, the principal rooms are the drawing-room (complete with minstrels' gallery), the ballroom and a cool recessed courtyard or cortile on the garden frontage. The outer walls are enriched with stone medallions of former governors.

Park Road leads north-east to Kirkee, a large cantonment area, once the regimental headquarters of the Bombay Engineers.

All Saints' Church (1841), formerly Christ Church, was consecrated by Bishop Carr. It is 45·7 m (150 ft) long from east to west and 22·8 m (75 ft) broad at the chancel. Over the west door are two regimental colours of the 23rd Bombay Light Infantry. There are some notable memorial tablets and brasses erected by regiments to officers and men who died on service in India. Note the plaque to the thirty officers of the 14th King's Light Dragoons who died or were killed in action between 1841 and 1859. The **Roman Catholic Chapel of St Ignatius** lies about 800 m (½ mile) to the south-east. To the north-east of this are the old cemeteries, close to the river.

The road to Pune crosses the River Mula via **Holkar's Bridge**. On the east bank, about 55 m (180 ft) from the bridge, is **Holkar's Tomb**. He was trampled to death by an elephant in 1802 and the adjacent temple of Mahadeo was erected in his memory.

The road continues past the **Deccan College** (1864), a long, handsome Gothic range in grey trapstone designed by Colonel Sir Henry St Clair Wilkins. The Library contains a collection of portraits of former principals, including Dr Wordsworth, a nephew of the poet, and Sir Jamsetjee Jeejeebhoy, the first Parsee baronet.

Deccan College Road leads to Fitzgerald Bridge, which crosses the Mula river to the pretty, six-acre Bund Gardens. On the north bank is Yeraoda. Here is the **Aga Khan's Palace** (1860), where Gandhi was held under house arrest. Today it is maintained as a memorial to him. Kasturba Gandhi, his wife, died here and her memorial tomb stands on the estate. Opposite the Bund is Bund Hill, where the British mounted artillery in November 1817 to secure the river crossing. The Purna Kuti Palace, built by Sir Vithaldas Thackersey, lies at the top of the hill.

The **Lloyd Bridge** (1922) provides access across the Mutha river for the Bombay Road. Opened by Sir George Lloyd, Governor of Bombay, it is 157 m (514 ft) long, crossing the river in a series of eleven spans into the heart of the city.

The **City** is divided into nineteen districts or peths. In general the streets are wide, with an interesting heritage of vernacular buildings. The road passes the Panchaleshwar Temple and the Shivaji Memorial Hall and Military School, founded in 1922. In front of the hall is a notable bronze equestrian **Statue of Shivaji**, over 9 m (30 ft) high, unveiled by Sir Leslie Wilson in June 1928. The sculptor was V. P. Karkomar.

On the right bank of the Mutha in a maze of narrow alleys and streets is the **Shanwar Wada** or Saturday Palace, built by Baji Rao, grandfather of the last Peshwa in 1736. Originally an imposing residence for the Peshwa, with guesthouses, gardens and fountains, it was gutted by fire in 1791, 1812 and 1828, so that today only the massive outer walls remain.

Although built in the mid-18th century, the quadrangular enclosure is designed on mediaeval lines, with high walls, towers, embrasures and loopholes. Faced in dressed stone and brickwork, there are four corner towers projecting well beyond the walls and one to the centre of each side. The walls have a continuous walkway protected by a loopholed parapet. The principal entrance is via the Delhi Gate, in the north wall facing

495

the river. The entrances are protected by huge doors studded with elephant spikes. Those on the Delhi Gate are over 30 cm (12 in) long.

The **Delhi Gate** is flanked by two powerful bastions, the central portion rising between them to form a balcony with rooms behind. It was from this balcony that the Peshwa Madhava Rao Narayan fell to his death in 1796. Here also in 1773 the young Peshwa Narayan Rao was murdered by his guards. It has a tall pointed archway 3·65 m (12 ft) wide, closed by spiked and studded teak doors, the spikes arranged in eight horizontal rows, each 15 cm (6 in) apart. Inside the gateway is a rectangular hall with recesses and guardrooms to each side. A recent discovery has been the Hazari Karanje or Fountain of a Thousand Jets, a lotus fountain from which issued 197 jets of water.

Near to the palace is a street where, under the last Peshwa, offenders were executed by being tied to the feet of an elephant to be trampled and crushed to death. One of the most notorious incidents involved Vithoji Holkar, brother of Jaswant Rao Holkar, who was killed in April 1802 in a public spectacle witnessed by the Peshwa Baji Rao II and his favourite, Balaji Kunjar.

In front of the palace is a **war memorial** to the Maratha soldiers who fell in the First World War.

In the nearby Budwar Peth is the **Visram Bagh**, a perfect example of a Maratha palace, with beautiful columns, a courtyard and wooden entrance porch.

On the outskirts of the town is **Parbati Hill**. The Singh Gadh road leads past the Hirabagh or Diamond Garden. In the cemetery here is the grave of the renowned African traveller Sir William Cornwallis Harris, a former Major of the Bombay Engineers, who died in 1848.

A long series of steps and ramps leads to the top of the hill, where there is a temple built by Peshwa Balaji Rao in about 1758. On the north-west side of

the perimeter wall is a Moorish window, where Baji Rao is alleged to have witnessed the defeat of his army at Kirkee in 1817.

A ruined palace of the Peshwas lies to the south-west. It was struck by lightning in 1817.

PURANDHAR

Purandhar lies 32 km (20 miles) south-east of Pune. Once one of the strongest forts in the Deccan, it later became a sanatorium for European troops. It really comprises two fortresses, Purandhar and

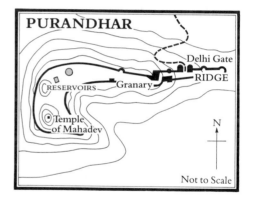

Wazirgarh, which command a passage through the hills, the former the stronger and more important of the two.

Both hills are crowned by ruins studded with impressive bastions. On a level terrace 305 m (1,000 ft) above the plain lies the old cantonment area within the fortifications. A winding path leads to the upper fort, perched on a basalt cliff, the approach to which is commanded by loopholed masonry walls. The walls run for over 42 km (26 miles), relieved by three gateways and six bastions.

On the approach, a sharp left turn is commanded by the Delhi Gate, flanked by two robust towers. The path passes two more gateways before it reaches a bomb-proof building.

On the summit of the hill is a temple of Mahadev. The return path passes two bastions called Fateh Burj and Konkani Burj. Adjacent to the latter is a bomb-proof chamber from which criminals, rolled in blankets, with their heads and feet uncovered, were hurled over the precipice as a punishment. To the north-west is a triple bastion resembling an elephant's head, called Hatti Burj.

The earliest fortifications date from 1350. For a time the site was held by Shivaji's grandfather. In 1665 it was invested by Mughal forces under the command of the famous Rajput general Raja Jai Singh, and in 1670 it was seized by Shivaji. In 1776, a treaty was signed here between the Peshwa and the East India Company, represented by Colonel Upton, who marched across central India and back for the purpose. In later years it became the chosen retreat of the Peshwas

in times of emergency. On 16 March 1818 the British under General Pritzler captured both forts, after which they fell into a state of decay, but the ruins are still impressive.

RAICHUR

Raichur is an old town and fort in the south-west corner of the former territory of the Nizam of Hyderabad, situated midway between the Kistna and Tungabhadra rivers. When Bijapur secured independence in 1489, Raichur was its first capital.

The **Fort**, about 2·4 m (1½ miles) from the station, is picturesque, with double lines of fortification rising 88 m (290 ft) above the plain. The North Gate, with flanking towers, is the most impressive. Outside is a huge stone elephant,

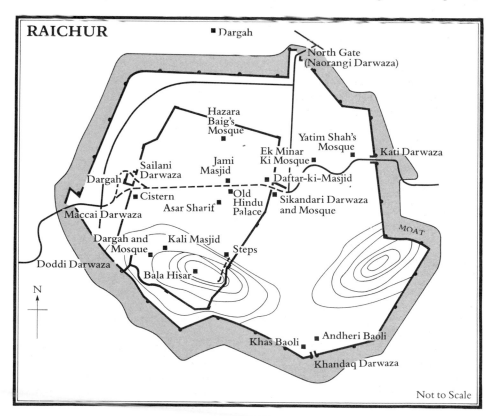

RAICHUR

Not to Scale

just under life-size. On the inner wall is a carved relief. The Kasba Darwaza, another gate, stands at right-angles. Adjacent to it is a tunnel out of which the garrison could come to close the massive gateway in times of emergency.

A short distance from the Sikandaria or West Gate is the old palace, with thick walls. The ascent to the **Citadel** begins by the North Gate. From the summit fine views of the plain below can be obtained. The walls of the citadel have no mortar. There is a row of cells and a stone pavilion overhanging the precipice. On the east side is the **Jami Masjid** (1577-8), a small mosque built, according to an inscription, by Abd al-Muhammad using earlier Chalukyan masonry. The mihrab is crowned by a dome enriched with a circular row of lotus petals. The eastern gateway is characteristic of early-15th-century gateways with its three domes, the centre one hemispherical on an octagonal drum. To the south lies a stone belfry.

Other buildings of consequence from this early period are the **Jami Masjid** in Sarraf Bazaar (1628–9), which although built of temple masonry, resembles the great mosques of Bijapur; the **Tomb of Pir Sailani Shah** (*c.* 1620); and the **Chawk Masjid** (*c.* 1560), with a central dome carried on pendentives and, unusually, with temple pillars supporting a flat porch roof.

The **Daftar-ki-Masjid** (*c.* 1510) is the earliest example of a mosque built of temple masonry in the Raichur district. All these mosques share a common theme of flat ceilings supported by Chalukyan pillars instead of masonry piers. The **Tomb of Shah Abu Taha Husayni** (*c.* 1490), the **Mosque of Hazara Baig** (1512) and the **Kali Masjid** (*c.* 1510), with four black basalt pillars, are also noteworthy.

The **Ek Minar Ki Masjid** (1513) cannot be mistaken, owing to its single minaret in the south-east corner of the courtyard, probably designed originally both as a victory tower and for use by the muezzin. It is crowned by a hemispherical dome in the Bahmani style.

RAIGARH

Known to early Europeans as the Gibraltar of the East, Raigarh or Royal Fort lies 51·5 km (32 miles) south-west from Pune, high in the Western Ghats, 869 m (2,850 ft) above sea level. It is one of the great strongholds of India, but its real importance came between 1664 and 1680, when it was the capital during the last years of Shivaji's reign.

In view of its remote location and difficult access, it is rarely visited. From a distance it is not particularly striking, as it stands against a higher range of hills which form a backdrop.

Raigarh, like most other hillforts, was the scene of complex dynastic squabbles. In the 12th century, Rairi, as it was known, was the seat of a family of petty Maratha chiefs who later paid tribute to the Vijayanagara princes and the Bahmani king. From 1479 to 1636 the fort passed to the Nizam Shahi rulers of Ahmadnagar, who in turn ceded it to the Adil Shahi dynasty of Bijapur, but it was under Shivaji, who acquired the fort in 1648, that it reached its heyday. The royal and public buildings are reputed to have numbered over 300 stone houses and structures. In 1648 Shivaji was crowned prince at Raigarh, and he died here in 1680. In 1690 Aurangzeb took control, but it reverted to the Marathas and was surrendered to the British under Colonel Prother in 1818.

The ascent begins at Wadi, past some ruined granaries. Above the pathway on a spur is the **Khublada** bastion, access to which is along a narrow pathway and past a gate called the Nana Darwaza. Ruins flank the path up until there is a sharp turn. Beyond is the **Maha Darwaza**, flanked by two massive bastions. Over the gateway is the shardula motif.

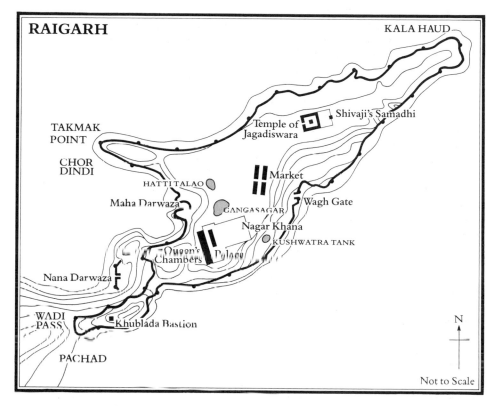

RAIGARH

KALA HAUD

TAKMAK POINT

Shivaji's Samadhi

Temple of Jagadiswara

CHOR DINDI

HATTI TALAO

Market

Maha Darwaza

GANGASAGAR

Wagh Gate

Nagar Khana

KUSHWATRA TANK

Queen's Chambers

Palace

Nana Darwaza

WADI PASS

Khublada Bastion

N

PACHAD

Not to Scale

At this level a high curtain wall and broad fosse enclose the north-west frontage. 61 m (200 ft) above are the remains of a second curtain wall; the same distance above this is a third line.

The hilltop is a plateau of about 2·4 m (1½ miles) by 1·6 m (1 mile) in an irregular wedge. To the west, south and east the hill is so sheer that there are no defensive walls. Among the ruins lie the tomb of Madar, a Muslim saint, near to which is an oval reservoir. There is another, the Ganga Sagar, near the citadel, close to which are two two-storey towers with pointed windows.

The **Palki Darwaza** leads to the **Bala Killi**. To the right are seven large apartments for the royal ladies; on the left are guardrooms. The main gate of the citadel is on the south wall. The walls of the king's court are still standing. On a low mound in the centre is the site of Shivaji's throne.

There are ruins of many other buildings – houses, magazines and cisterns – as well as the old market place, with two rows of twenty-two shops. To the north are the old elephant stables.

The **Temple of Jagadiswara** lies in a walled enclosure surrounded by a pond and the quarters of dancing girls. To the east is Shivaji's chatri, on an octagonal plinth.

RAIRI

Built on a rocky outcrop above a small navigable river, Rairi lies 361 km (225 miles) south of Bombay. The fort was built in 1662 by Shivaji, but later it fell into the hands of the local rulers of Sawantwari and became a stronghold of piracy, as a result of which it was stormed by the British in 1765, only to revert a year later. In 1819 it was ceded to the British permanently.

The **Fort** stands on a low hill and is enclosed by an irregular outer wall, which is reinforced by circular bastions, the largest being 6·1 m (20 ft) high, joined by a loopholed curtain wall 5·2 m (17 ft) high. The entrance road is crossed by a wall which links the citadel to the outer walls. A gateway leads to a square court, up a flight of steps to a third gate and the citadel, which is about 7·6 m (25 ft) high and surrounded by a ditch. The citadel walls are 3·6 m (12 ft) thick with semicircular towers every 55 m (180, ft), designed to carry artillery.

Nearby on Hasta Dongar Hill are sacred caves.

RAJAMUNDRY (RAJAMAHENDRI)

Rajamundry is the site of the ancient seat of the Vengi kings. In 1471 it fell to the Muslims, but in 1512 it was restored to the Orissa Rajas. In 1571 it fell to the Deccan Muslims under Rafat Khan and for the next 150 years it was the scene of bitter fighting, before it was granted to the French in 1753. De Bussy made his headquarters here between 1754 and 1757.

The town contains two churches, a museum and a provincial college. It is a good centre for visiting the beautiful Godavari Gorge, which is surrounded by some of the most attractive scenery in southern India. A few miles down-river are the headworks of the Godavari Delta Irrigation system, designed by Sir Arthur Cotton (1852), to whom there is a marble bust on the dam.

RANIBENNUR

This small town, 129 km (80 miles) south-west of Dharwar, was seized by Colonel Arthur Wellesley in 1800 while he was in pursuit of the Maratha freebooter Dhundia Wagh, in retaliation for having been sniped at by the local garrison. Later, in 1818, it was occupied by General Munro.

RAUZA (KHULDABAD)

Rauza or Khuldabad (literally the Heavenly Abode) lies 22·5 km (14 miles) north-west of Aurangabad. Situated 833 m (2,732 ft) above sea level, it is only 6·5 km (4 miles) distant from the spectacular caves at Ellora and is well worth a visit en route. (For details of the caves at Ellora, see Volume I.)

Rauza is of major religious importance to Deccan Muslims. Emperor Aurangzeb is interred here, together with his second son, Azam Shah, Asaf Jah, founder of the dynasty of the same name at Hyderabad, Abul Hasan Tana Shah, last King of Golconda, Nizam Shah, King of Ahmadnagar and numerous other minor figures.

Once an important and prosperous town, Rauza retains between fifteen and twenty fine domed tombs and over 1,400 plain sepulchres. The town is picturesque, enclosed by a high fortified wall built by Aurangzeb, with seven gates: the Nagarkhana, Pangra, Langda, Mangalpeth, Kunbi Ali, Hamdadi and a wicket called Azam Shahi.

The approach from Aurangabad is lined with ruins of mosques and tombs on all sides. A paved ascent, sections of which have collapsed, continues into the town. Midway between the north and south gates is the **Tomb of Aurangzeb** (1707), within a simple enclosure approached by a steep path. The gateway and domed porch were added in 1760. Within is a large quadrangle with open-fronted buildings. On the south side is a delightful Nakkar Khana or Music Hall. To the west is a mosque with scalloped arches. Opposite the north end of the mosque is a gateway leading to an inner courtyard, in the south-east corner of which is Aurangzeb's burial place.

The grave is simple, set in the centre of a stone platform on a marble floor and open to the sky. The marble screen was erected by Lord Curzon and the Nizam. To the right are the tombs of Azam Shah, his wife and daughter.

Between the tombs of Aurangzeb and Azam Shah lies the **Dargah of Sayyad Zain-ud-Din** (1370), a Muslim saint. It is set in the quadrangle with two gates inlaid with brass, silver and bronze and steps enriched with polished stones. The grave is richly embroidered, with a string of ostrich eggs suspended above it. In a small room in the angle of the courtyard is the Robe of the Prophet, which is exhibited once a year.

Opposite the tombs is another building, also with a large quadrangular courtyard and a Nakkar Khana. In the courtyard are two large drums. The west end is used as a school and leads to an inner courtyard. Facing the entrance is the **Tomb of Sayyad Burhan-ud-Din** (1344). The shrine is alleged to contain hairs from the Prophet's beard. The doors are richly ornamented with wrought silver inlay. A mosque stands in front of the dargah, and within the town are other dargahs to Muslim saints such as Muntajab-ud-Din and Sayyad Yussuf.

To the right of the mausoleum are the **Tombs of Asaf Jah I** (mid-18th century) and **Nasir Jang**, surrounded by a screen of red porphyry on a platform of white marble. Nasir Jang lies to the left.

To the west of this group of tombs is the **Maqbara of Bani Begum** (18th century), the consort of one of Aurangzeb's sons. It stands in a large garden enclosed by a handsome wall with corner kiosks carrying bulbous domes. The main entranced is via the north west. The Begum's tomb lies within the central enclosure, which is enriched with pavilions carried on slender pillars surmounted by Bengali-style domed roofs.

The **Lal Bagh** was built by Aurang-

zeb's foster-brother, Khan Jahan, in the late 17th century. It is similar in form to the Begum's maqbara, but is built of red porphyry and is smaller, with ornamental fountains.

North-west of the town is the **Dargah of Malik Ambar** (1626) and the tomb of his wife, Bibi Karima. They are raised on low platforms. The main tomb is enriched with cusped arches in stucco. A short distance away lies the open **Tomb of Abul Hasan Tana Shah** (late 17th century), last Sultan of Golconda. North of the town is the **Tomb of Nizam Shah Bhairi**, which was later converted by the British into a bungalow.

The **Dargah of Ahmad Nizam Shah** (1490–1509) stands on a raised platform with an open court around. It is square in plan, with a projecting stringcourse dividing the façade into two, the lower part having three compartments on each side, enriched with horseshoe arches. The upper cornice is carried on brackets, with a pierced parapet above, crowned by corner kiosks. The lower part of the dome is ornamented with lotus leaves.

Between here and the northern gate of the town is the Tomb of Zar Zari Bakhsh, which contains numerous relics, including a circular mirror of steel mounted on a pedestal presented by Tana Shah of Golconda. The earliest Muslim saint in the region, Ganj Ravan Ganj Bakhsh, is buried to the west of the town in a tomb with piers carrying pointed arches and a horseshoe dome, dating from the early 14th century. To the south of the town the mausolea of Abdul Halim and Kak Shah contain old Hindu masonry.

RAYADRUG

The hillfort of Rayadrug lies close to Bellary and comprises a citadel and lower fort, the latter containing the small town. The citadel, which has Jain antiquities in the form of ancient rock sculptures and three small cells, occupies the summit of a mass of granite rocks, rising over 366 m (1,200 ft). The south face is perpendicular and inaccessible. The lower fort has a triple line of works, from which a steep path leads up to the citadel. At intervals are gateways of solid masonry. About half-way up the path is the old palace (early 16th century).

SADASHIVGARH

6·4 km (4 miles) north of Karwar, Sadashivgarh Fort was built by a Sonda chief between 1674 and 1715. It is situated on a flat-topped hill 68 m (220 ft) high, overlooking the entrance to the Kali river, with a steep, inaccessible face on the riverside.

In 1752 the Portuguese carried the fort, which they greatly strengthened, but two years later returned it to the Sonda chief. In 1763 it was seized by Haidar Ali's general and twenty years later was garrisoned by the British, and later by Tipu. The fortifications comprise a granite and mortar wall 6 m (20 ft) high and 1·8 m (6 ft) thick, surrounded by a moat. There are three outworks guarding the outer approaches.

SATARA

16 km (10 miles) from Satara Road station, Satara lies in a shallow basin between two hills, near the confluence of the Kistna and Verna rivers. It is a pleasant and interesting town with a fine collection of historical relics associated with Shivaji.

The old **Cantonment** contains the **Residency** (1820) used by Sir Bartle Frere in 1849. Outside the north gate were the old British lines.

The Judge's Court occupies the Old Palace, a plain building of no great consequence. The **New Palace** was built by

the local British engineer Mr Smith between 1838 and 1844; he also built the bridges over the two rivers. The façade is unusual. It is enriched with several mythological pictures, now badly eroded by the weather. On the west side of the central courtyard is a hall carried on sixty-four teak pillars. The surrounding buildings are occupied as administrative offices.

About 182 m (591 ft) beyond is a **villa** containing the remarkable crown jewels of the Satara family, the famous sword of Shivaji – the Jai Bhavani – probably made in Genoa, and the waghnakh or 'Tiger's claws' with which Shivaji killed Afzul Khan. His shield, seal, coat and bejewelled dagger can also be seen.

The **Historical Museum** (1930) has an interesting collection of documents relating to Maratha history.

The **Fort of Wasota** can be reached via a path from the south side of the town. The entrance gate is formidable, with 12·2 m (40 ft) buttresses, but there is little of interest inside: a bungalow, a small temple and the ruins of the Raja's palace. The Fort, alleged to have been built in 1192, was stormed and carried by the British on 10 February 1818.

SECUNDERABAD

Today Secunderabad and Hyderabad are connected by ribbon development and the two cities are merged. Secunderabad is named after Nizam Sikander Jah (1803–29). It is one of the largest cantonments in India, laid out from 1806 for the British Subsidiary Force following the treaty of 1798 secured by Major James Achilles Kirkpatrick. As Secunderabad grew to become the largest British cantonment in India, it developed its own distinct identity.

The main thoroughfare and shopping centre is James Street. The plan is a typical cantonment grid pattern, with the large Brigade parade ground and race-course near the centre. Notable buildings include the King Edward VII Memorial Hospital, the United Services Club – a local landmark – and, on the road to Begampet, the buildings where Sir Ronald Ross identified the link between malaria and mosquitoes. **St John's Church** (*c.* 1860) is to a conventional classical design. St Mary's Cathedral lies nearby.

Near to the Boat Club, east of the Husain Sagar, is the **Tomb of Abdul Haq Diler Jung**, with elaborate carved jali screens. Within the compound of the Pulgani Palace, opposite the Police Lines, is a large **mosque** copied from a Spanish prototype and built in 1906. It has octagonal domes and minarets with Moorish arches. Just to the right of the entrance to the compound is the **Kuttay-Ki-Kabar**, a monument to a dog.

Near the Plassey Lines in Bowenpally is a **step-well**, reputedly haunted by the ghost of Lieutenant John Moore, killed with his favourite horse on 9 July 1807. The former country house of the British Resident at Bolarum lies 4·8 km (3 miles) north of the post office. Now the **Rashtra-pati Nilyam**, it is the official residence of the President of India, with fine interiors surrounded by manicured lawns.

At the village of Alwal, on the road to Amaravati, is the **Maharaja Chandulal's Temple** (*c.* 1830), which contains a silver idol to Lord Venkateshwara and which features in *Temple Confessions of a Thug* by Meadows Taylor (1916).

6·5 km (4 miles) west of Secunderabad is the **Shrine of Maula Ali**, with a mosque surrounded by more ancient remains, including an old citadel and an extensive prehistoric cemetery.

At Trimalgiri, 4·8 km (3 miles) north-east of Secunderabad, is a large entrenched camp surrounded by a stone ditch. The large castellated building, known locally as **Windsor Castle** (late 19th century), was a military prison. The station hospital lies south of the south east bastion.

In the Parade Ground Cemetery are a large number of British tombs and memorials. The Old Lancer Lines Cemetery is enclosed by a wall built in 1822 by HM 30th Regiment. St John's Church also retains many military memorials from 1818 onwards.

SHIVNER

The site of this hillfort, about 80·5 km (50 miles) north of Pune and close to Harischandragarh and the town of Junnar, rises over 305 m (1,000 ft) from the plain, commanding the main road. It is triangular in shape, narrowing from a southern base of about 244 m (793 ft) to a point of rock to the north.

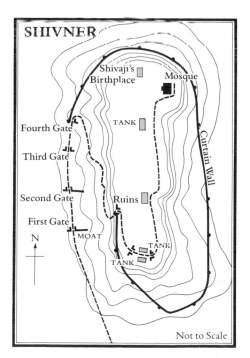

Shivner is of interest as it was the birthplace of Shivaji. In the 3rd century it was a great Buddhist centre. About fifty rock cells remain, particularly on the eastern

503

face. In 1599 the hillfort was granted to Shivaji's grandfather, Maloji Bhonsla, and Shivaji was born here in 1627. Possession of the fort ebbed and flowed with the fortunes of war. Shivaji himself was repulsed in an attack on the Mughal garrison in 1670.

SHOLAPUR

Situated on the plain of the Sina, Sholapur lies 241 km (150 miles) by rail from Pune. To the south-west, close to the city wall, lies the fort of Sholapur. To the south of the city is the **Siddhaswar Lake**, with a temple at the centre.

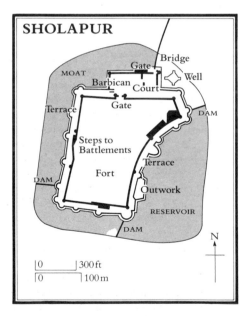

Originally, the city was enclosed by a wall 4 km (2½ miles) in circuit, but large stretches were demolished in 1872 to permit expansion. The **Fort**, which is of Muslim construction, is enclosed by a double line of fortifications with battlemented parapets reinforced by towers. The outer wall is 14th century; the inner wall and four great square towers, from the 16th and 17th centuries. The outer

walls are pierced for musketry and have four corner and twenty-three side towers, with embrasures and vaulted chambers for cannon.

In May 1818 Thomas Munro and General Pritzler marched against the remaining forces of Baji Rao and routed them under the walls of Sholapur, after which the fort surrendered.

The **King Edward VII Memorial Hospital** and **Government High School** are the most significant public buildings.

SINHAGARH (SIMHAGAD)

Sinhagarh or Lion's Fort lies about 19 km (12 miles) south-west of Pune. It is spread over a wide area on one of the highest points of the Bhuleshwar range, 1,317 m (4,322 ft) above sea level and 701 m (2,300 ft) above the level of the surrounding plain.

The fort was called Kondana until 1647, when its name was changed to Sinhagarh by Shivaji. In 1328 Muhammad Tughluq blockaded and captured the fort. It fell to Malik Ahmad, founder of the Ahmadnagar dynasty, on his capture of Shivner in 1486. In 1637 it was surrendered to Bijapur and, after repeatedly changing hands, it was the scene of one of the most daring exploits in Maratha history when it was retaken by Shivaji's forces under Tanaji Malusare. Between 1701 and 1703 it was besieged by Aurangzeb. Finally, the British under General Pritzler seized the fort on 2 March 1818, capturing a vast amount of treasure.

To the north and south are steep cliffs, from which rises a wall of basalt 12·2 m (40 ft) high, crowned by ruins. Two tortuous paths rise from the north-east and southwest. Each is defended at the top by three successive gates in a poor state of repair. The walls are built of roughly bonded dressed stone.

Pune Gate, the first on the north-east approach, is flanked by a conical tower on the outer side and by a section of a tower

against the cliff face. The gateway stands in a pointed-arched recess with central battlements pierced by loopholes. The second gate is similar, but more ruinous; the third is the most complete, with intact towers and a wing wall. On the west side a strong wedge-shaped wall seals the mouth of the gorge, the apex acting as a break-water for the river during heavy rain.

The upper surface of the fort is undulating and irregular and retains few buildings. Ruins of temples, tombs and towers are scattered about. Near the gorge is a **monument** (1937) commemorating the capture of the fort in 1670 by Tanaji, who became a national hero. There are numerous modern bungalows on the hill which were once used by Europeans from Pune (Poona) during the hot weather.

SIRUR

69 km (43 miles) from Pune is the deserted cantonment of Sirur. It is of interest because of the tombs in the local cemetery. The **Tomb of Colonel Wallace** (1809) is revered by the Hindus of the town and surrounding area. He is remembered as Sat Purush or the Holy Man. At harvest-time offerings of grain are made at the tomb as 'food for the saintly spirit'. The cemetery retains a number of other early European tombs.

TALIKOTA

96 km (60 miles) north-east of Kaladgi town and 40 km (25 miles) east of Bagalkot, near a bend in the Kistna, close by the village of Tondital, is the battlefield of Talikota.

Here on 23 January 1565 the power of the Hindu Vijayanagara Empire was crushed by a confederacy of Muslim kings of the Deccan. The small town of Talikota, from whence the allies marched to meet the Vijayanagara forces, lies 48 km (30 miles) from the epic field.

THANA

Thana, 34 km (21 miles) north-east of Bombay, reached its peak in the 13th century, when it was the capital of a great kingdom. In 1318 it was conquered by Mubarak Khalji and placed in the hands of the Muslim governor. In 1529 the Portuguese obtained local supremacy, and after the city was sacked, it was ceded to Portugal by treaty in 1533. Under Portuguese rule Thana achieved fresh prosperity, until in 1739 it fell to the Marathas. In 1744 the English preempted a Portuguese attempt to recover their possessions by storming the fort and seizing the town. In 1818 Trimbakji Danglia, minister to the last Peshwa, escaped from Thana while under guard with the aid of a Maratha syce or groom.

The **Anglican Church** was being built when Bishop Heber arrived in 1825, and on 10 July of that year it was consecrated by him.

Thana was the terminus of the Great Indian Peninsular Railway, the first in India, which in 1853 connected the town with Bombay.

TRIMBAK

Trimbak or Tryambak (literally the Three-eyed, a name for Mahadeo) lies 32 km (20 miles) south-west of Nasik town. The 17th- and 18th-century Fort, which is 1,295 m (4,248 ft) above sea level and about 549 m (1,800 ft) above the village, is situated on an impregnable outcrop of rock with steep scarps to each face varying between 61 m (200 ft) and 122 m (400 ft) sheer. There are only two gateways.

The main south gateway is the principal access point. The north gateway is only a single gate, approached by a narrow passage with steps cut from the rock, wide enough for one person only.

The **Temple of Trimbakeshwar** is a place of Hindu pilgrimage off the Nasik Road (see Volume I).

VADGAON (WARGAON)

This small village, 37 km (23 miles) north-west of Pune, was the scene of the gallant stand of a small British force under Lieutenant-Colonel Cockburn on 12 and 13 January 1779. It was here that General Carnac drew up a truce with the Marathas which entailed the surrender of all British conquests in the area since 1773. The treaty was later repudiated by Warren Hastings and the war continued until 1783.

VENGURLA

This old sea port and fort lies 46·5 km (29 miles) from Mormugao in Goa and 313 km (196 miles) from Bombay.

In 1638 the Dutch had a small trading settlement here, which was used for victualling ships during their blockade of Goa. In 1664 it was burned to the ground by Shivaji, and again eleven years later

by the Mughals. In 1772 a small factory was established here by the British, but forty years later the town was ceded in perpetuity to the Rani of Sawantwari.

At the northern point of the bay, 76 m (250 ft) above the high-water level, are the Vengurla port lighthouses, erected in 1869. The public offices in the town occupy the old Dutch factory.

VIJAYADRUG (VIZIADRUG)

Vijayadrug, situated 48 km (30 miles) south of Ratnagiri, has one of the best harbours and most interesting sea-forts on the west coast of India.

The **Fortress** is one of the strongest in the area, rising grandly 31 m (100 ft) from the river. It is an ancient site, enlarged by the rulers of the Bijapur, and again strengthened and enlarged in the mid-17th century by Shivaji, to whom it owes its triple line of fortifications, towers and massive inner buildings.

In 1698 Angria, the Maratha admiral and pirate, made Vijayadrug his headquarters and terrorized the European maritime powers with persistent naval raids on coastal shipping. In 1717 the English were repulsed from the fort with great loss. Three years later a joint Anglo-Portuguese expedition failed to take the fort, although it succeeded in destroying at least sixteen Maratha ships. In 1724 the Dutch tried, also without success. In 1738 the French ship *Jupitor* was seized offshore with 400 slaves. The fort finally surrendered to the English in 1818.

The fort is formidable, with twenty-seven bastions, three of which are magnificent, multi-storey bays. At the strongest point the walls mass up to a huge round tower. The west side is open to the sea. Inside the triple fortifications is a broad inner moat. The citadel is massive, with many good wells and storehouses. In 1682 the fort boasted over 278 guns.

VIJAYANAGARA (HAMPI)

Vijayanagara, the City of Victory, was the largest and strongest Hindu capital of the Deccan, dominating the region from 1336 until the catastrophic Battle of Talikota in 1565. Under the patronage of this powerful Hindu dynasty, the religious centre at Hampi on the Tungabhadra river was transformed into a fortified and magnificently appointed capital. (For a complete description of the ruins see Volume I.)

Although only a fraction of Vijayanagara's defensive system has survived, the remains suggest that the capital was conceived as a gigantic fortress. Granite walls rising to more than 6 m (20 ft) follow the tops of the ridges wherever possible. These walls were constructed of massive granite blocks with tightly fitting joints punctuated by rectangular bastions with look-out posts.

Defensive gateways, often elaborately constructed with upper chambers, are positioned along the ancient roads. Doorways are roofed with beams on

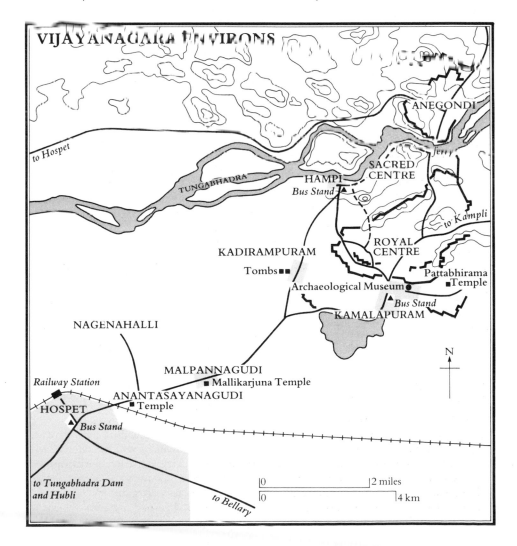

corbelled brackets. **Bhima's Gateway**, one of the best preserved, has ornamented corbels. Other examples have a dome raised high on four arches or façades with arched openings. Thick walls in front of the gateway demarcate squares with complex entrances.

Zone of Royal Performance

Within the enclosures to the east of the **Ramachandra Temple** lie the remains of structures associated with the ceremonial, administrative and military functions of the Vijayanagara rulers.

South-east of the temple is a large enclosure, known as the **King's Palace**, containing two significant monuments. One is a square platform with 100 column footings, probably the basement of a hall of justice. Nearby stands another platform, its multi-storey sides covered with lively friezes, including scenes of hunting and reception, and processions of musicians, dancers, elephants, horses and even camels. The Vijayanagara kings may have ascended this platform to witness the celebrations of the Mahanavami festival.

All around are the remains of smaller, columned structures, possibly for attending officers or guards. A subterranean chamber, now missing its roof, may have served as the state treasury.

Bathing was an important activity at the royal centre and several wells, aqueducts and tanks have been discovered here. These include one finely finished tank with stepped-stone sides and another almost 75 m (250 ft) long. Outside the enclosure to the south-east is a water pavilion, known as the **Queen's Bath**, built in an Islamic style. An empty square water basin is surrounded by a corridor with ornamental vaults. Elaborate balconies project gracefully over the basin.

North-east of the Ramachandra temple is another enclosure surrounded by high walls, mistakenly called the 'zenana'. This was possibly the residence of the king himself, or of the military commander. Standing in the middle of the enclosure is a two-storey pavilion on a stepped plan. Known as the **Lotus Mahal**, this is the finest example of Vijayanagara courtly architecture. Much of the delicately modelled plaster detail around the multilobed arches has survived. Nine pyramidal towers with eaves-like mouldings rise above. Built in a similar style are three watchtowers in the surrounding walls (in the north, north-east and south-east corners). The rectangular building with a gabled roof (north-west corner) may have served as a treasury or a storehouse.

Outside the enclosure to the east is a parade ground for military displays. Facing this are the celebrated **Elephant Stables**, the most impressive secular structure now standing in the royal centre. This has eleven chambers arranged in a row, with contrasting domed and vaulted forms symmetrically arranged around the double-storey pavilion in the middle. The adjacent structure has a raised verandah with multi-lobed arches and an inner colonnaded court. Athletic and military contests may have taken place here.

Zone of Royal Residence

To the west of the Ramachandra temple are the enclosures linked with the private activities of the king and his household. (Two of these are mistakenly called 'mint' and 'danaik's enclosure'.) Here there are several Islamic buildings, including a multi-domed watchtower (in the corner of one enclosure), an octagonal two-storey pavilion and a nine-domed reception hall. To the south is an octagonal fountain.

This zone also contains palace structures, the remains of which have recently been exposed by excavation. The typical palace had a symmetrical stepped plan with a sequence of rising levels in a 'U' formation. Private chambers were located at the highest level at the rear.

508

Only the stone basements, plaster floors and fragmentary rubble walls have been preserved.

Islamic Quarter

The presence of a Muslim community in this part of the capital is attested by a mosque and domed tomb, both dating from the 15th century. Numerous gravestones and small tombs are located nearby.

South of the village of Kadirampuram are two large Muslim tombs, only one of which retains its original dome.

VINUKONDA

This fortified hill site, about 72·5 km (45 miles) south-west of Kondavid, comprises a bare rock, 183 m (600 ft) high, bereft of vegetation and crowned by a temple to Shiva, known as Ramalingeshwaraswami. Ancient stone circles or dolmens can be seen in the area.

Access to the summit is via a steep staircase cut in the rock. Near the temple at the summit are two large reservoirs revetted with cut stone. The fortifications rise in three lines, one above the other, but the walls have been demolished and only traces remain. It was probably built by the Reddi dynasty. The foundations of magazines, granaries and defensive works can be seen.

At the bottom of the hill is a small ruined mud fort which once belonged to the Malraj Zamindar's family. There is a large representation of Hanuman, the monkey god, nearby.

VISHAKHAPATNAM (VIZAGAPATAM)

This town, known as Vizag, is now a major industrial centre and port, with a reputation for shipbuilding and a significant complex of oil refineries. Situated midway down the east coast of India, it includes the old resort of Waltair, the 'Indian Brighton', which has the finest beach in India.

Historically, the town is something of a backwater, having escaped many of the misfortunes and depredations which affected most other areas in the 18th century. In June 1757 the British surrendered the town to de Bussy, but in 1758 Colonel Forde landed with a small force and drove the French from the Northern Circars, which had been granted to them by the Nizam in 1753. With the exception of a minor Sepoy Mutiny in 1780, the town has enjoyed a long period of peace and prosperity.

Architecturally, there are few buildings or monuments of any note. At the small port of Bimlipatam, 29 km (18 miles) to the north-east, there is an interesting Dutch cemetery with some 17th-century tombstones of historical significance.

VIZIANAGRAM

Situated 27 km (17 miles) north-west of Bimlipatam, midway down the east coast, Vizianagram, the City of Vijaya, is the chief town of the district and famous as the seat of the munificent maharajas of Vizianagram.

The town was founded in 1712. The **Fort** is occupied by the **Maharaja's Palace** and its ancillary offices and quarters. The town is well built and maintained. The market commemorates the visit of the Prince of Wales to India in 1875. The Town Hall and Church are noteworthy. Most of the public buildings were donated by the Maharaja, who was also responsible for a fine Gothic drinking fountain erected in Hyde Park in London but now sadly demolished.

At Bobbili there is an obelisk (1891) commemorating the murder of an earlier Raja by four retainers of Raja Ranga Rao.

509

WARANGAL

Warangal was the ancient capital of the Kakatiyas, but only ruins and earthworks reflect its early importance. The carpets and cottons of Warangal were once highly valued and were praised by Marco Polo.

The town, 138 km (86 miles) northeast of Hyderabad in the Deccan, is first mentioned during a Muslim incursion by Ala-ud-Din Khalji in 1303. Six years later another expedition, under Malik Kafur, succeeded in capturing Warangal Fort after a long and costly siege. Warangal changed hands many times as the battle to stem the Muslim advance continued. The emergent Bahmani state collided with the Warangal Raja on numerous occasions, but by 1543 the state had been absorbed by the Qutb Shahi dynasty of Golconda. In 1688 Golconda fell before Aurangzeb's armies and Warangal waned into insignificance.

Excavations have revealed the foundations of several early temples (see Volume I). A thick earth rampart (8th century) encloses the city and citadel. Access is through a gateway with a barbican which has high walls and a wide passage with a right-angled turn and guardroom recesses at the inner end.

The inner wall around the citadel is formidable. Built of granite and rectangular in plan, it has bastions to each corner and also at regular intervals along the flanks. In the centre of each side is a gateway with mantlets protecting the outer entrance. The west gate has carved lions in relief on either side: the shardula motif. The gateway is typically Hindu, with a moulded architrave, flat lintel and Hindu pilasters carrying a moulded cornice.

Within the citadel is the **Kush Mahal** or **Audience Hall of Shitab Khan** (early 16th century), a fascinating building which appears to be a copy of the Hindola Mahal at Mandu. It is built to the same system, but is smaller in scale. The hall has six bays divided by plain, pointed transverse arches. Nearby are the ruins of a large temple with four monumental gateways.

YANAON

This tiny former French enclave of only 913·8 hectares (2,258 acres) was founded *circa* 1750. Its fortunes ebbed and flowed with the tide of French history in southern India. A mere 5·6 km (3½ miles) in extent, the French station was guaranteed by treaty in 1814–15 and was administered from Pondicherry.

SOUTHERN INDIA

THIRTEEN

SOUTHERN INDIA

Southern Andhra Pradesh, southern Karnataka, Tamil Nadu, Kerala

Introduction

For many centuries the palm-fringed shores of southern India have exerted a strong allure for Europeans and foreign traders. The exotic Malabar coast of Kerala, with its maze of backwaters and romantic shoreline, has been a major point of contact between Europe and India since the time of Christ. The Greeks visited the coasts of Karnataka in the pre-Christian era. The Romans also knew it well. They traded in spices, silks, ivory and fragrant woods and maintained a cohort of troops at **Calicut**. So when Vasco da Gama landed in the same spot in 1498, he merely restored a pattern of social and economic intercourse which had been enjoyed by the Ancient World but severed by the fall of Rome and the subsequent rise of Islam.

Ancient Syrian Christian communities settled in Kerala from the dawn of Christianity. **Cochin**, the oldest European settlement in India, was reputedly visited by Thomas Dydimus, St Thomas the Apostle, in 52. The Thoman tradition of Christianity is certainly very strong in south India. It is alleged that the Doubting Apostle sailed to Malabar with an envoy of the Parthian king. There he made his first conversions among the Hindu community, and also among the Jews, who had settled in the area as early as 567 BC. He is alleged to have founded seven churches on the Malabar coast before travelling to the Coromandel coast, where, in 72, he was martyred at Mylapore on the outskirts of modern **Madras**.

In the 15th century the Nestorian church in India declined, until in most places it totally disappeared, except for a lingering survival at St Thomas's Mount. This ancient regional Christian tradition received an enormous boost with the arrival of the Portuguese in the 16th century, and later from the expansion of other European powers such as the French in **Pondicherry**, the Dutch at **Nagapattinam**, the Danes at **Tranquebar** and the British at **Madras** and at other coastal settlements, now long since decayed, such as **Anjengo**.

In the 18th and 19th centuries European missionaries were active all over southern India. In Travancore and **Cochin** missionary groups and societies motivated by ethical and philosophical ideals made a considerable impact, not just in a religious sense but by the physical provision of hospitals, schools and dispensaries for the poorer classes.

The Islamic connection with southern India was important but sporadic. Muslim converts arrived in Kerala very early in the expansion of Islam. They founded numerous mosques and played an important but limited role in the cosmopolitan life of the region. However, in the early 14th century Muslim raids from the north began to have a significant effect on local life, dislocating the architectural traditions of the region and causing a temporary hiatus in the construction of the monumental temple buildings for which southern India was renowned.

Overleaf The fabled palm-fringed shores of Kerala

In 1324 **Madurai** fell to the Muslim hordes, but with the foundation of the great Hindu empire at **Vijayanagara** (Hampi) in 1336 and its subsequent expansion, a major bulwark was formed between the Muslim kingdoms of the Deccan and the predominantly Hindu lands of the south. For over 200 years Vijayanagara led a formidable confederacy of Hindu forces powerful enough to resist Muslim expansion. Over this period there were at least twenty-eight major clashes between Muslims and Hindus in the triangle of land formed by the Tungabhadra and Krishna rivers. At its height the Vijayanagara Empire extended from **Rajamundry** to **Tiruchirapalli** on the east coast and from **Tinnevelly** to Goa in the west. However, with its collapse after the Battle of Talikota in 1565, there was little Muslim conquest further south. In 1593 Bijapur seized **Seringapatam**, but domestic problems prompted a rapid withdrawal and no lasting impact was made.

Although the southern region has a rich heritage of ancient sacred architecture, with world-famous temples at **Madurai**, **Thanjavur**, Mamallapuram and Kanchipuram, historical examples of Hindu secular architecture are much harder to find. There are, however, a number of palaces of the 16th and 17th centuries which are important survivals of the period.

The earliest and simplest is the Lotus Mahal, a garden palace built at **Vijayanagara** in about 1575. Here the early impact of the Muslim style of the north on the Hindu architecture of the south may be seen to advantage. Owing to the very limited impact of Islam on southern India, there was a much more gradual penetration of Hindu secular architecture by Islamic principles of construction. The Lotus Mahal is a fascinating commingling of elements, with a tiered pyramidal roof adapted from local temple architecture combined with recessed, foliated arches taken from the Lodi tombs of Delhi. The pillars and concentrically recessed arches are Islamic, but the pyramidal roofs, chajjas and stucco ornament are Hindu in origin.

The three-storey palace at **Chandragiri**, built in the early 17th century, is a highly instructive, sophisticated exercise in the blending of the two traditions. The palace has a prominent pyramidal tower, but the arcaded façade is treated with a series of orthodox Muslim arches.

Unfortunately, this accomplished style did not persist in southern India. The palace of Tirumala Nayak at **Madurai**, although monumental in conception, is poorly integrated, uncoordinated and lacking in cohesion. This huge edifice contains an inner courtyard which is surrounded by massive round granite columns over 12 m (40 feet) high, derived from European sources, above which rise foliated arcades of brick and stucco. Although the scale and magnitude of the exercise are impressive, there is a fundamental lack of synthesis between the constituent parts.

The final example of Hindu secular architecture is the palace complex in the fort at **Thanjavur**, built about 1700, which portrays the same lack of discipline and cohesion as the palace at **Madurai**. The admixture of Hindu iconography, weak classical detail and an eccentric eight-storey tower creates a monument which expresses the decadent values of a more materialist age – in a similar manner to the extravagant fantasies of the Nawabs of Oudh at **Lucknow**, far to the north.

In Kerala the palace at **Padmanabhapuram**, a splendid exercise in Keralan architecture, and the Mattancherry Palace at **Cochin**, built by the Portuguese, are both significant. Both contain a fine series of murals depicting scenes from the Hindu epics and both are distinguished examples of secular palace architecture of the period.

After the collapse of the Vijayanagara Empire, the local viceroy at **Mysore** asserted his independence. Gradually, the state consolidated its borders. By the 18th century **Mysore** had become a local power of some importance, but the ruling Wadiyar family lost effective control to intriguing ministers. In 1761 Haidar Ali became master of Mysore. Together with his son Tipu Sultan, Haidar Ali dominated the political stage of southern India for almost forty years, until in 1799, after four separate wars, the British stormed the island fortress at **Seringapatam**, crushed Tipu and restored the Wadiyar family. With the collapse of **Mysore** as an effective independent power in the south and the defeat of the French by the forces of the East India Company, the British obtained paramountcy throughout southern India.

Madras was the first important English settlement in India. Founded in 1639, it remained the nerve-centre of English influence in the East until the rise of **Calcutta** in the late 18th century. Centred on Fort St George, the city developed a fine legacy of classical colonial architecture well adapted to the climate and arranged on a grid plan, the earliest example of English town planning in India. Later, with the establishment of greater security, charming garden houses were built in outlying areas, renowned for their elegant architectural style. Government House and its magnificent Banqueting Hall were notable examples of the public expression of rising British Imperial power.

Within the fort St Mary's Church, the oldest surviving Anglican church in the East, was the physical and spiritual focus of the city. Today it contains a remarkable concentration of early British monuments and artefacts. Outside the fort, St Andrew's Kirk and St George's Cathedral, erected in the early 19th century, are two of the finest classical churches in India, both based on the famous London prototype of St. Martin-in-the-Fields.

In the late 19th century the city developed a reputation for its Indo-Saracenic architecture, based on a highly inventive synthesis of European and local styles. A whole series of sumptuous public buildings arose along the waterfront, designed by local British architects such as Robert Fellowes Chisholm. They imparted an unforgettable romantic skyline to the city. Elsewhere in the south, British architects employing Indo-Saracenic styles were active, notably at **Mysore**, where the Maharaja's city palace was designed by Henry Irwin, the architect of Viceregal Lodge, Simla.

With its mild and healthy climate, the British developed **Bangalore** into a major military station and cantonment. As the town expanded, a strong classical tradition was maintained for the public buildings, while at a domestic level a delightful form of vernacular architecture evolved whereby pretty classical and Gothick bungalows were embellished with ornamental bargeboards and decorative trelliswork, known as monkey-tops.

After the consolidation of British power in the region, hill stations were founded for rest and recreation in the Nilgiri Hills at **Coonoor, Kotagiri** and **Ootacamund**, and in the Palni Hills at **Kodaikanal**.

With its long, liberal, spiritual tradition and ancient heritage of sacred architecture, the south has always attracted a wide range of religious organizations and cults. The world headquarters of the Theosophical Society is at **Madras**, set in serene gardens of remembrance with a series of buildings containing the shrines of all faiths. To the north of **Pondicherry** at **Auroville** is the Sri Aurobindo Ashram, founded in 1968 as an experimental international community. It is set in modernistic buildings. Men and women can live here in peace and harmony transcending all creeds, politics and nationalities, a contemporary expression of the strong spiritual currents which flow through the history of the region.

516

St Andrew's Kirk, Madras

Above left The Kalyana Mahal, Gingee

Below left The Palace at Cochin

Above Government House, Mysore

Left The Law Courts, Madras

Above Government House, Madras

Below The Council House, Fort St George, Madras

Left St Mary's Church, Fort St George, Madras

Above Clive's House, Fort St George, Madras

Below The High Court, Bangalore

Left The Law Courts, Ootacamund

Above St Stephen's Church, Ootacamund

Below The Amba Vilas Palace, Mysore

Palace of the Maharaja of Mysore, Bangalore

The Lalitha Mahal Palace Hotel, Mysore

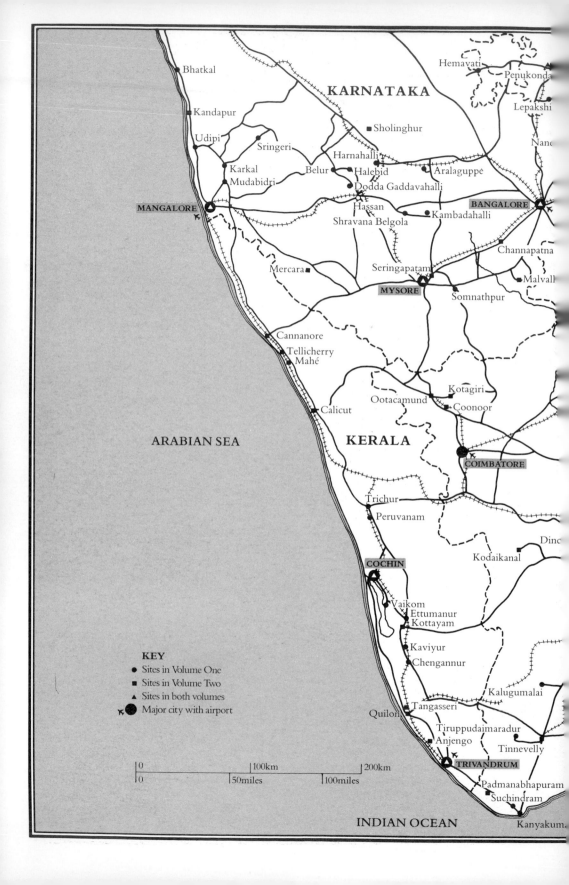

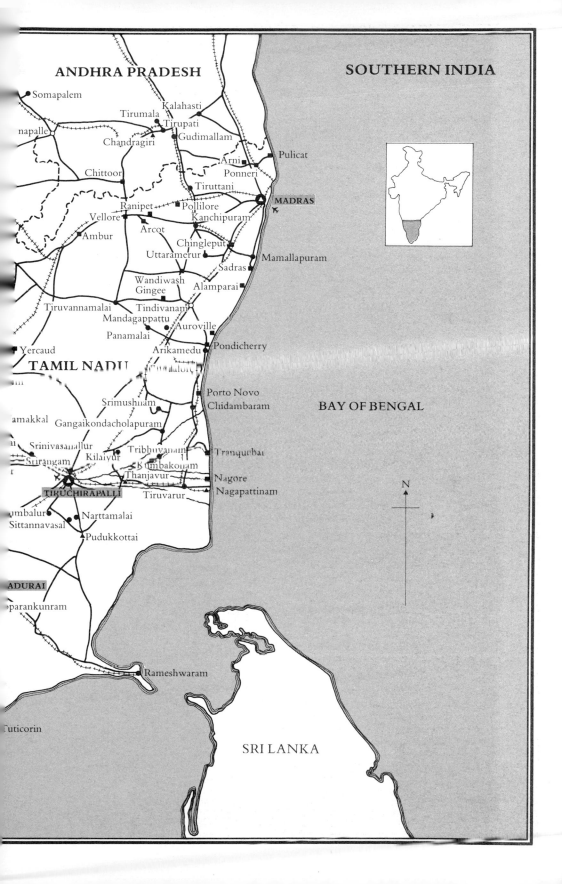

ALAMPARAI

This small coastal village, lying midway between Pondicherry and Chingleput, has an historical reputation out of all proportion to its size. Granted to Dupleix in 1750 by Muzaffar Jang, it was the scene of constant fighting during the struggle for local supremacy between England and France. In 1758 a severe naval engagement was fought offshore. Two years later the town and fort were seized by Sir Eyre Coote.

AMBUR

This small town, located 48 km (30 miles) from Vellore, at the foot of the Kadapanatham Pass on the Palar river, boasts a fine hillfort on the peak of Ambur Drug, which dominates the town.

The fort has been keenly contested. In 1750 the first significant battle in which European forces were employed in Indian warfare was fought under its walls when Muzaffar Jang defeated the Nawab of Arcot. In 1768 the stronghold was gallantly defended by the 10th Madras Infantry. Twenty years later Haidar Ali stormed and captured the fort, after which it was restored to British control by the Treaty of Mangalore. In both expeditions against Mysore in 1792 and 1799, the fort played a vital role in the British line of supply.

ANJENGO

Anjengo (literally Five Coconut Trees), a small coastal settlement between Quilon and Trivandrum, is the site of an old English factory established here in 1684 and abandoned in 1810.

There are a number of interesting build-ings and monuments, including an English cemetery with early-18th-century tombs, an extensive laterite fort and a Portuguese church. It is reputed to be the birthplace of Robert Orme (1728), the historian, and Eliza Draper (1744), the heroine of Laurence Sterne's *Sentimental Journey*, to whom there is a monument in the cathedral cloisters at Bristol.

ARCOT

Historically, Arcot is of very considerable interest, but few vestiges of its former power remain. Situated 105 km (65 miles) from Madras and 8 km (5 miles) from the railway station, the town lies on the bank of the Palar river. Once the capital of the grandiloquent Nawabs of the Carnatic, the town is now of little importance.

The Muslim presence is derived from Daud Khan, who was made governor by Zulfiqar Khan, Aurangzeb's general, after the fall of Gingee in 1698. In 1710 Saadat-ullah Khan assumed the title Nawab of the Carnatic and made Arcot his capital, but the tortuous dynastic feuding after his death drew in the British and French in support of the opposing factions. In 1751 Clive, then a young, unknown writer in the East India Company's service, was sent to Arcot to divert the enemy from the siege of Trichinopoly. The capture and subse-quent defence of Arcot by a handful of British troops and sepoys against enor-mous forces is one of the most remarkable feats of British arms in India. The siege lasted fifty days, until 15 November 1751, when reinforcements arrived from Madras.

Subsequently, in 1758, Arcot was sur-rendered to the French under Lally, but it was recaptured by Colonel Coote in 1760.

The old red-brick town walls were obliterated by Tipu Sultan in 1783, but the foundations can still be traced. On the river front the **Delhi Gate** survives and conveys some idea of the original fort. Over the gateway is **Clive's Room**. The road into the town passes the old **Taluk Cutcherry** and crosses the dry moat. Close to two small tanks are the **Tomb of Saadat-ullah Khan** (*c.* 1732) and, within the same compound, the **Jami Masjid**.

West, beyond the Jami Masjid, are the ruins of the **Palace of the Nawabs of the Carnatic**, situated on raised ground over the Nawab's Tank. The shell of the **Durbar Room** may still be seen. Opposite is the **Black Mosque** or Kala Masjid. Various tombs lie nearby, including one which is reputed to have sheltered the body of Subadar Nasir Jang, murdered at Gingee in 1750. Another in whitewashed brick is that of Tipu Auliya, a local saint, after whom Tipu Sultan took his name.

ARNI

This ruined fort played an important role in the wars of the Carnatic. Stormed by Clive in 1751 after the successful defence of Arcot, it was the scene of further fighting in 1782, when Sir Eyre Coote defeated the combined troops of Lally and Haidar Ali.

An imposing monument in the form of a 20-m-high (65 ft) column stands on one side of the old parade ground. It commemorates Captain Robert Kelly, who was shot in a duel by Colonel Urban Vigors. Apparently, in conversation with his wife, Vigors referred to Kelly as 'an old woman'. She repeated the comment to Mrs Kelly, who insisted that her husband should obtain satisfaction. He was then shot for his efforts.

There is an interesting old temple in the north-west angle of the enclosure.

BANGALORE *Map overleaf*

Bangalore (literally the Town of Bengalu, a type of bean) is one of the fastest-growing cities in India. It is being transformed from a relaxed military

station and cantonment into a bustling modern city of over 2,500,000 people, the capital of the state of Karnataka.

The town was founded by Kempe Gowda in the early 16th century, and it became an important fortress under Haidar Ali and Tipu Sultan in the late 18th century. With the storming of Seringapatam in 1799 and the demise of Tipu Sultan, the Wadiyar family were restored to power by Wellesley. In 1881 the state passed from British control to an adopted heir, although the large cantonment area was assigned to the British government for military use.

Bangalore resembles an English garden city in its layout, with spacious parks, wide streets and tree-lined avenues.

The cantonment was founded in the early 18th century as a more salubrious location for the British garrison than the malaria-ridden island at Seringapatam. By the end of the century Bangalore was a well-established and flourishing garrison town.

The **Cantonment** grew during the 19th century as a military and administrative centre, separated from the old town by a strip of open land. Today this distinction has been lost. The two areas have merged into a large conurbation, but the special character of the cantonment can still be discerned.

In the north-west lies the **Maharaja's Palace** (*c.* 1865; modified 1881 onwards). This is an extraordinary pile set in a large estate. It was built for a local British merchant, Mr Garrat, but was taken over and extended for use by the Maharaja of Mysore. In silhouette it is reminiscent of Windsor Castle, on which it is based, with a romantic skyline of machicolated and crenellated towers. Adjoining the entrance is a large semicircular bay crowned by an elegant cast-iron verandah. It is built of stone and, in spite of the expense lavished on it, the whole resembles a Disneyland parody of an English Gothic country house.

The inside has a steep staircase with a

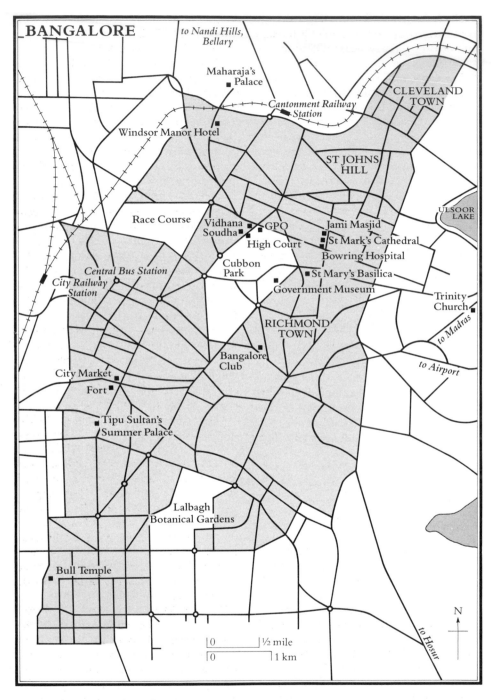

carved Gothic balustrade, enriched with bronze figures and overlooked by hunting trophies. The ballroom, reception rooms and bedrooms are well worth a visit, as is the splendid tiled multiple lavatory.

The Maharani's and Maharaja's Courtyards are delightful internal wells surrounded by arcaded cloisters, but the entire palace is sadly run down.

There is a Dower House in the extensive grounds, together with an interesting cast-iron conservatory.

The Indian Institute of Science and other research institutes lie to the north of the palace on the outskirts of the city. To the south-east is the opulent **Windsor Manor Hotel** (1985), designed in a classical colonial style, demonstrating the continuity of the classical tradition in India. On the east side of the cantonment is the large Ulsoor Tank, north-east of which lie the suburbs of Cleveland Town, Fraser Town and Richards Town. In Cleveland Town are **St Xavier's Roman Catholic Church** and **St John's Anglican Church**, in the cemetery of which is the **Tomb of General J. W. Cleveland**, after whom the area is named. Cleveland died in 1883, at the age of ninety-two, having served for seventy-three years in the Madras Army.

The famous Madras Sappers and Miners are based nearby. A memorial obelisk to the regiment can be found at Ulsoor. South of their lines is a whole series of civil and military buildings alongside the Parade Ground. These include St Andrew's Kirk (1864), the Main Guard, Bowring Civil Hospital and the Lady Curzon Women's Hospital. Just to the north lies Russell Market, in Indo-Saracenic style, and the Jami Masjid, the oldest mosque in the city. **St Mary's Basilica**, a frenetically ornate Gothic church, lies nearby. South of Ulsoor lie the Artillery Barracks, the old Cemetery, which contains some early graves from 1808 and 1809, the Mounted Parade and the YMCA buildings.

Trinity Church, off the Old Madras Road, contains some fine memorials. There is a half-length marble statue of General Clement Hill, who served through the Peninsular War and later commanded the Mysore Division, before his death in 1845. Immediately west of Trinity Church lie the Wesleyan Chapel, the Public Offices and **Mayo Hall**. This is a handsome Italianate stucco building with rusticated quoins and a typical crested roofline. Next is the Gymkhana on the General Parade Ground, which stretches over 1·6 km (1 mile) from east to west. To the south are St Joseph's College, the Gothic Roman Catholic Cathedral and All Saints' Church.

At the west end of the Parade Ground is **St Mark's Church** (mid-19th century). This is an interesting building, a distinguished stucco edifice with a shallow dome over the crossing and a domed apse. Inside is a memorial tablet to Lieutenant-Colonel Sir Walter Scott of Abbotsford (the second baronet), who died at sea in 1847.

West of the church lies **Cubbon Park**, one of the principal parks in the city, covering over 120 hectares (296 acres) and laid out by Sir Mark Cubbon in 1864. It contains some of the most interesting buildings in Bangalore.

The **High Court** (formerly the Public Offices) is a long, low, arcaded range enriched with Ionic porticos. Finished in Pompeian-red stucco, the building was designed by Colonel (later Sir) Richard Sankey between 1864 and 1868. Opposite is the **Vidhana Soudha**, a huge neo-Dravidian granite building which houses the Secretariat and State Legislative. It is one of the most impressive modern buildings in India. The huge door to the Cabinet Room is made entirely of sandalwood.

The **Sir Sheshadri Iyer Memorial Hall** contains the public library. The **Government Museum**, founded in 1866, is also located in the park. Here there are relics from Tipu's palace at Seringapatam and sections on geology, numismatics and art. Upstairs is a remarkable collection of stuffed animals and fish. (For details of the Museum see Volume I.)

North-east is the **Memorial Statue of Queen Victoria**, unveiled by the Prince of Wales (later George V) in 1906, and north again, a **statue of Edward VII**. There was a local outcry against recent proposals to remove them. Look out for the splendid cast-iron bandstand nearby. To the west are the **Public Offices**, a huge building in front of which is a statue of Sir Mark Cubbon, Commissioner of Mysore (1834–61).

Raj Bhavan, the former Residency (early 19th century), a low stucco building in a beautifully landscaped compound, lies 400 m (¼ mile) north of the Public Offices.

One of the greatest delights of the cantonment area is the concentration of fine colonial bungalows. Many of these are disappearing fast, as pressure for higher-density development increases, but some fine examples can still be found. Many have elaborately carved bargeboards and trelliswork, known as monkey-tops. This is an attractive local style which imparts a distinctive character to the cantonment. The area around Richmond Town retains a number. Here also is the **Bangalore Club**, an early-19th-century classical range. The pride of the club is an unpaid bill from Winston Churchill.

The city area of Bangalore is called the **Petta**, after the deep ditch and thorn hedge which protected the area until 1898. The **Fort** lies on Krishnarajendra Road, south of the Petta and the City Market. Built in 1537 by Kempe Gowda and originally a mud-brick structure, it was reconstructed in stone by Haidar Ali in 1761. It is oval in shape, 731 m (2,400 ft) from north to south and 548 m (1,800 ft) from east to west. Only the Delhi Gate remains. The fort contains an Arsenal and fragments of Tipu Sultan's palace, but little else of any consequence. It was captured by Cornwallis on 21 March 1791 after a fierce battle.

Outside are the Victoria Hospital and Minto Ophthalmic Hospital.

Tipu Sultan's Summer Palace, completed in 1791, is now a dilapidated ruin next to a temple at the junction of Krishnarajendra Road and Albert Victor Road.

2·4 km (1½ miles) east of the Petta, the **Lalbagh Botanical Gardens** lie on the southern edge of the town and cover an area of 96 hectares (237 acres). The gardens were laid out by Haidar Ali with tropical plants and shrubs. They are beautifully maintained. In the centre is a large iron and glass **conservatory** reputed to be modelled on the Crystal Palace, but in fact there is little resemblance. Among the lotus ponds, lakes and shaded avenues is a large outcrop of some of the most ancient rock in the world.

CALICUT

Calicut (literally Kolikotta or Cock Fort) is situated on the coast, 9·6 km (6 miles) north of Beypur, among palm groves. Historically, it is an interesting town, but there is not much to see.

Vasco da Gama landed here on 20 May 1498, but he was made unwelcome by the local Moplah traders. A memorial tablet records the event. In 1501 a Portuguese colony was destroyed by the Moplahs and a series of retaliatory raids took place over the next few years. In 1510 Albuquerque sacked the town, but was repulsed with heavy losses. Finally, the local Zamorins made peace and permitted the Portuguese to build a factory, in 1513. The English founded a factory in 1616, the French followed in 1722 and the Danes arrived thirty years later. The notorious pirate Captain Kidd ravaged the port in 1695 and when, in 1766, Haidar Ali invaded, the Zamorin set fire to the palace, dying with his family in the flames. Under the Treaty of Seringapatam the entire territory was ceded to the British.

The centre of the town has Roman

Catholic and Anglican churches. The remains of the old palace and a later palace are near to the Judges' Court. In the Moplah quarter, to the south of the town, are several mosques.

CANNANORE

This small town is an old military cantonment situated about 88 km (55 miles) north of Calicut. The Portuguese **Fort of St Angelo** (1505) stands on the headland, overlooking the bay.

Within the cantonment are the church and burial ground. The Portuguese factory (now the church) lies close to the seashore. There is an old Moplah quarter in the town with some picturesque if undistinguished mosques, the Raja's Palace and a fascinating maze of narrow lanes around the south end of the fort.

Historically, the town is notable. Vasco da Gama called here in 1498. Seven years later he erected a factory. In 1656 the Dutch expelled the Portuguese and subsequently sold the town to a Moplah family who claimed sovereignty over the Laccadive Islands. After associations with Tipu Sultan, Moplah rule was terminated by the British, who attacked and captured Cannanore in 1790.

CHANDRAGIRI

After the sack of Vijayanagara in 1565, the Hindu dynasty established itself first at Penukonda and then at this site, which it rapidly transformed into a royal centre. Until 1646 this was the site of the declining Vijayanagara Empire. Both the natural defences of Chandragiri, which is ringed by hills, and the proximity to the Venkateshvara shrine at Tirumala, 11 km (7 miles) to the north-east, were responsible for the decision to locate here.

The **Upper Fort**, reputed to date from 1000, stands on a 183 m (600 ft) outcrop of granite in an impregnable location

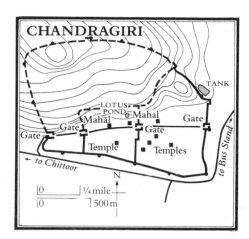

high over the valley. At its base is a fortified zone. This is divided into three enclosures with defensive gateways along an east-west road. Within the central enclosure are two well-preserved palaces, a tank and other civic structures.

Within the walls stand the remains of the **Palace of the Vijayanagara Rajas,** a notable example of early-17th-century south Indian architecture, characterized by a commingling of Hindu and Muslim styles. The palace is 45·7 m (150 ft) long, with a three-storey façade enriched with pointed arches and a skyline broken by pyramidal towers, the largest crossing the Durbar Hall. The hall is surrounded by a two-storey colonnade, which acts as a clerestory, allowing light to penetrate the space. The building is faced in stucco and the whole complex shows considerable ingenuity and flair. (See Volume I.)

It was in this palace in 1639 that Francis Day obtained a grant of land at Madras for the East India Company. The town fell to the Sultan of Golconda in 1646 and later to Haidar Ali, in 1782.

CHANNAPATNA

This small town, 56 km (35 miles) from Bangalore, has a ruined fort built by Jagadura Raja in 1580 as the capital of a territory bestowed on him by the Vijayanagara king for the defence of Penukonda in 1577. There are two large Muslim tombs north of the town, one of which is that of the religious preceptor of Tipu Sultan.

CHINGLEPUT

Chingleput, 56 km (35 miles) south of Madras, is of historical importance owing to its fort. The origin of its name is disputed: it is either the Brick Town or Singhala Petta, the Town of the Lotus.

The **Fort** stands beside a large tank. It was built at the end of the 16th century, probably by Timmu Raya, when the Vijayanagara Rajas held their court alternately here and at Chandragiri. Three sides are defended by a lake and swamps and the fourth has a double line of fortifications. In 1644 the fort passed to the Sultans of Golconda, by whom it was ceded to the Nawabs of Arcot, who in turn gave it over to Chanda Sahib in 1751. Clive secured the surrender of its French garrison in 1752 and it remained an important strategic centre until 1758, when it was temporarily abandoned. In 1780 a British force found refuge here after the defeat of General Baillie's column. In the ensuing wars with Mysore the fort was lost, recaptured and subsequently besieged unsuccessfully twice.

Today the fort is ruined and the railway passes through it. Two old buildings survive. The **Raja Mahal** or Ther Mahal was originally of five storeys, built in the form of the temple car of Kanchipuram, which was visible from the top. The building has arcades of pointed arches around a small inner room surmounted by a dome enriched with plasterwork.

Another Hindu temple provides the lower storey of the house of the Deputy Superintendent of the Reform School. It was built for the Prime Minister by the Raja and was subsequently modified by

the Muslims. A Hindu temple dedicated to Anjaneya, the monkey god, was transferred from the fort into the town in 1813.

Near the town the Pallava caves of Vallam have several very ancient inscriptions.

CHITTOOR

A **monument** marks the spot where Haidar Ali died, on 7 December 1782, at Narsingh Rayanpet outside Chittoor.

The **Cemetery** contains a number of interesting old tombs, including a large octagonal mausoleum to Mrs Waters. This has an iron door which opens on to two graves dated 1823 and 1828. It was known locally as the Meeting of the Waters, as the graves are supposed to be those of the two wives of George Jenkins Waters (1792–1882), the judge at Chittoor, the 'Bluebeard of the Civil Service', for he had no less than six wives in his ninety years. Their two coffins are reputedly suspended from the roof by chains.

COCHIN

Cochin is one of the most fascinating cities in India, a cosmopolitan melting pot of races and cultures. Portuguese, Chinese, Jewish, early Christian, Dutch and British influences can all be seen to advantage here.

Cochin is the oldest European settlement in India. Tradition asserts that St Thomas the Apostle visited the region in 52, leaving behind him the Moplahs as a Christian colony. The Jews are also said to have settled here at this time. There is evidence that both Jewish and Syrian Christian communities were well established by the 8th century. Later there were recorded visits by a friar, Jordanus, in 1347, Chinese travellers in 1409 and a Persian in 1442. In 1500 the Portuguese adventurer Cabral landed here and took

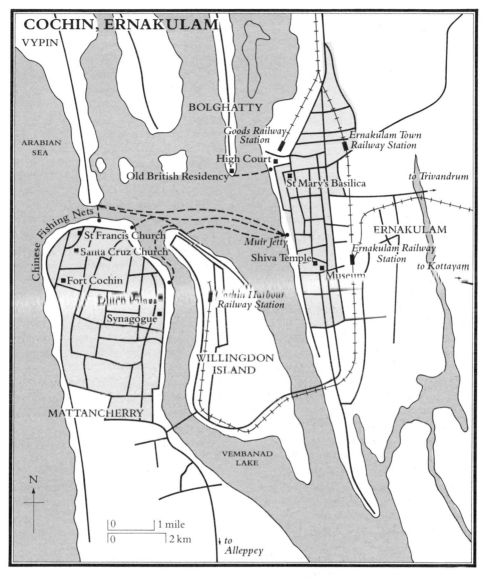

COCHIN, ERNAKULAM

home a consignment of pepper. He was soon followed by Juan de Noval Castelho and then by Vasco da Gama, who established a factory in 1502. A year later the Portuguese admiral Albuquerque arrived, helped the Cochin Raja and established a fort. Portuguese friars who travelled with him founded a chapel on the site of the Church of St Francis. From 1530 onwards St Francis Xavier preached here and made many converts. By 1557 the Church of Santa Cruz was consecrated a cathedral.

In 1635 the English founded a factory by agreement after earlier attempts at sedition had failed, but in 1663 the town fell to the Dutch, who did much to improve it. The Franciscan church was made into a Protestant chapel and the cathedral used as a warehouse. In 1778 Adrien Van Meens reconstructed the fort and built seven strong bastions. With the fall of Holland to France in 1795, the British seized the Dutch possessions in India. Cochin was captured on 20 October 1795 by Major Petrie. Nine years later the cathedral, most of the fort and the quays were blown up by the British.

Most of the historical sites are in Fort Cochin or Mattancherry. **St Francis Church** (*c.* 1546) is reputed to be the oldest European church in India. It is a plain, massive structure built by the Portuguese Franciscan friars who sailed with Pedro Alvarez Cabral. The original wooden church was replaced in stone in 1546. One inscription is dated 1562. Vasco da Gama died here on Christmas Day, 1524, and was buried in the church. What is alleged to be his tombstone can still be seen (but the coat of arms is not his). Later, his body was removed to Lisbon. After the occupation of Cochin by the British in 1795 the church became Anglican. Today it is used by the Church of South India. The earliest Portuguese tombs date from 1546, the Dutch from 1664.

Nearby, the Cathedral of Santa Cruz (20th century) should be visited.

Opposite Vypeen Island, along the tip of Fort Cochin, are cantilevered Chinese fishing nets introduced centuries ago by traders from the court of Kublai Khan. Others can be seen in the Malabar backwaters near Kottayam and between Quilon and Alleppey.

The **Mattancherry** or **Dutch Palace** was actually built by the Portuguese in 1557 and presented to the Cochin Raja as a gesture of goodwill to secure additional trading privileges. In 1663 it was renovated by the Dutch. It comprises a two-storey building set around a central quadrangle, which contains a Hindu temple. The principal hall at first-floor level was the Coronation Room of the Rajas. There is an interesting exhibition of court dress and other artefacts from the palace. The spectacular 17th-century frescoes in the bedchambers and other rooms are some of the finest in India,

depicting scenes from the Hindu epics and Puranic legends.

At the south end of the long main street in Mattancherry is the Jewish quarter, an atmospheric warren of old buildings haunted by the pungent aroma of cloves, cardamom and other local spices. There are two **Synagogues**: one belongs to the Black Jews, who trace their settlement here to 567 BC, the other to the White, who arrived much later. The synagogue of the White Jews, built in 1568, is the oldest in the Commonwealth. The building was destroyed by the Portuguese in 1662 but reinstated by the Dutch. It has a floor of white, willow-pattern Chinese tiles brought from Canton in the mid-18th century by Ezekial Rahabi, who was also responsible for the clocktower above. Among the possessions are the Great Scrolls of the Old Testament and copper plates recording the grant of privileges by King Ravi Varman (962–1020) to the Jewish merchant Joseph Rabban.

The **Cochin Museum** is housed in the old Durbar Hall, an enormous rambling building built in local Keralan style, and has an interesting collection of oil paintings, coins, sculptures, etc., as well as exhibits from the Cochin palace.

At Ernakulam open-air dance performances are held, the most spectacular display of dance drama in India, with origins which go back 400 years or more, based on the great Hindu epics the Ramayana and the Mahabharata.

On Bolghatty island, in the lagoon, is the old **British Residency** (1744), built by the Dutch and set in a beautiful landscaped garden. Some of the old paintings are still on the walls. It is now a Government Tourist Bungalow.

COONOOR

Coonoor is a pleasant hill station situated about 17·7 km (11 miles) from Ootacamund in the Nilgiri Hills. It was constituted a municipality in 1866. It is a small town with wonderful views over the plains, compared by Lady Charlotte Canning to the view of the Mediterranean from the corniche at Monte Carlo. Its function as a health resort has been reinforced by the Pasteur Institute for South India, which has been established here for some years. There are a hospital, four small churches, a library and numerous schools.

Sim's Park is a botanical garden of exceptional beauty with huge tree-ferns and giant rhododendron trees. The surrounding hills offer many rewarding walks – a place for peace and contemplation.

CUDDALORE

Cuddalore and Fort St David lie 19 km (12 miles) south of Pondicherry. In 1684 the East India Company obtained permission to settle here and Fort St David was constructed soon after. The Fort was seized by Lally in 1758 and destroyed. A ditch and some fallen ramparts are all that remain of the Fort, which lies near Devanampatnam.

A few simple European-style bungalows and offices lie in the Manjakuppam district. There are some interesting tombs in the churchyard.

DINDIGUL

Dindigul is renowned for its great rock fort, which lies about 87 km (54 miles) from Kodaikanal and 64 km (40 miles) from Madurai.

The **Fort** crowns a hill which rises 85 m (280 ft) out of the surrounding plain, 372 m (1,223 ft) above sea level. Strategically, it commands the passes between Madurai and Coimbatore, and in the past ownership was fiercely contested for this

reason. Between 1623 and 1659 it was the scene of many encounters between the Marathas and troops from Mysore and Madurai. In 1755 Haidar Ali seized control. It was taken by the British in 1767, lost a year later, retaken in 1783, returned to Mysore in 1784 under the Treaty of Mangalore, recaptured in 1790, and finally ceded in 1792.

The rock on which it stands is steeply scarped. The line of approach is commanded by strongly fortified walls and entrance gates. The parapets are pierced by embrasures to accommodate cannon of different calibres. The entrance gateway is defended by a robust barbican, a long passage and right-angled turn, commanded on all sides from the walls above. The steps cut into the rock are a later device to facilitate easier access, but originally, as a defensive position, the fort must have been formidable. The outer and inner gateways are 17th century, part of the first wave of fortifications built by the Nayakas of Madurai. The gates have flat pilasters crowned by urns, with decorative detailing between the arches and lintels. Inside, the building is in ruins. From the entrance gateway a flight of steps leads past the old guardrooms to the citadel.

GINGEE (JINJEE) *Map overleaf*

The great fort at Gingee, located 132 km (82 miles) south-west of Madras, covers three fortified hills – Krishnagiri, Chandragiri and Rajagiri – and the intermediate ground in a formidable array of walls and bastions. Now deserted, once it was one of the most impressive forts in India. It is also one of the most ancient.

Gingee was built during the Chola dynasty but was later reconstructed and strengthened by the Vijayanagara kings in 1442. In 1638 it was lost to Bijapur and in 1677 it fell to Shivaji. Thirteen years later Imperial troops were despatched from Delhi against Shivaji's son Raja

Ram, who was concentrating his forces at Gingee. The French under de Bussy and d'Auteuil succeeded in a night attack and held the rock fortress for eleven years, until it surrendered to the British in 1762.

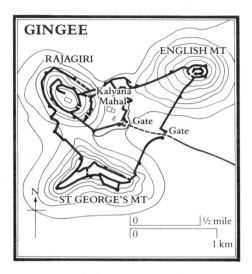

An outer curtain wall encloses the three hills. The citadel, which stands on the summit of the central peak, Rajagiri, over 152 m (500 ft) high, has three defensive lines, all with powerful gateways, two with triple arches. To the south-west a narrow defile is reinforced by three walls thrown across at different points in the ascent. The route to the citadel is defended by seven gateways; three of the gates in the second and fourth walls have large courtyards between them.

The first gate has a barbican and moat crossed by a drawbridge, but the courtyard walls are destroyed. Over the lintel of the second gate is a small circular carving of Kirtimukha – 'Mouth of Glory' – with a demonic head. The gateways in the curtain walls are staggered in the classic mediaeval pattern to enable the defence to delay an enemy advance.

Inside the fort, the most notable buildings are the Kalyana Mahal, two temples and various granaries and storehouses.

The **Kalyana Mahal** is a square courtyard surrounded by chambers with a large central tower of eight storeys resembling a beehive. Each storey, except the highest two, comprises a small room surrounded by an arcaded verandah.

There is a sophisticated system of water supply via earthenware pipes connected to large reservoirs. Other features of interest include the Raja's Bathing Stone, a large granite block near where the palace once stood, and a huge gun crowning Rajagiri. The Prisoner's Well is a gigantic boulder, pierced by a large opening, balanced on a rock and surmounted by a low, circular brick wall. It is alleged that prisoners were thrown in and left to die of starvation.

INJARAM

Injaram is a small town, 8 km (5 miles) south of Korangi. It is the site of one of the earliest British settlements on the Coromandel coast. The factory, renowned for its manufacture of fine cloth, was founded in 1708. In May 1757 it was captured by the French under de Bussy. Later restored, it remained a mercantile station of the East India Company until 1829. As the result of a disastrous cyclone in 1839, little of interest remains.

KANDAPUR

Kandapur is a small town, 88·5 km (55 miles) north-west of Mangalore. Once it was one of the ports of the Bednur Rajas, who ruled the area in the 16th century after the disruption of the Vijayanagara kingdom.

A 16th-century Portuguese fort commanding the entrance to the river remains, with a robust redoubt overlooking the sea. The local Collector's Office is now located here. It was from here that General Matthews started on his march against Bednur. In 1799 the town fell to the British.

KARUR

Karur is a small but busy market town on the Amaravati river which was once the capital of the ancient kingdom of Chera or eastern Kerala. With the rise of the Nayakas the town fell to the kingdom of Madurai. The fort was attacked repeatedly, until it was annexed by the kingdom of Mysore in the late 17th century.

In 1760 the British seized the town from Haidar Ali, but it was repossessed eight years later. In 1783 Colonel Lang held the town again for a short while and in 1790 it was captured by General Medows for the third time. It was finally ceded to the British in 1799 and abandoned as a military post in 1801. The ruins of the oft-contested fort and an old temple remain. An early Jesuit mission was established here in 1639.

KODAIKANAL

Kodaikanal (literally Forest of Creepers) is a popular hill station situated in a stunning location 2,197 m (7,209 ft) above sea level in the Palni Hills, an offshoot of the Western Ghats. To the west are breathtaking views of the Anaimalai hills. The station lies in and around

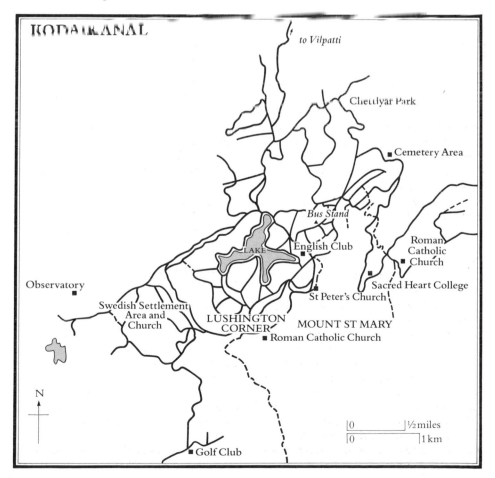

541

a natural amphitheatre of rolling, wooded hills which overlook a 28·3-hectares (70 acres) artificial lake.

The first European visitor was Lieutenant B. S. Ward, who was on survey work in 1821, but the first houses were not constructed until the American Mission arrived four years later. Its consolidation as a hill station was largely due to Sir Vere Henry Levinge, Bart, a Madras civil servant who retired there in 1867. He bore at his own expense the construction of the Bund at the north-east end of the lake, as well as major road improvements and the introduction of countless English flowers and species. On the edge of the lake by the municipal offices is a red granite cross to his memory. The inscription reads:

And thus he bore without abuse
The grand old name of gentleman!

There are many delightful walks and drives around the area. The principal buildings are **St Peter's Church** (1884) on Mount Nebo, with a stained-glass window dedicated to Bishop Caldwell, the club, the golf club and the observatory, removed from Madras in 1899. The old European houses are concentrated on the east and south shores of the lake. Below Coackers Walk is the Sacred Roman Catholic College, founded in 1895. On Lower Shola Road a granite **obelisk** marks the site of the first American Church and cemetery. At the junction with Violet Lane is an old **graveyard** with interesting tombstones. One, erected to the memory of Dudley· Sedgwick, recalls he was 'killed by a bison: 29 March 1875'. Another, to David Scudder, who drowned on 16 November 1862, is aptly inscribed on the reverse: 'He leadeth me by still waters.'

KOTAGIRI

This is a small hill station which enjoys a pleasant climate and magnificent views across the Nilgiri Hills from the Ootacamund Road. The first English cottage in the area, built in 1819, still survives at Dimhatti, just to the north of the main station, which was founded in 1830. There are a large number of European-style bungalows and a small church. Lord Dalhousie stayed at Kota Hall, the oldest house in Kotagiri, for three months in 1855. Lady Canning followed his example in 1858.

KOTTAYAM

Kottayam, a small town 72 km (45 miles) south-east of Ernakulam, is an old Syrian Christian centre where the Church Mission Society has operated since 1816. It is the seat of the Bishop of Travancore and Cochin.

The town lies on the bank of a small river running into the great Cochin backwater. There are several interesting old churches associated with the Syrian Christian community which are of considerable antiquity.

MADRAS

Madras was the first important settlement of the East India Company. It was founded in 1639 from the nearby factory at Armagaum by Francis Day on territory ceded by the Raja of Chandragiri. In 1644 a small fort was erected from which the city grew steadily and, until the emergence of Calcutta, it remained the nerve-centre of English influence in the East.

By 1690 the small fort had grown into a major city of over 300,000 people and its layout, on a distinctive grid pattern, represents the earliest example of English town planning on a large scale in India. The European settlement remained inside the fort, with Black Town outside

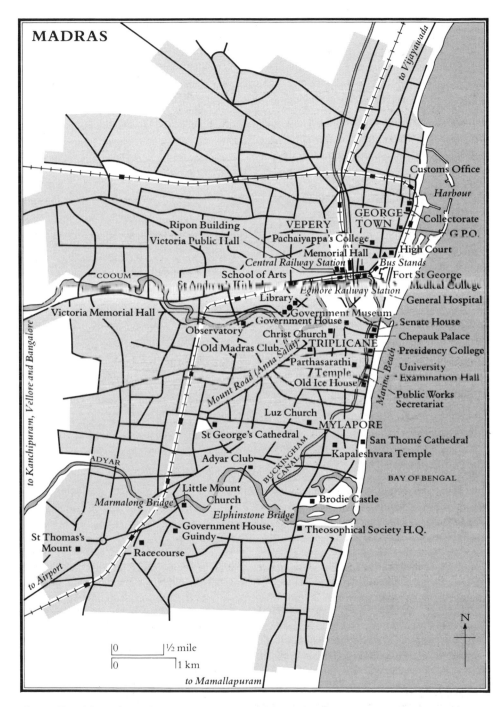

MADRAS

the walls, although with greater security in the 18th century Europeans bought estates outside the walls and built beauti-

ful garden houses, many of which still survive.

Madras has a fine legacy of colonial

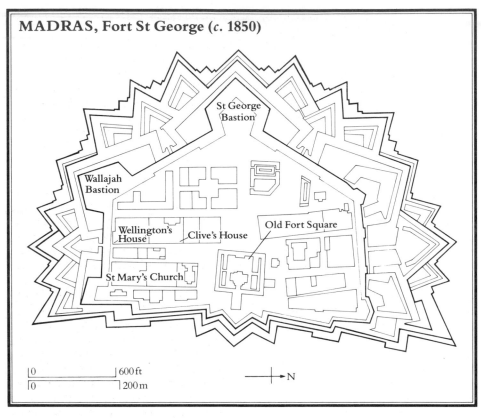

MADRAS, Fort St George (c. 1850)

St George Bastion

Wallajah Bastion

Wellington's House

Clive's House

Old Fort Square

St Mary's Church

architecture, ranging from the elegant classical houses of the 18th-century nabobs to the spectacular Indo-Saracenic buildings of the late 19th century.

Fort St George, the starting-point for any tour of Madras, lies on the seashore, immediately north of the island. The east face is separated now from the sea by the road and foreshore. Here is the Sea Gate. The west face is curved and set behind a fosse. It is crossed by drawbridges, which lead to the Wallajah Gate and St George's Gate. The San Thomé Gate is in the south wall, the North and Choultry gates are in the north wall.

The Fort was commenced in 1644. It was gradually converted into a formidable masonry structure by a series of incremental changes. In 1694 the original Fort House was demolished to make way for a new one. This now forms the nucleus of the Secretariat. In 1711 the inner Fort walls and corner bastions were pulled down and Fort Square was created. The Fort was lost to the French under Labourdonnais in 1746, but was restored to the British by the Treaty of Aix-la-Chapelle of 1748. As a result of this reverse, designs for its remodelling were prepared in 1750 by Bartholomew Robins, FRS, a mathematician. From 1755 until its completion in 1783, the work was supervised successively by Captain Brohier, Colonel Scott, Colonel Call and Colonel Ross.

The French besieged the Fort again in 1758 under Count Lally. At this time St Mary's Church was used as a look-out post and store, but the French withdrew when a British fleet arrived. In April 1769 Haidar Ali briefly threatened, prompting the transformation of the outer fortifications from a half-decagon to a semi-octagon in 1771.

544

At the heart of Fort St George lies **St Mary's Church** (1678–80), the spiritual and physical centre of the original settlement and the oldest surviving building in the East associated with the Anglican Church. It was built by Streynsham Master, the Governor, after a private appeal. Excavations began on Lady Day, 1678, hence the dedication to St Mary. The architect was probably William Dixon, Master Gunner of the Fort, and this accounts for its robust construction and simple plan. It is 24·3 m (80 ft) long by 17 m (56 ft) wide, with three aisles covered by semicircular roofs, built of solid masonry to withstand bombing, siege and cyclone. The outer walls are 1·2 m (4 ft) thick and carried on firm laterite foundations. The tower was completed in 1701 and a steeple added in 1710. The tower and belfry were detached from the main body of the church until 1760, when a link was made. Severely damaged during Lally's siege of 1758, the building was repaired and the distinctive fluted obelisk spire added in 1795 to the design of Colonel Gent. Other than the minor addition of two vestries at the east end of the aisles and a small 19th-century extension to the sanctuary, the church is remarkably faithful to its original design.

The interior is whitewashed, with plain raised rose ornaments in relief. The West Gallery has a carved teak balustrade depicting elephants, parrots and be-wigged gentlemen. This is original late-17th-century work, although the gallery was altered in 1761 and again in the early 19th century. The font of black Pallavaram granite is original. The three daughters of Job Charnock, founder of Calcutta, were baptized in it on 19 August 1689. The ornamental font cover was added in 1885.

The Altarpiece, a painting of the Lord's Supper, is by a pupil of Raphael, who actually painted the chalice. It was probably captured from the French in Pondicherry in 1761. The present organ, the fifth, was installed in 1894. The lectern and altar rails are both replacements but bear the original plaques. The church plate is also of interest. A silver alms dish was donated in 1687 by Governor Elihu Yale, the future benefactor of Yale University and the first to marry in the church. Robert Clive married Margaret Maskelyne here on 18 February 1753.

The church is crammed with evocative monuments which bear mute testimony to the glories of British India and warrant close inspection. The intramural interments include Lord Pigot (1777), Lord Hobart (1875), Sir Henry Ward (1860), the enlightened Sir Thomas Munro (1827), Sir Alexander Campbell (1824),

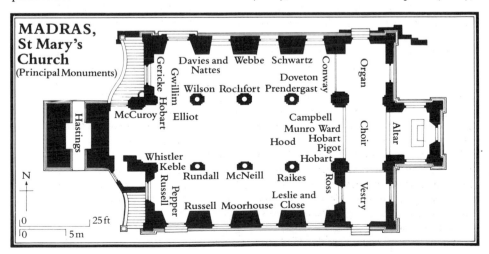

MADRAS, St Mary's Church
(Principal Monuments)

Sir John Doveton (1847) and Vice-Admiral Sir Samuel Hood (1814).

At the west end of the church lie four distinguished wives: the lovely Lady Elizabeth Gwillim (1807), Baroness Hobart (1796), Lady Elliot (1819) and Jane Amelia Russell (1808), to whom there is a monument by John Bacon, Jr, close to the font.

On the north wall there are four monuments. Close to the door is Flaxman's **Memorial to Rev. Christian William Gericke**, an associate of F. C. Schwartz, the distinguished Christian missionary. Gericke was frightened to death by monkeys at Vellore on 2 October 1803! On the other side of the door is a **monument** by Bacon to two officers who fell at the siege of Mallegaon (1818). Next is Flaxman's **Monument to Josiah Webbe** (1804). Beyond is the **Monument to Frederick Christian Schwartz**, by John Bacon, Jr, which is the finest in the church. Close to the organ is a **statue of Thomas Conway** (the soldiers' friend), by Ternouth (1837). Other notable monuments include, in sequence, a **brass to Sir Herbert Taylor Macpherson, VC** (1886); a **marble relief to Charles Robert Ross**, (1816), by John Bacon, bearing the pelican motif of self-sacrifice; a large **monument to Sir Barry Close** (1813), probably by Flaxman, depicting a British soldier and a sepoy in early-19th-century dress; a **memorial to Joseph Moorhouse** (1791), by C. Peart, with Britannia seated on a lion; a life-sized **statue of Hercules Henry Pepper** (1826), by G. Clarke, 'the Birmingham Chantrey'; and a **statue of George Gilbert Keble** (1811), by John Bacon, Jr, representing Friendship and Charity with masonic devices. There are six detached pillars within the church, all of which carry memorial tablets.

The churchyard is enclosed by iron railings. Along the north side of the church and extending round the east and west sides are a number of ancient grave-stones taken from the old graveyard and relocated here in 1763. The sepulchral tombs provided cover for Lally's troops during the siege of 1758, after which the stones were removed to the church. Many are worn or broken, but some inscriptions and dates may be discerned.

On the west side of Charles Street, leading to the San Thomé Gate, are the ruins of **Wellesley's House**, a late-18th-century building once occupied by Colonel Arthur Wellesley (later the Duke of Wellington). Parts collapsed in 1980. Its future remains uncertain.

South of St Mary's Church is the **Accountant-General's Office**, used as Government House until 1799. The house was purchased from an Armenian in 1749 as a residence for the Deputy Governor. It was extended in 1762 and again in 1778–80. **Clive's House** is marked by a small plaque which claims he resided here. There is a small museum to his memory in a corner of the Pay and Accounts Office.

Beyond is the **Arsenal** (1722), designed by Colonel Patrick Ross and built by John Sullivan. The first storey has inverted arches to create a bomb-proof structure. The courtyard has an impressive portico crowned by two lions in alto-rilievo carrying the East India Company's coat of arms.

The **Museum** was founded in 1944 by Lieutenant-Colonel D. M. Reid in the former Officers' Mess of the Madras Guards, once the Old Exchange. The Hall of Arms contains mediaeval artillery, regimental flags, weapons and armour. The ground floor also contains the cage in which Captain Philip Anstruther was imprisoned for over a year in China in 1840. The Prints Section has some early views of Madras, while other rooms retain correspondence from Clive, Pigot, Wellesley, Cornwallis, Bentinck and other notable figures. At the foot of the stairs is a **statue of Lord Cornwallis** (1800), by Thomas Banks, which once stood under the rotunda in Fort Square.

546

The first-floor Portrait Gallery contains collections from Government House, Guindy and Ootacamund. Notable portraits are those of Streynsham Master, George III, Queen Charlotte, Stringer Lawrence, Robert Clive and Henry Havelock.

The **Secretariat** is the oldest secular building in the Fort, the core of which incorporates the second Fort House, built in 1694. Wings were added in 1825, when the building became government offices, but the earlier structure can be traced inside. The Secretariat surrounds the **Legislative Council** (1910), the Upper House of the State Legislature. The building incorporates twenty black granite columns, which once formed a colonnade linking Fort Square to the Sea Gate built by Governor Pigot in 1752. A brass tablet records the fact. In the hall are busts of Edwin Montague, Sir P. Rajagopala Achariyar and Diwan Bahadur L. D. Swamikannu, the first elected President of the Council.

Outside the main entrance on the fortifications facing the sea is the **Flagstaff**, reputed to be the tallest in India and a local landmark for over 300 years.

In the Fort Square is an **Ionic rotunda**, erected in 1799 to accommodate the statue of Cornwallis which now stands in the Museum. Elsewhere throughout the Fort are numerous fine colonial barrack buildings of the late 18th and 19th centuries.

To the north of the Fort lies the **High Court** (1888–92), a spectacular complex of Indo-Saracenic buildings designed by J. W. Brassington but revised and completed by Henry Irwin and J. H. Stephens, the engineer. The four corner towers are crowned by Mughal domes, but the *tour de force* is the central tower, 48·7 m (160 ft) high, which forms a huge, bulbous-domed minaret with its upper stage designed as a lighthouse, visible for 32 km (20 miles) at sea. A plaque on the boundary wall commemorates the shelling of the building by the German cruiser

Emden in 1914. It is a wonderfully exuberant synthesis of Western Gothic forms and Eastern ornamental details.

The light tower is open to the public on most working days. The view from the top is stunning and worth the steep climb. In the crypt beneath the tower is a marble statue of Sri T. Muthasamy Iyer, the first Indian judge, by Wade. Near the compound walls is a statue of Dr Miller, the educationalist, who developed the Christian College which once stood opposite.

In the south–east corner is a huge fluted Greek Doric column 38·1 m (125 ft) high, constructed in hard Pallavaram granite on a firm laterite and brick base. This was the former **Lighthouse**, commenced in 1838 and completed in 1843 to the design of Captain J. E. Smith of the Madras Engineers, later superseded by the tower of the High Court. The earliest lighthouse was a rudimentary affair on the roof of the Old Exchange in the Fort, now the Museum

The south range of buildings is the **Small Causes Court** and to the west is the **Law College**. In the Court precincts there are two tombs from the old graveyard which lay here. The **Tomb of David Yale and Joseph Hynmers** is a square, pyramidal structure surrounded by a spire, visible from Esplanade Road. Access can be obtained from the High Court compound.

The **Powney Vault** close by is a typical square tomb surrounded by an iron fence. It contains at least six members of the family. Another tomb near the Medical College is that of Edward Bulkey, physician of the new hospital, who was buried in his own garden on 8 August 1714.

Opposite to the High Court stood the Madras Christian College, now the Mysore Bank; part of the old College buildings survive in Linghi Chatty Street. Next door is the YMCA, in red sandstone, presented by the Hon. W. Wanamaker, one time Postmaster-

General of the USA. A **statue of the Maharaja of Travancore** stands at the southern end of the Broadway, commemorating the lead he gave in opening temples to Harijans. Opposite is the **Annamalai Manram**, a modern theatre. In China Bazaar Road (now Netaji Subhas Chandra Bose Road), opposite the Clocktower and Telephone Exchange, is **Pachaiyappa's College** (1846–50), based on the Athenian Temple of Theseus, originally founded for the education of poor Hindu boys by Pachaiyappa Mudhiar, an interpreter working for the East India Company. It was opened by Sir Henry Pottinger, the Governor of Madras, in 1850. Today it is a high school, elevated on a podium over the pandemonium of the bazaar beneath.

The area to the north of the College is **George Town**, formerly Black Town, an intricate network of roads and alleyways marking the old native town which grew up outside the Fort walls. The basic grid pattern is the earliest example of English town planning in India. **Parry's Corner** is named after Parry & Co., located in the prominent building opposite the Law Courts at the junction of the Esplanade and First Line Beach. The latter is the main commercial artery and contains the **General Post Office**, an inventive piece of tropical Gothic with distinctive arcaded eaves and two 38·1-m (125 ft) towers. It was commenced in 1875 and completed in 1884 by Robert Fellowes Chisholm, the gifted consulting architect to the government of Madras. The **Collector's Office** (Bentinck's Building) is a long galleried range with odd intercolumniation and a bowed centrepiece. From 1817 it was used as the Supreme Court, but it is now in a precarious state of disrepair. Opposite is a fine octagonal pavilion dedicated to Lord Cornwallis. The **Customs House** (early 19th century) lies beyond.

Several banks and other institutions line the road and face the **Harbour**. This was commenced in 1875 to provide an all-weather facility to replace the colourful 'masula' boats which once constituted a shuttle service to the shore for passengers from boats anchored in Madras roads. Beach Railway Station lies beyond.

The **Armenian Church** (1772) is hidden behind tall walls and high black doors. It has a large white dome with a peal of six bells. In Portuguese Church Street is the Church of Assumption of Our Lady (1650), the first church built in British India.

Armenian Street, running parallel to First Line Beach, contains the **Mosque of Nawab Muhammad Ali** and the Roman Catholic Cathedral of St Mary of the Angels (1775). The date 1642 is inscribed on the door. Inside are some rare oil paintings of the Crucifixion and of St Mary Magdalene.

The Evening Bazaar is a continuation of the Rattan Bazaar, at the end of which is the **Memorial Hall** (c. 1855), by Captain Winscom, modified by Colonel Horsley, and built as a thanksgiving for the preservation of southern India from the Mutiny. It has a handsome Ionic portico inscribed with the name and date, beneath which is a verse from the 15th Psalm: 'The Lord hath been mindful of us. He will bless us.' The Biblical Society occupies the basement. The hall is used for public meetings, but it has fallen on hard times.

Across the road are the **Medical College** and **General Hospital** (1859). The latter bears a misleading plaque: 'Founded in 1753'. The original hospital buildings were erected in 1772, redeveloped in 1859 and then further altered in 1929. Opposite is the **Central Railway Station** (1868–72), two-storey Gothic arcaded ranges with corner pavilions disposed around a central clocktower 41 m (136 ft) high. It was designed by George Hardinge. The **Southern Railway Office** (c. 1916), across Walltax Road, is an elegant fusion of classical and Mughal motifs, executed in hard local granite.

Both the station and offices are festooned with coloured lights during festivals.

The Cochrane Canal was built by Basil Cochrane and opened by Clive. Until 1985, **Moore Market** (*c.* 1900) stood on its western bank, a low, red-brick, arcaded building in Indo-Saracenic style with cusped arches and hood moulds designed by R. E. Ellis and now sadly demolished. To the east is the **Victoria Public Hall** (1883–8), in Romanesque style by Henry Irwin, designed to commemorate Queen Victoria's Golden Jubilee with the aid of the donation from the Maharaja of Vizianagram. This is threatened with imminent demolition for a railway development. Nearby is the **Memorial to Sir Charles Trevelyan**, responsible for the **People's Park**, 47 hectares (116 acres), including the Corporation Stadium, Royal Swimming Pool, My Ladye's Garden, which is a showpiece of exotic Indian flowers, and the zoo.

The **Ripon Building** (*c.* 1900) by Harris accommodates the offices of the Corporation of Madras, inaugurated in 1688. It is a handsome three-storey stucco range in an Italianate style, reminiscent of Sancton Wood's Lancaster Gate in London but with a central clocktower. At the centre is a statue of Conran Smith, a former Commissioner. At the front are statues of Sir P. Theagaraya Chetty and Sri P. M. Sivagnana Mudaliar, former Corporation presidents. A statue of Ripon, former Governor and Governor-General, has been relocated here. To the west are the Everest Hotel and the **School of Arts**, founded by Dr Alexander Hunter in 1850.

Further west, beyond the viaduct, is **St Andrew's Kirk** (1818–21), by Major Thomas Fiott de Havilland and Colonel James Caldwell. This is the most accomplished neo-classical church in India, a magnificent building of considerable sophistication. It is modelled on St Martin-in-the-Fields, London, with a tall steeple and spire over a massive pedi-

mented Ionic portico, inscribed with the word Jehovah in Hebrew. The exterior of the chancel also carries a huge pediment, inscribed with the motto of the East India Company: '*Auspicio Regis et Senatus Angliae*'.

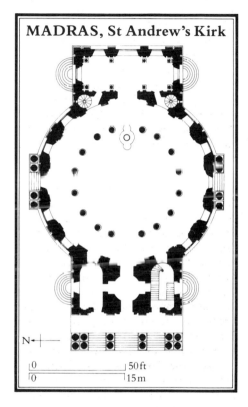

MADRAS, St Andrew's Kirk

The interior is circular in plan, with a delightful shallow self-supporting dome decorated with stars on a blue background and carried on fluted Corinthian columns. Note the cane pews and the louvred doors, which can be thrown open to allow a cool flow of air through the church. In the churchyard, close to the road, is a pleasant early-19th-century bungalow enriched with an Adamesque fan motif in raised stucco relief.

The footbridge next to the church leads to **Egmore Railway Station**, a splendid Indo-Saracenic pile, attributed to Chisholm.

Pantheon Road lies on the site of the Pantheon, a place of public entertainment and balls in the late 18th century. Today it is the main museum area. The **Government Museum** (1854) is a circular arcaded rotunda in an Italianate style, faced in red brick with a carved ornamental frieze. It was started in 1851 as a Museum of Practical Geology and Natural History and now contains an internationally famous collection of exhibits from the Pallava, Chola, Pandya and Vijayanagara periods. (For details of these fascinating exhibits see Volume I.) The ethno-industrial and art departments contain the statue of Brigadier-General Neill which was removed from Mount Road.

Part of the Museum complex houses the **Connemara Public Library** (1896), by Henry Irwin, which has a central hall crowned by a high stained-glass roof. The **Museum Theatre**, parts of which are 18th century, has a roof over the stage which is laid with iron grooves to allow heavy cannon shot to be rolled across to simulate the sound of thunder.

The **Empress Victoria Memorial Hall and Technical Institute** (1909), now the National Art Gallery, is the jewel in the Museum's crown. Designed by Henry Irwin in rich pink Tada sandstone, it is based on the Duland Darwaza at Fatehpur Sikri, a robust and vigorous composition of exceptional quality. The large inner hall is overlooked by balconies. It has a fine ceiling and marble floor. There is a wide collection of paintings of various south Indian schools and Rajput and Mughal art of the 16th to 18th centuries.

The road over Anderson's Bridge leads to Old College Road and the **Old College of Fort St George**, set behind a large arched gateway. Adjacent, in a pleasant building similar in style to the Police Station on North Beach Road by the Harbour, is the **Literary Society** (1877). Next door is the **Women's Christian College** and beyond, the old

Observatory (1793), founded by W. Petrie in 1787 and now used as a meteorological station. Madras had the first Western observatory in the East and set railway time for the entire subcontinent. The astronomical observatory moved to Kodaikanal in 1899.

A considerable distance further on, in Sterling Road in the district of Ningambakkam, is **Loyola College** (1925), which has a Gothic church with a fine steeple at the end of a long tree-lined vista.

From the Observatory the route runs south to the **Horticultural Gardens**, 8·9 hectares (22 acres), founded in 1836 by Dr Wright, and on to the **Cathedral Church of St George** (1814–16), by Colonel James Caldwell and Major Thomas Fiott de Havilland, with a steeple and spire 42·5 m (140 ft) high, modelled on St Giles-in-the-Fields, London. The cathedral is faced in dazzling white Madras chunam with Ionic porches to each flank and an imposing entrance portico. A double row of eighteen Ionic columns carrying an arched ceiling, which is decorated in raised plasterwork. The aisles have semicircular headed stained-glass windows over louvred doors. The chancel is apsidal, with a marble altarpiece of St George crowning a broken pediment.

The monuments include some fine neo-classical works. The **Memorial to Archdeacon John Mousley** (1823), by Flaxman, depicts Faith leaning on the Cross. Chantrey's sculpture of *Bishop Heber* (1830), author of the hymn 'From Greenland's Icy Mountains', who drowned in a bath at Trichinopoly in 1826, is a subtle mixture of naturalism and classicism. The **Memorial to Dr James Anderson** is also by Chantrey. Others of note are those to Bishop Corrie and the astronomer Norman Robert Pogson.

The burial ground lies to the northeast of the church and is approached through a pavilion crowned by an octagonal cupola. The first interment was Elizabeth de Havilland, the architect's wife, in March 1818. The cemetery is enclosed by a railing made from musket barrels, pikes and discarded weapons, allegedly brought from Tipu Sultan's arsenal at Seringapatam in 1799.

From the Cathedral the road to the south via Guindy runs through the suburbs, past the Teachers' College and Richard's Park on the banks of the Adyar river, to **Marmalong Bridge**, built by a devout Armenian merchant, Khoja Petrus Uscan, in 1726. It spans the river in a series of twenty-nine arches.

Beyond the bridge is a small village, **Little Mount**, an outcrop of rock associated with the martyrdom of the apostle St Thomas. It is alleged that the apostle founded some Christian communities on the west coast and came to Mylapore, where he was killed in 68 by outraged Hindus. The **Church** was built by Antonio Gonsalves de Taide, a Goanese, in 1612. Steps lead down to a cavern in the rock beneath the altar which is reputed to be the cave where he lived. An opening in one side is said to have been miraculously formed to permit his escape and certain marks are supposed to be his handprints. Behind the church is a small spring to which are attributed miraculous powers. To the north is a stone cross marking the spot where he preached. A fine view of the area can be obtained from the visitors' room in the parochial house.

About 3·2 km (2 miles) from Little Mount, south of Guindy railway station, is **St Thomas's Mount**, approximately 91·5 m (300 ft) high. The approach is via 132 steps, built by the Armenian Petrus Uscan, who built the Marmalong Bridge. On the main road is **St Thomas's Church** (1547), built by the Portuguese. An archway carries the date 1726 and several epitaphs can be traced. The main gate and portico were built by C. Zacharias in 1707. The central altar stone is alleged to be the one on which

the apostle was kneeling when attacked with a lance. Behind the altar is 'the Bleeding Cross', with a Nestorian inscription in Sassanian Pahlavi (c. 800) which reads: 'Ever pure is in favour with Him who bore the cross.' Tradition asserts that two red spots on it represent bleeding. The picture of the Virgin Mary is supposed to have been painted by St Luke and brought here by St Thomas.

Next door is the **Convent of Franciscan Missionary Nuns of Mary**, who run an orphanage and school.

At the base of St Thomas's Mount is the **Old Cantonment**, which still retains numerous Madras flat-tops, colonial-style bungalows. One was the former headquarters of the Madras Artillery and the home of Warren Hastings between 1769 and 1772. The **Anglican Church** is an elegant classical edifice containing numerous military monuments.

Close to Little Mount is the former **Government House** (1817; altered), now Raj Bhavan, the country residence of the Governor. It is a typical colonial bungalow, faced in bright white chunam and first used by Sir Thomas Munro. The hall has a bust of Wellington and some of the paintings which once adorned the Banqueting Hall have been rehung here. Adjacent is the **Gandhi Memorial Pavilion** (1956), designed in the manner of a south Indian temple. The central tower is Chola and the vimanas are Pallava in style. West of Government House is **Madras Racecourse**.

Elliot Beach Road leads to Adyar Bridge Road, where Elphinstone Bridge crosses the Adyar river. On the south bank are the **World Headquarters of the Theosophical Society**, set in 107·6 hectares (266 acres) of woodland. In the Headquarters Hall are statues of founders of the various religions. The famous Adyar Library, Museum, Chapel of St Michael and All Angels, Zoroastrian temple, Mosque, Besant Theosophical School and one of the largest banyan trees in the world are all here.

551

After crossing the bridge, built as a famine-relief measure in 1876-8, about 1·6 km (1 mile) to the west over the Buckingham Canal lies the **Adyar Club**, now the Madras Club. The club was founded in 1891 in a late-18th-century house originally owned by George Moubray, who arrived in Madras in 1771. The river frontage is embellished with a stately octagonal cupola over a semi-circular bay. The octagon room has an arcaded perimeter and trompe-l'oeil paintwork. The club stands in beautiful gardens which sweep down to the Adyar river.

Also in Adyar is **Brodie Castle** (1776), a white stucco garden house built on Quibble Island, a peninsula formed by two branches of the Adyar river. It has two castellated turrets flanking the frontage. The house is named after James Brodie, an East India Company servant who drowned in the river. Today it is the home of the College of Carnatic Music.

The **Chettinad Palace**, set in sprawling grounds by the Adyar river, has an old garden house, Somerford, on the estate. Ramalayam, the Maharaja of Travancore's garden house, now a school, is another notable example of colonial-style classical architecture in the same area.

South Beach Road leads to San Thomé or Old Mylapore, legendary burial place of St Thomas the Apostle. Nestorian Christians from Persia erected a chapel over the tomb and the site was renowned for centuries as a holy Christian shrine. The Portuguese arrived in 1522, built the chapel and founded a church nearby. The old cathedral was demolished in 1893 and the **New Cathedral** was opened in 1896. St Thomas's remains are alleged to rest beneath an altar in a subterranean niche. Adjacent is a small Anglican Church. San Thomé fell in 1672 to the French, who in turn were expelled by the Dutch in 1674. In 1749 the British occupied the site.

South of San Thomé Cathedral, in the grounds of 'Leith Castle', is an old circular fortification built in 1751. Further

inland is the **Luz Church** (1516), with a Franciscan coat of arms, reputedly built in honour of Our Lady of Light, who aided a Portuguese landing here during a fierce gale.

The **Marina**, running along the sea-front, is one of the most beautiful marine promenades in the world. It was planned by the Governor Grant Duff (1881–6). It runs from San Thomé right along the seashore, past Fort St George, and contains a series of impressive private and public buildings. Running northwards are **Queen Mary's College** and Lady Willingdon Training College (1917), then the former **Ice House** (1842), now Vivekanand House, a curious circular building with a roof pavilion capped by a slender pineapple. It was used by the Tudor Ice Co. to store blocks of ice imported from America. Later it was a home for Brahmin widows. It is now a hostel for the Lady Willingdon Training College.

Next is the **University Examination Hall**, a really excellent essay in the Indo-classical style, in the manner of Lutyens at New Delhi, with a distinctive helmet dome derived from a Buddhist stupa, all in warm red brick and crisp white stone.

The **Presidency College** comprises two separate blocks, the northern one relatively recent, the southern over 100 years old. The College began as a High School, founded in 1840 by Eyre Burton Powell, a Cambridge Wrangler. In 1855 it became the Presidency College and later gave birth to the University proper, which was founded in 1857. The older building is by Chisholm (1870), in the style of the French and Italian Renaissance. A statue of Powell (1882) stands below the central dome. The central portico, in pink sandstone, is a later addition by Harris, which detracts from Chisholm's original concept. The clock was installed to mark the centenary in 1940. Behind the College are the **Victoria Hostel** and **Kasthurba Hospital** (1885).

In Pycrofts Road is the **Amir Mahal**, the residence of the Prince of Arcot, originally the Police Court but used as a palace since 1876, with square corner towers in a simple Italianate style.

Next in line is the **Public Works Secretariat**, with curved corner turrets and a monumental arched entrance over a porte-cochère (*c.* 1870). Next comes the **Chepauk Palace**. The original buildings were designed by Philip Stowey in 1768 for Wala Jah, Muhammad Ali, the anglophile Nawab of the Carnatic. There were two blocks: the southern, the Khalsa Mahal, a two-storey pile with small domes, and the northern, a single-storey block containing the Humayun Mahal and Diwan Khana with the Durbar Hall. The title lapsed in 1805 and the buildings were acquired by the government as offices. The distinctive central tower was designed by Chisholm in 1870 to link the two blocks. A plaque in the south-west corner records its history. The Khalsa Mahal is now part of the Public Works Department buildings. The northern range is the Board of Revenue Offices.

The **Senate House** and University buildings form a famous landmark on the foreshore. The Senate House was designed by Chisholm and opened in 1873. It is a symmetrical composition in a Gothic-Saracenic style, with four polychrome corner towers which are capped by domes and linked by a giant arcade. Outside the south entrance is a Golden Jubilee **Statue of Queen Victoria** (1887) under an ornate cast-iron pavilion made by Macfarlane's of Glasgow. Facing the road on the east side are statues of Gokhale, Sri V. Krishnaswami Iyer and Judge Subramania Iyer. To the north are departmental buildings marked by a redbrick and stone tower in the same Indoclassical vein as the Examination Hall.

North of the University Buildings Napier Bridge crosses the sluggish Cooum river. Close by is the **Victory Memorial**, built in 1936 from public subscriptions in memory of the fallen of the First World War. A statue of George V stands nearby.

Mount Road leads to the Island. Beyond the Willingdon Bridge is Chantrey's famous bronze equestrian **Statue of Sir Thomas Munro** (1839), one of the most popular Englishmen to have served in India. In the south-west corner of the Island is the Gymkhana Club. Outside the entrance to old Government House, marked by huge iron gates, are statues of George V and, a little way off, **Judge Bodam**.

Old Government House lies in a large compound. Originally the house of a Portuguese merchant, Luis de Madeiros, it was acquired by the Governor in 1753. Damaged during the French wars, it was later repaired and extended before being extensively remodelled and enlarged by the astronomer John Goldingham in 1800. A drawing-room and dining-room were created on the upper floors, approached by a grand double staircase. An additional storey was added in 1860, the huge verandah in 1895.

A short distance from the house Goldingham erected the **Banqueting Hall** (1802), now Rajaji Hall, a magnificent monumental basilica designed for official entertainments and banquets. The main chamber is pedimented at either end with Tuscan-Doric three-quarter columns carrying an entablature with a frieze of urns and shields. Originally, the pediments were adorned with trophies commemorating British martial values – Seringapatam at one end and Plassey at the other – but these have been removed. Some of the power of the original composition was lost when an arcaded verandah was added to the outside in the remodelling of 1875. The resplendent sphinxes flanking the steps were replaced by a pair of Victorian urns at this time. The building is an important symbol of the growth of British Imperial power in India and the change of emphasis from mercantile to Imperial values in the early 19th century.

Internally, it is much as it was when the grand inaugural ball was held on 7 October 1802, although the pictures by famous artists which once adorned the walls now form part of the collection in the Fort Museum. Goldingham's plans for the government buildings were part of a wider Arcadian vision of an English country house set in its own estate, and the grounds were landscaped accordingly, with fountains, basins and other ornamental features. Little now survives of the original concept, but the compound is a pleasant oasis in the middle of the city.

Mount Road is the principal commercial thoroughfare of the city. Most of the shops, hotels and businesses are located here. The route leads south-west past the Munro statue. To the west of Bodam's statue is **Napier Park**. Next are the offices of the *Hindu* and the *Mail*, leading local English papers, and P. Orr & Sons, a quaint Gothic pile with a clocktower designed by Chisholm. The clocktower was connected to the Madras Observatory and once signalled Standard Time to the entire area. The roundabout is called **Round Tana**. Henry Irwin's South India Co-operative Insurance Building has just been demolished and replaced by a totally inappropriate modern block.

At the bend of the road is **Christ Church**. Opposite and further on lie **Higginbotham's Store** (1844), the US Information Office and **Government Arts College** (1934). **Spencer & Co.** (1897) is housed in a respectable Gothic pile punctuated by three gables with corner turrets. Adjacent is the arcaded range of Kaleeli Mansions. Situated in a small avenue immediately to the east is the former **Madras Club**. A few old garden houses linger on in a state of crumbling ruination behind Mount Road. The former Club is the finest.

Once the best residential club in India, the 'Ace of Clubs' was founded in 1831. One of the earliest additions was an octagonal 'divan' or smoking-room (1832) at the rear and this can still be seen. In 1842 the main house was recast. The fine north portico, added in 1865, gives the entire complex a focal point and overall cohesion. In 1882 Chisholm added a delightful Gothic card-room in timber and glass over a rear wing. Today the building is derelict and decaying; the main reception room is used as a squash court, although there are plans by Indian Express newspapers next door to use part as a theatre and offices.

Further down Mount Road is **Umda Bagh** (*c.* 1790), a handsome colonial-style house, formerly the home of the beautiful Khayrun Nissa Begum Sahiba, wife of the last Nawab of the Carnatic. In 1901 the house was purchased by the government. It is now a Women's College.

There are two major mosques in the city. The Big Mosque (1789) was funded by the Wallajah family. At the junction of Mount Road and Peters Road is the Thousand Lights Mosque, originally built in 1800 by Nawab Umdat-ul-Umara for use by Shia Muslims during Muharram mourning, but now redesigned.

MADURAI

Madurai, situated on the Vaigai river at a height of 135 m (442 ft), is one of southern India's oldest and most fascinating cities. Its main interest is the world-famous **Shree Minakshi Temple**, a riot of Dravidian architecture, but this and the other Hindu and Jain buildings fall outside the scope of this volume. (A full description can be found in Volume I.)

However, there are a few Islamic and British buildings of interest which should not be overlooked on any tour, even though they are only of secondary importance.

West of the main entrance to the People's Park is the **Jami Masjid**, which contains two tombs: that of Ala-ud-Din

554

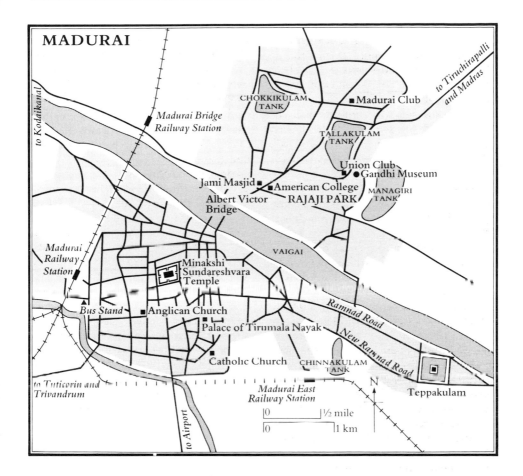

and his brother Shams-ud-Din. A pillar inside is inscribed with the date 1574 and describes the sanctuary as the 'Mosque of the Delhi Orukol Sultan'. The main feature of interest is the dome, cut from a single block of stone and measuring 6·7 m (22 ft) from base to apex and 21 m (69 ft) in diameter.

The **Tirumalai Nayaka Palace**, 1·2 km (¾ mile) south-east of the Great Temple of Shree Minakshi, was built in 1636, but only a single section of the once superb complex remains since it was dismantled between 1662 and 1682 by Tirumala's grandson in the transfer of the capital to Trichinopoly. What survives comprises two oblong blocks in Indo-Islamic style connected at one corner. The larger is built around a spacious open

courtyard, which is surrounded by an elegant arcade. The columns are over 12·2 m (40 ft) high, enriched with foliated brick arches of finely chased chunam. Behind the arcade, three sides of the quadrangle have cloisters 13·1 m (43 ft) wide, carved in triple rows of columns. Traces of the original turquoise, orange and red paint can still be seen on the capitals.

At the end of the courtyard the cloister deepens into a hall with five rows of massive pillars and three great domes, the last 18·3 m (60 ft) in circumference and over 21·3 m (70 ft) high. The main entrance portico was built to commemorate Lord Napier and Ettrick, the Governor of Madras from 1866 to 1872 who was responsible for its restoration.

To the west and opposite the main entrance is the **Celestial Pavilion** or Swarga Vilasam, once the throne-room. It comprises an arcaded octagon, covered by a dome 18·3 m (60 ft) wide and 21·3 m (70 ft) high.

North of this is another hall of cathedral-like proportions, 41 m (135 ft) long and 21·3 m (70 ft) high, covered by a pointed arched roof and reinforced with granite ribs which spring from a double series of arches, one above the other, carried on columns. In each corner is the carved figure of a warrior with a drawn sword. Above is a large gallery. Tradition asserts that this was Tirumala's sleeping-apartment, with the bed suspended by chains from the ceiling.

On the north side of the Vaigai river is the **Tumkum** or summer house (mid-17th century) built for fights between wild beasts and other sporting events. Situated on a four-sided mound and faced in stone, it has a domed roof carried on arches springing from square columns. The ceiling is formed as an inverted lotus blossom in painted chunam.

The **Anglican Church** (*c.* 1875) is of interest as it was designed by Robert Fellowes Chisholm, the Madras architect. It can be found in the middle of the town in an open space south-west of the Great Temple.

MAHÉ

Mahe was once the only French settlement on the west coast, a tiny enclave no larger than 6·5 sq km (2½ square miles) with a useful harbour about 6·4 km (4 miles) south of Tellicherry. The town is named after M. Mahé de Labourdonnais, who seized the territory for France in 1725. It was taken by the British under Sir Hector Munro in 1761, but was restored to the French four years later. It was captured again in 1779 and once more restored, in 1785. It fell for the third and final time in 1793, but was given back, together with a small French factory at Calicut, in 1816.

Once a town of considerable importance, its constant loss to the British in the late 18th century adversely affected its trading prospects and it decayed into a pleasant, picturesque backwater. There is a Roman Catholic church and a Mission House run by Basel missionaries on a nearby hill. The territory was ceded to the Indian government by France on 1 November 1954.

MALVALLI

3·2 km (2 miles) from this small village 45 km (28 miles) east of Mysore, the British army under General Harris defeated the army of Tipu Sultan on the march to Seringapatam on 27 March 1799. Colonel Arthur Wellesley (later the Duke of Wellington) commanded the British left flank.

MANGALORE

Mangalore is a coastal town of considerable importance separated from the sea by a backwater around two sides of a peninsula. It has a long historical reputation as the commercial centre of the region. In the mid-14th century there were over 400 Muslim merchants residing here. Even though it was sacked on three separate occasions by the Portuguese, from 1640 to 1763 Mangalore was the stronghold of the Bednur Raja, before succumbing to Haidar Ali, who made the town his naval headquarters. In 1768 the town was captured by the British for a short period, but the most famous episode was the lengthy siege of the British garrison from 6 May 1783 to 23 January 1784. The town was heroically defended against the entire

556

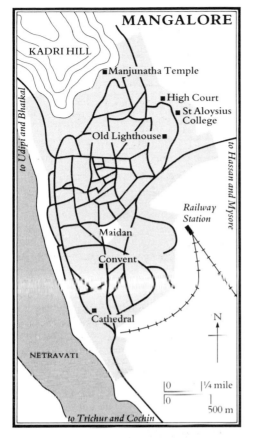

MANGALORE

KADRI HILL

to Udipi and Bhatkal

Manjunatha Temple

High Court

St Aloysius College

Old Lighthouse

to Hassan and Mysore

Railway Station

Maidan

Convent

Cathedral

N

NETRAVATI

0 | ¼ mile
0 | 500 m

to Trichur and Cochin

army of Tipu Sultan by Colonel John Campbell of the 42nd Foot with a small force of 1,850 men, of whom only 412 were British soldiers. Eventually it surrendered with full military honours. In 1799 it became British territory, after which the only serious disturbance was during the Coorg insurrection of 1837, when the public buildings were burned.

The town is picturesque, prosperous and pleasant, surrounded by groves of coconut palms. The principal buildings of interest are the **Government College** and the **Jesuit College of St Aloysius** (Museum). There is a large local Roman Catholic population with a European bishopric, several churches and a convent. From the hill on which the **Old Lighthouse** stands, a splendid view can be obtained of the coast and hills.

The **Old Burialground** is of great interest and includes an obelisk to the memory of Brigadier-General John Carnac, who died in 1800, aged eighty-four, after over sixty years of service in India.

(For details of the temple at Kadiri see Volume I.)

MERCARA

This interesting and prosperous old settlement was once the chief town of Coorg. It lies 120 km (75 miles) west of Mysore. The capital was established here by Madhu Raja in 1681.

The **Fort** stands on a rocky eminence surrounded by neighbouring hills. In shape it is an irregular hexagon set behind a ditch with a steep glacis to the north face. In 1773 Coorg was overrun by Haidar Ali and ten years later it was devastated by Tipu Sultan. In 1791 the fort was besieged by Vira Raja of Coorg, but was relieved by Tipu. By the Treaty of Seringapatam in 1792 Tipu was excluded from Coorg and the west coast. Later the subjects of Vira Raja complained of their ill-treatment. They sought British protection, which was secured by the unopposed annexation of Coorg in 1834.

The fort walls are well preserved. Within lie the palace, English church and arsenal. The former Commissioner's Residence lies within the eastern gateway. The **Palace**, erected by Linga Rajendra Wadiyar in 1812, has a local vernacular plan but European façades of two storeys faced in brick.

Within the old town are the **Mausolea of Dodda Vira Rajendra**, the hero of Coorg independence, **Linga Rajendra** and their respective queens. All are enclosed by a high embankment and are built in a local Muslim style with a central dome and corner minarets. The Hindu temple of Omkareshwara Devastana is similar in style.

The **Central School** is housed in a handsome building (early 19th century) erected by Dodda Vira Rajendra as a reception house for English visitors.

MYSORE

Quite simply, Mysore is one of the most beautiful cities in India, haunted by the pervasive aroma of sandalwood and incense. Situated about 138 km (86 miles) by road from Bangalore, it lies in a valley formed by two ridges. It has wide, spacious streets, numerous parks and is well kept, with a high standard of visual amenity. This is largely due to the energetic work of the City Improvement Trust Board in the 1930s and the enlightened outlook of the present municipal authorities. Under the Wadiyar family Bangalore was developed as the administrative centre and Mysore became the focus for state spectacles.

Modern Mysore is not particularly old; the entire town was levelled by Tipu Sultan in 1793 in order to build a new city. The old palace was reconstructed in the early 19th century along the lines of its predecessor, but this was never successful. In February 1897 it was severely damaged by fire. Today the centre of the city is dominated by the **Amba Vilas Palace**, which stands within the old Fort.

The new **Amba Vilas Palace** (1897) was designed by Henry Irwin, the versatile architect of Viceregal Lodge, Simla. It is a glorious Indo-Saracenic pile in grey granite dominated by a five-storey minaret with a gilded dome. On Sunday nights and during festivals the entire exterior is lit by over 50,000 light bulbs, like some sort of Oriental Harrods. The whole palace is a riot of domes, pinnacles and exotic ornament.

The palace is built around a courtyard. It is a building of extraordinary eclecticism, facing a large square, which is enclosed by ornamental walls and trium-

phal gateways. To the east is the Elephant Gate, 20 m (66 ft) high. On the north side are the armoury, library, lifts and staircases, above which lie the music room, ladies' drawing-room and bedrooms. On the west side of the inner courtyard lies what remains of the old palace of 1800 and the zenana. To the south is the beautiful peacock marriage pavilion and beyond, on the second floor, the great Durbar Hall, 47 m (155 ft) long and 13·7 m (45 ft) wide.

The **Durbar Hall** is one of the most exuberant rooms in India, a blaze of colour and sinuous forms, like a setting from *A Thousand and One Nights*. On the west wall are some decorative pictures from the Hindu epics painted by Ravi Varma and Raja Varma of Travancore. Between the pillars is fine Agra inlay work in jacinth and jasper, carnelian and carbuncle, amber and lapis lazuli. The ceiling is made of teakwood, enriched with spectacular stained glass. Every door has different details, which repay close inspection. One panel depicts the tiny Krishna kissing his baby toe. The throne, originally of figwood overlaid with ivory but now of gold and silver, is remarkable. According to palace legend, it may have been the ancient throne of the Pandus.

The **Peacock Pavilion** or Marriage Pavilion is octagonal in plan, with stained glass from Glasgow and a dome carried on triple iron pillars. A purdah gallery encircles the hall. The floor is enriched with elaborate geometric patterns.

The Armoury has a collection of over 3,000 weapons and several 'Tiger's claws', fearful iron talons used to tear an adversary to pieces. In the inner courtyard are eight enormous bronze tigers by Robert William Colton, RA. The Music Room has elaborate European plasterwork and furniture.

The **Jogun Mohun Mahal Palace** (1900) lies immediately to the west. It is in two parts: that on the east is a spacious

558

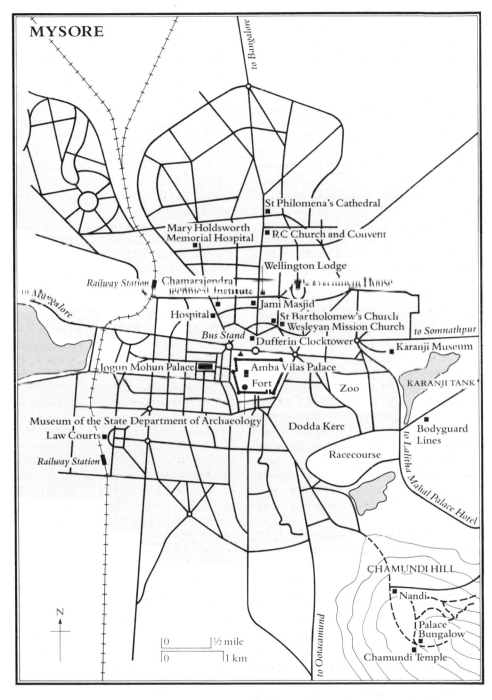

MYSORE

to Bangalore

St Philomena's Cathedral

Mary Holdsworth
Memorial Hospital

R.C Church and Convent

Wellington Lodge

Railway Station

Chamarajendra
Technical Institute

Government House

Jami Masjid

Hospital

St Bartholomew's Church
Wesleyan Mission Church

to Bangalore

Bus Stand

Dufferin Clocktower

to Somnathpur

Karanji Museum

Jogun Mohun Palace

Amba Vilas Palace

Fort

Zoo

KARANJI TANK

Museum of the State Department of Archaeology

Dodda Kere

Bodyguard
Lines

Law Courts

Railway Station

Racecourse

to Lalitha Mahal Palace Hotel

CHAMUNDI HILL

Nandi

Palace
Bungalow

Chamundi Temple

N

0 ½ mile
0 1 km

to Ootacamund

pavilion with massive carved doors, built
for the marriage of the then Maharaja and
scene of his installation by Lord Curzon

in 1902; the western building is the
Sri Chamarajendra Art Gallery and
Museum.

To the south lie the Municipal Offices, the entrance to which is flanked by two domed minarets. Nearby are the Palace Offices (1925), built in a complementary style to the main palace. Outside the north gate is the Chamarajendra Statue, beyond which is the **Dufferin Clock-Tower**.

Siyaji Rao Road is the main shopping centre. On the east side is the **Victoria Girls' School**, opened by Lady Robertson in 1902. Beyond is the **Krishna-rajendra Hospital**, rebuilt in 1918. Opposite is the **Chamarajendra Technical Institute**, completed in 1913. The Prince of Wales (later King George V) laid the foundation stone in 1906.

The **Mary Holdsworth Memorial Hospital** (1906) is a memorial to the Wesleyan missionary who devoted her life to the medical welfare of the city. From the east gate of the hospital it is a short walk to the **Azam Mosque** or Great Mosque (1799), one of over twenty mosques in the city.

On the south side of Railway Station Road is the **Jami Masjid** (1830). To the east over Church Road is a triumphal archway across the road. This marks one entrance to **Government House**. The house was begun in 1800 under Colonel Wilks and by 1805 it had been enlarged and completed. It is a fine example of a European-style house of the period, with extensive verandahs and a small, open, central courtyard. The Banqueting Hall was added in 1807 to the designs of Captain Thomas Fiott de Havilland, who created the largest room in south India with a roof unsupported by pillars after the construction of his famous experimental arch at Seringapatam. It is an elegant and tasteful room with Venetian arches to the flanks. The house is well maintained for state guests and retains a marvellous period atmosphere from the days of the Raj. The northern entrance to the estate is marked also by a triumphal gateway. To the east of the long main drive is the old Maidan, used for polo and as a parade ground.

Church Road, which runs along the western edge of the Government House estate, leads to the **Roman Catholic Church and Convent**, established by Abbé Dubois in 1799. Just beyond is the parish church of St Joseph. The whole group of buildings is designed in a pretty Gothic style. The new Cathedral of St Philomena is an imposing if rather eccentric example of the Gothic style, begun in 1931 and consecrated only in 1959. Its two peculiar spires are a local landmark.

Wellington Lodge, opposite the west gate to Government House, was the residence of the Commissioners of Mysore after the restoration of the Raja in 1799. A plaque testifies to the occupation of the house by the future Duke of Wellington, then Colonel Arthur Wellesley, between 1799 and 1801. To the south is the Government Training College. Opposite is the Wesleyan Mission Press and Church (c. 1870). Opposite again lies **St Bartholomew's** (1830–31), the Anglican Church instigated by Francis Lewis, an unprepossessing but historically interesting building.

On the outskirts of the town lies a splendid former palace of the Maharaja of Mysore, now converted to a hotel. The **Lalitha Mahal Palace** was designed by E. W. Fritchley in 1930. It has a pedimented, two-storey centrepiece behind which rises a huge dome, the design of which is derived from St Paul's Cathedral, London, but with long, attenuated wings of paired Corinthian columns culminating in secondary domed pavilions. Seen from a distance it resembles some evanescent dream palace rising from the dry plains around. The interior is well preserved, with stained glass, ornamental plasterwork and delightful suites of principal rooms. Afternoon tea is recommended.

The approach to the palace is via a long boulevard. On one side are the attractive lines of the Maharaja's Bodyguard. On the other is a good series of simple

Gothic bungalows, one of which was used in the TV series *Jewel in the Crown*. Between the Bodyguard Lines and the city is the Racecourse and to the north are the Zoological Gardens, which partly run alongside the Dodda Kere Lake. Just to the north of the Karanji Tank is the **Karanji Mansion**, built for the second sister of the Maharaja and distinguished by its many domes. 3·2 km (2 miles) south-east of the Fort is the commanding presence of Chamundi Hill. Access is either by road or on foot, but the going is precipitous, to a height of 1,173 m (3,849 ft). Two-thirds of the way up is a colossal statue of Nandi, the sacred bull of Shiva, hewn out of a single piece of solid basalt in 1659. At the summit is the **Palace Bungalow**, a substantial mansion with breathtaking views of the city and countryside. The house embraces the core of a building erected in 1822 by Sir Arthur Cole. (For the collections in the City Museum and details of Chamundi Hill see Volume I.)

To the west of the city lies Gordon Park and the University (1916). A statue of Sir James Gordon by Onslow Ford stands in front of the District Kacheri within the park.

NAGAPATTINAM

Nagapattinam (literally Snake Town) was known by Arab geographers as Malifattan and by the early Portuguese as the City of Choramandel. It is an old port and became one of the first Portuguese settlements on the east coast. It was seized by the Dutch in 1660 and later by the English in 1781.

There is an old lighthouse in the harbour. The Dutch Church and old tombs, dating from 1661, in the Karicop cemetery are noteworthy. Embedded in the walls of the old Salt Factory are some Dutch tombs from 1667 onwards.

(For the ancient Buddhist connections and the Hindu temples see Volume I.)

NAGORE

4·8 km (3 miles) north of Negapatam at the mouth of the Vetta river, Nagore was sold to the Dutch by the Raja of Tanjore in 1771, but was later wrested from them by the Nawabs of the Carnatic, assisted by the British. It was restored to the Raja, who granted it to the English in 1776.

The town is famous as a Muslim centre of south India. There is a celebrated mosque crowned by a 27·4 m (90 ft) minaret. The mosque houses the tomb of a Muslim saint, which has unusual inner doors dressed with silver ornament.

NANDI

Nandi (the sacred bull of Shiva) lies 50 km (31 miles) north of Bangalore. It comprises an impressive hillfort 1,478 m (4,851 ft) above sea level, at the summit of which is an extensive plateau with a tank fed by natural springs called the Amrita Sarovar or Lake of Nectar. Today it is a popular resort for visitors from Bangalore.

Access to the summit is via a steep footpath of 1,175 steps, but the less energetic may prefer the modern motor road which has been constructed recently. The fort stands on a huge outcrop of gneiss, with steep perpendicular sides 457 m (1,500 ft) high. It is protected by a double line of ramparts, most of which date from the time of Haidar Ali and Tipu Sultan, who believed the place impregnable. However, after a bombardment of twenty-one days it was stormed by the British army under Cornwallis on 19 October 1791 with only thirty casualties, chiefly due to stones rolled from above. At the summit is a large house in the European style built by Sir Mark Cubbon when he was Resident at Mysore in 1834.

(For details of the 9th-century temple at the base of the hill see Volume I.)

OOTACAMUND

Ootacamund, the 'Queen of Hill Stations', known popularly as Ooty, lies in the Nilgiri Hills at a height if 2,267 m (7,440 ft). The area was surveyed in 1818 by Whish and Kindersley, who returned with tales of a romantic lost world of open moorland teeming with game and wildfowl. On the strength of these reports, John Sullivan, the local Collector, explored the area and it was he who built the first house in 1823.

The town is surrounded by high hills. To the east is the highest, Dodabetta, at 2,578 m (8,460 ft), from which there is a superb panorama. To the south-east is Elk Hill, 2,465 m (8,090 ft); to the south of the lake is Chinna Dodabetta, 2,393 m (7,849 ft); in the west are Cairn Hill, 2,311 m (7,583 ft) and St Stephen's Church Hill, 2,264 m (7,429 ft); and to the north lie Snowdon, 2,529 m (8,299 ft) and Club Hill, 2,447 m (8,030 ft). The town itself is widely dispersed around a large artificial lake. The houses are reached by narrow, winding English lanes bordered by imported English shrubs and flowers, and plantations of eucalyptus.

Ooty rapidly became a popular sanatorium and retreat for invalids. In 1826 Sir Thomas Munro stayed with John

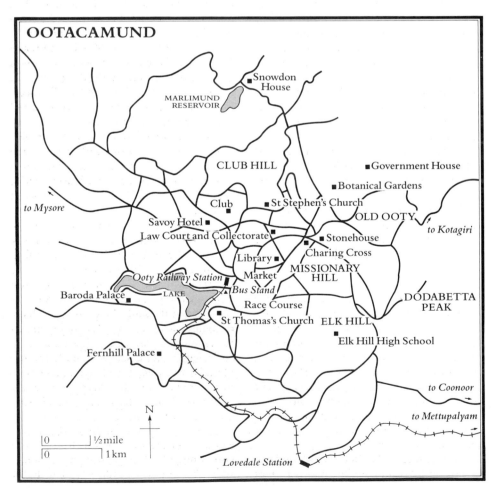

Sullivan. Stephen Lushington, who was later to be the Governor of Madras, became a regular visitor. The arrival of the miniature railway from Mettupalayam in the late 19th century improved access from Madras enormously. The journey through the hills is spectacular and should on no account be missed. Ooty was the summer headquarters of the government of Madras from 1861 onwards.

The best starting-point for a tour of the station is **St Stephen's Church** (1830), designed by Captain John James Underwood and consecrated by the Bishop of Calcutta. It is a pretty Gothic building with a low tower and crenellated parapets in cream stucco. The original teak timbers were taken from Tipu Sultan's Lal Bagh Palace at Seringapatam and reused here. The internal columns are salvaged teak, but plastered to resemble stone. There is a large projecting porte-cochère. The pews were added in 1842, the clock and bell in 1851. Inside there are some interesting brasses and memorial tablets.

Behind the Church is the picturesque **Cemetery**, crowded with tombs, which straggle back up the hill in great profusion.

Nearby is the **Club**. The building is a long, low, single-storey range with a pedimented Ionic centrepiece. It was built in 1831 as an hotel for the financier Sir William Rumbold under the supervision of his butler, Felix Joachim, who later ran the hotel. Here in 1834 Lord William Bentinck met Thomas Macaulay, author of the great Indian penal code. In 1843 the house was taken over by the Club. The interior is a perfect memorial to the days of the Raj, with animal trophies, tiger skins, old military and hunting prints and club furniture, all maintained beautifully. In 1875 Lieutenant Neville Chamberlain perfected the game of snooker here.

Stonehouse, the first house built in Ooty by John Sullivan in 1823, survives in a much-altered form, embedded in a later building used by the Government Arts College. It has a lovely garden, full of exotic shrubs of astonishing size. Other early buildings include the **School**, probably by Underwood, and Sylks Hotel, now the **Savoy Hotel**, built as a school for the Church Mission Society using salvaged teak beams, also by Underwood and, from 1841, his own house.

The principal shops lie around the vicinity of the Church, including a branch of Higginbotham's and also Spencer's. The **Law Courts** are contained in a red-brick range with steeply pitched corrugated-iron roofs and a needle tower and spire. Built in 1873 in perpendicular Gothic style, as Breek's Memorial School, it became the Civil Court in 1899. Nearby is the **Nilgiri Library** (1855), designed by Robert Fellowes Chisholm, with a lofty Reading Room lit by five arched windows and a tall Gothic window at the far end. It is faced in red brick with stucco dressings.

En route to **Charing Cross**, a major road intersection with a rather grotesque Victorian cast-iron fountain, the small Regency Gothick **Union Church** (1896) is passed; stylistically, it is sixty years out of date.

To the north-east of the town lie the **Botanical Gardens** (1840), beautifully laid out at the foot of Dodabetta Hill in broad terraces with a fascinating variety of species, including huge rhododendron trees. **Government House** (1880) is approached through the gardens. A half-timbered Arts and Crafts lodge marks the entrance to the estate. The house is in an Italianate style and was built for the Duke of Buckingham. The entrance portico is copied from the Duke's family seat at Stowe. Below the main house is Old Government House.

Of the outlying buildings the **Lawrence Memorial School** behind Elk Hill is notable. Designed in an Italianate style by Robert Fellowes Chisholm (*c.* 1865), it resembles Osborne House, Isle of Wight, with a tall campanile.

St Thomas's Church lies to the east of the lake, near Herbert Park and the Racecourse. To the south is **Fernhill Palace**, now a hotel, once the Palace of the Maharaja of Mysore. Faced in dark-red stucco with elaborately carved bargeboards, it was built in 1842 but extended in 1873, with large ballrooms and other suites for the Maharaja's own use. Behind in an outbuilding lies an indoor badminton court.

To the north-west, near the lake, is **Baroda Palace**, once the summer home of the Gaekwar. Other houses of note are The Cedars, used by the Resident at Hyderabad, Crewe Hall (1830–31), Lushington Hall (1827–8) and Elk Hill House, built by George Norton for his own use in 1836. **Aranmore**, to the north of the lake, was once the home of the Maharaja of Jodhpur. It is designed in a relaxed Arts and Crafts style, with an underground passage providing a direct link with the Maharani's quarters. **Woodside** (1850) has some handsome marble chimneypieces in the reception rooms which were taken from a palatial house built at Kaiti for Lord Elphinstone.

PADMANABHAPURAM

On the road to Kanyakumari, 53 km (33 miles) from Trivandrum, is the **Padmanabhapuram Palace**, a splendid example of ancient Keralan architecture and once the capital of the princely state. There are some splendid 17th- and 18th-century murals covering more than forty major panels. They depict scenes from the Hindu epics and are considered to be better than those at Mattancherry in Cochin.

It follows the typical palace plan, with a central courtyard and gabled tiled roofs. The woodwork shows delicate craftsmanship of exceptional quality. The perforated screens, foliated brackets

and dhatura-flower pendants are the best of their kind in existence. Inside, the ceiling beams are embellished with elaborate patterns in carved timber.

PENUKONDA

Penukonda or Big Hill lies outside Anantapur, which is situated 69 km (43 miles) from Guntakal. The hillfort contains a number of interesting antiquities. (For the sacred Hindu monuments see Volume I.)

Penukonda was the residence of the Vijayanagara Rajas from as early as 1354, and Tirumal Raya moved here after the disastrous Battle of Talikota in 1565. The ruins of the citadel crown the summit of the hill within the fort area, while the dilapidated remains of Hindu and Muslim buildings lie in great profusion. Some exhibit an incongruous mixture of styles and details.

The **Gagan Mahal** or Ancient Palace (16th century) has a basement of Hindu construction and a ground floor of elaborate Muslim detail, later altered to improve the relationship with the Hindu work. Built in the courtly style typical of the period, it is similar to several structures at Vijayanagara, with Islamic-style-arches, vaults and plaster decoration combined with temple-like elements. The upper level is capped with an octagonal pyramidal tower. An adjoining three-storey square tower with projecting balconies overlooks the approaches from the east. Nearby stands a small, square structure, also with a pyramidal roof.

The **Mosque of Sher Ali** (*c.* 1600) is a handsome building of dark-grey granite with jet-black stone mouldings of hornblende.

In the grounds of the Sub-Collector's house is a stone pillar 12·2 m (40 ft) high. A plaque on the Collector's office records the residence of Sir Thomas Munro. The Court House is known as Munro's Hall.

POLLILORE (PULLALUR)

Pollilore, 16 km (10 miles) north of Kanchipuram, was the scene of the defeat of Colonel William Baillie by Haidar Ali on 10 September 1780. Two lofty **Obelisks** mark the death of two officers during the engagement, which was a savage affair. 6,000 ill-equipped British troops were attacked by a force of over 100,000. After resisting continuous assaults, and on the brink of a spectacular victory, Baillie's ammunition tumbril exploded from a direct hit, devastating the British ranks. Baillie formed a last stand with 500 men on a sandy hillock, where he repulsed thirteen further attacks, by over 80,000 men, before surrendering.

Those who weren't killed were delivered into an appalling captivity at Seringapatam, from which only a handful survived. One of the survivors, Captain (later General Sir) David Baird, led the outstanding assault against the city of 4 May 1799 which finally crushed the power of the Mysore Rajas.

A further engagement was fought over the same ground on 27 August 1781 by Sir Eyre Coote.

PONDICHERRY *Map overleaf*

Pondicherry, 161 km (100 miles) south of Madras, is the capital of the Union Territory of Pondicherry, which is an amalgamation of all the former French settlements which were handed over to the Indian government in November 1854. The other territories – Mahé, Karaikal and Yanam – are administered from here. The French influence is still noticeable if superficial.

In 1672 Pondicherry was bought by the French from the King of Bijapur, but its subsequent history was one of endless disturbance and warfare. The old town was established by François Martin in 1674 as a trading settlement. In 1693 it fell to the Dutch, only to be restored four years later by the Treaty of Ryswick. After that it changed hands between the English and French no less than nine times. Under Dupleix from 1741 to 1754 it regained its former pre-eminence, but in 1761, during the Seven Years War, the British captured the town and razed its buildings. After repeated exchanges, the town was restored to the French in 1817. In 1940 it declared for the Free French.

The area of greatest French atmosphere is the waterfront. The present town, with its distinctive grid pattern set within a circular road, was laid out by Jean Law between 1756 and 1777. It is divided into White Town, near the waterfront, and Black Town beyond.

At the entrance to the **Pier** is a semi-circle of **eight pillars**, each 11·6 m (38 ft) high, brought from Gingee. On the third from the left is an astronomical plan which fixes the longitude of the town. In front of the pillars is a statue of Mahatma Gandhi. To the left of Gandhi Square is the **War Memorial**, a curiously lumpen affair erected to commemorate the French fallen in the First World War (1938). Nearby is a statue of Joan of Arc. Beyond is the lighthouse (1836) 27 m (89 ft) high. On rue Jawaharlal is a statue of Dupleix (1870).

Behind Dupleix's statue is **Raj Nivas**, formerly Dupleix's Palace (1752), a fine example of French colonial architecture. Opposite is Government Park, which contains numerous fountains and a fine neo-classical pavilion with pedimented façades and fluted Tuscan columns, crowned by a foliated urn. The **French Institute** on Dumas Street was established in 1955. The **Botanical Gardens**, off West Boulevard, were laid out by C. S. Perrotet in 1826, since when they have been well maintained.

The **Pondicherry Museum** occupies the former Government Library and has extensive collections on French India and

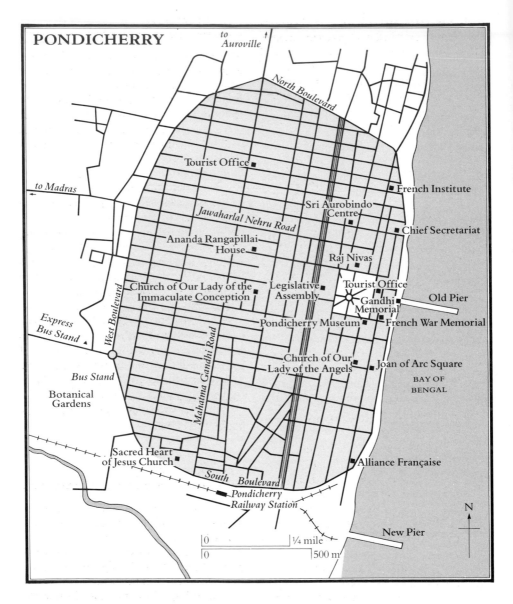

of sculptures, bronzes, arms, art and handicrafts; there is even a Roman-style sword found locally.

The interior is magnificently appointed in French style. The drawing-room, dining-room and bedroom are particularly noteworthy, with furniture, paintings and other pieces from various French homes in the town, including Dupleix's bed.

The churches in the town are well worth a visit. The **Church of the Sacred Heart of Jesus**, on South Boulevard, is in 19th-century Gothic style, with a large crocketed central gable flanked by two towers in white stucco with red dressings. The interior has some good stained glass.

The **Eglise de Notre Dame de la Conception** was commenced in 1691 and completed in 1765. On rue Dumas the **Eglise de Notre Dame des Anges** (1855) was designed by Louis Guerre and has a rare oil painting of Our Lady of Assumption presented by Napoleon III. Opposite, in the cemetery, is the **Tomb of Charles, Marquis de Bussy** (1785), the most enterprising of all Dupleix's followers.

At Villenour, outside the town, is the **Eglise de Notre Dame de Lourdes** (1876), in the style of the Basilica at Lourdes. The statue of Our Lady was given by the French Government a year later. The church is unique as a Catholic shrine in that it boasts its own tank. There is an annual festival here in June. The **Chapel of Our Sisters of Cluny** is a small 17th-century shrine. At Ariyankuppam, about 4 km (2½ miles) outside Pondicherry, is an 18th-century **chapel**, reputed to have been a favourite resort of Dupleix and his wife.

The town also boasts the homes of two notable Indian poets: 20 Easwaran Koil is the humble home of Subramania Bharathi; 95 Perumalkoil Street is the home of his disciple Bharathidasan. Both are preserved as museums.

69 rue Rangapillai is the house of **Ananda Rangapillai** (mid-18th century), the 18th century diarist. Described as 'the Pepys of India', he became Dupleix's protégé and his house is a fascinating mixture of Eastern and French colonial styles. It too is now a museum.

Today the main attraction of the town is the **Sri Aurobindo Ashram**, founded in 1926, one of the most popular and affluent in India, based on the teachings of the philosopher-poet Aurobindo Ghose. Outside the town, Auroville is a new city, an international community and education centre with fascinating buildings designed by the French architect Roger Anger in the International Modern style.

The European cemeteries south of the railway station are worth seeing.

PORTO NOVO

51·5 km (32 miles) south of Pondicherry, at the mouth of the River Vellar, is Porto Novo, an early trading station founded in 1575 by the Portuguese. It was lost to the Dutch in 1660, who abandoned their factory eighteen years later in favour of Pulicat. The English commenced trading in 1682.

There are no monuments of any consequence, but the town has important historical associations. On 1 July 1781 the indomitable Sir Eyre Coote fought a vital action at Porto Novo against the entire Mysore army of over 40,000 troops under Haidar Ali. The battle, which virtually saved the Presidency, was a key event in the history of Anglo-India.

Porto Novo is interesting also as the scene of an early English joint-stock venture. From 1824 efforts were made to establish an ironworks here. The Old Khan Sahib's Canal was dredged and deepened. A new canal was dug to facilitate transport of the iron ore, but after years of patient endeavour it was eventually abandoned.

PUDUKKOTTAI

Pudukkottai, 58 km (36 miles) from Thanjavur (Tanjore), is the capital of the small former state of that name. It is a clean, well-built town with a number of public buildings and a significant collection of paintings in the palace.

The ruling dynasty, the Tondaman Rajas, had a long history of cooperation with and support for the British, commencing with the supply of British troops before Trichinopoly in 1753 and later involving assistance against Haidar Ali and the French. As a result of this loyalty favourable consideration was given to Tondaman claims to the fort and district of Kilanelli.

(For the Museum see Volume I.)

PULICAT (PONNERI)

Pulicat, the first Dutch settlement in India, is situated 40 km (25 miles) north of Madras, close to a tidal lagoon. Today it is a backwater in every sense of the word.

In 1609 the Dutch built a fort here called Castel Geldria. Ten years later they permitted the English a share in the pepper trade with Java. The town became the chief centre of Dutch influence on the entire coast. It was in order to escape this that in 1626 the English traders moved to Armagaon, 64 km (40 miles) to the north, and later, in 1639, to Madras.

The town suffered from the usual see-saw of European political fortunes. In 1781 it was seized by the British, only to be restored to the Dutch four years later. It surrendered again in 1795. In 1818 Pulicat was handed back in accordance with the Convention of Allied Powers of 1814, but it was finally ceded to Britain in 1824.

The **Old Dutch Cemetery** is probably the most interesting of its kind in India. Many of the tombstones are over 400 years old. One tomb carries a representation of the original Dutch fort and others, Dutch coats of arms, so well executed that it has been suggested that they were sent from Holland. They owe their preservation to the work of Sir Charles Trevelyan, who saved many from decay.

The cemetery is entered via a quaint Romanesque lych gate bearing the date 1656. In front of each of the two gate-posts stands a sculpted stone skeleton, almost life size. One carries an hour glass on its head and the other a skull on a column. It is alleged that the former holds an eggshell and depicts a Dutch governor who, during a terrible famine, doled out eggshells of rice to the starving poor and made a fortune from their sufferings. His memory was so execrated that every passer-by used to spit at the effigy and a railing was therefore placed around it for protection. An old church and sundial adjoin the cemetery.

QUILON

Quilon is one of the oldest towns on the west coast of India, with an ancient history that can be traced back to the early days of the primitive Syrian church in India.

For centuries it was one of the great ports of the Malabar coast, and it remains a very attractive, prosperous resort. It is mentioned in early Christian manuscripts as early as 660, and appears in Arab records in 851, when it was a busy port trading with China. It is the 'Coilum' of Marco Polo. It remains an important sea port and centre for local Christians, and is reputed to be one of the seven churches founded by St Thomas himself.

In 1503 the Portuguese established a factory and fort here. These were captured by the Dutch in 1653. In 1741 it was besieged by Travancore. In the early 19th century British forces were garrisoned here.

There are few remains of any architectural importance, but the town is a pleasant, relaxing place to visit.

RANIPET

This is the European quarter of Arcot town, founded in 1771 by the Nawab of Arcot, in honour of the youthful widow of Desingh Raja of Gingee, who performed suttee on her husband's grave.

For many years it was a large cavalry cantonment. There are a number of churches in the town. The old cemetery has many interesting English tombs dating from 1791 onwards.

SADRAS

Sadras, 69 km (43 miles) south of Madras, to which it is connected via the Buckingham Canal, was an old Dutch trading settlement founded in 1647. An abortive peace conference between the English and the French was held here in January 1754.

The **Dutch Fort**, close to the shore, is now in ruins. Within it lies the **Old Dutch Cemetery**, with tombstones which date back to 1679. There is a small Lutheran Church and Wesleyan Mission in the town. Sadras was once famous for its printed cottons, but the industry has long since departed.

Sadras was taken by the British in 1781 and again in 1795. It was restored to the Dutch in 1818, but ceded to the British permanently in 1824 in exchange for Fort Marlborough and other possessions in Sumatra.

SAVANDRUG

This hillfort near Bangalore comprises an enormous mass of granite with a circumference of 13 km (8 miles). The summit is split by a chasm into two peaks: the 'kari' or black, and the 'bili' or white, each having their own water supply.

The original fortifications were erected in 1543 by Samanta Raya. At the end of the 16th century Immadi Kempe Gowda of Bangalore made the hill his stronghold, and it remained in the hands of his family until 1728, when it was captured by the Raja of Mysore, from whom it passed to Haidar Ali.

In 1791 Savandrug was stormed by Lord Cornwallis. Once a breach had been secured by artillery bombardment, the entire fort was carried within an hour without the loss of a single British life.

SERINGAPATAM (SRIRANGAPATNAM) *Map overleaf*

Seringapatam, 14·5 km (9 miles) from Mysore and about 120 km (75 miles) from Bangalore, is an island in the River Cauvery, 735 m (2,412 ft) above sea level. The name is derived from the ancient temple of Sri Ranganatha Swami which lies on the island. It is renowned as the capital of the Mysore Rajas Haidar Ali and Tipu Sultan and for the bloody struggles against the British in the late 18th century.

In 1610 the last of the Vijayanagara Viceroys, Tirumala Rayal, relinquished his power to the powerful Mysore ruler Raja Wadiyar. The Raja moved his capital to Shringapuram and Wadiyar and his three successors consolidated and extended the Mysore dominions. They were followed by a succession of weak puppet kings who fell increasingly under the influence of their diwans, until, in 1761, Haidar Ali, a Muslim trooper in the Mysore Horse, became diwan and virtual ruler of the state.

He not only usurped all power in the kingdom but asserted his independence in a series of struggles which established Mysore as a martial southern power feared and despised by both the Marathas and the Nizam of Hyderabad. Having won or bought peace from his rivals, he soon opposed a stronger combination from the English, who, trading peacefully from their isolated coastal enclaves, were forced by the internecine feuds throughout the country initially into protective measures, then into a series of defensive alliances, and finally into a protracted struggle for local supremacy. The Marathas and the Nizam of Hyderabad, both fearing the power of the rising Mysore state, allied with the English, and so began four separate wars between the Mysore Rajas and the English.

The first round was sparked off by Haidar's resentment of the capture of

569

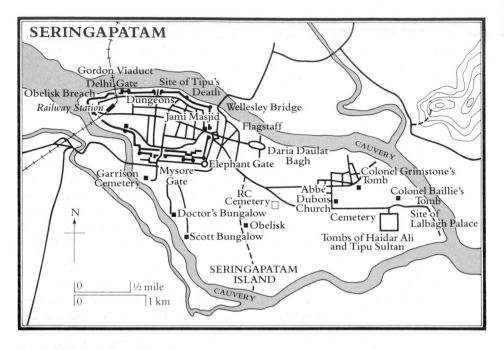

Mahé and led to the defeat of Colonel Baillie at Pollilore and the capture of British troops, who were imprisoned at Seringapatam from 1780 to 1784, and in some cases until 1799. In 1791 Lord Cornwallis captured Bangalore and attacked Seringapatam from the north, but owing to supply difficulties he was forced to retire. In 1792 he returned victorious and forced a humiliating peace on Tipu Sultan. The final struggle took place in 1799, when General (later Lord) Harris stormed the city and, in one of the most memorable British actions in India, destroyed the power of Tipu Sultan and restored the Hindu Wadiyars to the throne.

An understanding of the historical background and of the British operations in and around Mysore makes a visit here much more rewarding.

The road to Seringapatam from Mysore passes **Sultanpet**, scene of General Wellesley's only defeat, on 5 April 1799, when he was ambushed in the dark and narrowly missed capture. Wellesley was reputed to have been mor-

tified at the setback when he later discovered that the twelve British prisoners taken were executed by having nails driven into their skulls.

The road to the island crosses **Paschimavahirii** (literally Flowing to the West) **Bridge**, from which wonderful views of the riverside bathing ghats and temples can be obtained. At the east end of the bridge is a stone marked 'Skelly's Post, 26 April 1779'. Another nearby stone marks 'Major Wallace's post'. A rough cart-track leads west to a little temple erected in memory of Raja Wadiyar IX, who died here in 1796. Further west are two cannon, which mark the spot from where the storming party launched their assault under General Baird on 4 May 1799. Returning to the main road the **South Bridge** (1656), which serves as an aqueduct, leads to the island proper.

The chief southern entrance is the **Mysore Gate**, where about 10,000 captives seized the opportunity afforded by Cornwallis's advance in 1792 and broke out of the city. To the north-east is the

570

Flagstaff erected by Wellesley on the great cavalier. Near here the colours of the 23rd Regiment were shot down during the assault and replaced by a red infantry jacket hoisted by a gallant group of British privates.

Close by, to the west, is the picturesque **Elephant Gate** (1793), large enough to permit elephants and howdahs. The grooved channels bear witness to the drawbridge which once protected the gate. A marble slab carries a fulsome Persian inscription.

The circuit continues past a magazine, the old Racket Court and the simple tomb of General Sayyid Saheb, whose daughter was one of Tipu's wives. Next is the **Memorial Mandapa to H H Krishna Raja Wadiyar III** (1915) an unassuming building on the site of the ancient palace of the Vijayanagara Viceroys.

Beyond the mandapa is the former garden of Captain Thomas Fiott de Havilland. The famous de Havilland Arch, which was built as an engineering department experiment in 1801 with a flat span of 34 m (112 ft), fell in 1937 but the remnants can still be inspected. De Havilland was one of the most gifted military engineers of the period and he later used his experience of wide structural spans in the design of the Banqueting Hall at Government House, Mysore (1806–7) and at St Andrew's Kirk, Madras (1821).

The road leads on past the railway to the south-west rampart. To the right are the ruined cavalier, the old mosque of Mir Sadak and the site of the Garrison Hospital, built for the troops who occupied the fort after the siege. The **Obelisk Breach**, where Baird's troops broke into the fort on 4 May 1799, is marked by a plain monument.

The **Delhi Gate** led to the Delhi Bridge, which was dismantled by Tipu for defensive reasons, but the stone bases remain in the riverbed. The northern rampart leads to the **Sultan Battery** and,

beneath it, the **Dungeons**, where many of the British prisoners were confined for years in appalling conditions. Standing up to their necks in water they were chained with arms crossed facing the wall and compelled to eat like horses, the food being placed on the stone ledges still to be seen inset in the walls.

Beyond is the **Maidan** or parade ground and the **Temple of Sri Ranganatha Swami**, the core of which was built in 894, the scene of a great festival every January. Outside is a huge temple car (restored 1771). The **Narasimha Swami Temple** (c. 1700) contains a fine portrait statuette of an heroic scion of the Wadiyar dynasty.

The **Lal Mahal** or Palace of Haidar Ali and Tipu Sultan was originally a fine building with an open balcony overlooking the Maidan, but only a tablet marks the spot where it once stood. The circuit road leads on to the **Water Gate**, where Tipu Sultan is said to have died, though in fact the actual site is 182 m (591 ft) to the east on a spot marked by a small enclosure. Outside the Water Gate are some fine banyan trees sheltering a large number of inscribed stones. Further east along the ramparts is the Gateway of the Fallen Fortress or **Bidda Kote Bagalu**, with underground vaults which were also used as dungeons. The celebrated Maratha freebooter Dhondia Wahag was chained here for five years, before being released by British soldiers in 1799, after which he marauded around the territory committing depredations in every direction, until he was pursued and cut down by Wellesley in 1800.

The **Jami Masjid** (1787) lies close to the Ganjam or Bangalore Gate and was built by Tipu Sultan. It is a graceful affair with pierced minarets crowned by onion domes which contain narrow staircases. Within the embrasure of the gate is a small mound, the grave of Mir Muhammad Sadak, Haidar's appalling diwan, master of the most dreadful tortures and later Tipu's right-hand man.

To the north-west of the gate is **Wellesley Bridge** (1804). Outside the former fort area are a number of other sites of considerable interest. The **Daria Daulat Bagh** (1784) or Summer Palace of Tipu Sultan lies to the east. Now a Museum, it was built by Tipu and is covered in rich arabesque detail over every inch of wall, ceilings and multifoil arches. The west wall has a mural depicting the victory of Haidar Ali over Colonel Baillie at Pollilore in 1780. Restored by Wellesley, it was later whitewashed. Fifty years later it was crudely repainted by an Indian artist on the instruction of Lord Dalhousie. The palace stands in a beautiful garden area stocked with plants and shrubs brought by Tipu from all over India.

Across the river, below Karighatta Hill, is **Sibbald's Redoubt**, where Captain Sibbald, Major Skelly and a small contingent of 100 Europeans and fifty sepoys repulsed three fierce attacks in February 1792.

Ganjam, at one time a large town, was established by Tipu as an industrial suburb. The main interest is the small, whitewashed **Church** of the celebrated Abbé Dubois of the Missions Etrangères, who worked here from 1799 to 1823. The walls and ceiling of the transept remain as he built them. Dubois introduced vaccination to the state.

An obelisk not far from the church marks the **Grave of Colonel Grimstone**, a strict disciplinarian and governor of the cantonment jail. He was so unpopular that a high wall was erected around the grave to prevent its being defiled. Views of the grave can be obtained by mounting a step and looking through a hole in the wall.

At the end of the main Ganjam Road, outside the entrance to the Lalbagh, is a memorial to Colonel William Baillie (1816) erected by his brother, Colonel John Baillie, the Resident at Lucknow. William Baillie was captured at Pollilore and died a prisoner of Tipu in 1782. The memorial is a domed octagonal pavilion,

crowned by funeral urns, enclosed by whitewashed walls with a pillared porch. Adjacent is H M Cemetery, which contains many British graves.

The **Lalbagh** or Garden of Rubies marks the site of a palace laid out by Haidar Ali. Once alleged to be unparalleled in India, nothing now remains, although some of the timbers were salvaged and used in the building of St Stephen's Church, Ootacamund. Others were later used in the restoration of Holy Trinity, Ootacamund, in 1930.

The **Gumbaz** (1784) was laid out by Tipu at great expense and planted with ornamental trees from Kabul and Persia. A musicians' gallery or Naubat Khana stands over the gateway. Within the Gumbaz is the austere **Mausoleum of Haidar Ali and Tipu Sultan** (1799), a severe, square building crowned by a dome with corner minarets surrounded by a corridor carried on polished pillars of hornblende. It is approached via an avenue of tall sentinel cypresses. Around the main tomb are cloisters containing the remains of relatives and friends of the dynasty. The ebony and ivory doors were renewed at Lord Dalhousie's expense in 1855.

The tomb of Haidar Ali is in the middle, that of his consort, Fakhr-un-Nissa Seydani Begum, on the east and of their son, Tipu Sultan, on the west. Their bodies lie in the crypt below. The tombs are usually covered with shawls: red for Tipu as 'a martyr for the faith', black or purple for Haidar and pink for Seydani Begum. Tipu was interred with full military honours by the British to peals of extraordinary, apocalyptic thunder, so severe that two officers who survived the assault unscathed were struck dead by lightning.

At the extreme eastern end of the island, where the arms of the river reunite, is the **Tomb of Colonel Edward Montague**, the simple grave of the commander of the Bengal Artillery.

Returning from Ganjam to the Fort a

572

detour to the south passes the **Memorial Monument**, a large obelisk raised to the memory of officers of the 77th (Highland Light Infantry) and 12th (Suffolk) Regiments who died during the final assault on 4 May 1799.

The **Tomb of Mir Ghulam Ali Khan** commemorates one of Tipu's most gifted statesmen, although the graves within are probably those of his mother and two wives. The mausoleum is a grand affair with a magnificent dome.

South of the Mysore Gate a signpost points the way to **Scott's Bungalow**, which is invested with an aura of romantic melancholy. It is alleged that in April 1817 Colonel Scott returned home to find his wife and two daughters dead in bed with cholera, that mad with grief he drowned himself in the Cauvery river and that in his memory the Maharaja ordered that the house should remain evermore as it was that fateful morning. The bungalow does indeed remain preserved, together with a few vestiges of furniture, including a curious bed with a compartment beneath to hold a tiger taken from Tipu's palace and placed here in the late 19th century. But the story is untrue. Scott's wife and infant child lie in the Garrison Cemetery, having died during the birth. Scott returned to England, where he died at his home in Lovel Park, Berkshire, in January 1833.

The tomb in the garden is probably that of Akbar Pasha, Tipu's guru.

Between Scott's Bungalow and Garrison Cemetery is **Doctor's Bungalow**, occupied later by General (later Lord) Harris and one-time headquarters of the garrison commander. In 1812 Purniah, one of Tipu's ablest advisers and later, after the restoration, diwan to the young Raja, died here. A tablet on the wall records the connection with Lord Harris and Purniah.

3·2 km (2 miles) north of the road from Seringapatam to French Rocks is a simple granite column, the **Rana Khaubha**, erected by Purniah in memory of Josiah Webbe for his support to a claim of the Mysore revenues.

The circuit ends at **Garrison Cemetery** (1800) where a number of interesting graves can be seen, including those of Scott's wife, officers of the Swiss Regiment de Meuron (which served the East India Company) and many others. The cemetery is an appropriate place to contemplate the bloody history of the island and to end the tour. Piriyapatna Bridge provides a route back to the main road.

SHOLINGHUR

Sholinghur, 16 km (10 miles) from Dattavaram Station, was the scene of one of Sir Eyre Coote's greatest victories. On 27 September 1781 he defeated Haidar Ali and the young Lally. With vastly inferior numbers, he took the offensive and, for the third time within a few months, drove Haidar Ali's picked troops before him.

TANGASSERI

3·2 km (2 miles) from Quilon, Tangasseri was formerly a Dutch settlement comprising a Portuguese fort built in 1503 on a laterite peninsula jutting into the sea. Later it became an outlying British possession of a mere 39 hectares (96 acres). The headland is marked by a lighthouse. An old ruined Portuguese tower and belfry stand within the Protestant cemetery.

The fort is now in ruins. Most of it has fallen into the sea.

TELLICHERRY

21 km (13 miles) from Cannanore, Tellicherry is a picturesque old town set on wooded hills overlooking the sea among

delightful beaches and coastal scenery.

The East India Company established a factory here in 1683 for the pepper and cardamom trade. After a long period of quiet prosperity, it was blockaded by Haidar's general, Sardar Khan, in 1782, but the siege was raised by troops from Bombay, who combined with the garrison to repel the attackers.

The **Fort** lies close to the shore on the north side of the town. It is a compact, square laterite structure with corner bastions. To the north is another bastion on an overhanging cliff. The citadel was protected by a further wall, of which sections remain.

In 1783 the *Superb*, a great 74-gun ship of the line, went down here after hitting the offshore reef.

THANJAVUR (TANJORE)

The name Thanjavur is probably derived via Tanjore from 'City of Refuge'. It is a town of extreme antiquity, the ancient capital of the Chola kings, situated 346 km (216 miles) south-west of Madras. Its main interest lies in its fascinating heritage of sacred Hindu temples and sites (see Volume I). There are no Muslim buildings of any consequence, but the town was the centre of some of the earliest efforts of Protestant missionaries.

Schwartz's Church lies close by the Shivaganga Tank, adjoining an open landscaped square. The gate bears the date 1777, the façade 1779. Internally it is plainly treated. The west end, opposite the communion table, has a carved group of figures by Flaxman depicting the death of F. C. Schwartz, the distinguished Christian Missionary, in 1798; he is seen lying on a bed surrounded by three men and four boys. A flowing inscription encapsulates his achievements. The small house to the north-west is reputed to have been his home.

The **Nayaka Palace**, built partly by

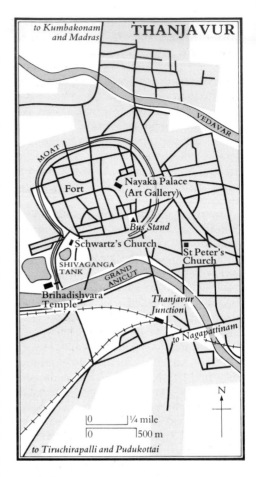

the Nayakas in about 1550 and later added to by the Marathas, lies in the Great Fort, which is to the east of the Little Fort. The palace is a vast masonry building disposed around a series of courtyards. On the south side of the third quadrangle is a huge eight-storey building resembling a gopura, over 58 m (190 ft) high. This was once the armoury.

East of this quadrangle is the **Durbar Hall** of the Nayaka kings. There is a black granite platform with carved panels in alto-rilievo on which stands a statue of Sarfoji, a pupil of the famous Schwartz. He is depicted at prayer wearing a pointed cap, the badge of the Tanjore princes in their last years. Opposite, across the quadrangle, is a remarkable

library with a magnificent collection of manuscripts and books in Sanskrit, Tamil and other languages.

St Peter's Cemetery contains a number of interesting tombs, including that of the tenth Lord Hastings, who died of fever while tiger-shooting with the Prince of Wales in 1875.

TINNEVELLY

Tinnevelly is renowned for its famous temple, part dedicated to Shiva and part to Parvati.

The town lies about 85 km (53 miles) from Kanya Kumari, at the southern tip of the Indian peninsula. It is one of the most Christianized areas of India and both the Society for the Propagation of the Gospel and the Church Missionary Society have important centres in the town.

St Francis Xavier (1506–52), the great Portuguese evangelist, began his preaching in India from here.

Outside Palmacotta, 4·8 km (3 miles) from the town, stands the **Church of the Church Missionary Society**, with a 33·5 m (110 ft) spire, which is a local landmark. St John's College nearby was erected in 1878.

TIRUCHIRAPALLI (TRICHINOPOLY) *Map overleaf*

Trichinopoly or 'City of the Three-headed Demon', now known more commonly as Tiruchirapalli, lies 404 km (252 miles) south-west of Madras and is dominated by the famous **Rock**, which can be seen from miles around. Chiefly famous for its great Hindu temples (see Volume I), there are a number of other buildings of note. Only a fragment of the once-formidable fort remains. The former moat is now a boulevard.

St John's Church (early 19th century), less than 5 minutes' walk from the station, is the burial place of Bishop Heber, who drowned in a bath here in 1826. His grave lies to the right of the communion table and is marked by a small brass tablet inset into the floor. Above, on the side wall, is a white marble tablet with black borders. Heber is best known today as the writer of the hymn 'From Greenland's Icy Mountains'.

The fatal **Bath** in which he drowned is near the Judge's House. A marble slab marks the spot. Nearby is a monument to Mr H. O. D. Harding, the local Sessions Judge, who was murdered outside his carriage on 22 February 1916.

The **Roman Catholic Cathedral**, consecrated in 1841, has beautiful frescoes by a French priest, Father de Noircourt.

North of the main tank or Teppakulam, en route to Sri Rangam, is **Christ Church** (1765), erected by Schwartz and paid for by the local British garrison. The cemetery is of considerable interest and includes the tomb of Mrs Rebecca Darke (1797), whose granddaughter married Sir Robert Peel, the British Prime Minister.

The **Mosque of Nathar Shah** is the most notable Muslim monument in the city. Here lie the body of Muhammad Ali and the headless remains of his rival for the Nawabship of Arcot, Chanda Sahib. The mosque is an important shrine and contains the tomb of the saint Sultan Saiyad Babayya Nathar Shah. Originally a Hindu temple, it is alleged to have changed hands when Nathar Shah wandered here as a fakir.

East of Teppakulam tank is a house marked by a plaque commemorating Clive's residence here in 1752, although this is uncorroborated. **St Joseph's College** stands near the Main Guard Gate and was transferred here in 1883. It is an impressive range of buildings. The College Church and Lawley Hall are notable.

Bishop Heber's College stands to the

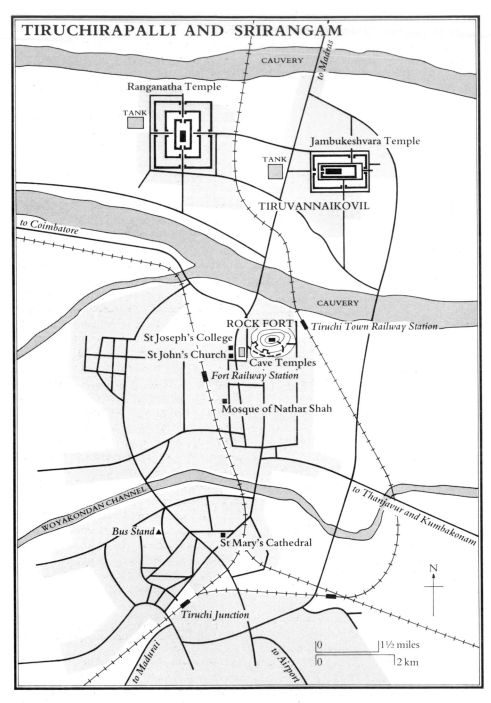

TIRUCHIRAPALLI AND SRIRANGAM

east of the Main Guard Gate, opposite the Teppakulam tank, and was developed from early schools founded by Schwartz and the Society for the Promotion of Christian Knowledge.

The bridge over the Cauvery river was

designed and built by Captain Edward Lawford in 1849. It carries a memorial plaque to four officers of the Madras army who served heroically during the defence of Trichinopoly between 1752 and 1754.

TRANQUEBAR

The old Danish enclave of Tranquebar, 35 km (22 miles) north of Negapatam, was purchased by the Danish East India Company from the Nayaka Tanjore in 1620. Four years later Tranquebar and a small piece of territory 240 km square (93 square miles) were transferred to the King of Denmark. In 1700 Haidar Ali exacted a fine from the Danes for supplying the Nawab of Arcot. Tranquebar was taken by the English in 1807, together with other Danish settlements in India, but restored in 1814. In 1845 it was purchased with Serampore for £20,000, after which it declined into insignificance.

The **Fort**, known as Dansborg, was built in 1620 by Ovo Gedde and was subsequently strengthened and extended in 1749 and in the 1780s. It is now a traveller's bungalow, a curious old place, square in plan and constantly eroded by the sea.

Within the town are a number of interesting Danish colonial buildings. **Zion's Church**, later the English Church, was built in 1701. It has a curious spiked dome, which is a local landmark. The bell is dated 1752. Within is a painting of the Last Supper in coloured relief on wood. Opposite is the **Lutheran Mission Church** (New Jerusalem), built in 1717 by Lieutenant Claus Krøckel on the plan of a Greek cross in a primitive Euro-Indian Baroque style. Both lie towards the east end of King Street.

Tranquebar was the first settlement of Protestant missionaries in India. The mission was founded by Ziegenbalg and Plütschau in 1706, and over the next century it spread its influence over the whole of southern India. The great F. C. Schwartz worked from here. In 1847 the Danes passed the work to the Leipzig Evangelical Lutheran Mission. There are interesting traces of older Christian relics, including five cemeteries with inscriptions in no less than nine European languages.

Tranquebar is interesting for its urban plan form. Unlike other European settlements, where houses were set in their own compounds, at Tranquebar they adjoin each other in continuous streets. The road into the town passes a gateway bearing the date 1792 and the coat of arms of the King of Denmark. A number of colonial houses and buildings survive, including the **Old Hospital** or Governor Hansen's House (late 18th century; altered), which lies beyond Zion's Church on the north side of the street. Almost opposite, the **'Convent'** (late 18th century) has similar characteristics but with a high square tower, known as John's Tower, after a local missionary. The **Tea Club** (early 19th century) is noteworthy for its simple Doric order. Many of the former Danish mansions warrant close inspection for their interesting details and distinctively Danish nuances.

Tranquebar was the birthplace of the future Princess of Benevento, the infamous Catherine Noël Werlée (1762–1835), who married G. F. Grand, almost ruined Philip Francis and later married Prince Talleyrand.

TRIVANDRUM *Map overleaf*

Trivandrum (literally Thiru Vananta Puram or Abode of the Sacred Serpent) was the state capital of Travancore, which in 1956 combined with Cochin to form Kerala. It is a large, rambling city dispersed across a series of lush forested

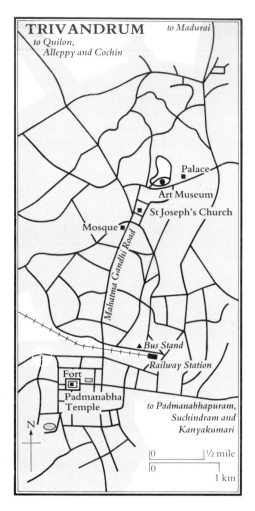

Map of Trivandrum showing to Quilon, Alleppy and Cochin; to Madurai; Palace; Art Museum; St Joseph's Church; Mosque; Mahatma Gandhi Road; Bus Stand; Railway Station; Fort; Padmanabha Temple; to Padmanabhapuram, Suchindram and Kanyakumari; ½ mile; 1 km.

About 800 m (½ mile) beyond the zoo, the **Maharaja's Palace**, now government offices, has a conference room and ballroom of some consequence. Enjoy the fine view from the terrace.

Most of the civic and legislative buildings are relatively modern. The Parliament House was built in 1939.

The **Fort** contains several palace buildings and an old Temple of Vishnu, known as the Padmanabha Temple.

TUTICORIN

Tuticorin was founded as a Portuguese settlement in about 1540 and it grew to be a thriving local centre. By 1700 the Jesuits referred to 50,000 people living here. In 1658 it was captured by the Dutch and in 1782 it was seized by the British. It was restored to the Dutch three years later, but reoccupied by the British in 1795. After reverting again to the Dutch in 1818, it was finally vested in the British in 1825.

The town is an old Christian centre and has a high proportion of Catholics. There are few buildings of any great consequence, but **Our Lady of the Snows**, the Roman Catholic Church, is an old Portuguese building with 17th-century fabric. The **Old Dutch Cemetery** has some fine early tombstones in the Baroque manner with carved armorial devices.

VELLORE

Vellore is situated 129 km (80 miles) west from Madras and about 24 km (15 miles) west from Arcot. Its main attractions are the old 16th-century Vijayanagara fort and the Jvarakandeshvara Temple inside the walls. The town is a typical rural centre, with chaotic bazaars and colourful street markets.

The **Fort**, built from granite blocks, was erected, according to tradition,

hills on the edge of the Arabian Sea. It retains a strong vernacular character, with red-tiled roofs and a common local architectural style. Its biggest attraction for tourists is the nearby Kovalam Beach.

There are few Islamic or European buildings of any great interest. The Napier Museum (1880), Zoological Gardens and Art Gallery form a complex in the park to the north of the city. The Museum has an interesting collection of bronzes, musical instruments and sculptures. The nearby Sri Chitra Art Gallery has some notable Rajput and Mughal paintings. (For details of these collections and the temples see Volume I.)

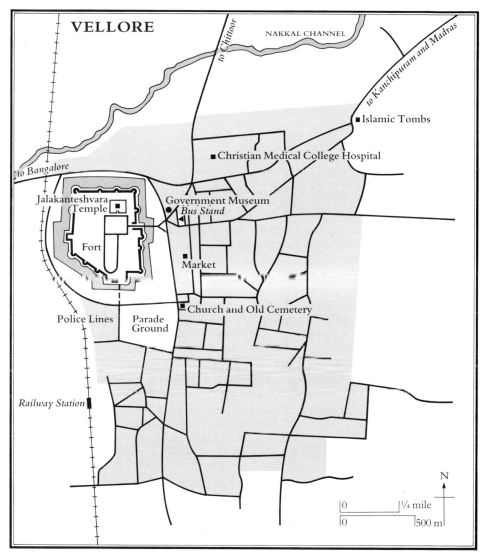

VELLORE

to Chittoor

NAKKAL CHANNEL

to Kanchipuram and Madras

Islamic Tombs

Christian Medical College Hospital

to Bangalore

Jalakanteshvara Temple

Government Museum

Bus Stand

Fort

Market

Police Lines

Parade Ground

Church and Old Cemetery

Railway Station

N

0 ¼ mile
0 500 m

between 1274 and 1283 by Sinna Bommi Reddi, although it is reminiscent of Italian fortifications of the period. Surrounded by a moat, the main rampart has circular bastions and square towers at intervals to provide clear fields of fire. The outer wall, which is lower than the inner, to which it is joined, provides a curtain of enormous thickness. The crenellated parapets have wide merlons for musket fire. On the south face the moat is crossed by a stone causeway which leads to a sally-port. Within the fort the parade ground is flanked by great mahals, two-storey houses with large internal courtyards. In 1676 the Marathas under Takaji Rao captured Vellore after a four and a half months' siege. In 1708 Daud Khan from Delhi in turn ousted the Marathas. It became the headquarters of Mortaza Ali, brother-in-law of the claimant to the Arcot throne, and in the 1740s it was renowned as the strongest fortress in the Carnatic.

In 1780 an English garrison held out against Haidar Ali for over two years. After the fall of Seringapatam in 1799 Tipu's family were detained here. The subsequent mutiny at Vellore in 1806 has been attributed to their intrigues, but it was more probably due to the orders of Sir John Cradock prohibiting the wearing of caste marks and beards. Sir Henry Newbolt's poem commemorates the dashing rescue of the besieged European soldiers by Colonel Rollo Gillespie.

To the right of the entrance to the fort is a small enclosure, the **Old Cemetery**. There is a low sarcophagus (1863–4) here, inscribed to the memory of the officers and men who were killed in the 1806 mutiny. There is a modern church nearby.

The **Jvarakandeshvara Temple** (c. 1566) is a beautiful example of Vijayanagara architecture, with fine stone carvings. It was rededicated in 1981, but non-Hindus may still enter the inner sanctum. The temple elephant can often be seen strolling around the market. The temple gateway has a seven-storey gopura on blue granite with rich ornamental carvings. (See Volume I.)

About 1·2 km (¾ mile) to the east of the fort are the **Tombs of Tipu Sultan's Family**, situated in a walled enclosure. To the right on entering is the tomb of Padshah Begum, Tipu's wife, who died in 1834. Next is Aftab Khan's tomb, beyond which is a large tank and two plain tombs of women attendants. The large granite pavilion contains the tomb of Mirza Raza, who married one of Tipu's daughters. At the end is a 6 m (20 ft) high mausoleum with a lofty dome to Bakshi Begum, widow of Haidar Ali, who died in 1806. To the left is a plain mosque.

After the Vellore Mutiny of 1806 Tipu's family were transferred to Calcutta, where they founded numerous mosques. The King of Kandy was also incarcerated here between 1816 and 1832.

The Christian Medical College Hospi-tal, founded in 1900, is a major medical centre.

WANDIWASH (VANDIVASU)

Wandiwash was the scene of the great battle on 21 January 1760 which destroyed French power in southern India. It was the most important victory ever won by the English over the French in India.

38 km (24 miles) north-west of Tindi-vanum station lies a ruined fort and 3·2 km (2 miles) beyond that, a rocky hill. Between these two landmarks several important operations were fought during the Wars of the Carnatic.

In 1752 the fort was attacked by Major Lawrence. Five years later Colonel Aldercom destroyed the town, but he was twice repulsed by the French. An attack by Monson in 1759 was also unsuccessful but, following a mutiny among the French soldiers, Sir Eyre Coote later captured the fort. In 1760 Lally appeared before the town and in the pitched battle which ensued only the European forces were engaged. The French were trounced and de Bussy was taken prisoner.

In 1781, in the war against Haidar Ali, the fort was defended by Lieutenant Flint against great odds. It was finally abandoned and blown up in February 1783.

YERCAUD

Yercaud is the oldest station in the Shevaroyan Hills, 1,471 m (4,828 ft) above sea level, and the regional headquarters, situated 22·5 km (14 miles) from Salem. It is a small, quiet town, ideal as a base for touring the magnificent scenery of the surrounding hills.

It is a typical British hill station, with a small club, church and other public buildings designed in a straightforward vernacular style.

HISTORICAL CHRONOLOGY OF KEY EVENTS

1612 First English factory at Surat

1615 Sir Thomas Roe, English ambassador to court of Jahangir

1628 Shah Jahan becomes Emperor

1631 Taj Mahal commenced

1639 Raja of Chandragiri cedes Madras to English

1646 Shivaji and Marathas attack Bijapur

1658 Aurangzeb deposes Shah Jahan

1659 Gol Gumbaz built at Bijapur

1665 Bombay transferred from Portuguese to English

1668 French East India Company founded

1677 Shivaji captures Gingee

1681 Aurangzeb transfers capital to the Deccan

1684 Submission of Mewar to Aurangzeb

1687 Aurangzeb conquers Golconda

1687 Pondicherry founded by French

1690 Job Charnock founds Calcutta

1698 Aurangzeb captures Gingee and Carnatic

1724 Asaf Jah declares independence at Hyderabad

1727 Jaipur founded by Sawai Jai Singh II

1739 Nadir Shah and Persians sack Delhi. Marathas conquer Malwa

1744 War of Austrian Succession

1746 Madras surrenders to Labourdonnais

1750 Balaji Rao, Maratha Peshwa assumes power. Wars of succession in the Deccan and Carnatic

1751 Siege of Arcot

1756 Calcutta falls to Suraj-ud-Daulah. Black Hole incident

1757 Calcutta recaptured. Battle of Plassey. Reconstruction of Fort William commenced.

1761 Third Battle of Panipat. Ahmad Shah Abdali and Afghans defeat Marathas

1764 Battle of Buxar. English supremacy established in Bengal

1765 Robert Clive becomes Governor of Bengal

1767 First Mysore War

1772 Warren Hastings becomes President in Bengal, later first Governor-General

1773–4 Rohilla War

1776 Treaty of Purandhar between Marathas and English

1778–83 Maratha War

1780 Second Mysore War between English and Haidar Ali

1784 Pitt's India Act

1788 Trial of Warren Hastings

1790–92 Third Mysore War between English and Tipu Sultan

1797–1805 Kirkpatrick ousts French influence from Hyderabad

1798 Wellesley builds Government House, Calcutta

1798–9 Fourth Mysore War. Seringapatam falls. Tipu killed

1803 Second Maratha War. Lord Lake takes Delhi

1804 War with Holkar

1806 Mutiny at Vellore

1809 Haileybury College opens

1815 War with Nepal

1817 Pindari Campaign. Pune (Poona) surrenders to British

1818 Rajasthani kingdoms accept British suzerainty

1824 War with Burma

1828 Bentinck becomes Governor-General

1829 Abolition of suttee in Bengal. Action against thugee

1833 Renewal of Company charter

1835 Macaulay's education minute

1839 Death of Ranjit Singh

1841 First tea planted at Darjeeling

1842 Retreat from Kabul

1843 Conquest of Sind

1845 First Sikh War

1848 Second Sikh War

1849 Annexation of Punjab

1852 Second Burmese War

1853 Annexation of Nagpur. Bombay to Thana railway opened

1854 First cotton mill opens in Bombay

1856 Annexation of Oudh by Dalhousie

1857 Outbreak of Indian Mutiny

1858 Government of India transferred to the Crown

1860 Macaulay's great Penal Code becomes law

1861 Indian cotton boom triggers expansion of Bombay

1863 Simla becomes summer capital of the Raj

1864 Bhutan War

1869 Opening of the Suez Canal

1877 Queen Victoria proclaimed Empress of India

1878 Second Afghan War

1883 Ilbert Bill

1885 Third Burmese War. First session of Indian National Congress

1886 Annexation of Upper Burma. World Headquarters of Theosophical Society founded
at Madras

Historical Chronology of Key Events

1887 Queen Victoria's Golden Jubilee
1891 Extremist agitation commenced by Tilak
1892 Indian Councils Act
1897 Queen Victoria's Diamond Jubilee. Plague in Bombay
1901 Coronation Durbar in Delhi for Edward VII
1905 Partition of Bengal
1906 Muslim League founded
1909 Morley–Minto reforms
1911 George V holds Delhi Durbar. Capital transferred from Calcutta to Delhi
1914 Outbreak of First World War
1915 Mahatma Gandhi returns to India from South Africa
1916 Home Rule League founded by Annie Besant
1918 Montagu–Chelmsford reforms
1919 Third Afghan War. Amritsar Massacre
1920 Elections to reformed Imperial Legislature
1921 Civil unrest in Bombay. Opening of Victoria Memorial in Calcutta
1922 Gandhi imprisoned for civil disobedience
1928 Simon Commission
1930 Gandhi's famous salt march. London Conference
1931 Inauguration of New Delhi. Gandhi attends London Conference
1932 Civil disobedience begins
1935 Government of India Act
1936 Nehru becomes President of Congress
1939 Second World War begins
1942 Fall of Singapore. Bose recruits Indian National Army for Japanese
1943 Bengal famine
1944 Battles of Imphal and Kohima turn the tide against Japan
1945 Attlee accepts case for Indian independence
1947 Partition. Independence for India and new Muslim state of Pakistan
1948 Gandhi assassinated by fanatic. Jinnah dies
1950 India becomes a republic within the Commonwealth

DYNASTIC TABLES

SULTANS OF DELHI

The Slave Dynasty   Date of Accession

Qutb-ud-Din Aybak	1206
Aram Shah	1210
Shams-ud-Din Iltutmish	1211
Rukn-ud-Din Firuz Shah I	1236
Jalalat-ud-Din Radiyya Begum	1236
Muizz-ud-Din Bahram Shah	1240
Ala-ud-Din Masud Shah	1242
Nasir-ud-Din-Mahmud Shah I	1246
Ghiyath-ud-Din Balban	1266
Muizz-ud-Din Kaiqubad	1287
Shams-ud-Din Kayumarth	1290

The Khalji Dynasty

Jalal-ud-Din Firuz Shah II	1290
Rukn-ud-Din Ibrahim Shah I	1296
Ala-ud-Din Muhammad Shah I	1296
Shihab-ud-Din Umar Shah	1316
Qutb-ud-Din Mubarak Shah	1316
Nasir-ud-Din Khusraw Shah	1320

The Tughluq Dynasty

Ghiyath-ud-Din Tughluq Shah I	1320
Ghiyath-ud-Din Muhammad Shah II	1325
Mahmud	1351
Firuz Shah III	1351
Ghiyath-ud-Din Tughluq Shah II	1388
Abu Bakr Shah	1389
Nasir-ud-Din Muhammad Shah III	1390
Ala-ud-Din Sikander Shah I	1393
Nasir-ud-Din Mahmud Shah II (first reign)	1393
Nusrat Shah	1395
Mahmud Shah II (second reign)	1399

The Sayyid Dynasty

Khidr Khan	1414
Muizz-ud-Din Mubarak Shah II	1421
Muhammad Shah IV	1435
Ala-ud-Din Alam Shah	1445

The Lodi Dynasty

Bahlul Lodi	1451
Nizam Khan Sikander II	1489
Ibrahim II	1517
Mughal conquest under Babur	1526

The Suris

Sher Shah Sur	1540
Islam Shah	1545
Muhammad V Adil Shah	1554
Ibrahim III	1554
Ahmad Khan Sikander Shah III	1555
Final Mughal conquest by Humayun	1555

The Mughal Emperors

Zahir-ud-Din Babur	1526
Nasir-ud-Din Humayun (*first reign*)	1530
Suri Sultans of Delhi	1540–55
Humayun (*second reign*)	1555
Jalal-ud-Din Akbar I	1556
Nur-ud-Din Jahangir	1605
Dawar Bakhsh	1627
Shihab-ud-Din Shah Jahan	1628
Murad Bakhsh (in Gujarat)	1657
Shah Shuja (in Bengal until 1660)	1657
Muhyi-ud-Din Aurangzeb Alamgir I	1658
Azam Shah	1707
Kam Bakhsh (in the Deccan)	1707
Shah Alam Bahadur Shah I	1707
Azim-ush-Shah	1712
Muizz-ud-Din Jahandar Shah	1712
Muhammad Farrukhsiyar	1713
Shams-ud-Din Rafi-ud-Darajat	1719
Rafi-ud-Daula Shah Jahan II	1719
Nikusiyar	1719
Nasir-ud-Din Muhammad	1719
Ahmad Shah Bahadur	1748
Aziz-ud Din Alamgir II	1754
Shah Jahan III	1760
Jalal-ud-Din Ali Jawhar Shah Alam II (*first reign*)	1760
Bidar Bakht	1788
Shah Alam II (*second reign*)	1788
Muin-ud-Din Akbar Shah II	1806
Siraj-ud-Din Bahadur Shah II	1837–58

PROVINCIAL DYNASTIES

1: Sultans of Bengal

In Eastern Bengal

Fakhr-ud-Din Mubarak Shah	1336
Ikhtiyar-ud-Din Ghazi Shah	1349–52

Conquest by Shams-ud-Din Ilyas Shah	1352

In Western Bengal and then in all Bengal

Ala-ud-Din Ali Shah	1339

Line of Ilyas Shah

Shams-ud-Din Ilyas Shah	1345
Sikander Shah I	1358
Ghiyath-ud-Din Azam Shah	1390
Saif-ud-Din Hamza Shah	1410
Shihab-ud-Din Bayazid Shah	1412
Ala-ud-Din Firuz Shah	1414

Line of Raja Ganesa

Jalal-ud-Din Muhammad Shah	1414
Shams-ud-Din Ahmad Shah	1432–6

Line of Ilyas Shah restored

Nasir-ud-Din Mahmud Shah II	1437
Rukn-ud-Din Barbak Shah	1460
Shams-ud-Din Yusuf Shah	1474
Sikander Shah II	1481
Jalal-ud-Din Fath Shah	1481–7

Line of Habashis

Sultan Shahzada Barbak Shah	1487
Sayf-ud-Din Firuz Shah	1487
Nasir-ud-Din Mahmud Shah	1490
Shams-ud-Din Muzaffar Shah	1490–4

Line of Sayyid Husain Shah

Sayyid Ala-ud-Din Husain Shah	1494
Nasir-ud-Din Nusrat Shah	1519
Ala-ud-Din Firuz Shah	1532
Ghiyath-ud-Din Mahmud Shah	1533–9

Line of Suri Afghans

Sher Shah Sur	1539
Khidr Khan	1540

Muhammad Khan Sur	1545
Khidr Khan Bahadur Shah	1555
Ghiyath-ud-Din Jalal Shah	1561–4

Line of Sulaiman Kararani

Sulaiman Kararani	1572
Bayazid Shah Kararani	1572
Dawud Shah Kararani	1572–6
Mughal conquest by Akbar	1576

2: The Sharqi Sultans of Jaunpur

Khwaja-i-Jahan	1394
Mubarak Shah	1399
Shams-ud-Din Ibrahim	1402
Mahmud Shah	1440
Muhammad Shah	1457
Husain Shah	1458–79
Conquest by Lodi Sultans of Delhi	1479

3: The Sultans of Gujarat

Zafar Khan Muzaffar I	1396
Ahmad I	1411
Muhammad Karim	1442
Qutb-ud-Din Ahmad II	1451
Daud	1458
Mahmud I Begada	1458
Muzaffar II	1511
Sikander	1526
Nasir Khan Mahmud II	1526
Bahadur	1526
Miran Muhammad I of Khandesh	1537
Mahmud III	1537
Ahmad II	1554
Muzaffar III (*first reign*)	1561
Mughal conquest by Akbar	1572
Muzaffar III (*second reign*)	1583
Final Mughal conquest	

4: The Sultans of Malwa

Line of Ghuris

Dilawar Khan Husain Ghuri	1401
Hoshang Shah	1405
Ghazni Khan Muhammad	1435
Masud Khan	1436

Line of Khaljis

Mahmud Shah I Khalji	1436
Ghiyath Shah	1469
Nasir Shah	1500
Mahmud Shah II	1510
Conquest by Sultans of Gujarat	1531

5: The Bahmani Sultans of the Deccan

Ala-ud-Din Hasan Bahman Shah	1347
Muhammad I	1358
Ala-ud-Din Mujahid	1375
Daud	1378
Muhammad II	1378
Ghiyath-ud-Din	1397
Shams-ud-Din	1397
Taj-ud-Din Firuz	1397
Ahmad I Wali	1422
Ala-ud-Din Ahmad II	1436
Ala-ud-Din Humayun Zalim	1458
Nizam	1461
Muhammad III Lashkari	1463
Mahmud	1482
Ahmad III	1518
Ala-ud-Din	1521
Wali-Allah	1522
Kalim-Allah	1525–7
Dissolution of Sultanate into five local sultanates	

6: Sultanates of the Deccan

The Imad Shahis of Berar

Fath Allah	1490
Ala-ud-Din	1504

Darya	1529
Burhan	1562
Tufal	1568–77

The Nizam Shahis of Ahmadnagar

Malik Ahmad	1490
Burhan	1509
Husain	1553
Murtaza Shah I	1565
Miran Husain	1586
Ismail	1589
Burhan II	1591
Ibrahim	1595
Bahadur	1596
Ahmad II	1596
Murtaza Shah II	1603
Husain Shah II	1630–3

The Barid Shahis of Bidar

Qasim I	1487
Amir I	1504
Ali	1542
Ibrahim	1579
Qasim II	1586
Amir Barid Shah	1589
Mirza Ali	1601
Ali Barid Shah	1609

The Adil Shahis of Bijapur

Yusuf Adil Khan	1490
Ismail	1510
Mallu	1534
Ibrahim	1534
Ali	1558
Ibrahim II	1580
Muhammad	1627
Ali II	1657
Sikander	1672
Annexed by Aurangzeb	1686

The Qutb Shahis of Golconda

Quli Shah	1512
Jamshid	1543
Subhan Quli	1550
Ibrahim	1550
Muhammad Quli Qutb Shah	1580
Muhammad Qutb Shah	1612
Abdullah	1626
Abul Hasan Tana Qutb Shah	1672–87

7: The Faruqi Sultans of Khandesh

Malik Raja Faruqi	1370
Nasir Khan	1399
Adil Khan I	1437
Miran Mubarak Khan I	1441
Adil Khan II	1457
Dawud Khan	1503
Ghazni Khan	1510
Alam Khan	1510
Adil Khan III	1510
Miran Muhammad I	1520
Ahmad Shah	1537
Mubarak Shah II	1537
Miran Muhammad II	1566
Hasan Shah	1576
Ali Khan, or Adil Shah IV	1577–8
Bahadur Shah	1597
Conquest by the Mughals under Akbar	1601

8: The Sultans of Kashmir

Line of Shah Mirza Swati

Shams-ud-Din Shah Mirza Swati	1346
Jamshid	1349
Ala-ud-Din Ali Shir	1350
Shihab-ud-Din Shirashamak	1359
Qutb-ud-Din Hindal	1378
Sikander But-shikan	1394
Ali Mirza Khan	1416
Zain-al-Abidin Shahi Khan	1420

Haidar Shah Hajji Khan	1470	Wajid Ali Shah	1847
Hasan	1471	Annexation by the East India Company	1856
Muhammad (*first reign*)	1489		
Fath Shah (*first reign*)	1490		
Muhammad (*second reign*)	1498	**10: Nawabs of Arcot**	
Fath Shah (*second reign*)	1499	Zulfiqar Ali Khan	1690
Muhammad (*third reign*)	1500	Dawud Khan	1703
Ibrahim I	1526	Muhammad Sayyid Saadat-ullah Khan I	1710
Nazuk (*first reign*)	1527	Dost Ali Khan	1732
Muhammad (*fourth reign*)	1529	Safdar Ali Khan	1740
Shams-ud-Din	1533	Saadat-ullah Khan II	1742
Nazuk (*second reign*)	1540	Anwar-ud-Din Muhammad	1744
Haidar Dughlat, Governor for Humayun	1540	Wala Jah, Muhammad Ali	1749
Nazuk (*third reign*)	1551	Umdat-ul-Umara	1795
Ibrahim II	1552	Azim-ud-Daula	1801
Ismail	1555	Azam Jah	1819
Habib	1557–61	Azim Jah Bahadur	1869–74
Line of Ghazi Khan Chak			
Ghazi Khan bin Chak	1561		
Nasir-ud-Din Husain	1563	**11: Nawabs of Bengal**	
Zahir-ud-Din Ali	1569	Murshid Quli Jafar Khan	1703
Nasir-ud-Din Yusuf	1579	Shuja-ud-Din	1727
Yaqub	1586	Sarfaraz Khan	1739
Submission to Mughal emperor Akbar	1589	Alivardi Khan	1740
		Suraj-ud-Daula	1756
		Mir Jafar	1757
		Mir Qasim	1760
9: Nawabs of Oudh		Mir Jafar	1764
Saadat Khan	1724	Najm-ud-Daula	1765
Safdar Jang	1739	Saif-ud-Daula	1766–70
Shuja-ud-Daula	1754		
Asaf-ud-Daula	1775		
Wazir Ali	1797	**12: Nizams of Hyderabad**	
Saadat Ali	1798	Mir Qamar-ud-Din, Nizam-ul-Mulk Asaf Jah	1724
Ghazi-ud-Din Haidar	1814	Mir Muhammad Nasir Jang	1748
Nasir-ud-Din Haidar	1827	Muzaffar Jang	1750
Ali Shah	1837	Mir Asaf-ud-Daula Salabat Jang	1751
Amjad Ali Shah	1842		

Nizam Ali	1762	Anand Rao	1800
Mir Akbar Ali Khan Sikander Jah	1802	Sayaji Rao II	1818
Nasir-ud-Daula	1829	Ganpat Rao	1847
Afzal-ud-Daula	1857	Khande Rao	1856
Mir Mahbub Ali Khan	1869	Malhar Rao	1870
Mir Usman Ali Khan Bahadur Fath Jang	1911	Sayaji Rao III	1875

The Holkars

Malhar Rao Holkar	1728
Ahalya Bai	1765
Tukoji I	1795
Jaswant Rao I	1798
Malhar Rao II	1811
Hari Rao	1834
Tukoji Rao II	1843
Shivaji Rao	1886
Tukoji Rao III	1903
Jaswant Rao II	1926–

PRINCIPAL MARATHA DYNASTIES

The Bhonslas

Shivaji	1674
Shambhuji	1680
Rajaram	1689
Tara Bai	1700
Shahu	1708
Ram Raja	1749
Shahu	1777
Pratap Singh	1810

The Scindias

Madhava Rao Scindia	1761
Daulat Rao Scindia	1794
Jankoji Rao	1827
Jayaji Rao	1843
Madhava Rao II	1886
Jivaji Rao	1925

The Peshwas

Balaji Viswanath	1714
Baji Rao	1720
Balaji Baji Rao	1740
Madhava Rao Ballal	1761
Narayan Rao	1772
Raghunath Rao	1773
Madhava Rao Narayan	1774
Baji Rao II	1796–1818

THE RAJPUT DYNASTY OF THE RANAS OF MEWAR

Hamir	
Kshetra Simha	$c.$ 1364
Laksha	$c.$ 1382
Mokala	$c.$ 1418
Kumbha	$c.$ 1430
Udaya Karan	1469
Rayamalla	1474
Sangrama	1509
Ratna Simha	1527
Bikramajit	1532
Ranbir	1535

The Gaekwars

Pilaji	1721
Damaji II	1732
Govind Rao	1768
Sayaji Rao I	1771
Fateh Singh	1771
Manaji	1789
Govind Rao	1793

Udaya Simha	1537	Raja Simha II	1754
Pratapa Simha I	1572	Ari Simha II	1761
Amara Simha I	1597	Hamir II	1773
Karan	1620	Bhim Simha	1778
Jagat Simha	1628	Jawan Simha	1828
Raja Simha I	1652	Sardar Simha	1838
Jay Simha	1680	Sarup Simha	1842
Amara Simha II	1699	Shambhu	1861
Sangrama Simha II	1711	Sujan Simha	1874
Jagat Simha II	1734	Fateh Simha	1884
Pratapa Simha II	1752	Bhopal Simha	1930

LIST OF GOVERNORS-GENERAL/ VICEROYS

Governors-General of Fort William in Bengal, 1774–1834

Warren Hastings	1774–85
John Macpherson (*acting*)	1785–6
Earl Cornwallis	1786–93
Sir John Shore (Baron Teignmouth)	1793–8
Earl of Mornington (Marquess Wellesley)	1798–1805
Marquess Cornwallis (*second time*)	(died at Ghazipur) 1805
Sir George Barlow (*acting*)	1805–7
Baron Minto	1807–13
Earl of Moira	1813–23
Baron Amherst	1823–8
Lord William Bentinck	1828–34

Governors-General of India, 1834–58

Lord William Bentinck	1834–5
Sir Charles Metcalfe (*acting*)	1835–6
Baron Auckland	1836–42
Baron Ellenborough	1842–4
Viscount Hardinge	1844–8
Earl of Dalhousie	1848–56
Viscount Canning	1856–8

Viceroys and Governors-General, 1858–1947

Viscount Canning	1858–62
Earl of Elgin and Kincardine	(died at Dharamsala) 1862–3
Sir John Lawrence	1864–9
Earl of Mayo	(assassinated at Port Blair) 1869–72
Baron Northbrook	1872–6
Baron Lytton	1876–80

Marquess of Ripon	1880–84
Marquess of Dufferin	1884–8
Marquess of Lansdowne	1888–94
Earl of Elgin and Kincardine	1894–9
Baron Curzon of Kedleston	1899–1904
Baron Curzon of Kedleston (*second time*)	1904–5
Earl of Minto	1905–10
Baron Hardinge of Penshurst	1910–16
Baron Chelmsford	1916–21
Marquess of Reading	1921–5
Baron Irwin of Kirby (Lord Halifax)	1926–31
Earl of Willingdon	1931–6
Marquess of Linlithgow	1936–43
Viscount Wavell	1943–7
Earl Mountbatten of Burma	1947

Governor-General

Earl Mountbatten of Burma	1947–8

GLOSSARY

Abacus, flat slab above the capital on a column

Acanthus, plant with thick, fleshy leaves used as carved ornament on some capitals

Acroteria, ornaments placed at the apex or ends of a pediment

Agnikula, born of the fire god

Aisle, lateral divisions running at the sides of a nave or main chamber

Annular arch, vaulted roof over a space between two concentric walls

Apse, curved or vaulted termination of a room or chapel

Arabesque, elaborate intertwining ornamental decoration

Arcade, range of arches carried on piers or columns

Architrave, moulded frame to a door or window surround; also part of an entablature comprising the beam over two or more columns

Arcuated, arched

Arris, corner or edge

Ashlar, hewn blocks of masonry

Atrium, inner court open to the sky

Attic, upper storey of a building above the main cornice

Bagh, garden

Bakhsheesh, alms

Baldachino, canopy over a throne, statue or altar

Bangaldar (bangla), curved roof or eaves derived from bamboo huts of Bengal

Bania, trader or moneylender

Baoli, step-well

Baradari, twelve-pillared portico or pavilion

Barbican, defensive outwork to a castle or fort

Bargeboard, projecting board on the edge of a gable, often decorated or carved

Barrel-vault, cylindrical form of roof or ceiling

Bartizan, battlemented parapet or projecting corner turret

Batter, slope or rake to a wall

Bazaar, market

Begum, Indian Muslim princess

Belvedere, summer house or small room on the roof of a house

Bhavan, building or house

Boss, ornamented knob covering intersecting ribs of a vault or ceiling

Brahmin, uppermost caste of society to which all Hindu and Jain priests belong

Budgeroe, river-boat

Bund, dam, embankment or causeway

Burj, bastion or tower

Campanile, Italian name for a bell tower

Cantonment, large planned estate or military station

Caryatid, sculpted female figure

Cavalier, defensive embankment

Chahar bagh, four-square garden

Chajja, thin sloping projection of stone resembling a cornice

Chala, Bengali curved roof form

Chandra, moon

Char-chala, Bengali roof form with crossed, curved ridges and curved eaves on a square or rectangular plan

Chatri, umbrella-shaped dome or pavilion

Chopar, landscaped space at intersection of two roads

Chowk, open space or court surrounded by ranges

Chunam, form of stucco made from burnt seashells which can be polished to resemble marble

Clerestory, upper part of main wall pierced by windows

Coffer, ceiling decoration comprising sunken square or polygonal panels

Corbel, bracket or block of stone projecting from a wall

Cortile, courtyard, usually internal and arcaded

Crocket, decorative feature projecting from the angles of a spire

Crore, ten million

Cutcha, built with sun-dried bricks; unreliable

Cutcherry, a judicial court

Dacoit, bandit

Dargah, Muslim shrine or tomb of note

Daulat khana, treasury

Decastyle, with ten columns

Dentil, small square block used as part of a cornice

Deval, memorial pavilion marking royal funeral pyre

Diaper, small floral pattern inlaid into a wall surface

Divali, festival of lights (September–October) usually marking end of rainy season

Divan (diwan), smoking-room; also a chief minister

Diwan-i-am, hall of public audience

Diwan-i-khas, hall of private audience

Do-chala, Bengali roof form with single curved ridge, curved side eaves and gabled ends, usually on a rectangular plan

Dodecastyle, with twelve columns

Durbar, Indian court or levée

Embrasure, splayed opening in wall or fortification

Engrailed arch, foliated or cusped, an arch with a serrated or indented edge

Entablature, upper part of an order incorporating architrave, frieze and cornice

Fakir, Muslim who has taken a vow of poverty

Fauwwara, fountain for ritual ablutions in a mosque

Festoon, ornament resembling a garland of fruit and flowers

Finial, crowning ornament on a gable, spire or pinnacle

Fiqh, Islamic jurisprudence

Firman, a royal order or grant

Flèche, a slender spire

Foliated, carved with leaf ornament

Gaddi, throne

Garh, fort

Ghat, landing place on a riverside with steps

Godown, warehouse

Gola, conical-shaped storehouse

Gopura, towered gateway in south Indian temple architecture

Groin-vault, formed by intersection of two tunnel vaults at right-angles

Guldasta, pinnacle

Gumbad, local name for a domed tomb in Delhi area

Gumbaz, dome

Guru, sage or teacher

Gurudwara, Sikh religious complex, generally with a temple and rest-house

Hadith, traditions related to the life of the Prophet

Hajj, pilgrimage to Mecca

Hammam, Turkish bath

Haveli, courtyard house

Hawa mahal, palace of the winds

Hexastyle, with six columns

Hijra, Muhammad's flight from Mecca to Medina in 622, from which the Muslim calendar is dated

Holi, spring festival (February-March) associated with Krishna

Hood mould, projecting moulding over an arch or opening

Howdah, seat on an elephant's back, sometimes canopied

Huzra, tomb chamber in a Muslim tomb

Hypostyle, pillared hall

Idgah qibla wall for prayers during Id festival

Imambara, tomb of a Shiite Muslim holy man

Impost, member at springing point of an arch

In antis, recessed portico

Intarsia, mosaic of tinted or natural wood, marble, etc.

Interlacing arches, arches which overlap each other

Jali, pierced ornamental screen to a window opening

Jalousies, slatted shutters or blinds

Jamb, vertical side slabs of a doorway

Jami masjid, a congregational mosque

Jampan, rickshaw

Jhilmil, projecting canopy over a window or door opening

Jihad, striving in the way of God; holy war against non-believers or base personal instincts

Johar, mass suicide by fire of women to avoid capture

Kacheri, see Cutcherry

Kadal, a bridge (Kashmir)

Kalasha, pot-like finial

Karma, present consequences of past lives

Keystone, central stone of an arch

Khamba, column

Khanqah, Muslim monastery for a particular brotherhood

Khind, pass

Kiosk, small pavilion generally on parapet or roof

Kothi, house

Kotla, citadel

Kund, well or pool

Lakh, hundred thousand rupees

Lat, column

Linga, Shiva as the phallic emblem usually mounted on a yoni pedestal

Liwan, pillared cloisters of a mosque

Loggia, gallery open to the air; arcaded verandah

Lunette, crescent-shaped fortification

Machicolation, projecting parapet carried on brackets

Madrasa, Islamic theological school or college

Maidan, large central open space in a town or city

Mandala, diagram illustrating cosmological ideas

Mandapa, columned hall preceding sanctuary in temple architecture

Mandir, room or palace; sometimes also a temple

Maqbara, mortuary chamber of a Muslim tomb

Maqsura, screen or arched façade of a mosque

Mardana, men's living-quarters and ceremonial rooms

Masjid, mosque; literally place of prostration

Memsahib, married European lady

Merlon, parapet battlements with pointed tops

Metope, the square space between the triglyphs on a Doric order

Mihrab, niche or arched recess in the western wall of a mosque towards which worshippers turn for prayer

Mimbar, pulpit in mosque

Minar, minaret, slender tower of a mosque from which the muezzin calls the faithful to prayer

Modillion, projecting bracket or scrolled console

Mofussil, the country or hinterland, as distinct from the town

Mohalla, quarter of a town inhabited by members of one caste

Moucharabya, carved elaborate latticework

Muezzin, mosque official who calls the faithful to prayer

Musallah, prayer carpet

Musnud, seat or throne of cushions used by an Indian prince

Mutule, projecting block above the triglyph in a Doric order

Nabob, weathy person from India

Nagar, town

Nakkar khana, naubhat khana, drum house; arched structure or gateway to announce arrival by beat of ceremonial drum

Nara durg, fort on a plain protected by men

596

Nave, central or main compartment of a building

Nirvana, enlightenment; literally, extinguished

Niwas, small palace

Octastyle, with eight columns

Oeil-de-boeuf, circular (bull's eye) window

Ogee, form of moulding or arch comprising a double curved line made up of a concave and convex part

Opus sectile, marble inlay of various colours

Oriel, projecting window

Pagoda, tall structure of several storeys

Palanquin, covered litter for one carried by four or six men

Pallia, stone monument commemorating a suttee or act of bravery

Palmette, fan-shaped ornament resembling a palm-leaf

Patera, a small flat circular ornament, usually a centrepiece to a ceiling

Patte d'oie, radiating vistas resembling in plan the imprint of a bird's foot

Pediment, triangular termination of a roof or similar ornamental feature in classical architecture

Pendentive, concave spandrel between the angle of two walls and the base of a circular dome by which the dome is carried over a square chamber

Peripteral, surrounded by a range of columns

Pietra dura, inlaid mosaic or ornament of hard or semi-precious stones

Pol, fortified gate

Polychromy, structural use of colour in building

Porte-cochère, a porch for vehicles to pass through

Portico, space enclosed between columns

Pukka, solidly built, reliable

Punkah, large suspended cloth fan worked by a cord

Purdah, seclusion of women from public view

Pylon, propylon, tall monumental gateway or gate towers

Qabr, grave

Qabristan, Muslim tomb

Qibla, direction for Muslim prayer

Qila, fort

Quatrefoil, four leaf-shaped curve formed by the cusping of a circle

Quoin, corner of a building

Quran, holy Muslim scriptures

Qutb, axis or pivot

Raj, rule or government

Raja, ruler, king (variations include rao, rawal); prefix 'maha' means great

Rajput, dynasties of western and central India

Ramayana, the epic story of Rama

Rana, warrior

Rang Mahal, painted palace

Rani, queen

Rauza, large Muslim tomb

Reredos, screen behind an altar

Rond-point, circular space with radiating streets or vistas

Rustication, masonry or stucco cut in incised blocks

Sabha, public audience hall

Sagar, lake

Sahn, open courtyard of a mosque

Sarai, halting-place; caravansarai

Sepoy, private soldier in Indian army

Seraglio, walled palace

Sgraffito, plaster decoration of incised patterns revealing a different coloured coat beneath

Shardula, carved lions in relief

Sharia, corpus of Muslim theological law

Sheesh mahal (shish mahal), palace apartment enriched with mirror work

Shikhara, temple tower

Shilpa-shastra, ancient Hindu texts on arts and crafts

Sileh khana, armoury

Singh, lion; also Rajput caste name adopted by Sikhs

Squinch arch, diagonally placed arches at the angles of a dome to connect square to round

Stambha, free-standing column

Stele, upright inscribed slab or pillar used as a gravestone

597

Stucco, plasterwork
Stupa, domed or beehive shaped Buddhist monument
Stylobate, a platform on which stands a colonnade
Sufi, ascetic Muslim mystic
Suttee (sati), widow-burning
Syce, groom

Tafsir, interpretation of the Quran
Talao, tank or reservoir
Tank, reservoir bounded by a dam wall, often with stepped sides
Tatties, cane or grass screens used for shade
Terracotta, burnt clay used as building material
Tetrastyle, with four columns
Tiffin, light lunch or meal; drink
Torana, gateway with two posts linked by curved architraves
Trabeated, building constructed on post and lintel principles
Tracery, ornamental perforated patterns in a window or door
Triforium, arcaded wall or passage facing the nave
Triglyphs, grooved blocks on a Doric frieze
Tulwar, razor-sharp Indian sabre
Tykhana, an underground room in a house in Upper India for use in hot weather
Tympanum, an area enclosed by the pediment or arch

Ulama, learned orthodox Muslims who believe in the authority of the Quran and sharia

Vav, baoli or step-well
Venetian arch or window, large central arched opening flanked by tall narrow square-headed openings
Vihara, Buddhist monastery with cells opening on a central court
Vilas, house or pleasure palace
Vimana, towered sanctuary in temple architecture
Volute, spiral scroll on an Ionic capital
Voussoir, brick- or wedge-shaped stone in an arch

Yoga, school of philosophy which concentrates on different mental and physical disciplines
Yoni, vulva; sexual emblem of Devi

Zamindar, landowner
Zarih, cenotaph in a Muslim tomb
Zenana, segregated women's apartments
Ziarat, holy Muslim tomb
Zimmis, protected non-Muslims

FURTHER READING

There is a vast bibliography on the art, history, culture and architecture of the Indian subcontinent in the period covered by this book. The following is a brief selective list of important or recent relevant titles which may assist the lay traveller to come to terms with the rich and complex tapestry of Indian history.

General

Charles Allen and S. Dwivedi, *Lives of the Indian Princes*, Century, London, 1984
Mark Bence-Jones, *The Viceroys of India*, Constable, London, 1982
Bamber Gascoigne, *The Great Moghuls*, Jonathan Cape, London, 1987
S. M. Ikram, *Muslim Civilisation in India*, University Press, Columbia, 1965
Philip Mason, *The Men Who Ruled India*, Jonathan Cape, London, 1985
Geoffrey Moorhouse, *India Britannica*, Collins, London, 1983
Geoffrey Moorhouse, *Calcutta*, Penguin, London, 1986
S. Muthiah, *Madras Discovered*, Madras, 1987
Francis Robinson (ed.), *The Cambridge Encyclopedia of India, Pakistan, Bangladesh and Sri Lanka*, Cambridge University Press, 1989
Romila Thapar, *The Penguin History of India, Vol. I*, London, 1986
Percival Spear, *The Penguin History of India, Vol. II*, London, 1986
Gillian Tindall, *City of Gold – The Biography of Bombay*, M. T. Smith, London, 1982

Islamic and Mughal Architecture

Percy Brown, *Indian Architecture – Islamic Period*, Delhi, 1942
S. Crowe, *The Gardens of Mughal India*, Thames & Hudson, London, 1972
A. S. Dani, *Muslim Architecture of Bengal*, Dacca, 1961
James Fergusson, *History of Indian and Eastern Architecture*, John Murray, London, 1899
E. B. Havell, *Indian Architecture*, John Murray, London, 1927
George Michell (ed.), *Architecture of the Islamic World*, Thames & Hudson, London, 1978
George Michell (ed.), *The Islamic Heritage of Bengal*, Unesco, 1984

Forts and Palaces

Prabhakar V. Begde, *Forts and Palaces of India*, New Delhi, 1982
Virginia Fass, *The Forts of India*, Collins, London, 1986
Gaekwad Fatesinghrao, Maharajah of Baroda, *The Palaces of India*, Collins, London, 1980
G. H. R. Tillotson, *The Rajput Palaces, The Development of an Architectural Style, 1450–1750*, Yale, 1987

Sidney Toy, *The Strongholds of India*, Heinemann, London, 1957
Sidney Toy, *The Fortified Cities of India*, Heinemann, London, 1965

European Architecture

Pat Barr and Ray Desmond, *Simla – A Hill Station in British India*, Scolar Press, London, 1978
Mark Bence-Jones, *Palaces of the Raj*, Allen & Unwin, London, 1973
Philip Davies, *Splendours of the Raj – British Architecture in India 1660–1947*, John Murray, London, 1987
Robert Grant Irving, *Indian Summer – Lutyens, Baker and Imperial Delhi*, Yale, 1981
Thomas R. Metcalf, *An Imperial Vision – Indian Architecture and Britain's Raj*, Faber and Faber, London, 1989
Jan Morris with Simon Winchester, *Stones of Empire*, OUP, Oxford, 1983
Sten Nilsson, *European Architecture in India 1750–1850*, Faber and Faber, London, 1968
Mollie Panter-Downes, *Ooty Preserved*, Century, London, 1985

INDEX OF SITES

Sites marked with an asterisk (*) also appear in Volume I.

PHOTOGRAPHIC CREDITS